MW00784088

Business and Society

Sara Miller McCune founded SAGE Publishing in 1965 to support the dissemination of usable knowledge and educate a global community. SAGE publishes more than 1000 journals and over 800 new books each year, spanning a wide range of subject areas. Our growing selection of library products includes archives, data, case studies and video. SAGE remains majority owned by our founder and after her lifetime will become owned by a charitable trust that secures the company's continued independence.

Los Angeles | London | New Delhi | Singapore | Washington DC | Melbourne

Business and Society

Ethical, Legal, and Digital Environments

Cynthia E. Clark
Bentley University

Kabrina K. Chang
Boston University

Sean P. Melvin
Elizabethtown College

Los Angeles | London | New Delhi
Singapore | Washington DC | Melbourne

FOR INFORMATION:

SAGE Publications, Inc.
2455 Teller Road
Thousand Oaks, California 91320
E-mail: order@sagepub.com

SAGE Publications Ltd.
1 Oliver's Yard
55 City Road
London, EC1Y 1SP
United Kingdom

SAGE Publications India Pvt. Ltd.
B 1/I 1 Mohan Cooperative Industrial Area
Mathura Road, New Delhi 110 044
India

SAGE Publications Asia-Pacific Pte. Ltd.
18 Cross Street #10-10/11/12
China Square Central
Singapore 048423

Copyright © 2021 by SAGE Publications, Inc.

All rights reserved. Except as permitted by U.S. copyright law, no part of this work may be reproduced or distributed in any form or by any means, or stored in a database or retrieval system, without permission in writing from the publisher.

All third party trademarks referenced or depicted herein are included solely for the purpose of illustration and are the property of their respective owners. Reference to these trademarks in no way indicates any relationship with, or endorsement by, the trademark owner.

Printed in the United States of America

Library of Congress Cataloging-in-Publication Data

Names: Clark, Cynthia E., author. I Chang, Kabrina K., author. I Melvin, Sean P., author.
Title: Business and society : ethical, legal, and digital environments / Cynthia E. Clark, Bentley University, Kabrina K. Chang, Boston University, Sean P. Melvin, Elizabethtown College.
Description: First edition. I Los Angeles : SAGE, [2021] I Includes bibliographical references and index.
Identifiers: LCCN 2020013368 I ISBN 978-1-5063-8810-6 (paperback ; alk. paper) I ISBN 978-1-5063-8808-3 (epub) I ISBN 978-1-5063-8809-0 (epub) I ISBN 978-1-5063-8811-3 (ebook)
Subjects: LCSH: Social responsibility of business. I Management—Social aspects. I Business—Social aspects. I Business ethics. I Business law.
Classification: LCC HD60 .C526 2021 I DDC 658.4/08—dc23
LC record available at https://lccn.loc.gov/2020013368

This book is printed on acid-free paper.

MIX
Paper from responsible sources
FSC® C008955

Acquisitions Editor: Maggie Stanley
Editorial Assistant: Sarah Wilson
Content Development Editor: Darcy Scelsi
Production Editor: Rebecca Lee
Copy Editor: Megan Markanich
Typesetter: Hurix Digital
Proofreader: Alison Syring
Indexer: Integra
Cover Designer: Dally Verghese
Marketing Manager: Sarah Panella

20 21 22 23 24 10 9 8 7 6 5 4 3 2 1

BRIEF CONTENTS

Preface   xix

Acknowledgments   xxi

About the Authors   xxiii

PART I • MANAGING IN TODAY'S BUSINESS WORLD   1

CHAPTER 1 • STAKEHOLDER AND SHAREHOLDER THEORIES OF THE FIRM   3

CHAPTER 2 • CORPORATE SOCIAL RESPONSIBILITY   23

CHAPTER 3 • ETHICS AND ETHICAL REASONING   44

CHAPTER 4 • ORGANIZATIONS AND PUBLIC POLICY   67

CHAPTER 5 • LIABILITY, BUSINESS AGREEMENTS, AND MANAGING RISK   90

CHAPTER 6 • GOVERNMENT REGULATION OF THE ORGANIZATION   114

PART II • BUILDING RELATIONSHIPS AND WORKING WITH STAKEHOLDERS   137

CHAPTER 7 • ENVIRONMENTALISM AND SUSTAINABILITY   139

CHAPTER 8 • EMPLOYEES AND THE CORPORATION   163

CHAPTER 9 • MANAGING A DIVERSE WORKFORCE   188

CHAPTER 10 • FINANCIAL SYSTEMS AND SOCIETY   209

CHAPTER 11 • INTERNATIONAL AND MULTINATIONAL ORGANIZATIONS   240

PART III • CONTEMPORARY BUSINESS ISSUES IN TODAY'S SOCIETY   261

CHAPTER 12 • SOCIAL MEDIA AND CITIZEN MOVEMENTS   263

CHAPTER 13 • BIG DATA AND HACKING   292

CHAPTER 14 • PRIVACY IN THE DIGITAL AGE   315

CHAPTER 15 • CORPORATE PERSONHOOD   340

CHAPTER 16 • GLOBALIZATION   363

Glossary   380

Notes   392

Index   415

DETAILED CONTENTS

Preface   xix
   Structure of the Book   xix
   Applicable Courses   xx
   Digital Resources   xx

Acknowledgments   xxi

About the Authors   xxiii

PART I • MANAGING IN TODAY'S BUSINESS WORLD   1

CHAPTER 1 • STAKEHOLDER AND SHAREHOLDER THEORIES OF THE FIRM   3
   ➡ **Learning Objectives**   3
Introduction   3
Defining *Stake* and *Stakeholder*   4
   ➡ **Key Takeaways:** Defining *Stake* and *Stakeholder*   5
Stakeholder Versus Shareholder Theories   5
   Stakeholder Theory   5
   Shareholder Theory   6
   ➡ **Key Takeaways:** Stakeholder Versus Shareholder Theories   8
The Stakeholder and Shareholder Debate   8
   The Stakeholder Arguments   8
   The Shareholder Arguments   9
   Is One Right and One Wrong?   10
   ➡ **Key Takeaways:** The Stakeholder and Shareholder Debate   12
Stakeholder Types: Interests, Issues, Legitimacy, and Power   12
   Market and Nonmarket Stakeholders   12
   Stakeholder Interests and Power   14
   ➡ **Case Study 1.1:** Juul's E-Cigarettes and Teens   15
   ➡ **Key Takeaways:** Stakeholder Types: Interests, Issues, Legitimacy, and Power   18
Managing Stakeholders   18
   ➡ **Key Takeaways:** Managing Stakeholders   19
   ➡ **Ethics in Context:** Competing Stakeholder Demands at Amazon   20
Summary   21
Key Terms   21
Review Questions   22
Manager's Challenge   22
   1.1: Stakeholder–Stockholder Debate   22
   1.2: Stakeholder or Shareholder Perspective?   22

CHAPTER 2 • CORPORATE SOCIAL RESPONSIBILITY — 23

    ➡ **Learning Objectives** — 23

Introduction — 23

Corporate Social Responsibility Defined — 24

    Origins — 24

    Corporate Social Responsibility Pillars — 25

    ➡ **Key Takeaways:** Corporate Social Responsibility Defined — 26

Corporate Social Responsibility as a Strategy — 27

    Branding and Reputation — 27

    ➡ **Case Study 2.1:** Dollar General Literacy Foundation — 28

    Reporting Corporate Social Responsibility Efforts — 28

    ➡ **Law and Society 2.1:** *Ramirez v. Exxon Mobil Corp.*, 334 F. Supp. 3d 832 (2018) — 29

    ➡ **Key Takeaways:** Corporate Social Responsibility as a Strategy — 31

Different Corporate Social Responsibility Views and Schools of Thought — 31

    The Narrow View: Profit First — 32

    The Moderate View: Shared Value — 32

    The Broad View: Good Corporate Citizenship — 33

    The Explicit and Implicit Corporate Social Responsibility Framework — 33

    ➡ **Ethics in Context:** Using Corporate Social Responsibility as a Business Strategy — 35

    ➡ **Key Takeaways:** Different Corporate Social Responsibility Views and Schools of Thought — 36

Corporate Social Responsibility and Its Limitations — 36

    Benefits and Costs — 36

    ➡ **Case Study 2.2:** Amazon Ups the Ante — 38

    ➡ **Key Takeaways:** Corporate Social Responsibility and Its Limitations — 38

Corporate Social Responsibility Strategies and Trends — 39

    Cause Marketing — 39

    Corporate Philanthropy — 39

    Strategic Partnerships — 39

    Volunteerism — 40

    Socially Responsible Business Practices — 40

    ➡ **Case Study 2.3:** Google's Corporate Social Responsibility Strategy and Project Maven — 41

    ➡ **Key Takeaways:** Corporate Social Responsibility Strategies and Trends — 42

Summary — 42

Key Terms — 42

Review Questions — 42

Manager's Challenge — 43

    Employee Participation in Corporate Volunteer Efforts — 43

CHAPTER 3 • ETHICS AND ETHICAL REASONING — 44

    ➡ **Learning Objectives** — 44

Introduction — 44

Morals, Ethics, and the Law — 45

➡ **Key Takeaways:** Ethics, Morals, and the Law 46

Motivations And Rationalizations **46**

Ethical Temptations 47

Ethical Dilemmas 48

Rationalizations 51

➡ **Case Study 3.1:** The University of Arizona: Innovative Use
of Technology or Ethical Dilemma? 53

➡ **Key Takeaways:** Motivations and Rationalizations 55

The Origin of Ethics **55**

Consequences-Based Approach to Ethics 57

Principles-Based Approach to Ethics 58

Virtue-Based Approach to Ethics 58

➡ **Key Takeaways:** Origin of Ethics 59

Organizational Ethics and Creating an Ethical Climate **59**

➡ **Law and Society 3.1:** *Peterson v. Hewlett-Packard,*
358 F.3d 599 (9th Cir. 2004) 60

Conflicts of Interest 62

➡ **Ethics in Context:** Profits Versus Ethics for Glassdoor Ratings? 63

➡ **Key Takeaways:** Organizational Ethics and
Creating an Ethical Climate 64

Summary **65**

Key Terms **65**

Review Questions **65**

Manager's Challenge **65**

3.1: Moral Intuition or Reason? 65

3.2: Ethics and the Law 66

3.3: Profitability and Ethics—Are They in Tension? 66

CHAPTER 4 • ORGANIZATIONS AND PUBLIC POLICY **67**

➡ **Learning Objectives** 67

Introduction **67**

Role of Business in Shaping Laws and Policy **68**

How Laws and Policy Are Made 68

➡ **Key Takeaways:** Role of Business in Shaping Laws and Policy 69

Evolution of Lobbying: Opportunities for Influence **69**

Business Involvement in Policy: From Necessary Evil
to Welcome Partner 70

Getting In On the Ground Floor: Elections 72

➡ **Law and Society 4.1:** *McCutcheon v. Federal Election Commission,*
134 S. Ct. 1434 (2014) 72

How Social Media Is Changing Access to the Political Process 73

➡ **Case Study 4.1:** Social Media and Access to the Government 74

➡ **Key Takeaways:** Evolution of Lobbying: Opportunities for Influence 75

Creating Public Policy **75**

➡ **Key Takeaways:** Creating Public Policy 79

Public–Private Partnerships **79**

➡ **Case Study 4.2:** Alphabet City to Zucktown 82

➡ **Key Takeaways:** Public–Private Partnerships 84

Ethical Dimensions of Influencing Policy **84**

Private Prisons   84

➡ **Ethics in Context:** Private Prisons   85

➡ **Law and Society 4.2:** *Minneci et al. v. Pollard et al.,* 132 S. Ct. 176 (2012)   87

➡ **Key Takeaways:** Ethical Dimensions of Influencing Policy   88

Summary   88

Key Terms   88

Review Questions   88

Manager's Challenge   89

Private Prisons   89

CHAPTER 5 • LIABILITY, BUSINESS AGREEMENTS, AND MANAGING RISK   90

➡ **Learning Objectives**   90

Introduction   90

Risk of Injury   91

Intentional Torts   92

➡ **Law and Society 5.1:** *Seaton v. TripAdvisor*, 728 F.3d 592 (2013)   94

➡ **Case Study 5.1:** Is Each Retweet a New Publication?   97

➡ **Law and Society 5.2:** Defamation, Tortious Interference, and E-Commerce: *Broadspring, Inc. v. Congoo*, 2014 U.S. Dist. LEXIS 116070   99

➡ **Case Study 5.2:** Privacy and Social Media   101

Negligence   102

➡ **Key Takeaways:** Risk of Injury   102

Respondeat Superior and Product Liability   103

Respondeat Superior   103

Product Liability   103

➡ **Case Study 5.3:** Can a Dating App be an Unreasonably Dangerous Product?   103

➡ **Key Takeaways:** Respondeat Superior and Product Liability   104

Contracts   104

Elements of a Contract   105

➡ **Law and Society 5.3:** *In re Zappos.com, Inc. Customer Data Security Breach Litigation*, 893 F. Supp. 2d 1058 (2012)   106

➡ **Case Study 5.4:** Embryos Are the New Frontier in Contracts   107

➡ **Key Takeaways:** Contracts   108

Limiting Risk Through Contracts   108

➡ **Ethics in Context:** Nondisclosure Agreements and Public Safety   110

➡ **Key Takeaways:** Limiting Risk Through Contracts   111

Summary   112

Key Terms   112

Review Questions   112

Manager's Challenge   112

Defamation and Public Figures   112

CHAPTER 6 • GOVERNMENT REGULATION OF THE ORGANIZATION   114

➡ **Learning Objectives**   114

Introduction   114

Anticompetitive Behavior and Antitrust Regulation   115

The Sherman Antitrust Act 115
The Federal Trade Commission Act 117
The Clayton Act 117
The Robinson–Patman Act 118
➡ **Ethics in Context:** Student–Athletes and Antitrust Law 118
➡ **Key Takeaways:** Anticompetitive Behavior and Antitrust Regulation 120

Protection of Consumers and Creditors **120**
Warranties 120
Unfair or Deceptive Sales Practices 121
Bait and Switch 122
Pricing and Price Gouging 122
➡ **Case Study 6.1:** Surge Pricing: Workforce Incentive or Price Gouging? 123
Food and Drug Safety 124
Credit Transactions 125
➡ **Key Takeaways:** Protection of Consumers and Creditors 125

Protecting Investors **126**
Securities Transactions 126
➡ **Case Study 6.2:** Caution and Crowdfunding 129
Securities Exchange Act of 1934 (Exchange Act) 130
➡ **Law and Society 6.1:** Insider Trading: *United States v. McGee,*
No. 13-3183 (3d Cir. 2014) 132
➡ **Key Takeaways:** Protecting Investors 133

Summary **133**
Key Terms **134**
Review Questions **134**
Manager's Challenge **134**
Consumer Protection 134

PART II • BUILDING RELATIONSHIPS AND WORKING WITH STAKEHOLDERS **137**

CHAPTER 7 • ENVIRONMENTALISM AND SUSTAINABILITY **139**
➡ **Learning Objectives** 139
Introduction **139**
Environmentalism: Definitions and Policy Objectives **140**
Environmental Justice 140
Environmental Activists 141
➡ **Key Takeaways:** Environmentalism: Definitions and
Policy Objectives 142

Green Management and Competitive Advantage **142**
➡ **Ethics in Context:** Green Management or Greenwashing? 143
Codes of Environmental Conduct 144
➡ **Case Study 7.1:** Eco-Branding 146
➡ **Key Takeaways:** Green Management and Competitive Advantage 146

Sustainable Development **146**
Circular Economic Theory 147
Global Standards for Sustainability 148
Sustainable Development Goals 149
➡ **Key Takeaways:** Sustainable Development 151

Global Environmental Trends: Climate Change 151

    Climate Change and Society 153

    Global Response 153

        ➥ **Case Study 7.2:** Voluntary Carbon Offsets 154

        ➥ **Key Takeaways:** Global Environmental Trends: Climate Change 155

Government Regulation and Protection 155

    Limiting Government Impact on the Environment 156

    Air and Water Quality 157

        ➥ **Law and Society 7.1:** The Oil Spill by the Oil Rig Deepwater Horizon in the Gulf of Mexico on April 10, 2010, MDL 2179, U.S. District Court, E.D. Louisiana (September 9, 2014) 159

    Citizen Interest Organizations 160

        ➥ **Key Takeaways:** Government Regulation and Protection 161

Summary 161

Key Terms 161

Review Questions 161

Manager's Challenge 162

    The Role of Business in Environmental Ethics 162

CHAPTER 8 • EMPLOYEES AND THE CORPORATION 163

        ➥ **Learning Objectives** 163

Introduction 163

The Employment Relationship 164

        ➥ **Case Study 8.1:** Gigs and Side Hustles 165

        ➥ **Key Takeaways:** The Employment Relationship 167

Employment at Will 167

    Public Policy Exception and Whistleblowers 167

        ➥ **Ethics in Context:** Whistleblower Bounty 169

        ➥ **Key Takeaways:** Employment at Will 171

Workplace Protections 171

    Worker's Compensation 171

    Fair Labor Standards Act 173

        ➥ **Law and Society 8.1:** *Braun et al. v. Wal-Mart Stores, Inc.,* 630 Pa 292, 106 A.3d 656 (2014) 175

        ➥ **Case Study 8.2:** To Tip or Not to Tip 177

    Unions and Concerted Activity 178

        ➥ **Law and Society 8.2:** *Karl Knauz Motors, Inc. d/b/a Knauz BMW and Robert Becker,* Case 13-CA-046452 180

    Leave 182

        ➥ **Key Takeaways:** Workplace Protections 183

Employee Privacy 184

        ➥ **Case Study 8.3:** Monitoring Employee's Personal Social Media 184

        ➥ **Case Study 8.4:** GPS Tracking Apps 185

        ➥ **Key Takeaways:** Employee Privacy 185

Summary 186

Key Terms 186

Review Questions 186

Manager's Challenge 186

    Hiring in a Start-Up 186

CHAPTER 9 • MANAGING A DIVERSE WORKFORCE   **188**

     ➡ **Learning Objectives**   188

Introduction   **188**

Diversity and Inclusion   **189**

     ➡ **Key Takeaways:** Diversity and Inclusion   190

Bias and Discrimination   **190**

     ➡ **Key Takeaways:** Bias and Discrimination   191

Intersectionality   **192**

     ➡ **Case Study 9.1:** Gender Pay Equity   193

     ➡ **Key Takeaways:** Intersectionality   194

Laws to Protect Against Discrimination   **194**

     Equal Pay Act   195

     Title VII of the Civil Rights Act   195

     ➡ **Case Study 9.2:** Stereotypes and Discrimination   196

     ➡ **Law and Society 9.1:** *EEOC v. Abercrombie & Fitch Stores, Inc.,*
     135 S. Ct. 2028 (2015)   201

     Age Discrimination in Employment Act   201

     ➡ **Ethics in Context:** Bias in Online Job Postings   202

     The Americans With Disabilities Act   204

     ➡ **Law and Society 9.2:** *Huber v. Wal-Mart Stores,* 486 F.3d 480 (May 30, 2007)   206

     ➡ **Key Takeaways:** Laws to Protect Against Discrimination   207

Summary   **207**

Key Terms   **207**

Review Questions   **208**

Manager's Challenge   **208**

     Discrimination and Grooming Codes   208

CHAPTER 10 • FINANCIAL SYSTEMS AND SOCIETY   **209**

     ➡ **Learning Objectives**   209

Introduction   **209**

Roles of Finance in Society   **210**

     Global Financial System   210

     ➡ **Case Study 10.1:** Microfinance   211

     ➡ **Key Takeaways:** Roles of Finance in Society   213

Main Street to Wall Street   **213**

     Financial Firms: Brokerage Houses and Banks   214

     Issuing Securities   214

     The Initial Public Offering   215

     Public Perceptions of the Financial Industry   218

     ➡ **Key Takeaways:** Main Street to Wall Street   219

The Global Financial Crisis   **219**

     Root Causes   220

     ➡ **Law and Society 10.1:** *U.S. ex rel. O'Donnell v. Countrywide Financial Corp and Bank of America, 822 F.3d 650 (2016)*   221

     Government Bailouts: Too Big to Fail   226

     TARP   226

     The Dodd–Frank Act   227

     ➡ **Case Study 10.2:** Occupy Wall Street   227

Ongoing Debates — 228
  ➡ **Key Takeaways:** The Global Financial Crisis — 229
Alternative Financing and Payday Loans — **229**
Auto Title Loans — 230
Payday Loan Regulation — 230
  ➡ **Ethics in Context:** Payday Loans: Parasites or Providers? — 232
  ➡ **Key Takeaways:** Alternative Financing and Payday Loans — 233
Financial Market Regulation — **233**
Expanded Jurisdiction and Enforcement — 233
Financial Stability Oversight — 235
  ➡ **Key Takeaways:** Financial Market Regulation — 237
Summary — **238**
Key Terms — **238**
Review Questions — **238**
Manager's Challenge — **238**
Community Microfinancing — 238

CHAPTER 11 • INTERNATIONAL AND MULTINATIONAL ORGANIZATIONS — **240**
  ➡ **Learning Objectives** — 240
Introduction — 240
Cultural Competence — 241
  ➡ **Key Takeaways:** Cultural Competence — 242
International Customs and Law — 243
Protecting Shared Values: The United Nations — 243
  ➡ **Case Study 11.1:** State Enforcement of International Human Rights — 245
  ➡ **Key Takeaways:** International Customs and Law — 247
Doing Business Around the World — 247
Foreign Corrupt Practices Act — 247
  ➡ **Case Study 11.2:** Is an Unpaid Internship a "Thing of Value"? — 248
Protectionism and the General Agreement on Tariffs and Trade — 250
  ➡ **Case Study 11.3:** Walmart de Mexico — 250
  ➡ **Law and Society 11.1:** *American Institute for International Steel and Sim-Tex et al. v. United States*, Slip Op. 19-37, United States Court of International Trade (March 25, 2019) — 252
Other Trade Agreements — 254
  ➡ **Ethics in Context:** Free Trade Zones — 256
  ➡ **Key Takeaways:** Doing Business Around the World — 258
Summary — **258**
Key Terms — **258**
Review Questions — **259**
Manager's Challenge — **259**
Foreign Corrupt Practices Act — 259

PART III • CONTEMPORARY BUSINESS ISSUES IN TODAY'S SOCIETY — **261**

CHAPTER 12 • SOCIAL MEDIA AND CITIZEN MOVEMENTS — **263**
  ➡ **Learning Objectives** — 263
Introduction — 263

The Evolution of Social Media   **264**
From Bulletin Boards to Instagram   264
Smartphones and Apps   267
➡ **Key Takeaways:** The Evolution of Social Media   269
The Business Model of Social Media   **269**
Selling Ad Space   269
Selling Data   270
➡ **Case Study 12.1:** Social Media, Our Data, and Trust   271
➡ **Ethics in Context:** Social Media Addiction   273
➡ **Key Takeaways:** The Business Model of Social Media   276
How Businesses Use Social Media   **276**
➡ **Case Study 12.2:** Got Influence?   278
➡ **Key Takeaways:** How Businesses Use Social Media   279
Society, Democracy, and Social Media   **279**
#OccupyWallStreet   280
#BlackLivesMatter   281
#JeSuisCharlie   282
#MeToo   283
#Hate   284
➡ **Case Study 12.3:** An Algorithm for Hate?   285
➡ **Key Takeaways:** Society, Democracy, and Social Media   286
What Rules Apply to Social Media?   **286**
➡ **Law and Society 12.1:** *Force v. Facebook*, 934 F.3d 53 (2019)   287
➡ **Key Takeaways:** What Rules Apply to Social Media?   289
Summary   **290**
Key Terms   **290**
Review Questions   **290**
Manager's Challenge   **290**
Access to User Data   290

CHAPTER 13 • BIG DATA AND HACKING   **292**
➡ **Learning Objectives**   292
Introduction   **292**
The Digital Revolution   **293**
Drivers of Technology   293
Positive Impacts on Society   294
Threats to Society   295
➡ **Case Study 13.1:** RFID Transponders and Paying Your Toll   297
➡ **Key Takeaways:** The Digital Revolution   298
The Digital Divide   **298**
Economic Disparities   298
Educational Disparities   300
Digital Readiness   300
➡ **Key Takeaways:** The Digital Divide   300
Big Data and the Organization   **302**
What Is Big Data?   302
Data Analytics and the Organization   303
➡ **Key Takeaways:** Big Data and the Organization   305
Digital Security and Safety   **305**
➡ **Case Study 13.2:** Ransomware That Made Managers "WannaCry"   306

Cyberterrorism   307

➡ **Law and Society 13.1:** *Michael Terpin v. AT&T Mobility,*
2019 U.S. Dist. LEXIS 121905   308

➡ **Key Takeaways:** Digital Security and Safety   310

Legal and Ethical Aspects of Big Data   **310**

Legal Issues and the Use of Big Data   310

Ethical Issues and the Use of Big Data   311

➡ **Ethics in Context:** Big Data and Insurance   312

➡ **Key Takeaways:** Legal and Ethical Aspects of Big Data   313

Summary   **313**

Key Terms   **313**

Review Questions   **313**

Manager's Challenge   **314**

Big Data and Codes of Ethics   314

CHAPTER 14 • PRIVACY IN THE DIGITAL AGE   **315**

➡ **Learning Objectives**   315

Introduction   **315**

What Is the Right to Privacy?   **316**

➡ **Law and Society 14.1:** Data Privacy and the Constitution:
United States v. Carpenter, 819 F.3d 880 (2016)   317

➡ **Key Takeaways:** What Is the Right to Privacy?   318

Collecting Personal Information: Benefits and Harms   **318**

Responsibilities of Individuals, Companies, and Governments   319

➡ **Ethics in Context:** Profits versus Privacy Protection   322

➡ **Key Takeaways:** Collecting Personal Information: Benefits and Harms   323

Right to be Forgotten, Right to Erasure, and Surveillance   **323**

The Right to Be Forgotten   323

➡ **Case Study 14.1:** Google and the Right to Be Forgotten   326

Right to Erasure   331

Surveillance   332

➡ **Key Takeaways:** Right to Be Forgotten, Right to Erasure,
and Surveillance   334

What Can Managers Do?   **334**

Best Practices   335

Risk Mitigation   335

Privacy Policies   336

Use Protocols   337

➡ **Key Takeaways:** What Can Managers Do?   337

Summary   **337**

Key Terms   **337**

Review Questions   **338**

Manager's Challenge   **338**

14.1: Biometric Data, Ethics, and the Law   338

14.2: Safety or Ethics?   339

CHAPTER 15 • CORPORATE PERSONHOOD   **340**

➡ **Learning Objectives**   340

Introduction   **340**

Corporate Personhood   **341**

How *Citizens United* and *Hobby Lobby* Shaped the Corporate
Personhood Debate   342

➤ **Law and Society 15.1:** Race and Corporations:
*Carnell Construction Corp. v. Danville Redevelopment &
Housing Authority*, 745 F.3d 703 (2014)   344

Public Accommodation   345

➤ **Case Study 15.1:** Public Accommodations and the First Amendment:
Can Business Be Art?   345

➤ **Case Study 15.2:** Is A Website a Place of Public Accommodation?   348

➤ **Key Takeaways:** Corporate Personhood   349

Regulation of Business Through the Commerce Clause   **350**

Evolution of the Commerce Clause   350

What Is Commerce?   350

What Is Commerce Among States?   350

The Commerce Clause and Marijuana   351

➤ **Law and Society 15.2:** *Gonzales v. Raich*, 545 U.S. 1 (2005)   352

➤ **Case Study 15.3:** If Not the Commerce Clause, Then What?   353

The Dormant Commerce Clause   354

➤ **Law and Society 15.3:** *Wal-Mart Puerto Rico, Inc. v.
Juan Zaragoza-Gomez*, 834 F.3d 110 (August 24, 2016)   355

➤ **Key Takeaways:** Regulation of Business Through
the Commerce Clause   356

Regulation Through the Tax and Spend Clause   **356**

Values, Justice, Taxes, and Commerce   357

➤ **Law and Society 15.4:** *National Federation of Independent
Businesses v. Sebelius*, 567 U.S. 519 (2012)   357

➤ **Ethics in Context:** Sin Taxes   359

➤ **Key Takeaways:** Regulation Through the Tax and
Spend Clause   361

Summary   **361**

Key Terms   **362**

Review Questions   **362**

Manager's Challenge   **362**

Dormant Commerce Clause   362

CHAPTER 16 • GLOBALIZATION   **363**

➤ **Learning Objectives**   363

Introduction   **363**

Globalization and Its Impact   **364**

➤ **Law and Society 16.1:** *Yahoo!, Inc. v. La Ligue Contra le Racisma et
L'Antisemitisma*, 433 F.3d 1199 (9th Cir. 2006)   368

➤ **Key Takeaways:** Globalization and Its Impacts   370

International Trade   **370**

➤ **Case Study 16.1:** Globalization and Brexit   371

➤ **Key Takeaways:** International Trade and Barriers   374

Human Aspects of Globalization   **375**

➤ **Ethics in Context:** Think and Act Globally   377

➤ **Key Takeaways:** Human Aspects of Globalization   378

Summary   **378**

Key Terms   **378**

Review Questions   379
Manager's Challenge   379
    Managing International Assignments   379

Glossary   **380**

Notes   **392**

Index   **415**

PREFACE

This first edition of *Business and Society: Ethical, Legal, and Digital Environments* is designed to fill a growing void in the business and society field, namely the parallel conversation occurring in many universities that separate ethics from the law. Or that preference of one over the other in combined courses. Yet every manager, or aspiring manager, must consider ethics and the law together in their efforts to be effective. At the same time, it is impossible to ignore the way in which technology has changed the business and society relationship. However, in most business and society textbooks, legal issues are either covered in a superficial manner or not at all, and the coverage of the digital environment is sparse.

In reality, managing multiple stakeholders and making multiple decisions every day, managers routinely face ethical challenges, legal requirements, and digital opportunities and challenges. Since our world today is not only global but increasingly digital as a result, these concerns must also be at the forefront of teaching future managers how to effectively manage a business *within* the society they are a part of.

Our mission is to prepare future managers so they understand appropriate business responses to the ethical, legal, and digital challenges they will undoubtedly face as they embark on their careers in today's global society.

STRUCTURE OF THE BOOK

The first six chapters focus on laying the groundwork for managers. Accordingly, we discuss stakeholder and shareholder perspectives of the firm, corporate social responsibility (CSR), ethics and ethical reasoning, public policy, liability, and business agreements. The next five chapters focus on unique stakeholders every manager must become familiar with in order to manage effectively. The remaining chapters focus on the topical issues in today's society—social media and citizen movements, big data and hacking, privacy, and globalization.

Nearly every chapter features the following sections:

- *Ethics in Context:* This section examines a relevant and thought-provoking ethical challenge that raises multiple issues for stakeholders. Students are asked to apply different ethical frameworks. Instructors will appreciate the in-depth coverage of related ethical issues throughout.

- *Case Study:* This section examines real-world situations in business and allows students to think critically about the events that occurred and asks them to challenge themselves to think about how they may have handled situations or if alternative outcomes may have been achieved if a different approach was taken. Instructors will appreciate the in-depth coverage of related ethical issues throughout.

- *Law and Society:* This section provides an in-depth summary of a recent legal case and asks students to think more broadly about the decision and how it might impact society and business. Instructors will appreciate the in-depth coverage of related legal cases.

- *Point–Counterpoint*: This section presents conflicting views or positions about a relevant chapter topic to illustrate that not every issue is clearly black and white. Students and instructors are able to investigate different positions stakeholders might hold about a relevant issue or concept and thus be better prepared.

- *Manager's Challenge:* This section enables students an opportunity to apply concepts from the chapter with a realistic business challenge. Instructors will be able to have students apply their knowledge to a real managerial challenge, enlivening the classroom discussion or serving as a useful assignment.

Some of these features include companies like Juul, Glassdoor, Uber, Facebook, TripAdvisor, Amazon, Abercrombie & Fitch, ExxonMobil, and Google, as well as topics like fintech, citizen surveillance, #MeToo, diversity and inclusion, GPS and employee tracking, the circular economy, artificial intelligence (AI), environmental footprint, sustainable development, and more.

APPLICABLE COURSES

This textbook is ideal for college and university courses that are titled Business and Society; Business and Its Environment; Organizations and Environment; Organizations, Society, and Responsible Management; The Legal and Ethical Environment of Business; Social Issues in Management; Business, Government, and Society; Stakeholder Management; Business & Technology; and Business Ethics.

This book is appropriate for either a required or elective course seeking to meet the requirements of the Association to Advance Collegiate Schools of Business (AACSB) for coverage of perspectives that form the context for business: legal, ethical, and global issues; the influence of political, social, legal and regulatory, environmental, and technological issues; and the impact of diversity on organizations. The book is primarily intended for undergraduate courses, but when supplemented with other materials it would be appropriate for graduate courses. It is global throughout all chapters, by design, as students are themselves global.

DIGITAL RESOURCES

At SAGE we know your time is valuable. To improve efficiency and effectiveness in teaching your classes and to help engage your students, we cultivate an impressive array of tools and resources for review, study, and further exploration, keeping both instructors and students on the cutting edge of teaching and learning. Please visit the product page for this book at us.sagepub.com to access those materials. Learning and teaching has never been easier!

ACKNOWLEDGMENTS

First, we would like to thank our reviewers, who gave us many insights into how to make each chapter read and educate more effectively. We would also like to thank Professor Rachel Spooner for her contribution and input on the book; Darcy Scelsi and Megan Markanich for invaluable editing and patience; and Maggie Stanley for her advice, guidance, and insight into all things publishing.

Second, we would like to express gratitude to our professional colleagues in the Academy of Legal Studies in Business, the North Atlantic Regional Business Law Association, the Social Issues in Management Division of the Academy of Management, the International Association for Business and Society, and the Society for Business Ethics. Many colleagues helped us provide a stimulating environment in which to discuss this book and its contents, and some are cited in this edition. We appreciate their work and recognize that our textbook is better for it.

SAGE wishes to thank the following reviewers for their valuable feedback during the development of this book:

David Bartlett, *American University*

Hossein Bidgoli, *California State University, Bakersfield*

Barry J. Brock, *Barry University*

Diane P. Caggiano, *Fitchburg State University*

Veronica Diaz, *Florida Atlantic University*

Jerry Gladwell, *Marshall University*

Bernie N. Hayen, *Kansas State University*

Johndavid Kerr, *Harris-Stowe State University*

John R. Lego, *Pennsylvania State University*

MarySheila E. McDonald, *La Salle University*

Frank J. Mendelson, *Savannah State University*

Amit Mukherjee, *Stockton University*

Jeffrey Muldoon, *Emporia State University*

Susan A. O'Sullivan-Gavin, *Rider University*

Fatma Pakdil, *Eastern Connecticut State University*

Steven Palmer, *Northwestern Oklahoma State University*

Kathy Parkison, *Indiana University Kokomo*

Jared L. Peifer, *Baruch College*

Michael R. Poretti, *William Paterson University*

Douglas Scripture, *Indiana University South Bend*

Joy Turnheim Smith, *Elizabeth City State University*

Lei Wang, *University of Texas Rio Grande Valley*

Christina L. Yoder, *Mount St. Mary's University*

ABOUT THE AUTHORS

Cynthia E. Clark is a professor of organization studies at Bentley University. She primarily teaches Organizations, Society and Responsible Management in the undergraduate program and Ethics, Social Responsibility and Corporate Governance in the MBA and PhD programs. She has conducted numerous training sessions for practitioners on topics such as ethical decision-making, activism, and optimal nominating and governance procedures to boards of directors. Professor Clark's research interests concern ethics and governance issues in organizations, such as conflicts of interest, shareholder activism, privacy breaches, and disclosing information, with a particular focus on how firms address them. Recently published work has appeared in *Harvard Business Review*, *Strategic Management Journal*, *Business Ethics Quarterly*, *Journal of Business Ethics*, *MIS Quarterly*, *Organization & Environment*, and *Business & Society*. Professor Clark serves on the editorial board of *Business & Society*. Additionally, she is an active member and Governance Fellow with the National Association of Corporate Directors (NACD), the Society for Governance Professionals, and 2020 Women on Boards. She has been widely cited in the media on governance issues, including the *Wall Street Journal*, the *Boston Globe*, CNN, *Fortune*, Reuters, and Bloomberg Radio. Prior to joining Bentley, Clark was a member of the faculty at Boston University, following a career in the banking and securities industry. She holds a PhD from the honors program at Boston University, a master's degree from Northwestern University, and a BA from Boston College.

Kabrina K. Chang is a clinical associate professor of business law and ethics in the Markets, Public Policy, and Law Department at Boston University's Questrom School of Business. She teaches Introduction to Business Law and Employment Law in the undergraduate program and Business Law in the MBA program. Professor Chang also developed and co-coordinated Business, Society, and Ethics, a gateway course for all Questrom School of Business students. She is the director of academic integrity initiatives for Questrom and is leading university-wide academic integrity initiatives. Professor Chang's research focuses on employment matters, in particular social media, and how that impacts employment and management decisions and also on corporate social advocacy. Her work has been published in academic journals and news outlets such at the *New York Times*, Quartz.com, Bloomberg, and the *Boston Globe* as well as in magazines such as *Forbes* and *Harvard Business Review*. Professor Chang has won several awards for her teaching and writing. Before her academic career, Professor Chang was a trial lawyer in private practice.

Sean P. Melvin is an associate professor of business law and has taught at Elizabethtown College since 2000. Professor Melvin is the author of five books (including two textbooks), has contributed to over two dozen scholarly and professional articles and case studies to various publications, and is a member of the Academy of Legal Studies in Business. His most recent textbook, *The Legal Environment of Business: A Managerial Approach*, was published by McGraw-Hill/Irwin in October 2010 and is in use at over 100 colleges and universities. His recent article *Case Study of a Coffee War: Starbucks v. Charbucks* won "Best Case

Study" and "Distinguished Proceedings" at the 86th Annual Meeting of the Academy of Legal Studies in Business and was published in the Spring 2012 volume of *Journal of Legal Studies Education*. Before his academic career, Professor Melvin was a corporate lawyer in a large Philadelphia-based law firm and went on to become vice president and general counsel at a publicly traded technology company in King of Prussia, Pennsylvania. Melvin earned his juris doctor degree from Rutgers Law School, where he was awarded the American Jurisprudence Award in Business Organizations.

PART I

MANAGING IN TODAY'S BUSINESS WORLD

CHAPTER 1: Stakeholder and Shareholder Theories
of the Firm

CHAPTER 2: Corporate Social Responsibility

CHAPTER 3: Ethics and Ethical Reasoning

CHAPTER 4: Organizations and Public Policy

CHAPTER 5: Liability, Business Agreements, and
Managing Risk

CHAPTER 6: Government Regulation of Business

STAKEHOLDER AND SHAREHOLDER THEORIES OF THE FIRM

Ethics in Context

Competing Stakeholder Demands at Amazon

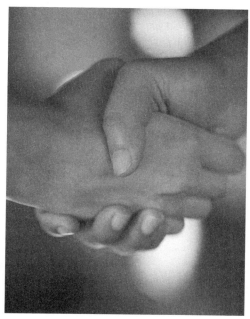

iStockphoto.com/ShotShare

Businesses have a vested interest in managing different stakeholder groups. Similarly, various stakeholders closely monitor what businesses do and how they treat them. While the interests of various stakeholders and businesses may not always align, some view managing stakeholders as an ethical issue. Does a person or a group have the moral right to be treated in a certain way by a company? Later in the chapter, in the Ethics in Context section, we will examine the ethical implications of conflicting stakeholder demands.

Learning Objectives

Upon completion of this chapter, the reader should be able to do the following:

1.1 Describe what is a stake and who is a stakeholder.

1.2 Explain the difference between shareholder and stakeholder theories of the firm.

1.3 Articulate the main issues in the stakeholder and shareholder debate.

1.4 Describe stakeholders in terms of issues, powers, and interests.

1.5 Assess the issues that may arise when businesses try to manage various stakeholder interests.

INTRODUCTION

The role and influence of a broader set of "stakeholders" of a business organization has become a very common theme in the business and society landscape. Often this perspective is juxtaposed to the "shareholder" perspective. There are many reasons for managers and researchers alike to think of these two perspectives as if coming from different camps. While there are differences in these two predominant theories of the firm, there are also similarities and overlaps. Each stakeholder has different powers, issues, and interests. And while most stakeholder groups are thought to have certain characteristics, a person can be a part of one or more stakeholder groups simultaneously. Managing multiple stakeholders at one time—something managers are routinely pressured to do—can be a challenge given there are also conflicts between these groups.

DEFINING *STAKE* AND *STAKEHOLDER*

LO 1.1   Describe what is a stake and who is a stakeholder.

stake: A kind of interest in or claim on something of value.

claim: A legal entitlement or a right to be treated in a certain way.

To understand the concept of a stakeholder, it helps to start with its root—a stake. A stake is a kind of interest in or claim on something of value.[1] For example, a person or a group who is affected by a certain decision has an *interest* in that decision. A claim could be a legal entitlement or a right to be treated in a certain way—or even a formal request.[2] In R. Edward Freeman's influential book on stakeholder management, "stakes" are multidimensional and represent stakeholders' issues of concern about the company.[3]

One additional idea to keep in mind is that multinational corporations (MNCs)—some of the largest of which are Microsoft, Google, FedEx, Diageo, and Marriott—operate in many and varying legal jurisdictions, so they often face additional pressures because the claims made on them may be numerous and therefore difficult to resolve, both for formal reasons, such as differences in legal institutions or competing legal requirements and jurisdictional conflicts, and for informal reasons, such as cultural differences. For example, Google has faced criticism for its practices resulting from differences in the privacy rights of stakeholders in Europe, China, and the United States. We will discuss globalization more in Chapter 16.

stakeholder: Any identifiable group or individual who can affect the achievement of an organization's objectives or who is affected by the achievement of an organization's objectives.

The term stakeholder was coined by the Stanford Research Institute in the early 1960s, but later, two academic scholars—Edward Freeman and David Reed—proposed a broad definition of stakeholder as "any identifiable group or individual who can affect the achievement of an organization's objectives or who is affected by the achievement of an organization's objectives."[4] They contrast this definition with a narrow sense of stakeholder as "any identifiable group or individual on which the organization is dependent for its continued survival."[5]

shareholder: A person, group, or organization owning one or more shares of stock in a corporation.

While the broad sense definition reveals the perception that multiple and varied groups affect and are affected by the firm, termed the *stakeholder perspective* or *theory*, the narrow sense definition can lead to interpretations that shareholders, as a stakeholder group, deserve primacy because they are the foundation of a firm's survival. Shareholders are directly relevant to the firm's core economic interest, which represents the *shareholder perspective* or *theory*.[6] A shareholder, or sometimes known as a stockholder or investor, is a person, group, or organization owning one or more shares of stock in a corporation.

Defining _Stake_ and _Stakeholder_

- A stake is a kind of interest in or claim on something of value.

- A stakeholder is any identifiable group or individual who can affect the achievement of an organization's objectives or who is affected by the achievement of an organization's objectives.

- A shareholder is a person, group, or organization owning one or more shares of stock in a corporation. A shareholder is also stakeholder.

STAKEHOLDER VERSUS SHAREHOLDER THEORIES

LO 1.2   Explain the difference between shareholder and stakeholder theories of the firm.

Theory provides a road map that allows us to make sense of unfamiliar terrain. Even when we think we are just using common sense, there is usually a theory guiding our actions. A theory is a set of propositions or concepts that seek to _explain or predict_ something.

Stakeholder- and shareholder-oriented theories are both what are called _normative_ theories of corporate responsibility—advocating for what a firm _ought_ to be—that is, its purpose.[7] Some theorists have suggested that one perspective should, or will, eventually replace the other[8] or even that the two are contradictory and incompatible.[9] Positioning these as distinct theoretical camps has resulted in overlooking the possibility that shareholder and stakeholder perspectives might complement one another.[10]

There are two critical questions when talking about theories of the firm. Stakeholder and shareholder theories or perspectives answer these questions differently.

- What is the purpose of the modern corporation?

- To whom, or what, should the firm be responsible?

> **theory:** A set of propositions or concepts that seeks to explain or predict something.

Stakeholder Theory

There is general consensus that **stakeholder theory** operates when management believes there is a moral obligation for a firm to work toward addressing the needs of customers, employees, suppliers, and the local community as well as shareowners, keeping these needs and interests in "balance" not simply so it will benefit the firm in the long run but because it is the right thing to do.[11] It is also generally acknowledged that managers need to engage in making trade-offs but must also be accountable to multiple stakeholder groups.[12]

There is a growing assertion that responsible management, which balances the legitimate stakes of internal and external constituencies, can lead to higher financial return. However, additional research requires a second look at the concern over any real trade-offs between shareholder objectives and social responsibility.[13]

> **stakeholder theory:** Creating value for society beyond a pure monetary benefit for shareholders, sometimes referred to as there being a moral obligation to work toward addressing the needs of customers, employees, suppliers, and the local community as well as shareowners, and keeping these needs and interests in balance.

While managers need to focus on generating profits in order to be sustainable, stakeholder theory emphasizes creating value for society beyond a pure monetary benefit for shareholders. Likewise, the obligation of managers extends to consider the interests of all stakeholders even if doing so reduces company profitability.[14]

There are three key questions for managers to consider with stakeholder theory:

1. If this decision is made, for whom is value created or destroyed?

2. Whose rights were enabled or not?

3. What kind of person would I be if I make this decision in a particular way?[15]

Multinational firms approach stakeholder theory a bit differently. They tend to add local stakeholder obligations as the process of globalization unfolds over time and most often manage these obligations centrally, at the firm's headquarters, but actively allocate responsibilities to subdivisions. This central coordination is most beneficial when it is integrated with already established multinational stakeholder groups which share the firm's goals (e.g., the United Nations Global Compact or the World Wildlife Federation).[16]

Shareholder Theory

The **shareholder theory** claims that managers should spend capital, given to them by shareholders initially, in ways that have been authorized by shareholders and act in the shareholders' interests.[17] In fact, some have argued that managers assume what is called a fiduciary duty to use various company resources in ways that have been authorized by the stockholders—regardless of any societal benefits or detriments.[18] **Fiduciary duty** involves trust that *one* party will act in the best interests of another, owing them a duty of loyalty and care.[19] Likewise, there is an underlying belief that shareowners' interests ought to take precedence over the interests of all other groups. In part, the theory and practice of corporate governance relies on this premise. **Corporate governance** is defined as the rules, processes, and procedures as outlined by an organization's board of directors to ensure accountability, fairness, and transparency among all parties with a claim on the organization.

The shareholder theory focuses on the firm's ability to provide long-term market value for shareholders[20] regardless of the benefits or detriments to other organizational or societal constituents.[21] The shareholder view also rests on the belief that a firm is better able to achieve competitive advantage because it allows managers to be unencumbered by other stakeholders' concerns.[22] This focus appeals to managers wanting to lower the cost of capital necessary for expansion and consequently gain better access to the capital markets—both of which some argue is the best reasoning for a global convergence of the stockholder form.[23]

Generally, this view supports the idea that firms must put shareholders' interests above all others because the firm is the property of its (share)owners. The owners' interests take precedence over the interests of all other groups because of the recognition of a special relationship between the firm and its shareholders.[24] Professor Cynthia E. Clark and her colleagues created a table comparing and contrasting some of the key elements of both perspectives, which is adapted in Table 1.1.[25]

In shareholder theory, managers must ask themselves the following:

1. How do we measure "better" versus "worse" with regard to what we are trying to do?

shareholder theory: A shareholder-oriented view of the firm's responsibilities claims that managers should spend capital, given to them by shareholders initially, in ways that have been authorized by shareholders and act in the shareholders' interests.

fiduciary duty: The trust that *one* party will act in the best interests of another, owing them a duty of loyalty and care.

corporate governance: The rules, processes, and procedures as outlined by an organization's board of directors to ensure accountability, fairness, and transparency among all parties with a claim on the organization.

2. How do we best maximize long-term value?

3. Who should decide value: managers or shareholders?[26]

Table 1.1 Stakeholder and Shareholder Theories

Characteristic	Stakeholder Theory	Shareholder Theory
Fiduciary relations	Multifiduciary—Obligations of loyalty and care are owed to multiple parties.[i]	Single fiduciary—Shareholders have a special role, and these obligations are owed only to them.[ii]
Moral claim	Shareowner's theory is morally untenable.[iii]	Stakeholder theory is morally inadequate.[iv]
Sources of legitimacy	Stakeholders' relationship with firm; nature of request	Shareholder primacy[v]
Sources of power	Access to resources[vi]	Residual risk bearers[vii]
Basis of strategy	Stakeholders have intrinsic value; management selects activities and directs resources to obtain benefits for legitimate stakeholders.[viii]	Direct resources and capabilities are toward shareholder value; management has free hand to direct externalities to society and even may have obligation to do so.
Governance mechanism	Nonshareholding stakeholders should have board representation.	Manager (agent) works on behalf of principal (owner); only shareowners have representation on board and voting rights; and shareholders ought to have control.[ix]
Attitude toward social responsibility or purpose	"The survival and continuing profitability of the corporation depend upon its ability to fulfill its economic and social purpose, which is to create and distribute wealth or value sufficient to ensure that each primary stakeholder group continues as part of the corporation's stakeholder system" (Clarkson, 1995, p. 110).[x]	"What does it mean to say that 'business' has responsibilities? Only people can have responsibilities. That responsibility is to conduct the business in accordance with their desires, which generally will be to make as much money as possible while conforming to the basic rules of the society, both those embodied in law and those embodied in ethical custom" (Friedman, 1970).[xi]

[i]For a discussion of both approaches, see Goodpaster, K. E. (1991). Business ethics and stakeholder analysis. *Business Ethics Quarterly*, 1, 53–73.

[ii]See Marcoux, A. M. (2003). A fiduciary argument against stakeholder theory. *Business Ethics Quarterly*, 13, 1–24.

[iii]This is mainly based on an article by Donaldson, T., & Preston, L. E. (1995). The stakeholder theory of the corporation: Concepts, evidence, and implications. *Academy of Management Review*, 20, 65–91; it is also based on related citations.

[iv]This is mainly based on an article by Marcoux (2003) and related citations.

[v]Shareholder primacy tends to regularly render legitimate all corporate efforts on behalf of shareholders and to render irregular those efforts on behalf of other constituents and, further, that such efforts need of some type of justification—cf. Boatright, J. R. (1994). Fiduciary duties and the shareholder-management relation: Or, what's so special about shareholders. *Business Ethics Quarterly*, 4, 393–407.

[vi]See Frooman, J. (1999). Stakeholder influence strategies. *Academy of Management Review*, 24, 191–205; Eesley, C., & Lenox, M. J. (2006). Firm responses to secondary stakeholder action. *Strategic Management Journal*, 27, 765–781.

[vii]See Boatright (1994).

[viii]See Donaldson & Preston (1995).

[ix]See Boatright, J. R. (2006). What's wrong—and what's right—with stakeholder management. *Journal of Private Enterprise*, 21, 106–130.

[x]Clarkson, M. B. E. (1995). A stakeholder framework for analyzing and evaluating corporate social performance. *Academy of Management Review* 20, 92–127.

[xi]Friedman, M. (1970, September 13). The social responsibility of business is to increase its profits. *The New York Times Magazine*, 32–33, 122, 124, 126.

Source: Adapted from Clark, C. E., Steckler, E. L., & Newell, S. (2016). Managing contradiction: Stockholder and stakeholder views of the firm as paradoxical opportunity. *Business and Society Review*, 121, 123–159.

KEY TAKEAWAYS

> ### Stakeholder Versus Shareholder Theories
>
> - Both theories are *normative* theories, and both advocate for what a firm *ought* to be: the purpose the firm plays in society.
>
> - The *shareholder theory* supports the idea that firms must put shareholders' interests above all others because the firm is the property of its (share) owners. The owners' interests take precedence over the interests of
>
> all other groups because of the recognition of this special relationship.
>
> - The *stakeholder theory* supports the idea that there is a moral obligation for a firm to work toward addressing the needs of customers, employees, suppliers, and the local community as well as shareowners not simply so it will benefit the firm in the long run but because it is the right thing to do.

THE STAKEHOLDER AND SHAREHOLDER DEBATE

LO 1.3   Articulate the main issues in the stakeholder and shareholder debate.

There is considerable debate about which theory is better at describing how a company should operate. This debate is ongoing and complex. There are descriptive, instrumental, normative, moral, and legal arguments in this debate.

The Stakeholder Arguments

In an attempt to clarify and justify the stakeholder theory over the shareholder theory, researchers Tom Donaldson and Lee Preston conceptualized the descriptive, instrumental, and normative arguments. These authors model these three aspects of the theory in a bull's-eye fashion, with normative at the core and descriptive at the outer edge (see Figure 1.1).

Stakeholder theory defined in a descriptive manner literally describes how firms operate, arguing that the stakeholder approach is more representative of how firms truly operate. There is little doubt that stakeholder language is very common; for example, corporate websites, brochures, and Instagram posts are filled with firm's using the word *stakeholder* or expressing their concern for stakeholders.

Stakeholder theory defined from an instrumental perspective is characterized by attempts to find evidence of connections between stakeholder management and positive financial performance. Stakeholders are a means to an end in that they contribute to achieving better performance overall. Here, firms are more likely to work toward the goal of better financial performance and see stakeholders as secondary.

Defining *stakeholder theory* from a normative perspective, stakeholders have value regardless of their instrumental use to managers or the firm. Adopting this view requires managers to endorse the attitude that all stakeholders have a legitimate stake in the firm, that they have *intrinsic* value. Here, firms work directly with stakeholders because they are a primary concern. In fact, Donaldson and Preston argue that stakeholder theory is fundamentally normative because of its guidance about what are right and wrong behaviors. In other words, a stakeholder approach should be adopted simply because it is the right thing

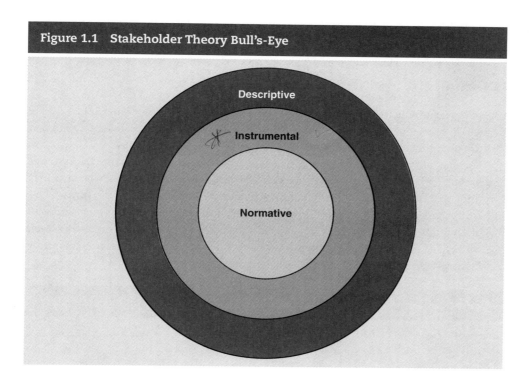

Figure 1.1   Stakeholder Theory Bull's-Eye

Descriptive

Instrumental

Normative

to do. What's more is they maintain that a shareholder approach to the firm, which treats one group as superior, is therefore not morally supportable.

The Shareholder Arguments

Some shareholder theorists, in turn, claim a lack of a moral foundation in stakeholder theory. The main criticism of stakeholder theory by shareholder theorists is that it appears morally and practically unworkable to orient firms' decisions that bear on the fiduciary duties of managers to anyone but stockholders. Because shareholders hold a special moral status in their relationship with managers, a stakeholder approach is morally inadequate.[27] This description of fiduciary duties refers to a prioritization, a commitment to advancing the interests of that special group over those of another party—very much like a doctor has to a patient. From this perspective, a firm simply cannot have multiple fiduciary duties (as stakeholder theory asserts) because if it did it would require trade-offs, compromises, and multiple loyalties that it cannot sustain because of the very meaning of the word *fiduciary*.[28]

Finally, a legal perspective on the debate is provided by Professor Lynn Stout, who observes that shareholder primacy is often granted as a result of ownership, which she noted is not quite accurate legally.[29] From a legal standpoint, she contends, stockholders do not own the corporation but merely a stock. This stock provides the stockholder with certain rights, which are limited. For example, Stout highlights that stockholders do not have the right to control the firm's assets or to decide on the distribution of the firm's earnings. Stout also notes that shareholder primacy is often granted on the premise that stockholders are the sole residual claimants of the firm, which, from a legal position, stockholders are only residual claimants in the case of bankruptcy. But even if the law cannot be counted on to enforce the shareholder theory, economic forces might drive the board of directors and thus the managers they oversee to embrace it.[30] Figure 1.2 is illustrative of each side of the debate.

Is One Right and One Wrong?

Given these contradictory arguments, some suggest the stakeholder and stockholder debate is based on a series of misrepresentations about what they stand for (see Table 1.2) and that they are not mutually exclusive.[31]

For one, numerous stakeholders can benefit from managers prioritizing the interests of shareholders. For example, some argue that all constituents are better off when the firm is run for shareholders because it forces an accountable management of the firm's assets and creates greater overall wealth.[32] Professor John Boatright thinks that "any successful corporation must manage its relations with all stakeholder groups, if for no other reason than to benefit the shareholders" by not necessarily serving each group's interest but by considering their interests "sufficiently to gain their cooperation."[33]

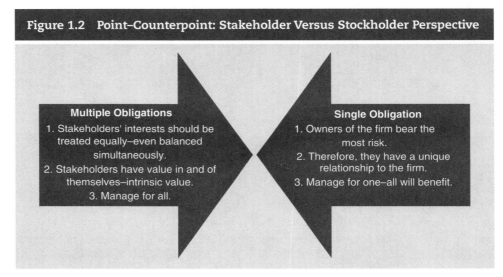

Figure 1.2   Point–Counterpoint: Stakeholder Versus Stockholder Perspective

Multiple Obligations
1. Stakeholders' interests should be treated equally—even balanced simultaneously.
2. Stakeholders have value in and of themselves—intrinsic value.
3. Manage for all.

Single Obligation
1. Owners of the firm bear the most risk.
2. Therefore, they have a unique relationship to the firm.
3. Manage for one—all will benefit.

Source: Adapted from Clark, C., Steckler, E., & Newell, S. (2016). Managing contradiction: Stockholder and stakeholder views of the firm as paradoxical opportunity. *Business and Society Review,* 121(1): 123–159.

Table 1.2   Misrepresentations of Each Theory

Shareholder Theory Misrepresentations

- Firms do anything to make a profit.
- Firms focus on short-term profits.
- Firms are prohibited from giving to charity or nonprofits.

Stakeholder Theory Misrepresentations

- There is no demand that firms make a profit.
- The theory can't be practically implemented.

Two, since most firms today have evolved from the traditional family-operated business to corporations with dispersed ownership, there are several subsets of specific interest groups even within the shareholder group. For example, shareholders can be long-term investors interested in a retirement income, short-term investors seeking to make a noticeable profit every quarter, or activists who acquired a share of the firm in order to press interests as varied as environmental preservation to women's rights or animal protection.[34]

Three, academics argue that a basis for both the shareholder and the stakeholder theories of the firm exists in the law through the concept of fiduciary duties. But while traditional American law posits firms as fiduciaries of their owners (the shareholders), many states have amended the law to allow managers to take into consideration a wider range of other stakeholders' interests, reflecting the increasing pressure by multiple stakeholders for firms to endorse responsibility and accountability for social issues as well as economic issues. Still, H. Jeff Smith believes managers and firms that do not achieve profitability, operating either under a stakeholder or stockholder framework, will likely be penalized for underperformance by being removed by the board of directors or taken over by a competitor.[35] In fact, recently the Business Roundtable, a group of large company CEOs and a powerful voice in Washington for U.S. business interests, called for a new purpose for corporations: to view each stakeholder as essential and deliver value for all of them. This departs from its former statement of purpose, which focused on an obligation to provide value for shareholders alone.[xii]

Lastly, others suggest that despite the persistence of these opposing theories, there are two key aspects where they complement one another: accountability and value.[36]

Shareholder theories argue managers should be held accountable for a single goal, such as shareholder value, and thus held accountable to shareholders for increasing the wealth of the firm's shareholders to the extent possible.[37] On the other hand, normative stakeholder theory suggests firms should manage with multiple and competing stakeholder interests in mind while not holding shareholder interests above others. And those adopting a stakeholder perspective would tend to argue that managers are accountable to all legitimate interests or to legitimate groups.[38]

As we mentioned previously, a fundamental question asked by both shareholder and stakeholder theory is this: For whose primary benefit is this firm managed? If we were to say the shareholders, we could equally say that we are all shareholders given the contemporary dependence on the financial markets for anything from retirement to routine banking to college savings. Likewise, we could say the firm is managed for stakeholders and recognize that employees, consumers, and suppliers can also be shareholders.

As you might guess, the term *value* has also been defined by both stakeholder and shareholder theorists. Recently, academics from the shareholder perspective have moved toward saying "maximizing total firm value" instead of "maximizing the value of the firm's equity" in recent years.[39] Further to the point, "total value created is the value created for all business model stakeholders (focal firm, customers, suppliers, and other exchange partners)".[40] This premise is complementary to the central idea of stakeholder theory: "focusing on stakeholders, specifically treating them well and managing for their interests, helps a firm create value along a number of dimensions and is therefore good for firm performance."[41] It is also complementary to the principle of shared value, which involves creating

[xii] Business Roundtable Redefines the Purpose of a Corporation to Promote "An Economy That Serves All Americans' Business Roundtable. (2019, August 19). Retrieved from https://www.businessroundtable.org/business-roundtable-redefines-the-purpose-of-a-corporation-to-promote-an-economy-that-serves-all-americans

economic value in a way that also creates value for society by addressing its needs and challenges.[42]

So do you think there is some overlap in these two perspectives?

KEY TAKEAWAYS

The Stakeholder and Shareholder Debate

- Stakeholder theory is described in normative, instrumental, legal, and descriptive ways. The instrumental version is very similar to shareholder theory. The debate centers on whether the purpose of the firm is to put stakeholders or stockholders first.

- Both theories emphasize the need for value and accountability by firms.

- The stakeholder versus stockholder debate is really based on a series of misrepresentations about what each stands for.

STAKEHOLDER TYPES: INTERESTS, ISSUES, LEGITIMACY, AND POWER

LO 1.4 Describe stakeholders in terms of issues, powers, and interests.

While the debate continues, managers are often faced with limited resources to allocate as well as multiple and competing demands from stakeholders—sometimes every day. So the question becomes who and what should managers pay attention to and in what priority? That is, which stakeholder groups or issues should take precedence over others?

Market and Nonmarket Stakeholders

While stakeholders can be *any* identifiable group or individual—public interest groups, protest groups, government agencies, trade associations, competitors, and unions, as well as employees, customer segments, shareowners, and other stakeholders[43]—they have increasingly been divided into two categories based on their value to the firm.[44]

While traditionally thought of as primary and secondary stakeholders, they have increasingly been categorized as market based and nonmarket based with the following characteristics:[45]

- Market stakeholders—Engage in economic transactions with the company as it carries out its primary purpose (see Figure 1.3).

- Nonmarket stakeholders—Do not engage in direct economic exchange with the firm but are affected by the firm or can affect the firm (see Figure 1.4).

From a firm-centric viewpoint as depicted in Figures 1.3 and 1.4, these sets of stakeholders can seem very separate from one another because of the categories they are placed in. However, researchers and managers alike have emphasized that they are interrelated

12 PART I • MANAGING IN TODAY'S BUSINESS WORLD

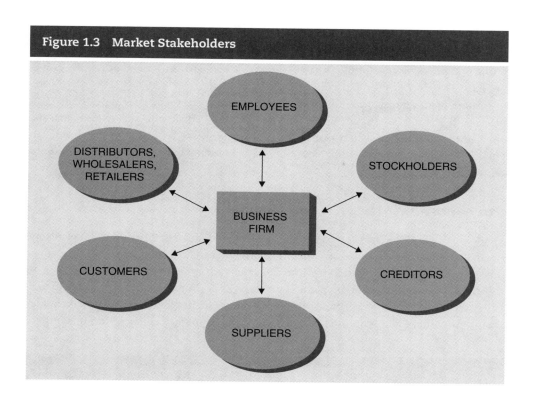

Figure 1.3 Market Stakeholders

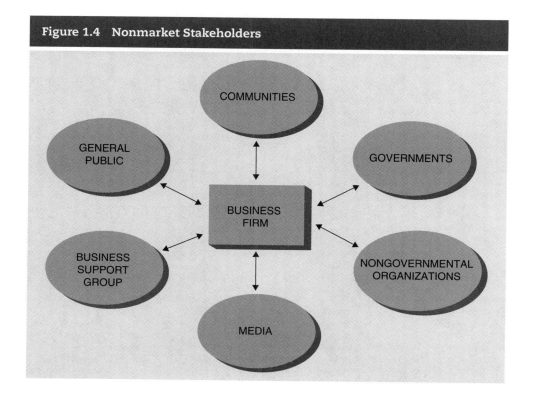

Figure 1.4 Nonmarket Stakeholders

and not always voluntary. For example, engaging with the nonmarket environment may be voluntary, such as when the firm adopts a policy of developing relationships with government officials, or involuntary when government regulates an activity or activist groups organize a boycott of a firm's product.[46]

Some managers advocate for products, services, or certain stakeholder groups to be placed at the center (see Figure 1.5); otherwise, this firm-centric approach tends to marginalize other stakeholders even if that is not the explicit intent.[47] Novo Nordisk, headquartered in Denmark and the leading developer of diabetes medication, places patients in the center of its activities.

Stakeholder Interests and Power

While there are different ways to categorize stakeholders, most firms find the challenge lies in how to prioritize and engage them. Determining what their interests are, what their power base is, and how salient to the firm they are is a common starting point.

Because stakeholders are dynamic by nature, they do not have the same characteristics, especially in terms of their power, legitimacy, issues, and interests. Stakeholder groups often have common interests and will form temporary alliances to pursue these

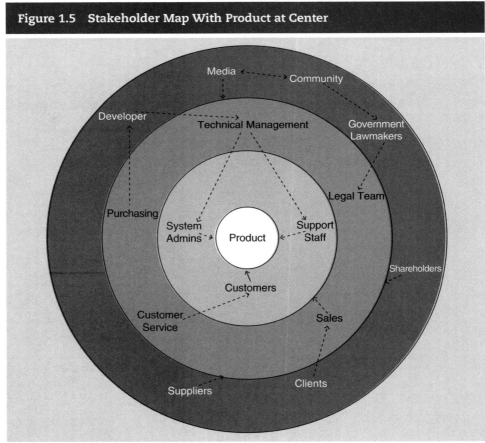

Figure 1.5   Stakeholder Map With Product at Center

Source: BAwiki | A Reference and Blog for Business Analysts. David Olson.

common interests. Analyzing stakeholder interests typically includes addressing two key questions.

1. What are the groups' issues or concerns?

2. What does each group want or expect from their relationship with the firm?

Issues are the basic unit of analysis when thinking about stakeholder identification and engagement and often result when there is a discrepancy between what is expected from a firm in terms of responsible management and what is actually provided—its performance on those expectations. It is important to differentiate between stakeholder issues, which are defined as the concerns that stakeholder groups nurture in regard to the firm's activities, and social issues, which pertain to the social context in which the firm exists, addressing economic, social, political, or technological concerns.

Both market and nonmarket stakeholders have issues they are concerned about. For example, with Juul Labs, Inc., the largest e-cigarette company, parents, physicians, and regulators have become increasingly concerned about underage use of its vaping products. All three are nonmarket stakeholders. However, they may be part of its adult customer base or they may not use the product. Its current adult customers who are not underage, versus its youth customers, are concerned about a potential shutdown of a company whose products are far less deadly than cigarettes and may offer them a way to eventually quit smoking. As the Juul example indicates, it can be challenging to put stakeholders in clearly defined groups because many overlap. In Case Study 1.1, we discuss these overlapping and conflicting stakeholder challenges in more detail.

Juul's E-Cigarettes and Teens

Juul Labs, Inc. is a San Francisco-based e-cigarette company started by two Stanford University graduate students in 2015. Adam Bowen and Adam Monsees set out to make a replacement for cigarettes that was both appealing and less risky to use. In fact, they thought of it as a sort of off-ramp for adult smokers, wanting "cigarettes to become obsolete," according to Monsees.[48] From that simple wish, Juul has become a high-growth enterprise in just a few short years. Today, the company mission is to improve the lives of the world's 1 billion smoking adults.[49] Juul's products are estimated to be 75% of a $2.5 billion e-cigarette marketing in the United States alone. According to the National Youth Tobacco Survey, reported in the *Wall Street Journal*, one out of every five of high school students use e-cigarettes, up 78% between 2017 and 2018, and 5% of all middle schoolers use them, up 48%.[50] In the summer of 2018, the company was valued at $16 billion and raised $1.25 billion from investors wanting to back the future success of this venture.[51] The company is not publicly traded. Altria Group owns a 35% stake in the e-cigarette maker.

In the fall of 2018, the company ran into intense pressure from parents, physicians, and regulators who had become increasingly concerned about underage use of its vaping products. The Food and Drug Administration (FDA) sought to curb this underage use while parents and physicians were concerned about the effects of vaping on young people whose brains are still developing into their 20s and are vulnerable to addiction, according to scientific research.[52] In mid-November 2018, in response to mounting pressure, Juul Labs shut down its Facebook and Instagram accounts, which were a large part of its growth.[53] It also stopped sales of most of its flavored e-cigarettes, particularly popular among teens, in retail stores earlier that month.[54] The FDA imposed restrictions on the sale of sweet-flavored

(Continued)

(Continued)

options like mango and cucumber, limiting them to stores that minors can't access or to online sales with age verifications. Mint-flavored e-cigarettes remained on shelves and made up about 35% of Juul's sales in 2018.[55]

In early September 2019, citing the surge in underage vaping, President Trump's administration said it planned to ban all e-cigarettes except those formulated to taste like tobacco.

On its website, Juul CEO Kevin Burns outlined the company's action plan and emphasized their common goal with the FDA. The CEO stated, "We don't want youth using the product," and it is an unintended consequence and serious problem. FDA commissioner Scott Gottlieb said, "I will not allow a generation of children to become addicted to nicotine through e-cigarettes." If sales of mint do not decline, he will "revisit this aspect." In September 2019, the Centers for Disease Control and Prevention (CDC) urged people to stop using electronic cigarettes and other vaping products while they investigate several deaths from a mysterious lung illness; it did not identify a certain brand of vaporizer.[56]

How Does It Work?

A Juulpod is the cartridge that clicks onto the top of the device, and it contains a proprietary nicotine e-liquid formula that creates the actual vapor. The vapor is created when the e-liquid is heated.

Source: https://www.juul.com/our-technology

Discussion Questions

1. Given Juul Lab's reaction to regulatory concern by the FDA, which theory of the firm is the company following to help resolve the widespread concern? Explain.

2. Adult consumers are one set of stakeholders impacted by Juul's decision. Are its consumers one group with the same interests? Who might also be a consumer of these products?

3. What other stakeholders might have been involved, and what were their interests? Did all stakeholders have the same interests?

Critical Thinking

Given that the company's mission is to improve the lives of the world's 1 billion smoking adults, it plans to prevent youth from using its products while at the same time marketing to adult consumers—especially its mint product popular among both groups. How can it strike that balance? Are you convinced? Explain.

It is very common to identify which stakeholders deserve attention based on three specific attributes making them salient to firms:

1. The power of the stakeholder to influence the corporation

2. The legitimacy of the stakeholder's relationship with the corporation

3. The urgency of the stakeholder's claim on the corporation

stakeholder salience: A stakeholder group's ability to stand out or apart from something else by possessing power, legitimacy, and urgency.

Possessing these three attributes is thought to result in higher perceptions of **stakeholder salience,** the ability to stand out or apart from something else—and ultimately bring about changes in the firm's performance or current activities (see Figure 1.6).

But not everyone is convinced that power, legitimacy, and urgency are the best ways to describe who and what matters to managers and that there is a need to better understand how legitimacy, power, and urgency are different.[57] Others have noted this focus essentially argues for a shareholder primacy model—that is, a shareholder has each of these qualities through the simple quality of owning a share.[58] Still, others argue that the very definition of stakeholders—those with the ability to affect or be affected by the firm's activities—means

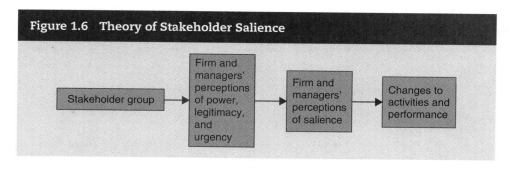

Figure 1.6 Theory of Stakeholder Salience

Stakeholder group → Firm and managers' perceptions of power, legitimacy, and urgency → Firm and managers' perceptions of salience → Changes to activities and performance

Source: Adapted from Mitchell, R. K., Agle, B. R., & Wood, D. J. (1997). Toward a theory of stakeholder identification and salience: Defining the principle of who and what really counts. *Academy of Management Review,* 22(4), 853–886.

they are legitimate and worthy of managerial attention.[59] And, finally, that urgency may not be as relevant for identifying stakeholders and instead the salience of stakeholders will vary as the degree of these attributes vary.[60] Still, it provides a useful tool to initially identify how important a stakeholder claim might be to a firm.

As we discussed earlier, the idea of a claim is central to the stakeholder perspective. Building on this idea, there are additional and interrelated concepts important to a stakeholder claim, such as its issue, its requested action, and the tactic used to make its issue and action known to management.

Some experts have argued that certain types of requested actions may be more successful than others as they provide less risk in terms of the costs and benefits associated with fulfilling the request. One example of a low-cost request is when a firm is asked to disclose information.[61] Also, certain stakeholder tactics are likely to receive more managerial attention—like those that impose greater risk to the continued survival of the firm, such as civil lawsuits rather than tactics that have little bearing on the firm's continued activities, such as letter-writing campaigns—because the latter fail to impose an economic burden on the firm while the former may create a sense of urgency.[62]

For these reasons, let's focus on stakeholder power and legitimacy and how they might interact.

What Is Stakeholder Power and Legitimacy?

Power is the ability or potential of a group to influence another and to secure a desired outcome. Power commands managerial attention in and of itself through the potential threat that it carries.[63] Power is context specific, meaning someone is not powerful or powerless alone but rather within the context of relationships with others. That is, power cannot be attributed to an issue, a request, or a tactic. **Legitimacy** represents some form of acceptance of a stakeholder's claim or of the group itself. Mark Suchman identified three primary forms of legitimacy: *pragmatic* occurs when the audience's self-interest is satisfied, *moral* is when the concerns over what ought to be are satisfied, and *cognitive* is based on whether something is taken for granted and well known or accepted (see Table 1.3).[64]

Many researchers have discussed the relationship between legitimacy and power. For example, Thomas Jones, Will Felps, and Gregory Bigley explored the dynamics between power and legitimacy by integrating an ethical perspective in the stakeholder salience debate. Using two types of values—other-regarding or self-regarding—the authors predict

power: The ability or potential of a group to influence another and to secure a desired outcome.

legitimacy: Some form of acceptance of a stakeholder's claim or of the group itself.

Table 1.3	Examples of Forms of Legitimacy
Type of Legitimacy	**Example of Type**
Pragmatic	Support for a new human resources (HR) policy based on its expected value for a particular group
Moral	Support for a new HR policy because it is the right thing to do
Cognitive	Support for a new HR policy because it would be unthinkable not to have it or because it is inevitable to do so

that firms will prioritize either the interests of stakeholders or their own because firm–stakeholder power relationships are determined by these two value orientations. They find that while self-regarding firms are more prone to exercise power over stakeholders to maintain their interests, they are also more responsive to stakeholders' power stemming from resources that are essential to their firm's operational performance. By contrast, firms that are other-regarding are more responsive to stakeholders with legitimacy as they respond more readily to moral appeals.[65]

KEY TAKEAWAYS

Stakeholder Types: Interests, Issues, Legitimacy, and Power

- Stakeholders are commonly categorized as market based and nonmarket based. The basis for these categorizations is whether or not they engage in economic transactions vital to the firm or not.

- A firm's perception of a stakeholder group's salience is based on the group's legitimacy, urgency, and power. These three attributes have different meanings, and these are important for managers to understand.

MANAGING STAKEHOLDERS

LO 1.5 Assess the issues that may arise when businesses try to manage various stakeholder interests.

Stakeholder management involves constantly monitoring and redesigning processes to better serve multiple and conflicting stakeholders. Companies may employ different strategies in terms of the degree of engagement with their stakeholders. Typically, engagement is most likely when (1) both the firm and the stakeholder recognize and share the same goal, (2) they are motivated to participate, and (3) the firm or the stakeholder have the knowledge and resources to effectively engage.[66] Given that many companies you've heard the names of are global, it's probably no surprise that stakeholder engagement has a global focus. For example, at Coca-Cola, an MNC, stakeholder engagement is carried out in a variety of formal and informal settings across the entire Coca-Cola system, including local, regional, and international stakeholders. At an international level, the company is involved in multistakeholder initiatives, such as the United Nations Global Compact and the World Economic Forum (WEF), so that it can address pressing global challenges.[67] In 2017, the company conducted workshops with more than 180 experts around the world to identify potential "impacts to people" associated with the company's activities and business relationships.

Firms can think of this in terms of four levels of commitment to practicing stakeholder management (see Table 1.4). Managers need to understand how the firm can make various stakeholders' benefit—making customers better off and simultaneously offering an attractive value proposition to employees, suppliers, communities, and shareholders (Level 1).[68] Today's competitive, economic, regulatory, and political environments are so dynamic they require firms to constantly revise their stakeholder perceptions—often upsetting the delicate balance in the basic value proposition to various stakeholders.

Managers must have a deep understanding of how these trade-offs affect each stakeholder, and they may wish to take positions on issues that are not always directly business related (Levels 2 and 3). Recent research points to a strong connection between ethical values and positive firm outcomes like long-term profitability and high innovation and motivation among employees.[69] Ethical leadership is possible when there is a deep understanding of the power, legitimacy, interests, and issues of concern of the stakeholders (Level 4).[70]

Table 1.4   Levels of Commitment to Managing Stakeholders

Level 1	Basic value proposition	How do we make our stakeholders better off? What do we stand for?
Level 2	Sustained stakeholder cooperation	What are the principles or values on which we base our everyday engagement with stakeholders?
Level 3	An understanding of broader societal issues	Do we understand how our basic value proposition and principles fit or contradict key trends and opinions in society?
Level 4	Ethical leadership	What are the values and principles that inform my leadership? What is my sense of purpose?

Managing Stakeholders

- Stakeholders have issues of concern that they bring to firms with the expectation that the firm will respond to them.

- Firms need to engage with stakeholders to know what their interests and issues are and to better manage conflicts among stakeholder groups. There are four levels of commitment to managing tensions.

KEY TAKEAWAYS

Competing Stakeholder Demands at Amazon

iStockphoto.com/ShotShare

Amazon, the publicly traded online retailer with extraordinary success and name recognition, announced in September 2017 a search for a second, equal headquarters to its home base in Seattle, Washington, known as the HQ2 decision. It stated the new location would house roughly 50,000 jobs and represent billions in investments. Amazon factored a number of qualifications for the selection of HQ2, including access to mass transit, proximity to an airport with direct flights to and from Seattle, and a pool of available tech talent nearby. In November 2018, Amazon decided to split HQ2 into two additional headquarters between New York's Long Island City and the Crystal City community in Arlington, Virginia—both located directly across from the major city centers. The company planned to evenly split the operations with as many as 25,000 employees in each location. Amazon intended to begin hiring employees for the new headquarters in 2019 and claimed the average salary for new employees would be $150,000 per year.

The Pros and Cons

There are a number of potential benefits and harms to a decision to locate a substantial headquarter in these two cities. For example, according to published reports,

Amazon's move to New York pits it against Google, its largest competitor, which is gearing up for its own expansion in the city. And it gives Amazon a major presence in three coastal hubs that politically lean left at a time when tech companies are under scrutiny for their perceived elitism and liberal social views.

On the other hand, Arlington, Virginia, could be a good fit for Amazon politically, as an important purple swing state that promises political clout no matter which party is in power. The company has faced critics ranging from President Donald Trump to Vermont senator Bernie Sanders, who have called out the company over issues like wages. In September 2018, Amazon raised its minimum wage to $15 per hour compared to the federally mandated minimum of $7.25 per hour at that time.

The Request for Proposal

Amazon's 2017 request for proposal for HQ2 was sent out to over 200 cities and mentioned incentives as part of its key preferences and decision drivers. For these communities, the announcement of a deal between local government and Amazon includes the promise of jobs but also $5 billion in new investments. In exchange, these communities offered tax breaks and other incentives. According to MarketWatch, Amazon was to receive $1.525 billion in performance-based incentives for creating jobs in Long Island City. In return, Amazon was to donate space for a tech incubator for artists and industrial businesses alike, and for a primary public school. In Arlington, Virginia, Amazon is to receive $573 million in performance-based incentives and a cash grant from the community of $23 million over 15 years based on incremental growth of a tax on hotel rooms. Virginia will invest $195 million in infrastructure in return.

After one large company receives a tax deal like this one, a state legislator or city council member will often need to make decisions about where to draw the line. For example, JPMorgan Chase CEO Jamie Dimon told investors that he would work to get HQ2 in New York in order to lobby legislators to give his company the same benefits as Amazon. This puts elected officials in the position of determining whether JPMorgan Chase and other companies should receive subsidies on par with Amazon.

Amazon's stock rose 2% after the HQ2 announcement. And analysts who rate the stock's performance estimated the stock price would soon reach $2,100 per share. It would seem, then, that Amazon's shareholders were pleased.

In February 2019, Amazon canceled its plans to build its headquarters in Long Island City due to "growing political opposition" in the area. The decision will cost the New York City borough an estimated 25,000 jobs for its community. Public protesters called it corporate welfare and felt the money could be used elsewhere in the community. According to the *Wall Street Journal*, Amazon's decision caught the deal's biggest government backers—Governor Andrew Cuomo and Mayor Bill de Blasio, both Democrats—by surprise. Lastly, Amazon's reputation more broadly took a hit, affecting consumers and employees. In August 2019, reports surfaced of a "burn book" where the company kept a list of negative statements and who said them, including tweets from the hashtag #scamazon.[71]

Discussion Questions

1. *Stakeholder–shareholder theories*: Who are the stakeholders affected by Amazon's HQ2 decision? How might its decision impact these stakeholders? Are there advantages and/or disadvantages for them by winning the bid? Do some stakeholders—like employees who are also shareholders—have conflicts by being a member of both groups?

2. *Ethical decision-making*: Why do some businesses receive incentives from communities and others do not? Do companies have a moral responsibility to treat stakeholders equally? Using a principles-based approach and a consequences-based approach, answer this question: How does Amazon choose benefits and harms to various stakeholder groups (including shareholders) in its HQ2 decision-making?

Take a Position

Issue: Should the community offer tax breaks to Amazon, or should it pay the same tax as other businesses? How does the cancellation of the Long Island City site change your view, if at all?

SUMMARY

As every manager eventually realizes, the interests of a firm's stakeholders do not always align with each other or with the business's goals. Effective stakeholder management remains a challenge for both business and society. We've discussed in this chapter how shareholders are one type of stakeholder and how shareholders sometimes stand on their own as a different class of stakeholder. We've also discussed that both share a concern for firm accountability and value creation. It's vital that managers understand each stakeholders' interests, power, and claim on the firm as a starting point for stakeholder management and engagement.

KEY TERMS

claim 4
corporate governance 6
fiduciary duty 6
legitimacy 17

power 17
shareholder 4
shareholder theory 6
stake 4

stakeholder 4
stakeholder salience 16
stakeholder theory 5
theory 5

REVIEW QUESTIONS

1. What are the differences and similarities of stakeholder and shareholder theories of the firm?

2. What are the primary arguments for managing the firm from either a stakeholder or shareholder perspective? What are the common misrepresentations of each?

3. What is stakeholder salience? Why does it matter to managers of firms?

4. What types of power and legitimacy do stakeholders have?

5. Do stakeholder interests conflict? Can a stakeholder be part of more than one stakeholder group?

6. What are the ways in which firms can manage conflicts among stakeholders?

MANAGER'S CHALLENGE

1.1: Stakeholder–Shareholder Debate

You are a mid-level manager at a company that is considering changing the focus of its annual report. In the past, the report has consisted of regulatory- and shareholder-focused information because annual reports are required by a regulatory body in most countries across the globe, like the U.S. Securities and Exchange Commission (SEC) in the United States, but attitudes about these reports are changing. Now, most are glossy stakeholder-oriented brochures that serve a broader purpose.

Framing Questions

1. How do managers go about integrating both stakeholder and shareholder perspectives?

2. What nonmarket and market stakeholders might read an annual report?

Assignment

Write a memo addressing how stakeholder and shareholder perspectives can be complementary and thus both used in the report. What arguments would you include? How would this dual-purpose benefit the company? Its shareholders? Its stakeholders?

1.2: Stakeholder or Shareholder Perspective?

Your company's products improve consumers' lives. Suppliers want to do business with your company because they benefit from this relationship. Employees really want to work for your company and are satisfied with their remuneration and professional development. And the company is a good citizen in the communities where you are located; among other things, you pay taxes on the profits you make. You compete hard but fairly. You also make an attractive return on capital for shareholders and other financiers.

Framing Questions

1. What are the hallmarks of running a firm using the stakeholder perspective? The shareholder perspective?

2. What are the misconceptions about each perspective?

Assignment

Prepare a one-page memo answering this question: Do you manage your firm from a shareholder or a stakeholder perspective?

Adapted from Freeman, R. E., Velamuri, S. R., & Moriarty, B. (2006). Company stakeholder responsibility: A new approach to CSR. *Business Roundtable Institute for Corporate Ethics, 19.*

CORPORATE SOCIAL RESPONSIBILITY

Ethics in Context

Using Corporate Social Responsibility as a Business Strategy

iStockphoto/juststock

For many Fortune 500 corporations, CSR has become a big business globally. Combined, such companies now spend billions of dollars doing good deeds and self-promoting those myriad efforts to the public. The expectation, of course, is that ethically minded consumers will prefer the products and services of these companies. But is it ethical for such companies to use CSR strategically? As you study this chapter, think about the ethical dimensions of using CSR as part of a business strategy. Should business and social responsibility mix in this way? Are there any ethical boundaries? Later in the chapter, in the Ethics in Context section, we use stakeholder and ethical lenses to examine the use of CSR by businesses as part of a branding strategy.

Learning Objectives

Upon completion of this chapter, the reader should be able to do the following:

2.1. State a working definition of *corporate social responsibility (CSR)*, and describe its four pillars.

2.2. Articulate the fundamental reasons why CSR is an effective organizational strategy.

2.3. Explain the three primary views of CSR and the explicit and implicit CSR framework.

2.4. Compare arguments for and against the use of CSR by businesses.

2.5. Identify current strategies used by businesses to achieve their CSR objectives.

INTRODUCTION

Organizations are embedded in a complex web of stakeholders with interests that can be both convergent and divergent. This chapter continues our discussion presented in Chapter 1 of the stakeholder and shareholder theories of the firm by focusing on how managers sometimes use either or both perspectives to carry out their daily operations by incorporating corporate social responsibility (CSR). Adopting CSR embraces the belief that businesses thrive when they consider societal and global interests together with their own. Organizations are faced with challenges that often require managers to take an integrated approach that balances legal, economic, ethical, and societal concerns. While many commentators and managers agree that integrating CSR is an important goal for any business, they debate the *degree* to which a business and its managers prioritize its societal objectives and the resources allocated to CSR initiatives. We begin by providing a working definition of CSR and briefly trace its historical underpinnings. Then we examine the primary schools of thought related to business's balance between economic success and its contribution to society and analyze the debate about how organizations should resolve conflicts when CSR values between various business constituents do not align. Finally, we conclude by reviewing current examples of various CSR strategies being used by organizations.

CORPORATE SOCIAL RESPONSIBILITY DEFINED

LO 2.1 State a working definition of *corporate social responsibility (CSR)*, and describe its four pillars.

While business ethics may be thought of as an application of ethics to the corporate sector and may be useful to determine responsibility in business dealings, corporate social responsibility (CSR) involves a broader-based identification of important business and social issues and a critique of business organizations and practices. Various definitions of CSR have been offered over the past 50 years. In fact, one study identified over three dozen CSR-related definitions from a variety of sources.[1] A generally accepted working definition of **corporate social responsibility (CSR)** is actions that appear to further some social good, beyond the interests of the firm and that which is required by law.[2]

> **corporate social responsibility (CSR):** Actions that appear to further some social good, beyond the interests of the firm and that which is required by law.

Origins

While one could trace the European origins of the social responsibility of business to before World War II, the 1950s is a logical starting point because its growth took a noticeable uptick at that time, especially in the United States, and continues to do so globally. Initially, this social responsibility took the form of corporate philanthropy and stewardship. From its origins, social responsibility was framed as a social benefit and rooted in moral obligation—that is, what *should* a manager do[3]—at a time when few social safety nets existed and corporations were under attack for being too powerful. Being a socially responsible business evolved significantly through the 1960s and 1970s as academics and businesses started to focus their CSR initiatives toward business strategy. The stakeholder model emerged in the 1980s as a response to a contrary view by a prominent economist, Milton Friedman, who believed the only social responsibility of business was to use its resources to increase its profits.[4] Most recently, corporate financial performance and the emphasis on measuring the impact of CSR activities reflects businesses' understanding of the strategic value of CSR.[5] The origins of CSR also illustrate why it is so difficult to define CSR in a global context. In other words, managers seeking to integrate CSR throughout the firm must align that strategy with contextual differences including national or regional culture, geography, or social and economic practices. How managers ultimately conceptualize their CSR strategy varies.

Corporate Social Responsibility Pillars

Although commentators, scholars, and executives use a variety of methods for explaining CSR, the building blocks for balancing multiple responsibilities begin with recognizing your company's economic, legal, ethical, and philanthropic responsibilities, which we call the *four pillars* of CSR (see Figure 2.1).[6] The pillars help us begin to ask the right questions when designing a CSR strategy.

- *Economic:* A fundamental ingredient of any CSR strategy is the recognition that for-profit organizations are created by shareholders or owners primarily for the financial benefit of its shareholders or owners. While economic expectations may not strike you as a social responsibility, it is understandable that a community expects (and their ability to thrive requires) business organizations to be able to sustain themselves through being profitable enough to sustain their operations. Although economic interests such as profitability are balanced with social interests such as environmental sustainability, it is important to understand the social benefit of an organization's economic success in and of itself.

- *Legal:* Through their government officials, society sets certain rules and restrictions that are viewed as necessary to justice, order, and reliability. In a sense, the law reflects society's view of a global ethical code in that these rules set out the minimum standards for business practices as established by lawmakers at federal, state, and local levels. Legal compliance may not be as easy as it appears at first glance. The law can be complicated, and courts can be unpredictable. Still, the other pillars hardly matter if an organization is engaged in illegal or fraudulent

Figure 2.1   The Four Pillars of Corporate Social Responsibility (CSR)

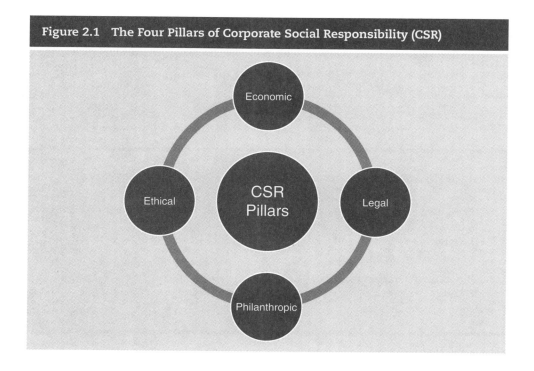

practices. Any CSR strategy should ideally have systems in place to be sure that internal or external wrongdoers are detected and that any illegal activity is halted and reported to authorities.

- *Ethical:* This pillar requires the CSR strategy to embrace the notion that a company will behave in an ethical manner and assume responsibility for its impact on social and environmental well-being beyond what is legally required. While laws and regulations set out minimum ground rules for business operations, societal expectations go beyond mere compliance. The distinction between legal and ethical expectations takes some thought, as you will see in Chapter 3. Integrating ethical responsibilities into your CSR strategy adopts the belief that certain activities, norms, standards, and practices that are legal still may not be ethical. Part of the ethical expectation is that businesses operations are guided not just by the precise statutes but also the substance (or "spirit") of the law. In cases where the law is silent on a particular aspect of a business practice, there is a societal expectation that businesses will carry out its economic interests in an ethical manner using the highest standards of conduct. The consequence-, principles-, and virtue-based approaches to ethical deliberations will be discussed in Chapter 3 and can be useful here.

- *Philanthropic:* This pillar recognizes that it's desirable on a number of levels for companies to be good corporate citizens. Organizations voluntarily choose to engage in practices that directly improve community and environmental well-being, including supporting or engaging in efforts to raise or distribute capital resources to relevant and appropriate social causes. Of course, since there is no mandate, the exact nature of these activities are guided by a business's desire to participate in certain social causes. Integrating this pillar into a CSR strategy provides the community (and its leaders) with the sense that a business is "giving back," and this may be an opportunity to showcase the businesses as a good citizen with an ongoing commitment to a given cause or social problem. Some commentators view a business's philanthropic efforts as part of a fulfillment of the social contract between business and society whereby the community citizenry expects businesses to be responsible corporate citizens just as individuals are.[7]

KEY TAKEAWAYS

Corporate Social Responsibility Defined

- CSR is defined as actions that appear to further some social good, beyond the interests of the firm and that which is required by law.

- The stakeholder model emerged in CSR as a response to a contrary view by prominent thinkers who believed that the only responsibility of business was to use its resources to increase its profits.

- Developing an effective CSR strategy requires a consideration of economic, legal, ethical, and philanthropic factors.

CORPORATE SOCIAL RESPONSIBILITY AS A STRATEGY

LO 2.2 Articulate the fundamental reasons why CSR is an effective organizational strategy.

Now that we have a solid understanding of the definition of CSR and its origins, the next natural question is *why* organizations are increasingly embracing CSR strategies. While some of a business's social responsibility reflects genuine concern for society and the environment, it would be naive to ignore that the CSR movement is driven partly by the public's perceptions that corporations are too powerful. According to the CNBC/Burson-Marstteller Corporate Perception Indicator, the first word that most Americans think of when they hear the word *corporation* is "greed," and more than half think of corporate power as a "bad thing." More than 70% of the survey's respondents believe that corporations take advantage of tax loopholes and do not pay their fair share.[8] Whether or not these perceptions are based in fact hardly matters. Managers must take these perceptions into account as part of their overall strategy, and CSR allows them to challenge and influence these perceptions.

CSR has also now developed as a strategic concept to the point where it has become as important to an organization as its financial strategy. In a study by McKinsey & Company, executives stated overwhelmingly that corporations must balance shareholder needs while making contributions that benefit society. Most even disagree with Friedman's assertion that companies' sole responsibility is to shareholders. CSR is viewed as a means to manage complex sociopolitical issues businesses face and reduce risk for their organizations. The range of issues affecting their organizations is overwhelming, which include challenging subjects such as climate change, health care, and human rights.[9] Edelman, an American public relations firm, surveyed a global group of high-level executives from 23 countries in their annual Edelman Trust Barometer survey and found the global business community sees CSR activities as a "requirement." In their view, a corporation's reputation is based on key factors such as transparency, honesty, and whether it treats employees well and is a good corporate citizen.

Branding and Reputation

Given the public's sentiment about corporate greed and increased awareness of the importance of CSR, it is not surprising that one of the ways that organizations use a CSR strategy is for purposes of promoting or strengthening their brand. When CSR is integrated into a business's operations, it becomes a strategic branding tool to manage customers' expectations. Indeed, studies have shown that a CSR strategy, tied to the societal needs of the community, presents an especially compelling brand image and spurs better firm performance.[10] The link between CSR strategy and positive brand image is well established and an important consideration in creating an effective CSR strategy.

Developing a CSR strategy also helps an organization build a better reputation among internal and external stakeholders. Through attracting talent, motivating employees, recruiting employees, and retaining employees, CSR can help build organizational reputation among customers and business partners alike. An enhanced reputation can also act as a

Dollar General Literacy Foundation

Dollar General, headquartered in Goodlettsville, Tennessee, is a leader in the low-cost housing goods marketplace with more than 15,000 retail stores in 44 states. The company's major CSR initiative is adult English literacy. To this end, the company has established the Dollar General Literacy Foundation to raise and distribute funding to local nonprofits providing adult literacy service in Dollar General's primary business market locations.

Over the past 25 years, the Dollar General Literacy Foundation has awarded more than $127 million in grants to nonprofit organizations and schools that have helped increase literacy throughout the United States. Approximately 8 million individuals have benefited from these grants, resulting in learning to read, preparing for the high school equivalency test, or learning to speak English. The end result has been a significant impact on literacy service provision as well as an increase in Dollar General's image as a good corporate citizen.

Dollar General believes its decision to enter the adult literacy service arena is a sound business decision as well as a demonstration of social responsibility. Dollar General feels it is contributing to the economic vitality of its work environment while building its customer base. Dollar General sees these activities as part of a long-term investment that will contribute to enhancing its employee base as well as growing its revenue.

Discussion Questions

1. Why did Dollar General chose adult literacy as a cause?

2. How can this cause enhance the attractiveness of the company for potential employees?

3. How can this cause expand Dollar General's customer base?

Critical Thinking

Critics of CSR warn these activities can distract companies from their core mission to increase profits, while supporters feel that well-chosen CSR efforts can contribute significantly to a company's bottom line.

1. What are the strongest arguments on each side of this issue? Which argument is most compelling? Explain.

2. What advice would you provide to corporate leaders on choosing an appropriate CSR initiative?

sort of insurance policy against accusations of corporate greed or negligence by countering the perceptions of corporate dishonesty and self-indulgence.[11] In Case Study 2.1, we examine a CSR strategy related to literacy. We discussed the ways companies can utilize CSR as a strategic initiative. This case study illustrates how a company can enhance their brand and develop their market through CSR activities.

Reporting Corporate Social Responsibility Efforts

Organizations with a CSR strategy typically record their efforts in some form ranging from disclosures in government compliance documents to including it in organizational mission statements and marketing materials. While some critics view CSR reporting as a form of publicity to improve company reputation, there is a clear expectation by stakeholders that companies will communicate CSR efforts. In fact, according to accounting firm KPMG, which provides assurance for these reports, disclosure of CSR activities by large, global firms has become a widespread practice.[12] The spike in issuing these reports is in direct response to pressure from consumers, regulators, employees, and shareholders who are demanding more social and environmental responsibility from companies than in the past. For the companies, the reporting serves as evidence of their adherence to CSR and sustainable development concepts. When reporting CSR activities, businesses must embrace the kind of transparency that clearly, fully, and publicly reports the information because doing so is essential to improving organizational contributions to society. By comparing the CSR strategy reporting of different organizations, this information can be used by companies to validate their commitment to sustainable activities, for measuring and benchmarking existing CSR programs, and monitoring CSR performance over time. The future challenge for companies' reporting CSR efforts is how to report to stakeholders not just their financial results—as in the traditional annual report to stockholders—but also their environmental and social impacts.

The Global Reporting Initiative (GRI) is the most widely used framework for CSR reporting. The framework, called the Sustainability Reporting Guidelines, "sets out the principles and indicators that organizations can use to measure and report their economic, environmental, and social performance." GRI is an independent international organization that has pioneered sustainability reporting since 1997. According to the GRI website, it received information from over 1,500 companies from 60 different countries voluntarily reporting on their social and environmental performance. It has become the official standard in global reporting.[13] Another growing trend is to tie together various aspects of the business such as those that effect people, profits, and the planet—or the **triple bottom line**. The International Integrated Reporting Council (IIRC), formed in 2010, has proposed a framework to integrate these types of financial and nonfinancial information metrics by taking a broader view of how firms create value. According to the IIRC, firms create value via six capitals: financial, manufactured, intellectual, human, social, and natural.

The pressure to commit to CSR comes from different stakeholders. In the Law and Society 2.1 section, we see one of the first cases to go to trial brought by shareholders claiming a company committed **securities fraud** when it misled them by underrepresenting the dangers of climate change and their carbon emissions to the financial health of the company. This suit highlights the inconsistencies between what a company says are its CSR priorities and what it actually does in terms of effectively managing the economic risks of complying with ever-increasing regulation.

triple bottom line: Financial, social, and environmental results, taken together as an integrated whole, constitute a company's triple bottom line.

securities fraud: Deception that induces an investor to make a purchase or sale decision based on a false or deceptive statement.

Ramirez v. Exxon Mobil Corp., 334 F. Supp. 3d 832 (2018)

Facts: Mr. Ramirez is a member of the Greater Pennsylvania Carpenters Pension Fund (Fund). He filed this securities fraud case on behalf of the Fund and all people who purchased Exxon Mobil stock between March 31, 2014, and January 30, 2017. The Fund claims executives at ExxonMobil made material misrepresentations or omissions in their securities filings about the dangers of climate change and its carbon emissions to the financial well-being of ExxonMobil.

On March 31, 2014, ExxonMobil released its report "Energy and Carbon—Managing the Risks" (Report), which addressed shareholder concerns regarding global energy demand and supply, climate change policy, and carbon asset risk. The Report stated that ExxonMobil considers the

(Continued)

LAW AND SOCIETY 2.1

(Continued)

impact on the business of possible government regulations on climate controls and carbon emissions by factoring in to its projections a virtual cost of compliance, called a proxy cost of carbon. On March 31, 2014, ExxonMobil also released a report titled "Energy and Climate," which stated ExxonMobil applied a proxy cost of approximately $60 per ton in 2030 and $80 per ton in 2040 as its cost of complying with environmental controls. The Fund alleges that despite this public statement, internal documents state the actual proxy cost for 2030 was closer to $40 per ton. This means that internally ExxonMobil was using a lower number when planning how much to invest in carbon reduction efforts.

In mid-2014, oil and gas prices began to fall worldwide; nevertheless ExxonMobil reassured investors that it had superior investment processes and project management that allowed it to continue operating without a loss. The Fund alleges these representations were materially misleading because ExxonMobil knew it could not survive the historic drop in oil and gas prices without losses. The Fund alleges ExxonMobil made these misrepresentations to maintain its AAA credit rating and allow it to move forward on its $12 billion public debt offering scheduled for March 2016. On January 31, 2017, ExxonMobil announced its fourth quarter and full-year financial results for 2016. In the announcement, ExxonMobil stated it would be recording "an impairment charge of $2 billion largely related to dry gas operations."

The Fund sued for securities fraud, and ExxonMobil filed a motion to dismiss, claiming the Fund did not allege enough facts to support the claim that ExxonMobil materially misled investors nor that ExxonMobil executives made any material misstatements with the intent to deceive or defraud investors.

Issue: Did the Fund have enough evidence to support the claims that ExxonMobil materially misled investors and that they did this with the intent to deceive them?

Decision: Yes, the Fund had enough evidence in their complaint to support the claims that ExxonMobil materially mislead investors and that they did this with the intent to deceive them. A complaint must allege facts upon which the claims are based and not simply recitations of the law they think has been violated. When determining whether statements amounted to material misstatements intentionally made to defraud investors, we must look at all of the statements taken together and not each individual statement read alone, and decide whether a reasonable person would be misled by those statements. A statement is material if a reasonable investor would have found the fact important in making her decision to invest.

ExxonMobil claims the Fund is confusing two separate proxy costs in its allegation—the proxy cost of carbon and the proxy cost of greenhouse gas emissions—and therefore cannot show they misrepresented the figure. Whether the different proxy costs represent two different costs or the same cost but with two different values as applied internally is irrelevant because ExxonMobil's public statements indicate to investors that only one proxy cost was used in making investment decisions, thus investors could have been materially mislead.

Next, ExxonMobil alleges that valuation of the proxy cost is more like an opinion than a statement of fact. If that is the case, the Fund must show that the speaker, in this case Chairman of the Board and CEO Rex Tillerson at the 2016 annual shareholder meeting, did not genuinely hold that opinion. As a member of the Management Committee, Tillerson extensively reviewed and discussed ExxonMobil's Report, which describes the company's investment planning for carbon emissions and greenhouse gases including the use of proxy costs to anticipate current and future government regulation. Thus, Tillerson would have had knowledge of the proxy cost of carbon and would have known that a different number than what was stated was actually used and therefore at the time he made the public statement he knew a different proxy cost was used internally.

Lastly, ExxonMobil claims the Fund cannot show that it intentionally misled investors by stating the carbon proxy numbers in the Report in order to maintain its AAA credit rating. ExxonMobil claims that all companies try to maintain a good credit rating, so ExxonMobil's desire cannot be used to show it intentionally misled investors. The Fund claims that at the time of the $12 billion debt offering, the company was in a dire financial condition, and this offering was "the single biggest offering in Exxon's history" and would allow the company to pay shareholder dividends. Because Tillerson was the chairman of the board and on the Management Committee, he received in-depth briefings on and actively engaged in discussions of ExxonMobil's financial position and the risks of climate change. Thus, he had the motivation to maintain the AAA rating by using a lower internal proxy cost in order to make the debt offering and pay dividends.

Law and Management Questions

1. The court found that ExxonMobil's use of different proxy costs internally could make the company's assets appear more financially secure than they actually were. Isn't the job of a CEO to advocate for his or her company? How did Tillerson's conduct cross the line?

2. Do you think the average investor would understand what a proxy cost of carbon represented? If not, how can this be securities fraud?

3. Is ExxonMobil's conduct an example of corporate irresponsibility or corporate hypocrisy? Why or why not?

4. How do you think other companies will react to the suit in terms of their CSR priorities and what they report to the public?

Corporate Social Responsibility as a Strategy

- Managers must take public perceptions about corporate power into account as part of their overall strategy, and CSR allows them to challenge and influence these perceptions.

- CSR has also now developed as a strategic concept to the point where it has become as important to an organization as its financial strategy.

- When CSR is integrated into a business's operations, it becomes a strategic branding tool to manage customer expectations.

- Reporting CSR activities embraces transparency that is essential to improving organizational contributions to society.

KEY TAKEAWAYS

DIFFERENT CORPORATE SOCIAL RESPONSIBILITY VIEWS AND SCHOOLS OF THOUGHT

LO 2.3 Explain the three primary views of CSR and the explicit and implicit CSR framework.

Most commentators and scholars view CSR in one of three general ways. The economic model recognizes that CSR can lead to differentiation and competitive market advantage for the business—something that can be branded for the present and future. Viewing profits as a sole outcome of social responsibility is considered a **narrow view**. Some researchers, like Professor John Hasnas, believe this type of social responsibility refers exclusively to expenditures that are not designed to help the business achieve the ends for which it was organized.[14] At the other end of the spectrum, some urge businesses to embrace a **broad view** of CSR in which the starting point is a socially defined goal rather than a business objective. In the middle, businesses that operate under a **moderate view** believe that social responsibility objectives are met through a combination of creating economic value, solving social issues, and obeying the law.

narrow view (CSR): Focusing on profits as a sole source of social responsibility.

broad view (CSR): View of CSR in which the starting point is a socially defined goal rather than a business objective.

moderate view (CSR): Social responsibility is a balance between being a good corporate citizen and creating economic value.

The Narrow View: Profit First

Nobel Prize-winning economist Milton Friedman proposed that the only responsibility a business has is to produce shareholder wealth.[15] Moreover, in his classic condemnation of the broad view of CSR, Friedman further argued managers who pursue social initiatives with corporate funds are violating their fiduciary duties to the owners of the corporation. This more narrowly defined view of CSR emphasizes a corporation's duties to its shareholders and views CSR as a way to create competitive advantage and, as a result, more profits. While individuals are free to act morally and behave in a socially responsible manner on their own time and with their own resources, managers are responsible solely to the shareholders to make a profit, within the prevailing legal and ethical guidelines. As for society's well-being, the argument goes, the "invisible hand" of the market will end up producing the most benefits overall to society. According to Adam Smith's famous "invisible hand" metaphor, the common good is best served when people and businesses pursue not the common good but rather their self-interest.

The Moderate View: Shared Value

Advocates of a more moderate view of CSR focus on the importance of "doing good to do well"[16] so that both business and society benefit from managements' actions—sometimes referred to as "shared value" by researchers Michael Kramer and Michael Porter. The shared value approach draws on stakeholder theory mentioned in Chapter 1. This moderate view looks to create economic value in a way that also creates value for society by addressing its needs and challenges, and it is typically highly integrated into the firm's overall strategy.

In this view, businesses are not responsible for all the world's problems, nor do they have the resources to solve them all. Rather, each company can identify the particular set of societal problems that it is best equipped to help resolve and from which it can gain the best competitive synergy. An integral part of the moderate CSR perspective is the focus on the triple bottom line mentioned earlier. Essentially, the triple bottom line emphasizes not only the conventional creation of economic value (profits) but also a company's creation (or destruction) of environmental and social value. The triple-bottom-line approach thus places a great deal more pressure on managers to perform, as it is not uncommon for these three sets of bottom-line issues to conflict. It is not enough, then, for managers to aggressively pursue a social agenda; they must also not lose sight of financial goals or environmental performance.

Consistent with this moderate view, the government's job is to establish legal and regulatory guidelines for business because the government already represents the aggregate moral views of the public. This view is especially common in Scandinavia and Europe. Under this view, a business's ethical responsibility is to comply with the law and pursue objectives that are legal, at a minimum. The regulatory hands of the law and the political process, rather than Adam Smith's invisible hand, provide the basis for ethical decision-making.

The Broad View: Good Corporate Citizenship

Business organizations committed to a broad view of CSR aim to achieve commercial success in ways that honor ethical values and respect people, communities, and the natural environment in a sustainable manner while recognizing the interests of stakeholders. A rich body of research argues that normative reasons—"doing good to do good"[17]—are the heart of CSR, as companies *ought* to be socially responsible. Stakeholders include investors, customers, employees, business partners, local communities, the environment, and society at large. The broad view of CSR also involves the notion of "corporate citizenship," which means a business is part of a social web, a citizen of the society in which it operates. As a member of this community, its profit motive does not trump its other ethical obligations to society. Furthermore, the broadest view of CSR is that corporations have a social responsibility and that profitability is secondary. Indeed, some business ethicists argue that corporations are allowed to exist only because they can serve some public good. These business ethicists also invoke the concept of a "social license to operate," which include the demands on, and expectations for, a business that emerge from environmental groups, community members, and other elements of civil society.[18] Businesspeople should realize that in some instances the conditions demanded by "social licensors" may be tougher than those imposed by regulation, resulting in a "beyond legal compliance" approach.

Others point to CSR being in the public's interest and a company's self-interest *and* that a company does well by employing socially responsible principles in its business operations. In this way, CSR may be thought of as a form of enlightened self-interest because the long-term prosperity of a firm depends not on short-term profits but on societal well-being.

Figure 2.2 summarizes the three schools of thought on CSR.

The Explicit and Implicit Corporate Social Responsibility Framework

Another framework has been developed to offer comparisons of CSR across international settings, by scholars Dirk Matten and Jeremy Moon.[19] Matten and Moon first introduced the concept of implicit versus explicit CSR as a way to compare and contrast the different forms of business responsibility to society. Based on the idea that practices of CSR are diverse across different country settings, they developed a theoretical framework of business responsibility. In this framework, they argue that national business systems help to define the explicit versus implicit nature of CSR because the country government, its corporations, and its markets define the norms, incentives, and rules of CSR. As such, the U.S.-style CSR is explicit; it is embedded in a system that provides incentive and opportunity for corporations to assume and take responsibility for social interests through voluntary programs and strategies to address issues considered to be the social responsibility of the company. The intent of explicit CSR is also different because it is deliberate, voluntary, and often strategic. Therefore, explicit CSR is reliant on firm-level discretion versus formal institutions like the government.

In contrast, CSR in Europe is implicit in that corporations in Europe do not normally articulate their own CSR agendas; rather, their country-level norms, values, and rules are the result of "coordinated approaches to economic and social governance" through mainly government–led partnerships.[20] The intent of implicit CSR is not reflective of a corporate decision; rather, it is a reaction to, or reflection of, the corporation's institutional environment such that codified norms, rules, and laws already reflect society's broader interests. Therefore, implicit CSR is reflective of the collective country obligations rather than of individual firms. Table 2.1 provides a comparison between explicit and implicit CSR.

Figure 2.2 Summary of Corporate Social Responsibility Schools of Thought

Narrow	Moderate	Broad
• Profit-driven • Competitive advantage alone	• Shared value-driven • Create economic value and solve social issues; integrated	• Society-driven license to operate • Business as a global citizen

Table 2.1 Explicit Versus Implicit CSR

Explicit	Implicit
Style practiced in the United States	Style practiced in Europe
Corporations take responsibility Incentives are provided Opportunities are provided	Country-level responsibility Government-led partnerships
Voluntary, strategic, and deliberate	Based upon social governance
Not formalized	Formalized through norms, rules, and laws

Using Corporate Social Responsibility as a Business Strategy

iStockphoto/juststock

For many Fortune 500 corporations, CSR has become a big business. Combined, such companies now spend billions of dollars doing good deeds and self-promoting those myriad efforts to the public. The expectation, of course, is that ethically minded consumers will prefer the products and services of these companies. But is it ethical for such companies to use CSR strategically? Should business and social responsibility mix in this way? Many companies now claim that their products are made with high ethical standards or eco-friendly production methods. Starbucks, for instance, recently declared it has invested over $70 million to promote sustainable coffee harvesting and that 99% of the coffee beans in its beverages are "ethically sourced." Meanwhile, other companies are starting to tout their living wage and health care policies. At Whole Foods, for example, the average hourly wage was $18.89 in 2013. As John Mackey, the company's cofounder and co-CEO, likes to say, "There's no inherent reason why business cannot be ethical, socially responsible, and profitable." But even if a company can be ethical and profitable at the same time, are Starbucks, Whole Foods, and other such ethically minded companies any more virtuous than their competitors?

Consider Starbucks's highly touted ethical-sourcing program. Although Starbucks has invested significant resources ($70 million) in this campaign, it's not clear how much of this money has been devoted to advertising. Also, for what it's worth, Starbucks generated well over $16 billion in revenue in 2014, the year before it announced it reached its 99% ethical-sourcing plateau. Critics argue that Starbucks has invested a mere 0.0003% of its annual revenue to do what it should be doing anyway.

For its part, Whole Foods claims that, "Buying organic supports the small, family farmers that make up a large percentage of organic food producers." But this claim is misleading at best. In reality, although there are a lot of small, family-run organic farmers, their share of the organic crop—and their share of the produce sold at Whole Foods—is minuscule. Whole Foods, of course, knows this, so its claim about the "small family farmers that make up a large percentage of organic food producers" is dubious, if not downright fraudulent.

Discussion Questions

1. *Stakeholder theories:* What is the impact of CSR on the internal and external stakeholders of businesses that deploy CSR as part of their business strategy? Could it backfire if consumers object to what appears to be using social responsibility as a marketing ploy? Can you think of other examples of CSR efforts by organizations as part of their branding efforts? Has it helped or hurt the public's perception of the business?

2. *Ethical decision-making:* Is it ethical to use CSR strategically to promote a company's "ethical brand" or attract new customers? What measures could managers use to ensure that companies are truly committed to social responsibility that they tout as part of their brand?

Take a Position: Corporate Social Responsibility as a Strategy

Issue: Should organizations integrate CSR into their overall strategic planning process?

Sub-Issues:

1. Are there any examples of CSR efforts that should stand alone and not be a part of a strategy?

2. Is CSR just a way for managers to "check a box" for stakeholders, or is there a genuine desire on the part of most managers to benefit society through their business operations?

KEY TAKEAWAYS

Different Corporate Social Responsibility Views and Schools of Thought

- There are three schools of thought that define CSR in practice: the narrow view, the moderate view, and the broad view.

- A narrow view of CSR emphasizes a corporation's duties to its shareholders.

- A moderate view of CSR focuses on a business's responsibility to create economic value and solve social issues at the same time.

- Businesses committed to a broad view of CSR aim to solve global social issues in ways that honor ethical values and respect people, communities, and the natural environment in a sustainable manner.

- Explicit CSR is different from implicit CSR; the former is more firm driven, and the latter is more culturally driven.

CORPORATE SOCIAL RESPONSIBILITY AND ITS LIMITATIONS

LO 2.4 Compare arguments for and against the use of CSR by businesses.

On its face, to some managers and researchers, the concept of CSR is straightforward and noncontroversial: Business should strive to contribute to various societal interests as well as to give back to society through philanthropy. Yet a more critical examination of CSR exists and focuses on its potential to be costly and perhaps even hypocritical. For example, could a company's CSR strategy harm its own shareholders? What are the costs of CSR, and who bears them? Let's consider some of the downsides to CSR alongside its benefits.

Benefits and Costs

corporate social irresponsibility: When the firm causes some social harm and should be held in contempt for the harm.

corporate hypocrisy: When a firm deceptively claims to be what it is not or to be doing something it is not.

While the majority of CSR conceptualizations are from a positive approach and are focused primarily on the benefit to society, there is a growing literature on **corporate social irresponsibility** and **corporate hypocrisy**.[21] And while reporting on a firm's positive acts is common, as mentioned previously, so is media coverage of socially irresponsible business practices—causing some doubt about the integrity of these socially responsible acts and leading to greater skepticism about corporate intentions. It likely goes without saying that firms want to steer clear of appearing hypocritical, or deceptively claiming to be what they are not, or issuing statements that are in fact false representations of the true reality.[22] Likewise, managers need to avoid the social harm caused by being irresponsible.

There are multiple benefits of a clear CSR strategy, and many of its proponents point to cost savings based on reforming internal and external practices as a justification for a CSR program. Often, these efforts result in less of a need for government regulation of business, saving both the company and society the costs associated with regulation. Doing so can also promote long-term profits and savings for the business. Let's suppose, for example, the management team at High Flyers Corp. start the planning phase for a new facility with the objective that its design and use is aligned with the company's commitment to a sustainable environment. However, implementing this policy may result in extra upfront costs during a new construction project. High Flyers' challenge is to focus on *long-term* cost savings yielded by energy efficiency practices, such as natural light design and use of smart systems to control power output. If the extra up-front costs reach a break-even point in the foreseeable future, then High Flyers ultimately returns long-term value to shareholders (via the energy cost savings) while reducing its pollution output and contributing to an overall reduction in environmental harm. One could argue these efforts result in better relationships with stakeholders too. In fact, as we have discussed earlier in this chapter, some managers see CSR strategy as an investment similar to investing in a marketing campaign that promotes and strengthens their brand.

Opponents of CSR argue that only large corporations have the luxury to engage in CSR strategies because they are costly to run, so they may not yield costs savings in the long-term and are not as feasible for certain businesses. As a practical matter, small and midsized businesses may not have sufficient assets to wait for a return, such as energy costs savings. Given this, one primary criticism of CSR is that it disproportionately favors wealthier companies over start-ups, small, and midsized businesses. Likewise, some stakeholders do not view CSR favorably. Consumers are often bearing the costs of the CSR program as the real cost is passed on to them through higher prices for products and services. And there is considerable subjectivity of how and when, for example, philanthropic CSR strategies should end—having achieved their intended impact—and how much of the firm's resources should be devoted to it at any given time.[23]

Others believe the onus of social responsibility is on the individual and not the corporation because the company has primary responsibilities to the shareholders, as discussed in Chapter 1 and earlier in this chapter. Some commentators also question the inherent ability of a management team to develop a CSR strategy in accordance with the moral standards of both the internal and external stakeholders.[24] Even in relatively small companies where managers and shareholders are one in the same, there can be a moral disconnect on how CSR resources should be allocated. Lastly, critics view CSR as potentially leading to perceptions of corporate hypocrisy at worst and CSR skepticism at best. Figure 2.3 illustrates primary arguments for and against CSR.

Figure 2.3   Point–Counterpoint: Corporate Social Responsibility

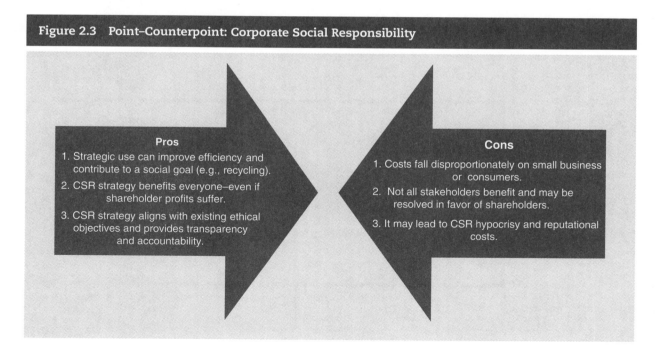

Pros
1. Strategic use can improve efficiency and contribute to a social goal (e.g., recycling).
2. CSR strategy benefits everyone–even if shareholder profits suffer.
3. CSR strategy aligns with existing ethical objectives and provides transparency and accountability.

Cons
1. Costs fall disproportionately on small business or consumers.
2. Not all stakeholders benefit and may be resolved in favor of shareholders.
3. It may lead to CSR hypocrisy and reputational costs.

Amazon Ups the Ante

As Amazon became only the second company in history to reach $1 trillion dollars in market during 2018, it remained haunted by press reports of low employee wages and poor warehouse working conditions. Despite having substantial CSR efforts such as the Amazon Career Choice Program that prepays 95% of tuition for employees to take courses for in-demand fields regardless of whether the skills are relevant to a career at Amazon, the public's perception of Amazon as a good corporate citizen was waning. After the *New York Times* published a report detailing Amazon's negative workplace culture and mistreatment of its workforce, the company, while denying the most serious allegations, increased its oversight of third-party providers and affirmed that the well-being of its employees was a top priority. Still, Jeff Bezos, Amazon's famous founder and CEO, had become a target of politicians and commentators that decried the wealth inequality between Amazon's executive management and their labor force and compared Bezos to the robber barons of a bygone era. Senator Bernie Sanders cosponsored a bill called the Stop BEZOS Act that would tax corporations for every dollar of public assistance that their workers received. Faced with criticism and a shortage of workers in retail generally, Amazon announced it would boost its minimum hourly rate to $15, surpassing all other major retailers and the highest minimum wage required by a state.

Discussion Questions

1. What factors were at work in Amazon's decision to raise its minimum wage?

2. Is $15/hour a fair wage? Should Amazon raise the wages of mid-level workers as well? Explain.

Critical Thinking

1. Use your favorite search engine to find Amazon's statements on CSR. Interestingly, despite the size and the scope of its business, Amazon does not release an annual sustainability or CSR report. The website remains the only source of information about the range of sustainability programs and measures initiated by the company. Why do you think Amazon doesn't follow the practices of others in reporting its CSR efforts?

2. Based on your Amazon CSR research, what type of CSR strategy does it employ? Could it be perceived as an example of CSR hypocrisy? Explain your answers.

Corporate Social Responsibility and Its Limitations

- *Advantages of CSR:* Cost savings, decreased need for government regulation, promotion of long-term profits, improved relationships with stakeholders, improvement in societal need

- Disadvantages of CSR: Favors larger businesses, higher costs to consumers, not all benefit equally, may have an adverse impact on brand and reputation

CORPORATE SOCIAL RESPONSIBILITY STRATEGIES AND TRENDS

LO 2.5 Identify current strategies used by businesses to achieve their CSR objectives.

CSR strategies vary widely because organizations are so different in terms of size, resources, culture, geography, and other factors that influence strategic decision-making. Workforces that are largely from the millennial generation tend to favor volunteerism over corporate giving. Smaller and midsized business have to be cost conscious, so they tend to favor low-cost strategies such as strategic partnerships. We discuss some of the current trends in CSR strategies here, but it is important to note that new strategies often grow from existing strategies.

Cause Marketing

Cause marketing is a form of CSR that raises awareness for a particular cause through the provision of marketing, sponsorship, and promotional activities. For example, the Subaru Loves Pets initiative is part of a cause marketing strategy because participating Subaru retailers across the country work alongside the automaker's established network of local animal organizations (e.g., the ASPCA) to collect supplies needed to keep animals healthy, happy, and ready to find homes. Retailers will also provide Subaru Loves Pets shelter supply kits, created in partnership with BarkBox.

Corporate Philanthropy

Philanthropy is the voluntary raising and distributing of money by an organization to a variety or focused set of business-relevant causes, most commonly through a re-grant program or direct partnerships with service providers in the community. For example, Alphabet (Google) provided a $2.4 million grant to GiveDirectly, a nonprofit organization that distributes direct monetary contributions to the poor. Table 2.2 provides an illustration of how much other corporations give as part of their CSR strategies.

Strategic Partnerships

Strategic partnerships are one of the most common methods for developing a CSR strategy. For example, Michelin's Uniroyal tires partnered with the World Wildlife Fund (WWF) to form the Tx2 alliance, which aims to reduce poaching and habitat loss for tigers in Asia and Africa. Their goal is to double the number of tigers in the wild by 2022, and the effort is funded through a Uniroyal tire rebate. For every Uniroyal tire rebate redeemed during the promotional period, Michelin donates $20 to the WWF wild tiger efforts, with no set limit. The Uniroyal rebate customer receives a WWF/Uniroyal co-branded "Save the Tiger" kit, which includes a plush tiger, a tiger decal, a species card, and a save-the-tigers-themed reusable tote bag.

Table 2.2 Largest Corporate Foundations by Total Giving

Name	Total Giving
Gilead	$446,700,000
Walmart	$301,000,000
Wells Fargo	$286,500,000
JPMorgan Chase	$250,000,000
Microsoft	$169,000,000
Goldman Sachs Group	$168,500,000
ExxonMobil	$168,500,000
Chevron	$168,500,000
Bank of America	$168,500,000
Alphabet (Google)	$167,800,000
Citigroup	$142,800,000
Merck	$132,500,000
Coca-Cola	$117,300,000

Source: The 13 Most Philanthropic Companies in the World, by Sion Phillpott, 16 July 2018. https://www
.careeraddict.com/corporate-philanthropy. Accessed October 16, 2019.

Volunteerism

Organizations deploy volunteerism as a CSR strategy by providing an incentive or permission for employees to volunteer for a business relevant cause. For example, Starbucks encourages its employees to volunteer in local community projects through its Volunteer-Match program. PriceWaterhouseCoopers (PwC) introduces new hires to their employee volunteer program during their orientation. New hires work together to build a bike that they then donate to a local youth organization.

Socially Responsible Business Practices

Socially responsible business practices as a CSR strategy involves an examination of current and planned business operations. As part of the planning process, managers aim to engage in specific socially responsible activities that are consistent with the values and preference of customers, suppliers, employees, or the local community. The goal is to ensure third parties, who represent the business, are aware of the business's CSR commitment and follow certain practices that align with the business's values. One example of a third party who regularly represents organizations are attorneys. As part of a holistic CSR strategy, some businesses have imposed guidelines on their outside attorneys in an effort to harmonize legal representation with social values. For example, Walmart has specific internal CSR guidelines that instruct its attorneys to behave ethically during litigation.

Google's Corporate Social Responsibility Strategy and Project Maven

The announcement by Google in June 2018 that it would not seek another contract for its work providing artificial intelligence (AI) for a U.S. Department of Defense project was a culmination of months of internal struggle that pitted shareholder interests against stakeholder interests. However, after a backlash from employees and other stakeholders, Google updated its CSR strategy to include specific policies on AI research. These policies include a specific prohibition of deploying Google technologies that "cause or are likely to cause overall harm." Nor will Google participate in developing "weapons or other technologies whose principal purpose or implementation is to cause or directly facilitate injury to people."[25]

The origins of Google's AI controversy began in September 2017 after its management team announced that Google was awarded a contract for $28 million to work with the Pentagon on a program dubbed "Project Maven." The project required Google to develop and support AI algorithms that the Department of Defense used to analyze footage from military drones. It was touted by Google as "a large government program that will result in improved safety for citizens and nations through faster identification of evils such as violent extremist activities and human right abuses." According to the *New York Times*, two sets of e-mails reveal that Google's senior leadership was enthusiastically supportive of Project Maven primarily because it would help pave the way for larger Pentagon contracts. Privately, though, the e-mails showed a deep concern about how the company's involvement would be perceived. Google's chief AI scientist urged colleagues in an internal e-mail to avoid "any mention or implication of AI" in public statements about the Pentagon contract and warned that it may become "red meat to the media" and ultimately damage Google.[26]

News of the Pentagon contract and Google's AI efforts fueled an extraordinary internal debate and protest. Employees feared the partnership would pivot toward developing weaponry and other offensive technology. Its top technical talent complained the Pentagon contract betrayed its principles, while profit-oriented officials at Google worried the protests would damage its chances to secure more business from the Department of Defense. Several AI scientists resigned in protest, while others called for the company to cancel the Maven contract. The growing protests resulted in a petition signed by about 4,000 employees who demanded a clear policy stating that neither Google nor its contractors will ever build warfare technology.

Discussion Questions

1. Given Google's reaction to the petition and protests, which CSR strategy did Google follow to resolve their dilemma? Explain.

2. Employees are one set of stakeholders impacted by Google's decision. What other stakeholders might have been involved, and what were their interests? Did all stakeholders have the same interests?

3. What did Google's chief scientist mean by warning her colleagues of AI being "red meat to the media"? How could the use of the term *AI* damage Google? Explain.

Critical Thinking

1. Critics of the protests and of Google's reaction point out that Google's actions will ultimately make no difference to society because plenty of other tech companies are waiting to fill Google's shoes with a Pentagon contract. Does that strike you as convincing? Explain.

2. Use your favorite search engine to find Google's current AI policies and principles. While it makes clear that although Google will not engage in contracts for use of its AI research to develop weapons, it also specifically affirmed that Google would pursue contracts with the Pentagon in the future so long as it was consistent with its principles. Is there any contradiction in their CSR strategy? Is it consistent with a broad-based view of CSR, a moderate view, or a narrow view? Explain.

Corporate Social Responsibility Strategies and Trends

Businesses put into practice a variety of strategies to achieve CSR objectives. Those discussed in this chapter are as follows:

- *Cause marketing*: Raising awareness for a particular cause through the provision of marketing, sponsorship, and promotional activities

- *Corporate philanthropy*: The voluntary raising and distributing of money by an organization to a variety or focused set of business relevant causes, most commonly through a re-grant program or direct partnerships with service providers in the community

- *Strategic partnerships*: Partnering with a social organization to raise funds for that organization

- *Volunteerism*: Incentivizing employees to volunteer time or services to a business relevant cause

- *Socially responsible business practices*: Establishing business operations standards that are in line with the business's values

SUMMARY

This chapter continues our discussion presented in Chapter 1 by focusing on how managers sometimes use stakeholder and shareholder perspectives to carry out their daily operations by incorporating CSR. Organizations are faced with challenges that often require managers to take an integrated approach which balances legal, economic, ethical, and societal concerns. While many agree that integrating CSR is an important goal for any business, some also debate the *degree* to which a business and its managers prioritize its societal objectives and the resources allocated to CSR initiatives.

KEY TERMS

broad view (CSR) 32
corporate hypocrisy 36
corporate social irresponsibility 36

corporate social responsibility
  (CSR) 24
moderate view (CSR) 32

narrow view (CSR) 32
securities fraud 29
triple bottom line 29

REVIEW QUESTIONS

1. In your own words, define *corporate social responsibility (CSR)*.

2. Give an example of a business practice that represents each of the four pillars of CSR.

3. Provide an example of how CSR can be an effective business strategy.

4. Describe and provide an example of each of the three views of CSR discussed in the chapter.

5. Explain how a CSR strategy can backfire on a company. Provide an example.

6. Choose one of the strategies discussed to achieve CSR objectives, and using a current company, provide an example of how they could implement that strategy.

MANAGER'S CHALLENGE

Employee Participation in Corporate Volunteer Efforts

Data Metrics, a privately held corporation, is in the process of planning a fundraising event in partnership with the American Heart Association. The event will consist of a 5K run along with a dinner whereby participants will be asked to pledge $150 per person to attend. The top management is very supportive of this cause and strongly encourages participation from the employees of Data Metrics. All employees have been given 20 hours of company paid time to work on organizing and promoting this event. However, not all of the employees are on board with this cause. Some feel that it is a very personal decision to participate in these types of charitable events and would rather not see this type of thing enter their workplace environment. In addition, other employees feel a closer allegiance toward other causes, such as breast cancer or diabetes. However, these employees fear they will be viewed negatively by management if they do not participate.

Source: Dawn R. Elm, PhD, David A. & Barbara Koch Distinguished Professor of Business Ethics and Leadership, University of St. Thomas, Opus College of Business. 2018 Global Business Ethics Teaching Workshop, Bentley University, 2018. Used with Permission.

Framing Questions

1. Should all employees be required to participate in Data Metrics's volunteer efforts?

2. How can managers ensure that Data Metrics's fundraising event will not distract employees from their "regular" work?

3. What things should management consider in selecting a cause that will be both acceptable to participating employees and impactful?

Assignment

Prepare a two-page internal communication plan that would help managers roll out this initiative in a way that encourages participation while discouraging employees from feeling forced to participate or is outside of their level of comfort. Be sure to include a checklist of specific actions that managers can take to implement this fundraising project.

ETHICS AND ETHICAL REASONING

Learning Objectives

Upon completion of this chapter, the reader should be able to do the following:

3.1 Define *ethics, morals,* and the *law.*

3.2 Explain the difference between an ethical temptation and an ethical dilemma.

3.3 Articulate the main issues regarding the debate over the origin of ethics.

3.4 Articulate the principles-based and consequences-based approaches to ethics and the integrity and compliance organizational ethics models.

3.5 Outline the ways in which organizations can create an ethical climate as well as some of the conflicts of interests (COIs) facing managers.

Ethics in Context

Profits Versus Ethics for Glassdoor Ratings?

iStockphoto.com/BlackSalmon

Companies seek publicity and spend millions of dollars annually to improve their image and reputation. Websites like Yelp, Glassdoor, and TripAdvisor are all in the business of rating companies for consumers. High ratings can make or break a company in terms of profitability. Should the companies being rated provide internal encouragement to employees for filling out the reviews? Should the ratings companies advise those companies being rated on how to improve their rankings when the rankings are designed to be objective?

Later in the chapter, in the Ethics in Context section, we will examine the tension between profits and ethics.

INTRODUCTION

Managing multiple stakeholders and making multiple decisions every day, managers routinely face ethical challenges. Many of these decisions are tough ethical dilemmas. We do not have to look far to find reasons to manage ethically. Businesses operating on sound ethical principles attract good employees, customers, and investors and avoid multiple pitfalls such as litigation, criminal fines, consumer boycotts, and complaints. There are, in fact, many reasons for businesses to be ethical. But despite these reasons, managers also face ethical temptations, pressures to meet compliance standards, legal issues, and COIs.

MORALS, ETHICS, AND THE LAW

LO 3.1   Define *ethics*, *morals*, and the *law*.

As we discussed in Chapter 1, managers need to aim toward achieving a high level of commitment to managing stakeholders, and the highest level of that commitment is to become an ethical leader—that is, asking yourself, What are the values and principles that inform my leadership? What is my sense of purpose? To understand your purpose and your values, you need to consider the concept of *ethics*, and it helps to start with differentiating it from *morals* and the *law*.

One's **morals** are an individual's determination of what is right and wrong. It is usually guided by your family, your religion, your peers, and the society in which you live—to name a few influences. So you probably have a moral compass that guides you in terms of what you will and will not do—your line in the sand so to speak. Think about what your line is and how it is formed.

Typically, there are cognitive, affective, and behavioral components to your morals. You have certain thoughts and beliefs about an issue: cognition. Also, you are likely to have an emotional reaction to an issue or situation; this is your affect. Lastly, you will act on or behave in a certain way when facing an ethical issue.

Ethics—more broadly—are the expectations of conduct regarding how a person should behave, based on moral principles or values. **Business ethics** applies these values to business decisions. Often, professional associations outline accepted guidelines of behavior for their membership. For example, the American Marketing Association[1] and the International Federation of Accountants[2] both have professional codes of ethics (see Figure 3.1), but they vary in terms of geographical scope and are specific to the functions of marketing and accountancy respectively.

The **law** is generally a society's codification of what it believes, its opinions, and customs.

Professor Lynn Sharp Paine believes there are similarities between ethics and the law. She states, "If we think about law and ethics not as defining classes of permissible or impermissible actions, but as defining methods of reasoning and justification...both ethical and legal thinking involve the interpretation and application of general principles."[3] It is in this way that our legal analysis provides facts and assumptions that may be necessary in order to conduct an ethical analysis. So the ethics office needs to work in tandem with the legal department. Further on in the chapter, there are additional considerations discussed about how ethics and the law can work together to create an ethical climate.

There is little doubt that ethics and the law inform a manager's interactions with stakeholders (a concept introduced in Chapter 1), but more importantly, a manager must manage their organization's ethical environment. It is not exactly easy to do—largely because of three things:

1. The different motivations and rationalizations for behaving ethically or not
2. The overall approach to ethics (principles-based vs. consequences-based) one is using
3. The manager's past and current work environment (integrity vs. compliance)

> **morals:** One's own determination of right and wrong.

> **ethics:** The expectations of conduct regarding how a person should behave, based on moral principles or values.

> **business ethics:** Applying personal values to business decisions.

> **law:** A society's codification of public opinion and belief.

Figures 3.1   Codes of Ethics

The code of ethics of the American Marketing Association:[i]

1. Do no harm. This means consciously avoiding harmful actions or omissions by embodying high ethical standards and adhering to all applicable laws and regulations in the choices we make.

2. Foster trust in the marketing system. This means striving for good faith and fair dealing so as to contribute toward the efficacy of the exchange process as well as avoiding deception in product design, pricing, communication, and delivery of distribution.

3. Embrace ethical values. This means building relationships and enhancing consumer confidence in the integrity of marketing by affirming these core values: honesty, responsibility, fairness, respect, transparency and citizenship.

The code of ethics for the International Federation of Accountants follows an overarching framework of[ii]

- Professional competence and due care

- Integrity

- Objectivity

- Confidentiality

- Professional behavior

- Independence

[i] https://www.ama.org/AboutAMA/Pages/Statement-of-Ethics.aspx

[ii] http://www.ifac.org/news-events/2018-06/iesba-overview-revised-and-restructured-code-ethics

KEY TAKEAWAYS

Ethics, Morals, and the Law

- Ethics, morals, and the law are different concepts. Ethics are the expectations of conduct regarding how a person should behave, based on moral principles or values. The law is generally a society's codification of what it believes, its opinions, and customs.

- Each of these terms interrelate, and managers need to use all three concepts to work effectively and promote sound business acumen.

MOTIVATIONS AND RATIONALIZATIONS

LO 3.2   Explain the difference between an ethical temptation and an ethical dilemma.

All decisions begin with motivations and end with consequences. Therefore, it is important to understand what your motivations are and if they come from one of a few common rationalizations or, instead, if they stem from your moral character. Doing so will help foresee some of the potential consequences.

Sometimes we throw around the phrase *ethical dilemma* when really we are experiencing nothing more than a temptation. Is there a difference? Try to answer these two questions before reading on:

1. What is an ethical temptation?

2. What is an ethical dilemma?

Values are often strong motivators and clearly important to today's managers. According to a 2016 survey of millennials by Deloitte—a provider of advisory services to more than 85% of the Fortune 500 companies—the top ranked influence on decision-making was "my personal values/morals." However, by its 2018 survey, there was a negative shift in millennials' feelings about business's motivations and ethics. Respondents were disappointed that business leaders' priorities did not appear to align with their own—but where they did align, the respondents' perceptions were that those companies are more successful, have more stimulating work environments, and do a better job of developing talent. Some 33% see "strong ethics/integrity" as essential skills.[4] Similarly, the 2019 chief compliance officer of accounting firm KPMG found 66% of compliance officers identified ethics as "one of the key regulatory and compliance obligations for 2019."[5]

Research across cultures and different time periods show there are five widely shared values: honesty, respect, responsibility, fairness, and compassion (see Figure 3.2).[6] Even still, most dilemmas fall into one of these sets of conflicting values:

- Truth versus loyalty
- Individual versus community
- Short term versus long term
- Justice versus mercy[7]

It is important to note these sets of conflicting values are not choices between having values and not having values. Instead, tension arises because there is a conflict between two important values.

Ethical Temptations

All human beings are motivated by temptations—the temptation to eat too many french fries, to drive too fast, or even to lie. According to a recent study, adults lie in order to protect their identity—who we think we are and how we want to be perceived.[8] And while protecting against threats to your identity is an understandable motivation, according to Rushworth Kidder, it is simply an ethical temptation.

An ethical temptation represents a tension between a clear right behavior and clear wrong behavior.[9] For example, cheating on your girlfriend may be tempting—and you may be adept at providing any number of rationalizations for doing it—but it is clearly wrong. Your motivation and the consequences that result carry the bulk of the ethical weight.

> ethical temptation: A conflict between a clear right behavior and clear wrong behavior.

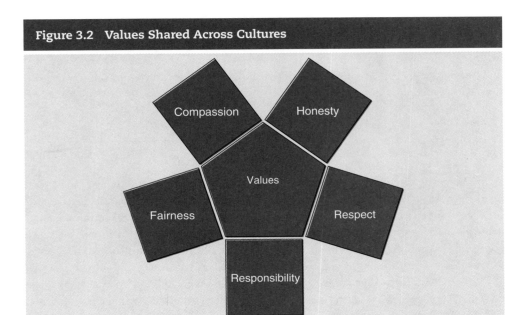

Figure 3.2 Values Shared Across Cultures

Compassion

Honesty

Values

Fairness

Respect

Responsibility

So while eating too many french fries may result in being overweight, it is not wrong; however, driving too fast is both unethical and illegal as you are likely to endanger yourself and others as a result.

On a deeper level, we need to ask ourselves this: Do we have the motivation to act consistently according to our moral character, and do we have the ability to self-regulate when we feel tempted to go off course? This question leads us directly to ethical dilemmas.

Ethical Dilemmas

ethical dilemma: A
conflict between two
right moral values.

A true **ethical dilemma**, in contrast, exists when there is a conflict between two right moral values. Let's consider Kidder's four types of values conflicts more closely.

- *Truth versus loyalty*: Truth generally involves honesty, candor, or integrity, whereas loyalty involves commitment, responsibility, or promise-keeping.

- *Individual versus community*: This tension can be restated simply as "us" versus "them," "one's self" versus "others," or the smaller group versus the larger group.

- *Short term versus long term*: Sometimes referred to as now versus then, this paradigm reflects difficulties arising from immediate needs versus future goals or prospects.

- *Justice versus mercy*: Justice generally reflects notions of fairness, equity, and sometimes an even-handed application of the law that often conflicts with compassion, love, and empathy, which are hallmarks of showing mercy.

Certainly, these values come in conflict. Do you find them on equal footing? Let's suppose that a parent catches her daughter drinking alcohol at a party, which violates the high

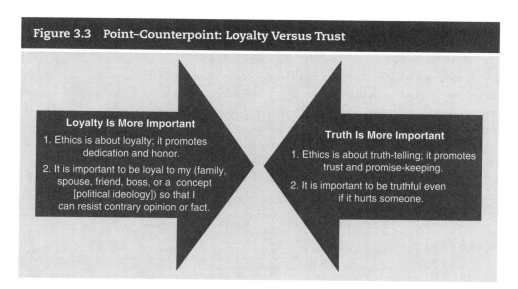

Figure 3.3 Point–Counterpoint: Loyalty Versus Trust

Loyalty Is More Important

1. Ethics is about loyalty; it promotes dedication and honor.
2. It is important to be loyal to my (family, spouse, friend, boss, or a concept [political ideology]) so that I can resist contrary opinion or fact.

Truth Is More Important

1. Ethics is about truth-telling; it promotes trust and promise-keeping.
2. It is important to be truthful even if it hurts someone.

school rules for athletes. She has a lacrosse playoff game tomorrow and is the star player. Should the parent tell the coach? What would justice guide the parent to do? What would mercy suggest? You need to choose, but you cannot do both. Take a look at the point–counterpoint in Figure 3.3 to explore the tension between truth and loyalty further.

Nowhere do values conflict more often than in company home versus host county norms. Global business ethics is a fact of life and remains a reality as does the globalization of business itself. How should a company behave when the standards followed are different, or lower, than those followed in the home country? Ethicists Tom Donaldson and Tom Dunfee use a social contract perspective to show how individual communities can be allowed to develop their own local standards as long as they do two things:

1. Meet certain standards involving acceptance by community members.

2. Do not violate broad, universal standards, called hypernorms.

Hypernorms are the result of a convergence of religious, political, and philosophical thought across a number of countries and cultures.[10] Examples include a country's citizenry being allowed to participate in some way in the direction of the country's political affairs and the common humanity that should be afforded to all people. Particular values of a corporation, as expressed through its actions and policies, serve to establish the integrity of the firm, allowing it to go beyond legal regulations to apply moral universalist norms and codes of conduct across all subsidiaries, often coordinated by company's home country headquarters.[11] Donaldson and Dunfee offer an instructive example: Companies in India sometimes promise employees a job for one of their children when the child is of age. Such a policy may be in tension with Western notions of egalitarianism and anti-nepotism, but it is consistent with India's traditional values of the importance of the extended family. A global manager could acknowledge the Indian company's policy is in tension with the norms of other economic communities around the globe—giving voice to a gray area—but stopping short of declaring it ethically impermissible so that a dialogue can begin around how to adapt this norm such that it

hypernorms: The result of a convergence of religious, political, and philosophical thought across a number of countries and cultures.

becomes more in line with the company policy over time.[12] More about cultural norms can be found in Chapter 11.

When we are motivated to do something by these values, it ideally results in good consequences, right? Yes, ideally. However, sometimes unintended consequences can be motivated by the best of intentions. For example, the e-cigarette from Juul Labs, Inc., discussed in Case Study 1.1, started out as a way for adult smokers to begin the process of quitting. What the company didn't expect was to create a new market for underage users—and intense pressure from parents, physicians, and regulators who had become increasingly concerned about underage use of its vaping products.

As ethicist Daryl Koehn explains in her book *Living with the Dragon*, unintended consequences result from actions that are typically within the control of the actor and result from actions that can be linked to a cause (e.g., choice, emotion, desire, policy, rule). Importantly, in bringing about these unintended consequences, she notes, the actor could have acted differently than they did.[13]

In other cases, people intentionally wish to cause harm resulting in bad consequences for the actor and the action's target. For example, an employee deliberately lies about her coworker's reason for being absent from work with the intention of getting the coworker fired. The Ethics Resource Center (ERC) annually surveys misconduct in the workplace—conduct that would appear intentional. In its 2018 survey it focused on outright abusive behavior, sexual harassment, and discrimination (see Figure 3.4). Most problems happened on multiple occasions (62%) and were deemed "serious" or even "very serious" by observers (61%). Equally troubling, many of those perpetrating the misconduct were middle or senior managers.[14]

One of the most compelling conflicts—a right versus right conflict—is between ethical performance and financial performance. The financial well-being of a company depends on employees, boards of directors, and executives appropriately serving the needs of customers, investors, and other employees. The integrity and culture of the organization relies on the ethical performance of the company. There is much compelling statistical evidence that this is a false choice. For example, a recent comprehensive study, a meta-analysis, was compiled of other studies that looked at the relationship between a firm's social performance (as measured by its social responsibility or citizenship) and its financial performance (as measured by its revenue after expenses). It concluded there is a positive relationship between the two; in fact, one caused the other (i.e., social performance caused the financial performance).[15] Furthermore, firms evaluated by JUST Capital outperformed the Russell 1000 index throughout the decade ending in 2016 within a range of 104 percentage points. The Russell 1000 is considered a bellwether index for how well or how poorly large U.S. companies perform financially. JUST Capital measures and ranks companies on important issues. These companies also do or did the following:

- Generated 3.5% higher 5-year return on invested capital

- Pay about 20% more workers a living wage

- Have almost 17% more women board members

- Created 1.8 times more jobs in America

- Provide more flexible working hours and paid time off

Figure 3.4 The ERC Survey of Misconduct in the Workplace

TYPE OF INTERPERSONAL MISCONDUCT	ABUSIVE OR INTIMIDATING BEHAVIOR	SEXUAL HARASSMENT	DISCRIMINATION
OVERALL OBSERVATION RATE	21%	12%	12%
FREQUENCY ■ Single Incident ■ Multiple Incidents ▨ Ongoing Patterns	33% / 24% / 43%	42% / 17% / 41%	44% / 19% / 37%
PERPETRATOR ▨ A Senior Leader ■ A Middle Manager ▨ A First Line Supervisor ▨ A Non-Management Employee ■ Someone You Work With Who Is Outside the Company ■ Other	1% 2% / 25% / 22% / 16% / 34%	3% 2% / 23% / 24% / 16% / 32%	3% 1% / 28% / 29% / 18% / 22%
SEVERITY ■ Very Serious ■ Serious ▨ Somewhat Serious ▨ Not Very Serious ■ Not Serious At All	3% / 29% / 29% / 26% / 13%	4% / 38% / 24% / 22% / 12%	9% 4% / 36% / 28% / 23% / 23%
SPECIFIC OBSERVATIONS	TYPE OF ABUSIVE BEHAVIOR Verbal 88% Physical 24%	TYPE OF SEXUAL HARASSMENT Unwelcome sexual comments 70%	DISCRIMINATION BASED ON: Race 58% Gender 49%

Source: © 2019 Ethics & Compliance Initiative. Used with permission of the Ethics Research Center, 2650 Park Tower Dr., Suite 802 Vienna, VA 22180, www.ethics.org.

- Recycle about 3 times more waste in percentage terms
- Are twice as likely to have sound supply chain policies
- Donate about twice as much of their profit to charity[16]

Rationalizations

Sometimes it is difficult to talk about our values and immediately change the behaviors of ourselves or others because, typically, our inner thoughts and emotions (i.e., cognition and affect) present us with a rather sophisticated set of rationalizations for either acting or not. Drawing on the actual experience of business practitioners as well as social science and management research, author Mary Gentile developed the Giving Voice to Values (GVV) framework to help managers combat rationalizations so they may voice their values.

Table 3.1 Common Rationalizations

Rationalization	Example
Standard practice or status quo	"Everyone does it."
Materiality	"It's no big deal."
Locus of responsibility	"I'm just following orders."
Locus of loyalty	"I know this isn't fair to the customer, but I don't want to hurt my boss."

According to Gentile, a manager must ask, "What *if* I were going to act on my values—what would I say and do?"[17] GVV provides a framework for answering this question so a manager can practice, script, and then act on their values in the workplace.

According to Gentile, there are four common rationalizations (see Table 3.1):

1. Standard practice or status quo

2. Materiality

3. Locus of responsibility

4. Locus of loyalty

The standard practice argument is best captured by the statement "Everyone does it." This argument assumes that an action is acceptable simply because the majority of the people engage in it or because it is something that has been done for a long period of time. This rationalization is powerful and many of us use it to avoid taking responsibility.

Second, the rationalization of materiality refers to the argument that an action is not material—or it doesn't matter, it is insubstantial, does not hurt anyone, or does not make a difference in the long run. Framing the question in terms of materiality shifts the focus from the action to its consequences, and it also minimizes those consequences. One could say here: "It's no big deal" or "It's not that important to the overall picture."

A third customary rationalization involves one's locus of responsibility. Responsibility refers to our sense of who we think should act in a situation or who is requiring us to act in a situation. We tell ourselves either "It is not my problem" or "I'm just following orders." This rationalization usually reduces your personal accountability because you think your actions result from some authority figure who has the control. Sometimes people claim they are not the appropriate person to handle the situation—or do not possess the requisite authority to remedy the issue—or are simply following directions. This rationalization can get extended to blaming the victim of harm for a variety of reasons: "It's their own fault."

Fourth, we justify actions that concern the locus of loyalty. As noted previously, our loyalties can conflict. We can, at the same time, not be fair to one person but also not want to harm another. This rationalization assumes that loyalty to one group necessarily means disloyalty to another group.

Each of these rationalizations can be identified and worked through. In doing so, it doesn't mean we will become free of personal bias or ethical temptations. It does mean we will recognize them more quickly and begin to implement change.

According to Joseph T. Hallinan, author of *Why We Make Mistakes*, we are all to some degree afflicted with biases in the way we see, remember, and perceive the world around us, which makes us prone to commit certain types of errors. Overcoming psychological biases are often the reason we make unethical decisions like stereotyping, ethnocentrism, and even overconfidence.[18] For example, researchers asked a group of people, Which city is farther north: Rome or New York? This test relies on the bias that most people tend to be—erroneously—confident in their knowledge. As a result, management policies based on erroneous information may prove harmful or simply fail. Also, we tend to stop searching for more information about a problem (before acting) as a result of overconfidence.[19]

CASE STUDY 3.1

The University of Arizona: Innovative Use of Technology or Ethical Dilemma?

The University of Arizona (UA) is a public university in Tucson, Arizona, founded in 1885. As a global leader in research, the school has a total enrollment of 43,625 students and offers 129 bachelor's programs, along with 137 master's and 94 doctoral degrees. The school is known for the employability of its graduates and brings Arizona an estimated $8.3 billion annually.[20]

The UA, along with many other schools in the United States, has turned its attention toward freshman retention rates. Students who drop out after their first year have impacts on prospective student recruiting and alumni donations, so preventing students from leaving supports the bottom line. For years, Arizona has struggled with freshman retention rates at their colleges and universities, with an average first- to second-year retention reaching as low as 59%.[21] In response to new goals set by the State of Arizona, the UA is determined to continue increasing their student retention.[22] The school has been successful in not only reaching but exceeding the goal of 83% set by the Arizona Board of Regents, with the first-year retention rate of the 2017–2018 school year reaching 86.5%.[23]

Sudha Ram, a professor of management information systems at the UA and director of the university's Center for Business Intelligence and Analytics in the Eller College of Management, saw an opportunity in tracking student IDs with the "CatCard."[24]

With retention rates in mind, Ram was testing to see if there was a relationship between card swipes and freshman students who would drop out after their first year. In this experiment, data was collected about the time and location of freshman students, based on where they were swiping their cards at over 700 locations on campus.[25] With this information, Ram and her team could make assumptions about the students' social interactions and daily routines. They found that those most at risk of leaving the school were students with a lack of routine and fewer social interactions, and the predictions could be made after just 4 weeks of the student's first semester.[26] With this implication of big data, the UA accurately predicted 85% to 90% of the freshman who would not return after their first year.[27]

The experiment highlights the implications of big data; however, the UA students' daily routines and social interactions were being closely analyzed, without student understanding of the research. Since the data collected was anonymized, the researchers could not see names, ID numbers, or anything that could be used to identify the student. However, if fully implemented, the research team plans on sharing the at-risk students' names with their advisers in order to prevent them from dropping out.[28] To do so, data could not be anonymized. Currently, the university states that a student's "University ID number is not included on

(Continued)

the card, but will be electronically encoded on your card, unless otherwise requested." The ID number is linked to the student's personal records and is used for "internal purposes such as student and/or personnel services," but there is no indication in the CatCard terms and conditions that students' data is collected and analyzed.[29] Therefore, with 60,000 active CatCards on campus, more explicit consent would be required in order to move forward with this data collection.[30]

The UA Acceptable Use of Computers and Networks requires students to "make only appropriate use of data to which you have access," going on to explain that "privileged access to data may only be used in a way consistent with applicable laws, University policies, and accepted standards of professional conduct."[31] However, the UA itself seems to have conflicting actions since the collection of CatCard data is nowhere to be found in their privacy policy or CatCard terms and conditions. In fact, their privacy policy suggests the opposite, stating that "UA does not obtain personal information about you when you visit our websites or other online services unless you provide us that information voluntarily."[32]

Collecting and analyzing data from students is not a new venture at the UA. Although the school currently does not use Ram's CatCard research, the UA has 800 data points including academic performance, financial aid, and other activity that work to identify the 20% of students in each college who are most likely to leave. With 73% accuracy, the names of those students are shared with the college and advisers to offer support and guidance. The university is also looking to utilize their 8,000 Wi-Fi hubs on campus in order to further analyze students' movement and behavior.[33] How far is too far in terms of student data collection?

The UA is not unique in its use of big data. Big data is big business. In 2017, it accounted for $35 billion a year in revenue, and experts expect the growth to continue.[34] Companies see the importance in collecting and analyzing data of consumers, yet the United States has few laws regarding individuals' privacy rights. The Federal Trade Commission (FTC) recommends that businesses offer consumers "greater disclosure…[and] simple "opt-out' tools," but there is no legislation enacted by Congress that enforces these practices. This lack of collaboration between the FTC and Congress are creating performance–expectation gaps between what citizens expect to be protected and what businesses are actually doing in regard to collecting data.

Unlike the uncertainty of consumer data collection in the United States, the European Union has recently placed strict regulations on businesses in regard to using big data. This law, called the General Data Protection Regulation (GDPR), prevents companies from collecting and processing any data that can be connected to an identifiable person without prior consent.[35] In addition, individuals have the ability to block companies from collecting their data and using it for profiling purposes.[36] Implemented in May of 2018, the GDPR has also imposed conditions on how the information is stored, and for how long.[37] If something similar were to be enacted in the United States, businesses like the UA would be forced to reconsider their collection of student data.

Discussion Questions

1. What is the main ethical issue in this case? Explain.

2. What are the benefits and costs of the UA collecting student data? What are the duties of the school with regard to students' data? What rights do student have over their personal data?

3. How are law and ethics intertwined in this case?

4. How would you feel about this research if you were a student at the UA?

Critical Thinking

Given the university's mission is to educate students and retention is a key element to that goal, how can the UA strike a balance between student rights and university duties? Explain.

This case was prepared by former undergraduate management student Holly Fiscus in consultation with Professor Cynthia E. Clark, both of Bentley University, Waltham, Massachusetts, USA.

Motivations and Rationalizations

- Motivations include personal values but also bad intentions. Motivations result in consequences, which are either intentional or unintentional.

- Ethical temptations are different from ethical dilemmas because dilemmas are situations

where right versus right moral values are in conflict.

- Rationalizations prevent us from exercising our values and speaking up. We can think through them and recognize them for what they are—false reasons to behave unethically.

KEY TAKEAWAYS

THE ORIGIN OF ETHICS

LO 3.3 Articulate the main issues regarding the debate over the origin of ethics.

LO 3.4 Articulate the principles-based and consequences-based approaches to ethics and the integrity and compliance organizational ethics models.

There is considerable debate about where, when, and *if* ethics originates in humans. This debate is ongoing and complex. There are four overarching categories to this debate, suggesting that people are born with these things:

1. Prior knowledge of right and wrong
2. Goodness
3. Badness or inherited sin
4. Moral neutrality

Philosopher David Sedley explains that to Socrates and Plato, prominent ancient Greek philosophers, people are born with a soul forming an inner essence and composed of personal emotions, the mind, and human desire. And it is with age and experience that individuals rediscover what they already knew at birth.[38]

Building on this notion, 17th-century philosopher Jean-Jacques Rousseau believed that children are born with a pureness, a goodness, and later may learn to be immoral from adults who themselves have become corrupt.[39] More recently, ethicist Jonathan Haidt wondered, similarly, where one's morality came from. In response, he articulated the notion of **moral intuition** to suggest that morality comes from a small set of intuitions built into the brain from evolution. Haidt defines *moral intuition* as the sudden appearance in one's consciousness of a moral judgment, including an affective valence (good–bad, like–dislike), without any conscious awareness of having gone through steps of searching, weighing evidence, or inferring a conclusion.[40]

One's moral judgment, Haidt argues, is caused by these quick, intuitive, and often automatic moral intuitions. For example, we tend to know immediately if some behavior makes us feel disgust or empathy, gratitude or guilt. Some would be disgusted by even

moral intuition: The sudden appearance in one's consciousness of a moral judgment, including an affective valence (good–bad, like–dislike), without any conscious awareness of having gone through steps of searching, weighing evidence, or inferring a conclusion.

the thought of eating horse meat, but others would not (see Manager's Challenge later in the chapter).[41]

These intuitions can be followed up by more consciously deliberated, typically slower, moral reasoning, but only when needed. Haidt's assessment of where morality comes from—moral intuition—has been one of the most compelling new ideas in ethics for some time. It is in direct contrast to what was thought to be a common approach to judging an act to be moral—the rational and conscious process of **moral reasoning**. Moral reasoning is a conscious mental activity that consists of transforming given information about people in order to reach a moral judgment.[42] American psychologist James Rest created a four-step process of moral reasoning:[43]

1. *Awareness* that there is a moral issue or ethical problem or that the situation has ethical implications (also referred to as "interpreting the situation," "sensitivity," or "recognition")

2. Leading to a moral *judgment* (also referred to as "moral evaluation," "moral reasoning," or as "ethical decision-making")

3. Establishing a moral *intent* (also referred to as the "moral motivation" to do what is right)

4. Resulting in taking *action* on these intentions through one's behavior (also referred to as "implementation")

However, as more research has been conducted on the human brain, we now know this type of reasoning is not as reliable as once thought. Haidt argues that, instead, people use their innate moral intuition to make moral judgments.

As we noted earlier, many people develop their moral compass from religion, and it is religious denominations that largely argue these origins of one's ethics. The common thread of most religions is that a person is born morally imperfect. For example, the Hindu and Buddhist religions believe that, though one is born morally imperfect, the soul is reincarnated from leaving a body at death and reentering another body at birth.[44] Catholics and Protestants believe that sin was inherited from Adam and Eve and their defiance of God's wishes. But by choosing to do good, Catholics and Protestants can absolve their sin. One need only to look at today's churches to see that worshippers still believe in the notion of sin.

Finally, Aristotle, an ancient Greek philosopher, argued that people are born more morally neutral, with an "unscribed tablet," but it was John Locke who gave the theory of tabula rasa—or blank slate—a more modern understanding. Locke thought people store their moral knowledge, based on life experiences and their cultural context, and in infancy we are not preprogrammed to be moral.

Based on a number of these contributions, moral philosophers divide ethics into two overarching categories—**teleological** and **deontological**. Teleological (consequences-based) approaches focus on the outcomes or consequences of a decision, the ends not the means. Utilitarianism is the major theory in this category. Deontological (principles-based) approaches focus on duties—like justice or rights—and therefore the means not the ends. Figure 3.5 summarizes each approach.

moral reasoning: A conscious mental activity that consists of transforming given information about people in order to reach a moral judgment.

teleological: An ethical approach focusing on the outcomes or consequences of a decision, the ends not the means.

deontological: An ethical approach focusing on duties—like justice or rights—and therefore the means not the ends.

Figure 3.5   Summary of Ethical Theories

Consequences-based Approach:

- My actions are to be judged right or wrong solely based on their consequences.
- Consequences are based on the amount of happiness or unhappiness created.
- Each person's happiness counts the same.

Principles-based Approach:

- There are principles, like justice and rights, that matter over consequences.
- One's duty, or the means to an end, is important.

Virtue-based Approach:

- What character traits make someone a good person?
- What specific personal virtues are important?

[handwritten margin notes: teleological → ends / utilitarianism]
[handwritten margin notes: deontological → means]

Consequences-Based Approach to Ethics

Some ethical decisions can be evaluated based on their utility, their overall consequences. Utilitarianism or consequentialism holds that a person's action—or a policy or rule—is morally good if it, and only if it, produces the greatest net utility or happiness for the largest number of people compared with alternative actions, rules, or policies. Philosophers Jeremy Bentham and John Stuart Mill articulated three main propositions:

1. Actions are to be judged right or wrong solely based on their consequences.

2. In determining the consequences, the only thing that matters is the amount of happiness or unhappiness created; everything else is irrelevant.

3. Each person's happiness counts the same.[45]

To a consequences-based mind, right actions are the same as those that are good, or produce the most good.

This approach involves first identifying alternative courses of action and then performing a sort of cost–benefit analysis for each of the parties or stakeholders assumed to be affected. As you might guess, it is difficult to account for every possible consequence because, as discussed previously, we do not always know the consequences of our actions— some are, in fact, unintended as well.[46]

Likewise, there are other challenges to the theory. First, what is happiness? Even though each person's happiness counts the same, it is unlikely that each would define *happiness* in the same way. For example, do you define *happiness* in the same way as your parents might? Second, are consequences all that matter? Consider this: If things other than consequences are important in determining what is right, then utilitarian thinking might be incorrect, or at least limited. In fact, this argument is precisely one that the principles-based approach of justice makes. Third, utilitarianism implies that certain actions are right—those that represent the greatest happiness for the largest number of people—when in fact they may violate another person's rights. The notion of a personal right is not a utilitarian concept because these rights place a limit on how an individual may be treated regardless of the happiness created or for whom.[47] People have rights that may not be trampled on merely because someone anticipates good results—even net positive results. This argument is precisely one the principles-based approach of rights makes. Finally, utilitarian thinking is focused on the ends that justify the means. And, as Daryl Koehn suggests, if an evaluator is already biased toward a particular outcome, then doing a cost–benefit evaluation will become a self-validating exercise only—one where the evaluator simply confirms his or her existing bias.[48]

Principles-Based Approach to Ethics

The *principle of justice* requires that we treat people fairly in accordance with their particular situation. But, as noted previously, Kidder suggests that justice implies an evenhanded impartiality that emphasizes equality and plays no favorites. To others it means that the benefits and burdens of some decision or action are distributed equally, according to some accepted rule. Philosopher John Rawls explains that, a just society is one in which the "liberties of equal citizenship are taken as settled; the rights secured by justice are not subject to political bargaining or to the calculations of social interests.[49]

The *principle of rights* is based on the idea that a person or a group is entitled to something or to be treated in a certain way. These types of rights include the right to due process, to worship freely, to one's privacy, and to one's safety. Philosopher Immanuel Kant believed that all of our duties can be summed up in one ultimate principle, which he called the categorical imperative. In his *Foundations of the Metaphysics of Morals*, he explains this principle as a way to tell if something is morally permissible. Kant's categorical imperative suggests the following:

1. When thinking about doing something, ask yourself what rule you are following.

2. Then ask whether you would be willing to have this rule become a universal law—one followed by all people at all times?

3. If the answer is yes, it is permissible; if it is no, it is not.[50]

Virtue-Based Approach to Ethics

The ethics of virtue stems from Aristotle's belief that virtue is a trait of character manifested in habitual action. The habit-forming aspect of this definition is important. For example, the virtue of honesty cannot be practiced occasionally to be correctly described as a virtue.[51] While virtues may differ from person to person, certain virtues will be needed by all people throughout time. Aristotle believed that courage, generosity, honesty, and loyalty are needed because people face the same basic problems and have the same basic needs (e.g., *courage* for the need to take risks, *generosity* for the need to recognize others are worse off than you, *honesty* to have reliable communications, and *loyalty* to have friends). Can you think of other necessary virtues?

Origins of Ethics

- There are different origins of ethics— some believe we have prior knowledge of right and wrong, are born with goodness and moral intuition, are born with inherited sin or badness, or that we are essentially blank slates.

- Two large camps of ethical theories are used today: consequences- and principles- based approaches.

- Consequences-based theories has origins in utilitarianism and principles-based theories have their origins in justice and rights.

- Virtue-based conceptions believe if a person has and maintains certain virtues they will be a good person.

- Any of these approaches can be used to think through ethical dilemmas.

ORGANIZATIONAL ETHICS AND CREATING AN ETHICAL CLIMATE

LO 3.5   Outline the ways in which organizations can create an ethical climate as well as some of the conflicts of interests (COIs) facing managers.

In addition to these approaches to ethics, managers must consider their work environment— namely whether it is integrity or compliance based. Doing so helps to determine what an organization is and what it stands for.

According to Professor Lynn Sharp Paine, managers must acknowledge their role in shaping organizational ethics and see it as an opportunity to create a climate that can strengthen the company's reputation and relationships. Paine views organizations as needing to move past a **compliance-based approach** where the goal is to protect and punish legal violations to one where exemplary behavior is fostered in order to create an ethical climate. An **integrity-based approach** to organizational ethics combines the concern for the law with an emphasis on managerial responsibility for ethical behavior.[52] Paine believes the organization cannot be a high-integrity organization without high-integrity individuals, so there is an essential link between organizational ethics and individual integrity. As seen in Figure 3.6, each approach to organizational ethics relies on different behavioral assumptions and uses different organizational methods to create that type of corporate culture.

compliance-based approach: The goal is to protect and punish legal violations.

integrity-based approach: Combines the concern for the law with an emphasis on managerial responsibility for ethical behavior.

Figures 3.6   Integrity-Based Versus Compliance-Based Approaches

Characteristics	Compliance-Based Approach	Integrity-Based Approach
Org. Methods	Education, auditing controls, penalties	Education, leadership, accountability, systems and decision processes, auditing and controls, penalties
Behavioral Assumptions	Autonomous beings guided by material self-interest	Social beings guided by material self-interest, values, ideals, peers

Source: Adapted from L. S. Paine, "Managing for Organizational Integrity," *Harvard Business Review* 72, no. 2 (1994), p. 113.

LAW AND SOCIETY 3.1

Peterson v. Hewlett Packard, 358 F.3d 599 (9th Cir. 2004)

Facts: Peterson was employed in the Boise, Idaho, office of Hewlett Packard (now known as HP) for almost 21 years prior to his termination. Peterson describes himself as a "devout Christian" who believes that homosexual activities violate the commandments contained in the Bible and that he has a duty "to expose evil when confronted with sin." The conflict between Peterson and HP arose when the company began displaying "diversity posters" in its Boise office as one component of its workplace diversity campaign. The first series consisted of five posters, each showing a photograph of an HP employee above the caption "Black," "Blonde," "Old," "Gay," or "Hispanic." Posters in the second series included photographs of the same five employees and a description of the featured employee's personal interests as well as the slogan "Diversity is Our Strength."

In response to the posters that read "Gay," Peterson posted two biblical scriptures on an overhead bin in his work cubicle. The scriptures were printed in a typeface large enough to be visible to coworkers, customers, and others who walked by. One of Peterson's postings was taken from Corinthians 10:12. The other featured the following passage from Isaiah:

> The shew of their countenance doth witness against them; and they declare their sin as Sodom, they hide it not. Woe unto their soul! For they have rewarded evil unto themselves. (Isaiah 3:9)

Peterson posted a third scriptural passage. This time he chose the well-known and highly controversial passage from Leviticus:

> If a man also lie with mankind, as he lieth with a woman, both of them have committed an abomination; they shall surely be put to death; their blood shall be put upon them. (Leviticus 20:13)

Peterson's supervisor removed the scriptural passages because she determined they could be offensive to certain employees and that posting them violated the HP policy prohibiting harassment. Over the course of several days after Peterson posted the biblical materials, he met with HP managers, and he and they tried to explain to each other their respective positions. Peterson explained that he meant the passages to communicate a message condemning "gay behavior." The scriptural passages, he said, were "intended to be hurtful. And the reason [they were] intended to be hurtful is you cannot have correction unless people are faced with truth." Peterson hoped his gay and lesbian coworkers would read the passages, repent, and be saved.

Peterson also claimed that the HP workplace diversity campaign was an initiative to "target" heterosexual and fundamentalist Christian employees at HP in general, and him in particular. Ultimately, Peterson and the managers were unable to agree on how to resolve the conflict. Peterson proposed that he would remove the offending scriptural passages if HP removed the "Gay" posters; if, however, HP would not remove the posters, he would not remove the passages. When the managers rejected both options, Peterson responded: "I don't see any way that I can compromise what I am doing that would satisfy both [HP] and my own conscience." He further remonstrated, "As long as [HP] is condoning [homosexuality] I'm going to oppose it...."

Peterson was given time off with pay to reconsider his position. When he returned to work, he again posted the scriptural passages and refused to remove them. After further meetings with HP managers, Peterson was terminated for insubordination. Peterson sued, alleging religious discrimination in violation of Title VII of the Civil Rights Act.[i]

Issue: Did HP discriminate against Peterson based on his religion?

---

[i] For a more complete discussion of Title VII of the Civil Rights Act, see Chapter 9.

Decision: No, HP did not discriminate against Peterson based on his religion. In order to prove that he was fired because of his religious beliefs, Peterson must show that his job performance was satisfactory and that his termination was discriminatory. The undisputed evidence shows that HP carefully developed its campaign during a 3-day diversity conference at its Boise facility in 1997 and subsequent planning meetings in which numerous employees participated. The campaign's stated goal was to increase tolerance of diversity. Peterson may be correct that the campaign devoted special attention to combating prejudice against homosexuality, but that is not unlawful. To the contrary, the HP efforts to eradicate discrimination against homosexuals in its workplace were entirely consistent with the goals and objectives of our civil rights statutes generally.

According to Peterson, HP managers harassed him in order to convince him to change his religious beliefs. However, the evidence shows that HP managers acted in precisely the opposite manner. In numerous meetings, HP managers acknowledged the sincerity of Peterson's beliefs and insisted that he need not change them. They did not object to Peterson's expression of his antigay views in a letter to the editor that was published in the *Idaho Statesman*—a letter in which Peterson stated that HP was "on the rampage to change moral values in Idaho under the guise of diversity" and that the diversity campaign was a "platform to promote the homosexual agenda." Nor did the HP managers prohibit him from parking his car in the company lot even though he had a bumper sticker stating, "Sodomy Is Not a Family Value." All the managers did was explain the HP diversity program to Peterson and ask him to treat his coworkers with respect. They simply requested that he remove the posts and not violate the company's harassment policy—a policy that was uniformly applied to all employees.

Peterson also claimed HP failed to reasonably accommodate his religious beliefs, as required by the law. An employer's duty to negotiate possible accommodations ordinarily requires it to take "some initial step to reasonably accommodate the religious belief of that employee." Peterson contends that the company did not do so even though HP managers convened at least four meetings with him. In these meetings they explained the reasons for the company's diversity campaign, allowed Peterson to explain fully his reasons for his postings, and attempted to determine whether it would be possible to resolve the conflict in a manner that would respect the dignity of Peterson's fellow employees. Peterson, however, repeatedly made it clear that he would accept only two options: either that (1) both the "Gay" posters and antigay messages remain or (2) HP remove the posters and he would then remove the antigay messages. Peterson's first proposed accommodation would have required HP to permit an employee to post messages intended to demean and harass his coworkers. His second proposed accommodation would have forced the company to exclude sexual orientation from its workplace diversity program. Either choice would have created undue hardship for HP because it would have inhibited its efforts to attract and retain a qualified, diverse workforce, which the company reasonably views as vital to its commercial success; thus, neither provides a reasonable accommodation.

The other alternative acceptable to Peterson—taking down all the posters—would also have inflicted undue hardship upon HP because it would have infringed upon the company's right to promote diversity and encourage tolerance and goodwill among its workforce. The Supreme Court has acknowledged in other cases that "the skills needed in today's increasingly global marketplace can only be developed through exposure to widely diverse people, cultures, ideas, and viewpoints." These values and good business practices are appropriately promoted by the HP workplace diversity program. To require HP to exclude

(*Continued*)

(Continued)

homosexuals from its voluntarily adopted program would create undue hardship for the company.

Law and Management Questions

1. Identify the management decisions made in this case by HP that reflect its values and an integrity-based approach to management.

2. Based on this case, is the Court saying that HP does not have to honor or value Peterson's religious beliefs? Why or why not?

3. If the answer to Question 2 is no, then why did the Court decide in the favor of HP?

---

ethical climate: Employees' shared perceptions of the ethical practices and procedures of a firm.

conflict of interest (COI): When a manager has to choose between his or her interests and the interest of another group.

An **ethical climate** is defined as employees' shared perceptions of the ethical practices and procedures of a firm.[53] A majority of corporate ethics research has focused on ethical climate as a critical antecedent of organizational outcomes.[54] So developing it is important for a manager. It is either developing or deteriorating, enriching itself or impoverishing itself. It needs constant care and attention.

Conflicts of Interest

Very often in making decisions in an organization, and even when working toward creating an ethical climate, managers face conflicts of interest (COIs). In broad terms, a **conflict of interest (COI)** is a situation in which a manager must choose between his or her interests and the interests of another group—essentially one of conflicting loyalties.

A COI is when the judgment of a professional is subject to undue influence, whether the risk arises from gifts or kickbacks; an individual's personal (generally financial) interests; or the interests of family members, colleagues, or current and former clients.[55] To be sure, expert and trustworthy judgment is central to many professions, and a COI makes that judgment unreliable while also threatening the good of that profession and its reputation.

COIs exist whether or not they are recognized by the party creating the conflict or the party harmed by it.[56] Researchers have noted there are two types of conflicts: the actual conflict, in which a party in a position of trust fails in its obligation to serve in another's interest, and a potential conflict, where there is a mere presence of a conflict to fulfill an obligation even though the party may or may not have failed in its obligation.[57] An actual conflict is a bit different; it is an initial, simple COI between two parties. A potential conflict, if committed, could represent a compound form where the presence of a conflict may be transferred among multiple parties who are unaware of the presence of that (simple) conflict, committing a further wrong.[58] Here's a scenario where this compound conflict applies:

- Fidelity is required to ensure that the employees' best interests are upheld in a 401(k) investment plan that it manages for one of its client companies—Insurance Company X—but Fidelity allows another firm, Company Y, to do the voting of the shares held in the plan.

- Company Y has no fiduciary duty to these employees of Insurance Company X with regard to the 401(k) investment plan (fiduciary duty is explained in

Chapter 1). The insurance company employees are unaware that Fidelity does not do the voting.

But potential conflicts—even if not made compound—are still troubling. Consider the example of a publicly traded firm (in Chapter 10, you will learn more about corporate governance and boards of directors). The vast majority of board members of these types of firms must demonstrate director independence from the company and management under stock exchange rules. But a company needs to consider whether there are factors that might imply this director is not independent. Let's use the example of Carnival Cruise Line:

- Carnival Corporation director Randall J. Weisenburger qualified as independent while working as CFO for advertising firm Omnicom Group, Inc.

- The cruise operator spent more than $34 million on Omnicom advertising and marketing services during the 5 years Mr. Weisenburger held both positions.

- Is there a conflict here? What type?

Often, we have choices as to whether we engage in COIs, but sometimes the very system we are working in is flawed. Effectively, a person may be participating in the situation because it is hard not to. For example, companies pay external raters of stocks and bonds to rate them. You may have heard of Moody's or Standard & Poor's ratings companies. How can the rating be objective if it is being paid for by the companies they are rating? All companies pay for the ratings.

Profits Versus Ethics for Glassdoor Ratings?

iStockphoto.com/BlackSalmon

Glassdoor is a website of more than 800,000 company rankings and each year ranks companies for its "Best Places to Work" award, which highly rated firms use in news releases because it helps recruiting efforts. According to Andy Challenger, vice president of placement firm, Challenger, Gray & Christmas, Inc., "Glassdoor is the most dominant company reviews website by far."

Just how are these influential ratings determined? Glassdoor ratings are driven by current and former employees who anonymously review companies and their management, according to Glassdoor's website. Users can post reviews and companies can respond for free. Glassdoor makes money by charging companies to customize their pages and promote open positions. The company boasts, "Glassdoor has millions of jobs plus salary information, company reviews, and interview questions from people on the inside making it easy to find a job that's right for you." A five-star rating is the highest.

To be sure, Glassdoor wants to make its ratings accurate and authentic. According to a 2019 *Wall Street Journal* investigation, these ratings can be manipulated by employers trying to sway opinion in

(Continued)

(Continued)

their favor. Since the site gets some 60 million users per month, according to web research firm SimilarWeb, these ratings are a powerful recruiting tool and, some say, a strong motivation for companies to inflate them.

According to the *Wall Street Journal*'s investigation, five-star ratings jumped in October, the month preceding the annual "Best Places to Work" assessment cutoff. And the analysis—8,500 posted reviews—found some 400 companies with unusually large single month increases in ratings. One-star reviews remained flat. Companies like SAP, LinkedIn, Anthem Health, and SpaceX admit to encouraging employees to post reviews, and some offer incentives like free company mugs for employees completing their reviews to make the "Best" list. Glassdoor says the reviews tend to jump for a variety of reasons like a hiring surge, a company event, or internal encouragement. According to the *Wall Street Journal*, Glassdoor "coaches clients on how to target groups [of employees] that tend to be more enthusiastic, such as new hires."

And while Glassdoor has human moderators and technology filters to detect abuses—such as fake accounts or offensive content—it has no completely accurate way to prevent people from gaming the system. Other ratings platforms, like Amazon, Yelp, and TripAdvisor, have all faced attempts to game reviews and ratings.

Yet, according to a spokeswoman, "The employee is just as powerful as the employer."

Discussion Questions

1. *Stakeholder–shareholder theories:* Who are the stakeholders affected by Glassdoor? How might its ratings impact these stakeholders? Are there COIs in the way Glassdoor works with its customers—client company or employee who posts reviews?

2. *Ethical decision-making:* Discuss whether the employee is just as powerful as the employer as Glassdoor states. Using a principles-based approach and a consequences-based approach, answer this question: What is the problem with companies providing internal encouragement to employees for filling out the reviews?

Take a Position

Issue: Should Glassdoor offer advice to companies on how to improve their rankings when the rankings are designed to be objective?

Source: Winkler, R., & Fuller, A. (2019, January 23). How companies secretly boost their Glassdoor ratings. *Wall Street Journal*; https://www.glassdoor.com.

KEY TAKEAWAYS

Organizational Ethics and Creating an Ethical Climate

- Managers have a significant role in shaping organizational ethics and must be proactive in creating an integrity-based climate.

- An integrity-based approach to organizational ethics combines the concern for the law with an emphasis on managerial responsibility for ethical behavior.

- COIs can be actual or potential. Expert and trustworthy judgment is central to many professions and conflict makes that judgment unreliable.

SUMMARY

This chapter investigates business ethics and why managers need to manage from a sound ethical footing because when managing multiple stakeholders and making multiple decisions every day, managers routinely face ethical challenges. There are sound reasons to manage ethically, which we discuss in this chapter alongside the challenges that may accompany them.

KEY TERMS

business ethics   45
compliance-based approach   59
conflict of interest (COI)   62
deontological   56
ethical climate   62

ethical dilemma   48
ethical temptation   47
ethics   45
hypernorms   49
integrity-based approach   59

law   45
moral intuition   55
moral reasoning   56
morals   45
teleological   56

REVIEW QUESTIONS

1. What are the differences and similarities of ethics, morals, and the law?

2. What is an ethical temptation? What is an ethical dilemma? Name four types of ethical dilemmas.

3. What are the primary arguments for a consequences-based approach to ethical reasoning? For a principles-based approach?

What are the common challenges to each approach?

4. What are the types of organizational ethics strategies? How can they be integrated?

5. What is an ethical climate and how is it fostered?

6. What types of COIs exist, and why are they a problem for managers?

MANAGER'S CHALLENGE

3.1: Moral Intuition or Reason?

You are a mid-level marketing manager at a large supermarket company considering offering horse meat, sometimes called chevaline, to its U.S. and U.K. customers. Horse meat is an inexpensive, very lean meat with more omega-3 fatty acids than salmon and more iron than steak. Despite its being a delicacy, some have called it inhumane and immoral. However, your boss believes the target market of males—ages 40 to 60—will be more convinced to buy the product based on reason, not emotion.

Framing Questions

1. How do people judge something as moral?

2. Where does morality come from? Does religion inform your ideas of whether it is right to eat horse meat?

Assignment

Write a memo addressing the arguments made by moral reasoning and moral intuition. What arguments would you include? How will you convince your boss one way or another?

3.2: Ethics and the Law

You work for a national medical insurance company that provides malpractice coverage to medical professionals. You are responsible for filing all confidential surgical malpractice notices for your firm and making the necessary notifications. At a recent get-together, you learned that a good friend of yours is seriously ill and needs major, complicated surgery. He mentioned the name of the surgeon he is planning to have do the procedure. You happen to know from your job that the surgeon he has chosen has had numerous claims against him. All of the claims were found to be indefensible because of poor surgical technique. Your firm is currently considering nonrenewal of this surgeon's insurance due to the risk level.

Source: Dawn R. Elm, PhD, David A. & Barbara Koch Distinguished Professor of Business Ethics and Leadership, University of St. Thomas, Opus College of Business. 2018 Global Business Ethics Teaching Workshop, Bentley University, 2018. Used with Permission.

Framing Questions

How do you balance the ethical and legal aspects of this decision?

Assignment

Do you tell your friend? If so, what arguments would you include? How would you speak to the ethics and the legalities of this situation?

3.3: Profitability and Ethics—Are They in Tension?

Visit the student companion site: edge.sagepub.com/clark1e. Watch the video on B corporations, and read the article.

Write up your analysis of the B corporation concept from the video. How does it help ease the tension between profitability and ethics? Do you think this type of governance is the missing link in corporate social responsibility (CSR)? Why or why not?

Framing Questions

1. What are the hallmarks of the B corporation concept from the video?

2. How does it help ease the tension between profitability and ethics?

Assignment

Prepare a one-page memo answering this question: Do you think this type of way a company is governed is the missing link tying ethics to profits? Why or why not?

ORGANIZATIONS AND PUBLIC POLICY

Ethics in Context

Private Prisons

Businesses have a vested interest in the policies and laws created by our government (both federal and state). Similarly, our government cares what businesses do and often depends on private business to help it accomplish its goals in serving society. However, sometimes the interests of the government and business do not align. Think about how the government serves the public, from collecting taxes, to building roads, and to maintaining our safety. Are there some government functions we should not leave in the hands of private business? Later in this chapter, in the Ethics in Context section, we will examine the ethical implications of for-profit businesses operating prisons.

iStockphoto.com/Rattankun Thongbun

Learning Objectives

Upon completion of this chapter, the reader should be able to do the following:

4.1 Understand how laws and policy are made.

4.2 Explain how the relationship between the government and business is shaping laws and creating public policy.

4.3 Describe public–private partnerships (3Ps), and critique their influence on the duties of government and values of a community.

4.4 Analyze and critique the rise of corporate social advocacy (CSA) as a means of influencing policy.

4.5 Identify and assess the ethical issues that may arise when business and government work together.

INTRODUCTION

The role of business in our government and shaping public policy has evolved from reluctance to proactive, sophisticated engagement. There are many reasons for this change. Lobbying, one method of advocating for policy changes, is not a surprising phenomenon; it is a logical result of our form of democracy. There are many points in the legislative process for education and influence. More recently, the role of social media and motivation of CEOs has created a much more public, and some say equally effective, form of advocacy. The day-to-day struggles of running the government, whether federal, state, or local, also create opportunities for businesses and governments to work together to provide much-needed services and infrastructure for the community. No matter the avenue, the role of business in our government is not always smooth sailing, as customers and constituents may have different priorities.

ROLE OF BUSINESS IN SHAPING LAWS AND POLICY

LO 4.1   Understand how laws and policy are made.

To understand the role of business in government and its influence in shaping laws and public policy, it is important to remember how laws and regulations are made in this country. In its most basic form, a law is the codification of a society's beliefs, values, and opinions. An idea for a law can come from anywhere. Sometimes ideas come from events that elected officials and the public want to make sure never happen again. For example, in 2001, Enron Corporation, an energy company from Houston, Texas, filed for bankruptcy. Just before its bankruptcy, *Fortune* magazine ranked Enron the fifth largest company in America.[1] Enron collapsed as a result of internal fraud, including creating complex off-the-book entities and inflating financial reports. At the time, its $63.4 billion bankruptcy was the largest in U.S. history until 2002 when communication company WorldCom, with $107 billion in assets, filed for bankruptcy also due to internal fraud.[2] As a result of these bankruptcies and other corporate fraud, Congress quickly passed the **Sarbanes–Oxley Act (SOX)**. SOX expanded oversight of auditors and lawyers as well as established corporate controls and rules issued by the U.S. Securities and Exchange Commission (SEC) and created new New York Stock Exchange (NYSE) listing standards in an effort to make sure such wide scale corporate fraud could not happen again.[3]

Sarbanes–Oxley Act (SOX): Federal law that increases transparency in public company reporting requirements. The law protects employees of publicly traded companies who report violations by their employers of SEC regulations.

bill: A draft of a proposed law.

committee: A legislative suborganization in the U.S. Congress or state legislature that handles subject matter.

direct democracy: When people are allowed to vote directly on a law.

referendum: A vote by registered voters on whether to approve or reject an existing law.

How Laws and Policy Are Made

The journey from idea to law can have many starts and stops. In order for SOX to have become a law, for example, it first started as a bill sponsored by Senator Paul Sarbanes and Representative Michael Oxley. The bill then was assigned to an appropriate committee for research and debate. The committee might make some changes to the bill and then vote to release the bill to the full chamber (either the House of Representatives or the Senate depending on where it started). If the full chamber votes to pass the bill, it moves to the other chamber and goes through a similar committee process and full vote. Both houses must vote on the same version of the bill and then it moves to the president's desk for signature or veto. The process is substantially similar in every state. President Bush signed SOX into law in 2002.

About half of the states also use referendum and initiative processes (see Figure 4.1). These are sometimes referred to as **direct democracy** because they allow people to vote directly on laws.

A **referendum** is a vote by registered voters on whether to approve or reject an existing law. Sometimes the state legislature sends a proposed bill straight to the public for

Direct Democracy.

Figure 4.1   Types of Referenda and Initiatives

Referendum → Legislative → Popular

Initiative → Direct → Indirect

a vote (**legislative referendum**), or the public can vote to repeal a law after it has been passed (**popular referendum**). An **initiative** is a proposal for a new law or a constitutional amendment. A **direct initiative** is a petition with a required number of signatures supporting the issue put on the ballot for a vote. An **indirect initiative** is the same, but the measure goes to the legislature for a vote. Of the states that use referenda and initiatives, California is the most prolific: Between 1996 and 2016, the average number of issues for vote on the ballot was 18; in the 2016 election, Californians voted on 17 ballot propositions. Some issues that have been decided by referendum or initiative in California include the legalization of marijuana, gun control, single-use plastic bags, and the repeal or rule changes of the death penalty.[4]

> **legislative referendum:** When the state legislature sends a proposed bill straight to the public for a vote.
>
> **popular referendum:** When the public can vote to repeal a law after it has been passed.
>
> **initiative:** A proposal for a new law or constitutional amendment.
>
> **direct initiative:** A petition with a required number of signatures supporting an issue can be put on the ballot for a vote.
>
> **indirect initiative:** A petition with a required number of signatures supporting the issue can go to the legislature for a vote.

KEY TAKEAWAYS

Role of Business in Shaping Laws and Policy

- Ideas for laws can come from events that elected officials want to prevent from happening again.

- Laws can start as bills, referenda, or initiatives.

EVOLUTION OF LOBBYING: OPPORTUNITIES FOR INFLUENCE

LO 4.2   Explain how the relationship between the government and business is shaping laws and creating public policy.

Given the nature of how laws are made in this country, there are many opportunities for education and influence in the journey of our democratic process. There are also points in our legislative process for checks, such as committee votes, full chamber

lobbying: Influencing or advocating on an issue making its way through the legislative process.

votes, veto power, and veto override. Lobbying is influencing or advocating on an issue making its way through the legislative process. Its roots are in the First Amendment: Congress cannot limit people from petitioning the government. Prior to the 1970s, businesses did not have a significant political presence, and few had their own lobbyists. Business's slow acceptance of their need to pay attention to the government began in the 1970s as a reaction to several federal labor laws and the creation of new federal agencies.

Business Involvement in Policy: From Necessary Evil to Welcome Partner

During World War II, American industries switched to defense production to meet the demands of wartime. That switch created a permanent arms industry that coincided with a vast increase in military spending and readiness.[5] Lobbying on behalf of the defense industry grew in power and influence. After the end of the Cold War, the industry and its influence did not disappear; it simply reorganized. By the 1980s, with the exception of the defense industry, most businesses' attitude toward the government was "stay out." Gradually, that attitude changed to "how can we make them our partner?" As more companies and trade associations employed lobbyists, the strategies changed from reactive to proactive. For example, Medicare is the federal health insurance program for people over 65. For years, legislators wanted the program to cover the cost of members' prescriptions; however, many pharmaceutical companies opposed covering that cost because that would give the government strong bargaining power to negotiate cheaper bulk drug prices. Industry lobbyists developed a strategy that added a prescription drug benefit to Medicare but also included a prohibition on discount bulk sales, resulting in a $205 billion profit for pharmaceutical companies over 10 years.[6]

In 2014, corporations spent over $2.6 billion a year lobbying the federal and state governments; that was more than the operating budgets of both the House of Representatives ($1.8 billion) and the Senate ($860 million).[7] The largest corporations have approximately 100 lobbyists working for them at all times. According to Opensecrets.org, in 2018 the defense industry spent $126 million on 774 lobbyists working on its Washington agenda. The pharmaceutical industry spent $155 million, followed by the electrical manufacturers at $81 million.[i] Individually, the largest corporate spender was insurer Blue Cross Blue Shield, followed by Google parent Alphabet, AT&T, and Boeing. The amount a business spends on lobbying can change year to year depending on the issues it is facing, such as a decrease in military spending by the government, immigration and visa issues, autonomous driver technology, or privacy breaches by social media companies.

This relationship isn't all about money; high-profile government staff take jobs with the companies that used to lobby their offices and vice versa. This revolving door can create an appearance of undue influence or access. As companies' political

revolving door: Reference to the circumstance where former public officials take jobs with the companies that used to lobby their office, or when former lobbyists or corporate officials take jobs with the government agencies they used to lobby.

---

[i] Colleges, universities, and schools spent almost $79 million.

strategies and priorities, and lately technology companies' political strategies and priorities, get more complicated, having someone familiar with their agendas and how the government works at a high level is critical. Although laws limit what issues former government workers can participate in, knowledge of larger administration agendas is valuable in the private sector. For example, 10 of the 34 former George W. Bush cabinet secretaries have registered as lobbyists or joined consulting firms. Others sit on boards of companies their agencies used to regulate.[8] Dozens of officials from the Obama administration have taken jobs in Silicon Valley. David Plouffe, former Obama campaign manager and White House adviser, joined Uber in 2014 as senior vice president of policy and strategy, eventually becoming a board member. Uber faced numerous regulatory challenges in multiple U.S. (and non-U.S.) cities, and Plouffe was instrumental in developing a strategy whereby now Uber is welcome in most U.S. cities.[9] In January 2017, Facebook CEO Mark Zuckerberg hired Plouffe to run the Chan Zuckerberg Initiative, a philanthropic vehicle created by Zuckerberg and his wife Dr. Priscilla Chan. Part of the mission of the initiative is to cure diseases and provide personalized education, impressive goals that will need government help to succeed.[10]

Traditional industries for lobbying include those that have been part of our market system the longest: defense contractors, fossil fuel, banks, insurance, and pharmaceuticals. The technology industry is the newest player in our system of lobbying. A common misconception is that all technology companies share the same issues in terms of laws and political priorities. The reality is that companies like Apple and Google have vastly different regulatory priorities than IBM and HP. Like all lobbying, technology lobbyists aim to educate elected officials and their staff about the regulatory and political priorities of their clients. Many elected officials want to learn about the newest technology, how it works, and its impact. More than traditional industries like fossil fuel and tobacco, technology is generally a bipartisan topic: Elected officials on both sides of the aisle are interested and ready to learn. That doesn't mean that there are not politically divisive technology issues, but interest in the industry is shared by both political parties. Many technology companies have only known one president and one White House administration. They have no experience dealing with an administration of another political party and do not have the decades of experience on which to draw in developing strategies and contingencies. Nevertheless, like all industries, they must start from scratch with every new administration, educating elected officials about the issues and priorities that most impact their business.

Because lobbying is couched in the First Amendment, states and the federal government must be careful when passing laws that limit the political speech of lobbyists and others that seek access and advocacy. Over the past 40 years, courts have held that avoiding corruption or the appearance of corruption in our government is a permissible goal to achieve through laws and regulations. For example, lobbyists must comply with the registration, contribution reporting, and disclosure requirements of the **Lobbying Disclosure Act.** But government regulation cannot target the general gratitude an elected official may feel toward those who support her or the political access support might create. As Justice Kennedy said in *Citizens United*, "Ingratiation and access…are not corruption."

Lobbying Disclosure Act: Legislation that is meant to bring increased accountability to federal lobbying practices and that requires certain compliance with registration, contribution reporting, and disclosure.

Getting In On the Ground Floor: Elections

dark money: Money donated by a business to a nonprofit or a trade association that will then contribute to a candidate the donor supports but will not have to reveal the identity of the donor when making the contribution.

Bipartisan Campaign Reform Act (BCRA) of 2002: A federal law that regulates the financing of political campaigns.

base limits: Restriction on donations to a specific candidate.

aggregate limits: Restrictions on how much money a donor may contribute in total to all candidates and committees.

Not all advocacy relationships are between businesses and representatives or agencies. More and more, businesses are advocating in elections. In 2010 the Supreme Court decided in *Citizens United* to lift limits on how much money can be given to and spent by outside groups like political action committees (PACs) or politically active nonprofits (like the Chamber of Commerce) for political campaigns (more on this in Chapter 15). If a business doesn't want to reveal that it is supporting a specific candidate, it can donate an unlimited amount to a nonprofit or a trade association that will make contributions to the candidate and will not have to reveal its donors. This type of contribution is often referred to as dark money.

Corporate and individual spending on state and federal elections has risen sharply since 2010: the year *Citizens United* was decided. There are laws that limit campaign donations and require the disclosure of donors. For example, according to the Bipartisan Campaign Reform Act (BCRA) of 2002, donations to a particular candidate, called base limits, are restricted, as is how much money a donor may contribute in total to all candidates and committees, called aggregate limits. Congress imposed limits to prevent corruption and the appearance of corruption in our democratic system. In *Citizens United*, the Court struck down BCRA provisions that prohibited corporations and unions from using their general treasury funds to pay for TV or radio ads that mention a specific candidate (electioneering communications). The Supreme Court revisited campaign finance limits in 2014—this time deciding whether the aggregate spending limits violate the First Amendment.

LAW AND SOCIETY 4.1

McCutcheon v. Federal Election Commission, 134 S. Ct. 1434 (2014)

Facts: In the 2011–2012 election cycle, Shaun McCutcheon contributed the maximum base limit to federal candidates and noncandidate political committees. He wanted to contribute more but because of the aggregate spending limits could not. McCutcheon sued, claiming the aggregate limits violated the First Amendment. The district court dismissed his case, holding that because the base limits are constitutional as they serve the interest of preventing corruption in our democratic system, the aggregate limits are also constitutional because they prevent evasion of the base limits and serve as a coherent system rather than a collection of individual limits. McCutcheon appealed.

Issue: Do the aggregate spending limits in the BCRA violate donors' First Amendment rights?

Decision: Yes, the aggregate spending limits in the BCRA violate donors' First Amendment rights. Contributing money to a candidate is a statement of an individuals' political expression and political association and thus falls under the First Amendment. In 1976 when this Court first looked at political contribution limits, we decided that the purpose of placing limits on contributions was to prevent quid pro quo corruption—money in exchange for a specific act—and that aggregate limits served to prevent circumvention of the base limits.

If a donor complies with the base limits, they are prohibited from contributing to more than 10 candidates. To cause one person to contribute at lower levels just so they can contribute to more candidates or causes penalizes that person for "robustly exercising" his First Amendment rights. Moreover, donating large sums of money to campaigns does not, by itself, give rise to quid pro quo corruption. The problem with the aggregate limits is that once they kick in, a donor is banned from making *any* contributions regardless of the amount. If the aggregate limits were put in place to prevent circumvention of the base limits, there are stricter anticircumvention rules in place today, such as prohibiting donating to a specific candidate and to a single-candidate committee. The advancement of technology and social media means that disclosure offers better protection against corruption than it did in 1976. As a result, we find that the aggregate limits do little, if anything, to protect against quid pro quo corruption while significantly restricting participation in the democratic process. The line between quid pro quo corruption and general influence must be respected to prevent suppression of protected speech. Money in politics may appear unseemly but so too is much of what the First Amendment protects.

Law and Management Questions

1. The Court mentions the difference between quid pro quo corruption and general influence. How might influence impact our democratic system that depends on a person's right to engage in free political expression?

2. Before this case, campaign spending increased dramatically, and there were more PACs than ever (2,700 nonaffiliated PACs during the 2012 election). What does that tell you about the effectiveness of base limits?

3. Republican senator John McCain said this of the impact of money in our democracy: "At a minimum, large soft money donations purchase an opportunity for the donors to make their case to elected officials." How might this opportunity affect the impact of First Amendment political speech? Whose speech reaps the benefit of this effect?

Many feel that because the Supreme Court in *McCutcheon* limited the definition of corruption in election financing to quid pro quo corruption, such as bribery, that erasing contribution limits altogether is not far away. The role of corporate money in elections is different in other advanced democracies due to campaign rules and cultural norms. For example, in the United States, most candidates spend the majority of their money on television advertising—much of it negative.[11] In the 2012 presidential election, Barack Obama and Mitt Romney both spent more than $400 million on TV ads. In Germany, where technically there are no limits on contributions, each political party creates just one 90-second ad for the entire election, and the number of times the ad runs on TV is in proportion to the number of votes that party got in the prior election. Culturally, Germans do not tolerate attack ads, and a candidate that used that strategy would lose. Moreover, the entire campaign season in Germany lasts only 6 weeks.[12]

How Social Media Is Changing Access to the Political Process

Social media brings unprecedented levels of transparency to lobbying and the political process: Anyone can check the status of a bill, keep updated on what their elected official's office is doing, or find videos of elected officials making contradictory statements. As a result, elected officials can no longer rely on backroom deals or campaign donations as justification for voting a certain way. Social media has emphasized the importance of facts and a more logical rationale to justify votes while also, some say, reducing the impact of lobbying and the importance of money in the lobbying equation. Mail and television advertising were the typical avenues for communication, but they are expensive; thus, only the biggest players could afford to get their messages out to the voting public. Social media has changed that. Now anyone with Twitter or Facebook accounts can raise awareness and attempt to influence opinion and voting in a more affordable and precise manner.[13]

Social Media and Access to the Government

So important is social media in our lives that the U.S. Supreme Court was asked to decide whether we have a First Amendment right to use it. In *Packingham v. North Carolina*, Lester Packingham, a registered sex offender, was arrested 6 years after serving his sentence for a post he made to Facebook. In that post, Packingham expressed gratitude for not getting a parking ticket. Posting to Facebook violated a North Carolina law that prohibits registered sex offenders from using social media. Packingham claimed the law violated his First Amendment rights, and in 2018 the U.S. Supreme Court agreed. In describing the vital role of social media in our lives in terms of expressing our ideas and opinions, getting the news, and participating in civic society, Justice Kennedy stated that "these websites (social media) provide perhaps the most powerful mechanisms available to a private citizen to make his or her voice heard." As proof, the Court pointed out that governors in all 50 states and almost every member of Congress have social media accounts to engage with constituents.

That makes sense. But what happens when your elected official blocks you from their social media account? President Trump has been criticized for blocking people like author Stephen King and model Chrissy Teigen, among others, from his @realDonaldTrump Twitter account. People across the country are being blocked from their elected officials' social media accounts. For example, J'aime Morgaine, a U.S. Army veteran, was blocked from her congressman's Facebook page after she posted comments critical of his positions. A central Texas congressman has blocked so many constituents from his social media accounts that a local activist group has started selling "My Congressman Blocked Me on Twitter" T-shirts. In early 2017, the American Civil Liberties Union (ACLU) asked Maryland governor Larry Hogan to stop deleting critical comments and blocking people from posting on his Facebook page. Honolulu, Hawaii, and San Diego County, California, were sued when the police and sheriff's departments, respectively, deleted critical comments and banned members of the public. An ethics complaint was filed against former Atlanta mayor Kasim Reed for blocking people, including journalists.

The U.S. Supreme Court considers social media the new public square from which we cannot be denied. Is blocking a constituent from Twitter denying them a voice in the public square? A court in New York says yes. In *Knight v. Donald J. Trump*, six people and the Knight First Amendment Institute at Columbia University sued the president and his social media director for blocking them from @realDonaldTrump. The court found that the interactive space on @realDonaldTrump where users can engage with the content of the president's tweets is a public forum because it is controlled by the president. Although the Twitter account was created before he became president, since he took office the president has used that account to engage with foreign political leaders, promote his administration's legislative agenda, and announce personnel changes before they have been announced to the public through official channels.

Discussion Questions

1. In *Packingham*, why would North Carolina pass a law prohibiting sex offenders from using social media? What stakeholders are impacted by this law?

2. What does the court's ruling in New York mean for the users who have been blocked from elected

officials' social media in other parts of the country?

3. In *Packingham* the Court said that social media was the new public square. Does that mean that *all* censorship of social media is unconstitutional? Does the *Knight* ruling put limits on speech in the public square?

Critical Thinking

The Court in *Packingham* held that the law, N.C. Gen. Stat. Ann. §14-202.5, was overbroad because the definition of *social media* excluded too many sites that had no relation to the state's goal. Look up the law. Can you think of ways to make the law more specific, and therefore constitutional, while still achieving the state's goals?

KEY TAKEAWAYS

Evolution of Lobbying: Opportunities for Influence

- The relationship between business and government has changed considerably over the years through lobbying and revolving-door jobs.

- Businesses advocate for their priorities through lobbying and more recently through political contributions to election campaigns.

CREATING PUBLIC POLICY

LO 4.3 Analyze and critique the rise of corporate social advocacy (CSA) as a means of influencing policy.

We have seen two different ways businesses can influence policy: lobbying and contributing to election campaigns. More recently, an increasing number of CEOs and executives have spoken out on issues they believe are important. According to Howard Schultz, executive chairman of Starbucks, "You can't create emotional attachment if you stand for nothing."[14] For Starbucks and many other companies, having a social conscience now includes speaking up on important and controversial social and political issues such as LGBT rights, gun control, and race. Isn't this what they hire lobbyists to do? Not exactly. When the chairman of Starbucks speaks out on an issue like race, he is branching out on a topic that does not fit squarely with his business or industry, unlike fair trade issues or minimum wage for example. This type of advocacy, called **corporate social advocacy (CSA)**,[15] is different from traditional lobbying. In traditional lobbying, businesses, through their hired lobbyists, work with legislators to draft bills or amendments to bills that are subject to debate, revision, and opportunities for veto. CSA uses a different strategy, typically involving the CEO or other high-level executive speaking directly with the public and/or an elected official about a current social topic, yet it has the potential to influence legislation and policy

> **corporate social advocacy (CSA):** When a CEO or other high-level executive of a business speaks directly with the public and/or an elected official about a current social topic that is outside the scope of their core business. CAS has the potential to influence legislation and policy in the same manner as lobbying.

in the same manner as lobbying. And unlike the multiple layers of the legislative process, social media has provided a direct line from CEOs and other leaders to the voting and buying public.

Marc Benioff, CEO of Salesforce.com, has been a vocal opponent of several state bills many felt would allow religious groups to discriminate against gay people. In late 2014 and early 2015 the Indiana legislature was debating their Religious Freedom Restoration Act (RFRA). Salesforce.com employs between 2,000 to 3,000 people in Indiana, and Benioff felt compelled to speak on their behalf. When both houses passed the bill, Benioff took to Twitter (see Figure 4.2).

When then governor Mike Pence signed the bill into law, Benioff responded (see Figures 4.3 and 4.4).

One week later, Governor Pence signed a revised version of the bill that expressly forbids discrimination on the basis of sexual orientation and gender identity. Shortly thereafter, Arkansas governor Asa Hutchinson signed his state's RFRA after he asked the legislature to make changes to address sexual orientation and gender identity.

In 2016 the Georgia legislature passed House Bill 757: the Free Exercise Protection Act. Both chambers of the Georgia legislature passed the bill; however, several businesses expressed their opposition to the value statement made by the bill. Disney and Marvel stated, "[We] are inclusive companies, and although we have had great experiences filming in Georgia, we will plan to take our business elsewhere should any legislation allowing discriminatory practices be signed into law."[16] Marc Benioff tweeted in response to the bill (see Figure 4.5).

Less than a week later, Georgia governor Nathan Deal vetoed House Bill 757, stating, "I do not think we have to discriminate against anyone to protect the faith-based community in Georgia."[17] Marc Benioff was not the only CEO to publicly oppose the bills. Companies and CEOs as diverse as Tim Cook from Apple, Panera Bread, Walmart, and the NBA made public comments in opposition to one or more state RFRA bills.

There is a downside to CSA and CEO involvement in public political issues: It creates an expectation among the public and customers that a business will take a stand. If the

Figure 4.2   Marc Benioff Protesting the Religious Freedom Restoration Act in Indiana via Twitter

Marc Benioff ✓
@Benioff

We are forced to dramatically reduce our investment in IN based on our employee's & customer's outrage over the Religious Freedom Bill.

6:32 PM · Mar 25, 2015 · Twitter for iPhone

1.7K Retweets   **1.5K** Likes

Source: Twitter/@Benioff

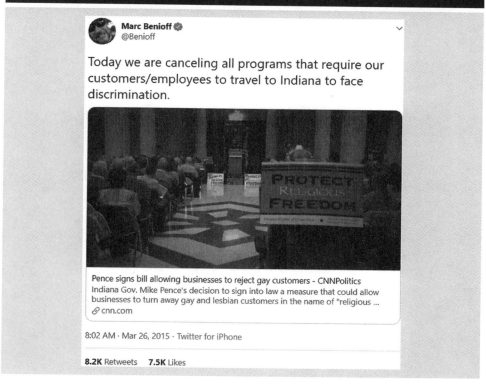

Marc Benioff ✓
@Benioff

Today we are canceling all programs that require our customers/employees to travel to Indiana to face discrimination.

Pence signs bill allowing businesses to reject gay customers - CNNPolitics
Indiana Gov. Mike Pence's decision to sign into law a measure that could allow businesses to turn away gay and lesbian customers in the name of "religious ...
⊘ cnn.com

8:02 AM · Mar 26, 2015 · Twitter for iPhone

8.2K Retweets   **7.5K** Likes

Source: Twitter/@Benioff

business does not, employee and customer frustration may become public. For example, in 2018 Georgia, along with many other southern states, passed a strict abortion law that would essentially ban almost all abortions in the state. Georgia also has a well-established movie production industry, and many celebrities and filmmakers urged studios to boycott Georgia. However, former Georgia state representative Stacey Abrams urged those opposing Georgia's new law to instead invest in groups in the state that are trying to make legislative change. According to Abrams, not only do boycotts punish innocent workers but they are not long-term solutions to a legislative issue. In this instance the ban on abortions is a concerted legislative effort among several states, and a boycott in one state will not impact the results in another.[18]

The government has done its part in fostering a relationship with industry by encouraging business involvement in addressing social issues. For example, in 1996 President Clinton held a Corporate Citizenship Conference to challenge the corporate sector to meet social problems while avoiding the legislative process. The conference highlighted companies that help working families with benefits like on-site daycare, flextime, and parental leave. These companies were meant to serve as role models to encourage other companies to adopt similar policies because there are no laws in the United States mandating parental leave—the United States is the only country of 41 industrialized nations not to offer any paid parental leave.[19]

Figure 4.4   Marc Benioff's Tweet Rallying CEO Opposition to the New Indiana Law

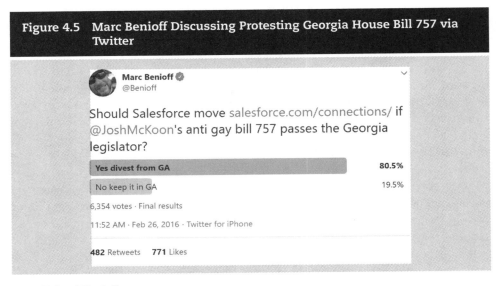

Marc Benioff ✔
@Benioff

Calling other tech CEOs and tech industry leaders to please take a stand.

Salesforce CEO Says Company Is 'Canceling All Programs' In Indiana Over LGBT …
Salesforce CEO Marc Benioff says he doesn't want his employees subjected to discrimination as part of their work for the San Francisco-Based company, and h…
🔗 sanfrancisco.cbslocal.com

11:00 AM · Mar 26, 2015 · Twitter for iPhone

846 Retweets   **746** Likes

Source: Twitter/@Benioff

Figure 4.5   Marc Benioff Discussing Protesting Georgia House Bill 757 via Twitter

Marc Benioff ✔
@Benioff

Should Salesforce move salesforce.com/connections/ if @JoshMcKoon's anti gay bill 757 passes the Georgia legislator?

| Yes divest from GA | 80.5% |
| No keep it in GA | 19.5% |

6,354 votes · Final results

11:52 AM · Feb 26, 2016 · Twitter for iPhone

482 Retweets   **771** Likes

Source: Twitter/@Benioff

KEY TAKEAWAYS

Creating Public Policy

- Businesses engage in CSA when the CEO (or other executive) speaks publicly on a social or political issue not related to their core business.

- CSA creates an expectation among customers and the public that a business will take a stand on a social or political policy issue.

PUBLIC–PRIVATE PARTNERSHIPS

LO 4.4 Describe public–private partnerships (3Ps), and critique their influence on the duties of government and values of a community.

While lobbying and, to some extent, CSA are a natural part of our democracy in terms of businesses' opportunities to influence public policy, governments and businesses have been working together for years to run the business of government. For example, a standard part of building infrastructure and providing services is **outsourcing**: When a highway or a new school needs to be built, the government will contract with private businesses, architects, construction companies, etc., to do the actual design and construction work. This relationship should be mutually beneficial: The government (and we the public) benefits from the expertise and efficiencies of private industry, while the private business gets the revenue from the job.

Sometimes, this mutually beneficial relationship can move beyond simply outsourcing and become a partnership. A **public–private partnership (3P)** is a relationship between a public sector agency—either federal, state, or local—and a private business. Through a contract the parties agree on the nature and scope of the work, delivery of services, and the balance of risks and rewards. In a 3P both parties share the resources, risks, and rewards of a project.

Let's consider an example from Washington, D.C. Running a red light at an intersection is a bad idea: It's against the law and it's dangerous. D.C. had the distinction of being one of the top 20 worst cities in the United States for fatalities from car crashes as a result of running a red light, and it wanted to do something about it. So it partnered with Lockheed Martin IMS (now known as Lockheed Martin) to implement a red light enforcement program. IMS bought over 50 cameras and installed them at strategic intersections throughout the District to take pictures of vehicles, including license plates, while in the act of running a red light. The company handles all aspects of the program: processing images, identifying vehicle owners, issuing notices, and collecting fines ($75 per violation). According to the partnership agreement, IMS also covers all up-front costs and capital expenses like buying, installing, and maintaining the cameras and

outsourcing: When the government contracts with a private business to complete municipal work.

public–private partnership (3P): A relationship between a public sector agency—either federal, state, or local—and a private business with a contract containing agreed-upon terms and conditions. Both parties share the resources, risks, and rewards of a project.

underground sensors. In return, IMS gets paid a percentage of every fee it collects from violators. In 2000, IMS mailed 133,732 notices and collected $6,104,839 in fines for the district. Most importantly, red light violations were down 47% with some intersections seeing an 86% drop in violations.[20]

As cities and states deal with budget cuts and crumbling infrastructure, 3Ps can make a lot of sense. This type of relationship is more common in Asia and the United Kingdom: Tokyo's train and Metro system is privatized, as is the Oyster travel smartcard system in London. It is less common in the United States because governments generally have money put aside for infrastructure projects, and if they need financing, a strong municipal bond market provides tax-free financing. However, funding for infrastructure has been cut dramatically, and our public transit infrastructure earned a grade of D from the American Society of Civil Engineers. 3Ps are one solution: balancing the policy objectives of the government with the cost structure of a private project. However, not everyone is convinced. Many feel when the government "privatizes" a public highway, for example, they are selling public spaces to the highest bidder. As a result, when the public travels on that highway and pays a toll, they are increasing the profit of the company rather than paying the state to maintain the highway. And because the private company is in charge of maintaining that highway, many feel there is no accountability for the private business to the public should maintenance slip. Figure 4.6 compares the advantages and drawbacks of 3Ps.

Only 23 states have legislation allowing 3Ps for public transit projects. The public transit system in Boston, Massachusetts, is the oldest in the United States, dating back to 1631. Although pioneers in mass transit, the Massachusetts Bay Transportation Authority has its share of struggles maintaining and updating a very old system amid budget cuts and staggering debt. So when the multinational company New Balance announced in 2015 that it planned a $500

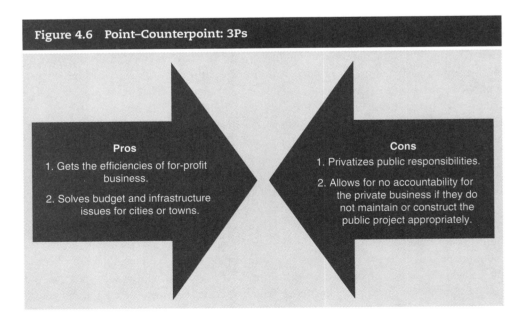

Figure 4.6   Point–Counterpoint: 3Ps

Pros
1. Gets the efficiencies of for-profit business.
2. Solves budget and infrastructure issues for cities or towns.

Cons
1. Privatizes public responsibilities.
2. Allows for no accountability for the private business if they do not maintain or construct the public project appropriately.

The train station opened in Brighton, Massachusetts, in partnership with New Balance.

million expansion[ii] of its headquarters in the Boston neighborhood of Brighton, residents were worried about the traffic impact on a neighborhood that desperately needed public transit service. Rather than wait for the state to appropriate money and build a train station, New Balance decided to build one itself. The partnership between the company and the state included supervision and design approval by the state, but New Balance paid the almost $20 million cost of construction and will maintain the stop for the first ten years after it opens. In order to address stakeholder concerns, the company sought neighborhood input on the design, accessibility, and impact on parking. New Balance sees this as a win-win-win: the train station and expansion will make New Balance a better place to work, its 700 employees and the public can take public transit rather than drive to the many properties in the complex owned by New Balance, and the community now has train service.[21] The station opened in May 2017.

For Boston and New Balance, a 3P can make sense. But when an employer will have as many employees as residents of the town (like Facebook in Menlo Park, California), or occupies the same amount of office space as the city's next 40 biggest employers combined (Amazon in Seattle, Washington), a 3P seems inadequate to handle the impact on the city's infrastructure and residents. The upsides of growth are many: decreased unemployment, and increased salaries, economic activity (like restaurants, retail, entertainment), diversity, and taxes. However, the downsides are also significant. For example, traffic congestion: Seattle has the third highest concentration of mega-commuters—people traveling at least 90 minutes each way to work. Home prices in East Palo Alto, California, a historically African American and Latino community neighboring Menlo Park, rose by almost 76% from 2012 to 2014. Balancing the need for economic growth and residents' concerns about that growth have led to varied solutions.

[ii]Including an ice rink open to the public (when the Boston Bruins aren't practicing on it), a practice facility for the Boston Celtics basketball team, and open space.

Alphabet City to Zucktown

One concern about the explosive growth of tech companies is the rising "app culture" where tech employees take a private bus to work, get off the bus, eat lunch at the work cafeteria, get back on their bus, go home, and order dinner from an app. So while workers live in a community, they are not engaging with the community. This lack of engagement has economic consequences for local business likes cafés and restaurants. To combat this, Mountain View, California, one of the new homes of Facebook, passed a law prohibiting companies from fully subsidizing meals. San Francisco, home to Google and Twitter, proposed a similar law that would prohibit the construction of on-site eating facilities in new office buildings. Harry Glaser, cofounder of tech company Periscope Data said to *Business Insider* that he thinks "it's reasonable for the community to expect us to engage" whether by voting, volunteering, or buying lunch.[22]

Perhaps the most dire impact of tech growth is soaring housing prices and growing homelessness. East Palo Alto was the most affordable community left in Silicon Valley, and many who live there supply the low-wage labor to affluent suburbs like Menlo Park. Infrastructure and housing inventory have not increased in line with population growth, and residents are either getting forced out because of unaffordable rents or moving to areas that have fewer job opportunities. Seattle is the eighteenth largest city in the United States but has the third largest homeless population. The economic surge coupled with the disappearance of affordable housing has changed the stereotype of the homeless as unemployed; now many homeless are retail clerks, plumbers, janitors, baristas, and teachers who go to work, sleep in their car, and join a gym to use the showers. Ten local governments on the West Coast have declared states of emergency to help fund solutions for their growing homeless population.

Do businesses have a responsibility to address different stakeholder concerns when their presence dominates a community? In 2011, when Apple proposed building Apple Park, a $5 billion campus in Cupertino, California, that was not near public transportation and had parking spaces for 11,000 cars, the Cupertino City Council asked Steve Jobs how residents would benefit from the new building. Jobs' reply was this: Apple pays taxes. Apple's chief design officer stated, "We didn't make Apple Park for other people...it wasn't made for you."

Not all tech companies are taking the same approach. Amazon has developed a relationship with Mary's Place, a nonprofit network of homeless shelters in Seattle. Amazon has promised that their new building would also house a new Mary's Place, which will be the city's largest homeless shelter; has provided the nonprofit with one of its unused buildings in another part of town; and also started offering Mary's Place free food from its nearby Amazon Go store. While generous, some feel that funding a homeless shelter is not a sustainable solution as shelters offer only temporary, emergency relief and cannot address the underlying economic problems causing displacement.

Google and Facebook, among other tech companies, have gone beyond philanthropy and 3Ps by reinventing the company town, a concept that has had mixed success in the United States. In 2017, Google won approval from the city council of Mountain View, California, to create three new residential neighborhoods: Joaquin, Shorebird, and Pear. Google owns 58% of the land that will be used for the neighborhoods, which will include 10,000 homes, offices, shops, businesses, and a public park. Google's vice president of real estate development said Google agrees with the community that "development should be done in a way that is open to everyone, including varying levels of affordability...while helping to alleviate traffic congestion... and housing imbalance." One member of the city council raised concerns that because Apple did not build any housing when it built Apple Park, some of the 12,000 Apple workers would move to the new Google neighborhoods. The city council views the development plan as a "living document," something Google and the city of Mountain View will revisit and adjust along the way. Google's development goals reach internationally as well. Alphabet, Google's parent company, has committed $50 million of an expected $1 billion for the first phase of development of Quayside, a high-tech neighborhood on Toronto's waterfront. The neighborhood will include apartment buildings, bikeshares, bus lines, and parks.

Facebook bought 54 acres in Belle Haven, California, a neighborhood between Menlo Park and East Palo Alto. Their new community, called Willow Village, will have 1,500 apartments, 225 available at below-market rents, retail, a grocery store, and a drug store. While many Facebook employees will most likely live in Willow Village, it is a public community complete with parks, plazas, bike paths, a revamped rail line, and a pedestrian bridge. The company is already embedded in the community: the Chan Zuckerberg Initiative has given $3 million to an East Palo Alto legal services group that helps low-income residents with housing and immigration issues, and it has given $7 million to create an elementary school in the community. In 2014, Facebook paid $200,000 to build a new police substation next to its campus, pays the annual rent for the station, and also pays the $173,146 salary and benefits of an officer. When Facebook offered the city $9 million over 5 years to fund police training, a Menlo Park city councilman stated, "I'm not on board…[it is] bad public policy to accept gifts for basic city services."

Like the councilman, having a community run by a private company worries some. According to a Belle Haven community activist, "Corporations are paying for things the city or county used to pay for…they have a lot of money…more than the city does. And a lot more power." Instead of owing a duty to the public, many worry public servants will be beholden to a private company. Others worry about the relationship between employees and employers if their boss is also their landlord. If a worker leaves Facebook, will they also have to leave their home? According to Facebook, their goal is to strengthen the community by providing spaces where people can engage more; Willow Village is just the starting point.

Discussion Questions

1. Patti Fry, the former chairwoman of the Menlo Park City Planning Commission, agrees that Facebook is doing more than most companies in terms of mitigating its impact on the community; yet "most of what they do serves them…I do not expect a company to have as a priority providing community services that a real community needs. They're in business to be in business." What does she mean by this? Do you agree with her? Explain your answer.

2. Cecilia Taylor, a Belle Haven community activist, claims that Facebook is very smart because "they have money in every problem. Immigration. Housing. Transportation. Education." Why is this a smart strategy for Facebook? What potential problems can you see for the community with this strategy?

3. Some worry that people literally living where they work will create insularity that will stymie innovation and the start-up culture of Silicon Valley, an area built by people jumping from job to job. How could living where you work discourage innovation? Can where you live actually impact an entire industry? Explain your answer.

Critical Thinking

In a company town, the private business takes over many of the public services. Thinking about Google's neighborhoods and Facebook's Willow Village, who are the stakeholders impacted by the creation of these privately run communities? What could be some long-term consequences of company towns for the community as well as local and state governments?

Public institutions are only as strong as the public that holds them accountable. Given your previous answer, what might be the impact of the rise of company towns on public institutions? Is this a trade-off you think we should be willing to accept?

KEY TAKEAWAYS

Public–Private Partnerships

- 3Ps are an effective way to provide solutions for cities and towns with tight budgets.

- 3Ps privatize what typically is a public function, like building a train station.

ETHICAL DIMENSIONS OF INFLUENCING POLICY

LO 4.5 Identify and assess the ethical issues that may arise when business and government work together.

In many situations, 3Ps can provide alternatives to public infrastructure or other projects: cost savings for budget-strapped government agencies, access to private sector expertise, and dependable revenue for businesses. However, should a public project be handed over, even partially, to a private business whose interests are not always aligned with those of the larger society the government serves? Are there some public projects that should not be subjected to the profit and loss calculations of the private sector?

Private Prisons

Private prisons provide an example of how in a 3P the interests of the government (and the public) and the interests of a private, for-profit business can collide—with human beings caught in the middle. Since the 1980s, incarceration rates in the United States have more than tripled, resulting in a federal prison population increase of over 800%—far faster than existing facilities could keep up. [23] In order to accommodate the growing inmate population, the Federal Bureau of Prisons entered into 3Ps with private prison corporations to house and manage federal prisoners. By 2013, the peak of inmate population growth, the federal government was housing 15% of its prisoners (30,000 people) in privately run prisons, but as of late 2016 that number was down to 14,200 people. [24] Twenty-nine states now use private prisons, and while some states do not use them at all, a few states make extensive use of privately run facilities. For example, nearly 44% of all New Mexico prisoners are held in private prisons. [25] The partnership focuses generally on low-security inmates designated "criminal aliens," non-citizens who have committed a crime, with less than 8 years left on their sentence. Nationally, the two largest private prison corporations, CoreCivic and the Geo Group, own and operate almost all of the U.S. Immigration and Customs Enforcement (ICE) detention facilities. [26] Advocates of private prisons argue that competition and freedom from bureaucratic constraints allow private companies to run prisons efficiently without sacrificing effectiveness. But because private facilities do not have to release as much information as public facilities, not much is known about their cost-effectiveness, and because they can choose which types of inmates they will house (healthy, nonviolent, etc.), comparing the efficiency and effectiveness of private facilities with public facilities is not an apples-to-apples comparison.

Private Prisons

iStockphoto.com/Rattankun Thongbun

The number of private prison companies has shrunk since 1999 when there were 12 companies competing for government partnerships; now there are 6. Core-Civic and Geo Group, both publicly traded, account for 55% and 30%, respectively, of all private prison beds. The consolidation of the industry and the rise of two dominant players encourage both companies to lobby for favorable legislation. The two private prison companies spent nearly $3 million combined lobbying Congress in 2018. Over 70% of migrants are held in ICE detention facilities run by CoreCivic and Geo Group. In its 2018 10-K Annual Report filed with the SEC, CoreCivic stated that the company's future is subject to the uncertainties associated with "changes in occupancy levels…the public acceptance of our services…continued utilization of the South Texas Family Residential Center by U.S. Immigration and Customs Enforcement."[27] Because the success of the private prison business model depends on people to fill the facilities, many 3P contracts include mandatory occupancy rates.

The goals of the government in punishing and incarcerating people are many, including deterrence, rehabilitation, and retribution. When a person commits a crime, they are engaging in conduct that society has determined is threatening. Thus, if a person is deprived of their liberty by going to jail, many believe that decision should only be made by a body that represents the people. A criminal sentence is a by-product of a social contract (and laws) between person and state and should not be delegated to a private entity because the identity of the punisher is key to achieving the goals of punishment: deterrence from harming society and the state. The goals of a for-profit private prison company are different; as for-profit businesses, they have a fiduciary duty to maximize shareholder value that is usually achieved through reducing costs and increasing profit.

In the case of private prisons, this means increasing the inmate population while reducing costs. Because about 65% to 70% of operating costs for private prisons are salaries, the primary cost reduction strategy is paying lower salaries—on average, correctional officers in private prisons earn $7,000 less than those in a public facility. Moreover, private prisons tend to hire fewer officers (1 officer per 6.9 inmates in a private facility versus 1 officer per 4.9 in a state facility). The combination of lower pay and lower staffing may explain the high turnover rate. A 2008 Texas report found that the turnover rate among the seven private prisons in the state was 90%, compared to 24% for public facilities.

New Mexico provides a telling example of the conflicting impact private prisons can have on a community. CoreCivic has operated a prison in Estancia, New Mexico, for nearly 30 years. In order to stay open, the facility needs at least 700 inmates; however, due to a declining inmate population, the prison currently houses only 580 prisoners. If the facility closes, 200 people will lose their jobs. In a town of only 1,500 and a county of 15,000 people, the possible closure has the attention of elected officials who do not want to see their constituents lose their jobs and must figure out a way to increase the inmate population to break-even levels.

Not everyone will miss the facility, or private prisons generally, if it closes. CoreCivic has been sued many times for sexual assault, physical assaults, harassment, deficient medical care, and civil rights

(Continued)

(Continued)

violations. In Idaho, CoreCivic operated the state's largest prison, nicknamed "Gladiator School" because of the rampant violence due to chronic understaffing. In 2014 the Federal Bureau of Investigation (FBI) opened an investigation into whether CoreCivic defrauded the government by falsely documenting staffing levels for financial gain. After 15 months, the agency did not bring charges because the false staffing records were created by low-level employees and the company got paid by the state based on the number of inmates, not the number of employees. Thus, even though false, the records were not for financial gain. The violent conditions in the prison were not part of the investigation.

In August 2016, Sally Yates, then U.S. assistant attorney general, wrote a memo to the Bureau of Prisons suggesting that it was time to phase out the use of private prisons. According to Yates, although private prisons served a very important purpose at the time, conditions have changed—for example, a decline in the federal inmate population and changes to sentencing laws. Moreover, Yates stated that private prisons do not provide the same savings, adequate levels of safety and security, nor effective rehabilitation and educational programs as public facilities. In February 2017, U.S. attorney general Jeff Sessions said the federal government would continue to use private prisons.

Discussion Questions

1. *Stakeholder theories:* Who are the stakeholders effected by our criminal justice system? How might using private prisons impact these stakeholders? Are there advantages and/or disadvantages for them by having something as critical as punishment linked to profit?

2. *Ethical decision-making:* Why is the identity of the punisher key to achieving the goals of punishment? Using a principles-based approach and a consequences-based approach answer: Does it make a difference who punishes a person for committing a crime or just that they are punished?

Take a Position

The day after Donald Trump won the presidential election, the stock of CoreCivic was up 43% and the Geo Group's up 21%.

Issue: Should the government build more prisons, or should we use private prisons to house and manage our inmate population? Explain your answer.

If you are an inmate in a prison facility run by a private company and you feel your legal rights have been violated, to whom do you look for accountability: the state that sentenced you and contracted with the private prison, or the company running the prison? To answer this, we must first answer the question: are employees of a private business in a 3P with a government agency considered part of the government? This is an important question because, as we will learn in Chapter 15, constitutional protections apply only when there is a government actor involved and there are limits on government liability for personal injury.

The Eighth Amendment and Private Prisons

The Eighth Amendment provides protection from the government for cruel and unusual punishment. When it comes to conditions in a public prison, this means that the court must determine whether the conditions were cruel: Did an official actually know of and disregard a substantial risk of serious bodily injury or deprive a prisoner of a basic human need? For example, denying meals as retaliation, poor air quality when it poses a serious danger to health such as secondhand smoke or extreme heat, or lack of sanitary toilet facilities. The U.S. Supreme Court has held that inmates in federal facilities may only sue agency employees, not the agency itself, for Eighth Amendment violations. Why? If the goal is to deter violations of the Eighth Amendment, suing the federal agency does nothing to deter individual employees in the prisons from violating the law. What does that mean when you are an inmate in a private prison?

Minneci et al. v. Pollard et al., 132 S. Ct. 176 (2012)

Facts: Richard Pollard was an inmate in a federal prison operated by Wakenhut Corrections Corporation, a private company. In 2001, Pollard sustained injuries when he tripped on a cart left in the doorway of the prison butcher shop. The prison staff x-rayed his arms and, thinking he might have fractured both elbows, transported Pollard to an outside medical facility and arranged for his surgery. Pollard claimed that despite telling the guard that he could not straighten his arms, the guard made him wear a prison jumpsuit for transport to the medical facility, causing him "excruciating pain." During several visits to the outside medical facility, prison staff made Pollard wear arm restraints that caused "excruciating pain." Prison medical and other personnel failed to follow medical instructions and provide Pollard with a posterior arm splint; failed to provide him with required physical therapy; failed to provide alternative arrangements for his meals, resulting in Pollard having to auction off personal items to raise the funds to buy food at the commissary. In addition, prison staff failed to provide Pollard with basic hygiene care to the point where he couldn't bathe for 2 weeks.

Pollard sued prison staff for damages, claiming they deprived him of adequate medical care in violation of the Eighth Amendment's prohibition against cruel and unusual punishment. The prison staff claimed that Pollard could not sue them for damages under the Eighth Amendment because, among other reasons, they are employees of a private business and not employees of the government.

Issue: Can an inmate of a private prison sue prison staff for damages as a result of inadequate medical care under the Eighth Amendment?

Decision: No, an inmate of a private prison cannot sue prison staff for damages as a result of inadequate medical care under the Eighth Amendment.

Prior case law tells us that constitutional violations by a federal officer may give rise to a claim for damages. The decision whether to recognize such an action requires a two-step analysis: First, is there any alternative, existing process for protecting Mr. Pollard's interests (compensating him for his injuries) that would convince us not to create a new type of legal claim? Next, even if there isn't an existing legal claim, courts must exercise prudent judgment before they authorize a new kind of federal litigation. We conclude that Pollard cannot assert a claim for damages under the Eighth Amendment because his claim focuses on conduct that typically falls within state tort law (physical and related emotional injury). Because the prison staff are private employees, state tort law provides an adequate process for Mr. Pollard to sue and get damages. In California, where any state claim would be filed in this case, state law provides tort claims for negligence, lack of ordinary care or skill, and negligent failure to diagnose or treat. Although Mr. Pollard may get less in damages by suing the guards for torts than he would for an Eighth Amendment constitutional claim, this does not render the state process inadequate.

Law and Management Questions

1. Does the threat of a tort lawsuit provide enough incentive in this case for Wakenhut employees to follow the law? Keep in mind the last sentence of the decision.

2. Why wouldn't Mr. Pollard sue the guards individually? How do you think that would impact his daily life in prison?

3. Can you think of management policies that could incentivize correctional staff to follow proper procedure? What about accountability policies?

Ethical Dimensions of Influencing Policy

- Incentives and fiduciary duties may cause a private company in a 3P to work against the interests of the public.

- Liability for injury is complicated when a 3P is involved.

SUMMARY

The relationship between private business and the government has evolved. Today, more companies are getting involved in social and political issues, and more customers demand that involvement. While efficiencies can be realized by partnering with private business, accountability for injury may become murky.

KEY TERMS

aggregate limits   72
base limits   72
bill   68
Bipartisan Campaign Reform Act (BCRA) of 2002   72
committee   68
corporate social advocacy (CSA)   75

dark money   72
direct democracy   68
direct initiative   69
indirect initiative   69
initiative   69
legislative referendum   69
lobbying   70

Lobbying Disclosure Act   71
outsourcing   79
popular referendum   69
public–private partnership (3P)   79
referendum   68
revolving door   70
Sarbanes–Oxley Act (SOX)   68

REVIEW QUESTIONS

1. Describe the process by which a bill becomes a law and how that process provides opportunities for influence.

2. Explain the difference between lobbying and CSA.

3. What are the pros and cons of CSA for the business and for elected officials?

4. How does a 3P work? Explain the advantages and disadvantages of a 3P for the public.

Private Prisons

Lena is the assistant director of her state's Department of Corrections. She has spent her career, thus far, in law enforcement. The new governor has proposed slashing her department's budget by almost 30%; this would mean no new facilities to help alleviate the already-crowded conditions in local jails. Lena wants to pursue a 3P with a private prison company but is wary of the problems that can arise in the relationship.

Framing Questions

1. What are some of Lena's goals entering into a 3P with a private prison company?

2. How would those goals change if she were dealing with a female inmate population? Juvenile population?

3. Could Lena structure the payments made under the contract to help her better achieve her goals?

Assignment

You are Lena's new deputy assistant director, and she has asked you to draft a memo addressing how you would structure your 3P contract with a private prison company to better meet your goals. What clauses would you include? How would you define *breaches*? Thinking about the incentives created by getting paid based on capacity, how could you structure payments to avoid those incentives? What would you consider "effectiveness"?

LIABILITY, BUSINESS AGREEMENTS, AND MANAGING RISK

Learning Objectives

Upon completion of this chapter, the reader should be able to do the following:

5.1 Identify and interpret risk and potential damages exposure in light of torts.

5.2 Assess business conduct that might increase or decrease risk using tort theories.

5.3 Explain the elements of a contract.

5.4 Analyze how businesses can use contracts to limit liability risk.

Ethics in Context

Nondisclosure Agreements and Public Safety

Contracts provide predictability: They set out the rules of a transaction and what might happen if a party breaks those rules. Such clarity creates trust because each party knows what to expect. Nondisclosure agreements (NDAs), once only found in the tech industry to protect confidential information, are now used regularly in employment contracts to prevent current and former employees from speaking about toxic cultures, sexual harassment, and other information important for public safety that might be damaging to a business. Do

iStockphoto.com/powerofforever

NDAs create distrust? Are they more harmful, under certain circumstances, to the public than they are helpful to the business? Later in the chapter, in the Ethics in Context section, we will examine the ethical and justice implications of widespread use of NDAs.

INTRODUCTION

Business is risky for the entrepreneur who puts their heart, soul, and frequently their last penny into their business and hopes the market likes it, or for the manager who goes out on a limb to introduce a new business line. But there is also the everyday risk of liability when you provide a service, sell a product, or have employees. What if your product injures a customer?

What if your star employee leaves to work for your competitor, taking her knowledge of your confidential operations with her? Despite your good faith and ethics-based leadership, risk and liability are unavoidable in business. However, there are ways to limit exposure through carefully worded contracts.

RISK OF INJURY

LO 5.1 Identify and interpret risk and potential damages exposure in light of torts.

When someone is injured by another, either physically or financially, they have the right to compensation for their injuries. This is the world of civil justice and torts. A **tort** is a civil wrong that causes harm to another; that could be an injury from a defective product, damage to your car from an accident, or something less tangible like harm to your reputation from false statements made about you online. There are two broad categories of torts: intentional torts and negligence. Tort law not only allows an injured party to seek compensation for their injuries but also holds people and businesses accountable for their actions. Accountability can incentivize behavior that is good for society, like making products safer, driving carefully, and speaking truthfully.

> **tort:** A civil wrong that causes harm to another.

For example, Johnson & Johnson faces more than 14,000 civil tort lawsuits claiming its baby powder contained the carcinogen asbestos and caused ovarian cancer and mesothelioma, a rare cancer linked to asbestos exposure. How do the injured people determine how much to ask the court for in damages? The goal of **compensatory damages** is to make the injured person whole, restoring them to the position they were in before the injury. Compensatory damages achieve this by replacing costs such as lost wages, out-of-pocket medical expenses, any future medical expenses, and also compensation for damaged property. In the Johnson & Johnson lawsuits, a jury awarded Ms. Olson, a Delaware resident, $25 million in compensatory damages for her mesothelioma and the impact that has had on her life, marriage, family, etc.[1] **Punitive damages**, on the other hand, serve a broader purpose: They are intended to punish the defendant for reprehensible conduct and deter others from engaging in the same type of conduct (see Figure 5.1). Although intended to punish the defendant, the injured party receives the money. For this reason, punitive damages can be controversial and more powerful in terms of incentivizing ethical conduct and accountability. The jury in Ms. Olson's case ordered Johnson & Johnson to pay her $300 million in punitive damages. Ms. Olson claimed Johnson & Johnson knew for years that some of its powders contained asbestos but hid that from regulators and the public.[2] Figure 5.2 compares compensatory and punitive damages.

> **compensatory damages:** Money awarded to the plaintiff, or injured person, that is intended to restore them to the position they were in before the injury.

> **punitive damages:** Damages, in addition to compensation for the injury, that are intended to punish the defendant for reprehensible conduct and deter others from engaging in the same type of conduct.

Compensation for damages is an important component of fairness and justice: two concepts of global importance. Many European countries have tort laws similar to the United States, including compensation for injuries and losses. Although we have 50 different states in the United States, state legal systems and tort laws are similar. Thus, although there are differences from state to state, by and large resolution of tort claims and awarding of injuries is consistent across the country. The same cannot be said for the European Union.

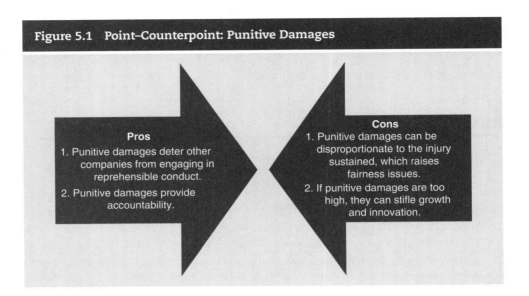

Figure 5.1 Point–Counterpoint: Punitive Damages

Pros
1. Punitive damages deter other companies from engaging in reprehensible conduct.
2. Punitive damages provide accountability.

Cons
1. Punitive damages can be disproportionate to the injury sustained, which raises fairness issues.
2. If punitive damages are too high, they can stifle growth and innovation.

Figure 5.2 Comparison of Compensatory and Punitive Damages

Compensator Damages	Punitive Damages
• To make the injured person whole	• To punish the defendant
• Medical expenses	• For reprehensible conduct
• Lost wages	• To deter others
• Pain and suffering	

Legal systems among member states vary a great deal more than the state legal systems in the United States. For example, there are fundamental differences in common law in Ireland and England. Member states have been independent countries for centuries, with their own distinct tort systems; however, the European Union is moving toward harmonizing civil law of member states.[3]

In China, on the other hand, contemporary tort law is a more recent development. After the Cultural Revolution of the 1970s, the first written set of tort law was introduced in 1987, and the Tort Liability Law, a more organized and comprehensive set of laws, was enacted in 2009. Chinese tort law includes concepts of fault and both compensatory and punitive damages.[4]

Intentional Torts

intentional tort: Harm caused by deliberate conduct.

An **intentional tort** is harm caused by deliberate conduct. This does not mean that a person intended to harm another—only that the person intended to engage in the conduct. Figure 5.3 lists some intentional torts most related to business. A plaintiff must prove each element of her tort claim in order to prevail.

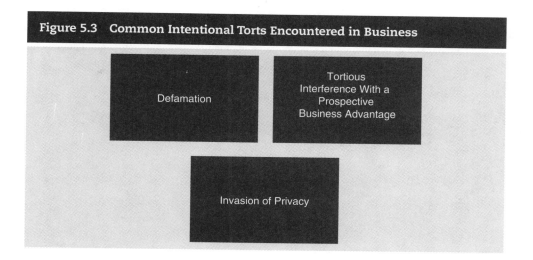

Figure 5.3   Common Intentional Torts Encountered in Business

Defamation

Tortious Interference With a Prospective Business Advantage

Invasion of Privacy

Defamation

Defamation involves injury to one's reputation. In business, a company's reputation can be one of its most valuable assets and vigorously defended. The elements of defamation are as follows:

- The statement is defamatory; this is a factual statement that is likely to hurt someone's reputation.

- The statement is false.

- The statement is communicated to someone other than the plaintiff.

- The statement causes injury.

Injury for defamation is generally injury to your reputation—how others think of you and what they believe about you. So, in order to sue for defamation, other people had to have heard the statement. This can cause embarrassment, humiliation, anxiety, lost clients, lost business, etc.

Defamation in the United Kingdom is very similar to that in the United States. However, the United Kingdom had a "no win, no fee" contingency, and damages awarded were generally much higher than in the United States and other countries. Because of this, the United Kingdom was known as the "libel tourism" capital of the world: non-U.K. citizens or companies would attempt to use U.K. courts for defamation cases because U.K. law at the time favored plaintiffs. However, the 2013 U.K. Defamation Act attempts to curb this trend by barring non-U.K. parties from filing defamation cases in the United Kingdom unless they can prove serious harm and a more systematic connection with the country.[5]

In the case *Seaton v. TripAdvisor*, there is no doubt that the reputation of the Grand Resort Hotel and Convention Center was damaged, but does that mean they will win their defamation suit?

> defamation: Intentional tort; defamatory statement that is false, communicated to someone other than the plaintiff, and causes injury.

Seaton v. TripAdvisor, 728 F.3D 592 (2013)

Facts: Kenneth Seaton was the sole proprietor of the Grand Resort Hotel and Convention Center in Pigeon Forge, Tennessee. Seaton operated the Grand Resort since 1982 and established it as a valuable business in the state and for tourists traveling to the Great Smoky Mountains. TripAdvisor, a worldwide company in the business of conducting surveys on hotels and restaurants throughout the world, conducted a survey in 2011 of its users that was titled "The 2011 Dirtiest Hotels as Reported by Travelers on TripAdvisor." Number one on this list was the Grand Resort in Pigeon Forge, Tennessee. Included with the survey was a photo of a ripped bedspread along with a quote: "There was dirt at least ½ inch thick in the bathtub which was filled with lots of dark hair." It also had a thumbs-down image next to this statement: "87% of reviewers do not recommend this hotel." Seaton sued TripAdvisor for $10 million for defamation and lost business. TripAdvisor claimed that Grand Resort's placement on the list was protected speech under the First Amendment to the U.S. Constitution because the list does not make any factual claims.

Issue: Whether TripAdvisor's list claiming the Grand Resort is the dirtiest hotel is a statement of fact and therefore defamatory?

Ruling: No, TripAdvisor's list claiming the Grand Resort is the dirtiest hotel in America is not a statement of fact. Because TripAdvisor considers itself providing "the world's most trusted travel advice," Seaton claimed that placement on this list connotes a statement of fact. We disagree. First, TripAdvisor's use of the word *dirtiest* is a loose, hyperbolic term because it is the superlative of an adjective. No reader of TripAdvisor's list would understand the Grand Resort to be, objectively, the dirtiest hotel in all of the Americas. Thus, it is clear to us, as it would be to any reader, that TripAdvisor is not stating that Grand Resort is the dirtiest hotel in America as an actual assertion of fact.

The general tenor of the list supports this conclusion. On the webpage where the list appears, TripAdvisor clearly states the list is "reported by travelers on TripAdvisor." The implication is clear: The rankings are based on the subjective reviews of TripAdvisor users, not on objectively verifiable facts. Based on this, readers would know that TripAdvisor did not conduct a scientific study to determine which 10 hotels were objectively the dirtiest in America but instead would understand the list to be the opinions of travelers who use TripAdvisor.

Discussion Questions

1. Who generates most of the content on TripAdvisor?

2. How does a site like TripAdvisor make money? Do you think its business model contributed to its decision to run a list like this?

3. Who are the stakeholders in a decision to run a list like the one run by TripAdvisor?

Critical Thinking

Do you think the Grand Resort lost business because of the list? Does it seem fair that it should suffer from TripAdvisor's list and not be able to recover any damages from the company? Explain your answer. What other strategy could TripAdvisor have used to generate traffic and not get sued for defamation?

Defamation and Social Media

The prevalence of social media as a method of communication has caused courts to consider how the context and structure of the platform impacts whether we expect people to tell the truth when communicating online. Social media by its nature encourages exaggeration and emotion; it also encourages people to republish what they read. More on the impact of social media will be discussed in Chapter 12, including the incentives created by the business model of most social media companies. The platforms make money by user engagement, and extreme and shocking content increases user engagement. This has important ramifications for liability for defamation.

For example, Sandals Resorts learned of several widely disseminated e-mails sent by an unknown author to several undisclosed recipients containing critical and allegedly defamatory comments about the resort's hiring practices. In order to pursue a defamation action, Sandals asked a court to require Google to release the e-mail account holder's identity. In denying Sandals' request, the court explained that for Sandals to be entitled to this information, it must show that its reputation was damaged by the statements made in the e-mail, and Sandals could not do that. Looking at the overall context of the e-mail, the court said it was an "exercise in rhetoric,"[6] raising questions in the reader's mind rather than making assertions of fact. Moreover, according to the court, the culture of Internet communications (the court treated the anonymous e-mail sent to undisclosed recipients the same as a social media post) encourages "free-wheeling, anything goes"[7] writing that is often casual, emotional, and replete with grammatical mistakes. And because anyone with an Internet connection can post their thoughts online, readers give less credence to social media than traditional forms of media.

The casual and emotional characteristics of communication on social media was reiterated in a defamation case against President Trump brought by Cheryl Jacobus, a political strategist and commentator, for tweets by the president (see Figure 5.4).

In denying her defamation suit, the court said the culture of Internet communications, unlike traditional print media, is such that even fiery rhetoric and epithets are seen as expressions of strident opinion rather than fact. Even though the court recognized that the tweets were meant to belittle and demean Jacobus, given the context in which the statements were made, no reasonable reader would think less of her and her work.[8]

Does that mean that nothing said online can be considered defamation? Not quite; statements must be viewed holistically, looking at the overall context and not just the specific words that were used. So when computer software company ESG sued computer support network Bleeping Computer for posting defamatory comments about the business and products of ESG, the court considered whether a reasonable reader would take Bleeping Computer's statements as true. Bleeping Computer has a live chat feature where its experts advise customers about products on the market. Through the live chat, one Bleeping Computer expert referred to the ESG product SpyHunter as "a rogue product...[that] has since been delisted" and as a "dubious program with a high rate of false positives" and alleged that ESG did this purposely to provide unnecessary services to unsuspecting customers. Looking at the overall context, the court stated a reasonable reader

Figure 5.4   Then Candidate Trump's Tweet at Issue in *Jacobus v. Trump*

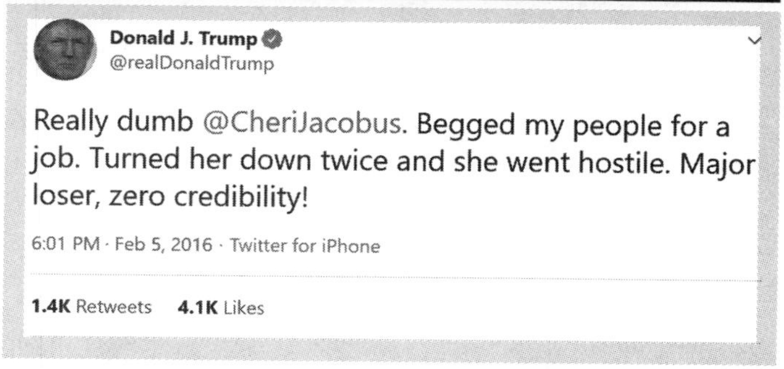

Donald J. Trump ✓
@realDonaldTrump

Really dumb @CheriJacobus. Begged my people for a job. Turned her down twice and she went hostile. Major loser, zero credibility!

6:01 PM · Feb 5, 2016 · Twitter for iPhone

1.4K Retweets   **4.1K** Likes

Source: Twitter/@Benioff

would consider these statements true. The speaker was an expert of Bleeping Computer, whose business is to provide support and advice; the speaker used specific facts and referred to specific conduct and then characterized those facts and that conduct as a "deliberate... scam." The intermittent use of "my personal recommendation" and "in my opinion" do not transform the statements into opinion because the overall context of the live chat is expert, fact-based advice, and if a Bleeping Computer expert was giving a customer a recommendation, the customer would assume that recommendation was based on facts.[9]

In another example, a court in Virginia included hashtags used in a Twitter feed as part of the overall context of the statements. AvePoint, Inc., sued Power Tools (Axceler) for defamation based on several of Power Tools' tweets, such as "U know things are bad when the Evil Avenue's customers are dumping out of 3 year deals in year 2 to buy Axceler's ControlPoint!" The court found this tweet was a factual statement because it could be proven true or false. It also found that hashtags used by Axceler, such as #MadeinCHINA, which followed critical tweets about AvePoint were implied facts that could also be used as evidence of defamation since AvePoint is a military contractor, and any allegation that its products are not made in the United States harms its reputation.[10]

A person suing for defamation must prove that the false statement was communicated to others, and when the defamation is in print (libel) the communication is called **publication**. Is publication in traditional media such as a newspaper the same as publication online? When a defamatory statement is in the newspaper, each sale of a paper does not constitute a new claim for defamation. Under the **single publication theory**, the alleged defamatory statement was communicated once—when it was published in the newspaper. However, if the alleged defamatory statement were in the morning edition, and the paper also ran an evening addition that contained the same alleged defamatory statement, the evening edition would be considered a republication because it is meant for a different audience.

Social media has called single publication into question with the advent of retweets and reposting. The **Communications Decency Act (CDA)** provides some guidance on this issue. The CDA, passed in 1996, was the first attempt to regulate pornography on the Internet. Although many of the provisions dealing with specific content were struck down, **Section 230** remains. Section 230 of the CDA protects providers and users of interactive computer services from liability for what others say and do online. This means that platforms such as YouTube, Vimeo, Craigslist, Facebook, and Twitter will not be liable for material posted by users. Section 230 also provides protection to bloggers, considered "intermediaries" under the law, from liability for comments left by readers, guest bloggers, or information received through RSS feeds.

If a public official or public figure is suing for defamation, they must prove the extra element of **actual malice**; that is, the speaker knew the statement was false and published it anyway or acted with a reckless disregard for the truth. Why this extra burden? Criticism of the government falls squarely within First Amendment protection; our democracy depends on free and open conversation and criticism of public officials. If someone criticizing the government had to make sure that everything they said was true, they would never criticize the government and we would lose much public debate. Public figures, like celebrities and professional athletes, have this extra burden because they invite attention and comment and possess persuasive power and influence. So if a public figure or official wants to sue for defamation, he or she has to prove the statement was defamatory and false as well as

publication: In libel, print communication.

single publication theory: States that the alleged defamatory statement was communicated once—when it was published in the newspaper.

Communications Decency Act (CDA): Passed in 1996, the CDA was an attempt made by U.S. Congress to regulate pornography on the Internet.

Section 230: Part of the CDA; protects providers and users of interactive computer services from liability for what others say and do online.

actual malice: Must prove if a public official or personality is suing for defamation; the defendant published a statement that was either (1) false and published it anyway or (2) acted with a reckless disregard for the truth.

Is Each Retweet a New Publication?

Unless the original tweet was substantially altered, thus far the answer is no. Courts have also decided that leaving a statement up on a website is not republication unless the original statement was substantially altered; disemminating material to Twitter or Facebook using a "share" button is not republication as the share button is a technical enhancement of the site, not a directive; and providing a hyperlink to material is not republication either—the hyperlink does not present the defamatory material but merely provides easy access.

The CDA is unique to the United States. The vast majority of other countries, even those with high Internet use such as much of Europe, Japan, and Canada, do not have similar protections. Like in the United States, under Canadian law, a person may be found liable for defamation based on their statements on social media. However, in Canada a person may also be liable for the republication of their statements and for defamatory comments made by third parties based on the original defamatory statement.

Consider the Facebook posts of Ms. Van Nes. The Van Nes and Pritchard families were next-door neighbors whose relationship deteriorated when the Van Neses installed a fish pond with a waterfall in their backyard. The Pritchards claimed the waterfall ran 24 hours a day and kept the family up at night—especially in the summer when they had their windows open. According to the Pritchards, the Van Neses also had late-night parties, blocked their driveway, and let their dog go to the bathroom in their backyard.

In June 2014, Ms. Van Nes made several posts to her Facebook page about Mr. Pritchard, a popular music teacher at the local middle school, accusing him of using a system of cameras and mirrors to keep her backyard, and her children, under 24-hour surveillance. The posts, available to Ms. Van Nes's 2,000 Facebook friends, generated over 50 comments that described Mr. Pritchard as a "creep," "#creeper," and "pedo" and motivated one friend to send an e-mail to the middle school principal describing Ms. Van Nes's statements. The natural meaning and innuendo of the posts and comments was that Mr. Pritchard was a pedophile. At no time did the Pritchards have video surveillance, and the mirror referred to was a decorative accessory on their back deck consistent with a feng shui aesthetic.

Mr. Pritchard claimed the impact of the posts on him and his family was significant: He became constantly guarded during interactions with students and no longer helped them adjust their fingers on their instruments; he cut back on his extracurricular activities; and when a job opening at a private school became available, Mr. Pritchard did not apply for it, knowing that with these allegations he would never be hired to teach again. In general, Mr. Pritchard felt awkward, humiliated, and stressed out when he went out in public and frightened for his family's safety given some of the posts suggested physical confrontations. The Pritchards sued Ms. Van Nes for defamation, claiming that not only did Ms. Van Nes defame Mr. Pritchard with her post but also that she was liable for the republication of her defamatory post by her Facebook friends and for the defamatory comments her Facebook friends made in response to her defamatory post.

The court agreed. It was clear that Ms. Van Nes defamed Mr. Pritchard in her posts. Moreover, republication of Ms. Van Nes's original post was the expected result because distribution of information is fundamental to the use of social media. Facebook facilitates republication through its architecture: Posts on a users' own page are automatically shared with friends; as friends comment, those comments may be spread automatically to friends of friends. Regarding the e-mail sent to the school principal, the court found that because Ms. Van Nes did nothing to discourage her Facebook friends from republishing her allegations, she should have known that her defamatory statements would spread using other forms of communication. Ms. Van Nes was also

(Continued)

(Continued)

liable for the defamatory comments her Facebook friends made in response to her post. Given the timing of the posts, it was clear that Ms. Van Nes was constantly monitoring her Facebook page and thus was aware of the defamatory comments and failed to delete them or her original post. The defamatory comments of her friends were not unprovoked reactions; they were part of a conversation in which Ms. Van Nes participated and failed to stop. This failure, according to the court, allowed what may have started off as thoughtless "venting" to snowball into a perceived call to action including offers of interventions, confrontations, and public shaming—all with devastating consequences.

Discussion Questions

1. Why do you think courts consider traditional media, such as newspapers, more reliably truthful than social media posts? What is it about the nature and structure of traditional media that might make this so?

2. It is clear that Ms. Van Nes did not give much thought to the long-term consequences of her Facebook post. Why do you think her friends joined with some raising the stakes in their comments?

3. If you were one of Ms. Van Nes's Facebook friends and you saw her post, what, if anything, would you do? Can you make an argument that doing nothing is not an option?

Critical Thinking

The court stated that an accusation of pedophilic behavior is a guaranteed way to destroy the reputation and career of a teacher, not to mention the devastating impact on their life and dignity. Mr. Pritchard was awarded $65,000 in damages for defamation and republication. Had this case been tried in the United States, Mr. Pritchard would have most likely only been awarded damages for the original post.

Why do you think U.S. courts take such a hard line on republication on social media? In thinking about your answer, factor in that several of the top social media companies like Facebook, YouTube, and Twitter are located in the United States. Why might this be an important fact?

communicated to a third party, caused injury, and that the speaker knew the statement was false and made it anyway or acted with a reckless disregard for whether the statement was true. This is a very high standard.

Tortious Interference With a Prospective Business Advantage

A business's reputation may be one of its most valued assets. As we saw in the *TripAdvisor* case, statements made on social media can hurt business. However, the free market system of the United States thrives on competition; competition is good for business, and it is good for consumers by giving us more choices, better quality, and lower prices. There are some limits on our free market; for example, when competition crosses the line into unlawful conduct. **Tortious interference with a prospective business advantage** is a tort based on unlawful conduct in competition. The elements of that claim are as follows:

tortious interference with a prospective business advantage: A tort based on unlawful conduct in competition.

- The plaintiff had a business relationship (or a prospective business relationship) with a third party.

- The defendant knew about this relationship.

- The defendant maliciously interfered with that relationship.

- The interference caused injury to the relationship between the business and the third party.

The case *Broadspring, Inc. v. Congoo* demonstrates how tortious interference with a prospective business advantage can easily result from defamation.

Defamation, Tortious Interference, and E-Commerce: *Broadspring, Inc. v. Congoo*, 2014 U.S. Dist. LEXIS 116070

Facts: Broadspring and Congoo are bitter rivals in the online advertising industry. They each operate online advertising networks that connect advertisers with websites (publishers). Online advertising networks place their advertiser's ads on publisher's websites; generate revenue from the advertisers; and, in turn, pay publishers for the space. This dispute centers on a webpage an executive from Congoo created. Using a pseudonym, Congoo created a page (lens) on the topic of online advertising and stated, among other things, "Broadspring was formerly Mindset, a notorious spyware company. Mindset was eventually shut down by the FTC in 2005 and Sanford Wallace, their founder... was banned from online activity for 5 years."[11] Congoo disseminated this lens by posting a link to it in discussion threads on other websites under false names and e-mailing links to the lens directly to publishers such as Geology.com.

Geology.com ran Congoo and Broadspring ads on its site, but a few days after reading the lens, Geology.com terminated its dealing with Broadspring because the founder was concerned about what he had read. Broadspring sued Congoo for defamation and tortious interference with a prospective business advantage based on the Geology.com termination. Congoo claimed the lenses were statements of opinion, and any factual statements were true.

Issues:

1. Were Congoo's statements defamation?
2. Did Congoo maliciously interfere with the business relationship between Broadspring and Geology.com?

Ruling: Yes and yes. Generally, statements of opinion are constitutionally protected speech while false statements of fact are not. Telling the two apart can be tricky; one must ask whether a reasonable fact finder (juror) could conclude that the statement declares or implies a provably false fact. Here, there is no question that Congoo's statements about Broadspring imply provably false facts. For example, whether the FTC ever shut down Broadspring or Mindset is easily provable. Congoo also claims its statements are true and therefore cannot be defamation. Truth is another defense to defamation, and if the defendant raises this defense, they have the burden of proving its statements are factually true. The evidence submitted indicates Congoo's statements were false. The FTC never shut down Mindset; Wallace was merely investigated by the agency. Moreover, Wallace is not the founder of Broadspring or Mindset; he was a third-party vendor that did business with the company.

Broadspring also claims that Congoo interfered with its business relationship with Geology.com. There is no doubt that a business relationship existed between Broadspring and Geology.com, and Congoo

(Continued)

(Continued)

knew of this relationship. Here, a reasonable juror could conclude that Congoo improperly interfered with Broadspring's relationship with Geology.com by disseminating defamatory statements in the lenses, and this defamatory information was the reason Geology.com terminated its relationship with Broadspring.

Law and Management Questions

1. Why did Congoo publish the defamatory material in the lens?

2. If you worked in the marketing department at Congoo and your boss asked you to create this lens, how would you respond?

3. Did Geology.com have any alternatives to ending their relationship with Broadspring after it read Congoo's lens? Explain your answer.

Invasion of Privacy

The line between work life and private life is increasingly blurred—especially with the availability of new technology. Flexible work schedules, working from home, social media, and 24/7 access via e-mail and text have given businesses myriad ways to support and develop valuable talent and have given workers multiple avenues by which to pursue their career. It has also given businesses a foot into our private lives, whether we want them there or not. Many claim this connectivity allows workers to bring their whole selves to work, which helps to create a culture based on honesty and acceptance. Others worry that conduct in their private lives might be used against them at work; plus, there are certain parts of their lives they don't want to share with their coworkers. There are three claims based on privacy that might provide a remedy when someone crosses the line: intrusion into seclusion, public disclosure of embarrassing facts, and appropriation of name or likeness.

intrusion into seclusion: Occurs when one intrudes into another's private affairs and that intrusion would be highly offensive to a reasonable person.

public disclosure of embarrassing facts: Revealing truthful information that the public has no legitimate need to know.

appropriation of name or likeness: Also known as the right of publicity; occurs when someone uses another's name or likeness without their permission for personal benefit.

- **Intrusion into seclusion** happens when someone intrudes into another's private affairs, and that intrusion would be highly offensive to a reasonable person. When a department store employee's locker, including her purse in the locker, was searched without her knowledge or consent, she sued for intrusion. The court found that because she provided her own lock for the locker, and because employees were never informed of the possibility of their lockers being searched, the employee had a valid claim for intrusion into seclusion.

- **Public disclosure of embarrassing facts** is revealing truthful information that the public has no legitimate need to know. For example, you agree to participate in an anonymous study about illegal drug use administered by a medical school. The researcher assures you that your name will not be used and the results are only intended for use within the medical school. Several weeks later, the researcher has published the results of his study in the local newspaper, using your first and last name.

- **Appropriation of name or likeness** is also known as the right of publicity and occurs when someone uses another's name or likeness without their permission for personal benefit. In 2012, Kim Kardashian settled a lawsuit against retailer Old Navy for using a look-alike model in an ad campaign. Kardashian's suit claimed that Old Navy was unauthorized to use her likeness, "which is a valuable commercial asset… for which [she] receives substantial financial offers" for permission to use.[12]

Privacy and Social Media

When it comes to an employer's interest in your social media, everything counts: posts, tweets, photos, and likes. In many ways, searching our social media footprint is merely an expansion of an employer's existing duty to prevent negligent hiring—a tort recognized in every state.

But aren't our social media posts private—especially if we have the settings turned to private? Probably not; unlike traditional journals, social media posts are written for others to read. What happens when there is an unintended reader, such as your boss? This question is critical for managers because often disgusted coworkers blow the whistle on employees who embarrass the company or reveal lies told to their employers. Consider Deborah Ehling's Facebook posts. Ms. Ehling was a paramedic in New Jersey. After news coverage that an 88-year-old had killed a security guard at the U.S. Holocaust Memorial Museum in Washington, D.C., Ms. Ehling posted the following to her Facebook News Feed: "An 88 yr old sociopath white supremacist in the Washington D.C. Holocaust Museum this morning shot and killed an innocent guard (leaving children). Other guards opened fired. The 88 yr old was shot. He survived. *I blame the DC paramedics.* I want to say 2 things to the DC medics. 1. WHAT WERE YOU THINKING? and 2. This was your opportunity to really make a difference! WTF!!! And to the other guards…go to target practice."

Of her 300 Facebook friends that saw this post, one was also a paramedic coworker and the real-life friend of their manager. That Facebook friend forwarded a screen shot of the post to the manager who then forwarded it to the executive director. Ultimately, Ms. Ehling was suspended with pay and given a written reprimand that stated she showed a "deliberate disregard for patient safety." Ms. Ehling sued for, among other things, invasion of privacy, claiming her employer invaded a private sphere of her life (*Ehling v. Monmouth-Ocean Hosp. Service Corp*). The court disagreed. Intrusion is a fundamental element of the tort, and here the employer did not access Ms. Ehling's Facebook page; a coworker provided the information. Therefore, there was no intrusion: The employer was a passive recipient of information that it did not ask for.

Discussion Questions

1. Many will agree that Ms. Ehling's post does show a disregard for patient safety. Why else is her employer concerned about her post?

2. Given the context and circumstances in which Ms. Ehling made her post, do you think her employer has bigger issues to worry about by keeping Ms. Ehling on staff?

3. Based on your answer to Question 2, should the employer have disciplined her more harshly, or does the punishment fit the infraction?

Critical Thinking

1. What the court in the *Ehling* case did not comment on (because it didn't need to) was whether Ms. Ehling's Facebook posts were private even though 300 people could read them and none of them had any obligation to keep the posts private. What are the strongest arguments for why our social media posts should not be considered private? Should be considered private?

2. What are the long-term consequences of both outcomes?

negligence: Careless conduct and accidents that cause injury to another person or to property. Elements of negligence include (1) duty of due care, (2) breach of duty, (3) factual cause, (4) foreseeable harm, and (5) injury.

duty of due care: An element of negligence; a level of responsibility to act as a reasonable person with care in a circumstance.

breach of duty: An element of negligence; the defendant failed to act as a reasonable person with care in a circumstance.

factual cause: An element of negligence; the defendant's conduct caused the plaintiff's injury.

foreseeable harm: An element of negligence; it was foreseeable that the defendant's conduct could cause this type of harm.

injury: An element of negligence; a physical injury or measurable loss.

Negligence

Unlike intentional torts, **negligence** is the world of careless conduct and accidents: Someone's carelessness caused injury to another person or to property. This sounds simple, but the reality of negligence is much more complicated. Generally, conduct is measured against a standard of a reasonable person: Did the defendant act as a reasonable person in the situation? Should a court impose liability for an accident? And if so, who should be responsible? For example, Andy owns a barbecue restaurant that gets a big lunchtime crowd. Reese, a customer, slipped and fell on spilled barbecue sauce on her way to the restroom, injuring her ankle. Should Andy's restaurant be liable for her injury?

Does it make a difference if Reese was texting as she was walking to the restroom? What would be the long-term consequence of Andy's restaurant *not* being responsible for Reese's injury?

There are five elements of negligence that a plaintiff must prove

- **Duty of due care:** The defendant owed a duty to the plaintiff to act as a reasonable person in the circumstance. Andy owed a duty to Reese (and all of his customers) to act as a reasonable restaurant owner.
- **Breach of duty:** The defendant failed to act as a reasonable person in that circumstance. Andy failed to act as a reasonable restaurant owner because there was a slippery spill left on the floor during lunch hour rush.
- **Factual cause:** The defendant's conduct actually caused the plaintiff's injury. Because Andy did not clean up the spill immediately, Reese was injured when she slipped and fell on the sauce on the floor while walking to the restroom.
- **Foreseeable harm:** It was foreseeable that the defendant's conduct could cause this type of harm. It is foreseeable that if sauce is spilled on the floor and not cleaned up immediately during the lunchtime rush, someone will slip and fall on it.
- **Injury:** The plaintiff suffered an actual injury or a measurable loss. Reese injured her ankle.

KEY TAKEAWAYS

Risk of Injury

- Intentional torts like defamation, tortious interference with a prospective business advantage, and invasion of privacy can impact our personal and professional lives.
- Negligence is based on reasonable conduct and incentivizes careful conduct of both people and businesses.

RESPONDEAT SUPERIOR AND PRODUCT LIABILITY

LO 5.2 Assess business conduct that might increase or decrease risk using tort theories.

It is not difficult to see how negligence and accidents apply to our everyday lives. But how does this impact businesses? Two theories make this tort particularly important for businesses:

- Respondeat superior
- Product liability

Respondeat Superior

Under the theory of **respondeat superior,** an employer is liable for the negligence of its employees if the employee was acting within the scope of her employment at the time of the injury. For example, Andy did not spill the barbecue sauce, or fail to clean it up, because he was in the kitchen all day and did not see it. However, Ellen, an employee of the restaurant, dropped the sauce as she was clearing a table and did not wipe it up. Andy's restaurant would still be liable for Reese's injury because Ellen was acting within the scope of her employment at the time.

Product Liability

Businesses that manufacture and sell products could be liable under **product liability** for injuries caused by their products if the product was designed poorly so that it was unreasonably risky (**negligent design**); something happened during the manufacturing of the product, such as a failure to inspect, that caused a dangerous product to leave the manufacturing facility (**negligent manufacturing**); or the business did not warn consumers of the reasonable dangers associated with the normal use, and even foreseeable misuse, of the product (**negligent failure to warn**).

> **respondeat superior:** A theory that states an employer is liable for the negligence of its employees if the employee was acting within the scope of her employment at the time of the injury.
>
> **product liability:** Businesses that manufacture and sell products are responsible for injuries caused by their products if the product has (1) negligent design, (2) negligent manufacturing, or (3) negligent failure to warn.
>
> **negligent design:** A type of product liability; the product was designed poorly so that it was unreasonably risky.
>
> **negligent manufacturing:** A type of product liability; something happened during the manufacturing of the product, such as a failure to inspect, that caused a dangerous product to leave the manufacturing facility.

Can a Dating App Be an Unreasonably Dangerous Product?

In October 2016, Matthew Herrick was standing outside his apartment building in New York City when a man walked up and buzzed his apartment. The man asked Herrick if he had been the person just messaging him through the hookup app Grindr and had invited him over. Herrick said no; he hadn't been on Grindr for weeks. The man then showed Herrick a Grindr profile that included a picture of Herrick taken from his Instagram account. In the 5 months that followed, over 1,100 men would show up at Herrick's home and workplace in response to a spoofed profile on the app, with the interactions growing increasingly hostile and sometimes violent. The profile included false and dangerous statements like Herrick was HIV positive and that if they show up and Herrick denies the account or resists interaction not to give up because the conduct was "part of an agreed upon rape fantasy or role play."[13] During that same time period, Herrick filed over 100 complaints to Grindr, flagging the fake profile, but the company only responded with a generic "Thank you for your report" and never took the profile down. Herrick accuses his ex-boyfriend of

CASE STUDY 5.3

controlling the spoofed profile to harass him by using a GPS spoofing app to manipulate the geophysical settings to make it look like Herrick was using the app from his apartment or from work.

The CDA generally bars Internet or computer service providers from liability for publishing harmful content generated by a third-party user. As a result, Grindr cannot be liable for the content of the spoofed account. In April 2017, Herrick's attorneys sued the app for product liability, claiming Grindr availed itself as an unreasonably dangerous weapon used to destroy Herrick's life. Grindr knew less dangerous alternatives were available because other dating apps such as Scruff took the spoofed profile down as soon as Herrick complained and used technology to ban the same device or IP address from creating new accounts. Also, image recognition software used in the industry made identifying specific images easy to implement. In January 2018, a federal court in New York dismissed Herrick's suit holding that all of his product liability claims relate back to the content of the spoofed account, something for which Grindr cannot be held liable under the CDA.

Discussion Questions

1. Section 230 of the CDA protects providers of interactive Internet services such as Facebook, Tindr, and Grindr from liability for torts arising from content posted by a third party. How does this provision help this industry in the short term and the long term?

2. What impact could this ruling have on users of platforms such as Facebook, Instagram, Snapchat, and Tindr that have third-party generated content?

Critical Thinking

In 2013 attorneys general from 47 states wrote a letter to Congress requesting that the immunity provisions in Section 230 be removed. The American Civil Liberties Union (ACLU) opposed this request in its own letter, stating that if the immunity provisions were removed "it wouldn't take long for the vibrant culture of free speech to disappear from the web."[14] What is at stake for the attorneys general and the population at large according to the ACLU? Should our priority be protecting people like Matthew Herrick or protecting free speech? Do we have to give up one to protect the other?

KEY TAKEAWAYS

Respondeat Superior and Product Liability

- Respondeat superior imposes liability on a business when its employees cause injury.

- Product liability imposes liability on a business when its products cause injury.

negligent failure to warn: A type of product liability; the business did not warn consumers of the reasonable dangers associated with the normal use, and even foreseeable misuse, of the product.

CONTRACTS

LO 5.3 Explain the elements of a contract.

Businesses face myriad risks through tort theories like respondeat superior and product liability but also just by doing business. As we read in Chapter 10, good faith is universally recognized as an international standard; parties intend to honor their promises. However, sometimes things happen that make honoring a promise impossible despite your good faith. For example, you own a catering company and are catering a party where the customer has ordered, among other things, lobster salad and grilled salmon. Unfortunately, your regular seafood supplier was late with her delivery of the salmon, and as a result, you had to serve grilled haddock at the party. Your contract with your customer spells out what happens in this type of situation, as does your contract with the seafood supplier. But that doesn't change the fact that you did not fulfill your promise to your customer despite your good faith and best efforts.

Contracts can help provide predictability and transparency and can reduce risk. We are all parties to several different contracts: our cell phone service agreements, credit card agreements, terms of use for every social media platform and online retailer, gym memberships, residential leases, mortgages, school loans—you name it. Whether we read them is another story. Contracts are based on our freedom to make promises, subject to the rules that we establish in the agreements and any state laws that may apply. This means we can make contracts for all sorts of things. Provided the agreement meets the required elements, parties are very much left to themselves to honor—or not—their contracts.

Elements of a Contract

What is a contract? A **contract** is a promise that the law will enforce. But not all promises are contracts. In order for a promise to be legally enforceable as a contract it must contain the following:

- An **agreement**, which includes making a definite *offer* and that offer was *accepted*.

- **Consideration**, which is bargaining that leads to an exchange. In other words, what are you giving up to get what you want? Consideration can be almost anything: money, provision of services, or the exchange of goods. Consideration also includes promising to do something like using best efforts to promote a product or promising to refrain from doing something like suing, working for a competitor, or disclosing confidential information. Margot's hairdresser, Joe, wants to buy her computer for $300. In exchange for the computer, Joe will cut Margot's hair for free for a year. Both parties have given consideration: Margot is selling Joe her computer for $300 (she thinks she could have gotten a little more), and Joe is giving Margot haircutting services for a year (which he normally charges for).

- The agreement must be for a **legal purpose**, so if Joe knows Margot got her computer by stealing it from Adrienne, that agreement is not for a legal purpose.

- All parties to a contract must have the **capacity** to make the promise, which usually means they are both over 18 years old.

contract: A promise that the law will enforce.

agreement: An element of a contract; includes making a definite offer and that offer was accepted.

consideration: An element of a contract; bargaining that leads to an exchange.

legal purpose: An element of a contract; the contract must be compliant with the law of the land and public policy.

capacity: An element of a contract; one's authority under law to engage in certain actions or undertakings.

Contract law is similar in many countries around the world. This makes sense in a global marketplace. For example, like in many other countries, in Japan contract law is based on the manifestation of intent through offer and acceptance. Generally, contracts do not need to be in writing in Japan and when there is a dispute as to terms not in the written contract, evidence of oral agreements as well as other types of evidence are relevant in the analysis.[15]

In the case *In re Zappos.com Inc. Customer Data Security Breach Litigation*, the court must decide whether a user agreed to Zappos terms and conditions just by browsing the site.

LAW AND SOCIETY 5.3

In re Zappos.com, Inc. Customer Data Security Breach Litigation, 893 F. Supp. 2d 1058 (2012)

Facts: In mid-January 2012, a computer hacker attacked the Zappos.com website and attempted to download files from a Zappos.com server containing customer information. On January 16, 2012, Zappos.com notified customers via e-mail that their personal information had been compromised as a result of the hack.

Several customers sued for damages resulting from the security breach. Zappos.com filed a motion to compel arbitration, saying when customers use their website, they agree to the terms of use, which state that the parties agree to resolve all disputes through arbitration. The customers claimed they never saw the arbitration agreement and therefore never agreed to it.

Issue: Were the terms of use so inconspicuous that users of Zappos.com would not reasonably see them?

Ruling: Yes, the terms of use were inconspicuous, and no reasonable user would see them. The Federal Arbitration Act says that arbitration agreements are valid and enforceable unless there is a legal reason to revoke the contract. This law indicates Congress' intent to favor arbitration agreements provided they meet the requirements of a contract.

Zappos' arbitration agreement is found in the terms of use on the Zappos.com website and states that "ACCESSING, BROWSING OR OTHERWISE USING THE SITE INDICATES YOUR AGREEMENT TO ALL THE TERMS AND CONDITIONS IN THE AGREEMENT." This type of agreement is a "browsewrap" agreement whereby a website owner seeks to bind users to terms and conditions by posting the terms, typically accessible through a hyperlink, somewhere on the website. A "clickwrap" agreement, by contrast, requires users to indicate their assent by clicking an "I accept" button. Browsewrap agreements are suspect because they do not require any affirmative action by the user other than using the website in order to be bound by its terms.

The hyperlink for Zappos' terms of use is between the middle and bottom of the page and is inconspicuous because it is in the same size, font, and color as most of the other nonsignificant links. The website does not direct a user to the terms of use when creating an account, logging in to an existing account, or making a purchase. Without direct evidence that a customer clicked on the terms of use, we cannot conclude that they assented to the terms of use. No reasonable user would have reason to click on the terms of use, and as a result, we find that there was no acceptance by the customers, no meeting of the minds, and no manifestation of intent as required by law.

Law and Management Questions

1. Think back to the last time you were online. How were you made aware of the terms of service of the website?

2. Read the terms of service of your favorite site—it could be an online retailer, media site like CNN.com or ESPN.com, or a blog. What terms surprised you the most and why?

3. Using your answer to Question 2, what interests are the business trying to protect? What risk is it trying to avoid by using those terms?

Technology moves much faster than the law, and sometimes courts are left to apply traditional laws to new-age events. In the *Zappos* case, the court decided whether by browsing a website a user has agreed to the terms of use of the site. In Case Study 5.4, a court has to apply traditional contract law to cutting-edge medical technology.

Embryos Are the New Frontier in Contracts

On February 14, 2017, *Modern Family* star Sofia Vergara filed suit against her ex-fiancé, Nick Loeb, asking a court to prevent him from using the frozen pre-embryos (frozen fertilized ova) the couple created while still together. A court dismissed Loeb's request for full "custody" of the pre-embryos in order to bring them to term, but he later filed a right-to-live suit on behalf of the pre-embryos. Who controls the destiny of pre-embryos if a couple splits is a novel legal question. Like so many couples using advanced reproduction technology, Vergara and Loeb signed a contract with the fertility clinic that stated that neither party (Vergara/Loeb as a couple and the clinic) could use the pre-embryos created without the express written consent of the other party. Vergara's suit claims Loeb would be in violation of the contract if he gained custody of the pre-embryos. But the contract that Vergara claims Loeb violated is a contract between the clinic and the couple, not between Vergara and Loeb.

Use of reproductive technology has doubled in the past 10 years, and companies like Citigroup, JPMorgan Chase, Netflix, Apple, Microsoft, and others offer egg freezing as another employee benefit, along with subsidized food and paid vacation. Advances in the technology have made it more affordable for couples to freeze eggs, leading to more disputes over ownership if the couple splits. However, the law has not caught up. Fewer than 12 states have addressed this issue, and among them there are no consistent rulings. In 2010 when a Chicago doctor learned she had lymphoma and had to begin chemotherapy immediately, she asked her boyfriend to help her create frozen pre-embryos because her treatment would leave her infertile. Within a week, they signed an informed consent with the fertility clinic and created the pre-embryos. The couple hired a lawyer to draft a coparenting

agreement for themselves, but they never signed it, and a few months later they split. The doctor sued for control and use of the pre-embryos. In 2015 the Illinois Appellate Court ruled that the conversation between the couple at the time they decided to create the pre-embryos was an oral contract in which the boyfriend said he wanted to help her have a child; thus, the doctor was entitled to control of the pre-embryos.

Later the same year, the opposite was decided in a California court. In that case, a husband and wife decided to freeze pre-embryos after the wife's cancer diagnosis. The couple signed a contract with the fertility clinic that stated the embryos would be destroyed in the event of divorce. When the couple divorced, the ex-wife sued for custody of the pre-embryos, claiming they were her only chance to have a biological child because her treatment left her infertile. The judge, while sympathetic, ruled that the plain language of the contract overrode the ex-wife's desires.

Discussion Questions

1. In the Chicago case, where the court said his conversation with his girlfriend created an oral contract, the boyfriend argued that he agreed to help his girlfriend during a phone call that he had to dash into the bathroom at work to take; within days they were at the fertility clinic, and then immediately after she started treatment. Their sense of urgency was spurred by the uncertainty of whether she would survive treatment. Under these conditions, he said, he could not think straight. Why should this matter?

2. In the Vergara and Chicago cases, the only written contracts were with the clinics; there were no contracts between the couple outlining the status of the pre-embryos in the event they

(Continued)

(Continued)

split. If a court were to rule the contracts with the clinics invalid, what impact might that have on the assisted reproduction industry?

3. Many say the law is ill-equipped to deal with these kinds of issues; they are deeply personal and emotional and cannot be adequately expressed in contract terms. If that is the case, what is the alternative when, like in the three cases we read, the couple splits, leaving pre-embryos?

Critical Thinking

In the Chicago case, the boyfriend argued that he had a right to control when and how he becomes a father, and therefore his rights would be violated if the doctor had a child from their pre-embryos. In the California case, the ex-wife argued that the pre-embryos were her only chance of having biological children. Both lost their cases. Had the courts ruled in their favor, what stakeholders would have been impacted? How would they have been impacted?

KEY TAKEAWAYS

Contracts

- Contracts are used to provide predictability to business transactions and reduce risk created by tort law and other exposure.

- Technological advances push the limits of traditional contract law by presenting novel issues that courts must decide using standard contract theories.

LIMITING RISK THROUGH CONTRACTS

LO 5.4   Analyze how businesses can use contracts to limit liability risk.

Businesses use contracts for all sorts of things: buying goods, inventory, supplies, and equipment; hiring and firing employees; merging with other companies, etc. One key value of contracts is to limit risk. As we saw, torts create a multitude of risks for business; those risks can be mitigated through carefully worded contract clauses. One risk that can be managed is the risk of being sued. In a 2015 survey of 803 companies in 26 countries, 29% reported that their litigation (suing people or getting sued) spending through 2013 was between $1 and $5 million. Almost 20% reported their litigation spending to be over $10 million. Looking at U.S. companies specifically, 34% said their litigation spending was between $1 and $5 million, and 25% had litigation spending over $10 million during the same time period.[16] Reducing litigation costs is a priority for many businesses; reducing risk and discouraging litigation through contracts can be part of the solution.

One way to reduce costs is to discourage litigation in the first place. A **forum selection clause** in a contract states that the parties agree that any litigation will be resolved in a specific state (forum). For example, the terms and conditions for using Apple Media Services (including iTunes, iBooks, the App Store, and Apple Music) state that all users (except those living in specifically listed non-U.S. countries) agree to resolve any dispute arising from using Apple Media Services in Santa Clara County, California.[17] Thus, if you live in Florida, for example, and use iTunes, you must travel to Santa Clara County, California, to access the courts to resolve any dispute you have with Apple due to using iTunes. This is probably not likely to happen given the expense compared to potential damage award. A **choice of law clause** in a contract states that the parties have agreed to what state's laws will apply to their agreement. In the Apple Media Services terms and conditions, users have agreed that the laws of California will apply to their dispute.

Another method of reducing risk and costs is a **limitation of liability clause.** This clause limits the amount of exposure a company faces in the event of a lawsuit. In the terms and conditions for using Apple Media Services, Apple (the licensor) has limited its liability exposure. By using iTunes, we have agreed that Apple will not be liable to us for the following:

> LIMITATION OF LIABILITY. TO THE EXTENT NOT PROHIBITED BY LAW, IN NO EVENT SHALL LICENSOR BE LIABLE FOR PERSONAL INJURY OR ANY INCIDENTAL, SPECIAL, INDIRECT, OR CONSEQUENTIAL DAMAGES WHATSOEVER, INCLUDING, WITHOUT LIMITATION, DAMAGES FOR LOSS OF PROFITS, LOSS OF DATA, BUSINESS INTERRUPTION, OR ANY OTHER COMMERCIAL DAMAGES OR LOSSES, ARISING OUT OF OR RELATED TO YOUR USE OF OR INABILITY TO USE THE LICENSED APPLICATION, HOWEVER CAUSED, REGARDLESS OF THE THEORY OF LIABILITY (CONTRACT, TORT, OR OTHERWISE) AND EVEN IF LICENSOR HAS BEEN ADVISED OF THE POSSIBILITY OF SUCH DAMAGES

A **nondisclosure agreement (NDA)** is a contract, or a clause in a larger contract, that prohibits one or both parties from speaking about certain things typically under the threat of financial penalty. Historically, NDAs were used by big tech companies like IBM to protect trade secrets and proprietary information like algorithms and processes. By the 1980s, NDAs began appearing in various types of agreements like employment agreements and legal settlements. Today it is estimated that over one third of the U.S. workforce is subject to an NDA.

In many ways, NDAs are a valuable method of managing risk: Businesses of all kinds can protect trade secrets and research and development from leaking. For businesses whose largest assets are intellectual property (IP), this is a must-have document. However, NDAs also raise important ethical issues. Often NDAs are broadly worded to prevent employees or parties to a settlement agreement from speaking about a wide range of topics, including issues of public safety.

forum selection clause: A section of a contract that states that the parties agree that any litigation will be resolved in a specific state (forum).

choice of law clause: A clause in a contract where the parties agree what state's law will apply to the agreement.

limitation of liability clause: A section of a contract that limits the amount of exposure a company faces in the event of a lawsuit.

nondisclosure agreement (NDA): A contract, or a clause in a larger contract, that prohibits one or both parties from speaking about certain things typically under the threat of financial penalty.

Nondisclosure Agreements and Public Safety

iStockpoto.com/powerofforever

Jeffrey Wigand, the former vice president of research and development for tobacco giant Brown & Williamson, signed an NDA as part of a severance agreement when he left the company. In 1995 when Wigand began working with the news program 60 *Minutes* to reveal the tobacco industry's efforts to hide research proving the harmful effects of smoking, Brown & Williamson threatened Wigand with, among other things, legal action based on his NDA and also threatened to sue CBS for interfering with the company's NDA with Wigand. (This standoff was the basis for the movie *The Insider*.)

In 2011, prosecutors in Boston pressured local Roman Catholic archdioceses to release victims of clergy sex abuse from their NDAs. The archdiocese in Los Angeles also released victims of sexual abuse from their NDAs. In 2002, the U.S. Conference of Catholic Bishops established a policy prohibiting American dioceses from requiring victims to enter into NDAs when they reached a financial settlement with the church. In 2018, the Catholic diocese of New Jersey released all victims from NDAs signed prior to 2002; they can now speak publicly about their experiences.

Gretchen Carlson, former news anchor at Fox News, broke her NDA with the company when she filed a sexual harassment suit in 2016 against former Fox CEO Roger Ailes. Because Ailes had been with Fox for 20 years, many wondered why more women had not come forward. Once Carlson spoke out, many women feared speaking publicly because they also had NDAs with Fox that included nondisparagement clauses—they could not say anything that

would reflect badly on the company. This included consulting an attorney on potential legal claims against Fox. Shortly after Carlson's suit was filed, 21st Century Fox waived the NDAs to allow women to speak publicly.

In 2017 when news broke of Hollywood producer Harvey Weinstein's years of alleged sexual harassment and abuse, many questioned the role NDAs and nondisparagement clauses played in covering up the abuse. Weinstein employees had to sign nondisparagement clauses, and those who complained of sexual harassment and settled their legal claims had to sign an NDA as part of the settlement. This combination, according to many, allowed Weinstein to continue to abuse unsuspecting women and silenced those who contemplated speaking up.

As we will learn in Chapter 9, Title VII of the Civil Rights Act (and criminal law) prohibits sexual harassment and assault at work. Moreover, according to the National Labor Relations Act (NLRA), employees are allowed to join together to discuss the terms or conditions of work. This means that employers cannot prevent employees from speaking among themselves about sexual harassment, sexual assault, or any other topic related to their work. In 2016, the U.S. Court of Appeals for the D.C. Circuit found an NDA and nondisparagement clause used in employment agreements at Quicken Loans violated the NLRA because it prevented employees from gathering information needed to pursue union activity and because it forbade them from making any negative comments about the company, its leadership, and its policies.

Several states have acted to prohibit the use of NDAs to silence victims of sexual harassment and abuse. Six states have passed laws restricting the use of NDAs by private employers in harassment cases. New York's new law prohibits the use of NDAs in sexual harassment settlements unless the person who brought the complaint wants the provision. Arizona now allows victims of sexual misconduct to talk with police and testify in court despite having signed an NDA. California has introduced two bills: The first, supported by Gretchen Carlson, would prohibit employers from requiring NDAs related to sexual harassment as a condition of getting or keeping a job, and the other would prohibit settlements in sexual harassment cases that require keeping the circumstances secret.

There are some downsides to banning the use of NDAs in sexual harassment cases. First, victims might be worried that a former employer would disparage them in public or hamper their efforts to find a new job. Also, many victims might not want the financial terms of any settlement revealed for fear of public backlash. For many victims, their silence is important leverage in negotiating a settlement, and without it, financial terms may not be as favorable. Because of the devastating effects harassment can have on a person's career and life, financial compensation can be a crucial component to any settlement.

Discussion Questions

1. *Stakeholder theory:* Who are the stakeholders impacted by a company's use of NDAs in employment contracts? What is at stake for them? Who are the stakeholders impacted by a company's use of an NDA in the settlement of a sexual harassment complaint? What is at stake for them? Looking at the proposed laws in California, what stakeholder concerns are most effectively addressed by each bill?

2. *Ethical decision-making:* Is banning NDAs better for society but potentially devastating to individuals? Using a principles-based approach and a consequences-based approach, answer this question: Should the goal of employment protections like banning NDAs in sexual harassment cases be to create a future of better and safer working conditions? Or should the law focus on providing individuals with legal recourse and compensation? Explain your answers.

Take a Position

Many states that have passed laws addressing the use of NDAs specifically in sexual harassment claims have not banned their use in settlement agreements.

Issue: Should NDAs be banned when used in a settlement agreement for sexual harassment claims? Explain your answer.

The existence of a contract does not guarantee a party will honor their promises. A **breach** occurs when a party to a contract does not fulfill one or more of their promises. Breaches may be intentional or inadvertent, like the catering company. With a contract, parties can provide clear remedies in case one party breaches. For example, the contract mentioned at the beginning of this section between the catering company and the customer may say that the caterer may substitute items, but if a substitution is made, the customer is entitled to a 10% discount on that cost.

breach: Of a contract; when a party to a contract does not fulfill one or more of its promises.

KEY TAKEAWAYS

Limiting Risk Through Contracts

- Businesses can reduce tort liability risk through contracts and specific contract clauses.

- NDAs reduce public relations risks and the loss of confidential information by prohibiting former employees from speaking about certain topics.

SUMMARY

Risk in business is unavoidable. For some, that is the lure of going into business: taking risks on products or services that you believe in. Understanding how torts encourage careful behavior and how contracts impact risk helps a business predict and prepare for exposure. Like with other aspects of business, thinking broadly about the consequences of liability and contracts will help limit some unintended consequences that may conflict with your values and those of society.

KEY TERMS

actual malice   96
agreement   105
appropriation of name or likeness   100
breach   111
breach of duty   102
capacity   105
choice of law clause   109
Communications Decency Act
    (CDA)   96
compensatory damages   91
consideration   105
contract   105
defamation   93

duty of due care   102
factual cause   102
foreseeable harm   102
forum selection clause   109
injury   102
intentional tort   92
intrusion into seclusion   100
legal purpose   105
limitation of liability clause   109
negligence   102
negligent design   103
negligent failure to warn   103
negligent manufacturing   103

nondisclosure agreement (NDA)   109
product liability   103
public disclosure of embarrassing
    facts   100
publication   96
punitive damages   91
respondeat superior   103
Section 230   96
single publication theory   96
tort   91
tortious interference with
    a prospective business
    advantage   98

REVIEW QUESTIONS

1. Explain the torts of defamation and tortious interference with a prospective business advantage.

2. How do respondeat superior and product liability impact risk exposure for businesses?

3. Discuss negligence and how the tort is proven.

4. Describe three ways businesses can use contract clauses to limit their liability and risk of getting sued.

5. What are the ethical implications of NDAs?

MANAGER'S CHALLENGE

Defamation and Public Figures

On November 14, 2014, *Rolling Stone* magazine published a story titled "A Rape on Campus" about an alleged gang rape of a female student at a fraternity on the campus of the University of Virginia (UVA). The story depicted Nicole Eramo, then the associate dean of students, who also served as the head of the UVA Sexual Misconduct Board, as "callous" toward sexual assault victims and not willing to move forward with the alleged victim's case because she didn't want to harm the reputation of the school. Almost a year later, *Rolling Stone* retracted the article after police found no credible evidence that a sexual assault ever happened, and the reporter admitted to journalistic failings in confirming sources and facts. Ms. Eramo sued the magazine for defamation, and in 2016 a jury awarded her $3 million in damages.

Framing Questions

1. Apply the elements of defamation to the previously stated facts to make Ms. Eramo's claim.

2. The court ruled that Ms. Eramo was a public figure because she was head of the school's sexual misconduct board. Does this change what she must prove in order to win her defamation claim? If so, how?

3. What was Ms. Eramo's injury? How do you think that injury impacted her life? Given your answer, do you think $3 million is an appropriate damage award?

Assignment

In response to criticism and doubt about the facts of the published story, *Rolling Stone* asked the dean of the Columbia School of Journalism to conduct an independent investigation of how they could have gotten the story so wrong, and the magazine retracted the story. Who are the stakeholders impacted by the publication of the erroneous story? Draft a one-page public statement on behalf of *Rolling Stone* that speaks to the stakeholders you have identified and expresses the magazine's intent to never let something like this happen again. What do you need to say to rebuild trust and credibility?

GOVERNMENT REGULATION
OF THE ORGANIZATION

Learning Objectives

Upon completion of this chapter, the reader should be able to do the following:

6.1 Articulate the standards used to protect consumers from deceptive sales or advertising, unsafe products, and unlawful credit or collection practices.

6.2 Identify examples of government regulations that prevent anticompetitive behavior.

6.3 Explain two primary provisions of securities law that protect investors from fraud.

Ethics in Context

Student–Athletes and Antitrust Law

Antitrust law is designed to encourage competition and protect consumers from predatory practices by big businesses. In fact, the first antitrust law, the Sherman Antitrust Act, was enacted in response to concerns about the consolidation of the oil industry into one big and powerful company. But should we be concerned about the impact of consolidation on stakeholders other than consumers? Later in the chapter, in the Ethics in Context section,

we will examine the ethical and justice implications of the lack of competition in the collegiate sports industry and the refusal of the National Collegiate Athletic Association (NCAA) to pay its athletes.

iStockphoto.com/RBFried

INTRODUCTION

Regulation has become a fact of life. In every country around the globe, governments attempt to make markets and businesses fair and transparent. Chapter 11 introduces us to international regulation of business. In this chapter, we begin by surveying the U.S. version of regulations that protect consumers and creditors from deceptive practices and anticompetitive behavior. We then turn to the rights of shareholders and laws that protect investors from fraud. To learn more about regulations of employees as stakeholders, please read Chapters 8 and 9. Although organizations play a significant role in influencing public policy, the government has the responsibility of creating and enforcing laws and regulations that make up a body of public policy. Here, we examine instances where organizations encounter regulation by the government and how the government's efforts to carry out regulations can impact the organization and its stakeholders.

ANTICOMPETITIVE BEHAVIOR AND ANTITRUST REGULATION

LO 6.1 Articulate the standards used to protect consumers from deceptive sales or advertising, unsafe products, and unlawful credit or collection practices.

The creation of the railroad in the second half of the 19th century provided the opportunity for businesses to grow beyond local entities and reach a national market. John D. Rockefeller, entering the oil industry around this time, used the railroad to create a national business by buying up small refineries, oil fields, and pipelines. Rockefeller and his partners transferred the stock of these smaller companies to one they had created: Standard Oil Trust. Soon enough, Standard Oil Trust controlled the oil market in the United States. Congress became concerned about the concentration of market power in one company and worried this type of consolidation could happen in industries beyond oil. In response to these concerns, it passed the Sherman Antitrust Act in 1890. In 1914, Congress passed the Clayton Antitrust Act to prohibit anticompetitive behaviors not specifically prohibited by the Sherman Act. In that same year, Congress created the Federal Trade Commission (FTC) by passing the Federal Trade Commission (FTC) Act, adding another enforcement mechanism against unfair trade practices and anticompetitive conduct. The Clayton Act was amended in 1936 by the Robinson-Patman Act to prohibit price discrimination without justification of differing expenses. The U.S. Department of Justice (DOJ) enforces antitrust laws other than the FTC Act, which is enforced by the FTC.

The antitrust laws prohibit restraints of trade. Because every simple agreement can be a restraint of trade—by agreeing to sell my widgets to you I am not selling them to your friend—the courts have interpreted the statutes to prohibit only *unreasonable* restraints of trade. In determining whether an action is an unreasonable restraint, courts apply different standards depending on the conduct: *per se* or rule of reason. Conduct that is inherently anticompetitive and harmful to the market is analyzed under the **per se standard**. If conduct is per se illegal under the Sherman Act, the conduct automatically violates the law. Examples include agreements between competing companies to fix prices or a conspiracy to create a monopoly. Defendants cannot defend themselves from per se violations with evidence that competitors or consumers are not harmed. By contrast, **rule of reason** violations are illegal only if the conduct has an anticompetitive impact. Defendants may provide evidence that their conduct does not harm competitors or consumers to escape liability.

per se standard: Conduct that is inherently anticompetitive and harmful to the market is analyzed under this standard to determine whether an action is an unreasonable restraint.

rule of reason: Conduct that is illegal only if it has an anticompetitive effect.

The Sherman Antitrust Act

The Sherman Antitrust Act, or Sherman Act, was originally aimed at large businesses that had too much economic power. It was under this theory that the Supreme Court in 1911 used the Sherman Antitrust Act to break up the Standard Oil Company and force the smaller companies that made up Standard Oil to compete with each other.[1] The Sherman Antitrust Act has two major provisions: Section 1 prohibits all agreements "in restraint of trade," and Section 2 bans all "monopolization."

Section 1: Unreasonable Restraints of Trade

unreasonable restraints: Include conduct that restrains competition.

The Sherman Act prohibits a business from unreasonably restraining trade, meaning engaging in conduct that restrains competition. **Unreasonable restraints** of trade can take many forms, including price fixing. In 2012, the United States filed a lawsuit against Apple, alleging that it had conspired with five publishing companies to fix the prices on e-books in violation of Section 1 of the Sherman Antitrust Act.[2] The lawsuit alleged that the publishing companies, upset about the low price that Amazon charged for e-books, had their CEOs meet regularly to discuss Amazon's pricing policies. In late 2009, Apple representatives met with publishers to discuss Apple's entrance into the e-book market. Apple adopted a price strategy with pricing higher than Amazon's and decided to use its App Store for distribution of e-books. This agency model let publishers control the price of e-books, with Apple receiving a commission. Amazon complained to the FTC that many publishers had signed agency model agreements with Apple simultaneously. The court concluded that Apple and the publishers had engaged in a per se violation of Section 1 of the Sherman Act. By simultaneously agreeing to agency model agreements with Apple, the publishers and Apple committed illegal price fixing. After the U.S. Supreme Court refused to hear Apple's appeal, it settled with the United States for $450 million.

Section 2: Monopolies

monopoly: Occurs when a company or its products dominate a particular market.

market: One in which buyers view two products as close substitutes.

Section 2 of the Sherman Act makes it illegal to monopolize or attempt to monopolize a market. A **monopoly** occurs when a company or its products dominate a particular market. Sometimes monopolies occur by legal means. For example, a company may receive a patent on its product, and therefore have an exclusive right to use it, or there may be high barriers to entry into the market. To determine whether a monopoly is illegal, the courts must define the market, consider whether the accused company controls it, and then determine whether the control was acquired improperly. A **market** is one in which buyers view two products as close substitutes. Geography is also relevant; the court will consider the areas where the same product can be purchased. A company controls the market if it has at least a 50% market share and the long-term ability to exclude competitors or raise prices.

Monopolies are illegal only if obtained by improper means. Improper conduct occurs when the company suppresses competition with anticompetitive conduct. In the 1990s, Microsoft was accused of violating Section 2 of the Sherman Act by using its dominance in the personal computer operating system market to limit competition in Internet browsers. Microsoft was accused of bundling its Windows operating system with its Internet browser, making it impossible for PC manufacturers to uninstall Microsoft's Internet browser. After trial, Microsoft was found in violation of Sections 1 and 2 of the Sherman Antitrust Act and ordered to split the company into two units—one to produce the operating system and the other to produce other software. Microsoft appealed, and the trial court's legal conclusions were overturned. The DOJ and Microsoft later settled. The Microsoft antitrust case is a good example of how the law tries to protect consumers from anticompetitive behavior that may harm them while still encouraging innovation and investment by companies.

Figure 6.1 The Sherman Antitrust Act and the Federal Trade Commission Act

Sherman Antitrust Act	Federal Trade Commission Act
• Bans unreasonable restraints of trade	• Bans false or deceptive advertising
• Bans illegal monopolies	• Bans deceptive business practices
• Bans price fixing	

The Federal Trade Commission Act

The FTC Act bans "unfair methods of competition" and "unfair or deceptive acts or practices." The goal of the act is to ensure fair competition among businesses and also to protect consumers from fraudulent business practices. This law overlaps with the Sherman Act but is enforced by the FTC. The FTC Act also reaches other practices that harm competition but are beyond the reach of the Sherman Act, such as banning false or deceptive advertising. The act further protects consumers by banning deceptive business practices in areas such as credit reports, debt collection, and payday loans. Figure 6.1 compares the two acts.

The Clayton Act

The Clayton Act prohibits specific conduct that was not clearly addressed by the Sherman Act. It prohibits anticompetitive mergers—those that may substantially lessen competition in a market. For example, nearly every publicly traded company in the United States is listed on either the Nasdaq or the New York Stock Exchange (NYSE). So, in 2011 when the competitors proposed a merger, the DOJ blocked the merger and stated, "The acquisition would have removed incentives for competitive pricing and high quality of service and innovation in the listing, trading, and data services"[3] on which the investing public reply.

The Clayton Act also prohibits predatory pricing, where a business sets their prices artificially low to drive out competition. Low prices are good for consumers, unless those prices are so low that competitors quit rather than compete and then the business raises prices to above-market levels for a prolonged period of time to recoup their losses. In 2019, the EU antitrust regulator fined Qualcomm $271 million for predatory pricing: Qualcomm sold 3G chipsets to smartphone makers at below cost to freeze out competitor Icera.[4]

The U.K. version of the FTC is called the Competition and Markets Authority (CMA). Like the FTC, the CMA works to promote competition and reduce anticompetitive behavior. The CMA also investigates mergers between businesses to make sure the merger and resulting entity do not harm competition. For example, Deliveroo is a U.K.-based food delivery service similar to Uber Eats and Grubhub in the United States. It offers takeout from local restaurants and delivers via bikes and motorcycles. Deliveroo is one of the most successful start-ups in the United Kingdom, but like Uber in the United States, it has faced criticism for its categorization of delivery people as independent contractors instead of employees. In July 2019, Amazon announced a $575 million investment in Deliveroo, which raised concerns at the CMA that the two companies would merge. A merger would give Amazon access to Deliveroo's on-demand delivery network, solving Amazon's "last mile" problem of getting packages to their final destination. The CMA initiated a "Phase 1" investigation, meaning it will examine the impact of a potential merger on competition and how that might affect consumers. If the CMA finds the deal anticompetitive, it will move into a "Phase 2" investigation that could either stop the deal altogether or force Amazon to divest of certain assets in order for the deal to move forward.[5]

The Robinson–Patman Act

price discrimination: Offering products at different prices to competitors.

The Robinson–Patman Act amended the Clayton Act to prohibit **price discrimination**. It makes it illegal for a company to offer its product at different prices to competitors. The same product may only be offered at different prices if the costs of serving a buyer are lower or the seller is meeting competition. The Robinson–Patman Act was passed in response to large chain stores driving smaller local stores out of business by negotiating better prices on the same products.

Antitrust laws emerged, and have continued to be applied, in response to the formation of large businesses controlling an important market: oil, computers, books. What if the market is less of a traditional business, such as college athletics? Should antitrust laws apply to restraints of trade in college athletics? Who is harmed if college sports unreasonably restrain trade?

ETHICS IN CONTEXT

Student–Athletes and Antitrust Law

iStockphoto.com/RBFried

Professional and collegiate sports have been the center of antitrust disputes dating back to the infamous Major League Baseball exemption recognized by the U.S. Supreme Court in 1922. Both players and third-party vendors have pursued claims that league rules and policies amount to a restraint of trade and are anticompetitive. In 2010, the National Football League policies related to licensing contracts for merchandising of its team's logos were found to violate antitrust laws because all 32 teams colluded in an exclusive agreement with a single vendor. More recently, college athletes have pursued antitrust claims against the NCAA. The NCAA had revenues in

excess of $1 billion in the 2017–2018 academic year. It is a consolidated industry of 347 Division I colleges and universities. Yet NCAA athletes—the source of NCAA revenues—are unpaid because they are considered students, not employees. On the other hand, student–athletes receive generous scholarships. Is a broader stakeholder approach required to protect the athletes? In a recent lawsuit against the NCAA, college athletes have alleged that NCAA-imposed limitations on athletic scholarships violate antitrust laws. Second, certain athletes have argued that licensing college athletes' names or likenesses for video games without consent or payment was a restraint of trade.

A federal judge recently approved a $208.7 million settlement stemming from a 2014 lawsuit by Shawne Alston, a West Virginia football player. Alston's lawsuit, which was ultimately combined with similar cases, alleged that former and current athletes' scholarships were limited by league rules to tuition, books, and room and board. Alston's theory was that the cap was an illegal restraint because it did not account for the "full cost of attendance" expenses such as travel, clothing, and off-campus meals. A 2013 study by the National

College Players Association found that 86% of college athletes live below the poverty line. The lawsuit led the NCAA to alter its scholarship limits by allowing for the full cost of attendance starting in 2015. The additional amount is calculated by each university and usually comes to between $3,000 and $6,000 each year.

In a related case, all-American basketball player Ed O'Bannon sued the NCAA while he was a student–athlete at UCLA after he saw a video game with an avatar of himself—a virtual player who visually resembled him and wore a UCLA jersey with his number. O'Bannon alleged the NCAA "amateurism" rules that banned student athletes from being compensated for use of their names, likenesses, or images were an illegal restraint of trade. The O'Bannon case resulted in victories for both sides. The trial court ruled that certain NCAA amateurism rules with regard to an athlete's name, image, and likeness violate federal antitrust laws. When all the colleges in the NCAA get together and agree that they will prevent college athletes from being paid for endorsements or other use of their name, likeness, or images, that is an unreasonable restraint of trade. On appeal, the trial court's remedy of limited payment for athletes during college, with the balance coming after they leave, was rejected. Ultimately the appellate court tied educational expenses to athlete compensation.

In every antitrust challenge, the NCAA has argued that its amateurism rule—treating athletes as student–athletes, not employees—keeps it from becoming an illegal monopoly. There cannot be a restraint of trade when there is no trade. The NCAA emphasizes the advantages that a free or subsidized education provides to student–athletes. But do student–athletes really get an education? Consider the hours of practice, travel, and community appearances required of a Division I NCAA athlete. A typical Division I athlete devotes about 40 hours per week to his or her sport. A recent scandal at University of North Carolina involving fake classes in which many athletes enrolled exposed a darker side of the "education" many Division I athletes receive. Fewer than 2% of NCAA student–athletes go on to be professionals, so a future professional career is not the answer for most. Who benefits

from the $1 billion the NCAA receives in revenue? Should alumni or fans care about how student–athletes are treated?

Discussion Questions

1. What other "full costs of attendance" expenses might be included in a scholarship other than travel to or from home and clothing? Is the $3,000 to $6,000 cost allocation too much, too little, or about right?

2. If the NCAA licenses O'Bannon's image for (hypothetically) $1 million dollars and UCLA awards O'Bannon a 4-year full cost of attendance scholarship for (hypothetically) $200,000, is that sufficient "alternate" compensation? Why or why not?

3. *Stakeholder theory:* The NCAA has 24 different sports, many with both men's and women's teams. Only a handful of those sports—predominantly football and men's basketball—contribute to the NCAA revenue in a meaningful way. What is at stake for all athletes if the NCAA decided to compensate its athletes beyond the cost of attendance of college? How can the revenue be shared fairly?

4. *Ethical decision-making:* Aside from any antitrust issues, is it ethical for colleges and universities to prevent students from benefiting financially from their skills and fame? Are there other students who are compensated for their skills and fame while remaining students? Does a principles-based approach suggest athletes should be treated differently than, for example, a music student who is paid for playing in a band? What if that question is analyzed using a consequences-based approach?

Take a Position

Should Division I athletes be paid? If yes, what form should the payment take: increased costs of attendance, a salary while in college, or allowing student–athletes to profit from the endorsements, jerseys, and autographs? Explain your answer.

KEY TAKEAWAYS

Anticompetitive Behavior and Antitrust Regulation

- Antitrust law focuses on conduct that restrains competition, such as monopolies and price fixing.

- Mergers will be reviewed if they substantially lessen competition in the market.

- The FTC plays a role in ensuring fair competition by banning false advertising and deceptive business practices.

PROTECTION OF CONSUMERS AND CREDITORS

LO 6.2 Identify examples of government regulations that prevent anticompetitive behavior.

Businesses exist to provide services, sell products, and make profits. As Milton Friedman famously stated, "There is one and only one social responsibility of business: to use its resources and engage in activities designed to increase its profits. ..."[6] Some businesses, however, leave out the second half of Friedman's most famous sentence, which requires businesses to increase profits "within the rules of the game, which is to say engages in open and free competition without deception or fraud."[7] Because there are businesses and employees that act deceptively and defraud consumers, Congress created several federal agencies that are charged with protecting consumers, including the FTC and the Consumer Financial Protection Bureau (CFPB). These agencies take a broader view of the purpose of business than free market advocates and attempt to protect all stakeholders.

The FTC mission is to protect consumers from anticompetitive or deceptive conduct without unduly burdening businesses. It seeks to build a "vibrant economy."[8] As with all government regulation, consumer protection law balances the needs of business with those of the consumer.

Warranties

Some consumer protections are found in common law, rather than statutes or administrative rules. Contracts are governed by law created by judges through a series of cases unless they are a special type of contract that is otherwise regulated, such as a credit card agreement. Because case law varies by state, which made doing business difficult and unpredictable, a group of legal scholars, judges, and lawyers came together in the middle of the 20th century to develop the **Uniform Commercial Code (UCC)**. The UCC is just what its name implies: a set of uniform rules to govern commercial transactions.

The UCC protects stakeholder interests by providing predictability for all parties to a transaction. One way in which the UCC protects consumers is through warranties. A **warranty** is a legally binding promise that goods will meet certain standards. Some warranties are expressly provided, such as when a merchant promises the product meets

Uniform Commercial Code (UCC): A set of uniform rules to govern commercial transactions.

warranty: A legally binding promise that goods will meet certain standards.

a standard of quality. Others are implied by the merchant's conduct; the merchant creates the warranty through actions or words that describe the product as having certain qualities, like "This frying pan is nonstick," or through a demonstration of the product as part of the sale, such as sliding a fried egg off of a frying pan. A warranty provides grounds for a remedy should a consumer be harmed—physically or financially—by defective goods. An advertisement, a pitch on the sales floor, or photos of the product can all create a warranty if they purport to state facts. Expressions of opinion by a salesclerk are considered "puffery" and do not create a warranty. For example, if a salesclerk tells you that a tennis racquet will only need to be restrung once a year, those words create a warranty. On the other hand, if that clerk tells you that the racquet will have you playing like Serena Williams, the clerk's words are mere puffery and do not create a warranty. The seller may expressly disclaim a warranty created orally by stating in the sales contract that all oral promises are disclaimed. Written warranties cannot be disclaimed.

Implied warranties apply regardless of the merchant's actions or words; these promises apply automatically to the sale of goods in order to protect consumers. The most important implied warranties are the implied warranty of merchantability and the implied warranty of fitness for a particular purpose. The **warranty of merchantability** promises the goods will be fit for the ordinary purposes for which they are used. The goods do not have to be fit for any purpose, just the purpose that is considered normal. The seller can exclude or modify this warranty by selling goods "as is." The **warranty of fitness for a particular purpose** is implied if the seller knows the buyer wants to use the product for a particular purpose. The warranty promises the product will be fit for that purpose as long as the seller knows that the buyer is relying on the seller's skill or judgment with regard to whether the product is fit for that purpose. For example, Rachel goes to her local paint store to buy weatherproof stain for her deck. She explains to the salesclerk that she wants weatherproof stain for her outdoor deck, and the clerk recommends a brand of stain. If Rachel buys the stain and it is in fact not suitable for outdoor use, the store has violated the implied warranty of fitness for a particular purpose. While the salesclerk never expressly stated the stain was fit for outdoor use, they provided the stain in response to Rachel's request.

implied warranties: When a merchant creates a warranty through actions or words that describe the product as having certain qualities.

warranty of merchantability: Promises the goods will be fit for the ordinary purposes for which they are used.

warranty of fitness for a particular purpose: Promises the product will be fit for that purpose as long as the seller knows that the buyer is relying on the seller's skill or judgment with regard to whether the product is fit for that purpose.

Unfair or Deceptive Sales Practices

In addition to enforcing antitrust laws, the FTC prohibits unfair and deceptive acts or practices in advertising. Essential to fair trade and business is complete information. Under **Section 5 of the Federal Trade Commission (FTC) Act**, an advertisement is deceptive if it contains an important misrepresentation or omission that is likely to mislead a reasonable consumer. We have all seen advertisements that promise health benefits, weight loss, or other highly desirable outcomes. Under Section 5, the companies making these products must be able to substantiate those promises with randomized and controlled human clinical trials. For example, when Skechers advertised that its toning shoes would help people lose weight, build muscle, and get in shape, the FTC brought a Section 5 violation. Although Skechers had some studies to back up their claims, the FTC found that the company had selectively chosen results that supported their claims and touted endorsements of doctors without disclosing their relationship to the company. Skechers paid $40 million to settle the false advertising case with the

Section 5 of the Federal Trade Commission (FTC) Act: An advertisement is deceptive if it contains an important misrepresentation or omission that is likely to mislead a reasonable consumer.

FTC and offered refunds to customers who had bought the shoes.[9] Similarly, when POM Wonderful advertised that its pomegranate juice could "help prevent premature aging, heart disease, stroke, Alzheimer's, even cancer" the court ruled that without randomized and controlled human studies to support these claims, the company was misleading consumers in violation of Section 5 of the FTC Act.[10]

In hindsight, perhaps these claims are too good to be true. Shoes that make you skinnier? A juice preventing so many terrible diseases? But many people bought these products, and the FTC recognizes that advertising is a powerful force. Companies can use advertising to put their products in the best light, but making false claims, especially as to specific medical benefits, is prohibited.

Less blatant but perhaps equally powerful are advertisements on social media by so-called influencers. In Chapter 12 we will learn more about social media and influencers like Kylie Jenner, with 130 million Instagram followers, who reportedly receives $1 million per post to advertise a product on social media. You do not need millions of followers to be an influencer. Individuals with 10,000 or more followers can make thousands of dollars per post. Recognizing the reach of social media influencers and the dangers of deceptive advertising, the FTC now regulates social media advertising. If an individual has a financial relationship with the advertiser, the social media post must indicate as such. A simple #ad or #sponsored fulfills the FTC rules and puts the consumer on notice that the influencer is being paid. Of course, the FTC Act ban on misleading advertisements also applies to social media ads.

Bait and Switch

bait and switch: A technique used by companies to lure the consumer into buying a product of a higher price by initially advertising a product at a low price but in actuality selling a different product at a higher price.

The FTC Act also prohibits companies from advertising one product with the intent to sell another, usually more expensive, product instead. This practice, referred to as **bait and switch**, typically starts with an alluring advertisement of a product at a great price. Once the consumer arrives at the store, or clicks in the case of online sales, the consumer finds that the company is really selling a different product at a higher price. A common technique is to advertise the product at a low price and then claim to be out of inventory when the customer arrives at the store. At that point, the seller offers a similar product at a higher price.

More recently, the FTC has brought cases against companies that engaged in bait and switch online. For example, an online business that offered to pay "top dollar" for consumers' used smartphones, laptops, or tablets, only to later refuse to pay more than a few dollars, was charged with violating the FTC Act. Laptop & Desktop Repair, LLC, had several websites where consumers could receive an instant quote for their used devices. The defendant promised that consumers would "receive the cash promised in your quote." Once the consumer mailed in the device, Laptop & Desktop Repair lowered its offer significantly, often to 3% to 10% of the original quote. The FTC received a court order banning this bait and switch buyback scheme.[11]

Pricing and Price Gouging

price gouging: A seller steeply increases the price of goods or services, usually after a demand or supply shock.

Price gouging refers to when a seller steeply increases the price of goods or services—usually after a demand or supply shock (see Figure 6.2). A common example is the steep price increase of gas or water after a hurricane. There is no federal law prohibiting price gouging, but several states prohibit it during emergencies. For example, during an emergency in California, it is illegal to raise prices of a consumer good or service more than 10%.[12] Advocates of strong anti-price gouging laws argue that raising prices on essentials during an emergency is immoral and creates an unfair windfall for businesses. On the other hand, anti-price gouging laws may encourage hoarding—for example, buying all your gas before the hurricane strikes—and may discourage businesses from increasing inventory in anticipation of an emergency. A new pricing strategy, surge pricing by ride-sharing services, has raised new questions about price gouging.

Figure 6.2   Point–Counterpoint: Price Gouging

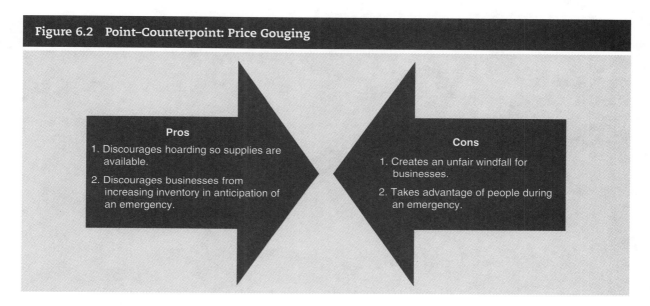

Pros
1. Discourages hoarding so supplies are available.
2. Discourages businesses from increasing inventory in anticipation of an emergency.

Cons
1. Creates an unfair windfall for businesses.
2. Takes advantage of people during an emergency.

Surge Pricing: Workforce Incentive or Price Gouging?

Surge pricing occurs when companies that operate ride-sharing services (e.g., Uber and Lyft) dramatically increase fares during peak times to incentivize drivers to be available. Surge pricing is never a surprise to riders because the smartphone app clearly displays what the price increase is before a customer accepts the ride offer. Lyft applies a similar model with its "Personal Power Zones," formerly "Prime Time." The Personal Power Zone feature shows drivers where there is high demand and charges riders more for rides in that zone. The practice has angered critics who say the technique is equivalent to price gouging. Surge pricing ignites controversy during incidents involving emergencies and natural disasters. For example, in a recent case, Uber began charging customers more than 4 times the normal rate during a hostage crisis in downtown Sydney, Australia. Following backlash on social media, Uber refunded customers their money and offered free rides. Uber faced similar scrutiny in New York and New Jersey for surging prices during and after Hurricane Sandy. New York's attorney general accused the company of price gouging, and Uber agreed to cap its surge pricing during emergencies and natural disasters and pledged to apply the same cap to its service across the United States. Uber's public response has always been to champion the policy as a careful balance between the goals of transportation availability with community expectations of affordability during disasters. They consistently defend the surge pricing practice with a basic economic argument:

(Continued)

(Continued)

Surge pricing helps supply meet demand. Consumers have fought back by filing a lawsuit against Uber, alleging that the company's business model amounts to a conspiracy to fix prices and take a cut of the profits. The suit does not question the company's practice of determining and coordinating the price of app-ordered car rides but rather takes aim at surge pricing specifically as the most favorable grounds for a challenge. If the court finds that Uber's business model is a form of vertical restraint—that is, an agreement between Uber and its drivers—their fate may hinge on whether its surge pricing ultimately benefits or harms consumers under the rule of reason.

Discussion Questions

1. Is surge pricing anti-consumer? Why or why not?

2. Explain whether you find Uber's argument about supply and demand compelling. Does that also include surge pricing during a natural disaster? Why or why not?

Critical Thinking

1. Price surging is one example of how the cyber economy may conflict with government regulation. Some tech companies, such as Uber, have come under criticism for deploying profit strategies skirting employment, antitrust, and antidiscrimination laws.

2. Is that a good public policy? Some argue the Uber conundrum calls for the creation of a third "independent worker" category of employment that gives it the control it needs to make its business model work, while safeguarding the flexibility its drivers prize. Explain whether you agree or not.

3. If courts and policymakers agree on an independent worker model, it would effectively carve out a tech-sector exception to the regulatory principles governing the economy since the New Deal era (1933–1941). Are current employment, antitrust, and antidiscrimination laws out of date? If so, how would you reform them?

Food and Drug Safety

The Food, Drug, and Cosmetic Act of 1938 created the Food and Drug Administration (FDA). The FDA is one of the oldest administrative agencies in the United States. It has been working to ensure the safety of agricultural products since 1848 and moved into protecting our food supply and drugs in 1906. The Food, Drug, and Cosmetic Act of 1938 was passed in response to a tragedy. A doctor reformulated an elixir used to treat a common illness. Without being tested for toxicity, the elixir was prescribed throughout the country. Unfortunately, the elixir contained small amounts of antifreeze and eventually killed 107 people, including children.[13] In response, Congress gave the FDA the power to test and approve drugs as well as regulate our food supply. Today, the FDA is responsible for protecting public health through regulation of food, drugs, cosmetics, and medical devices. The FDA also regulates tobacco products.

FDA Food Safety Processes

According to the FDA, about 48 million people in the United States get sick each year from foodborne diseases.[14] Food safety is a grave public safety issue: Of those sickened by food each year, 128,000 are hospitalized and 3,000 die. The Food Safety Modernization Act was signed into law in 2011 to address the changing threats to our food supply. The law's goal is to prevent foodborne illness rather than merely respond to it. The FDA has passed many rules to enforce this law, including standards for manufacturing practices and sanitary transportation for food, and growing, harvesting, packing, and holding of produce. The FDA enforces its rules through inspections, fines, and recalls.

Credit Transactions

After the financial crisis of 2008, Congress created the **Consumer Financial Protection Bureau (CFPB)** to regulate consumer financial transactions, including credit cards, home mortgages, and bank accounts. The goal of the CFPB is to ensure that consumers are treated fairly. Under the **Dodd–Frank Act (DFA)**, it is unlawful for any provider of consumer financial products or services to engage in any unfair, deceptive, or abusive act or practice.[15] The CFPB also has the authority to make rules to enforce consumer protection statutes (see Chapter 10 for more information on DFA and the financial industry as a whole).

Other laws that protect consumers in financial transactions include the **Truth in Lending Act (TLA)**, which focuses on disclosure by requiring that lenders disclose all of the loan information clearly, including the amount financed, the total of payments, the finance charge, and the annual percentage rate (APR). Home mortgages are also included in the TLA. A **mortgage** is a loan secured by real estate. After the financial crisis of 2008 resulted in huge numbers of homeowners being unable to pay their mortgages, which caused foreclosures and the collapse of the housing market, Congress amended the TLA with regard to mortgages. The law prohibits unfair, abusive, or deceptive home mortgage lending practices. Lenders must be responsible in deciding how much money to loan to the borrower. Qualified mortgages under CFPB rules prohibit features harmful to consumers such as balloon payments. The CFPB also requires that companies that service mortgages provide adequate disclosures such as clear monthly statements. The TLA also gives consumers the right to rescind a mortgage for up to three business days after the signing.

The **Fair Debt Collection Practices Act** governs communications between debt collectors and debtors to prevent harassment and abuse by collectors. For example, the law prohibits debt collectors from calling before 8:00 a.m. or after 9:00 p.m.; it also bans visits to the debtors' workplace if the employer prohibits these visits. More generally, it makes it illegal for debt collectors to make any false, deceptive, or misleading statements. The statute also regulates the debt collector's communications with the debtor's acquaintances. The debt collector may contact the acquaintance only once and cannot tell that person that the debtor is in debt.

Consumer Financial Protection Bureau (CFPB): An agency created to regulate consumer financial transactions, including credit cards, home mortgages, and bank accounts.

Dodd–Frank Act (DFA): Under this act, it is unlawful for any provider of consumer financial products or services to engage in any unfair, deceptive, or abusive act or practice.

Truth in Lending Act (TLA): Requires lenders disclose all of the loan information clearly, including the amount financed, the total of payments, the finance charge, and the APR.

mortgage: A loan secured by real estate.

Fair Debt Collection Practices Act: Regulates communications between creditors and debtors and prohibits creditors from making false, deceptive, or misleading statements.

Protection of Consumers and Creditors

- A warranty is a legally binding promise that goods will meet certain standards. Some warranties are expressly provided in contracts and others are implied by the merchant's conduct. A warranty provides grounds for a remedy should a consumer be harmed—physically or financially—by defective goods.

- Under the FTC Act, an advertisement is deceptive if it contains an important misrepresentation or omission that is likely to mislead a reasonable consumer.

- The FDA is responsible for protecting public health through regulation of food, drugs, cosmetics, and medical devices. This responsibility includes promulgating rules for food recalls.

- The TLA protects consumers borrowing money through mortgages by requiring that a lender disclose all information clearly, including the amount financed, the total of payments, the finance charge, and the APR.

KEY TAKEAWAYS

PROTECTING INVESTORS

LO 6.3 Explain two primary provisions of securities law that protect investors from fraud.

In Chapter 1, we saw how shareholders, directors, and officers govern organizations internally, and in Chapter 10 you will see how securities and other laws shape and influence the financial industry. Here, we focus on *external* governance intended to protect shareholders and investors when the principals of an organization wish to raise capital for its operations or expansion. Organizations raise capital from the general public by either (1) selling a percentage of ownership of the venture, known as **equity**, to investors who are interested in receiving a return on their investment based on the success of the business, or (2) issuing **debt instruments** to public investors who wish to receive a fixed rate of return regardless of the profitability of the business entity. Equity and debt instruments are called **securities** and are highly regulated by federal and state securities law.

Fundamentally, all securities regulation has the same rationale: to protect investors and ensure public confidence in the integrity of the securities market. Note that securities laws are not meant to provide insurance for losses or to punish a venture's principals simply because the business does not earn a profit. The underpinnings of all securities regulation are *disclosure and transparency*. Much of the regulation concerning fraud or securities sales boils down to whether the seller or issuer has made truthful and sufficiently full disclosures about the security itself. Securities law is primarily a matter of federal statutes and regulations, but all states have similar disclosure and fraud laws for transactions within state borders.

Securities Transactions

Securities are regulated in two types of transactions: (1) original and reissuance of securities by a business to raise capital (known as the **primary market**) and (2) the purchase and sale of issued securities between investors (known as the **secondary market**; see Figure 6.3). Both of these markets are governed by federal and state securities law and regulations. Various securities regulations require registration and disclosures and prescribe certain procedures intended to give confidence to investors in the value of a particular security and to prevent fraud.

In the primary market, issuers raise capital by selling securities in **public markets** (to the general investment community) or in **private placements** (to limited groups of investors, such as venture capitalists or institutional investors). Issuing securities to the public markets for the first time is known as an **initial public offering (IPO)**. A company is said to "go public" when it decides to sell its voting common shares for the first time to outside investors through use of public markets such as the NYSE. The sale is made using a mandatory registration statement that discloses important facts about the offering to potential investors. Not all securities offerings and transactions are subject to the full burden of the federal and state regulatory schemes. Some securities transactions are exempt from full registration, and the law allows a fast-track system for securities that fall into the category of relatively small offerings or private placements. These exemptions are not automatic. The issuer or trader of a security must structure the security transaction in such a way that it qualifies for an exemption according to federal and state laws. The federal

equity: An ownership percentage of a venture.

debt instruments: Assets that have a fixed rate of return (e.g., bonds and mortgages).

securities: Includes equities and debt instruments and other types of tradeable financial assets.

primary market: Original and reissuance of securities by a business to raise capital.

secondary market: The purchase and sale of issued securities between investors.

public markets: Markets open to the general investing community.

private placements: The limited groups of investors that issuers sell securities to (e.g., venture capitalists or institutional investors).

initial public offering (IPO): The first time securities are issued to the public markets.

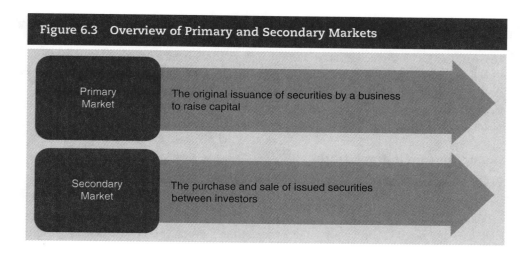

Figure 6.3 Overview of Primary and Secondary Markets

Primary Market — The original issuance of securities by a business to raise capital

Secondary Market — The purchase and sale of issued securities between investors

laws, regulations, and exemptions governing the primary market are found in the **Securities Act of 1933 (or Exchange Act).** More information on the process of an IPO can be found in Chapter 10 on financial systems.

In the secondary market, the trading of already-issued securities does not raise capital for the issuing business. Rather, investors sell to other investors to make a profit or prevent a loss. Once a company has sold shares to the public, it becomes subject to extensive reporting requirements to federal regulators. In theory, this secondary market provides cash flow for investors to continue their investments in primary markets. The secondary market is largely regulated through the **Securities Exchange Act of 1934 (or Exchange Act)**.

Securities Exchange Act of 1934 (or Exchange Act): Regulates the secondary market for securities.

Misrepresentation and Fraud Under the 1933 Act

All the disclosure rules in the Securities Act would be meaningless if not accompanied by regulations requiring that the information disclosed is accurate, not misleading, and not fraudulent. Section 11 of the 1933 Securities Act prohibits material misrepresentations or omissions in the registration statement. Anyone who purchased the security can sue anyone who signed the registration statement for violations of Section 11. The potential list of those responsible include the company, and its directors, executives, attorneys, underwriters, auditors, or any other experts that contributed to the registration statement. A plaintiff need not show that it relied on the erroneous information in deciding to purchase; Section 11 only requires proof of a material misrepresentation and a loss. **Material** means information that would be important to an average investor. The lawyers, underwriters, auditors, board members, and other experts can avoid liability if they can show they had a reasonable belief based on reasonable investigation that the registration statement was true.

material: Information that would be important to an average investor.

More broadly, Section 12(a)(2) of the Securities Act prohibits material misstatements or omissions, oral or written, in connection with the offer or sale of a security. While Section 11 protects investors only from being misled by the registration statement, Section 12(a)(2) protects investors from misleading or incomplete statements made in press conferences, interviews, at meetings, or in any other context. Facebook made costly errors in its IPO that resulted in lawsuits for violation of Sections 11 and 12(a)(2). The lawsuits alleged that Facebook did not disclose prior to its May 17, 2010, IPO that it had learned a trend of increasing mobile usage negatively impacted Facebook's advertising business, and in turn its revenue. These concerns were discussed with a small group of institutional investors before the IPO, but the lawsuit argued that the registration statement was not adequately amended to disclose the extent of the concern to all potential investors. The Securities Act requires that *all* potential investors have access to the same information before making an investment decision. Facebook learned that lesson the hard way, ultimately settling the lawsuits for $35 million.[16]

Exemptions From Registration

The procedures for issuing securities to the public under the Securities Act are onerous, time-consuming, and expensive. While it will always be worthwhile for tech giants such as Google and Facebook to undertake an IPO, how does a relatively smaller company raise capital? Through legislation and new U.S. Securities and Exchange Commission (SEC) rules, the U.S. government has acknowledged this challenge and incentivized smaller companies to issue securities by creating transaction exemptions to the Securities Act IPO requirements. There are several options, depending on the size of the company, the number and type of investors sought, and the amount of capital the offering seeks to raise. No matter how the company issues its securities, it is always subject to the anti-fraud provisions in the Securities Act.

Private and Small Transactions: Regulation D

Regulation D: Exempts small transactions from the registration requirements of the 1933 Securities Act.

Rule 504: Transactions where no more than $5 million is being raised, there is no advertising, and only restricted securities are sold is exempt from registration requirements.

restricted securities: Securities that cannot be resold on a public market.

Rule 506: Sets limitations on the type of investor that can buy the security but no limit on the dollar amount of the offering.

Regulation D allows small transactions to be exempt from the registration requirements of the Securities Act. Under **Rule 504,** if a company wants to raise no more than $5 million, it may do so without filing a registration statement. The company can only sell **restricted securities**, meaning those that cannot be resold on public markets, and there is no general advertising allowed.

Also, under Regulation D, a private placement under **Rule 506** has limitations on the type of investor that can buy the security but no limit on the dollar amount of the offering. Rule 506 allows for sales to an unlimited number of accredited investors but only up to 35 nonaccredited investors. An accredited investor, defined in the statute, is a sophisticated investor, either an institution or an individual with high net worth. In formulating Rule 506 offerings, the SEC sought to provide more access to capital from investors who are less likely to need the full disclosures required by the Securities Act, while still protecting the average "Main Street" investor.

Regulation A+

Regulation A+ offers another exempt transaction. It allows the company to raise up to $50 million in any 12-month period. Although exempt from the registration requirements, the company must file an offering circular with key disclosures. The investments are limited for nonaccredited investors to avoid an unsophisticated investor investing their life savings without adequate information. Regulation A+ is available only to nonreporting companies, meaning first-time issuers.

Crowdfunding

The Internet provides new ways to reach investors, especially when compared to how a company would obtain investors when the Securities Act was passed in 1933. Crowdfunding is an example of how technology has changed the opportunities for companies seeking capital. In 2012, Congress enacted the **JOBS Act**. As the name implied, this law was intended to stimulate economic activity. The JOBS Act created exemptions to existing securities regulations in order to ease the process of obtaining capital, especially for small- to medium-sized companies. In 2016, the SEC promulgated **Regulation CF**, which provided that entrepreneurs and other small businesses can raise up to $1 million from any investors using an online platform. Unlike Regulation D and A+ offerings, which are predominantly open to wealthy investors because of accreditation rules, crowdfunding allows the average person to invest in a company through an easy online process. The company must file a form with basic disclosures before crowdfunding. There are limits on the amount an individual can invest in any company's crowdfunding campaign that vary based on income and net worth. Finally, a company can only sell restricted securities, meaning the securities cannot be resold.

Exempt offerings, whether private placements under Regulation D or crowdfunding, balance business growth with protection of investors. The effort to achieve this balance pervades all of securities regulation, with the goal of maintaining public confidence in our markets without stifling economic growth.

> **JOBS Act:** A law that created exemptions to existing securities regulations in order to ease the process of obtaining capital, especially for small- to medium-sized companies.
>
> **Regulation CF:** Entrepreneurs and other small businesses can raise up to $1 million from any investors using an online platform by selling restricted securities, and maximum investments vary depending on income.

Caution and Crowdfunding

Take a moment, and think of crowdfunding in brick-and-mortar terms: You overhear a stranger at a coffee shop discussing a start-up business venture with another stranger and the business venture piques your interest. You approach the strangers and express your interest and voilà—as it turns out, they have a video on their laptop they would love to show you (and any other potential investors). The video is a multimedia extravaganza, and after a discussion where you are impressed by these strangers' creativity and command of numbers, you write them a check for $1,000. They write you an official-looking receipt and, to your surprise, offer you a T-shirt with the company logo once they have launched. Foolish? Certainly, yet this is precisely what happens in some crowdfunding transactions.

Indeed, despite recent SEC-mandated disclosures, a relatively blind trust is still at the core of a crowdfunding campaign. In the past, initial start-up capital depended on an entrepreneur's network of friends, family, and associates who held the principals accountable to prevent fraud. Now, the principals of a venture solicit money from strangers for their projects or ventures, usually through online platforms like Kickstarter, Indiegogo, or GoFundMe. In return,

they usually offer both a share of the profits and other rewards, like a sample product, T-shirt, or digital download. The FTC began a crackdown on crowdfunding fraud in 2015 by charging Erik Chevalier with fraud for his "The Doom That Came to Atlantic City" board game campaign on Kickstarter. According to the FTC, he raised more than $122,000 from 1,246 backers to whom he promised rewards, like a copy of the game or specially designed figurines. Although Chevalier represented in a number of updates that he was making progress on the game, he eventually announced he was canceling the project and refunding his backers' money. Despite Chevalier's promises, he did not provide the rewards nor did he provide refunds to his backers. In fact, according to the FTC, Chevalier spent most of the money on unrelated personal expenses like rent, moving himself to Oregon, personal equipment, and licenses for a different project.

What recourse do the 1,246 investors have? Not much. Chevalier agreed to an FTC settlement order with a $111,793.71 judgment against him, but the judgment is suspended because of his inability to pay. The full amount will only become due if he is found to have misrepresented his financial condition. The Kickstarter terms of use say, "Campaign Owners

(Continued)

CASE STUDY 6.2

are legally bound to perform on any promises and/or commitments to Contributors," but it does not include a strict timeline for meeting those commitments. Moreover, although it advises contributors that they "can use our Terms of Use in a US court… should you choose to take any legal action against the campaign," it also makes clear that Kickstarter is under no obligation to become involved in disputes between campaign owners and contributors.

Discussion Questions

1. Should Kickstarter bear more responsibility for getting investors their money back? Why or why not?

2. Should the investors have exercised more caution? What steps could they have taken to reduce their investment risk?

Critical Thinking

Crowdfunding has increased sharply in the past few years. Crowdexpert.com maintains a crowdfunding database and estimates that the amount of transactions will continue to rise as much as 75% year over year. In 2012, Congress gave crowdfunding a significant boost in the JOBS Act as part of an overall strategy to increase economic growth in response to the financial crisis that began in 2008. The law required the SEC to carve out a special exception in securities laws to allow crowdfunding as a tool for small businesses to raise capital.

1. Should crowdfunding be treated differently from other forms of fundraising by corporations in terms of disclosures and transparency to investors? Why or why not?

2. What effect does the increased use of crowdfunding have on the overall economy? Are there drawbacks? If so, what are they? If not, why not?

Securities Exchange Act of 1934 (Exchange Act)

The Exchange Act regulates issuers, which means that once a company goes public, it has ongoing obligations under the Exchange Act. The Exchange Act governs the secondary market, whether it is ensuring that issuers adequately disclose the status of the company or preventing market manipulation scams. Like the Securities Act, the Exchange Act's goal is to maintain public confidence in the markets through disclosure and fraud prevention, not to ensure that you make a profit from your financial investments.

Disclosure Under the Exchange Act

Remember our list of information that you would want to know before you decide to buy securities in an IPO? Whether it is months or years later, you would want the same type of information when deciding whether to buy or sell those securities on the secondary market. The Exchange Act recognizes the need to protect shareholders and potential shareholders through transparency. If you have invested—or are considering investing—in a company, our laws protect your right to know what is happening in that company. The Exchange Act's disclosure laws play an important part in corporate governance; a board of directors of an issuer knows that it is accountable to the public on a regular basis, which should shape the board's conduct.

The Exchange Act's disclosure requirements are implemented through a series of form disclosures that are filed with the SEC: the annual 10-K, quarterly 10-Q, and the 8-K form for any significant events that occur between quarterly reports. Under **Section 18(a)** of the Exchange Act, anyone who purchased or sold a security in reliance on a false or misleading filing can sue for money damages. Like the anti-fraud provisions of the Securities Act, Section 18 and its broader counterpart Section10(b), which is discussed next, are important tools in maintaining confidence in our markets through protecting shareholders from fraud or misrepresentation.

Rule 10b-5 is the primary anti-fraud provision in securities law. Rule 10b-5 was created by the SEC to enforce Section 10(b) of the Exchange Act. The history of Section 10(b) is illustrative of its purpose. In 1942, the Boston Regional Office of the SEC found out that a company president was making pessimistic statements about the company's earnings while purchasing shares. The Securities Act prohibited fraud in the sale of securities, but there was no regulation that prevented fraud in the purchase of securities. Alas, Section 10(b) was born. Rule 10b-5 prohibits fraud in the purchase or sale of securities. It allows the SEC to pursue civil violations against a wrongdoer; a shareholder to bring a civil claim for money damages; and, in some cases, the federal prosecutors to pursue criminal charges for willful violations.

Section 18(a): Allows anyone who bought or sold securities in reliance on a false or misleading filing to sue for money damages.

Rule 10b-5: Prohibits fraud in the purchase or sale of securities; the SEC can pursue civil and criminal claims against violators.

Insider Trading

While there are many ways to violate Rule 10b-5, one of the most pernicious is insider trading. **Insider trading** is the buying or selling of securities for a profit based on information not available to the public. It is a violation of civil and criminal law. Insider trading is illegal, and many consider it unethical because it violates the fundamental goal of regulation of securities: fairness. Insider trading gives an unfair advantage to those privileged enough to be on the "inside" or know someone who is. It also creates market inefficiencies because of asymmetric information. The mere perception of insider advantage will discourage average investors from participating in our financial markets. Insider trading law comes from the broad prohibition in Rule 10b-5 on fraud and what is considered illegal insider trading has evolved through common law on a case-by-case basis. The result of this evolution is a confusing tangle of rules about what is illegal and what is not.

What is clear is that so-called classical insider trading is illegal. **Classical insider trading** occurs when an individual who owes a fiduciary duty to the company—usually an employee or director—learns nonpublic information and breaches its fiduciary duty by trading the securities of that company. An insider includes **constructive insiders**, such as attorneys, accountants, consultants, and other third parties who have a temporary fiduciary duty to the company because of their jobs.

The **misappropriation theory** applies insider trading prohibitions to outsiders. Charles O'Hagan was a partner in a law firm whose client was Grand Metropolitan. Grand Metropolitan was considering a takeover of the Pillsbury Company. Obviously, it would be a breach of O'Hagan's fiduciary duty to his firm's client, and classical insider trading, if he traded in shares of Grand Metropolitan. Instead, O'Hagan purchased shares of Pillsbury and sold those shares for a profit once the transaction was announced. The SEC brought an insider trading case against O'Hagan, arguing that by misappropriating confidential information from his client he breached his fiduciary duty to that client regardless of the company in which he traded. The Supreme Court ultimately agreed with the SEC, ruling a person who uses insider information in trading securities has committed securities fraud against the source of the information.[17]

insider trading: The illegal act of buying or selling of securities for a profit based on information not available to the public.

classical insider trading: The illegal act of an individual that owes a fiduciary duty to the company—usually an employee or director—learns nonpublic information and breaches its fiduciary duty by trading the securities of the company.

constructive insiders: Attorneys, accountants, consultants, and other third parties who have a temporary fiduciary duty to the company because of their jobs.

misappropriation theory: Postulates that a person who uses insider information in trading securities has committed securities fraud against the source of the information.

tippees: Those who receive nonpublic information from insiders and then trade.

tipper: The insider.

In life and for insider trading, no man (or woman) is an island. Insiders often share their nonpublic information with family, friends, or those willing to pay them for it. These **tippees**—those who receive nonpublic information from insiders and then trade—do not fit the classical form of insider trading because they owe no duty to the company in which they trade. The Supreme Court has held that a tippee is committing illegal insider trading if the tippee knows that the **tipper** (the insider) is breaching a fiduciary duty by providing that nonpublic information. The tipper must also receive a "personal benefit" in exchange for the tip. The tipper can commit insider trading without trading; if an insider passes on nonpublic information in breach of a duty in order to receive a personal benefit, that tipper has violated insider trading law without trading.

The Supreme Court has provided guidance as to how to define the required "personal benefit" to a tipper, but questions remain. In *Salman v. United States*,[18] a tipper disclosed nonpublic information about mergers and acquisitions to his brother with the expectation that his brother would trade. Then the brother tipped the information to Salman, who traded. No money or gifts were provided to the tipper, and Salman argued that there was no personal benefit received by the tipper. The Court held that "a gift of confidential information to a trading relative or friend"[19] is a sufficient benefit to the tipper to create liability. In other words, there is no requirement that the tipper receives a financial benefit. The *Salman* case involved brothers with a close relationship, where the tipper wanted to help out his brother in difficult financial times by passing along the insider information.

Regardless of the unanswered questions about the complexities of insider trading law, the courts have made clear that using an unfair advantage to profit, or help others to profit, violates the spirit and purpose of our securities laws. As Law and Society 6.1 shows, the courts have been willing to extend insider trading liability well beyond the business world if the individual involved appears to take advantage of a relationship of trust.

LAW AND SOCIETY 6.1

Insider Trading: *United States v. McGee*, No. 13-3183 (3d Cir. 2014)

Facts: Timothy McGee, a financial adviser with more than 20 years of experience, first met Christopher Maguire while attending Alcoholics Anonymous (AA) meetings. For the better part of a decade, McGee was Maguire's sponsor in AA. They shared intimate details about their lives to alleviate stress and prevent relapses. Given the sensitive nature of their communications, McGee assured Maguire that their conversations would remain private. During this same time, Maguire was a member of executive management of a publicly traded company and was closely involved in negotiations to sell the company. During a conversation in which McGee was trying to convince Maguire to return to AA, Maguire blurted out inside information about the imminent sale of his company, telling McGee that he was under extraordinary pressure and that "we're selling the company... for three times book [value]." After this conversation, McGee purchased a substantial amount of the company's stock that eventually yielded him a $292,128 profit. After a jury found him guilty of insider trading, McGee appealed, arguing that he could not be guilty of insider trading unless he (misappropriator) had a fiduciary relationship with Maguire (inside source).

Issue: Is McGee's relationship as an AA sponsor sufficient to trigger insider trading laws?

Ruling: Yes. The court ruled against McGee and upheld his conviction. The court rejected McGee's defense that the misappropriation theory required a fiduciary duty between McGee and Maguire and held that the U.S. Supreme Court's precedent cases did not define the relationship so narrowly. Rather, any duty of loyalty, confidentiality, trust, or confidence would suffice for "recognized duties" to establish a violation of the law. For almost a decade McGee mentored Maguire, who entrusted "extremely personal" information to McGee. It was both men's understanding that information discussed would not be disclosed or used by either party. McGee encouraged Maguire to use his services as a financial adviser, telling him, "I know everything about what you're going through from an alcohol perspective. You can keep your trust in me." Based on this, a rational juror could find that there was a relationship of trust between the two men.

Law and Management Questions

1. Why is a relationship of trust the heart of this crime?

2. If McGee's conviction had not been upheld, what would be the cumulative effect of this ruling on the secondary market?

KEY TAKEAWAYS

Protecting Investors

- External governance in the form of securities regulation is the primary method for protecting the rights of shareholders and investors when an organization raises money for launching or expanding their venture.

- Securities issued by organizations in the form of equity (ownership) or debt (fixed rate of return) are regulated by the Securities Act of 1933.

- The Securities Exchange Act of 1934 governs the purchase and sale of already-issued securities.

- Offerings to "sophisticated" or wealthy investors are typically exempt from full registration but are not exempt from full disclosures about risk.

- Crowdfunding has a congressionally created carve-out from full securities registration and disclosure.

- Insider trading occurs when an insider uses nonpublic information to profit in a securities transaction. Non-insiders who use nonpublic information obtained from insiders also violate insider trading laws.

SUMMARY

Almost every business in the United States is regulated. The regulations discussed in this chapter strive to protect consumers, investors, and other stakeholders from unfair business practices and false or misleading statements.

Although they may increase the cost of doing business through mandatory disclosures, safety and security measures, and transparency, regulations play a crucial role in keeping business and our markets fair and open.

KEY TERMS

bait and switch   122
classical insider trading   131
constructive insiders   131
Consumer Financial Protection
     Bureau (CFPB)   125
debt instruments   126
Dodd–Frank Act (DFA)   125
equity   126
Fair Debt Collection Practices
     Act   125
implied warranties   121
insider trading   131
JOBS Act   129
market   116
material   127
misappropriation theory   131

monopoly   116
mortgage   125
per se standard   115
price discrimination   118
price gouging   122
primary market   126
private placements   126
public markets   126
Regulation CF   129
Regulation D   128
restricted securities   128
Rule 10b-5   131
Rule 504   128
Rule 506   128
rule of reason   115
secondary market   126

Section 18(a)   131
Section 5 of the Federal Trade
     Commission (FTC) Act   121
securities   126
Securities Exchange Act of 1934
     (Exchange Act)   127
tippees   132
tipper   132
Truth in Lending Act (TLA)   125
Uniform Commercial Code
     (UCC)   120
unreasonable restraints   116
warranty   120
warranty of fitness for a particular
     purpose   121
warranty of merchantability   121

REVIEW QUESTIONS

1. What are the differences between the 1933 Securities Act and the 1934 Exchange Act?

2. Describe the different types of private offerings.

3. What are the goals of the three main antitrust laws? How do they achieve those goals?

4. What is a warranty? Describe the different types.

5. How does the FTC Act protect consumers?

MANAGER'S CHALLENGE

Consumer Protection

Cyber Garden, LLC, is an online retailer of garden tools and supplies. The leadership team is creating a new marketing strategy to boost sluggish sales, and they are considering several options. One potential strategy is to create Internet traffic by sending targeted e-mails to their primary buying demographic with daily, limited-time flash sales of 50% off of a particular product. Once a user is drawn to the discount item via the flash sale link, she would be presented with options for other products at full price. The primary concern of the group, however, is about the profitability in the event that most users opt only for the discounted item. One manager, Lewis, offered a solution of simply limiting supply of the number of discounted products to 10 on the assumption that, even if the product were sold out, the user would opt to buy other items at regular price for convenience. Another manager, Winston, offered a different solution by creating an e-mail design and content intended to entice discount shoppers to purchase products at regular price by implying that

Figure 6.4 Draft of E-Mail Campaign

Cyber Gardens, LLC "Your One-Click Garden Shop"

FLASH SALE

HALF OFF: A-1 Weedkiller
Now only $5 per bottle
You must order in the next two hours!

Clearance!
Tectonic Brand Rakes
Only $10 each

Act Now! Warehouse Price!
Utility Wheelbarrows
$50

the product was discounted. He submitted the draft in Figure 6.4 to the team.

Framing Questions

1. Could Lewis's proposed solution be considered a bait and switch? Why or why not?

2. Is there anything in Winston's proposed e-mail design that runs afoul of consumer protection law? If so, what?

3. What ethical issues should the management team consider when creating the flash sale campaign?

Assignment

Design an e-mail campaign for Cyber Garden's flash sale campaign that balances marketing objectives and consumer protection law within the context of corporate social responsibility (CSR).

PART II

BUILDING RELATIONSHIPS AND WORKING WITH STAKEHOLDERS

CHAPTER 7: Environmentalism and Sustainability

CHAPTER 8: Employees and the Corporation

CHAPTER 9: Managing a Diverse Workforce

CHAPTER 10: Financial Systems and Society

CHAPTER 11: International and Multinational Organizations

ENVIRONMENTALISM AND SUSTAINABILITY

iStockphoto.com/natrot

Ethics in Context

Green Management or Greenwashing?

One of the topics we discuss in this chapter is how organizations use green management as a source of competitive advantage. As you study this chapter, think about the ethical dimensions of green management as well. Which green management practices strike you as ethical, and what kind of green practices would be unethical? Later in the chapter, in the Ethics in Context section, we use stakeholder and ethical lenses to examine a practice known as greenwashing.

Learning Objectives

Upon completion of this chapter, the reader should be able to do the following:

7.1 Define the terms and policy goals related to environmentalism and sustainability.

7.2 Explain how organizations deploy green management as a competitive advantage.

7.3 Explain global standards of sustainable development and the implementation of sustainable development goals (SDGs).

7.4 Describe climate change and its impact on society.

7.5 List the major sources of environmental policy.

INTRODUCTION

Our global focus on environmentalism and sustainability has sharpened in both importance and prominence among stakeholders and society at large. In this chapter, we define *environmentalism* and *sustainability*, analyze green management practices and ethics, and use sustainability as a context to examine the roles and expectations of stakeholders regarding an organization's environmental practices. Finally, we outline the environmental regulatory systems and examine the regulatory impact on business and society.

ENVIRONMENTALISM: DEFINITIONS AND POLICY OBJECTIVES

LO 7.1   Define the terms and policy goals related to environmentalism and sustainability.

Although the terms *sustainability* and *environmentalism* are sometimes used interchangeably, they represent two different concepts. **Environmentalism** is the study of the interaction between various components within the environment (e.g., internal and external factors that affect the environment) to look for solutions for environmental problems. As a scientific term, **sustainability** refers to the ability of systems and processes to endure. In the context of business and industry, sustainability is typically known as *sustainable development* and is used to describe meeting the needs of the present without compromising the ability of future generations to thrive. Sustainable development is discussed in detail later in this chapter.

> **environmentalism:** The study of the interaction between various components within the environment to look for solutions for environmental problems.
>
> **sustainability:** The ability of ecosystems and processes to endure through future generations.

To be sure, governments all over the globe have become involved in how people and organizations affect the environment. In this effort, governments can take one of several approaches. Here are a few examples:

- In some countries, governments offer minimal protection for the environment.

- Some set common standards in an attempt to take the cost of pollution control out of competition.

- Governments can also provide economic incentives for people and organizations.

- Some mandate criminal and civil enforcement (e.g., fines or even prison).

- Some encourage information disclosure (i.e., also called regulation by publicity or regulation by embarrassment).

The European Union has actively pursued environmental criminals, and in the United States there are guidelines for sentencing environmental wrongdoers by the U.S. Sentencing Commission. We will discuss environmental policy approaches more fully at the end of the chapter.

Environmental Justice

It may not be a surprise that environmental benefits and burdens are not shared equally by all. We learned about justice, more generally, in Chapter 3. The term *environmental justice* is similar. It is a movement that grew from the recognition of this disproportionate number of environmental burdens in certain communities. According to the U.S. Environmental Protection Agency (EPA), **environmental justice** is the fair treatment and meaningful involvement of all people regardless of race, color, national origin, or income with respect to the development, implementation, and enforcement of environmental laws, regulations, and policies. Scholar David Schlosberg lays out four specific tenets that recognize when environmental justice is in place:

> **environmental justice:** The fair treatment of all people with respect to the development, implementation, and enforcement of environmental laws, regulations, and policies.

- Equitable distribution of environmental risks and benefits

- Fair and meaningful participation in environmental decision-making

- Recognition of community ways of life, local knowledge, and cultural difference

- Capability of communities and individuals to function and flourish in society[1]

It is important for managers to recognize the signs of a lack of environmental justice as they work to implement sustainability and environmental management programs.

Environmental Activists

Environmental activists play a critical role in shaping environmental policy and can help to inform the conceptualization of an organization's environmental programs. Environmental activist and writer Alex Steffen identified three *activist categories* according to how invested someone is in the green movement:

1. *Light greens* are into protecting the environment and see it as a lifestyle choice, like eco-consumerism, rather than any kind of political activism. If your environmental efforts are centered around buying organic food and air drying your clothes, you're probably light green.

2. *Dark greens* fall at the other end of the spectrum; they are all about radical political change to solve our environmental problems. They believe industry and capitalism caused these problems, and until society embraces a postmaterialism and post-technology world, we'll never be able to stop harming the planet.

3. *Bright greens* fall somewhere in the middle; they also want radical change—eco-consumerism is not enough—but they think the best way to do it is by overhauling and improving the existing political and economic systems, rather than doing away with them entirely like the dark greens. Bright greens also embrace making better designs, creating innovative technologies, and actively looking for ways to change the way we do things.

iStockphoto.com/ArtMarie

Light green activities include buying natural and organic products as a lifestyle choice.

KEY TAKEAWAYS

Environmentalism: Definitions and Policy Objectives

- Environmentalism and sustainability, though complementary, are different concepts. Environmentalism is the study of the interaction between various components within the environment and is geared toward solutions to environmental problems. Sustainability is the ability of systems and processes to endure, in other words, sustainable development.

- Environmental justice is the fair treatment and meaningful involvement of all people regardless of race, color, national origin, or income with respect to the development, implementation, and enforcement of environmental laws, regulations, and policies.

- Environmental activists are sometimes identified by being in the light green, dark green, and bright green categories according to their personal investment in the green movement.

GREEN MANAGEMENT AND COMPETITIVE ADVANTAGE

LO 7.2   Explain how organizations deploy green management as a competitive advantage.

green management: Describes an organization's efforts to incorporate environmentalism and sustainability into its business model and practices.

Green management is a phrase generally used to describe an organization's efforts to incorporate environmentalism and sustainability into its business model and practices. It is best thought of as an organizational process that brings together corporate social responsibility (CSR) and economic concerns. Green management policies are also a prime example of the ways that external and internal stakeholders influence organizations to take a more long-term global perspective in their business planning and day-to-day operations. Equally important, *competition* can be a key factor in driving choices related to environmental impact and sustainability. In fact, recent research has shown that an organization is *more likely* to undertake enhanced green practices if their rivals improved their own environmental performance in the previous year.[2] This research reveals that environmental performance has become a valuable source of competitive advantage, and companies who fall behind do so at their own peril. In fact, there has been a greening of management itself over the past two decades whereby companies see viable reasons to go beyond mere environmental compliance. Such reasons include

- gaining a competitive advantage—either by saving money from reductions in energy, hazardous wastes, or electricity or by differentiating their products from others on the market;

- enhancing their legitimacy among consumers; and

- adhering to a moral commitment to be environmentally responsible.

Still, a growing concern continues to be those companies that try to appear to be practicing substantive environmental management but in reality do so superficially. When companies are superficially engaged, they are practicing what is known as greenwashing. The Ethics in Context section deals with the practice of greenwashing.

Green Management or Greenwashing?

iStockphoto.com/jnatrot

The *Oxford English Dictionary* defines *greenwashing* as "disinformation disseminated by an organization so as to present an environmentally responsible public image,"[3] but it was a ponytailed environmental activist in 1986, named Jay Westerveld, who first coined this term.[4] During a trip to the South Pacific, Westerveld noticed a small card in his hotel room. The card was decorated with three green arrows—the universal recycling symbol—with a message to the guest:

> Save Our Planet: Every day, millions of gallons of water are used to wash towels that have only been used once. You make the choice: A towel on the rack means, "I will use again." A towel on the floor means, "Please replace." Thank you for helping us conserve the Earth's vital resources.[5]

Westerveld began to question the true motives of this "Save Our Planet" policy. Specifically, was the card in his hotel room really about the hotel's commitment to protecting the environment, or was it more about the hotel wanting to save money by having to wash fewer towels? Collectively, hotels consume massive amounts of energy and water. Hotels require large amounts of water to provide amenities

expected by tourists, such as swimming pools, landscaped gardens, and golf courses. The washing of towels, by contrast, uses up a small amount of water relative to these other uses—but not having to wash as many towels saves the hotel both labor and materials. Westerveld thus coined the term *greenwashing* to describe marketing campaigns designed to manipulate consumers into believing that a company's products, aims, or policies are environmentally friendly.[6]

Discussion Questions

1. *Stakeholder theories*: Today, many major multinational firms like BP, Shell, and ExxonMobil spend millions of dollars in advertising campaigns touting their commitment to the environment. Who are the internal and external stakeholders affected by greenwashing? How might an organization's use of greenwashing impact these stakeholders? Can you think of other examples of greenwashing by organizations that impact stakeholders?

2. *Ethical decision-making*: Analyze greenwashing using a principles-based approach versus a consequences-based approach. What measures could we use to ensure that companies are truly committed to protecting the environment beyond mere compliance with legal standards?

Take a Position

Issue: Should the government regulate the practice of greenwashing, or should it be left to market competition?

Sub-Issues:

1. What form of government regulation would be effective? Explain your answer.

2. What market forces would incentivize organizations (e.g., consumers, competitors)? Explain your answer.

Codes of Environmental Conduct

While many organizations may have a formal code of ethics and conduct (see Figure 7.1), too often these codes do not include sustainability elements beyond a vague statement such as a commitment to practice recycling. Depending on the organization, a code of environmental ethics may be expressed as part of its code of ethics or as a stand-alone code. To be sure, environmental concerns and ethics are often related. In fact, **environmental ethics** is the discipline in philosophy that studies the moral relationship of human beings to, and also the value and moral status of, the environment and its nonhuman contents.[7] The definition of environmental ethics rests on the principle that there is an ethical relationship between human beings and the natural environment.

Creating an effective policy around the environment requires business organizations to explore several aspects such as global concerns, implementation, and measures for success.

> **environmental ethics:** The discipline in philosophy that studies the moral relationship of human beings to, and also the value and moral status of, the environment and its nonhuman contents.

Global Concerns

Although some industries have a specific environmental concern, in general all firms need to consider what the primary global environmental and sustainability issues are along with those most important to its internal and external stakeholders. Here are some specific questions firms need to ask themselves:

- What is our carbon footprint?
- What are our water and air pollution levels?
- Do we meaningfully commit to the conservation of resources?
- How much do we contribute to noise pollution in our communities?

Figure 7.1   The Purpose of Codes

According to the Ethics and Compliance Initiative, a code of conduct serves at least three important purposes:

- **Compliance**: Corporate boards or organizational leaders are legally required to implement codes or to provide justification for not having them.
- **Marketing**: A public statement of a commitment to high standards and right conduct; informs the public of what the company stands for.
- **Risk Mitigation**: Implementation of generally accepted codes of ethics reduce financial risks in the form of fines as a result of ethical conduct by showing a good faith effort was made to prevent illegal behaviors.

Source: Ethics & Compliance Initiative, 2650 Park Tower Drive, Suite 802, Vienna, VA 22180, www.ethics.org.

And last, but not least, should we become a part of a reporting framework like the Carbon Disclosure Project (CDP), Sustainability Accounting Standards Board (SASB), or the Global Reporting Initiative (GRI)—all of which are designed to illustrate our progress on environmental issues of concern? How will we adjust our approach as these standards become more aligned? See Figure 7.2 for comparisons of these frameworks.

Implementation

What methods should our company use to implement these policies, and how can we be sure that an environmental code of ethics is integrated through all levels of our organization? Is there a danger that employees may follow the letter of the policy but not the spirit of the policy? Have we engaged with external stakeholders—like employees and the community—to get feedback on our plan and its implementation?

Measures

How do we measure the effectiveness of an environmental ethics code, and how will we know when to update or revise it? If we choose a reporting framework, can we dedicate enough human capital to ensure our reporting is done properly?

In Case Study 7.1, we consider the practice by some corporations known as eco-branding.

Figure 7.2	Differences in Reporting Frameworks
CDP (Carbon Disclosure Project)	A disclosure system allowing companies and governments to track greenhouse gas emissions, use of water resources, and use of forest lands. The information is made available to investors, companies, cities, and states around the globe. This is a not-for-profit organization. It was formerly known as the Carbon Disclosure Project.
Global Reporting Initiative (GRI)	Was the first corporate sustainability reporting framework. It focuses on the significant impacts a company has on the environment, society, and the economy due to its products, activities, and services. It collects a wide range of data made available to investors and employees as well as other stakeholders. More than half of companies reporting their sustainability information use these standards.
The Sustainability Accounting Standards Board (SASB)	It focuses on the impacts on the organization by the environment, society, and the economy. It is working to develop standards for sustainability information of interest to investors.

Source: Keramida, "CDP, GRI, and SASB Working Together to Align Standards," November 7, 2018.

Eco-Branding

For many Fortune 500 corporations, ethics has become an integral part of their strategy. The expectation is that ethically minded consumers will prefer the products and services of these companies. According to *Forbes*, they do, especially millennials who more often buy from corporations with ethical business standards or prosocial messages.[8] But is it ethical for such companies to use ethics so strategically? Many companies now claim that their products are made with high ethical standards or eco-friendly production methods. Starbucks, for instance, recently declared it has invested over $70 million to promote sustainable coffee harvesting and that 99% of the coffee beans in its beverages are "ethically sourced."[9]

Although Starbucks has invested a significant amount of money in this campaign, it's not clear how much of this money has been devoted to advertising. At the same time, Starbucks generated well over $16 billion in revenue in 2014—the year before it announced it reached its 99% ethical-sourcing plateau. One might argue that Starbucks has invested a mere 0.0003% of its annual revenue to do what it

should be doing anyway. In 2018, Starbucks's revenue reached $25 billion, up 10% from 2017.[10]

Discussion Questions

1. Is the effort by Starbucks an example of eco-branding? Or, do you think it's legitimate marketing? Why or why not?

2. Should government regulatory agencies intervene in certain eco-branding campaigns in order to protect consumers?

Critical Thinking

1. We discussed the meaning of the terms *ethics* and *morals* in Chapter 3. Using these definitions, is Starbucks practicing ethics? Is it ethical to use ethics in this way to promote a company's "ethical brand" to attract new customers?

2. Are there any other examples of branding by an organization that is linked to a social cause or concern?

Green Management and Competitive Advantage

- Green management describes an organization's efforts to incorporate environmentalism and sustainability into its business model and practices.

- Practicing environmental ethics rests on the principle that there is an ethical relationship between human beings and the natural environment.

- Many companies practice environmental management as a competitive advantage, but some go too far and practice greenwashing.

SUSTAINABLE DEVELOPMENT

LO 7.3 Explain global standards of sustainable development and the implementation of sustainable development goals (SDGs).

Sustainable development is not a new concept, but its importance and prominence among the world's nation-states has focused their attention more sharply on the impact that social and environmental factors have on economic development and poverty. Many experts use the UN General Assembly report *Our Common Future* in 1987 as a starting point for understanding the modern notion of sustainable development. The report defines sustainable development as "development that meets the needs of the present without compromising the ability of future generations to meet their own needs."[11] This definition makes note of one's generational responsibility by recognizing that unsustainable development will be a burden on future generations.

Sustainable development is a much broader topic than just the environmental aspects. It also encompasses human rights, labor force regulations, and corruption. In this chapter, we focus primarily on the environmental aspects. The World Bank, a source of financial and technical assistance to developing countries around the world, provides data in the form of indices on these various aspects by country for comparison and other information.[12] Its environment-related indicators look into, for example, urbanization and the loss of biological diversity, agricultural output and declining forest area, freshwater withdrawals and freshwater growing scarcity, and greenhouse gas emissions. The indicators also reveal the progress that countries have made on many of the environment targets set by the UN in *Transforming Our World: The 2030 Agenda for Sustainable Development*. Some of the data the World Bank collects can be seen in Figure 7.3, for the Latin American country Argentina.

Circular Economic Theory

The **circular economic theory** underlies much of the objectives of sustainable development. Since the Industrial Revolution, companies and consumers have largely adhered to a linear model of value creation that begins with extraction and concludes with end-of-life disposal.[13] Resources are acquired, processed using energy and labor, and sold as goods—with the expectation that customers will discard those goods and buy more. Contemporary trends, however, have exposed the wastefulness of such take–make–dispose systems. The same trends have also made it practical to conserve assets and materials, so maximum value can be derived from them. Deloitte illustrates the difference between a linear value chain and how to move to a closed loop value chain (see Figure 7.4).

> **circular economic theory:** Describes an economy that goes beyond the pursuit of waste prevention and waste reduction to inspire technological, organizational, and social innovation across and within value chains.

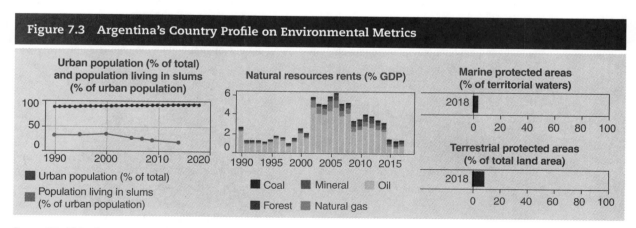

Figure 7.3 Argentina's Country Profile on Environmental Metrics

Source: World Bank Group. 2016. "Argentina Country Environmental Analysis." World Bank, Washington, DC. © World Bank. https://openknowledge.worldbank.org/handle/10986/25775 License: CC BY 3.0 IGO.

Figure 7.4 What Is a Circular Economy?

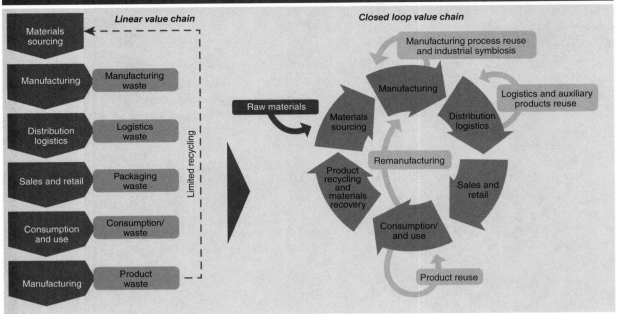

Source: Deloitte. (2017). *Circular economy: From theory to practice.* Available at https://www2.deloitte.com/content/dam/Deloitte/fi/Documents/risk/Circular%20economy%20FINAL%20web.pdf

Developing products for a circular economy offers another point of view on how to eliminate waste and create value: that of designers and engineers. It isn't easy to create products that are lasting, simple to reuse or recycle, and profitable. With digital technologies and novel designs, items can be tracked and maintained efficiently, which makes it easier to extend their useful lives. Governments are imposing new restrictions on pollution and waste that apply along entire product life cycles. These developments mean that it is increasingly advantageous to redeploy resources over and over, often for the same or comparable purposes. This is the organizing principle of circular economies, and the benefits that come from following it can be substantial. According to the research by the McKinsey Center for Business and Environment, a circular economy could generate a net economic gain of approximately $2 trillion per year by 2030 in Europe alone.[14] The building sector, for example, could reduce construction costs with industrial and modular processes. Car sharing, autonomous driving, electric vehicles, and better materials could lower the cost of driving by 75%.

Global Standards for Sustainability

One of the first comprehensive attempts to address environmental management was the International Organization for Standardization (ISO), which was created in 1992. It was designed as a phased approach allowing firms to establish, implement, maintain, and improve an environmental management system to enhance their environmental performance according to their own circumstances.[15] ISO has published more than 22,000 international standards all over the world that represent globally recognized guidelines and frameworks based on international collaboration; these form a solid base on which to create public policy that helps further the United Nations Global Compact (UNGC) Sustainable Development Goals (SDGs).[16]

UNGC, begun in 2000, originally addressed the growing need for a common set of principles that could guide business in a meaningful way across the world. The compact initially set out eight principles—called the Millennium Development Goals (MDGs)—that addressed a variety of ideals related to sustainable development including three principles specifically tied to environmental responsibility:

1. Businesses should seek to understand their current approach to environmental challenges.

2. Businesses should undertake initiatives to promote greater environmental responsibility.

3. Businesses should encourage the development and diffusion of environmentally friendly technologies.

Sustainable Development Goals

Building on the MDGs, a new comprehensive set of 17 Sustainable Development Goals (SDGs) were set out in *Transforming our World: the 2030 Agenda for Sustainable Development*. It is most commonly referred to as the 2030 Agenda (see Figure 7.5). The 2030 Agenda differed from the MDGs in three significant ways. First, the agenda contemplates a role for both *developed* and *developing* countries instead of just developed economies that were the primary target in the MDGs. Second, the SDGs are more comprehensive and detail 169 specific targets that if met, in theory, would achieve the 17 goals. The broad goals are interrelated though each has its own targets to achieve. These voluntary principles were intended to be aspirational and at the same time comprehensive, going beyond solely environmental issues to recognize sustainability as an interconnected part of other important global objectives such as eradicating extreme poverty and hunger, which define "the world we want—applying to all nations and leaving no one behind" according to the UNGC.

However, it also holds them accountable by requiring companies to make clear statements of support in their public documents (e.g., annual shareholders' report) and "delists" companies who do not comply with the principles. In 2019, there were over 10,000 companies in 164 countries that were signatories to the compact.[17] According to the UNGC, a total of over 800 companies have been delisted as of fall 2019.[18] Over the years, the UNGC increased its scrutiny of companies upon entry into the initiative including instituting new exclusionary criteria for companies involved in certain high-risk sectors like the production and manufacture of tobacco products as well as nuclear, chemical, or biological weapons.[19]

Third, the SDGs are implemented through a process called localizing the SDGs in which the planet, individual people, universities, governments, institutions, and organizations work on several goals at the same time. Individual nation-states have agreed to translate the goals into national legislation, develop a plan of action, and establish implementation budgets.

Figure 7.5   17 Sustainable Development Goals

1. End poverty.

2. End hunger.

3. Achieve good health and well being for all.

4. Achieve quality education for all.

5. Achieve gender equality.

6. Achieve clean water and sanitation for all.

7. Achieve affordable and clean energy.

8. Decent work and economic growth.

9. Promote and build industry, innovation, and infrastructure.

10. Reduce inequality.

11. Build sustainable cities and communities.

12. Promote responsible consumption and production.

13. Combat climate change.

14. Conserve and sustainably use water sources.

15. Conserve and sustainably use land sources.

16. Implement peace and justice in institutions.

17. Create partnerships to achieve these goals.

Localizing the SDGs can prove challenging, especially in underdeveloped countries. For example, SDG Goal 6 is designed to provide access to clean water and sanitation and has been localized in communities in sub-Saharan Africa, South Asia, East Asia, and Southeast Asia. In sub-Saharan Africa over US$360 million have been spent on implementing the infrastructure; however, once the building is complete, the water supply sites are not maintained and fall into disrepair. Now more than one third to one half of all water points are nonoperational. Unfortunately, the cost of maintenance to keep the water sources operational were not factored into the plan. The local peoples do not have the financial resources or training to maintain the water points after they are built.[20]

Criticism and Responses: 2030 Agenda

The approach embraced in the 2030 Agenda has been met with criticism that has largely centered around feasibility and clarity of the SDGs approach. The *Economist* blasted the SDG approach as "sprawling, misconceived" compared to the earlier MDGs. It pointed to the inadequate resources in achieving the SDGs since experts estimated that alleviating poverty and achieving the other SDGs will require about $2 to $3 trillion per year for the next 15 years.[21] Some critics also cited contradictory goals (e.g., seeking high levels of global GDP growth might undermine ecological objectives) as a flaw to the effort.

Yet, the UNGC believes this seeming contradiction is exactly what companies face in reality. Likewise, analysts from the World Economic Forum (WEF) argued that the world is complex and efforts to improve it must reflect a more complex approach set out in the SDGs. The complexity inherent in the targets allows serious people doing the difficult work of solving global challenges to "accurately communicate what needs to be done while still aligning to a set of common global targets."[22]

Sustainable Development

KEY TAKEAWAYS

- Sustainable development is a broad topic going beyond the environmental aspects. It also encompasses human rights, labor force regulations, and corruption.

- The circular economy is a new way to think about reusing and redesigning products in a closed loop fashion, creating less waste.

- There are a number of environmental standard setters like ISO and UNGC that help guide companies in their sustainability efforts globally.

GLOBAL ENVIRONMENTAL TRENDS: CLIMATE CHANGE

LO 7.4 Describe climate change and its impact on society.

Perhaps more than any other global environmental trend, climate change affects business and society on multiple levels. The Intergovernmental Panel on Climate Change (IPCC), a scientific body that reviews and assesses scientific, technical, and socioeconomic data and established by the UN Environment Programme and the World Meteorological Organization, has summarized the following effects of climate change:

- The increase in species extinctions

- Reduction of coral reefs, mangrove forests, and tropical rainforests

- Threats to small island states in the Pacific as sea levels rise

- Increased drought threats in Africa

- More severe flooding in densely populated river deltas in Asia

- More severe weather in hurricane prone zones

IPCC notes the major causes of these effects are due to "discernable human influences" and "observed increase in greenhouse gases."[23]

Similarly, in a large-scale study of scientific literature on climate change, a group of scholars found that 97% of the scientific literature agrees that (1) the earth's average surface temperature is rising and (2) human activity is the overwhelmingly predominant factor in that trend.[24] There is also some consensus on the detailed effects of climate change—for example, that the earth's average surface temperature rose by approximately 2 °F in the period from 1880 and 2012. The rate of warming almost doubled in the last half of that period. It is important to keep in mind that although climate change is often cast in terms of land temperature, it may be more accurate to think of its most significant impact as being on oceans. Experts on climate change caution us not to miss the importance of the fact that most of the additional energy stored in the climate system since 1970 has accumulated in the oceans of the world. The rest has melted ice and warmed the continents and the atmosphere.[25] The rate at which ice is melting in Greenland is currently 4 times what was originally thought, according to a 2019 study in the Proceedings of the National Academy of Sciences of the United States of America, contributing even further to the rise in sea levels.[26]

However, scientists do disagree about climate change—just as some disagree about evolution.[27] Not surprisingly, not everyone agrees with the 97% consensus of scientists figure often quoted. The main reason cited for disputing the study is its methodology. According to Climate Change Dispatch, there are 97 articles refuting the study as poorly conceived, designed, and executed. Are you a climate change skeptic? Take a look at the website, and decide for yourself. The link can be found on the companion website: **http://edge.sagepub.com/clark1e**.

The increased awareness of climate change has also brought with it increased use of data analysis in an attempt to understand how climate change has impacted our weather and ecosystem and to understand how to prevent conditions from getting worse. Scientists who have studied extreme weather events from 1960 until 2010 suggest that droughts and heat waves appear simultaneously with increased frequency. Extremely wet or dry events within the monsoon period have increased since 1980. Moreover, climate models indicate

iStockphoto.com/aluxum

Jokulsarlon Lagoon in Iceland has increased in size due to the melting of local glaciers.

that future extreme weather events are likely to increase in frequency and severity especially for heat-related extreme events, such as heat waves. In addition to extreme events, climate change is also causing gradual changes in our ecosystem as the combination of increased carbon emissions and higher temperatures are linked with the extinction of many species and reduced diversity of ecosystems.

Climate Change and Society

While ecologists and environmentalists have measured the impact of climate change on weather and the ecosystem, so too have social scientists studied the existing and potential impact of global warning on society and the economy. Our overall climate is directly related to crop output, which impacts our food chain, and scientists fear that crop failure will be a significant obstacle to developing countries, which may increase poverty, hunger, and homelessness. In terms of other health and welfare issues, researchers studying the connection between temperature and violence concluded in a 2014 study that each degree of temperature rise will increase violence by up to 20%, which includes fistfights, violent crimes, civil unrest, or wars.[28] The combination of these destabilizing forces can have profound impacts on developed countries as well. As one example, waves of refugees fleeing poverty, violence, and flooded coastal cities would overwhelm governments and generate fear and hording among the population.

Global Response

The first major, comprehensive, global response to climate change was a UN treaty in 1992. The United Nations Framework Convention on Climate Change (UNFCCC) was ratified by a majority (though not the United States) of member states at the so-called Earth Summit.[i] Each year the UNFCCC hosts the Conference of the Parties (COP), a convening of these member states to discuss progress as well as setbacks. The treaty committed signers to reduce atmospheric concentrations of greenhouse gases with the goal of "preventing dangerous anthropogenic interference with Earth's climate system." Although the treaty included developing nations such as India, the treaty allowed those countries a sort of safe harbor if their financial resources would not allow reductions. In essence, the treaty made clear that "social development and poverty eradication are the first and overriding priorities of the developing country."[ii]

The Kyoto Protocol and Paris Agreement

Although the UNFCCC was a major step toward a multilateral greenhouse gas reduction agreement, it lacked some specifics that were needed to make an impact on the problem. In 2011, the treaties' participants gathered to consider a common course of action. Underlying the difficulties of coming to an agreement was the economic impact on developed economies versus developing countries. The most developed nations were reluctant to commit to reforms that might dampen their economy while major polluters such as China were not bound by any agreement. Ultimately, the parties to the UNFCCC treaty agreed to develop

---

[i] 1992 United Nations Conference on Environment and Development (UNCED) in Rio de Janeiro.
[ii] Article 4(7).

a strong protocol and "other legal instruments" to enforce its carbon output domestically. Developed countries were required to reduce their emissions in two phases: 5% below the 1990 level from 2011 to 2013, and, more controversially, parties to the treaty were required to reduce the emissions by 18%. These protocols became known as the **Kyoto Protocol**.[iii] By 2015, the UNFCCC had 196 signature member states that convened for the UN Climate Change Conference in Paris. The parties agreed to a similar reduction in emissions as agreed upon in Kyoto (i.e., limit the future increase in global mean temperature to below 2°C), but the Paris Agreement attempted to answer concerns about the contribution of developing nations by blurring the divide between developed and developing nations. As part of the program, all the nations under the UNFCCC treaty have to outline and commit to their own domestic emission reduction targets. In a June 2017 speech, the Trump administration announced its intent to leave the agreement, stating it "punishes" the United States while imposing "no meaningful obligations" on major polluters, such as China and India, which will take advantage of the United States' supposed sacrifice.[29]

The 25th convening (COP25) took place in December 2019 in Madrid, Spain, but was initially slated for Brazil, which pulled out after the election of Jair Bolsonaro as president. Bolsonaro spoke before the UN in September 2019, defending Brazil's sovereign right to develop the Amazon rainforest. According to the *Wall Street Journal*, he claimed much of the Amazon is practically untouched, and many of the fires that sparked global dismay in August were set by local, indigenous communities who should have the right to exploit the richness of the land. However, environmental experts blamed President Bolsonaro for the rainforest's destruction, saying it was due to budget cuts at Ibama, the government's environmental protection group, and his recent speeches they say incited loggers to cut down the forest.[30]

Kyoto Protocol: Treaty protocols requiring developed countries to reduce their emissions in two phases.

CASE STUDY 7.2

Voluntary Carbon Offsets

Voluntary "carbon offset" credits have become attractive to both businesses and consumers. According to Ecosystem Marketplace, its latest data shows the volume of offsets reached a record high in 2017, or an equivalent of *not* consuming almost 150 million barrels of oil.[31] Consumers can offset their emissions by purchasing carbon credits, which are generated by reducing emissions elsewhere (e.g., planting trees or building a wind farm). While there are a lot of greenhouse gases—carbon dioxide (CO_2), methane, nitrous oxide, perfluorocarbons, and hydrofluorocarbons—people generate CO_2 the most.[32] And travel by air is one of the leading ways of putting carbon into the atmosphere. For business organizations, carbon emissions may be in the form of pollution from manufacturing or business operations. Of course, airplane travel by employees

on business would also contribute to enlarging the organization's carbon footprint. Purchasing carbon offsets allows a traveler to reduce that footprint because the money is used to support projects that reduce carbon in other ways.

Discussion Questions

1. Is the word *offset* a misnomer intended more as marketing than reality? Consider this: If an organization sends its sales force flying all over the globe but purchases carbon offsets, does it erase the emissions?

2. Offsets may be purchased from for-profit and nonprofit organizations. Is it ethical for stakeholders of a firm selling carbon offsets to profit from the sale of offsets? Why or why not?

[iii] Formally known as the "Durban Platform for Enhanced Action."

3. Should certain projects, such as assistance to developing countries, have priority? Use a search engine to look up various carbon offset firms such as TerraPass or Carbonfund.org. Are there any projects you think would be less of a priority?

Critical Thinking

Critics of carbon offsets argue it is simply a way for individuals to relieve their own guilt on climate change but has very little impact in the overall reduction of greenhouse gases. Use of the offsets by corporations allows them to check a box on the socially responsible checklist without any further commitment that amounts to a license to pollute and may lead to more carbon in the atmosphere.

1. Is carbon offsetting an effective method for reducing greenhouse gases or just corporate greenwashing?

2. How might carbon offsets actually increase the amount of carbon emissions?

KEY TAKEAWAYS

Global Environmental Trends: Climate Change

- Climate change is a timely, but also a contentious, issue for both business and society.

- Many scientists have made note of the human influence of climate change and the increasing use of greenhouse gases.

- There are numerous impacts from climate change, like the warming of the earth's atmosphere, more severe weather, and the melting of the ice caps, causing water levels to rise.

- The chorus of climate change skeptics has grown in the past few years.

- Carbon offset credits have both proponents and opponents.

GOVERNMENT REGULATION AND PROTECTION

LO 7.5 List the major sources of environmental policy.

Since pollution does not respect state or country boundaries, both federal laws and global initiatives like the Paris Agreement are useful ways to achieve environmental protections. Modern environmental protections are provided through a patchwork of global, federal, state, and local laws and regulations. In the European Union, for example, the European Environment Agency helps all European member states to make informed decisions about how to improve the environment and sustainability. Environmental regulation is wide-ranging but are primarily designed to achieve these five objectives:

1. Ensure that government agency decisions have a real impact on the environment.

2. Promote clean air and water through regulation and permits.

3. Regulate the use and disposal of solid and hazardous waste.

4. Clean up property or waterways that are contaminated with hazardous waste.

5. Protect wildlife and endangered species.

In the United States, for example, federal environmental laws are primarily administered, implemented, and enforced by an overarching government agency called the EPA. The EPA, created in 1970, works in tandem with other administrative agencies in handling a broad range of environmental concerns at the federal level. For example, the U.S. Fish and Wildlife Service primarily enforces statutes protecting endangered species. Through the European Environment Agency, the European Union has put in place a broad range of environmental legislation by working with over 300 institutions across all of Europe.[33] A major part of its recent 2020 environmental program, called "Living Well, Within the Limits of Our Planet," is specifically designed to improve environmental integration and policy coherence.[34]

Like many administrative agencies, the European Environment Agency and the EPA have broad powers to implement and enforce environmental laws by promulgating rules, issuing advisory opinions, and investigating and evaluating federal environmental protection policies as well as using traditional enforcement tools such as administrative fines and penalties; civil suits; and, in egregious cases, criminal complaints.

In addition to a federal agency, each local area typically has its own environmental department in order to implement and enforce environmental statutes related to that particular area. In certain municipalities, a local environmental agency may exist to enforce local ordinances, such as illegal dumping, proper trash removal and recycling, or the like.

Limiting Government Impact on the Environment

Many of the first environmental laws came into effect in the mid to late 1960s across the globe due to activism on the environment and commissioned reports following the 1962 publication of Rachel Carson's *A Silent Spring*. Carson spent years documenting her analysis about how humans were misusing powerful chemical pesticides before knowing the full extent of their potential harm to the whole ecosystem. Carson's main concern in the book is with the future of the planet and all life on Earth. She calls for humans to act responsibly, carefully, and as stewards of the living earth.[35]

One of the first attempts at comprehensive legislation to address environmental regulation was the National Environmental Policy Act (NEPA) enacted in 1969. The NEPA law was intended to serve as a national charter for environmental regulation, but its focus is one of planning and prevention rather than achieving a certain result (such as cleaner water) according to scientific standards. It established a process that must be followed by federal agencies in making decisions that have the potential to have a significant impact on the environment. The NEPA also created the Council on Environmental Quality to oversee the NEPA procedures and to make periodic progress reports to U.S. Congress and the president. The NEPA procedures are triggered when a federal agency takes any action that may be reasonably considered as having an impact on the environment. This action may be in the form of an agency issuing a permit or license or engaging in rulemaking. Note that actions by private individuals, businesses, and state and local governments are *not* regulated by the NEPA. However, all states have enacted parallel statutes (laws similar to the NEPA statute but covering a wider range of parties) to cover state and local government actions as well. Federal agencies are required to incorporate the NEPA procedural steps into their decision-making process at the earliest possible opportunity by identifying the purpose of and need for a promised project, possible alternatives, and the environmental impact of certain actions.

Air and Water Quality

Air and water quality are central components to government regulation and protection of the environment, and many countries have laws that protect them. EU legislation has long been focused on air, water, and soil pollution. The United Kingdom claims its tap water is ranked as some of the cleanest in the world.[36]

In contrast, according to the World Health Organization, 1 in 10 people drink water from an unprotected source, and almost half of those people live in sub-Saharan Africa. In Bangladesh, Nepal, Ghana, and Congo, many people use a water source that is protected from contamination, but the bacteria E. coli has been detected.[37]

In the United States, two major federal laws that protect air and water quality are the U.S. Clean Air Act (CAA) and the U.S. Clean Water Act (CWA). Each has an extensive set of federal regulations as well. The CAA focuses on stationary sources of air pollution, such as an industrial manufacturing plant, and mobile sources of air pollution, such as motor vehicles. Water quality standards are set primarily by and regulated through the CWA.

Focus on the U.S. Clean Air Act and Market-Based Incentives

Enacted in 1963, the CAA is a complex law aimed at improving outdoor air quality in the United States. The law has been amended several times since its original passage, most recently in 1997 to expand its coverage and provide a system of **market-based incentives** intended to encourage businesses to create their own solutions through voluntary compliance with clean air standards. Under a market-based incentives approach, businesses are more self-regulatory and can choose how they reach their pollution reduction goals, including pollution allowances that can be traded, bought, and sold. In that same vein, a business may be allowed to expand its pollution output in one area as long as it is offset by reducing another pollutant in greater measure than the one being expanded.

> **market-based incentives:** Approach in which businesses have certain choices as to how they may reach their pollution reduction goals, including pollution allowances that can be traded, bought, and sold.

A good example of a market-based solution is the voluntary emission-trading scheme that embraces the idea that overall pollution reduction will result if businesses have an economic and competitive incentive, rather than a mandate, to invest in modern equipment and plants. Proponents argue this approach will result in businesses investing in more efficient plants that yield clean air units that can then be sold or traded to out-of-compliance buyers. As emitting pollution becomes more expensive, every company will be forced to modernize to stay competitive in the market. Critics of this approach argue it results in clean air being treated as a commodity rather than as a natural resource. Opponents of market-based solutions argue the government could achieve greater reductions in pollution through the use of gradual statutory mandates to improve pollution control and government-sponsored loans to help companies purchase equipment.

Figure 7.6 provides a summary of arguments for and against market-based approaches in a point–counterpoint format.

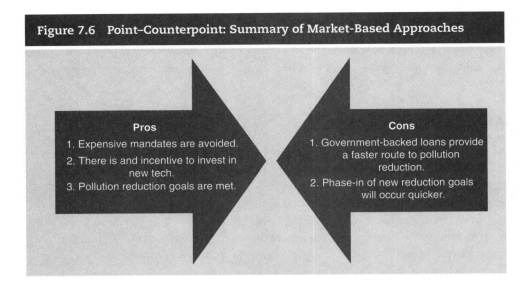

Figure 7.6   Point–Counterpoint: Summary of Market-Based Approaches

Pros

1. Expensive mandates are avoided.
2. There is and incentive to invest in new tech.
3. Pollution reduction goals are met.

Cons

1. Government-backed loans provide a faster route to pollution reduction.
2. Phase-in of new reduction goals will occur quicker.

Opponents of market-based solutions might argue that the government could achieve greater reductions in pollution more quickly using government-backed loans to help companies upgrade its technology. Companies purchasing upgraded equipment allows the government to more aggressively improve pollution control from all sources.

Focus on the U.S. Clean Water Act

The pollution of waterways is one of the biggest challenges facing environmental policymakers across the globe. Waterways take the form of surface water (i.e., lakes or rivers) or groundwater (i.e., subsurface water, such as that used for wells). Because water travels through jurisdictional boundaries and may be subject to various legal property rights, water pollution and conservation regulation is necessary via a combination of federal, state, and local statutes and rules. For example, the U.S.-based water quality standards are set primarily by and regulated through the CWA.[38] Much like the CAA, the CWA has been amended in significant ways to stem pollution from industrial, municipal, and agricultural sources. The CWA also contains important enforcement provisions. Any pollution discharge that violates the CWA triggers enhanced penalties if it was a result of gross negligence or willful misconduct.

U.S. Water Quality Regulation

Each state in the United States sets water quality standards, subject to EPA review, for the navigable waterways within the state's borders. State agencies set scientifically measurable standards consisting of several criteria intended to improve the quality of surface water. The standards are set according to the designated use of the water source. Sources in which the designated uses are swimming or fishing must have the highest quality standards. Once the state has set its standards, it must monitor whether its water sources are meeting those standards and disclose the results through a mandatory reporting system. If progress toward achieving the standards is too slow or nonexistent, the state will propose a new strategy to meet the quality standards. The EPA must approve any new strategies and may step in and impose its own strategy if it determines the state is out of compliance with the CWA.

The Oil Spill by the Oil Rig Deepwater Horizon in the Gulf of Mexico on April 20, 2010, MDL 2179, U.S. District Court, E.D. Louisiana (September 9, 2014)

Facts: The Deepwater Horizon was a 9-year-old semi-submersible, mobile, floating, dynamically positioned drilling rig that could operate in waters up to 10,000 feet deep. The rig was owned by Transocean, Inc., and was chartered and operated by BP from March 2008 to September 2013. It was drilling a deep exploratory well roughly 41 miles off the Louisiana coast of the United States when high pressure methane gas from the well expanded into the drilling riser and rose into the drilling rig, where it ignited and exploded, engulfing the platform with 126 crew members on board. Eleven people were killed and 17 others were injured. The Deepwater Horizon sank 2 days after the explosion. Subsequent investigations revealed that BP managers misread pressure data, failed to administer appropriate tests for integrity of the well, and gave their approval for rig workers to replace drilling fluid in the well with seawater. However, the seawater was not heavy enough to prevent gas that had been leaking into the well from firing up the pipe into the rig and causing the explosion. While acknowledging responsibility for the accident, BP argued the blame should be fully shared with Transocean, the owner of the Deepwater Horizon oil rig, and Halliburton, a contractor that oversaw a critical step in closing up the well. Transocean and Halliburton denied any liability. The government charged BP, Transocean, and Halliburton with, among other charges, a violation of the CWA and Oil Pollution Act (OPA). It also asked the court to impose enhanced penalties based on the "recklessness" and "willful conduct" provisions of the CWA and OPA. The impact of such a finding would result in BP being liable for 4 times the maximum penalties.

Issue: Did the conduct by BP amount to being reckless or willful?

Holding: The court ruled that BP had acted with conscious disregard of known risks. The court pointed to the actions of BP employees at the time of the incident and found they took risks that led to the environmental disaster. In particular, the court ruled the evidence indicated that the results of a pressure test should have prompted quick action to prevent an impending blowout. The court ruled BP was reckless and determined several crucial conversations between BP employees indicated a willful course of conduct that fit squarely into the statutory definitions of *reckless* or *willful* in the CWA and OPA. The court also found that Transocean and Halliburton's conduct was negligent but not reckless.

Aftermath: Despite the initial promise by BP to appeal, BP, the U.S. Department of Justice (DOJ), and five Gulf Coast states announced the company agreed to pay a record settlement of $18.7 billion in 2015. To date, the cost for BP for the cleanup, environmental and economic damages, and penalties has reached $54 billion.

Law and Management Questions

1. While the BP case is one of epic proportions, there are several areas of the law that provide for enhanced penalties for reckless or willful corporate crimes. What systems can management put in place to be sure that decision-making—by management or employee teams—does not trigger an enhanced penalty based on reckless conduct?

2. In some cases, the DOJ criminal charges can be leveled at executive management for environmental disasters that result in serious bodily injury or death. Given the fact that these executives did not contribute to, or perhaps didn't know about, the disaster, should Congress insulate them from criminal charges?

3. What is the most effective way to deter organizations from engaging in reckless conduct?

Citizen Interest Organizations

citizen interest organizations: An individual or group with the authority to file enforcement lawsuits by virtue of citizen suit provisions.

Perhaps more than in any other area of the law, citizen interest organizations (also called watchdog groups) have contributed to the enforcement of environmental statutes and policy. These **citizen interest organizations** and individual citizens are statutorily authorized to file a lawsuit against either a polluter who is in violation of environmental statutes or regulations or a government agency or unit that is not taking legally mandated steps to carry out environmental law enforcement. Individuals and groups derive this authority to file enforcement lawsuits by virtue of citizen suit provisions that are a part of many federal and state environmental statutes. When an environmental statute authorizes citizen suits, it generally requires that notice of a citizen suit be given to the agency with jurisdiction over the matter. Citizen suits may not be commenced against a polluter if the government agency is already prosecuting the same violator. Some of the more common initiators of environmental law citizen suits include the Sierra Club, the Natural Resources Defense Council, and the Environmental Defense Fund. Local environmental watchdog groups in different regions of the world tend to focus on a particular concern unique to the region (e.g., Amazon Watch in Brazil or the Spotted Owl Defense League of Oregon State). Many of these organizations take to Twitter to get attention.[39]

Kari Goodnough/Bloomberg via Getty Images

Many environmental laws allow watchdog groups such as the Sierra Club to enforce the statute.

Government Regulation and Protection

- The European Environment Agency is the regulating body on environmental issues in the European Union as the EPA is in the United States.

- The focus of NEPA is on the planning and prevention of environmental impact issues.

- The CAA is a complex law aimed at improving outdoor air quality in the United States.

- The CWA sets standards for water quality to reduce effects of pollution.

- Citizen interest groups have played a significant role in enforcing environmental standards.

KEY TAKEAWAYS

SUMMARY

This chapter discusses various environmental approaches to sustainable development. It outlines the major standards set globally for business to follow in order to create a more sustainable society. Noting the major challenges for business and society, we discuss the various regulatory and market-based approaches to solving these vexing environmental challenges. Special attention is given to the circular economy and climate change.

KEY TERMS

circular economic theory 147
citizen interest organizations 160
environmental ethics 144

environmental justice 140
environmentalism 140
green management 142

Kyoto Protocol 154
market-based incentives 157
sustainability 140

REVIEW QUESTIONS

1. Explain the purpose of green management. How do firms use green management to gain a competitive advantage?

2. What is the difference between environmentalism and sustainable development?

3. Explain the two major global standards for sustainable development.

4. What is the circular economy, and why is it important to business and society?

5. How do the EPA and the EEA oversee large-scale environmental issues like clean water and clean air?

The Role of Business in Environmental Ethics

Challenge: Colgate-Palmolive is a 200-year-old global company serving hundreds of millions of consumers worldwide. In 2018, it launched a campaign called "Every drop counts" and previewed a video during the Super Bowl football game, watched by millions around the world, to educate people about running water while brushing their teeth. Colgate-Palmolive sells toothbrushes and toothpaste, among other items. It highlighted that a single person can save 64 cups of water every time they brush. Globally, people's actions in response to its campaign have led to the potential reduction of 99 billion gallons of water. On its website, it asks consumers to pledge to save water and join the conversation on Twitter at #EveryDropCounts.[40] Its corporate code is as follows:

> The company cares about people: Colgate-Palmolive people, customers, shareholders and business partners. Colgate-Palmolive is committed to act with compassion, integrity, honesty and high ethics in all situations, to listen with respect to others and to value differences. The Company is also committed to protect the global environment, to enhance the communities where Colgate-Palmolive people live and work, and to be compliant with government laws and regulations.[41]

Framing Questions

1. Do you think Colgate-Palmolive's "Every drop counts" effort is effective? Responsible? What other environmental issues could the company be concerned about? Is the company a UNGC signatory, or does it subscribe to any other sustainability standards?

2. What are some of the possible positive and negative reactions consumers or regulators might have?

3. What changes or additions should be made to Colgate's core values statement?

Assignment

Research businesses that have an environmental component in their code of ethics, mission, vision, or values statements. Individually or in groups craft a two-page code of environmental ethics and sustainability for your chosen company. Start with a "statement of objectives," and build the policy from there. It should include a practical method for applying the code to the day-to-day operations of the business and should address both global environmental and sustainability issues as well as ones which are unique to your business or industry.

One of the most comprehensive statements is from IKEA; a link to it can be found on the companion site at **http://edge.sagepub.com/clark1e.**

The International Chamber of Commerce has a model for such codes; please see the link on the companion site.

8

EMPLOYEES AND THE CORPORATION

Ethics in Context

Whistleblower Bounty

An inclusive workplace includes empowering employees to do the right thing without fear of retaliation. That can be hard to ensure when an employee blows the whistle on corporate wrongdoing. Many laws account for the sacri-

iStockphoto.com/djmilic

fice of whistleblowers by offering them a bounty for their information. Can financial incentives to report wrongdoing have unintended consequences? Later in the chapter, in the Ethics in Context section, we will explore different bounty programs and whether their benefits outweigh their costs.

Learning Objectives

Upon completion of this chapter, the reader should be able to do the following:

8.1 Identify the different employment relationships and the legal and management issues raised.

8.2 Understand the theory of employment at will and the public policy exception.

8.3 Discuss workplace protections and impacts of employment regulation on employers and employees.

8.4 Explore workplace privacy issues and how the use of technology may impact the employment relationship.

INTRODUCTION

Most people will spend approximately one third of their lives at work[1]—as employees and many also as managers, supervisors, or executives. As a result, it is critical that workers understand their rights and obligations—whether you are an entry-level employee, a mid-level manager, CEO, or hiring for the first time for your new start-up. Employment law is a dynamic area of law that is multifaceted and evolving, which means as employees and managers, we must stay on top of what the law requires because the decisions we make every day at work will be impacted.

163

THE EMPLOYMENT RELATIONSHIP

LO 8.1 Identify the different employment relationships and the legal and management issues raised.

You and your roommate are tight on cash, so you both decide to get part-time jobs. You find a part-time job at the school bookstore, and your roommate starts delivering food for a delivery app. You are both employees, right? The answer to this question will determine your legal rights at work.

Whether a worker is an **employee** or an **independent contractor** generally depends on the amount of control the company has over the worker; the more control, the more likely a person is an employee. For example, does the company control what the worker does and how he or she does it? Who provides the tools and supplies for the job? Does the company control how the worker is paid or reimburse the worker for expenses? Is the worker economically dependent on their work for the company? Depending on the nature of the work, some factors may weigh in favor of one designation or the other. The key is to look at the entire relationship and the degree of control. Generally, independent contractors can work for more than one company at the same time, do not receive benefits or paid time off, and do not have taxes withheld from their pay. However, employees work for one employer, at the direction of their employer, may receive benefits like health insurance, access to a retirement fund, and paid leave, and have taxes withheld from their pay. Some businesses require workers to sign an agreement known as an **independent contractor agreement**, laying out the terms of the work and usually including a statement that the agreement is not an employment contract. While useful, courts have recognized that having an independent contract or agreement in place may not be the end of the analysis.

employee: Employment status where the worker works for one employer, at the direction of his or her employer, and may receive benefits like health insurance, access to a retirement fund, and paid leave as well as have taxes withheld from his or her pay.

independent contractor: Employment status where the worker can work for more than one company at the same time, does not receive benefits or paid time off, and does not have taxes withheld from his or her pay. Also, most employment laws do not apply to independent contractors.

independent contractor agreement: Contract establishing independent contractor status for the worker. The agreement usually lays out the terms of the work and usually includes a statement that the agreement is not an employment contract.

iStockphoto.com/rez-art

Someone who is working in a café is more likely to be an employee rather than an independent contractor.

Working part-time for the bookstore, you must wear the company logo on your shirt, taxes are deducted from your paycheck, you are entitled to two paid sick days, and at the start of every shift your manager gives you a list of tasks to complete by the time you punch out. Chances are, you are an employee. Your roommate, however, simply downloaded the delivery app, has no set schedule, can pick up deliveries whenever he wants, uses his own car to make the deliveries, pays for his own gas, and does not have taxes deducted from his pay. Chances are, your roommate is an independent contractor. Understanding and properly classifying workers as employees or independent contractors is important: Many of the workplace protections you will learn about in this chapter do not apply to independent contractors.

portable benefits: Benefits that move with a worker from job to job.

CASE STUDY 8.1

Gigs and Side Hustles

According to a January 2018 Marist College/NPR Poll, one in five Americans relies on contract work for income. This might include your Uber driver, your dog walker, the emergency room doctor who looked at your broken arm, and your favorite faculty member. This group also includes those working full-time who take on extra jobs for things like paying bills, building a safety net in case of emergencies, or perhaps putting a child through college.

One thing many contract workers have in common is that they have been misclassified. The U.S. Department of Labor (DOL) estimates that millions of workers each year are misclassified as independent contractors when they should be classified as employees. The distinction makes a difference. Unlike workers in many other countries, in the United States most social safety net programs, such as Social Security, unemployment insurance, disability insurance, and health insurance, are tied to work and not to citizenship. Independent contractors are not entitled to many of these programs, nor do businesses have to offer them, and they are not protected by many laws, making them cheaper labor for businesses than employees.

Misclassification is also risky. Microsoft routinely added a pool of independent contractors to its core of employees. These workers were hired to test software, proofread, edit production, and format. Although Microsoft had these workers sign independent contractor agreements that stated they would receive no benefits from the company, Microsoft treated them like employees. Many workers worked on the same site as employees, shared the same supervisor, performed the same functions, and worked the same hours as regular employees for more than 2 years. The workers claimed they were entitled to participate in Microsoft's employee stock discount purchase program because under the terms of the program they would be considered employees. After 8 years of litigation, Microsoft settled the case in 2000 for $97 million. Approximately 8,000 to 12,000 current and former workers qualified for an award under the settlement. At the time, the Microsoft settlement was the largest ever for a misclassification suit. That changed in 2016 when FedEx settled a suit for $240 million. In the suit, drivers from 20 states claimed FedEx labeled them independent contractors so it could shift costs for things like FedEx-branded trucks, FedEx-branded uniforms, FedEx scanners, fuel, maintenance, and insurance to the drivers. Meanwhile, drivers were not entitled to overtime or pay for missed meals or breaks. The year before, FedEx settled a similar lawsuit in California for $226 million. Misclassification lawsuits have been on the rise covering a wide range of industries such as Uber drivers, engineers, nail salon workers, and exotic dancers.

There are other lesser-known impacts of having millions of workers depend on contract work. Because so few workplace protection laws apply to independent contractors, there is no data available about the prevalence of discrimination or harassment because workers are not allowed to file complaints. While independent contractors can include anti-harassment and antidiscrimination clauses in an independent contractor agreement, workers have no real way of knowing the nature or culture of a workplace beforehand. And because they are

(Continued)

(Continued)

not employees of the company, if they do confront a workplace issue they have no human resources (HR) department they can turn to for advice.

Income can fluctuate month to month when you are a contractor. Irregular hours make it difficult to predict income, pay bills, take a vacation, or plan for the future. According to the Marist/NPR Poll, while many people enjoy the freelance lifestyle, the unpredictability can lead to anxiety. Over 50% of independent contractors do not receive health insurance or retirement benefits because they do not work for one company. That means that independent contractors must pay out of pocket for health expenses and save on their own for retirement—both of which are difficult to do. The toll of financial insecurity and lack of a social safety net on mental health is compounded by the lack of legal protections.

Several states are trying to change this reality for independent contractors by experimenting with **portable benefits** models—that is, benefits that move with the worker from job to job. Take, for example, New York's Black Car Fund (BCF). Although the BCF is no longer an experiment (New York implemented the fund in 2000), several states are experimenting with systems based on the success of the fund. The BCF was created by New York's legislature to provide workers' compensation benefits for contract drivers injured on the job but has recently expanded to provide a $50,000 death benefit to families of drivers and reimbursement for participation in wellness programs. It is funded by a 2.5% customer surcharge on rides and covers about 125,000 drivers from traditional taxis to Uber and Lyft drivers. Many believe the key to success for BCF is that participation is required by law. Washington and New Jersey are considering similar bills. In 2017, Virginia senator Mark Warner and Washington congresswoman Suzan DelBene introduced legislation creating a $20 million fund to experiment with portable benefits. The fund would award grants to state and local governments and nonprofits that want to pilot a portable benefits program. Although the bill enjoys bipartisan support, it has not made much progress in Congress.

Technology might provide one solution. In early 2018, with the help of a grant from Google, Fair Care Labs, part of the National Domestic Workers Alliance, began testing an app called Alia primarily for use by house cleaners. Alia pools voluntary contributions from clients (at least $5 per cleaning), and each cleaner can use their pool to redeem benefits such as life insurance, disability insurance, and paid time off. The app does not yet include health insurance, but the alliance is hoping to add that benefit soon.

Discussion Questions

1. According to a 2012 U.S. Treasury Department study, Illinois loses $300 to $400 million a year in income taxes, unemployment insurance taxes, and workers' compensation premiums due to misclassification of workers.[2] A 2009 Report of the Ohio Attorney General on the Economic Impact of Misclassified Workers for State and Local Governments in Ohio estimates that Ohio loses $890 million annually in state unemployment taxes, workers' compensation premiums, and state and local income taxes.[3] Based on this data, what other stakeholders are impacted by worker misclassification and how are they impacted?

2. Across the country, exotic dancers have won lawsuits alleging misclassification. Many dancers claimed clubs exerted control by requiring dancers to pay "tip outs" to other club employees such as the DJ, the "house moms," the emcees, security workers, and valets. Other suits allege club owners controlled all aspects of their work—when they danced, how they danced, and what they wore—as well as exclusively handled their advertising and promotions and required that dancers pay rent. Can you think of other industries that use a similar business model that might be vulnerable to similar suits?

Critical Thinking

Lyft and Uber have partnered with a technology firm to help their drivers save for retirement. What are the pros and cons of private businesses offering this benefit for independent contractors rather than a state-mandated portable benefits plan?

KEY TAKEAWAYS

The Employment Relationship

- Understanding the difference between employees and independent contractors depends on the amount of control the business has over the worker.

- Proper classification is crucial because many workplace protection and discrimination laws do not apply to independent contractors.

EMPLOYMENT AT WILL

LO 8.2   Understand the theory of employment at will and the public policy exception.

For those workers who are employees, what are the terms of their employment? In the United States, there aren't many terms. **Employment at will** is the premise of American labor law; unless there is a contract that says otherwise, employees are hired at will—they can leave for any reason and can be fired for any reason or no reason. The United States is one of only a small number of countries where employment is at will. In most countries, employers can dismiss employees only for cause. For example, in the EU, employment is indefinite and companies must follow specific procedures to fire employees. Even if an employer follows the procedures for firing, they usually must pay the now-former employee severance pay. Because of employment at will, U.S. employers are reluctant to enter into written employment contracts with employees; however, the EU requires written employment agreements called **statements of employment particulars**, which cover topics like pay, title, and expected hours of work.

Public Policy Exception and Whistleblowers

Employment at will is one of the oldest employment theories in the United States. Over the years, laws have been passed, making certain actions unlawful, and courts have identified exceptions to this blanket theory. For example, a court found the firing of an at will employee because he refused to commit perjury violated public policy—that is, his firing harmed the public interest.[4] Other **public policy exceptions to employment at will** include serving on a jury, exercising a legal right like filing a claim for a workplace injury, or refusing to break the law.

The public policy exception to at will employment serves as the foundation for protecting whistleblowers. A **whistleblower** is a person, often an employee or former employee, who reports illegal or fraudulent activity by an employer, government, or organization. Employees may risk retaliation from their employers for making a report, giving rise to state and federal protection. The public benefits from exposure of crimes, and the cooperation of those with knowledge of a crime is crucial to public safety and therefore is not outweighed by an employer's right to fire an employee at any time.

---

employment at will: Unless there is a contract that says otherwise, employees are hired at will—they can leave for any reason and can be fired for any reason or no reason. Employment at will is one of the oldest employment theories in the United States.

statements of employment particulars: Written employment agreements in the EU, covering topics like pay, title, and expected hours of work.

public policy exceptions to employment at will: Exceptions to the at will employment doctrine for reasons that harm the public interest, such as refusing to break the law, refusing to commit perjury, exercising a legal right, and serving on a jury.

whistleblower: A person, often an employee or former employee, who reports illegal or fraudulent activity by an employer, government, or organization.

retaliation: "Getting back at" a person. It could include firing or demoting or in any way discouraging someone from reporting violations of law or enforcing their rights.

bounty program: A monetary award for whistleblowers in order to incentivize reporting of wrongdoing.

False Claims Act (FCA): Federal law protecting a person or entity who reports, with evidence, fraud against any federal program or contractor. A whistleblower under the FCA can sue the wrongdoer on behalf of the U.S. government and recover up to 25% of any court award.

Internal Revenue Service (IRS): Federal agency that enforces the IRC. The IRS has a bounty program for whistleblowers who report persons who fail to pay their taxes. Whistleblowers can collect up to 30% of what the IRS collects.

Office of the Whistleblower: Office within the SEC created by the DFA to enforce whistleblower provisions of the law.

There are 22 federal laws that protect whistleblowers from **retaliation** such as firing or demoting as a way of "getting back at" the person for reporting suspected wrongdoing, or otherwise discouraging a person from reporting wrongdoing. Nevertheless, whistleblowers often face social and financial risk when they report wrongdoing. In order to acknowledge the risks and to incentivize reporting, several laws with whistleblower protections include a **bounty program** a monetary award for whistleblowers (see Figure 8.1). Bounties vary, as do the requirements for eligibility. The **False Claims Act (FCA)** has one of the strongest whistleblower protection clauses. Under the FCA, any person or entity with evidence of fraud against any federal program or contract can sue the wrongdoer on behalf of the U.S. government and recover up to 25% of any court award.

Similarly, the **Internal Revenue Service (IRS)** pays a bounty to any person who blows the whistle on persons who fail to pay their taxes due under the Internal Revenue Code (IRC). If the IRS uses the information provided by the whistleblower, that person could collect up to 30% of what the IRS collects. The Sarbanes–Oxley Act (SOX) protects employees of publicly traded companies who report violations by their employers of U.S. Securities and Exchange Commission (SEC) regulations. Those that report under SOX can be awarded damages in court. The Dodd–Frank Act (DFA), passed in 2010 in response to the financial crisis of 2008, also includes broad whistleblower protection and bounties. Under the DFA, a whistleblower who provides original information about a securities or commodities law violation to the SEC is entitled to between 10% and 30% of sanctions imposed by the SEC that exceed $1 million. The DFA also created the **Office of the Whistleblower** within the SEC to administer and enforce the whistleblower provisions of the law.

Whistleblowing is far less common in the EU and covered in a fragmented and inconsistent manner. In Europe, if a whistleblower's identity is revealed, they often lose their job and can face lawsuits, which is one reason it is less common than in the United States. However, in October 2019, the EU adopted broad new rules for whistleblowers, requiring

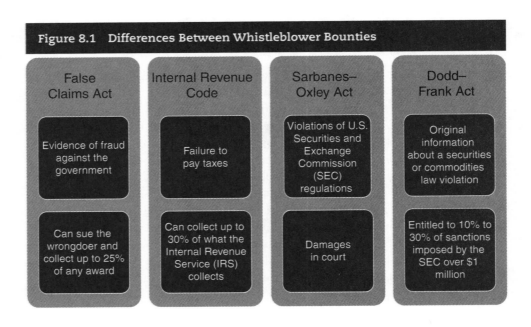

Figure 8.1 Differences Between Whistleblower Bounties

False Claims Act	Internal Revenue Code	Sarbanes–Oxley Act	Dodd–Frank Act
Evidence of fraud against the government	Failure to pay taxes	Violations of U.S. Securities and Exchange Commission (SEC) regulations	Original information about a securities or commodities law violation
Can sue the wrongdoer and collect up to 25% of any award	Can collect up to 30% of what the Internal Revenue Service (IRS) collects	Damages in court	Entitled to 10% to 30% of sanctions imposed by the SEC over $1 million

the creation of safe channels for reporting and greater protection against retaliation both for the whistleblower and those who assist them in reporting. Member states have 2 years to implement the new rules into their national laws.[5]

Whistleblower rewards and bounties are not part of the new EU rules. According to the European Commission, the rewards are seen "as shifting the purpose of the reporting away from the public interest to the personal gain of whistleblowers, thus making whistle-blowing appear as a commercial transaction."[6] Korea is the only other Organization for Economic Cooperation and Development (OECD) member nation to have a financial reward for whistleblowers. Korea's Anti-Corruption and Civil Rights Commission (ACRC) is mandated by law to provide a bounty to whistleblowers who report internally within their company or to the ACRC directly. Under Korean law, whistleblowers can also request compensation for their expenses, medical or psychological treatment, costs associated with a job transfer, and legal fees.[7]

ETHICS IN CONTEXT

Whistleblower Bounty

iStockphoto.com/djmilic

Historically, whistleblowers have been considered "rats." More recently, popular media has helped change the image of whistleblowers, now considered honorable or heroic. For example, movies like *The Insider* and *Erin Brockovich* and *Time* magazine's 2002 Persons of the Year cover with Coleen Rowley (Federal Bureau of Investigation [FBI]/pre-September 11, 2001, intelligence), Sherron Watkins (former vice president of Enron), and Cynthia Cooper (former vice president of internal audit at WorldCom) highlight the moral courage of whistleblowers.

The FCA, IRC, and the DFA have bounty provisions to acknowledge the risk and sacrifice many whistleblowers face. But what if the whistleblower is part of the scheme they report? Do they qualify for a bounty? In many cases, yes. The theory behind this policy is that information from participants in the scheme would involve details that would otherwise be very difficult for law enforcement to obtain. For example, the FCA bounty is premised on motivating coconspirators to turn on each other. Also, there is some evidence to suggest that the IRS receives tips from people after a relationship has soured; the disgruntled person usually has inside information they are now willing to share with law enforcement.

The IRS has awarded bounties since the late 1800s. It wasn't until 2006, when the code was amended, that Section 7623(b) was added. Part of that section states that if the claim for a bounty was brought by someone who "planned and initiated" the scheme, their award may be reduced based on the level of their involvement in the planning and initiating. If the person making the claim for a bounty was *convicted* for planning and initiating the scheme that gave rise to the bounty, that person collects nothing (see Figure 8.2). The case of Bradley Birkenfeld provides an example.

Birkenfeld is an American who worked as a private banker at the UBS headquarters in Geneva, Switzerland. His job was to develop and acquire new U.S. clients. Through his job, Birkenfeld knowingly

(Continued)

(Continued)

Figure 8.2   Point-Counterpoint: Whistleblower Bounties

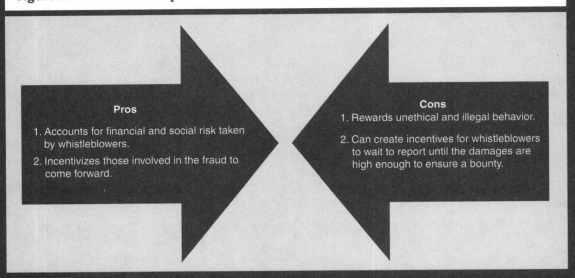

Pros

1. Accounts for financial and social risk taken by whistleblowers.

2. Incentivizes those involved in the fraud to come forward.

Cons

1. Rewards unethical and illegal behavior.

2. Can create incentives for whistleblowers to wait to report until the damages are high enough to ensure a bounty.

participated in a tax evasion scheme facilitated by UBS whereby bankers would help U.S. clients hide their assets in offshore accounts held by sham entities in Switzerland. Ultimately, the bank helped 19,000 customers hide almost $19 billion from U.S. tax authorities. In 2007, Birkenfeld alerted U.S. authorities of the scheme; however, during his cooperation with U.S. authorities Birkenfeld failed to disclose his relationship with a client for whom he helped hide $200 million in offshore accounts. As a result, Birkenfeld plead guilty to conspiracy to commit tax fraud and was sentenced to 40 months in prison.

Birkenfeld's inside information about the UBS fraud scheme was critical in helping the United States uncover the fraud and recover billions of dollars in unpaid taxes. Lawyers from the National Whistleblower Center described Birkenfeld as "the single most important informant in the U.S. probe of tax evasion and secrecy at UBS and other banks." When he was released from prison, Birkenfeld was awarded the largest-ever whistleblower bounty: $104 million. Neither his involvement in the fraud nor his conviction disqualified him under the law from receiving the award.

Birkenfeld would not have been eligible for an award under the DFA whistleblower program administered and enforced by the SEC. The goal of the DFA is to promote transparency and accountability in the financial system since the crisis of 2008 through improving the whistleblower protections under SOX and creating a new bounty program for whistleblowers who provide "original information" regarding a violation of federal securities laws. Unlike the IRS program, according to the SEC system whistleblowers who are convicted of an underlying crime related to the scheme they report are not eligible for the bounty. Therefore, Birkenfeld would not have received a bounty had he reported a violation of DFA. For whistleblowers who are complicit in the crime they report, they are still eligible for an award, but it will be reduced by, among other criteria, the level of their involvement and how forthcoming they are with information.

Discussion Questions

1. *Stakeholder theory:* Identify stakeholders in the government's decision to amend the IRC to include those who are convicted of a crime (just not the crime of planning and initiating the fraud they report) as eligible for a bounty. What is at stake for each group? How does the amendment address, if at all, any of those concerns?

2. *Ethical decision-making:* Many feel that whistleblowers, whether they are involved in the fraud or not, are usually the only people who can expose wrongdoing, and without them, the fraud would never be exposed. However, others believe that the serious issues raised by allowing those culpable of the fraud they report to receive a bounty will cause bigger problems. What issues, both short term and long term, are raised by allowing those culpable for the fraud they report to be eligible for a bounty?

Take a Position

The SEC whistleblower program under the DFA defines a *whistleblower* as a person who "provides the Commission with information" relating to suspected securities-law violations. The U.S. Supreme Court recently interpreted this definition to mean that if a person suspects securities fraud violations at their work and they report it internally to their supervisor and not to the SEC, they are not a whistleblower under the law and therefore not protected from retaliation.

Issue: What is the impact of the requirement to report first to the SEC on the reporting employee, the culture of the organization, the efforts of businesses to root out wrongdoing, and the overall need to fight crime? Should the definition of whistleblower be changed to include those who report wrongdoing internally as well as those who report to the SEC? Explain your answer.

Employment at Will

- Employment at will is the foundation of U.S. labor law.

- Exceptions to employment at will include reasons that violate public policy, such as serving on a jury and exercising a legal right.

WORKPLACE PROTECTIONS

LO 8.3 Discuss workplace protections and impacts of employment regulation on employers and employees.

Workplace laws have evolved to meet the needs of the labor force at the time. Most workplace protections were created by statute—not by the courts. States can pass their own laws, which means some protections can vary depending on the state in which the employee works.

Worker's Compensation

One of the challenges of management is worker health—how to encourage healthy habits and maintain a safe workplace to reduce absenteeism and increase productivity and morale. Injured workers struggle with the financial difficulties of missing work and often wages

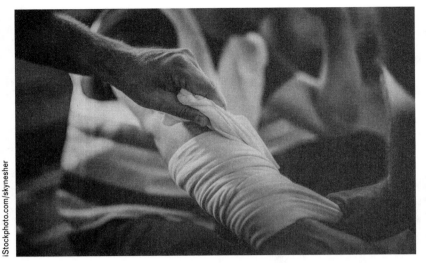

iStockphoto.com/skynesher

during their recovery. Imagine you work in an office building and take the stairs down to the cafeteria to get a cup of coffee. While in the stairwell, you trip and break your wrist. Your injury will require surgery and months of physical therapy, which means missing work. Think about the financial impact on your life because of this injury. **Workers' compensation** is a type of insurance program that compensates employees for lost wages and medical care after sustaining an injury or illness that is work related. Injured employees receive a certain portion of their wages while they are out of work for treatment of their injury and reimbursement for covered medical treatment. The program is mandated by the state, and each state establishes different rules. Workers' compensation is no fault, meaning it does not matter whether the worker was at fault for their injury. For many injuries, workers' compensation is a worker's only remedy if they are injured; they cannot sue in court for their injury. Although complicated and imperfect, a modern system of workers' compensation is so ultimately vital to society that all industrialized nations have some form of compensation for worker injury.

workers' compensation: Type of insurance program that compensates employees for lost wages and medical care after sustaining an injury or illness that is work related.

Determining what conduct could reasonably be expected as part of the job and therefore covered by workers' compensation can be tricky. For example, high school teacher Wanda Jones was sitting at her desk when the assistant principal stood in her office door holding a snake. Ms. Jones jumped out of her chair, started screaming, and ran into the concrete wall behind her chair, injuring her knee. The assistant principal claimed that a student brought the snake to school for a science class project, and she wanted to show it to office personnel. Jones sued the school board for her injuries, but the board said workers' compensation was Jones's only recourse because her injury happened at work. The court agreed; the assistant principal's conduct was not so far removed from what would typically be expected by an assistant principal so as to be outside the scope of her employment.

Determining what injuries are eligible for workers' compensation coverage is another complication with the policy. On December 2, 2015, San Bernardino County Department of Public Health worker Syed Farook and his wife, Tashfeen Malik, entered the Inland Regional Center in San Bernardino, California, during an office holiday party for the department and began shooting, killing 14 and injuring 22 people. Many of the injured victims are suing the State of California over workers' compensation coverage for their injuries—both physical and mental. There is no question the attack qualified as a "workplace injury," but the law is not clear about coverage for injuries from a terror attack. Like many states, California has cut back on workers' compensation coverage over the years to save money, and the state claims it does not cover everything the victims' doctors say they need to recover.

Fair Labor Standards Act

During the Great Depression, income inequality created devastating and life-threatening conditions for many Americans. In 1935, President Roosevelt signed the **Social Security Act** into law to create a federal financial safety net for elderly, unemployed, and disadvantaged workers. **Social Security** is funded by a tax on workers' earnings. That money is then pooled in the Social Security Trust Fund and paid out monthly to eligible recipients. Those 62 years old and older or disabled workers are eligible to collect Social Security benefits. How much an eligible worker collects depends on how much money they earned during their working life and their age when they start collecting benefits. Social Security disability benefits are based on a person's eligible lifetime average earnings.

The **Fair Labor Standards Act (FLSA)** was signed into law just 3 years after the Social Security Act to combat worker exploitation and "labor conditions detrimental to the maintenance of the minimum standards of living necessary for health, efficiency, and well-being of workers."[8] This included regulating child labor, establishing a minimum wage, and requiring premium pay for overtime. The FLSA has been amended 22 times since then, raising the minimum wage 22 times, reducing the standard work week to 40 hours, and requiring equal pay for women. While many view the FLSA as a living document, changing as the nature of our work and workforce changes, others fear that because the FLSA only applies to employees, the law cannot address the more pressing issues raised by the growing segment of contract workers in our new economy. In addition, fewer brick-and-mortar workplaces, coupled with growing use of technology and globalization, make it increasingly difficult to pinpoint whom is responsible for compliance with the FLSA.

Under the FLSA, employers are required to pay covered employees a **minimum wage**. While the federal minimum wage remains $7.25 per hour, many states have chosen to increase the rate, others (those depicted as having no minimum wage) comply with the federal rate, and Georgia and Wyoming pay those employees not covered by the federal minimum wage a lower rate (see Figure 8.3). The United States isn't the only country with a legally mandated minimum wage; most of Europe has a minimum wage that varies from country to country. Australia has the highest minimum wage at 9.47 euros (US$10.78) while Russia has the lowest: 1.64 euros (US$1.87).[9] In 2019, Spain raised its minimum wage by 22%, the largest increase in more than 40 years, from €736 to €900 (approximately $835–$997) just days after France announced they were raising their minimum wage by €100 (approximately $111).[10]

In response to states increasing their minimum wage, 24 states have passed **pre-emption bills** that either abolish or roll back state wage increases. Birmingham, Alabama, was the first southern city to raise its minimum wage for anyone employed within the city—primarily benefiting fast-food and retail workers. Shortly thereafter, the Alabama legislature passed a law that abolished that wage increase. In 2018, a group of civil rights groups sued the state, claiming passage of the law was "tainted by racial animus" given, among other things, Birmingham's predominantly black workforce and the fact that all of the state legislators who voted for the rollback were white.[11]

Private businesses have stepped in to fill some of the wage gap. Companies as diverse as JPMorgan Chase, Ben & Jerry's, Target, Bank of America, and Facebook have all raised their minimum wages well above the federal minimum and most above states' minimum wages.[12]

Social Security Act: A law to create a federal financial safety net for elderly, unemployed, and disadvantaged workers.

Social Security: A financial safety net for retired, disabled, and disadvantaged workers funded by a tax on workers' earnings.

Fair Labor Standards Act (FLSA): Passed in 1938, regulates child labor, establishes a minimum wage, and requires premium pay for overtime.

minimum wage: Minimum hourly wage required by FLSA, currently $7.25 per hour. States may have a different minimum wage.

pre-emption bills: Laws passed by states to roll back or abolish state increases to the minimum wage.

Figure 8.3 2019 Minimum Wage

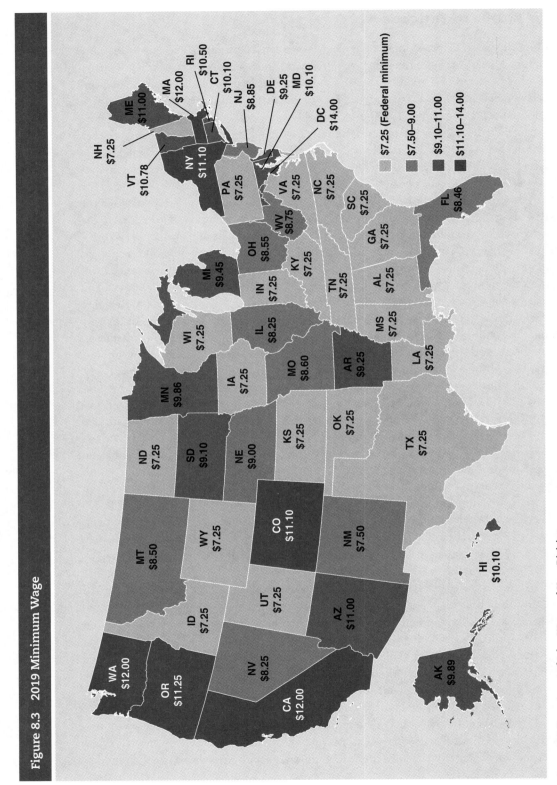

ME $11.00
NH $7.25
VT $10.78
MA $12.00
RI $10.50
CT $10.10
NY $11.10
NJ $8.85
PA $7.25
DE $9.25
MD $10.10
DC $14.00
WV $8.75
VA $7.25
OH $8.55
MI $9.45
IN $7.25
KY $7.25
NC $7.25
SC $7.25
GA $7.25
FL $8.46
WI $7.25
IL $8.25
TN $7.25
AL $7.25
MS $7.25
MN $9.86
IA $7.25
MO $8.60
AR $9.25
LA $7.25
ND $7.25
SD $9.10
NE $9.00
KS $7.25
OK $7.25
TX $7.25
MT $8.50
WY $7.25
CO $11.10
NM $7.50
HI $10.10
ID $7.25
UT $7.25
AZ $11.00
WA $12.00
OR $11.25
NV $8.25
CA $12.00
AK $9.89

$7.25 (Federal minimum)
$7.50–9.00
$9.10–11.00
$11.10–14.00

Source: U.S. Department of Labor Wage and Hour Division.

Braun et al. v. Wal-Mart Stores, Inc., 630 Pa 292, 106 A.3d 656 (2014)

Facts: This is a lawsuit brought by all current and former employees of Walmart and Sam's Club stores from 1998 to 2005 for denial of rest and meal breaks in violation of the FLSA. The employees claim that Walmart managers were pressured to decrease payroll by understaffing stores. Because of chronic understaffing, employees were denied promised paid rest and meal breaks or forced to work through them and to work once they had clocked out for their shift. Walmart's own internal audits indicated widespread rest break violations: In one week in 2000 across 127 stores, more than 60,000 rest break violations occurred. Using available records and extrapolating for breaks not recorded, experts testified that employees had been denied over $71 million in paid breaks.

After the audit, Walmart eliminated its "swipe" policy, which required employees to swipe out and back in for rest breaks. The company also instituted a "lockout" system whereby no employee who was off the clock could log in to and use a cash register. However, that system allowed managers to override the lockout, and it did not prevent off-the-clock employees from logging in under another (on-the-clock) employee's name. Thus, according to Walmart, it is impossible for the workers to prove how many breaks were missed and accurately assess damages.

A jury found for Walmart on all claims relating to missed meal breaks but found for the workers on all claims relating to rest breaks and off-the-clock work and awarded them $187,648,589 in damages. Walmart appealed, claiming it was subject to a "trial by formula" because the workers could only prove damages for the claims for which there were records. It then used the average damage amount for those claims to determine damages for the entire class without looking specifically at those remaining claims and allowing Walmart to defend each claim.

Issue: Did Walmart have a fair opportunity to defend itself against all FLSA claims?

Ruling: Yes. Walmart had a full and fair opportunity to defend itself against the FLSA claims. The trial by formula did not address *whether* the workers were entitled to damages because Walmart violated the FLSA—only *how much* they were owed. Moreover, by Walmart's own admission, its records were not complete or reliable for several of the years covered by the class action. Whether this was purposeful or by accident, it cannot be denied that Walmart enjoyed the benefit of the work performed by its employees and cannot now deny paying them because it failed to keep accurate records.

Law and Management Questions

1. In another case against Walmart, the company's own audit of their rest and meal break records showed the company failed to keep records for 325,188 shifts and failed to keep time records for off-the-clock employees 69,710 times. Yet, managers took no action to correct this. Can you point to similar bad management decisions in the *Braun* case that might have given rise to this lawsuit? Can you think of alternative courses of action?

2. The judge in the *Braun* case speculated whether Walmart's conduct was "purposeful or by accident." At the time *Braun* went to trial (2008), it was one of 70 ongoing cases across the country in which employees accused Walmart of making them work while off the clock. For example, a judge in a Minnesota case during this period ruled that Walmart owed 56,000 employees $6.5 million because it failed to give them rest breaks at least 1.5 million times. In that case the judge noted that managers were eligible for a bonus based on their store's profitability. What does this evidence say to you about Walmart's intent? Should that matter?

tipped employee: Someone who works in a job in which they customarily and regularly receive more than $30 a month in tips.

federal tipped minimum wage: Required by the FLSA, the employer must pay at least $2.13 per hour in direct wages. If an employee's tips combined with the employer's direct wages of at least $2.13 per hour do not equal the minimum hourly wage, the employer must make up the difference. States may have their own tipped minimum wage.

tip pooling: An arrangement whereby servers pool their tips at the end of a shift and share them with other staff.

The FLSA also established strict record keeping requirements that if not followed could harm a business sued for violations of the law. In the case *Braun et al. v. Wal-Mart Stores, Inc.*, Walmart's faulty record keeping and bad management decisions supported the workers' claim of rest break and off-the-clock work violations that cost the company $187 million in damages.

Approximately 4.3 million Americans work for tips, and almost 60% of them are food servers and bartenders.[13] Under the FLSA, a **tipped employee** is someone who works in a job in which they customarily and regularly receive more than $30 a month in tips. Unlike the regular minimum wage, the **federal tipped minimum wage** has not increased since 1996. The employer may consider tips as part of wages, but the employer must pay at least $2.13 per hour in direct wages (see Figure 8.4). If an employee's tips combined with the employer's direct wages of at least $2.13 per hour do not equal the minimum hourly wage, the employer must make up the difference. Many states pay more than the federal $2.13 minimum, and eight states have eliminated their tipped minimum wage, which means all workers in those states will be subject to the same minimum regardless of whether they earn tips. Tipped employees must retain all of their tips except to the extent that they participate in a valid tip pooling or sharing arrangement.

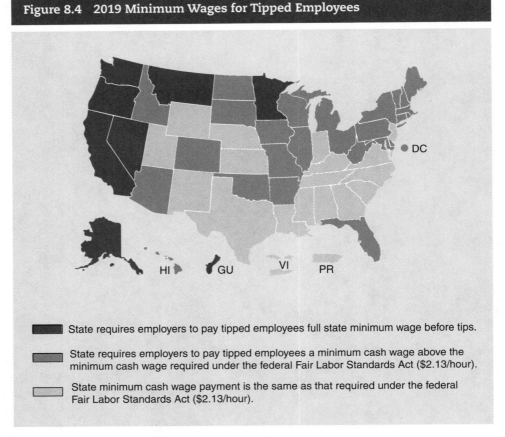

Figure 8.4   2019 Minimum Wages for Tipped Employees

State requires employers to pay tipped employees full state minimum wage before tips.

State requires employers to pay tipped employees a minimum cash wage above the minimum cash wage required under the federal Fair Labor Standards Act ($2.13/hour).

State minimum cash wage payment is the same as that required under the federal Fair Labor Standards Act ($2.13/hour).

Source: U.S. Department of Labor, Wage and Hour Division.

To Tip or Not to Tip

The federal minimum wage has not changed from $7.25 per hour since 2009. While several states have increased their minimum wages, many workers still struggle to make ends meet while working full time. One industry particularly sensitive to wage increases is the restaurant industry. Increases in wages drive labor costs up. One restaurateur said his labor costs went from one third of total costs in the 1980s to over 45% today. On top of this, the cost of rent, food, and energy continue to rise. Additionally in states like California where the minimum wage is $12.00 per hour before tips, labor costs can prove to be too much for some businesses.

Another impact of increases to minimum wage on the restaurant industry is increased pay disparity between servers and back-of-the-house workers such as dishwashers, sous chefs, chefs, and other employees who do not regularly receive tips. **Tip pooling** can help alleviate this inequity. According to the FLSA, a tip pool is an arrangement whereby servers pool their tips at the end of a shift and share them with other staff like bartenders and bussers. In 2011, the DOL amended its regulations to allow for tip pooling only among staff who were paid more than the federal minimum tipped wage and who regularly received tips. The amendment prohibited businesses from requiring that staff share their pooled tips with back-of-the-house staff. This led to several lawsuits and inconsistent court decisions around the country.

In 2018, the DOL amended the FLSA again to allow employers who paid workers the full minimum wage to include back-of-the-house staff in their tip pools. However, because of the unsettled case law, there is little predictability of outcome for tip pooling.

Some businesses are taking tipping into their own hands. In 2015, the Union Square Hospitality Group (USHG) announced that it would eliminate tipping at its 15 restaurants, including Union Square Cafe and Gramercy Tavern. The new "Hospitality Included" pricing model would reduce the pay disparities between servers and kitchen staff and allow raises in pay consistent with the increase in cost of living. Danny Meyer, CEO of USHG, offset the elimination of tips with a 21% increase in menu prices used to increase the hourly pay of servers. Other restaurants around the country had already begun eliminating tipping, and many more followed the trend. However, since the rollout of the new pricing model at USHG, Meyer says 40% of longtime waitstaff have left because their pay decreased without tips. Veteran workers could work several busy shifts on Thursday, Friday, and Saturday nights and rely on good tips to make a living. Without tips, there is little variation in shifts and less variation in pay between senior waitstaff and newer hires. Eliminating the incentive of tips has also changed the culture of the USHG workplace: The structure more resembles an office, where cooks and waiters can only get a raise in pay if they ask for it and pass written tests on their knowledge of food, wine, and service.

Other restaurants that have eliminated tipping have noticed that people do not order as much food. Joe's Stone Crab, the largest chain to test a no-tipping policy in 18 of its 100 locations, lost 8% to 10% of customers during the pilot phase. As a result, the company has reverted back to tipping at 14 of the test locations.

Unlike most other countries, tipping is a tradition and deeply ingrained in U.S. culture. Some say tipping provides an incentive for waitstaff to provide good service. Others claim tipping is just an opportunity for waitstaff to upsell diners on side dishes, drinks, and desserts. Because customers traditionally tip a percentage of the total bill, the most significant driver of a tip is the amount of the bill, not the level of service. Either way, Americans are hard-pressed to abandon this practice. Michael Lynn of Cornell University studied the effects of Joe's Stone Crab's test run of no tipping. According to his research, online reviews of the restaurants were higher when customers could tip than in the locations where they could not tip and service was included in the price, indicating less customer satisfaction in locations with a no-tipping policy. Lynn also claims that psychologically, customers see separate pricing (meal and tip) as cheaper than bundled pricing (tip is included in the price of the meal). And although tipping is ingrained in society, it is technically voluntary, and service charges that include gratuity take that option away.

(Continued)

(Continued)

To complicate it further, many question the social value of tipping. Lynn's research indicates racial disparities in tipping. Both black and white customers tip white servers more than black servers, and this discrepancy may be attributed to implicit biases. Moreover, the larger the group dining, the greater the disparity in tips: White servers got a bigger tip, and black servers received a smaller tip than those paid by groups of two. According to Lynn, this can be attributed to aversion racism: Most people try to avoid obvious racism, so they point to a reason other than race for their conduct. In the case of a group setting, the assumption may be that a diner does not have to leave a good tip because someone else in the group will leave a good tip.

Tipping also shifts the balance of power, where the customer wields more power in a server's income than the business. This imbalance can lead to servers enduring behavior that in another setting would not be tolerated. According to Equal Employment Opportunity Commission data from 1995 to 2006, more sexual harassment claims were filed in the restaurant industry than any other industry. Professor Stefanie Johnson of the University of Colorado and Professor Juan Madera of the University of Houston followed 76 female college students as they worked in the restaurant industry over 3 months. Once a month the women completed questionnaires asking them to identify from a list of sexually harassing behavior any incidents they had experienced on the job. Over the 3 months, the women reported 226 incidents of sexual harassment: 112 involved coworkers, 29 involved managers, and 85 involved customers.

Raising the minimum wage and eliminating tips, many feel, would reduce the incidence of sexual harassment by shifting the balance of power, creating more of a team atmosphere at work, and empowering managers to stand up for their employees without the fear of risking the server's tip.

Discussion Questions

1. What are some of the management issues that can arise due to the pay disparity between servers and back-of-the-house employees?

2. Erin Wade, the owner of Homeroom, a mac and cheese restaurant in Oakland, California, devised a system for addressing sexual harassment of servers by customers. The Management Alert Color System (MACS) gives servers three alert options: yellow if a customer has a "creepy vibe" or leers, orange if the customer makes a verbal comment on the server's appearance or makes a sexual comment, and red if there is an "overtly sexual" act. For yellow alerts, the server can ask a manager to take over the table; for orange, the manager takes the table automatically; and for a red, the customer is asked to leave. What are the pros and cons of the MACS system? If you were a manager at Homeroom, how would you ensure that everyone is on board with this system?

Critical Thinking

Would you be willing to pay more for your next restaurant meal if you knew that you did not have to tip the server? Why or why not?

Unions and Concerted Activity

National Labor Relations Act (NLRA): Guarantees the right of employees to organize, form unions, and bargain collectively with their employers.

The **National Labor Relations Act (NLRA)**, passed in 1935, became one of the most important legacies of the New Deal. Prior to the NLRA, workers had the right to organize and form unions, but employers also had the right to fire them for union activity and often retaliated against them or blacklisted them from other jobs. The NLRA shifts the balance of power and guarantees the right of employees to organize, form unions, and bargain collectively with their employers. The law ensures that workers have a choice on whether to belong to a union and promotes collective bargaining to ensure peaceful industry–labor relations. Importantly, the law requires employers to bargain in good faith with unions. The act also created a new **National Labor Relations Board (NLRB)** to arbitrate deadlocked labor–management disputes, guarantee democratic union elections, and penalize employers for unfair labor practices. Overall, the goal of the NLRA is to protect and encourage collective bargaining, ensuring most Americans a right to form a union. A **union** is an organized group of workers who cooperate to make decisions about the terms and conditions of work. Not all workers can form or join a union. Under the NLRA, railroad, airline,[i] government workers, farm workers, independent contractors, supervisors, and managers are excluded from the protection of the law.

If workers who are covered by the law want to form a union, their employer cannot interfere with that process, threaten retaliation, or coerce employees not to join. Workers can form a union in one of two ways: (1) their employer can voluntarily agree to recognize a union based on signed representation cards that show that a majority of employees want the union to represent them, or (2) if at least 30% of employees sign a petition saying that they want the NLRB to hold an election and a majority vote to form a union, the NLRB will certify the union as the representative of that unit for collective bargaining. A **bargaining unit** is a group of employees who do similar work and share similar issues and concerns when it comes to working conditions. A bargaining unit can make up the entire union, or a bargaining unit can be one small part of a larger union composed of many bargaining units. The bargaining unit negotiates a **collective bargaining agreement (CBA)** with the employer that covers all of the terms of employment for the members of that unit, such as pay, hours, conditions for promotion, employee discipline, raises, termination, health insurance, benefits, and vacation time. Once the CBA is executed, the employer cannot change any of the terms without first renegotiating with the union representative. If a member believes the employer is not enforcing a term of the CBA, that member may file a **grievance**, which is a procedure for internal dispute resolution involving the employee, union representation, and the employer's management team. If the grievance cannot be resolved internally, parties may proceed to **arbitration** to resolve the dispute. Arbitration is a private proceeding using a neutral third party to render a binding decision in a dispute.

The NLRA empowers union members to "engage in other **concerted activities** for the purpose of collective bargaining or other mutual aid or protection."[14] **Strikes**, included among "concerted activities," are a mass work stoppage usually in response to employee grievances. The law places restrictions and qualifications on how and why members may strike. The law creates two broad categories of strikes: lawful and unlawful. **Lawful strikes** are either **economic strikes**—usually involving economic issues like higher wages or better working conditions—or **unfair labor practices**, which is a practice that violates the NLRA, such as retaliating against an employee for joining a union. An **unlawful strike** is one in which the purpose violates the NLRA.

Unions would like to protect against **free riders**—those workers who benefit from the services of the union but do not join the union or pay dues. To protect against free riders, some unions and businesses agree that the union can require eligible employees join or that the employer will collect dues on behalf of the union. **Union security agreements** like this ensure that all workers pay dues. Not everyone supports union security agreements. Twenty-seven states, mostly in the south and Midwest, have passed **right-to-work laws** that prohibit union security agreements.

---

[i] The Railway Labor Act, 45 U.S.C.

National Labor Relations Board (NLRB): Created by the NLRA to arbitrate deadlocked labor–management disputes, guarantee democratic union elections, and penalize employers for unfair labor practices.

union: An organized group of workers who work together to make decisions about the terms and conditions of work.

bargaining unit: A group of employees who do similar work and share similar issues and concerns when it comes to working conditions.

collective bargaining agreement (CBA) Negotiated with the employer, a contract that covers all of the terms of employment for the members of a bargaining unit, such as pay, hours, conditions for promotion, employee discipline, raises, termination, health insurance, benefits, and vacation time.

grievance: A procedure for internal dispute resolution involving an employee, union representation, and the employer's management team.

arbitration: A private proceeding using a neutral third party to render a binding decision in a dispute.

concerted
activities: The right
of all employees
guaranteed under the
NLRA, regardless of
union membership,
to act together to
improve their working
conditions for mutual
aid and protection.

The NLRA also guarantees all employees, regardless of union membership, the right to act together to improve their working conditions. This type of action also falls within concerted activity. Concerted activity doesn't have to be a large sophisticated plan; it could mean two workers talking about whether they will get a raise, or one worker posting on Facebook concerns about her boss and other workers posting their support.[15] The key is whether the activity touches upon wages, hours, or working conditions and is for "mutual aid and protection."

LAW AND SOCIETY 8.2

Karl Knauz Motors, Inc. d/b/a Knauz BMW and Robert Becker, CASE 13-CA-046452

Facts: Knauz owned Knauz BMW, which sold new and used BMW vehicles. Knauz also owned the adjacent Land Rover dealership. Robert Becker began working as a salesperson at the Land Rover dealership in 1998, later moving to the BMW dealership in 2004. Like all salespeople at Knauz, part of Becker's compensation is a 25% commission on all sales. In June 2011, Knauz was to host the Ultimate Driving Event to introduce the redesigned 5 Series model to the public. Everyone at Knauz considered this event significant because the 5 Series was the BMW bread-and-butter model.

Leading up to the event, salespeople met with Knauz management to discuss expectations and logistics for the event. Phillip Ceraulo, Becker's supervisor, explained that because the event is important, food will be served: hot dogs from a hot dog cart, cookies, chips, and bottled water. The salespeople were concerned that such casual food did not reflect the importance of the event nor the level of luxury indicative of the 5 Series and the BMW brand. Ceraulo responded that the event was not a food event but an event to showcase the car. After the meeting, the salespeople continued to discuss the food selection; one salesperson claimed that the local Mercedes dealership served hors d'oeuvres. All agreed that for a luxury brand, perception was important and were worried that the event would not meet the impeccable perception of BMW. Becker

worried that their commission would be impacted because the casual nature of the event would turn customers away from the brand.

On the day of the event, Becker took pictures of salespeople holding hot dogs, small bottles of water, and snack-sized bags of chips provided by the dealership. He told them he was going to post the pictures to his Facebook page. A few days after the event, there was an accident at the adjoining Land Rover dealership: A salesperson was showing a customer a car and let the customer's 13-year-old son sit in the driver's seat with the door open. The boy must have stepped on the gas because the car rolled down an embankment, over the customer's foot, and into an adjacent pond. The salesperson was thrown into the water but not hurt. Becker could see the incident from the BMW dealership, and he took pictures of the car in the pond.

Later that day, Becker posted several comments and pictures critical of the event to his Facebook page, including the following:

I was happy to see that Knauz went "All Out" for the most important launch of a new BMW in years...the new 5 series...will generate tens in millions of dollars in revenue...the...chips, and the $2.00 cookie plate from Sam's Club...were such a nice touch.

Becker posted a picture of a salesperson with his arm around a woman serving hot dogs.

Becker also posted pictures of the Land Rover in the pond; one had this caption: "This is your car: This is your car on drugs." The picture shows the front end of the car in the pond, the salesperson with a blanket around her sitting next to a woman, and a young boy holding his head. Becker wrote the following:

This is what happens when a sales Person. . . allows a 13 year old boy to get behind the wheel of a 6,000 lb. truck...the kid drives over his father's foot and into the pond...OOOPS!

By the next day, management at Knauz saw the posts and asked Becker to remove them, which he did. Becker met with Ceraulo and higher management. When the president of Knauz asked him "What were you thinking?" Becker's response was "It's none of your business." The president told Becker that Knauz received calls from other dealerships, his posts embarrassed the dealership and all of his coworkers, and the management team needed time to think about how best to address his conduct. Five days later, Becker was fired.

Becker sued claiming his firing violated the NLRA protection for concerted activity.

Issue: Was Becker's conduct protected concerted activity?

Decision: One post was protected concerted activity and one post was not protected concerted activity. Regarding the Ultimate Driving Event post, evidence clearly proved that the salespeople were concerned that the quality of refreshments at the event betrayed the luxury and price point of the car and the brand. Because of this, several employees voiced their frustration at the planning meeting before the event. Employees worried that their commission would be impacted by fewer sales. Although only Becker posted about the event, concerted activity does not require that two or more people act in unison to protest or protect their working conditions. When a single employee tries to initiate, induce, or prepare for group action or voice group complaints, that action is concerted if it logically stems from prior concerted activity. Becker's post about the event was protected concerted activity.

Regarding the accident at the Land Rover dealership, Becker's posts clearly had no connection to the terms or conditions of work; they were posted without any discussion with any other employees and were made in a mocking tone. These posts were not protected concerted activity.

The question left is this: For which post was Becker fired? Becker testified that the president told him the posts embarrassed the company and his coworkers. Ceraulo testified that management agreed that the posts about the food were "comical" and they laughed about them, but the posts about the accident were far more serious, involving injury to a customer. They considered those posts not only damaging to the company but also to the customer and his son and was the basis for their decision to fire Becker. The court found that Becker was fired for his posts about the Land Rover accident and therefore was not a violation of the NLRA.

Law and Management Questions

1. In response to management questions, Becker claimed that what he posts on his Facebook page is none of their business. Do you agree with him? Why or why not?

2. Becker worked for Knauz for 13 years before he was fired for his Facebook posts. Presumably he was a good employee; management never mentioned any prior incidents of Becker's bad behavior or otherwise failing to meet expectations. Could this lawsuit have been avoided? Explain your answer. If you were Becker's manager, how could you have handled this issue differently?

strikes: Mass work stoppages usually in response to employee grievances.

lawful strikes: Strikes based upon economic issues or unfair labor practices.

economic strikes: Usually involving economic issues like higher wages or better working conditions.

unfair labor practices: Practices that violate the NLRA, such as retaliating against an employee for joining a union.

unlawful strike: The purpose of which violates the NLRA.

free riders: Those workers who benefit from the services of the union but do not join the union or pay dues.

union security agreements: Agreements between unions and businesses whereby the union can require eligible employees to join or that the employer will collect dues on behalf of the union.

right-to-work laws: Present in states that prohibit union security agreements.

Leave

Worker benefits like paid time off are an important way to balance family and work. According to the Holmes–Rahe Stress Scale, personal illness, illness of a close family member, and adding a new family member are major life stressors. Although the majority of U.S. workers are parents,[16] the United States does not have mandatory paid leave. In fact, the United States ranks last among industrialized countries in terms of paid leave laws (see Figure 8.5).

Some states and Washington, D.C., have passed mandatory paid maternity leave (California, New Jersey, New York, Rhode Island, and Washington) and sick leave (Arizona, California, Connecticut, Massachusetts, Oregon, Vermont, and Washington). City governments are also stepping in: Pittsburgh, Pennsylvania; Kansas City, Missouri;

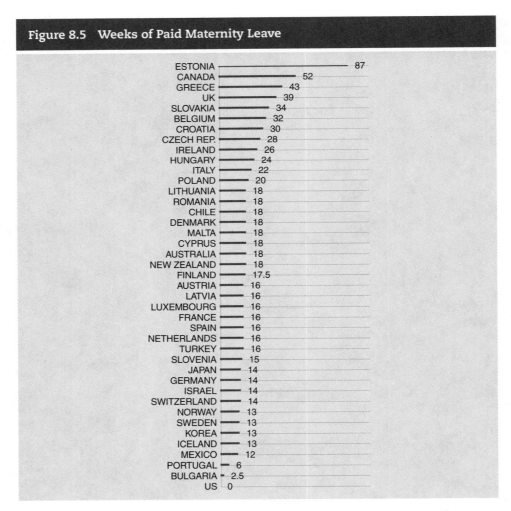

Figure 8.5   Weeks of Paid Maternity Leave

Country	Weeks
ESTONIA	87
CANADA	52
GREECE	43
UK	39
SLOVAKIA	34
BELGIUM	32
CROATIA	30
CZECH REP.	28
IRELAND	26
HUNGARY	24
ITALY	22
POLAND	20
LITHUANIA	18
ROMANIA	18
CHILE	18
DENMARK	18
MALTA	18
CYPRUS	18
AUSTRALIA	18
NEW ZEALAND	18
FINLAND	17.5
AUSTRIA	16
LATVIA	16
LUXEMBOURG	16
FRANCE	16
SPAIN	16
NETHERLANDS	16
TURKEY	16
SLOVENIA	15
JAPAN	14
GERMANY	14
ISRAEL	14
SWITZERLAND	14
NORWAY	13
SWEDEN	13
KOREA	13
ICELAND	13
MEXICO	12
PORTUGAL	6
BULGARIA	2.5
US	0

Source: OECD Family Database, https://www.oecd.org/els/soc/PF2_1_Parental_leave_systems.pdf.

Austin, Texas; New York City, New York; and Washington, D.C., all offer some form of paid parental leave.

The majority of workers who do have paid time off receive that benefit from their employer: About one third of all private businesses offer paid parental leave, and 68% offer paid sick leave to full-time workers. A greater number of private businesses have begun offering paid parental leave. In 2015 and 2016, Etsy, EY, Coca-Cola, American Express,[17] Facebook, Microsoft, Netflix, Johnson & Johnson, and Amazon, among others, announced paid parental leaves.[18] Hourly workers are hit the hardest by the lack of paid leave,[19] but many companies are changing their policies to reflect all workers' need for family leave: Starting in 2018, Walmart provides the same paid parental leave benefits for its full-time salary and hourly workers, as does Wells Fargo, JPMorgan Chase, and Amazon.[20]

The United States did make some movement toward a national leave policy, albeit unpaid. The **Family and Medical Leave Act (FMLA)** was the first law signed by President Clinton after his election in 1993. The law was designed to support working families in times of serious medical conditions. Under the FMLA, employees who work for an employer with 50 or more employees and have worked there for at least 1,250 hours for the preceding 12 months (about 24 hours a week) are entitled to 12 weeks of unpaid leave (the leave does not have to be taken all at once) for the birth, adoption, or foster care placement of a child; to care for themselves or their spouse, child, or parent with a serious medical condition; or any qualifying emergency situation arising out of the employee's spouse, child, or parent being on active military duty; or 26 weeks of leave to care for a covered service member's serious medical condition (military caregiver leave).

The eligibility requirements immediately disqualify 40% of the workforce from FMLA leave.[21] That figure does not include those workers who cannot afford unpaid leave. Most leave taken is for the employee's own illness (55%). Leave for pregnancy or a new child, and for illness of a spouse, child, or parent, is less common (21% and 18% respectively). Leave for other qualifying reasons, including military reasons, is quite rare (2%). Most leave is short. Nearly half of all leave events last 10 days or less (42%); less than a fifth (17%) last more than 60 days.[22]

> **Family and Medical Leave Act (FMLA):** Law designed to support working families in times of serious medical conditions.

KEY TAKEAWAYS

Workplace Protections

- Workers' Compensation, Social Security, and the FLSA provide eligible workers financial protections in case of injury, overtime, disability, and retirement.

- Under the NLRA, workers can join unions or simply work together to improve the terms or conditions of work.

- Although the United States does not have mandatory paid leave laws, FMLA provides 12 weeks of unpaid leave for the birth or adoption of a child, or the serious medical condition of the worker or their child.

EMPLOYEE PRIVACY

LO 8.4 Explore workplace privacy issues and how the use of technology may impact the employment relationship.

Technology is a paradox for workers: More methods of communication provide us flexibility as we no longer have to be in the office to get work done. On the other hand, more methods of communication also mean we are reachable 24/7. As a result, the line between work life and private life has become increasingly blurred; it can be difficult to see where one ends and the other begins. Think back to Chapter 5 when we learned about liability and invasion of privacy; now ask yourself this question: Do we give up our privacy when we take a job? In order to answer this, we must ask more questions. For example, do we work for the government or for private business? We know the constitution will control many aspects of our rights if we work for the government. If we work for a private business, do we use employer-provided services and devices such as e-mail, Internet access, servers, computers, tablets, smartphones, etc.? If we do, then chances are we do not have much privacy in the communications that take place using those services and devices.

CASE STUDY 8.3

Monitoring Employee's Personal Social Media

In 2016, 78% of Americans had a social media profile. Most of us really like using it: the majority of all U.S. Facebook (76%) and Instagram (51%) users say they visit the sites once a day. Employers like using social media too. According to a 2016 CareerBuilder survey, 60% of employers use social media sites to research job candidates, and 41% of employers said they use social media sites to research current employees.

Because we reveal so much about ourselves on them, social media sites have become reliable predictive tools for employers; they can find clues in online activity that may predict job success. For example, in a study of 100 college students, login frequency, duration, status updates, and photo sharing predicted the user's narcissistic tendencies off-line. In another study published in the *Journal of Applied Social Psychology*, researchers correlated the "Big Five" personality traits (conscientiousness, emotional stability, agreeableness, openness to experience, and extroversion) as judged from a subject's Facebook page with hireability and job performance. What makes this information more valuable to employers is the speed with which a reviewer can identify the personality traits. For the study, the researchers hired three evaluators: a 46-year-old man with 8 years of work experience and two 22-year-old college seniors proficient in Facebook. After a 2-hour training session, the evaluators spent an average of 5 minutes looking at a profile before assigning a Big Five trait and hireability rating called the Facebook score.

Discussion Questions

1. Think about your three most recent posts on social media: What traits could a potential employer learn by looking at and reading those posts? What else could they learn? Would you want your potential or current employer knowing that about you? Why or why not?

2. What sorts of positive things could an employer learn about someone from social media posts? Qualities or characteristics that might be beneficial to getting a job?

Critical Thinking

Some of what an employer learns by looking at a person's social media pages might be relevant to that person's on-duty potential, but much may not. What are some dangers for employers if they monitor employee social media use?

Another method of monitoring employees is using GPS to track their whereabouts. Tracking employees has many benefits for a business: It can make delivery and travel routes more efficient and ensure compliance with safety and overtime regulations. However, tracking employees can also cross the line into an illegal search or invasion of privacy. The Supreme Court addressed this issue in *U.S. v. Jones* and held that law enforcement installing a GPS device on a private individual's car, without a warrant, for purposes of tracking that individual and obtaining information about his whereabouts, constituted an illegal search under the Fourth Amendment.[23] Because the U.S. government is the largest employer in the United States, the *Jones* case has far-reaching implications.

CASE STUDY 8.4

GPS Tracking Apps

Many states have laws regarding using GPS devices to track employees, and it is well settled that when an employer attaches a GPS device to an employer-owned car, the employee driving that car cannot claim an invasion of privacy when the employer tracks their whereabouts.

What if your employer required you to download a GPS app to your smartphone? That is what happened in 2015 to Myrna Arias when she worked for Intermex Wire Transfer as a sales associate. Intermex is a money remittance service, moving money through wire transfers between 45 American states and 16 Latin American countries. In May 2014, Intermex asked Arias and other employees to download Xora onto their personal smartphones. Xora has a GPS function that allows users to track the phone's whereabouts. Arias asked John Stubits, the regional vice president, whether the app would be used to track employees off duty as Intermex employees had to keep their phones on around the clock to answer client calls. Stubits said that not only would they be tracked during nonwork hours but also that he could

see how fast Arias was driving at specific times. Arias objected to being tracked off duty and deleted Xora from her smartphone. The next month she was fired.

Arias sued Intermex for invasion of privacy and wrongful termination in violation of public policy. In November 2015, the parties settled the case out of court.

Discussion Questions

1. If you were the CEO of Intermex, why would you use a GPS app to track your employees? What risks are you trying to mitigate?

2. If you were an employee of Intermex, what concerns would you have about your employer's use of GPS to track your whereabouts?

Critical Thinking

What other stakeholders are impacted by whether a private business uses GPS to track employees' locations, on duty and off duty? Given your answers, how would you design a policy for GPS tracking?

KEY TAKEAWAYS

Employee Privacy

- Use of technology and more flexible work arrangements blur the line between work and personal life.

- If we use employer-provided technology, chances are the employer has a right to monitor activity on those devices.

SUMMARY

Understanding your rights and obligations both as an employee and as a supervisor or employer are crucial to effective management and sound decision-making. And because you will most likely need to make management decisions quickly, you will not always have the time (or the money) to seek legal advice. Spotting potential legal issues before they become a problem will save you time, money, and aggravation.

KEY TERMS

arbitration 179
bargaining unit 179
bounty program 168
collective bargaining agreement (CBA) 179
concerted activities 179
economic strikes 179
employee 164
employment at will 167
Fair Labor Standards Act (FLSA) 173
False Claims Act (FCA) 168
Family and Medical Leave Act (FMLA) 183
federal tipped minimum wage 176
free riders 179

grievance 179
independent contractor 164
independent contractor agreement 164
Internal Revenue Service (IRS) 168
lawful strikes 179
minimum wage 173
National Labor Relations Act (NLRA) 178
National Labor Relations Board (NLRB) 179
Office of the Whistleblower 168
portable benefits 166
pre-emption bills 173
public policy exceptions to employment at will 167

retaliation 168
right-to-work laws 179
Social Security 173
Social Security Act 173
statements of employment particulars 167
strikes 179
tip pooling 177
tipped employee 176
unfair labor practices 179
union 179
union security agreements 179
unlawful strike 179
whistleblower 167
workers' compensation 172

REVIEW QUESTIONS

1. What is the difference between an independent contractor and an employee?

2. Explain employment at will and how whistleblowers are protected under federal laws.

3. How do workers' compensation, the FLSA, and the NLRA provide protection for workers?

4. What is the FMLA? What protections does it provide, and how effective is the law?

MANAGER'S CHALLENGE

Hiring in a Start-Up

Parking in the city where you live is tight. You and your roommate are developing an app that helps users locate empty parking spaces in your city and reserve an empty spot. In order to have a complete picture of parking in the city, you need people to help you map the city and parking spaces, and programmers to help you write code for the app. As with many start-ups, funding for your business is limited; you are hoping as you make progress, more investors will become interested. Your first priority is to hire the right people to help you get your business off the ground.

Framing Questions

1. What are the pros and cons of classifying those you hire as independent contractors or employees?

2. Given your answer to Question 1, is there a way to structure your hiring so that some workers are employees and others independent contractors? If so, who will be which and why?

Assignment

Draft a strategy memo for the company outlining your hiring model that includes an independent contractor agreement and accounts for your goal of creating longer-term employment relationships and a happy and productive workplace.

MANAGING A DIVERSE WORKFORCE

Learning Objectives

Upon completion of this chapter, the reader should be able to do the following:

9.1. Understand the difference between diversity and inclusion.

9.2. Discuss bias and discrimination and how both impact managing diverse teams and legal risk.

9.3. Discuss the framework of intersectionality and how this perspective impacts management decisions.

9.4 Analyze the legal prohibitions on discrimination and how they can shape decision-making.

Ethics in Context

Bias in Online Job Postings

Over 2 billion people use Facebook every month. If you were a business with a job to fill, listing that position on Facebook is a good place to start. The social media platform collects data on users while they are on the platform, on Instagram, or on other apps, allowing businesses to specifically target their audience for the listing. Why pay to have your posting for an entry-level customer service representative shown to grandmothers and grandfathers who would never apply for that position? Microtargeting can be an efficient use of a limited recruitment budget but can also cross the line into unlawful discrimination. Later in the chapter, in the Ethics in Context section, we will explore the impact of Facebook's microtargeting feature when used to exclude certain age groups from learning of employment opportunities.

iStockphoto.com/luchezar

INTRODUCTION

The benefits of diversity are many: Research shows that diverse groups are more innovative[1] and more productive.[2] A diverse workforce may better reflect the experiences of customers and improve the educational experience of college students because students see faculty like themselves. Companies now stress diversity and inclusion in their recruiting practices in order to attract the best talent and foster an inclusive and welcoming culture in order to keep that talent. According to global health care company Eli Lilly, diversity means "understanding, respecting, and valuing differences."[3] Israeli sparkling water company SodaStream promotes "diversity by connecting people from various ethnic, religious, and social-economic backgrounds."[4] Managing diverse teams presents unique challenges and opportunities. Understanding the laws that apply can help managers fulfill their responsibilities and employees know their rights.

DIVERSITY AND INCLUSION

LO 9.1   Understand the difference between diversity and inclusion.

Diversity includes all differences, not just the categories protected by law—race, gender, color, national origin, religion, age, and disability (see Figure 9.1)—but also diversity of background, experience, opinion, and culture. Companies embrace diversity not just to satisfy the law but also to create a competitive advantage. Research shows that having a diverse workforce can increase productivity and profitability.[5] Consulting firm McKinsey has found a global link between gender and ethnic diversity and profitability.[6] A 2017 Boston Consulting Group study found that diverse teams produce 19% more revenue and develop more relevant products because they are more in tune with customer needs.[7]

Creating a diverse workforce is an intentional work in progress; businesses need to keep assessing and adjusting to get the most impact. But a diverse workforce is not enough; creating a workplace where diverse employees feel welcome and want to stay is equally important. An inclusive workplace means a workplace that makes all people feel welcome and helps them thrive. Diversity is who is sitting around the table, and **inclusion** is how you

diversity: A reflection of all differences in people, not just the categories protected by law—race, gender, color, national origin, religion, age, and disability—but also including culture, background, and experience.

inclusion: A workplace that makes all people feel welcome and helps them thrive.

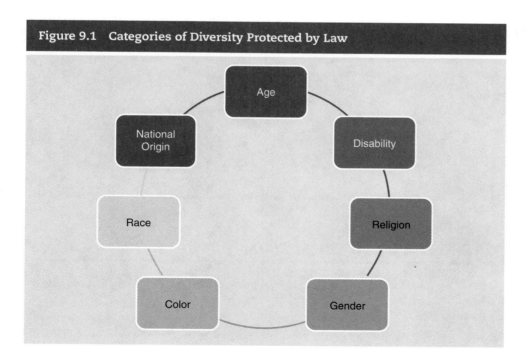

Figure 9.1   Categories of Diversity Protected by Law

Figure 9.2 Tips for Managing a Diverse Workforce

- Do the hard work of learning about your team rather than burdening them with teaching you.

- Listen to the experiences of your staff working in your organization, and work to examine any negative feedback.

- Use consisent training and education around diversity and inclusion so that staff are always learning and growing.

embrace those people and motivate them to produce results. Many management experts believe the more inclusive the workplace, the more attractive it will be for diverse talent.[8] According to Harvard professor Francesca Gino, although our decisions are impacted by biases, "it's possible to change the context of decisions by architecting the composition of decision-making teams for more diverse perspectives."[9]

One of the many benefits of diversity is that there is no magic formula; every team will look unique. This can also make managing diverse teams challenging. Reaping the most benefit from diverse teams and an inclusive workplace culture requires a long-term commitment from leadership, including leading by example. Inclusivity, making different people feel welcome and able to thrive, comes down to management style and good decision-making. Figure 9.2 offers some tips for managing a diverse workforce.

KEY TAKEAWAYS

Diversity and Inclusion

- Diversity is more than just racial and gender differences; it also includes diversity of backgrounds, experiences, and cultures.

- Diversity is not successful without also creating an inclusive workplace—

somewhere people feel welcome and able to thrive.

- Productivity and profitability increase with more diverse teams.

BIAS AND DISCRIMINATION

LO 9.2 Discuss bias and discrimination and how both impact managing diverse teams and legal risk.

While on a flight from Detroit to Houston, a passenger became unresponsive. His wife screamed for help, and the flight crew asked for a doctor. When Dr. Tamika Cross raised her hand, the flight attendant said, "Oh wow, you're an actual doctor? Let me see your credentials." Dr. Cross, who is African American, told the flight attendant that she was an obstetrician–gynecologist but did not show any credentials. A white male passenger approached the flight attendant and said he was also a doctor but did not show any credentials either. The flight attendant told Dr. Cross, "Thanks for your help, but he can help us, and he has credentials."[10]

Dr. Cross described her experience in a Facebook post that was shared more than 38,000 times and spawned the hashtag #Whatdoctorslooklike. Many comments were by minority professionals who shared their experiences fighting assumptions about their qualifications.[11]

Everyone has biases; it is unavoidable as a human being. Most of us understand what our biases are; however, science has shown that we also have unconscious biases.[i] Unconscious bias, known as **implicit bias**, includes our stereotypes and attitudes that affect our understanding in an unconscious way. A **stereotype** is framework through which we judge other people based on their social category, such as age, gender, or ethnicity, and then we view that person as interchangeable with any other person in that category. When we stereotype, we lose sight of the individual. We are all susceptible to implicit biases—even those whose job it is to be impartial, such as judges. The trouble arises because we all want to see ourselves as good people, not someone who would make a decision based on an unfair bias. But, according to research, the human reflex is to maintain our identity as a good person, regardless of whether we actually do good things. This impulse makes it hard for us to recognize when we do bad things.[12] **Discrimination** arises when we act on our biases and stereotypes—whether that means not sitting next to someone on the train, treating customers differently, or holding someone to higher standards than others. While our implicit biases and stereotypes may not align with our conscious beliefs, discrimination can have very real-world implications in areas such as criminal justice; education; and, as we will discuss here, employment.

> **implicit bias:** Stereotypes and attitudes that affect our understanding in an unconscious way.
>
> **stereotype:** Framework through which we judge other people based on their social category, such as age, gender, or ethnicity.
>
> **discrimination:** Acting on our biases and stereotypes in decision-making.

KEY TAKEAWAYS

Bias and Discrimination

- Implicit biases can infect decision-making in an unconscious way.

- Discrimination happens when we act on our biases or stereotypes, which leads to decisions that do not align with our values and beliefs.

---

[i] To test your inclination for different kinds of unconscious biases, take the Implicit Association Test at https://implicit.harvard.edu/implicit/education.html.

INTERSECTIONALITY

LO 9.3 Discuss the framework of intersectionality and how this perspective impacts management decisions.

Employees do not fall into just one category; we are not just our gender, or our race, or our religion (or absence of religion). We are all of those things and more and thus can be impacted by discrimination and bias on more than one level. **Intersectionality** recognizes that identities do not exist independently from each other—e.g., "woman" and "Jewish" for a Jewish woman—and therefore, bias can be more complex and informed by multiple issues.

Columbia law professor Kimberlé Crenshaw first coined the term *intersectionality* in 1989 in an article she wrote describing the reality of African American women in both feminist and antiracist politics. According to Crenshaw, based on case law and theory at the time, the standard for racism and racial discrimination was based on the black man's experiences. Similarly, in gender discrimination case law and feminist theory, the standard was the white woman's experience. African American women did not fit into either category. Crenshaw used intersectionality as a framework for understanding how different identities lead to different experiences of bias and discrimination.[13]

An easy way to see how intersectionality works is by looking at pay disparities. Disparities in pay exist, called the **pay gap**. While many factors contribute to the pay gap, such as education, experience, seniority, and industry, once you control for all of the differences, a pay gap exists between men and women. But the gap is not the same for all women, and not all men are paid the same. According to the 2017 Gender Wage Gap report from the Institute for Women's Policy Research,[14] the pay disparity breakdown is as follows.

- White man: $1.00

- Asian woman: $.85

- White woman: $.77

- Black man: $.74

- Black woman: $.61

- Native American woman: $.58

- Latina: $.53

The differences make it clear that gender is not the only issue facing most people when it comes to equal pay. Thus, while all women earn less than white men, a black woman's experience is different than a Latina's experience, which is different than a white woman's experience. Intersectionality helps us recognize that our multiple levels of identity can shape our experiences and treatment. A manager trying to create an inclusive culture, encourage and maintain a productive team, and comply with the law must understand how intersectionality impacts her employees.

intersectionality: Identities do not exist independently from each other, and our multidimensional identities shape our experiences of bias and discrimination.

pay gap: Disparities in pay.

Gender Pay Equity

According to the Institute for Women's Policy Research, women make up almost half of the U.S. workforce. In addition, they are the sole or co-breadwinner in half of American families with children, and they receive more college and undergraduate degrees than men. Yet on average in 2017, full-time, year-round working women earned less than 80 cents for every dollar earned by men.

The tech industry has come under increasing scrutiny over its pay practices. In January 2017, the U.S. Department of Labor (DOL) filed suit against Google over the tech company's failure to turn over compensation data requested by the DOL. Google is a federal contractor, which means it must allow the DOL to inspect and copy records about its compliance with equal opportunity laws. As part of a compliance review, the DOL requested employee compensation data from Google, and while the company did turn over many documents, it did not fully comply with the request. Based on the documents it did supply, the DOL claims that Google has "systemic compensation disparities against women." Google disagrees with this conclusion and in a blog post stated that it conducts rigorous analyses of its pay practices and claims it has closed the gender pay gap globally among its workforce.

The same year, Google was also in the news for the "Google Memo," written by former Google software engineer James Damore. Among the many topics in his memo, Damore rationalized much of the pay gap at Google, and in the tech industry more broadly, using gender stereotypes based on bias and unproven science, such as women do not take high stress jobs because they are too anxious. There is a link to the full memo on the student companion website: http://edge.sagepub.com/clark1e.

Google is not alone in facing scrutiny over pay equity. In September 2016, the DOL filed suit against Palantir, a data analytics firm, alleging it systematically discriminated against Asian job applicants. And in January 2017, the department sued Oracle, claiming it paid white men more than others, which led to pay discrimination against women and black and Asian employees.

The focus on pay equity is coming from many different directions. Shareholders at Apple, Microsoft, and Intel have submitted shareholder proposals that ask the companies to show their commitment to gender pay equity. In 2017 in response to a proposal submitted by Arjuna Capital, Starbucks released data on gender and pay that, according to Starbucks, showed that women and men who perform substantially similar work at the company are paid within 99.7% of each other. In 2018, the company announced it has reached 100% pay equity.

State and city legislatures are passing their own strict gender pay laws. In 2016, Massachusetts became the first state in the country to pass a law prohibiting employers from asking applicants about their salary history until after they make an offer that includes compensation. This law also requires that employers pay men and women the same not just when they do the same work, but also when their work is comparable.

California's Fair Pay Act, passed in 2016, prohibits employers from paying men and women differently for substantially similar work. In 2017, a provision of the act went into effect that requires employers to do the same between one race or ethnicity and those of another. In 2017, New York governor Andrew Cuomo signed two executive orders toughening pay equality: The first requires state contractors to regularly disclose job titles and salary information, and the other prevents state agencies from asking about salary history prior to making a job offer. Other states, like Alabama, make it illegal to refuse to interview, hire, employ, or promote a person based on their refusal to provide their salary history. While in cities like New Orleans, Louisiana, and Louisville, Kentucky, city departments cannot ask applicants about their salary history.

Discussion Questions

1. How do the laws in Massachusetts, California, and New York differ from the federal law?

2. Why pass a law banning asking about salary history? How does that help reduce the gender pay gap?

(Continued)

(Continued)

Critical Thinking

In 2019, 28 members of the world champion U.S. women's soccer team who sued their employer, U.S. Soccer, for gender discrimination. The players claim that not only were they paid less than the men's soccer team but they were also treated less favorably when it came to where and how often they played, how they train, medical treatment and coaching, and how they travel to matches. Direct comparison between men's and women's pay is difficult because each team has their own collective bargaining agreement (CBA) and the structures are different, but most agree the women's team has been outperforming the men's team for years. One discrepancy that is easy to see is the World Cup payout: Total prize money for women in 2019 was $30 million, split among the teams. Our 2019 U.S. women's champion team took $4 million. For men, the 2018 total payout was $400 million, the winning team getting $38 million. U.S. Soccer claims the difference in pay is because FIFA, the sport's global governing body, sets the World Cup payout pools, and U.S. Soccer merely passes the money along to the players.

If U.S. Soccer's defense is successful, what will be the impact on U.S. Women's Soccer? Does their defense address all of the women's claims? Why or why not? Can you think of other industries and jobs where such a defense might impact gender pay disparities?

KEY TAKEAWAYS

Intersectionality

- The framework of intersectionality helps us see others' experiences through the multiple dimensions of their identity.

- Understanding intersectionality helps managers make more informed decisions about workplace policies, leading to a more inclusive workplace.

LAWS TO PROTECT AGAINST DISCRIMINATION

LO 9.4 Analyze the legal prohibitions on discrimination and how they can shape decision-making.

While diversity and inclusion involve more than what the law requires, the law plays a critical role in workplace policies and treatment of employees. Today's diversity policies have their roots in prohibited discrimination based on race, gender, color, religion, national origin, age, and disability in all facets of employment. As we discussed, acting on biases may result in unlawful discrimination. In the 1960s, Congress passed three laws aimed at dispelling stereotypes and biases: the Equal Pay Act, the Civil Rights Act, and the Age Discrimination in Employment Act (ADEA). Together, the goal of these laws was to break down barriers and increase opportunity for participation in American life and the workforce.

Equal Pay Act

The **Equal Pay Act** was passed in 1963 at a time when women earned 60 cents for every $1 earned by a man. The law requires that men and women be paid equally for equal work. Pay includes salary, bonuses, stock options, vacation and holiday pay, travel reimbursements, and the like. Equal work does not mean identical work. To show **equal work**, one needs to show that the job content (not job title) is substantially similar in skill, effort, and responsibility.

Title VII of the Civil Rights Act

Among the most important achievements of the civil rights movement in the United States was the passage of the Civil Rights Act of 1964. This act, and its later amendments, banned segregation based on race, religion, color, national origin, and gender in public places like parks, restaurants, courts, hotels, and sports arenas. It also prohibited the use of federal money for any discriminatory purpose; prohibited unequal voting requirements; and insured equal opportunity in education, housing, and financing. **Title VII of the Civil Rights Act** prohibits discrimination based on race, religion, sex, national origin, or color in all facets of employment.[ii] Think broadly when considering all facets of employment—not only hiring and firing but also recruiting, applying for a job, promoting, demoting, having access to opportunities, receiving work assignments, and the like. The law also established a new federal agency, the **Equal Employment Opportunity Commission (EEOC)**, with the authority to investigate claims of employment discrimination, mediate disputes, and sue on behalf of injured parties.

Many countries have antidiscrimination laws. The Mexican Federal Labor Law (MFLL) prohibits discrimination in employment based on more protected categories than Title VII: race, nationality, sexual preference, immigration condition, religion, civil status, social condition, age, gender, and disability.[15] Similarly, the French Labor Code prohibits discrimination in employment based on origin, gender, sexual orientation, morals, age, marital status, religious beliefs, nationality, ethnic or racial origin, political opinions, trade union activity, physical appearance, name, medical condition, or disability.[16]

There are several different legal claims under Title VII. **Disparate treatment** is intentionally treating someone less favorably because of their protected trait. For example, in 2018, there were 12 women executives at Wells Fargo Bank who reported that although equally qualified, they were denied promotions based on their gender.[17] An employer can defend their decision by proving there was a legitimate, nondiscriminatory reason for the treatment, such as the women were not equally qualified because they did not meet certain sales goals required of all candidates for promotion. For an employee to win, they must show the reason was a pretext for discrimination—the real reason was because of their gender.

In a **disparate impact** claim, the worker is saying there is a rule or policy that doesn't look discriminatory, but in practice, it discriminates against a group of people based on a protected trait. For example, in 1965, Duke Power instituted a policy requiring all applicants for certain positions to have a high school diploma or passing scores on an intelligence test. The impact of this new policy was that far fewer black workers met the requirement as they were much less likely, at the time, to have a high school diploma and scored worse on the test.

Equal Pay Act: Passed in 1963, it requires that men and women be paid equally for equal work. Pay includes salary, bonuses, stock options, vacation and holiday pay, travel reimbursements, and the like.

equal work: Means the job content (not job title) is substantially similar in skill, effort, and responsibility.

Title VII of the Civil Rights Act: Prohibits discrimination based on race, religion, sex, national origin, or color in all facets of employment.

Equal Employment Opportunity Commission (EEOC): Created by Title VII, it is a federal agency with the authority to investigate claims of employment discrimination, mediate disputes, and sue on behalf of injured parties.

disparate treatment: Legal claim under Title VII, ADEA, and ADA; intentionally treating someone less favorably because of their protected trait.

disparate impact: Legal claim under Title VII, ADEA, and ADA; when a rule or policy doesn't look discriminatory, but in practice it discriminates against a group of people based on a protected trait.

[ii] The word *title* in this case refers to a subset of a larger law. The Civil Rights Act contains 11 titles. For an overview of each title, see http://www.loc.gov/exhibits/civil-rights-act/epilogue.html

Figure 9.3 Disparate Treatment Versus Disparate Impact

Disparate Treatment	Disparate Impact
• The employee was treated differently because of a protected trait. • The employer claims there was a legitimate, nondiscriminatory reason for the treatment. • The employee shows that reason is a pretext for discrimination.	• A neutral work policy or rule adversely impacts a disproportionate number of employees based on a protected trait. • The employer claims the work policy or rule is job related. • The employee shows that policy or rule is a pretext for discrimination or that there is a less discriminatory way of achieving the same result.

Moreover, the new requirements had nothing to do with measuring a worker's ability to perform the job. As a result, the sought-after positions went to white workers. African American workers at the plant sued, claiming the requirements were discriminatory and violated Title VII. The Supreme Court agreed; while Title VII does not prohibit the use of relevant testing, the tests must measure "the person for the job and not the person in the abstract."[18] Otherwise, such tests would serve as an unnecessary obstacle to employment opportunity that is based on discrimination. Figure 9.3 highlights the difference between disparate treatment and disparate impact.

In passing Title VII, Congress "made the simple but momentous announcement" that race, color, national origin, religion, and gender could not be factors in employment decisions. The goal of Title VII was to take characteristics that had nothing to do with a person's ability to do a job out of that process, forcing the decision-maker to focus on qualifications only. But decision-making is a complicated process, fraught with unconscious bias and other influences like stereotypes. However, Title VII protects individuals from discrimination; thus, acting on stereotypes may lead to legal liability. Although Congress has amended Title VII over the years to include pregnancy and age discrimination, courts have spoken about the dangers of stereotyping.

CASE STUDY 9.2

Stereotypes and Discrimination

In 1989, the U.S. Supreme Court heard Ann Hopkins's case against her employer Price Waterhouse (*Price Waterhouse v. Ann Hopkins*; Price Waterhouse now known as PriceWaterhouseCoopers [PwC]).[19] Ms. Hopkins worked at Price Waterhouse 5 years before partners proposed her for promotion. Of the 88 people proposed for partnership, Ms. Hopkins was the only woman. At the time at Price Waterhouse, candidates for promotion were proposed to a committee, who then decided which candidate to rec-ommend to the Policy Board. The Policy Board then voted, without any guidelines or objective criteria, either to promote, reject, or put on hold the candidate's application. Many believed Ms. Hopkins was an ideal candidate for partner: She worked diligently over 2 years to secure a $25 million contract with the State Department; no other candidate for partner had such an accomplishment. Clients loved her work, describing Ms. Hopkins as "extremely competent, intelligent…productive, energetic and creative."

Ms. Hopkins worked long hours, met deadlines, and had high expectations of her team. However, some staff members described Ms. Hopkins as abrasive, unduly harsh, and difficult to work with. Some of these comments were issues long before Ms. Hopkins was recommended for promotion. The committee, in their written comments passed on to the Policy Board, described Ms. Hopkins as "macho" and "overcompensating for being a woman." Some suggested she take a course in charm school, criticized her use of profanity because a lady should not swear, and noted that she had "matured" from being a tough-talking masculine manager into a "much more appealing lady ptr [sic] candidate." In explaining why her candidacy was put on hold, partner Thomas Beyer said to Hopkins that she should "walk more femininely, talk more femininely, dress more femininely, wear make-up, have her hair styled, and wear jewelry."

Ms. Hopkins sued for gender discrimination in violation of Title VII. According to the U.S. Supreme Court, while an employer may not take gender into account in employment decisions, it is free to decide against a woman for other, legitimate reasons. However, as in this case, an employer who acts on the belief that a woman cannot or should not be aggressive has acted on the basis of gender. "We are long beyond the day when an employer could evaluate employees by assuming or insisting that they matched the stereotype associated with their group." The Court held that in prohibiting discrimination based on gender, Congress meant to eliminate all forms of discrimination including that resulting from sex stereotypes. An employer who holds aggressiveness against a woman, yet the position requires this quality, puts women in an impossible situation: out of a job if they are aggressive and out of a job if they are not. According to the Court, it doesn't take a psychologist to understand that if an employee's interpersonal skills can be fixed with lipstick and a pastel suit, it is her gender and not her interpersonal skills that has drawn the criticism.

In 1995, Antonio Sanchez sued his employer, Azteca Restaurant Enterprises, for gender discrimination for a "relentless campaign of insults, name-calling, and vulgarities" over the course of the 4 years he worked at the restaurant (*Nichols v. Azteca Restaurant Enterprises, Inc.*).[20] According to Sanchez, his male coworkers and a supervisor repeatedly called him "she" and "her" both in English and Spanish, mocked him for walking and carrying his tray "like a woman," called him "f*gg*t" and a "f**ing female wh*re." This conduct happened at least every day. According to Sanchez, the abuse was based on the perception that he is effeminate and failed to conform to a male stereotype, and therefore was based on his sex. According to the court, the *Price Waterhouse* case applies equally to a man who is discriminated against for acting too feminine as it is to a woman who acts too masculine. In finding for Sanchez, the court held that the systematic abuse he endured reflected his coworkers' belief that he did not act as a man should act and had, according to them, feminine mannerisms. Thus, the conduct was because of Sanchez's gender.

In 2002, the same court made a similar ruling in a case against the MGM Grand Hotel (*Rene v. MGM Grand Hotel, Inc.*).[21] In that case, Medina Rene worked for the hotel as a butler on the 29th floor, serving high-end and famous guests. All of the workers on the 29th floor, including his supervisor, were men. Rene, an openly gay man, testified that he endured harassment by his coworkers such as whistling; blowing kisses; calling him "sweetheart"; telling crude, sexually oriented jokes; and even physical conduct of a sexual nature such as hugging, grabbing his crotch, and poking their fingers in his anus through his clothing. Rene believed the harassment was because he was gay. When he sued the hotel, the district court dismissed his complaint because discrimination based on sexual orientation is not protected under Title VII. The appellate court saw it differently. According to the appellate court, Rene's harassers "did not grab his elbow or poke their fingers in his eye"; they grabbed his crotch and poked their fingers in his anus. This conduct is clearly of a sexual nature. It has long been held that the physical sexual assault of a woman is sexual harassment under Title VII. In no case did the court ask whether the victim was a lesbian because her sexual orientation was irrelevant. If sexual orientation is irrelevant for a female victim, it is also irrelevant for a male victim. It is clear the harassment Rene suffered was because of his sex; "why the harassment was perpetrated is beside the point."

Aimee Stephens also faced discrimination by her employer because of her gender. Ms. Stephens
(*Continued*)

(Continued)

was born biologically male.[22] While presenting as a man, she worked for Thomas Rost, owner of R.G. & G.R. Harris Funeral Homes, as a funeral director from 2008 to 2013. In July 2013, Ms. Stephens gave Rost a letter explaining her struggle with gender identity and that she intended to have sex reassignment surgery. The first step in that process is to live openly as a female for 1 year. Several days later, Rost fired Ms. Stephens because "he was no longer going to represent himself as a man. He wanted to dress as a woman" and stating to Ms. Stephens that "this is not going to work out."

Ms. Stephens filed a gender discrimination claim. According to the court, although transgendered status is not a protected category under Title VII, Ms. Stephens does have a claim that she was fired for failing to conform to the funeral home's gender stereotypes. In relying on the *Price Waterhouse* case, the court stated that gender must be irrelevant to employment decisions, and failure to conform to gender stereotypes was no less prohibited than discrimination based on the biological differences between women and men. Here, Rost admitted that he didn't fire Ms. Stephens for any performance-related issues but that she no longer was going to represent as a man. Transgender discrimination, said the court, "is based on the non-conformance of an individual's gender identity and appearance with sex-based norms and expectations." Thus, discrimination because of a person's transgendered status is always based on gender stereotypes. The funeral home appealed this case up to the U.S. Supreme Court, but in 2019 the Supreme Court refused to hear the case; therefore, the lower court decision stands.

Discussion Questions

1. At trial, Rost testified that he worried if Ms. Stephens presented as a woman that she would cause a distraction and inhibit Rost's ability to serve families in their time of need. The EEOC claimed that this assumption was based on presumed bias. What do you think of Rost's argument? What is the presumed bias the EEOC is worried about? What if, instead, Ms. Stephens were African American and Rost made the same argument?

2. Rost also claimed that based on his Christian beliefs, he sincerely believes that a person's sex is an "immutable God-given gift and that it is wrong for a person to deny his or her God-given sex." Thus, said Rost, he could not be forced to allow Ms. Stephens to work at the funeral home and allow her to dress as a woman. The court said that while Rost may have sincere religious beliefs about gender, tolerating her understanding of her gender identity and sex is not the same thing as endorsing it. What does that mean? Provide other examples of this: Tolerating something does not mean endorsing it.

Critical Thinking

One judge in *Rene* stated that in the *Nichols* case it was clear Mr. Sanchez was being treated differently because he supposedly did not meet the masculine stereotypes of his coworkers. However, in *Rene*, Mr. Rene made it clear that he was discriminated against because he is gay, not because he failed to meet a stereotype. Regardless of how distasteful and unfortunate his treatment may have been, sexual orientation is not a protected category under Title VII. If sexual orientation is to be protected under the law, only Congress can make that change, not the courts. Did the holding in the *Price Waterhouse* case open the door for interpretation of "stereotype," or is the court exceeding its power and creating new protected categories? Explain your answer.

Harassment

Not long after Brittany Hoyos started her job at McDonald's, her manager began touching her hair and texting her about her appearance and even tried to kiss her after offering her a ride home. Ms. Hoyos was 16 years old at the time and told her parents about the conduct. When her parents complained to Ms. Hoyos's supervisor, Ms. Hoyos claims she was demoted from her position as a crew trainer.[23] Ms. Hoyos sued McDonald's for sexual harassment. **Harassment** is a form of discrimination and prohibited by Title VII. Harassment includes unwelcome conduct that is based on a protected category, when enduring the conduct becomes a condition of your job, or the conduct is so severe or pervasive that it creates a work environment that a reasonable person would find intimidating or abusive.[24] This does not include petty slights, annoying coworkers, or lack of manners. The U.S. Supreme Court tells us that Title VII is not a "general civility code for the American workplace"[25] and only conduct that is so abusive and intimidating that it alters the conditions of work is actionable. And that conduct must be based on a protected category. Ms. Hoyos sued McDonald's for **sexual harassment**, which is harassment based on gender and can include unwelcome sexual advances, requests for sexual favors, and other verbal or physical conduct of a sexual nature.[26] Like with harassment based on the other protected categories, sexual harassment becomes actionable when enduring the conduct becomes a condition of your job or rejection of the request or advances is used against you, or the conduct is so severe or pervasive that it creates a work environment that a reasonable person would find intimidating or abusive.

Similar to the United States, the French Labor Code prohibits sexual harassment. But the French law also prohibits "moral harassment." Moral harassment at work became a recognized condition in 1998 when a book published by psychiatrist Marie-France Hirigoyen stated that it "is possible to destroy a person with words, looks, and innuendos."[27] At work, moral harassment is defined as "any abusive conduct, in particular behavior, words, actions, gestures, or texts capable of violating the personality, dignity, or physical or psychological integrity of a person, jeopardizing their employment, or deteriorating the working environment."[28] Figure 9.4 compares harassment and sexual harassment.

Ms. Hoyos also sued McDonald's for retaliation when the company demoted her after her parents complained about her treatment. Retaliation under Title VII includes

harassment: Includes unwelcome conduct that is based on a protected category. Becomes discrimination prohibited by law when enduring the conduct becomes a condition of the job or is so severe or pervasive that it creates a work environment that a reasonable person would find intimidating or abusive.

sexual harassment: Harassment based on gender; includes unwelcome sexual advances, requests for sexual favors, and other verbal of physical conduct of a sexual nature.

Figure 9.4 Harassment Versus Sexual Harassment

Harassment	Sexual Harassment
• Unwelcome conduct	• Unwelcome sexual advances, requests for sexual favors, or other verbal or physical conduct of a sexual nature
• Based on a protected category	
• When enduring it becomes a condition of your job	• When enduring it becomes a condition of your job or rejection is used against you
• Conduct is so severe or pervasive that it creates a hostile work environment	• Conduct is so severe or pervasive that it creates a hostile work environment

punishing or in any way discouraging someone from asserting their rights under the law or resisting discrimination. This can include not only complaining about discriminatory behavior you experienced but also refusing to participate in such behavior, intervening to protect others, answering questions during an investigation, or requesting an accommodation.[29]

Religion

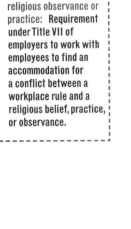

reasonably accommodate a religious observance or practice: Requirement under Title VII of employers to work with employees to find an accommodation for a conflict between a workplace rule and a religious belief, practice, or observance.

When it comes to religion under Title VII, it is not just our religious beliefs that are protected but also our religious practices and observances. However, some room is given to employers if a religious practice or observance interferes with the workplace. Thus, under the law, an employer must **reasonably accommodate a religious observance or practice** unless doing so would cause an undue hardship to the employer. For example, a worker claims her eyebrow piercing is part of her religion even though it violates the company's dress code. The employer has an obligation to offer a reasonable accommodation, perhaps keeping the piercing in but covering it up with a bandage, or replacing the piercing with a clear plastic retainer.[30] This conversation must be an interactive process—both the employer and the employee trying to reach a compromise (see Figure 9.5). If the employee refuses those accommodations, her employer most likely can fire or otherwise discipline her for failing to comply with the company dress code. The employer need only offer a reasonable accommodation, not the employee's first choice.

A dress or grooming code can be helpful in establishing a brand image such as a uniform with the company logo on it or suits and close-toed shoes. However, they can also raise discrimination issues if not written clearly and enforced consistently. The Law and Society 9.1 section is an example of a conflict between a dress code meant to reflect the "look" of the brand and religion.

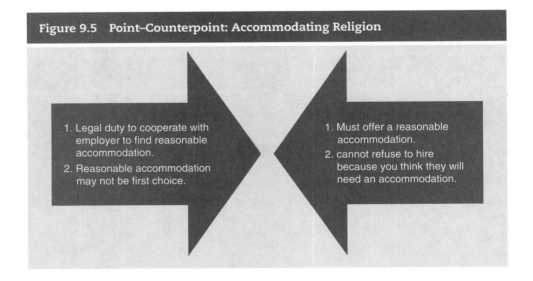

Figure 9.5   Point–Counterpoint: Accommodating Religion

1. Legal duty to cooperate with employer to find reasonable accommodation.
2. Reasonable accommodation may not be first choice.

1. Must offer a reasonable accommodation.
2. cannot refuse to hire because you think they will need an accommodation.

EEOC v. Abercrombie & Fitch Stores, Inc., 135 S. CT. 2028 (2015)

Facts: Abercrombie & Fitch (A&F) operates a chain of retail stores with a certain "look." Consistent with this look, A&F imposes a "look policy" on its employees: They must dress a certain way so as to positively reflect the brand and the "look." The look policy prohibits "caps," which is not defined in the policy, because they are considered too informal.

Samantha Elauf is a practicing Muslim, and in accordance with her religious requirements, she wears a head scarf. Elauf applied for a position at A&F and was interviewed by Heather Cooke, the store's assistant manager. According to the usual A&F system for scoring applicants, Elauf scored high enough to be hired. Concerned that Elauf's head scarf conflicted with the company's look policy, Cooke asked her manager whether the headscarf was a "cap." The manager could not answer the question, so Cooke asked the district manager, Randall Johnson, telling him that she believed Elauf wore the head scarf for religious purposes. Johnson informed Cooke that the head scarf, like any other headwear, would violate the look policy and told Cooke not to hire Elauf.

The EEOC sued A&F on Elauf's behalf, claiming the store refused to hire Elauf because of her religion in violation of Title VII. A&F claimed they could not be liable for intentionally discriminating against Elauf because she never told them that she would need an accommodation, in this case an exemption from the look policy.

Issue: Is an employer liable for disparate treatment even if an applicant does not inform them of their need for an accommodation?

Decision: Yes. An applicant only needs to show that their need for an accommodation was a motivating factor in the employer's decision not to hire them. The disparate treatment claim prohibits certain *motives*, regardless of whether the employer has actual knowledge. Thus, an employer who acts with the motive of avoiding accommodating an employee violates Title VII even if he only has a suspicion, and no actual knowledge, of that employee's need for an accommodation. Here, A&F knew Elauf wore a head scarf for religious purposes; it is irrelevant whether they knew this because Elauf told them or another A&F employee told her manager. A&F cannot make Elauf's religious practice, confirmed or otherwise, a factor in employment decisions.

Law and Management Questions

1. Many employment lawsuits are triggered by bad management: managers treating workers with disrespect or unprofessionally. If you were Cooke's manager or the district manager, how would you have handled this situation?

2. According to the Court, it is clear that the A&F manager's actions were unlawful. Few management decisions are clear, however. What should the owner of a bakery do if a Christian employee says that she cannot work on Sundays to observe her Sabbath, but Sundays are the bakery's busiest days?

Age Discrimination in Employment Act

In 1967, Congress passed the **Age Discrimination in Employment Act (ADEA)** to address unfounded assumptions and biases that age impacted a person's ability to do a job. The law requires an employer to look at an individual's ability rather than rely on assumptions about age more generally when making employment decisions. Today's older workers

Age Discrimination in Employment Act (ADEA): Passed in 1967, prohibits discrimination based on age (40 years old and older). Allows for disparate treatment, disparate impact, and harassment claims.

are far more educated and diverse than those in 1967; they are healthier and working and living longer. Age discrimination impacts all kinds of workers: white-collar, blue-collar, service and tech industries, and in rural and urban areas of the country. And despite research disproving a connection between age and ability, many employers still default to outdated stereotypes about older workers.[31]

In many ways, the ADEA was modeled on Title VII of the Civil Rights Act: The goal is to eliminate discrimination, and its prohibitions were taken verbatim from Title VII, including a narrow exception for a bona fide occupational qualification. Under the law, workers over 40 years old are protected from discrimination based on age in all facets of employment. Like Title VII, the ADEA provides *disparate treatment*, *disparate impact*, and *harassment* claims. Importantly, discrimination can occur even when both workers are over 40, and the law does not protect workers under age 40.[32] One difference between Title VII and the ADEA arises in a disparate impact claim. As we know, under Title VII if an employee alleges that a work policy or rule adversely impacts a disproportionate number of members of a protected class, the employer can defend its rule by showing that it is job-related. In 2008, the U.S. Supreme Court held that in a disparate impact claim under the ADEA, an employer can defend a claim by showing that the adverse impact was attributable to a **reasonable factor other than age**, meaning a non-age factor that seems objectively reasonable to an employer.[33] In that case, the Jackson, Mississippi, police department granted raises to all police officers and dispatchers in an attempt to bring their salaries up to the regional average. According to the new pay plan, those officers with less than 5 years' service received larger raises than those with more than 5 years of service. Most of the officers with more than 5 years of service were over 40 years old. Those officers sued, claiming the new pay plan had a disparate impact on officers over 40.[34] The U.S. Supreme Court held that for this claim, the ADEA is narrower than Title VII. The ADEA allows an otherwise prohibited action if the differentiation is based on a reasonable factor other than age. In this case, the city of Jackson said the different raises for younger and older officers was based on a need to make the junior officers' salaries competitive with the market. This, according to the Court, is a reasonable factor other than age.[35]

reasonable factor other than age: A non-age factor that is objectively reasonable to an employer.

Bias in Online Job Postings

iStockphoto.com/luchezar

How will you find a job for after graduation? Online, of course. Hopefully you will use other methods too, but there are thousands of job boards and job search engines that make it quick and efficient for job seekers to find openings and for employers to find talent. Many of the sites take different approaches. For example, Monster, Dice, and CareerBuilder are traditional job boards; other sites, like Indeed.com, allow you to search thousands of job boards, career sites, and classified ads; and LinkedIn allows you to network, look at job postings, and interact with employers. Online recruiting and job searching is big business: According to research from IBISWorld, revenue for this industry has grown at an average rate of 14.6% over the past 5 years and is predicted to hit $6.4 billion in 2022. Although LinkedIn has 575 million users and is the most popular social media network for professionals, Facebook and Google have entered the space, leveraging their membership size and troves of data to further specialize job searches and recruitment. In February 2017, Facebook released a new functionality for Pages where businesses can post open positions and job seekers can easily search and apply for them. According to Facebook, "this new experience will help businesses find qualified people where they're already spending their time on Facebook and on mobile." In July 2018, Google entered the job search market using, not surprisingly, machine-trained algorithms to categorize jobs already available online. Google for Jobs is not a jobs board but a search engine that scrapes and optimizes jobs already posted. Candidates can set preferences and alerts, and businesses looking for talent can optimize their postings by using Google's structured vocabulary to index listings. Because both Facebook and Google have amassed voluminous data on all of its users, they can offer businesses more targeted placement of job postings much the same way they do with ads.

While targeted ad placement is a distinguishing feature of Facebook's business model, their ability to show job postings to specific audiences can conflict with discrimination laws. In 2017, ProPublica and the *New York Times* investigated online job postings on Facebook, Google, and other sites and found that many companies posted job listings that excluded older workers. For example, according to the investigation, Verizon placed a posting on Facebook to recruit applicants for a financial analysis position. The posting included a picture of a young woman at her computer and was shown to users aged 25 to 36 who lived in the Washington, D.C., area and expressed an interest in finance. Facebook users older than 36 did not see the listing. The investigation revealed that many companies, including Amazon, Goldman Sachs, Target, UPS, State Farm, and even Facebook, placed job listings targeted to specific age groups.

Google and LinkedIn instantly approved listings that excluded users over 40; however, when contacted by ProPublica, LinkedIn changed its system to prevent such targeting in their job listings. When asked about excluding specific older workers form seeing their listings, Target, State Farm, and UPS defended their practice as only one part of a broad recruitment strategy reaching candidates of all ages. When Facebook learned of ProPublica's findings, Rob Goldman, VP of ads, posted a blog to the social media platform that rejected all allegations that their placement was discriminatory because their placements were also part of a broader recruitment strategy and also because simply showing ads to a certain group on Facebook, by itself, is not discriminatory. What matters, said Goldman, is that their broader strategy is inclusive.

In December 2017, the Communications Workers of America (CWA) filed a class action lawsuit on behalf of its members and Facebook users over 40 who may have been denied a chance to learn about job listings. The lawsuit alleges that T-Mobile, Amazon, Cox Communications, and other "similarly situated employers" routinely exclude older workers from receiving their job listings on Facebook and thus deny workers over 40 job opportunities because of their age. Facebook, according to the plaintiffs, "has turned its powerful ad platform into a conduit for age discrimination." In January 2019, Amazon filed a motion to dismiss the lawsuit, claiming, among other things, that nowhere do the plaintiffs allege that Amazon discriminates in its overall recruitment strategy, but that they merely claimed it uses Facebook to target certain age groups, which Amazon asserts is lawful.

Facebook originally fought the charges, claiming that under the Communications Decency Act (CDA), they were immune from liability for what third parties post on their platform. However, in the CWA lawsuit, plaintiffs allege Facebook is not a passive platform; they act more like an employment agency or marketing firm by proactively helping the employer create their listing, providing data on Facebook users, coordinating with employers to develop recruitment and marketing strategies, and collecting a fee for these services In March 2019, Facebook agreed to pay $5 million to settle the CWA suit and four other lawsuits that allege the advertising platform was used to exclude racial minorities and women. The settlement creates a partnership with the CWA, the National Fair Housing Alliance, and the American Civil Liberties Union (ACLU) to work collaboratively with the tech company to prevent future discrimination. Facebook agreed to build a separate portal for advertisers to create employment ads, which will not allow microtargeting by age, gender, zip code, or other categories prohibited by law. For the new portal to be successful in eliminating discrimination, employers also have to be on board because the new portal will not prevent companies from uploading their own list of people to target, which could include unlawful discrimination.

Discussion Questions

1. *Stakeholder theories*: Many companies defended their use of Facebook and other platforms for targeting job listings based on their overall recruitment strategy and limited budgets. Why pay for a listing to be posted to people who, experience has shown, will never apply for the job? In addition, marketing departments and businesses have many different groups looking at the finances. Identify the stakeholders in the decision whether to use targeted advertising as a cost-effective means of recruitment. What is at stake for each?

2. *Ethical decision-making*: Many feel that using targeting job postings on platforms such a Facebook is no different than placing a job listing in *Teen Vogue* or *AARP The Magazine*. What is the difference between targeting a specific age group for a job posting on Facebook and posting the listing in *Teen Vogue* or *AARP The Magazine*? How does using Facebook's microtargeting differ from recruiters coming to college campuses? What are critical issues, both short term and long term, of using Facebook's microtargeting job listing platform?

Take a Position

Many Facebook users claim that the result of Facebook's microtargeting is you don't know what you don't know. You don't know whether you have missed a job opportunity if you don't know there is an opportunity. Businesses claim that using Facebook is just one part of a multipart recruitment strategy designed to reach as many people as possible.

Issue: If the goal of all discrimination laws in the United States is to promote equal opportunity, does Facebook's, and other platform's, microtargeting deprive certain groups of opportunity?

The Americans With Disabilities Act

Americans with Disabilities Act (ADA): A federal law that prohibits discrimination against an otherwise qualified individual based on his or her disability, including disparate treatment, disparate impact, harassment, and failure to accommodate.

People with different mental and physical abilities have long been stigmatized. In the United States, our treatment of people with different abilities evolved from institutionalization, to indifference, to more paternalistic policies to "help the handicapped."[36] Unlike the civil rights movement, advocates for equal opportunity for those with disabilities were not unified under a larger banner; most were viewed by their affliction or ability: the blind, the deaf, those with diabetes. Things started to change after WWII and the Korean War when soldiers returned with injuries that left them disabled. Society and lawmakers saw the need to get the veterans back to work. The rehabilitation and occupational therapy industries grew to provide the needed services to help reintegrate veterans back into mainstream life and hopefully employment. When the **Americans with Disabilities Act (ADA)** was signed into law in 1990, President Bush stated what many disability rights groups had advocated for years: "Let the shameful walls of exclusion finally come tumbling down."[37] The law made clear that people living with disabilities are entitled to legal protections, equal opportunity, and the chance to contribute to society.

While the U.S. law is based on equal opportunity (also in Australia, England, and Canada), other countries approach employment discrimination against those with disabilities differently. The Japanese approach is based on an employment quota system: private sector employers must hire people with disabilities at a rate of 1 per 56 employees. Employers who do not meet this ratio are fined ("levied") a set amount per person with a disability they have not employed. That money is then used to fund grants awarded to employers who employ a higher number of people with disabilities than legally required.[38] While many EU countries also use a quota system, the trend in Europe is to move closer to a balance of both equal opportunity and quota approaches.[39]

The ADA bans discrimination on the basis of a disability in employment, public accommodations, public services, transportation, and telecommunications. A **disability** is defined as a physical or mental impairment that substantially limits a major life activity. As with Title VII, employment under the ADA is a broad term and includes hiring and firing, and also compensation, training, application, and other terms, conditions, or privileges of employment.[40] And like Title VII, the ADA provides disparate treatment, disparate impact, and harassment claims. The law was amended in 2008 and changed, among other things, the definition of a disability to include episodic impairments or impairments in remission; if the impairment would substantially limit a major life activity when active, it meets the definition of a disability.[41] An employer cannot discriminate against a person with a disability who is **otherwise qualified** to do the job. Whether a person is qualified includes whether they have the required skills, experience, and education for the position and can perform the essential functions of the job with, or without, a **reasonable accommodation.**[42] As with religion, the discussion of what would be a reasonable accommodation must be interactive. However, the ADA gives more guidance to employers, as their obligation to accommodate disability is much different than their obligation to accommodate religion. Under the ADA, a reasonable accommodation could include making facilities accessible and usable by those with disabilities, providing modified work schedules, acquiring or modifying equipment or training materials, or providing readers or interpreters.[43] There are limits on the requirements of employers; employers do not have to provide an accommodation if doing so would create an **undue hardship**. Factors to consider in determining whether an accommodation poses an undue hardship include the cost of the accommodation relative to the finances, size, and operation of the business; the location of the business's facilities; and the composition and functions of its workforce.[44] The following case against Walmart illustrates a different type of hardship.

disability: A physical or mental impairment that substantially limits a major life activity.

otherwise qualified: An employee has the requisite skills, education, and experience for the position and can perform the essential functions of the job with, or without, a reasonable accommodation.

reasonable accommodation: Requirement under the ADA for an employer to work with a disabled employee to find an accommodation that would enable the employee to perform the essential functions of the job.

undue hardship: Under the ADA, an accommodation is not reasonable if it creates an undue hardship for the employer; this may include cost of the accommodation relative to the finances, size, and operation of the business; the location of the business's facilities; and the composition and functions of its workforce.

HUBER V. WAL-MART STORES, 486 F.3D 480 (MAY 30, 2007)

Facts: Pam Huber worked for Walmart as an order filler, making $13.00 an hour. While working, Ms. Huber sustained a permanent injury to her arm and hand and could no longer perform the essential functions of the order filler job. Because of her disability, she wanted as an accommodation reassignment to an equivalent, vacant router position; however, Walmart would not agree to automatic reassignment because it had a policy of hiring the most qualified applicants for vacant positions. As a result, Ms. Huber had to apply and compete for the job. Although Ms. Huber was qualified for the new position, she was not the most qualified applicant, and she was not hired. Ms. Huber was placed in a maintenance position at another facility, earning $7.97 an hour. Ms. Huber sued under the ADA, claiming she should have been reassigned to the vacant router position as a reasonable accommodation. Walmart claimed it had a legitimate, nondiscriminatory policy of hiring the most qualified applicant for all job vacancies.

Issue: Is Walmart required to reassign a qualified disabled employee to a vacant position for which she is not the most qualified applicant for the position?

Decision: No, Walmart is not required to reassign a qualified disabled employee to a vacant position for which she is not the most qualified applicant. To make a reasonable accommodation claim under the ADA, a plaintiff has to show that (1) she is disabled under the law, (2) she is qualified, and (3) she suffered an adverse employment action as a result of her disability. To be qualified, a plaintiff must have the requisite skills, education, and experience for the position, and she must be able to perform the essential function of the job with or without a reasonable accommodation.

In this case, the only element of her claim in dispute is whether giving Ms. Huber preference for the vacant router position is a reasonable accommodation. Walmart claims that because it had an existing, nondiscriminatory policy to hire the most qualified candidate, automatic reassignment would be an undue hardship. Other circuit courts have reached inconsistent results. In the Tenth Circuit, reassignment under the ADA should automatically go to the qualified disabled employee. However, in the Seventh Circuit, reassignment under the ADA does not automatically go to the qualified disabled employee when there is a more qualified applicant if the employer has a policy to hire the most qualified candidate. Requiring automatic reassignment turns the ADA into an affirmative action law, mandating a preference that would be inconsistent with the goals of the ADA as a nondiscrimination statute, and an unreasonable imposition on businesses. Here, Walmart is not required to reject a superior candidate in order to give the job to Ms. Huber as a reasonable accommodation. By requiring Ms. Huber to compete for the vacant router position, Walmart was not discriminating against her; it was treating her like any other employee. The maintenance position may not have been Ms. Huber's perfect solution or preferred alternative, but the law requires only a reasonable accommodation, not an ideal accommodation.

We find that the ADA does not require automatic reassignment—only that the qualified disabled applicant be allowed to apply and compete for the job.

Law and Management Questions

1. In a similar case, the U.S. Supreme Court held that is was not a reasonable accommodation to give a disabled employee a higher seniority status so that she could retain her job if doing so would violate an existing, bona fide seniority system. In the *Huber* case, the court said that the automatic reassignment of Ms. Huber is not

reasonable because Walmart had an existing policy to hire only the most qualified candidate. What management lessons can you draw from these cases? How would you draft a policy that required your business to hire only the most qualified candidates for vacant positions?

2. An employer cannot discriminate against an employee based on his or her disability if that employee can perform the essential function of the job with, or without, a reasonable accommodation. The ADA does not define accommodation, but *Merriam-Webster* defines it as "an adjustment or settlement, a reconciliation of differences." Based on this definition, is allowing Ms. Huber to compete for the vacant router position on the same terms as other applicants an accommodation? If so, why? If not, why not?

KEY TAKEAWAYS

Laws to Protect Against Discrimination

- Discrimination claims usually result from poor decision-making by managers either engaging in prohibited conduct or not intervening when they have notice of prohibited conduct.

- Workplace policies that appear neutral might have unintended discriminatory impacts.

- Managers and employees must work together to find accommodations for religious conflicts and disability needs.

SUMMARY

We will spend about one third of our adult life at work,[45] and for managers, much of that time will be spent managing people. Embracing diversity and creating an inclusive work environment can lead to increases in morale and productivity. Although managing a diverse workforce has challenges, understanding the legal protections that apply to us at work is a good place to start.

KEY TERMS

Age Discrimination in Employment Act (ADEA) 201
Americans with Disabilities Act (ADA) 204
disability 205
discrimination 191

disparate impact 195
disparate treatment 195
diversity 189
Equal Employment Opportunity Commission (EEOC) 195
Equal Pay Act 195

equal work 195
harassment 199
implicit bias 191
inclusion 189
intersectionality 192
otherwise qualified 205

pay gap 192
reasonable accommodation 205
reasonable factor other
    than age 202

reasonably accommodate a religious
    observance or practice 200
sexual harassment 199
stereotype 191

Title VII of the Civil Rights Act 195
undue hardship 205

REVIEW QUESTIONS

1. What is the difference between diversity and inclusion? Why are they important management concepts?

2. How does Title VII prohibit discrimination in employment?

3. How do the ADEA and the ADA add to the prohibitions in Title VII?

4. Explain sex stereotyping and why it is a violation of Title VII?

MANAGER'S CHALLENGE

Discrimination and Grooming Codes

Julia has been a cocktail waitress at Fowler's Grille and Pub for the past 20 years. She is loved by her customers—many of whom are long-term regulars—and by her coworkers because she is hardworking and a team player. The new management at Fowler's instituted a grooming code in order to have the waitstaff appear more professional and polished. According to this new code, men could not have hair below the collar of their shirt, visible tattoos, or wear makeup, and they must be clean-shaven. Women could not have visible tattoos; had to wear their hair curled or styled; wear makeup, including foundation, blush, mascara, and lipstick; and have their nails polished either with clear polish or light-colored polish.

Julia never liked to wear makeup because it made her feel objectified. She especially didn't like to wear makeup to work because she felt it diminished her authority when dealing with drunk customers. Julia explained her reservations to the new management, but they were unimpressed; they told her she had to follow the new code or find another job. Julia refused to follow the new grooming code and was fired.

Framing Questions

1. Does Julia have a legal claim against her employers? If so, what is the basis for that claim?

2. What defense does the employer have for instituting the grooming code?

3. If you were in management at Fowler's, how would you have responded to Julia's concerns?

Assignment

Draft a grooming code for Fowler's and a one-page memorandum to management about the risks associated with grooming codes and how they can minimize those risks.

10

FINANCIAL SYSTEMS AND SOCIETY

Ethics in Context

Payday Loans: Parasites or Providers?

One of the most controversial forms of financing is called payday loans. These loans, as the name implies, typically require a borrower to pay the loan back in full on her next payday. Retail payday loan outlets now outpace the number of stores operated by McDonald's and Starbucks combined. Critics of payday loans call it predatory lending because those taking out these loans typically need more and more loans to pay off the original one—a circular debt cycle—which may be encouraged by payday lenders themselves. However, some argue that payday loans serve an important underserved market for low-income workers who have no alternatives when an unexpected financial obligation hits them (i.e., an unexpected health care bill). Is offering a payday loan ethical? Do lenders have an ethical responsibility to verify that borrowers have the means to pay the loan back? Should the government ban or regulate payday lending practices? Later in the chapter, in the Ethics in Context section, we use stakeholder and ethical lenses to examine whether payday loans are predators or providers.

iStockphoto.com/Shaun Wilkinson

Learning Objectives

Upon completion of this chapter, the reader should be able to do the following:

10.1 Identify primary and secondary stakeholders in the global financial system.

10.2 Describe the financial roles of Main Street versus Wall Street as well as the changes brought by fintech.

10.3 Articulate the events and factors leading to the global financial crisis.

10.4 Compare and contrast ethical dilemmas surrounding use of payday loans.

10.5 Explain the main provisions of various legislative acts like the Dodd–Frank Act (DFA).

INTRODUCTION

One of the many lessons of what economists have dubbed the global financial crisis, triggered by the financial crisis of 2008, was how interconnected and fragile the global financial infrastructure really is. Even a decade after the crisis, according to economist Susan Lund, governments all over the globe

209

provide financial support to the banking system and other critical industries. All of that has made these institutions more indebted and interconnected than ever before.[1]

But for some, it is still hard to fathom what happened in 2008. In a period of weeks (not months), multibillion-dollar financial firms around the world went bankrupt or were in crisis; the working public saw their retirement investments drop nearly 30% in value, and foreclosures on residential real estate skyrocketed. The underlying foundation for the financial system, including the institutions, information, technologies, rules, and industry standards, which enabled the financial market to thrive for nearly a century, had failed. It also underscored the importance of finance in our global society generally and how our specific goals as a society sometimes conflict with each other. In this chapter, we examine the components of the global financial infrastructure, the role of finance and its stakeholders in society, and the unique blend of self-regulation and law in the financial markets. We also focus on conflicting objectives between the financial community (sometimes referred to as Wall Street) and the public at large (sometimes referred to as Main Street) and ethical considerations related to global financial transactions.

ROLES OF FINANCE IN SOCIETY

LO 10.1 Identify primary and secondary stakeholders in the global financial system.

The World Economic Forum (WEF) identifies several categories of stakeholders in the financial system at large. The primary stakeholders are *financial consumers* (e.g., individual investors). Secondary stakeholders include the following:

- *Financial industry leaders*: Executives and investors that run financial services firms, banks, and other finance-related businesses

- *Financial policymakers*: Lawmakers at all levels of government and regulatory officials at local, state, and federal agencies

- *Economists and academics*: Those who study financial trends and look for risks and opportunities to improve the global financial infrastructure.

- *Advocates:* Stakeholders who advocate for consumer rights that may come from nonprofit watchdog groups or labor unions.[2] They come in a variety of forms.

Figure 10.1 provides an illustration of the stakeholders in the financial system.

Global Financial System

global financial system: A set of formal and informal agreements that are intended to promote economic stability and access to money for investment and new venture financing.

In a very broad sense, the **global financial system** is a set of formal and informal agreements that are intended to promote economic stability and access to money for investment and new venture financing. It includes all institutions, information, technologies, rules, and standards that enable financial transactions (such as credit) and financial security (such as a guaranteed savings rate). These key elements are vital to facilitating greater access to finance, improving transparency and governance, while safeguarding stability in global financial markets.[3] The global financial system centers on central banks, multilateral treaties, and international organizations in an effort to achieve growth for developed nations and to provide access for underdeveloped nations.

The global system depends on several **international financial institutions** that were created by one or more nations post–World War II. The two largest (and perhaps best well known) are the World Bank and the International Monetary Fund (IMF). The World Bank provides large, long-term loans to countries for capital projects or those facing a financial crisis. More recently, the World Bank has taken a more active role in the reduction of poverty in developing nations. As of November 2018, the largest recipients of World Bank loans were India ($859 million in 2018) and China ($370 million in 2018).[4] The IMF is a UN agency with a stated mission of ensuring "the stability of the international monetary system—the system of exchange rates and international payments that enables countries (and their citizens) to transact with each other." It works to foster global growth and economic stability by providing policy, advice, and financing to its member countries to help them achieve macroeconomic stability and reduce poverty.[5]

> **international financial institutions:** Institutions created after World War II by one or more nations to facilitate development and ensure financial stability.

Figure 10.1 Financial System Stakeholders

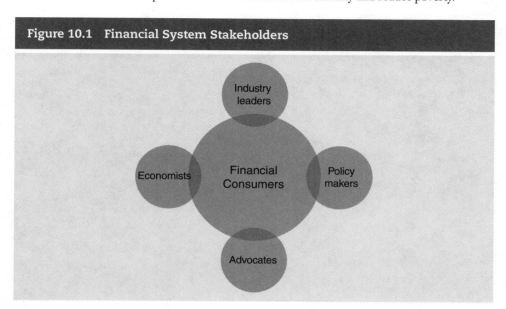

Microfinance

Microfinance harnesses the power of the free market to solve societal problems such as poverty, hunger, and inequality. In the past 10 years, the world of microfinance has changed dramatically. The field has moved rapidly from its origins of microcredit, which provided innovative loans to help poor entrepreneurs start businesses. Today, we consider microcredit to be part of a larger vision of creating entire microfinancial systems that work for the poor. Microfinance has proven to be an effective tool for reducing poverty and helping poor people to improve their lives. Yet many societies still lack access to an array of financial services—not just credit to start or enhance a business but also a safe place to save, the ability to transfer funds to family members, insurance against sickness or other household disasters, and other ways to mitigate risk in vulnerability.

Grameen Bank

Nobel Prize-winning economist Muhammad Yunus was among the pioneers in microcredit who were catalysts for a shift in financial thinking about society and credit. Realizing that traditional lenders would always opt to make fewer loans but for larger amounts to people with lots of collateral, Yunus created a separate bank for those who could not rely on traditional banks for access to credit. In 1983, Yunus helped

(Continued)

(Continued)

to create Grameen Bank in Bangladesh, his home country, which would provide loans to poor borrowers without collateral or credit histories. This shift in thinking meant citizens would not be shut out of the very resource needed to lift them out of poverty: credit. As Yunus reports in his book *Creating a World Without Poverty*, the idea was met with incredulity as critics predicted a certain collapse of Grameen because there was no incentive for borrowers to pay the money back. More than 30 years later, the Grameen Bank continues to thrive and has provided over $6 billion in loans with a repayment rate of 98.6%. Grameen is owned by its borrowers, who receive dividends from the bank, and is largely self-reliant (i.e., it no longer needs the support of donors to cover its expenses), and today has over 7.5 million borrowers.[6] Grameen Bank's website explains that it "takes deposits from borrowers and non-borrowers which are sufficient to fund its operations."[7] The bank also works with many corporate partners helping it to set up banks in various communities (e.g., its support from East West Bank) and tap into existing technologies (e.g., its support from Apple).[8]

Sixty-four percent of Grameen's borrowers who have been with the bank for 5 years or more have crossed over the poverty line.[9]

Microfinance in Action

Following Yunus's lead, humanitarian organizations such as Catholic Relief Services have created microfinance programs in India and Africa focused on microsavings, which are then used to make loans. In one reported case, a woman living in desperate poverty in the Central African Republic used microcredit to purchase land to build a house. Residents of her small village gathered regularly and deposited tiny sums (typically less than a dollar) into a savings pool. The pool was then used as a source for microlending for purchasing land, starting a business, or making agricultural practices more effective. As the loan is paid back, it provides resources for other borrowers and helps existing borrowers establish credit.[10] Experts also cite another significant benefit to the microfinance societies: community. Savings groups promote social cohesion and trust among community members. London School of Economics professor Sohini Kar calls this societal phenomenon the "domestication of microfinance." Domestication involves bringing finance under the control of the family as well as to turn it into something of value to the family. Kar concludes that microfinance relationships enhance everyday community kinship because "asking people to affirm particular relationships to gain access to credit" is now directly related to a "collective better life for their families."[11]

Microfinancing in America

In 2008, Dr. Yunus and several corporate sponsors, including Citi Foundation and Capital One, launched Grameen America in New York. Since then, Grameen has been serving the poor, mainly women, throughout four of the city's five boroughs (Bronx, Brooklyn, Manhattan, and Queens) as well as Omaha, Nebraska, and Indianapolis, Indiana. In 4 years, Grameen America has facilitated loans to over 9,000 borrowers, which is valued over $35 million. It has, as Grameen CEO Stephen Vogel notes, "a 99 percent repayment rate."[12] Since then, it has opened 23 branches in 15 U.S. cities, disbursing some $1.32 million to more than 124,000 low-income women.[13]

Discussion Questions

1. Why was Grameen Bank created?

2. What's the difference between microcredit versus microsavings?

3. What are the societal benefits of microfinance? Are there any drawbacks?

Critical Thinking

The Grameen Bank was based on a model of social business. A social business is a for-profit entity that provides a social benefit. Some have suggested that this model could be expanded beyond just banks. For example, a social business that sells high-quality, nutritious food products at very low prices to a targeted market of poor and underfed children is a sort of Grameen Supermarket.

1. What other businesses could use this model to provide a social benefit like Grameen Bank? Is it possible to be profitable by selling low-priced goods? Explain.

2. Could social businesses be part of a firm's corporate social responsibility (CSR) practices? What advice would you provide to corporate leaders incorporating the Grameen Bank model as a CSR initiative?

Roles of Finance in Society

- Stakeholders in the financial system at large include financial consumers (primary) as well as industry leaders, policymakers, economists, and advocates (secondary).

- The global financial system is a set of formal and informal agreements that are intended to promote economic stability and access to money for investment and new venture financing. It includes all institutions, information, technologies, rules, and standards that enable financial transactions and financial security.

MAIN STREET TO WALL STREET

LO 10.2 Describe the financial roles of Main Street versus Wall Street as well as the changes brought by fintech.

The terms **Main Street** and **Wall Street** are used colloquially by economists to describe the two interdependent parts of the global economy. When these terms are used by critics and scholars, they are most often focused on their differing goals, knowledge levels, long-term interests, and political power.[14] Main Street, sometimes called the *real economy*, is the workers who generate savings primarily through their own labor—rather than generating income primarily through investing—and then seek ways to invest their earnings, which provide a return on their investment. In a sense, Main Street is shorthand for individuals, small- and medium-sized business owners, and the overall economy. It can also include small investment firms and community-based banks that are intended to serve investors whose assets are relatively modest. Main Street investors are typically saving for long-term goals such as retirement, college funding, and real estate ownership.

Wall Street, on the other hand, means individuals and global firms that make the financial markets function by generating revenue primarily using financial markets rather than labor. These large, globally recognized firms create and deploy dozens of methods that are intended to serve the needs of high-wealth individuals and companies that have multimillion-dollar assets.

Fundamentally, these two categories depend on each other's success. Main Street depends on Wall Street to provide investment opportunities that will generate revenue at a higher rate of return on their savings than their traditional deposit accounts and achieve their financial goals more quickly. The various offerings for investment by Wall Street to Main Street investors also offer the opportunity for Main Street investors to control the *level of risk* involved with investing. Wall Street depends on Main Street for a steady flow of fees and capital that comes from Main Street investors and community banks. At the same time, it is also important to understand there is not necessarily a correlation of success between the two streets. During any given period, economists point out that unemployment rates

Main Street: In the context of finance, Main Street is sometimes called the real economy because it is shorthand for individuals, as well as owners of small- and medium-sized businesses, who generate savings primarily through their own labor (rather than generating income primarily through investing) and then seek ways to invest their savings in ways that provide a return on their investment.

Wall Street: Individuals and global firms that make the financial markets function by generating revenue primarily using financial markets rather than labor.

iStockphoto.com/BobHemphill

and low wage growth, which put pressure on the Main Street economy, may occur at the same time as high returns in the stock market boosting Wall Street.

Financial Firms: Brokerage Houses and Banks

The global financial system depends on **financial firms** to act on behalf of investors. These firms are centered on the sale of investments known as *securities*. Perhaps the most common form of a security is the stock of a company, which is listed on the exchange of a public market. The New York Stock Exchange (NYSE) is one of the best known and largest stock exchanges around the world, but there are many others—London, Tokyo, and Euronext—some 60 in total (see Table 10.1).[15] While stocks are one example of a security, there are other types of securities apart from stocks (e.g., bonds), with each having its own benefits and drawbacks. Financial firms, whose names have become familiar brands to many, hold significant interests in the global financial markets: Goldman Sachs, BNP Paribas, and JPMorgan Chase, among others. These firms have many divisions, and chief among them are brokerage, trading, research, and asset management. In some cases, these financial firms are called brokerage firms. These firms provide financial advice to their clients, who range from individual investors, called retail investors, to large institutional investors such as managers of pension funds, higher education endowments, or mutual funds. Much of the advice provided to their clients comes from the research arm of a brokerage house, which publishes reports and recommendations on which securities to buy, which to hold, and which to sell.

financial firms: Sometimes called brokerage houses—firms that act on behalf of investors in buying and selling securities.

Issuing Securities

Imagine you are deciding whether to purchase shares of a company. What would you want to know about that company? Your answer would likely include the company's financial results, its leadership, what assets it owns, what debts it is carrying, and other pieces of information relevant to its future success. These are exactly the types of information that companies are required to disclose through the registration process. The main objective is to require that investors receive financial and other significant information concerning securities being offered for public sale. For example, the U.S. Securities and Exchange Commission (SEC) accomplishes this objective through an extensive registration and disclosure process.

In a time where large amounts of information about most companies is at our fingertips—through our keyboards and smartphones—the Securities Act's registration process may seem superfluous. It is important to remember that the Securities Act was passed in 1933, in response to the stock market crash of 1929 and the Great Depression that followed. At that time, the public had much more limited means for obtaining information

Table 10.1   Global Stock Exchanges

Name of Exchange	Size (in trillions)	Continent
NYSE	$20T	North American
NASDAQ	$10T	North American
TMX Group	$2T	North American
London Stock Exchange	$5T	Europe
Euronext	$5T	Europe
Deutsche Börse	$2T	Europe
SIX Swiss Exchange	$2T	Europe
NASDAQ OMX Nordic Exchange	$2T	Europe
Shanghai Stock Exchange	$10T	Asia
Japan Exchange Group	$10T	Asia
Shenzhen Stock Exchange	$5T	Asia
Hong Kong Exchanges and Clearing	$5T	Asia
Korea Exchange	$2T	Asia
National Stock Exchange of India	$2T	Asia
BSE India Limited	$2T	Asia
Australian Securities Exchange	$2T	Australia

Source: Adapted from Desjardins, J. (2016). All of the World's Stock Exchanges by Size. http://money.visualcapitalist.com/all-of-the-worlds-stock-exchanges-by-size/.

about companies selling their securities. The Securities Act ensures that the information provided through the registration process has been vetted by the SEC. The Securities Act also requires public disclosure of the registration information, protecting the investors on "Main Street" from being disadvantaged by lack of insider information. By ensuring that everyone has access to the same information at the same time, the Securities Act tries to increase investor confidence in our markets.

The Initial Public Offering

Commonly referred to as "going public," an initial public offering (IPO) is where a previously unlisted company sells its securities (new or existing) to the public for the first time. Prior to an IPO, a company is considered private. Being a **private company** means that the company's securities have only been sold to early investors like the founder, family or friends, or to accredited investors such as a venture capital company. Deciding to go public is a big decision, as an IPO is time consuming and expensive as well as subjects the company to ongoing regulation.

private company: A company that has only sold securities to early investors that are not offered on the public markets.

underwriter: Usually an investment bank, advises the company throughout the IPO process, helping the company determine its value and its initial share price.

best efforts: A contractual agreement that the underwriter does not guarantee the price for the securities but markets and sells the securities on behalf of the company for a commission.

firm commitment agreement: When the underwriter purchases all the issued securities at a negotiated price and then resells the shares to the public.

prospectus: A document that discloses financial details about the company, such as risk factors, a business plan, and/or pending or threatened litigation.

The first step in an IPO is selecting an **underwriter**. An underwriter, usually an investment bank, advises the company throughout the IPO process. The underwriter helps the company determine its value and its initial share price. The underwriter also acts as a broker between the company and the investors. An underwriter can be hired by the company on a "best efforts" or a "firm commitment" basis. **Best efforts** agreements hold that the underwriter does not guarantee the price for the securities but markets and sells the securities on behalf of the company for a commission. In a **firm commitment agreement**, the underwriter purchases all of the issued securities at a negotiated price and then resells the shares to the public. Any increase in price is the benefit to the underwriter, and the company receives a guaranteed amount of money from the IPO.

The next step in the IPO process is drafting the registration statement, which must be distributed to all investors who buy the security. The **prospectus** must include important disclosures about the company, including risk factors for the company, how the company will use the proceeds of the IPO, the company's business plan, description of the company's properties, any pending or threatened litigation, inventory, and other information that would be relevant to the average investor. The SEC, and other global regulators, have specific rules requiring disclosure of audited financial statements. The registration statement must be reviewed and approved by the SEC or other governing body.[i] The responsibility for complete and accurate disclosure lies with the company, its underwriter, auditor, and lawyers. It is a back and forth process. For example, the SEC evaluates the registration statement from the perspective of a potential investor and provides comments to the company where the SEC believes company can improve its disclosure. The company responds to those comments and, often after several rounds of revisions and comments, the SEC declares the registration statement effective as of a certain date. The day before the effective date, the underwriter and company agree on an offer price. When the IPO goes effective, the sale of the security may begin.

Marketing of Securities in an IPO

The ability to market the securities is dependent on the timeline of the IPO. The IPO is divided into three separate time periods: (1) prefiling or "quiet" period, (2) the waiting period, and (3) post-effective period.

prefiling or quiet period: The period of time between when the company decides to go public and when the registration statement is publicly filed with the SEC.

Prefiling or quiet period begins when a company decides to go public, usually by hiring an underwriter, and ends when the registration statement is publicly filed with the SEC. During this time frame, laws prohibit any person from engaging in any activity that could be construed as making an offer of the company's securities (e.g., U.S. Section 5(c) of the U.S. Securities Act). Violations are often referred to as "gun-jumping." For example, the Securities Act prohibits gun-jumping because offers conveyed before the registration statement is public might reflect incomplete or misleading information.

Several forms of communication with the investing public are considered a violation of the quiet period; for example, with the U.S. Section 5(c), advertisements, e-mails to

---

[i] The SEC does not evaluate the merits of any investment; nor does it guarantee that the disclosure is complete and accurate.

customers, media interviews, and social media posts are considered violations. In 2011, the founders of Google gave an interview to *Playboy* magazine during what should have been the quiet period of Google's IPO. The interview was far-reaching, the founders never discussed the security, and *Playboy* is certainly not a financial publication. But the SEC ruled the interview was gun-jumping because a reader could be influenced by what the founders said about Google, rather than just relying on the registration statement. The SEC required that Google (1) revise its prospectus to include a risk factor warning that the *Playboy* interview may have violated Section 5, (2) include the full text of the *Playboy* article in the prospectus, and (3) address certain discrepancies between statistics in the article and prospectus.[16]

The **waiting period** is the time between public filing of the registration statement and the effective date of the IPO. Offers of the security are allowed during the waiting period, but sales cannot occur until the effective date. An offer is limited in form and subject to strict requirements. During the waiting period, the company often goes on what is referred to as a **road show**, which is one type of offer allowed under the Securities Act. A road show is when the company's executives and underwriters travel around the United States to makes presentations about the company to investment banks and institutional investors. The company can also publish a tombstone ad during the waiting period. A **tombstone ad** is a simple ad containing basic information about the offering: the amount and type of security, the underwriter, and the price.

The **post-effective period** begins once the SEC declares the registration statement effective; then the company, through its underwriters, may make sales of the securities. They must deliver a final prospectus, and there are limitations on publicity by the issuer for several weeks after the effective date.

Banks and other financial institutions play a pivotal role in the global financial structure. You are likely already familiar with traditional *commercial banks* that offer community-based services such as checking or savings accounts as well as low-yield investment instruments such as a certificate of deposit (CD). Commercial banks also offer consumer and small business loans for vehicles, mortgages on real estate, and credit cards. *Investment banks* are financial institutions that advise large companies on acquisitions, mergers, and IPOs. Financial firms and brokerage houses exist under a relatively complicated regulatory array that combines self-regulation with federal and state laws. Regulation is discussed in greater detail later in this chapter.

However, the traditional financial and banking systems have been meaningfully disrupted by financial technology or fintech. **Fintech** is the term used to refer to innovations in the financial and technology crossover space and typically refers to companies or services that use technology to provide financial services to businesses or consumers.[17] Payment apps like Venmo, Paypal, Square, or Zelle are only increasing in popularity—and expected to increase by 14% every year.[18] As of December 2018, 40% of the adult population across the whole world, from North America to Africa and from Asia to Europe actively use a digital platform for banking.[19] Other trends disrupting banking are

- chatbots, which facilitate communication between the bank and the online consumer;

waiting period: The time between public filing of the registration statement with the SEC and the effective date of the IPO.

road show: Occurs during the waiting period when the company's executives and underwriters travel around the United States to present the company to investment banks and institutional investors.

tombstone ad: A simple ad containing basic information about the offering: the amount and type of security, the underwriter, and the price.

post-effective period: The time after the SEC declares the registration statement effective, allowing for the sales of securities through the company's underwriters.

fintech: Term used to refer to innovations in the financial and technology crossover space and typically refers to companies or services that use technology to provide financial services to businesses or consumers.

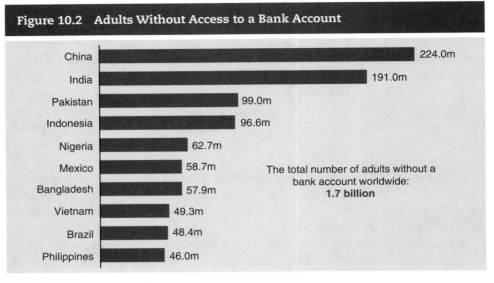

Figure 10.2 Adults Without Access to a Bank Account

Country	Adults without bank account
China	224.0m
India	191.0m
Pakistan	99.0m
Indonesia	96.6m
Nigeria	62.7m
Mexico	58.7m
Bangladesh	57.9m
Vietnam	49.3m
Brazil	48.4m
Philippines	46.0m

The total number of adults without a bank account worldwide: **1.7 billion**

Source: The World Bank via Statista, CC BY-SA 4.0

- banking as a service (BaaS), designed to extend services beyond working hours and provide value-added research and knowledge (often through accelerated programming interfaces—application programming interfaces (APIs)—or blockchain for secure data sharing); and

- cashless transacting, like Apple Pay, and use of cryptocurrencies like Bitcoin or Libra.[20]

These technologies help not only those with immediate access to numerous banking options, but also the billions who do not. Data released by the World Bank in 2018 notes that 1.7 billion worldwide do not have access to bank accounts (see Figure 10.2). China still has 224 million inhabitants without a bank account. In India, it's 191 million, while in Pakistan, it's 99 million.[21] This lack of access compromises the ability for people to make day-to-day living less complicated as well as allowing them to build up their assets.

Public Perceptions of the Financial Industry

The financial services industry relies heavily on trust as it is a relationship-based business. In fact, many bank names include the word *trust*. The 2019 Edelman Trust Barometer, focusing on financial services, indicates trust in the sector is at its highest level since Edelman started measuring it in 2012. But at 57%, trust in financial services, among the general population, remains the least-trusted sector measured by the Edelman Trust Barometer. It is a similar story across the globe.

Also, a recent survey in the *Economist* magazine revealed that 48% of the Americans surveyed responded that U.S. financial systems *hurt* the economy. The Chicago Booth/Kellogg School Financial Trust Index survey confirmed the skepticism of the American public when it found 58% of Americans *disagree* that financial innovation boosts economic growth. While this perception existed before the global financial crisis (discussed in detail in the next section), Americans' trust toward financial firms dropped precipitously during the crisis and has been slow to fully recover.[22]

The WEF has spearheaded efforts to repair trust by publicizing improvements that have been made by various stakeholders to the global financial system to help prevent future financial shocks. Part of this process involves establishing a set of goals for what a financial system *should* provide to society.

- *Financial resilience:* Financial systems stakeholders should strive to develop robust mechanisms to contain a financial crisis in one sector (e.g., housing) from creating a crisis in another sector (e.g., the stock market).

- *Safeguard savings:* For both developed and developing nations, the ability to safely save money for future needs and have immediate access to those funds are crucial.

- *Access to capital and payment systems to support growth:* Both individuals and businesses should have avenues for borrowing money for current needs and for expansion. Government organizations need access to capital to finance large infrastructure projects such as rail systems and public transportation.

- *Collect and analyze financial data for better decision-making:* Financial firms and government entities should work together to collect financial data for public use and to offer households financial advice om savings, investments, and other major financial decisions.

KEY TAKEAWAYS

Main Street to Wall Street

- The terms *Main Street* and *Wall Street* are used colloquially by economists to describe the two interdependent parts of the global economy.

- Main Street, sometimes called the real economy, means the workers that generate savings primarily through their own labor and then seek ways to invest their savings, which provide a return on their investment.

- Wall Street means the individuals and global firms that make the financial markets function by generating revenue primarily using financial markets rather than labor.

- Despite some of the obvious benefits of a healthy financial market, the perception of society tends to view the financial markets with less trust.

THE GLOBAL FINANCIAL CRISIS

LO 10.3 Articulate the events and factors leading to the global financial crisis.

The most significant event in recent economic history was the global economic downturn that took place between 2007 and 2010. Most economists mark the beginning of the recession as December 2007 and the end in June 2009, but the impact of the recession remained for many years. The IMF concluded the overall impact was the most severe since the Great

global financial
crisis: An 18-month
economic downturn
from 2007 to 2009 that
the IMF concluded
was the most severe
recession since the
Great Depression in the
1930s.

Depression in the 1930s, and this led media commentators to dub the 18-month-long downturn as the Great Recession, or the **global financial crisis**.[23] Extraordinary economic events such as recessions do not have a single cause, and the ebb and flow of economic cycles also plays a part. The financial crisis of 2008[ii] intensified the impact of the Great Recession not only in the United States but also globally, and it significantly curtailed economic recovery, which caused the recession to linger.

While the seeds of the financial crisis were planted over the period of many years, the crisis reached seismic proportions in September 2008. Within 1 week's time, two icons of the financial world were on the brink of failure. Lehman Brothers, the fourth largest financial services firm at the time and a venerable Wall Street player, filed for bankruptcy after a frantic last-minute search for a financial backer failed. It was the largest bankruptcy in U.S. history, and to the astonishment of Wall Street and Main Street alike, the 158-year-old firm was wiped out forever. Soon thereafter, auditors for American International Group (AIG), a massive financial services firm with $850 million in assets and 116,000 employees across the globe, revealed the collapse of AIG was imminent. The panic in the investment community over the failure of Lehman and the impending collapse of AIG caused the stock market to plummet. The panic quickly spread to Main Street as unemployment rose sharply soon after the Lehman bankruptcy. On average, the economy shed 651,000 jobs *per month* over the last quarter of 2008 and 780,000 jobs *per month* in the first quarter of 2009. In total, economists estimate that 8.8 million Americans lost their jobs in less than one year.[24] The crisis had a devastating effect on the Main Street economic sectors: new vehicle sales slumped, small businesses failed because of lack of cash flow, and upscale restaurants suffered downturns.[25] During that same time, total retirement assets, Americans' second-largest household asset, dropped by 22% from 2006 to 2009. Savings and investment assets (apart from retirement savings) lost $1.2 trillion while pension assets lost $1.3 trillion. Home prices dropped 32% from their peak in 2006 to their low point in 2009 and about 22% of homeowners faced mortgage foreclosure.[26] American policymakers were faced with two painful alternatives: risk a total collapse of the U.S. economy and a potential spread to other global markets or inject trillions of taxpayer dollars into the financial systems, including bailing out large banks and companies.

Root Causes

While a narrative of the financial crisis is evocative and useful in understanding the human dimension, the obvious question centers on *how*. How could a developed economy with low unemployment, a rising stock market, and abundant amounts of available credit ever shatter in such a short period of time? How could financial system stakeholders have missed the signs that a crisis was coming? As you may imagine, there are a variety of diverse views as to the causes and effects of the financial crisis, but most economists agree on certain fundamental root causes. We discuss them separately, but it is important to understand that they were all interconnected. Some commentators called these factors the perfect storm of the global financial crisis, but others blame regulators and other stakeholders, including consumers and investors alike, for their lack of oversight and prudence.[27] Some believed

---

[ii] Although the financial conditions leading to the crisis began in 2007 and ended in 2009, we refer to the entire period as the financial crisis of 2008 for clarity's sake.

U.S. EX REL. O'DONNELL V. COUNTRYWIDE FINANCIAL CORP AND BANK OF AMERICA, 822 F.3D 650 (2016)

Facts: This case arises in the context of the financial crisis. Prior to 2007, Countrywide Financial's Full Spectrum Lending Division specialized in subprime loans. After the collapse of the subprime market, Countrywide reorganized this division to focus on prime loans, selling them to government-sponsored Freddie Mac and Fannie Mae mortgage entities.

The government, on behalf of O'Donnell, a former Countrywide employee and whistleblower in this case, alleged Countrywide committed fraud under the Financial Institutions Reform, Recovery, and Enforcement Act (FIRREA) when it sold loans to both Freddie Mac and Fannie Mae that it knew were not investment quality. Specifically, in the contracts to sell the loans, Countrywide represented to Freddie Mac and Fannie Mae that the loans were "investment quality," but individuals from Countrywide knew the loans did not meet this quality standard and thus intended to defraud them. Countrywide claims the government has no proof of fraud—only that they breached their contract.

Issue: Does the government have proof that Countrywide committed fraud?

Decision: No, the government does not have proof that Countrywide committed fraud. According to FIRREA, anyone who conspires to violate federal mail or wire fraud statutes in a manner "affecting a federally insured financial institution" may face civil penalties. Fraud, for mail or wire fraud violations, includes "any scheme to defraud." According to case law, fraud under these circumstances turns on when the representations were made and the intent of the promisor at that time. Here, where the allegation is fraudulent statements made in a contract, we must determine the intent of the promisor at the time they made the contract. A representation in a contract is fraudulent only if it was made with the contemporaneous intent to defraud: The promisor knew *at the time they made the statement* that it was false or never intended to perform it and made it with the intent to induce the

other party to enter into the contract. Thus, there must be proof of deception at the time the contract was made, not just proof of a later breach of contract.

Here, the contract between the government and Freddie Mac and Fannie Mae states that Countrywide warrants that future transferred loans will be investment quality "as of" the delivery date. The government does not have proof of deception at the time the loans were sold (the delivery date) to Freddie Mac and Fannie Mae. Although the government alleges that some key individuals at Countrywide knew the loans they sold were not investment grade, those individuals were not part of the contract negotiations with Freddie Mac or Fannie Mae. Thus, the government cannot prove that at the time the contracts were executed that Countrywide never intended to perform its promise of investment quality loans or that any quality guarantee was made with fraudulent intent. Nor did it prove that Countrywide made any later representations from which fraudulent intent could be found.

Law and Management Questions

1. The decision in this case overturned a $1.27 billion jury verdict against Countrywide where the jury found it had committed fraud by lying to Freddie Mac and Fannie Mae about the loans. However, the appeals court said there was no technical fraud, but it does not dispute that some people at Countrywide knew they were selling bad loans. Should this matter? What might be the impact of this case on future fraud cases brought against financial institutions?

2. This case was one of the very few that resulted from the financial crisis, and the multibillion-dollar verdict was overturned. Analyze the impact this decision might have had on the millions of people and businesses that lost money in the crisis.

moral hazard: An information failure where one party to a transaction has greater material knowledge than the other party.

bubble: Term used by economists to describe a long-lasting deviation of the price of some assets from their fundamental value (e.g., housing bubble).

initially this crisis was due to a situation called **moral hazard**—essentially an information failure where one party (i.e., mortgage lenders) to a transaction has greater material knowledge than the other party (i.e., those taking out the loans).[28]

Housing Bubble

Economists use the term **bubble** to describe a large, long-lasting deviation of the price of some assets from their fundamental value. While experts in financial markets agree on the definition of a bubble, they do not always agree on when a bubble exists in the economy at a given moment in time. As early as 2001, economists such as Paul Krugman and Dean Baker warned of a housing bubble in the *New York Times* and other financial publications such as *Barron's* and *Forbes*. The National Commission on the Causes of the Financial and Economic Crisis (NCCFC) concluded that a housing gold rush spread quickly across America, and it was fueled by low mortgage interest rates and skyrocketing home values where housing prices increased 152% between 1997 and 2006.[iii] Wall Street and Main Street alike were seeking safer investments after experiencing the burst of the tech sector bubble in 2000 where many investors suffered significant losses. According to Susan Lund, McKinsey Global Institute economist, the "epicenter" of the global financial crisis was really the housing market. It started in the United States, but similar housing bubbles were building in other countries (e.g., the United Kingdom, Spain, and Ireland). Simply put, consumers were borrowing more than they could afford. Banks were giving out loans at very low introductory interest rates.[29]

Although it may seem irrational in hindsight, many homeowners believed the value of their property would *never* fall and acted accordingly by effectively using their home as an ATM and borrowing money based on the equity in their home. While some of the equity was produced from these consumers paying down their mortgage, home equity values skyrocketed because homeowners were seeing their homes double in value as housing prices continued to climb.[30]

The speed and intensity of the burst of the gold rush bubble took homeowners by surprise. By December 2009, the housing market plummeted, and the media popularized a new term to describe homeowners who now owed more on their home than it was worth: *under water*. Combined with rising unemployment and financial losses in their retirement funds, homeowners had greater difficulty in making their mortgage payments and were facing foreclosure. The pressure was so intense that some homeowners were willing to destroy their creditworthiness by simply abandoning their houses as the foreclosure process took its course. Of course, any collapse of the housing market has a direct impact not only on home valuations but banks and mortgage lenders, home builders, real estate brokers, home supply retail outlets, and others that depend on home buyers as customers. Figure 10.3 shows how quickly mortgage foreclosures spread in the United States.

Irrational Leveraging Throughout the Economy

leveraging: In the context of investing, borrowing money to invest with the objective of producing a higher level of return.

Homeowners weren't the only ones who had an overly optimistic view of the economy. Banks and financial firms increased their profits through transactions that relied on **leveraging**. In this context, leveraging is essentially borrowing money in order to invest

---

[iii] Based on the Case–Shiller Real Estate Index.

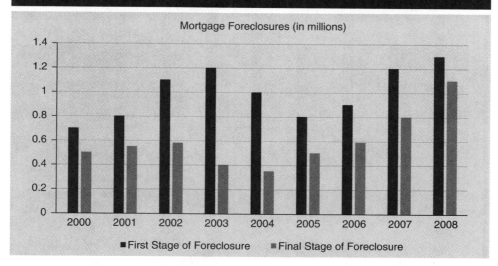

Figure 10.3 Mortgage Foreclosures in the First and Last Stages of Foreclosure (2000–2008)

Source: Based on data from the Federal Reserve and *The Financial Crisis Inquiry Report* (2011).

it and produce a higher level of return. So long as the investments yield positive returns, the borrower pays back the money and keeps the profit. The catch is that if the investment *loses* money, the borrower has no funds to pay the money back, and both the lender and borrower suffer catastrophic losses. That is precisely what happened in 2008—highly leveraged banks bet heavily on sophisticated investments related to homeownership and started to lose money on their investments as the housing bubble burst. The names of the complex investment transactions used by financial firms before the crisis, such as a collateralized debt obligation (CDO), a credit default swap, or commercial paper plays, became part of a new financial vocabulary. While a detailed discussion of these products is outside of the scope of this book, suffice it to say they all depended on the fragile real estate market.

To understand how investors use the power of leveraging, consider the example of two hypothetical investors who each want to invest $5,000 of their savings into an investment that they believe will yield approximately 15% return in one year. The first investor, Sarah Safety, does not want to use leverage because it is too risky. She invests $5,000, and at the end of the year her investment has earned $750—a tidy sum. Our second investor, Rhonda Risky, is an investor willing to leverage her $5,000 investment by borrowing an additional $20,000 at an interest rate of 6% per year. Rhonda invests the entire $25,000 (her initial $5,000 plus the borrowed $20,000) and earns a whopping $3,750 on her investment in one year. Even after she has paid back the loan and $1,200 in interest, Rhonda pockets $2,550—a 51% rate of return on her initial $5,000 investment. Rhonda's return was substantial, but so was her risk. If the investment *doesn't* return enough to cover the interest rate, Rhonda may actually *lose* money while Sarah would still come out ahead. Table 10.2 and Figure 10.4 provide a comparison between our two hypothetical investors.

Table 10.2   Investor Comparison

Investor	Sarah Safety	Rhonda Risky
Philosophy	Non-leveraged	Leveraged
Initial investment	$5,000	$5,000
Borrowed (interest rate per yr.)	0	$20,000 (6%)
Total investment	$5,000	$25,000
Year 1 return	$750	$3,750
Interest paid for borrowed funds	0	$1,200
Gain ($)	$750	$2,550
Return on Initial Investment	15%	51%

Figure 10.4   Understanding Leverage

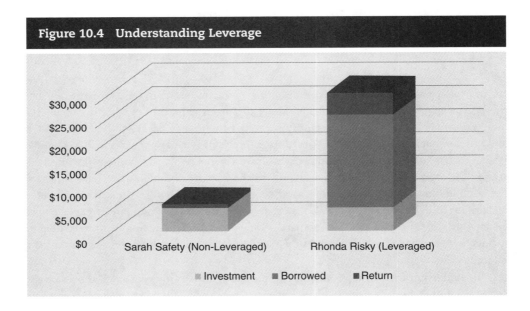

Unethical Lending Practices Via Subprime and Other Risky Mortgage Loans

subprime mortgages:
Mortgages that allow borrowers to have initial lower payments that increase over time.

The overwhelming consensus of experts agree that **subprime mortgages** were a center-piece of the housing bubble and contributed significantly to the crisis. Subprime mortgages were originally designed in the early 1990s for borrowers who would have a difficult time obtaining a traditional mortgage because of a low credit score. The original idea was a noble one: Provide mortgage credit for borrowers who were suffering some temporary financial setbacks such as a medical emergency or a sudden drop in business for self-employed borrowers. These loans had certain features allowing a borrower to have lower payments for an initial period of time, and eventually the payments would increase as the "borrower got back on her feet."[31] As housing prices went up, more borrowers discovered these loans as mortgage lenders enticed potential home buyers with attractive subprime mortgage products. Between 1998 and 2006, subprime lending swelled from 8% to over 20% of all new mortgages.[32]

A good example of such unethical practices is the case of Goldman Sachs, one of the largest investment banking firms. In 2007, Goldman engaged in a deal with Paulson & Co., a hedge fund firm, in which Paulson & Co. would select the bonds that Goldman repackaged into CDOs; its fund was called Abacus. CDOs are collections of unrelated debt instruments, like bonds, that are pooled together and sold to investors wanting to buy shares in the pool. During the housing boom in the United States, these pools were filled with mortgage-backed securities—which were themselves built on pools of personal mortgages—and were packaged together into highly complex CDOs. These CDOs were sold in tranches based on their creditworthiness. In the Abacus deal, Paulson selected the securities and then bet against them, with Goldman's knowledge, and Moody's rated the deal AAA, its highest rating. In April 2010, the SEC filed civil charges against Goldman for its role in the Abacus deal, charging it with "defrauding investors by misstating and omitting key facts about a financial product tied to subprime mortgages as the U.S. housing market was beginning to falter."[33] The SEC announced in July 2010 that Goldman Sachs should pay $550 million and reform its business practices to settle the charges that Goldman misled investors. In agreeing to the largest-ever SEC penalty paid by a Wall Street firm, Goldman also acknowledged that its marketing materials for the subprime product contained incomplete information.

Loans such as *pick-a-pay* mortgages where the borrower decided how much interest and/or principal to pay back and the lender adds any unpaid interest into the principal became increasingly popular. Nearly one third of subprime mortgages were either *no-doc* or *low-doc* mortgages that were marketed to borrowers whose income varied over time (e.g., jobs related to sales where a performance bonus was a substantial part of household income). These loans became known as "liar loans" because they required none of the traditional asset verification required for a traditional mortgages such as payroll stubs, tax returns, or savings account statements.[34] Giving in to the gold rush mentality mentioned earlier, borrowers believed that rising home prices would provide a more than adequate cushion until they could qualify for a traditional mortgage, and many borrowed more than they could afford at the time. Mortgage brokers generated fees based on the number of mortgage loans they closed and had no incentive to be concerned about whether the borrower could afford the loan.[35] The NCCFC report captured the mood of the gold rush:

> An advertising barrage bombarded potential borrowers, urging them to buy or refinance homes…Dancing figures, depicting happy homeowners, boogied on computer monitors…One percent loan! (But only for the first year.) No money down! (Leaving no equity if home prices fall.) No income documentation needed! Borrowers answered the call, many believing that with the ever-rising prices, housing was the investment that couldn't lose.[36]

Not surprisingly, subprime borrowers were among the first to fall when the housing bubble burst. By January 2008, approximately 21% of subprime were either 90 days' delinquent or the lender had begun foreclosure proceedings. By May 2008 it was 25%—one in four homes with subprime mortgages were nearing foreclosure and wreaking financial disaster on homeowners and their communities.[37]

Poor Regulatory Oversight

There is no question about the failure of government and industry regulatory authorities who are charged with ensuring the safe and sound operation of banks and other financial institutions. The disputed questions center on *why* regulators were so reluctant to halt the risky practices by financial institutions. Some cite a regulatory bias toward an unfettered free-market policy and an unwillingness to be perceived as constraining economic growth. The NCCFC reported that both the Clinton and Bush administrations made increased home ownership among low-income families an important part of their public policies, and both the Congress and administration officials were pressured to ease any regulation that may tamp down homeownership rates. Policymakers were convinced that even if the housing market crashed, the global financial system could outlast any temporary crisis.[38]

Government Bailouts: Too Big to Fail

As the housing bubble burst and the highly leveraged financial firms were brought to the brink of bankruptcy, banks were scrambling to recover their own assets and became unwilling to lend to financial firms or to individual borrowers effectively causing the credit markets to seize. Subprime borrowers were stuck with high monthly payments because banks were unwilling to lend or refinance their mortgage loans as housing prices plummeted. As the crisis spread throughout the nation's financial firms, banks, and mortgage lenders, it became clear that government intervention was necessary to prevent a global financial collapse. Dubbed by media commentators as "too big to fail" bailouts, government officials from the U.S. Treasury Department and the Federal Reserve invoked emergency powers to handle each major financial institution with individually crafted loans and guarantees that provided a lifeline of cash and, in most cases, avoiding bankruptcy and preventing the crisis from engulfing the world economy. The five largest U.S. investment banks, with combined liabilities or debts of $4 trillion, either went bankrupt (e.g., Lehman Brothers), were taken over by other companies (e.g., Bear Stearns and Merrill Lynch), or were bailed out by the U.S. government (e.g., Goldman Sachs and Morgan Stanley) during 2008.[39] Washington Mutual was seized in September 2008 by the Office of Thrift Supervision (OTS), and regulators arranged a merger of Wells Fargo and Wachovia after it was speculated that Wachovia was also going to fail.

Although the government had attempted to hold back the recessionary pressures with a $168 billion economic stimulus package in early 2008, most economists agree that it was too small to have been effective given the intensity of looming financial crisis. As the Wall Street bailouts continued, the White House and Congress faced public pressure to help bail out Main Street.

TARP

Realizing that the government's bailout efforts were only a temporary solution, Congress passed the Emergency Economic Stabilization Act of 2008, which included a $700 billon fund designated for the Troubled Asset Relief Program (TARP). These TARP funds were intended to stabilize financial institutions and eventually spread to other important segments of the economy, including $181 billion for automobile manufacturers General Motors and Chrysler. In exchange, TARP fund recipients agreed to give the government partial ownership of the company and to abide by certain internal financial controls and oversight. These restrictions led several recipients to repay the funds relatively soon. TARP recipients are required to apply for release from the program after showing that their financial condition is sufficiently stable. Within a year of passage of TARP, more than 50 banks were approved to pay back TARP funds, including a $25 billion payment from JPMorgan Chase and a $3.6 billion payment from Capital One Financial. In 2009, the Bush presidency came to an end, and the Obama administration faced continuing economic pressures to provide relief to Main Street, leading to the American Recovery and Reinvestment Act of 2009, which was intended to provide jobs by injecting government funds into national infrastructure projects ranging from fixing crumbling bridges to upgrading rail systems.

The Dodd–Frank Act

The financial crises destabilized American life and created a sort of national anxiety that spawned citizen movements such as "Occupy Wall Street," resulted in a popular anger at the government, and increased the perception that the system was rigged in favor of the

Occupy Wall Street

New York Times columnist Tom Friedman described the devastation of the financial crisis on ordinary citizens as a "collective congestive heart failure" as the result of losing the foundations of American life: their jobs and their houses.[40] There was also a growing sense that a corrupt political system was bailing out a financial system rigged to favor society's wealthiest at the expense of the middle-class and poor. While Congress was creating bailout plans, passing safeguards, and providing cash for projects to create jobs, activist groups and advocates became increasingly frustrated about the lack of prosecutions by state and federal officials. Nearly 2 years after the crisis, not a single criminal case had been brought against top figures in financial firms whose recklessness brought the global financial system to the brink of disaster.[41] Partially spurred by lack of prosecutions and concern over corporate influence in politics, a small group of activists began to call for a "Million Man March on Wall Street" in the summer of 2011.

We Are the 99%

As organizers began to create a social media presence and an advertising campaign, word spread among millennials and eventually to the wider community, such as labor unions. On September 17, 2011, a group of a few hundred protesters marched down the heart of New York's financial district with signs "We are the 99%" that many mark as the beginning of the Occupy Wall Street movement. Citing the financial crisis as Exhibit A, the 99% campaign stemmed from the root of the protesters' belief that the political and financial systems are rigged in favor of the top 1%. The protesters eventually were permitted to set up a tent city in nearby Zuccotti Park, and they began to organize and articulate more specific grievances and demands. While the movement itself clearly struggled under the weight of rapidly growing size and growing internal strife, some common points of grievances did emerge. A centerpiece was income inequality. Protesters grounded their

(Continued)

CASE STUDY 10.2

(Continued)

grievance on studies and economic data that indicated that the richest 1% in America has increased their wealth dramatically over the period of the past 40 years and that the financial crisis has actually made the inequality worse. Other common grievances included eliminating corporate influence on public policy, reform of the banking industry, prosecutions in the subprime mortgage crisis, and relief for debtors from home loans and student loans. Those grievances clearly touched a nerve in the American populace as a larger Occupy movement spread to over 1,000 locations across the United States.[42]

The Abrupt End and Impact

After 2 months of skirmishes with New York City officials and neighborhood residents about the impact of the protests on health, sanitation, and safety, Mayor Michael Bloomberg evicted the protesters. The NYPD cleared the park on November 11, 2011, and arrested 240 protesters. Attempts to reoccupy the park or other financial district locations were met with resistance from the police who continued to arrest groups of protesters around the city. Despite the splintering of the Occupy movement in the early part of 2012, organizers point to modern movements that used the Occupy Wall Street movement as a model for effective protests including Black Lives Matter and the Fight for $15 movement to increase wages for workers in the mega food chains such as McDonald's.[43]

Discussion Questions

1. What were the primary factors that caused the Occupy Wall Street movement? What does the "99% movement" represent?

2. What can primary and secondary stakeholders of the financial system learn from the Occupy Wall Street movement? Explain.

3. In what ways was the Occupy Wall Street movement successful, and in what ways did it not succeed? Did they influence any of the policies that were the subject of their grievances?

Critical Thinking

Who were the protesters? *HuffPost* reported on a study that revealed those who described themselves as actively involved in the Occupy movement were "overwhelmingly white, highly educated, and employed." Citing a report from the Joseph F. Murphy Institute for Worker Education and Labor Studies at the City University of New York, they found that although protesters ranged in age from 23 to 69, most were in their 20s or 30s. Other findings include that the majority were white, about 60% were men, 90% had college degrees, and 30% had postgraduate degrees.[44]

1. Do the demographics of the Occupy movement surprise you? How does it square with their 99% message? Explain.

2. Where does the Occupy Wall Street protester fall in terms of a stakeholder category? Are the demographics of the Occupy Wall Street movement related to its core values? Are all movements related to the demographics of its protesters?

wealthiest Americans who could rely on the government to bail them out of their excessive greed. As the economy stabilized, the focus shifted to the egregious conduct of the financial stakeholders that caused the crisis. Ultimately, Congress settled on the Dodd–Frank Wall Street Reform and Consumer Protection Act (commonly called the Dodd–Frank Act [DFA]) as the legislative solution to preventing future failures through a comprehensive set of regulations and oversight mechanisms (see Chapter 6 for more information on how DFA protects consumers). The DFA is explained in more detail later in this chapter.

Ongoing Debates

Both at the time of the crisis and in the aftermath, economists and commentators debated whether the bailouts were the best solution. For example, as Congress launched the bailout packages, Harvard economist Jeffrey Miron decried the bailouts as a form of corporate welfare that rewarded wrongful conduct and exorbitant risk. Miron favored bankruptcy over the bailouts, arguing that "bankruptcy does not mean the company disappears; it is just owned by someone new (as has occurred with several airlines)." Bailouts, he pointed out, are a transfer of wealth from taxpayers to those who took excessive risks and therefore generated "enormous distortions in an economy's allocation of its financial resources."[45] On the other hand, Alan Blinder, an economist, claimed that, all things considered, the bailouts were necessary to prevent a global financial disaster and that the bailouts "worked—probably better than anyone expected," and in the end it "cost the taxpayer almost nothing."[46] Others wonder if the meltdown was due to a market failure or a government failure, or both.[47] Market failure is when the marketplace fails to adjust prices for the true costs of a firm's behavior. Perhaps ironically, it is one of the reasons for government regulation to become necessary.

KEY TAKEAWAYS

The Global Financial Crisis

- The most significant event in recent economic history was the global financial crisis that took place between 2007 and 2009.

- While the seeds of the global financial crisis were planted over the period of many years, the crisis reached seismic proportions in September 2008.

- Most economists agree there were several root causes: (1) a gold rush housing bubble, (2) irrational leveraging throughout the economy, (3) unethical lending practices via subprime and other risky mortgage loans, and (4) poor regulatory oversight.

- The five largest U.S. investment banks either went bankrupt (Lehman Brothers), were taken over by other companies (Bear Stearns and Merrill Lynch), or were bailed out by the U.S. government (Goldman Sachs and Morgan Stanley) during 2008.

- Both at the time of the crisis and in the aftermath, economists and commentators debated whether the large bank bailouts were the best solution.

ALTERNATIVE FINANCING AND PAYDAY LOANS

LO 10.4 Compare and contrast ethical dilemmas surrounding use of payday loans.

One of the most controversial forms of financing is called **payday loans**. These loans, as the name implies, typically require a borrower to pay the loan back in full on her next payday. Payday loans were introduced in the early 1990s, increased steadily over the next decade, then exploded during the financial crisis of 2007–2008. According to the Pew Charitable Trusts, 12 million Americans per year now use payday loans. Retail payday loan outlets outpace the number of stores operated by McDonald's and Starbucks combined.[48] Payday loans are unsecured, short-term cash loans that range in size from $100 to $1,500 (the maximum amounts are set by individual state statutes), and the average loan term is 2 weeks. The loans must be paid back with interest in one lump sum on the borrower's next payday. Most people who use payday loans do so because they don't have enough credit or assets for a traditional bank loan. Payday lenders typically do not

payday loans: Controversial financing method that requires a borrower to pay a loan back with interest in one lump sum on her next payday.

Table 10.3 Rates and Fees Charged by the Five Largest Publicly Held Payday Lenders

Lender	Loan Amounts	Cost of a 2-Week Loan for $500	Resulting APR
Dollar Financial	Up to $1,500	$77.50	404.11%
Cash America/Payday 1	$100–$1,000	$112.50	587.00%
QC Holdings (now QCHI)/Tremont	$250–$500	$150.00	782.00%
Advance America	$100–$1,500	$125.00	651.00%
EZCORP	Up to $1,000	$150.00	782.00%

Source: Table composed by author based on SEC filings, Consumer Federation of America 2015 *Survey*, and Public Accountability Initiative's (PAI) *Report on Payday Lenders* https://public-accountability.org/wp-content/uploads/2011/09/payday-final-091410.pdf.

check the borrower's credit so long as the borrower can show that she is employed and has a bank account in good standing. Loans are available at retail outlets, online, and even through mobile apps. For the convenience, immediacy, and flexibility of a payday loan, borrowers pay a heavy price in interest (see Table 10.3). Payday lenders characterize their finance charge as a fee and charge from $15 to $30 per $100 borrowed. This means the effective annual percentage rate (APR) may range from 390% to 780% or more.[49] In contrast, other forms of unsecured credit, such as using a credit card, incur an average APR of 17%.[50]

Auto Title Loans

Payday loans have a close cousin called an auto title loan. They are similar in terms of access, convenience, and no check on the borrower's credit. They also carry triple-digit interest rates as well. The primary difference between an auto title loan versus a payday loan is that the borrower is pledging the title of his or her vehicle as collateral for the loan so that the loan is considered secured in case the borrower defaults. Auto title loans often are for an amount that is 25% to 50% of the value of the car. Because the loan is secured by the auto title, lenders are willing to provide larger loan amounts than for payday loans.

Payday Loan Regulation

Consumer protection regulations are often within the jurisdiction of state governments, and the result has been a patchwork of state regulation of payday loans. In

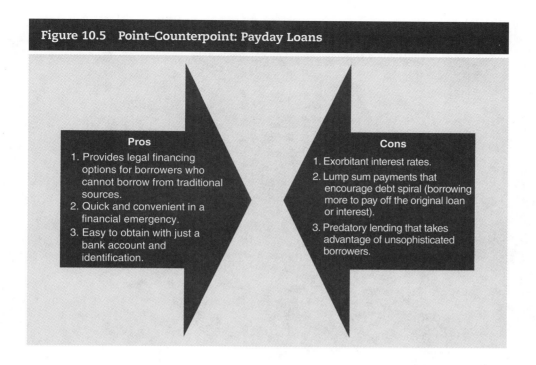

Figure 10.5 Point–Counterpoint: Payday Loans

Pros

1. Provides legal financing options for borrowers who cannot borrow from traditional sources.
2. Quick and convenient in a financial emergency.
3. Easy to obtain with just a bank account and identification.

Cons

1. Exorbitant interest rates.
2. Lump sum payments that encourage debt spiral (borrowing more to pay off the original loan or interest).
3. Predatory lending that takes advantage of unsophisticated borrowers.

response, the Consumer Financial Protection Bureau (CFPB) proposed new federal rules intended to protect payday loan borrowers. The centerpiece of the federal rules focuses on the frequency and amount of payday loans by setting a single loan maximum at $500. More importantly, lenders can only make a payday loan if the borrower has no other outstanding loans. These rules require lenders of any short-term loan (any loan in which repayment is due in less than 45 days) to take steps necessary to reasonably determine that consumers can repay the loans. This includes verifying the borrower's income and calculating a debt-to-income ratio for each borrower.[iv] As one would expect, the CFPB payday loan rule was met with harsh criticism by lenders, and the rule is currently being challenged in federal courts. In October 2018, the CFPB announced that they were reconsidering the rule.[51] In 2019, in her first move as the new director of the CFPB, Kathleen Kraninger proposed eliminating nearly all of the regulation's substantive requirements, including the "ability to repay" mandate, citing "insufficient evidence and legal support."[52] However, according to CFPB data, using payday loans can be a hard cycle to break; half of all payday loans result in needing 10 consecutive loans.[53] Figure 10.5 summarizes the arguments for and against payday loans.

[iv] A debt-to-income ratio compares total debt from all creditors to a borrower's sources of income.

Payday Loans: Parasites or Providers?

iStockphoto.com/ShaunWilkinson

Payday loans are the subject of intense debate. The *Washington Post* referred to payday lending as "legalized parasitism" in an editorial condemning the payday loan industry.[54] Critics of payday loans point to the circular debt cycle encouraged by payday lenders. Because the entire principal and interest of the loan must be repaid in one lump sum and in a short period of time, some borrowers find it impossible to repay the loan on their next payday and are forced to borrow even more to pay off the original loan. In fact, payday loan borrowers spent an average of $520 in interest for loans where the average amount borrowed was only $375. The same Pew Charitable Trusts survey cited earlier concluded that only 14% of borrowers can repay the average payday loan. This debt spiral is particularly burdensome on the most unsophisticated borrowers who may be left with no legitimate alternatives and are willing to look past the oppressive terms to receive the cash immediately. Some states have banned payday lending completely as a predatory lending practice, and others have regulated the loans by requiring more disclosures, capping fees, or mandating that all loans be installment loans that are paid over time rather than as one lump sum. As a result, payday lenders in certain states offer longer-term payday installment loans but require the borrower to authorize the lender to electronically withdraw multiple payments from the borrower's bank account, typically due on each pay date.[55]

At the same time, some argue that payday loans serve an important underserved market for low-income workers who have no alternatives when an unexpected financial jolt hits their household. Even consumers who are homeowners with steady incomes can be caught short when an urgent financial need arises. Defenders of payday loans cite studies that indicate the access to payday loans lowered the likelihood of home foreclosure after natural disasters by over 20%.[56] Payday loans also increased during the financial crisis of 2007–2008 as more and more consumers found themselves with increasing household debt while banks tightened the amount of available credit via loans and credit cards. Without payday loans, borrowers starved for cash may turn to illegal alternatives such as loan sharks. Payday lenders justify the exorbitant interest rates as necessary to cover the risks associated with high rates of borrower defaults on payday loans. Experts also warn that restricting payday lending may bring unintended consequences. One economist cautioned that it is important for policymakers to understand "both the potential benefits of restricting payday lending as well as the potential costs." These restrictions could hinder economic growth if bankruptcy or loan default rates increase and could potentially impact social services costs for the poor and people in need of medical care.[57]

The debate over the usefulness of auto title loans is similar to the debate over payday loans. In fact, most of the lenders that offer these products also offer payday loans.

Discussion Questions

1. *Stakeholder theories:* Identify the stakeholders in a payday loan transaction. What is the impact of payday loans on those stakeholders? Do their interests align? Why or why not? Should the government do more to protect payday loan consumers? If yes, what regulations would you propose? If no, why not? Do lenders have an ethical obligation to verify a borrower's assets before approving a loan? Explain.

2. *Ethical decision-making:* What measures could payday lenders use to ensure that consumers do not get caught into the circular debt cycle? How could a payday lender use CSR to guide its practices?

Take a Position

Issue: Should the federal government regulate payday lenders so that consumers have more uniform protections as opposed to state laws which vary widely? What should it do about the decision by the CFPB?

Sub-Issues:

1. Is government regulation necessary, or could the industry set up some type of self-regulatory body similar to the systems used by brokerage firms (discussed earlier)?

2. Could government regulation actually harm consumers who need a payday loan to cover an unexpected financial event? How?

KEY TAKEAWAYS

Alternative Financing and Payday Loans

- One of the most controversial alternative forms of financing are payday loans. These loans, as the name implies, typically require a borrower to pay the loan back in full on her next payday.

- Microfinancing has advanced from simple micro loans to a more comprehensive concept intended to use the free market to lift people out of poverty.

FINANCIAL MARKET REGULATION

LO 10.5 Explain the main provisions of various legislative acts like the Dodd–Frank Act (DFA).

Following the global financial crisis and its effect on consumers, governments across the globe began to implement policy aimed at protecting the consumer more fully for a broad range of financial services products (e.g., loans, mortgages, credit).

Expanded Jurisdiction and Enforcement

In the United States, the **U.S. Securities and Exchange Commission (SEC)** is an independent agency consisting of five commissioners appointed by the president of the United States. The other major stock exchanges around the world are overseen by similar government entities. The SEC only has the power to enforce federal securities laws; it also has the authority to regulate all aspects of U.S. capital markets, including the issuance and trading of securities on primary and secondary markets. In particular, companies that issue publicly traded shares have to submit quarterly and annual reports to the SEC. These mandatory disclosures are essential to many investors who use the information in these reports to make crucial decisions before investing in capital markets. Moreover, a firm that makes material misstatements on its reports or that is involved in other fraudulent activities could be subject to an SEC enforcement action and to lawsuits by investors (see example of Goldman Sachs).

> **U.S. Securities and Exchange Commission (SEC):** An independent agency consisting of five commissioners appointed by the president of the United States.

Broadly speaking, the objectives of these disclosure requirements are usually as follows:

- *Confidence:* Creating confidence in financial markets

- *Stability:* Maintaining the integrity and stability of financial markets

- *Investor protection:* Securing the appropriate degree of protection for investors—largely through disclosure of information

The SEC strongly believes that giving shareholders more and better company information, is the best way to safeguard investor interests. In fact, the right of a shareholder to obtain relevant and material information on the corporation on a timely and regular basis is a right held by much of the world's largest stock exchanges according to the Organization for Economic Cooperation and Development (OECD), an organization working in partnership with governments, policymakers, and citizens in 37 countries to establish international norms.[58]

The requirement to disclose information was the main reason the SEC was created in 1934 and remains an important aspect of its recent rulemaking. For example, in 2002, Congress enacted the Sarbanes–Oxley Act (SOX) to provide assurance about the accuracy and completeness of financial statements in the wake of a variety of accounting scandals involving Enron and Arthur Andersen, among others. It applies to U.S. and non-U.S. companies listed on a U.S. stock exchange. The intention was to provide investors and shareholders with confidence in a company's financial reporting—and this was not simply a U.S. phenomenon. The 8th EU Company Law Directive is considered the European version of the SOX. The Financial Instruments and Exchange Law is the Japanese version. It is unofficially called J-SOX, and there are requirements similar to the SOX Sections 302 and 404 (management certification and management evaluation and report on internal controls). Similarly aimed at disclosure, in July 2019 the proposed Climate Risk Disclosure Act of 2019 would direct the SEC to tailor disclosure requirements to different industries and to impose additional disclosure requirements on fossil fuel companies, including direct and indirect greenhouse gas emissions and the total amount of fossil fuel-related assets that the company owns or manages.[59]

In the United States, the DFA expanded the jurisdiction of the SEC and provided it with a powerful set of new tools for the investigation and enforcement of securities law violations. These new tools include the following:

- *Secret investigations:* Under the DFA, the SEC is no longer required to disclose its records or any other information related to its ongoing investigations or inquiries, including surveillance, risk assessments, or other regulatory and oversight activities (except for judicial or congressional inquiry). The effective result of this major change is that the federal Freedom of Information Act (FOIA) no longer applies to the SEC, so the SEC can refuse to supply documents it deems as being part of its regulatory and oversight activities.

- *Fiduciary duty of broker–dealers:* The DFA authorizes the SEC to impose a fiduciary duty on brokers and dealers when providing personalized investment advice to retail customers—the same standard that is applicable to investment advisers.

- *Hedge funds:* Advisers to hedge funds and private equity funds must register with the SEC as investment advisers and provide information about their trades and portfolios necessary to assess systemic risk.

President Obama signs the Dodd–Frank Act (DFA) into law with Senator Dodd (center) and Representative Frank (right) looking on.

- *Credit ratings agencies:* A specific office created at the SEC with expertise and its own compliance staff and the authority to fine agencies. The SEC is required to examine nationally recognized statistical ratings organizations (NRSROs) at least once a year and make key findings public. NRSROs rate bonds and stocks for their creditworthiness and are influential regulations on Wall Street and Main Street.

Financial Stability Oversight

At the Cannes Summit in 2011, the leaders of the largest 20 countries globally (the G20) endorsed the implementation of an integrated set of policy measures to address the risks to the global financial system from systemically important financial institutions (SIFIs) and the timeline for implementation of these measures. Specific measures focus on global SIFIs to reflect the greater risks that these institutions pose to the global financial system.

Globally, the Financial Stability Board (FSB) was created to bring together senior policymakers from ministries of finance, central banks, and supervisory and regulatory authorities for the G20 countries, plus four other key financial centers—Hong Kong, Singapore, Spain, and Switzerland. In addition, it includes international bodies, including standard-setters and regional bodies like the European Central Bank and European Commission. The goal of the FSB is to get all the players who set financial stability policies across different sectors of the financial system at one table.[60] Recently, the FSB has warned G20 bankers about the risks posed by cryptocurrency such as Facebook's Libra, namely privacy risks, money laundering, and tax evasion, because it has the potential to become systemically important over time.[61]

Cryptocurrency is digital cash. It shares some similarities with regular cash: You can use cryptocurrency to buy things, and you can transfer it electronically. However, cash retains its value based on our confidence in the government, whereas cryptocurrency retains its value based on supply and demand. And unlike money, cryptocurrency is managed by a network of open source computers instead of the government. Its unique management is also a vulnerability; cryptocurrency accounts can be hacked.

In the United States, in addition to expanding the SEC investigation and enforcement powers, the DFA also created a Financial Stability Oversight Council (FSOC), a new and independent body with a board of regulators to address dangerous risks to global financial markets posed by risky investments or the actions of large, interconnected financial institutions. The FSOC monitors the stability of the U.S. financial system and responds to emerging threats to that system.

The FSOC is chaired by the secretary of the Treasury and consists of 10 voting members who are the heads of various agencies involved in the financial system. The FSOC voting members include, among others, the secretary of the Treasury, the chairman of the Federal Reserve, the Comptroller of the Currency, the director of the CFPB, the chairman of the SEC, and the chair of the Federal Deposit Insurance Corporation (FDIC). The FSOC possesses statutory authority to designate certain "too big to fail" (as they are colloquially known) financial companies for additional regulation in order to minimize the systemic risk that such a company's financial distress will threaten the stability of the American economy. The FSOC also has five nonvoting members, representing the FSOC research arm and state level financial and insurance regulators.

In summary, the FSOC exercises its oversight function over financial markets in three ways:

1. *Risk analysis:* Assessing and reducing "systematic risks" to financial markets and preparing annual reports to Congress

2. *Early warning:* Identifying any emerging threats to the overall stability of financial markets and sounding the alarm when such threats emerge

3. *Identifying financial risk in firms:* Identifying nonbank financial institutions that pose a risk to the stability of the U.S. economy and designating them as SIFIs

Being designated as a SIFI subjects the institution to heightened scrutiny by the Federal Reserve and other regulators around the globe, like the FSB. Their role in identifying financial firms that pose a grave threat to financial stability and determining what action should be taken to break up such firms. These institutions have been dubbed by commentators as "too big to fail" and were a central issue in the financial crisis of 2008. See Table 10.4 for the 2018 list of the global SIFIs compiled each year by the FSB.[62]

Once a bank has been designated a nonbank financial institution as a SIFI, in the United States the DFA empowers the Federal Reserve to assume oversight and impose heightened standards on SIFIs. In addition, banks with over $50 billion in assets are subject to the Federal Reserve's tougher capital requirements and must undergo annual *stress tests* that are designed to test whether a bank has sufficient capital to continue operating and lending to households and businesses, even during times of economic and financial market stress.[63] The DFA also requires that all financial institutions follow certain prudent practices that discourage speculative investing practices. The stress test is a forward-looking quantitative evaluation of bank capital that demonstrates how a hypothetical set of stressful economic conditions developed by the Federal Reserve would affect the capital ratios of large firms.[64]

The DFA is not without criticism. Some have suggested it slowed the recovery without making banking safer, and others cited the expenses for the borrower that significantly increased due to the act's requirements for banking systems and fees that were passed on to the borrowers themselves.[65] Recently there has been much discussion of the act because many of the law's original congressional supporters are no longer in office and the urgency of the 2008 financial crisis has largely faded from public view. Stay tuned to see what the future holds as various lawmakers, along with those in the financial services industry, seek to have rules delayed, watered down, or revoked.[66]

Table 10.4 SIFI Banks Around the Globe	
Agricultural Bank of China	ING Group
Bank of America	JPMorgan Chase
Bank of China	Mitsubishi UFJ Financial Group
Bank of New York Mellon (BNY Mellon)	Mizuho Financial Group
Barclays	Morgan Stanley
BNP Paribas	Royal Bank of Canada
China Construction Bank	Santander Group
Citigroup	Société Générale
Crédit Agricole Group	Standard Chartered
Credit Suisse	State Street Corporation
Deutsche Bank	Sumitomo Mitsui Banking Corporation
Goldman Sachs	UBS
Groupe BPCE	UniCredit
HSBC	Wells Fargo
Industrial and Commercial Bank of China Limited	

KEY TAKEAWAYS

Financial Market Regulation

- Many countries passed regulation in response to the global financial crisis, most notably the United Kingdom, Japan, and the United States.

- Major financial institutions around the globe are now categorized by size and interconnectivity and called SIFIs.

- Securities markets all over the world are governed by laws and regulations

intended to safeguard those who invest their money, but like all regulation, there are benefits and costs.

- The right of a shareholder to obtain relevant and material information on a company to invest in, on a timely and regular basis, is a right held by much of the world's largest stock exchanges.

SUMMARY

In this chapter, we examined the interconnected global financial infrastructure, the role finance and its stakeholders in society, and the unique blend of self-regulation and law in the financial markets. We also focused on conflicting objectives between the financial community and the public at large along with ethical considerations related to global financial transactions and products.

KEY TERMS

best efforts 216
bubble 222
financial firms 214
fintech 217
firm commitment agreement 216
global financial crisis 220
global financial system 210
international financial institutions 211

leveraging 222
Main Street 213
moral hazard 222
payday loans 229
post-effective period 217
prefiling or quiet period 216
private company 215
prospectus 216

road show 217
subprime mortgages 224
tombstone ad 217
underwriter 216
U.S. Securities and Exchange
   Commission (SEC) 233
waiting period 217
Wall Street 213

REVIEW QUESTIONS

1. Which financial institution provides large long-term loans to countries for capital projects or those facing a financial crisis?

2. Name the primary stakeholders in the financial system, according to the WEF.

3. What are the rights of shareholders?

4. What is the global financial crisis? Name one of the root causes of the global financial crisis.

5. What is the role of the global FSB?

MANAGER'S CHALLENGE

Community Microfinancing

UltraWidgets Corporation is a profitable manufacturing and distribution business located in a suburban community. With solid growth and an annual revenue of $50 million, their facilities are environmentally sound, their workforce is well paid, and the company's management believes in a stakeholder approach with a well-designed CSR plan. Some of the top managers had a nagging feeling that they were too isolated in their suburban headquarters so, as part of their CSR strategy, they regularly allowed employees paid time off from UltraWidgets to work in community soup kitchens and homeless shelters in the city. After a stint at the soup kitchen, one top executive proposes a radical idea: Use UltraWidgets's substantial assets to launch a microbank similar to Grameen Bank.

Framing Questions

1. How does the fact that UltraWidgets embraces a stakeholder approach impact their planning for a microbank?

2. Is it ethical to use assets of UltraWidgets for such a risky venture? Is a microbank risky? Explain.

3. How could UltraWidgets integrate microfinancing into their CSR?

Assignment

Individually or in groups, prepare a two- to three-page microfinance plan. First, use a search engine to identify low-income neighborhoods near you that may benefit from microfinancing. Then do some research on Grameen America to learn best practices and processes. Finally, given what you know about UltraWidgets, sketch out a brief budget and timeline for the project.

INTERNATIONAL AND MULTINATIONAL ORGANIZATIONS

Learning Objectives

Upon completion of this chapter, the reader should be able to do the following:

11.1 Discuss cultural norms, and identify factors that contribute to cultural competence.

11.2 State what comprises the body of international law.

11.3 Discuss the treaties and organizations that ensure stable global markets.

Ethics in Context

Free Trade Zones

Free trade zones (FTZs) can help developing and emerging markets create industries, increase exports, and decrease unemployment in the local community by, in some cases, reducing tariffs and streamlining administrative procedures. For some industries in FTZs, workplace conditions and treatment of employees decreases as competition for their goods increases. Later in the chapter, we explore the impact of FTZs and learn about a factory that is leading the way in doing well and doing good.

iStockphoto.com/Rawpixel

INTRODUCTION

Becoming an international or multinational business has never been easier. Thanks to the Internet and social media, even the smallest entrepreneurial endeavor can go global. Social media influencing, blogging, and online retailing through eBay and Amazon require almost no technical experience and very little start-up capital. Success as a multinational business, no matter the size, requires more than an Internet connection. Besides knowing your business and your customers, you must also effectively navigate different cultures. Cultural competence includes not only successfully interacting with those of different cultures but also understanding the legal and political frameworks in which you do business. International law is not easy to recognize because there is no central global government with policymaking and law enforcement powers. Despite this, many countries understand that it is in their best interest to work together with other nations even though there is no central authority enforcing compliance. Complicating this further are the different cultures and values of each country. Because of this complexity, international law is practiced and enforced in different ways.

CULTURAL COMPETENCE

LO 11.1 Discuss cultural norms, and identify factors that contribute to cultural competence.

We learned in Chapter 3 that managing multiple stakeholders and avoiding ethical pitfalls requires constant vigilance of managers and employees. This task is made more difficult when stakeholders are from different parts of the world or different cultures. Research indicates that it is not enough for workers to have knowledge of a different culture. For example, most people understand that Mexico is a religious country and religion plays a significant role in daily life there. However, a culturally competent business or manager would also recognize how that impacts managing people and be willing to make change: allowing Mexican employees to display religious images in their work spaces.[1]

The cultural competency of a business and its employees helps business succeed in a globalized market by improving communication and relationships and by understanding cultural nuances.[2] **Cultural sensitivity** is the desire to learn and understand different cultures. This leads to the development of cultural competence. Developing cultural competence is a work in progress; it requires a mindset in addition to knowledge and skills and the motivation to use those features in cross-cultural situations. Whether managing a culturally diverse workforce, welcoming international customers, or opening an overseas location and transferring employees from the home location abroad, research indicates one important factor for international success is the ability of employees to work effectively with or in another culture.[3] **Cultural competence** for business and employees means a person's effectiveness in drawing upon their knowledge, skills, and personal traits in order to successfully work with people from a different culture, whether that happens among culturally diverse workers or customers at home or in a different country.[4]

Most knowledge of and skills adapting to different cultures can be acquired through education and training (see Figure 11.1). Knowledge of different cultures includes a general knowledge about cultural differences, the components of culture, and frameworks for assessing different cultures. Cultural knowledge also includes understanding a specific country's culture, including its political and legal systems, history, and customs.[5] For example, a retail business trying to enter the French market must know that in France the government determines when retailers (both online and brick and mortar) can hold sales, called *les soldes*. The periods are typically in the summer and winter and total no more than 6 weeks. But the company must also understand how the French culture impacts buying decisions, such as the priority of entertainment and food in everyday French life.[6]

Another component of cultural knowledge includes conceptual knowledge about value systems and how values are reflected in behaviors. This type of knowledge, according

cultural sensitivity: The desire to learn and understand different cultures. This leads to the development of cultural competence.

cultural competence: A person's effectiveness in drawing upon their knowledge, skills, and personal traits in order to successfully work with people from a different culture, whether that happens among culturally diverse workers or customers at home or in a different country.

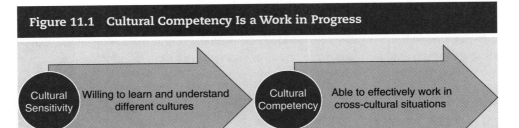

Figure 11.1 Cultural Competency Is a Work in Progress

Cultural Sensitivity — Willing to learn and understand different cultures

Cultural Competency — Able to effectively work in cross-cultural situations

to researchers, is not something that can be taught in a lecture but more *tacit knowledge* that is informal and hard to communicate to others. Tacit knowledge is accumulated over time from exposure to people of different cultures through diverse student bodies and teams, diverse workforces, and travel. The *skill* component of cultural competency includes things that can be developed over time with practice, like speaking the language and adapting to different **cultural norms**. Cultural norms are the standards we live by and are shared by people within a social group. These shared expectations are learned and reinforced by family, friends, and leaders in the society. Some societies are very strict in enforcing their cultural norms (cultural tightness), while others are more relaxed. For example, culturally tight societies tend to have more formal interpersonal interactions at work and school, and people in that society may be more cautious, while societies that are more culturally loose accept a wider range of behavior.[7] Personal traits that might make cultural competency easier for one person to attempt than another include, among others, curiosity, ambition, enthusiasm, judgment, and tolerance for ambiguity.[8]

We do not develop cultural competency in a vacuum; students are exposed to it in school, and employees are exposed to it through work in a business. Thus, to some extent, cultural competency can be limited or supported by the values and competencies of the organization.[9] For example, a culturally competent employee of a Spanish company is transferred to Canada to run the new Canadian location of her business. If the company insists she run and manage the new location according to Spanish norms and values, this will inhibit her ability to work effectively in the new culture and with her Canadian employees.

cultural norms: The standards we live by and are shared by people within a social group.

KEY TAKEAWAYS

Cultural Competence

- The cultural competence of a business and its employees improves communication and relationships within the business and with customers.

- General knowledge of cultural differences and tacit knowledge of value systems and behaviors contribute to an employee's cultural competency.

INTERNATIONAL CUSTOMS AND LAW

LO 11.2 State what comprises the body of international law.

For multinational corporations (MNCs) and their employees, developing cultural competency requires knowledge of and appreciation for different cultures, legal systems, and economic structures. Understanding the foundation of relationships between countries and governments is crucial to developing that knowledge. And like a country's laws, some of the foundations of international relationships are based on shared cultural values. Although there is no one body of international law, a collection of principles is seen as a framework for relations and interactions among and between countries.

Treaties, for example, are consensual agreements between the countries who sign them. Treaties can address any kind of issue, such as trade, like the United States–Mexico–Canada Agreement (USMCA; formerly NAFTA); nuclear weapons, like the Treaty on the Non-Proliferation of Nuclear Weapons; the use of air space by surveillance planes, like the Open Skies Treaty; or the flight path of birds in the Migratory Bird Treaty Act.

Less formal are customs. A **custom** is a practice that people of that state would consider illegal to break. Customs are usually not written down, but some are so universal that many regard them as laws called **customary international law (CIL)**, recognized by the International Court of Justice. For example, most countries recognize that intentionally killing civilians during wartime is a violation of international law. Because customs are different from country to country, they are harder to enforce. The value of CIL in terms of established and reliable law is up for debate. Some say because there are no reciprocal or retaliatory punishments, CIL offers little incentive for compliance. Others believe that CIL and treaties are practically the same thing, and the only difference is that in a treaty you can specify what actions you want included or excluded.

A third source of international law is based on general principles of **natural law**, a set of instinctual beliefs that some acts are right and some acts are wrong. For example, many countries' legal systems recognize the concept of "good faith," which means that parties intend to honor promises they have made. Because so many countries recognize and value good faith, it is understood as an international standard.

Protecting Shared Values: The United Nations

Although there is no global government and law enforcement entity, the **United Nations** is a step in that direction: a global body made up of many nations seeking to work together to ensure peace, security, and cooperation.

The precursor to the United Nations was the **League of Nations**, created in 1919 during the First World War under the Treaty of Versailles. The role of the League of Nations was to promote international cooperation and work toward peace and security. Under similar circumstances, the United Nations was established in 1942 during World War II. President Franklin D. Roosevelt and 26 nations pledged to work together to fight the Axis powers. These "United Nations" eventually grew to 50.[i] In 1945, they signed the Charter of the United Nations. Today there are 193 sovereign state members, and the UN Charter

---

treaties: Consensual agreements between the countries who sign them.

custom: A state practice that people of that state would consider illegal to break.

customary international law (CIL): Customs that are accepted universally as international law.

natural law: A set of instinctual beliefs that some acts are right and some acts are wrong.

United Nations: A global body made up of many nations seeking to work together to ensure international peace and security, provide humanitarian aid, promote sustainable development, uphold international law, and protect human rights.

League of Nations: Precursor to the United Nations; intended to promote international cooperation and work toward peace and security.

---

[i] Poland signed later, bringing it to 51 nations.

iStockphoto.com/luxiangjian4711

consists of 111 articles, covering everything from membership and composition of the UN, powers of the General Assembly and the National Security Council, actions with respect to peace and aggression, to international economic and social cooperation.[10] Like the League of Nations, the main mission of the UN is to maintain international peace and security and also to provide humanitarian aid, promote sustainable development, uphold international law, and protect human rights.[11]

How can a global body protect human rights when many of its members have different values, cultures, and ideas about human rights? In 1947 the UN established the **UN Commission on Human Rights** chaired by Eleanor Roosevelt. The job of the commission was to develop a set of rights to which all human beings on the planet are entitled. The world did not want the atrocities of World War II to happen again, and a basic set of human rights would galvanize the global community. A global team was organized including representatives with different legal and cultural backgrounds, including countries such as Lebanon, France, the United Kingdom, USSR (former Soviet Union), China, Australia, Chile, Canada, and the United States. The United States was represented by Mrs. Roosevelt. Each drafter used their strengths to negotiate and draft a common declaration: John Humphrey from Canada wrote a very inclusive first draft; René Cassin from France was a key player throughout the deliberations; Peng-chun Chang from China excelled at forging compromises where none were apparent; Charles Malik from Lebanon, a believer in natural law, was able to refine basic conceptual issues; and Roosevelt used her considerable prestige and authority with the superpowers to guide the drafting and negotiation process.[12] So grueling was the process that the delegate from Panama "begged Mrs. Roosevelt to remember that UN delegates have human rights, too."[13]

At 3:00 a.m. on December 10, 1948, the UN General Assembly adopted the **Universal Declaration of Human Rights (UDHR)**. The rights outlined in the UDHR begin with the premise that "all human beings are born free and equal in dignity and rights." Zeid Ra'ad Al Hussein, the UN High Commissioner for Human Rights, states that the UDHR is "not a reward for good behavior. They are not country-specific, or particular to a certain era or social group. They are inalienable entitlements of all people, at all times, in all places."[14] Such inalienable rights include, among others, the right to equity, freedom of thought and expression, freedom from slavery, freedom from discrimination, and the rights to life, liberty, and personal security. Today the UDHR is available in 360 languages and is the most translated

UN Commission on Human Rights: Established in 1947 with the goal of developing a set of rights to which all human beings on the planet are entitled.

Universal Declaration of Human Rights (UDHR): A declaration of "inalienable entitlements of all people, at all times, in all places."

International Covenant on Civil and Political Rights: Encompasses rights established in the UDHR and everyday rights such as the right to life; equality before the law; the right to individual liberties such as religion, expression, and assembly; the right to work; and the right to education.

document in the world. The declaration is the goal to which nations aspire and the standard by which they are measured; it has influenced constitutions and legislatures of many countries and has inspired more than 80 international human rights treaties and declarations—many of which are more specialized and have identified specific groups requiring protection.[15]

Building on the foundation of the UDHR, in 1976 the UN adopted the **International Covenant on Civil and Political Rights** and the **International Covenant on Economic, Social, and Cultural Rights**. These two conventions encompass the rights established in the UDHR and establish everyday rights such as the right to life, equality before the law, the right to work, and the right to education. All three documents comprise the **International Bill of Human Rights**. Today, all UN members have ratified some parts of the treaties, and 80% have ratified four or more core human rights treaties, making these values truly universal.[16] The UDHR is clearly influential, but enforcing the rights guaranteed in the declaration requires individual countries to take concrete action. By signing the declaration, countries promise to respect, protect, and fulfill human rights. In order to achieve this, governments must establish domestic measures and laws to meet these obligations, which means domestic legal systems become the main vehicle for enforcing the UDHR under international law. Regional and international procedures can help fill gaps left by domestic systems that fail to address human rights abuses.

International Covenant on Economic, Social, and Cultural Rights: Encompasses rights such as the right to work for fair wages, to a safe work environment, to social security, to an adequate standard of living, to the highest achievement of physical and mental health, and to participate in cultural life and the benefits of science.

International Bill of Human Rights: Composed of the UDHR; the International Covenant on Civil and Political Rights; and the International Covenant on Economic, Social, and Cultural Rights.

State Enforcement of International Human Rights

Can a global human rights system dependent on local governments to ensure and respect those rights be effective? For example, if a country does not have a legal system that is comprehensive enough to adequately address an allegation of a human rights abuse, may the victim use the justice system of another country to resolve their claim?

In the United States, the **Alien Tort Statute (ATS)** gives U.S. federal courts jurisdiction to hear "any civil action by an alien for a tort only, committed in violation of the law of nations or a Treaty of the United States." (See Chapter 5 for more on torts.) Passed as part of the Judiciary Act of 1789, the ATS was originally directed at pirates and was hardly used until a case in 1980 brought it back to life. In that case a Paraguayan father and daughter filed suit in the United States against a former Paraguayan police officer alleging the police officer kidnapped and tortured to death his son (her brother) in retaliation for the father's opposition to the Paraguayan government. The family argued that the ATS gave U.S. courts jurisdiction to hear the

suit because torture violated the law of nations. The U.S. Court of Appeals for the Second Circuit agreed.

Since that suit, the ATS has primarily been used to hold foreign corporations and individuals accountable in the United States for human rights abuses overseas. But a recent court decision may make it more difficult to bring foreign corporations to the United States to answer for human rights abuses. In 2013, the U.S. Supreme Court decided *Kiobel v. Royal Dutch Petroleum*, a case in which a group of Nigerians claimed that they or their relatives had been the victims of torture, execution, and other crimes against humanity by the Nigerian government with the active cooperation of Royal Dutch Petroleum. The crimes were allegedly in retaliation for the group's protesting the environmental impacts of the company's exploration and production in their region. The Court held that there is a presumption against the United States having jurisdiction to hear the group's suit because the ATS was not meant to cover human rights violations that have no connection to

(Continued)

CASE STUDY 11.1

the United States. Chief Justice Roberts stated, "It is implausible that the First Congress wanted their fledgling Republic—struggling to receive international recognition—to be the first nation to serve as the moral custodian for the world." According to the Court, there is a presumption against jurisdiction for suits alleging wrongdoing abroad unless the claims "touch and concern" the United States with "sufficient force." Although the Court was unanimous in its decision, it was divided in its reasoning and did not definitively state whether a corporation can be held liable under the ATS, thus leaving open the possibility that jurisdiction might be appropriate in some cases involving allegations of human rights abuses abroad committed by corporations.

One case many thought might test this ambiguity was *Jesner v. Arab Bank*. Arab Bank, one of Jordan's biggest banks, was sued by 6,000 non-U.S. citizens for its role in facilitating terrorism. They alleged that the bank helped Hamas finance international terror attacks and distributed millions of dollars in "martyrdom payments" to families of suicide bombers. According to the victims and their families, the history and purpose of the ATS makes clear that corporations can be liable. The law was passed to ensure that U.S. federal courts had jurisdiction to hear suits alleging violations of the laws of nations and there is no reason to think Congress just meant violations by individuals and not also corporations. If that were the case, there would be no method of deterring corporations from violating international laws nor a vehicle to compensate victims for those violations.

Whether the alleged wrongdoing "touches and concerns" the United States with "sufficient force" is another question. The bank argues that just because it used U.S. dollars as currency and that some of the transactions were automatically routed to their U.S. branch's clearing system does not mean that the bank's activities subject it to U.S. jurisdiction under the ATS. The victims argue that the bank was not merely using "banking services" in the United States but was actively facilitating money transfers for known Hamas leaders.

The U.S. Supreme Court heard this case in April 2018 and ruled against the victims. According to the Supreme Court, one of the many goals of the ATS is to avoid foreign entanglements by ensuring a federal forum for claims where without one a foreign country might hold the United States liable for an injury to a foreign citizen. In *Jesner*, said the Court, we have foreign nationals seeking millions of dollars against a foreign corporation for injuries suffered from terrorist attacks in the Middle East. The only connection to the United States was the bank's use of an automated system to clear dollar-denominated currency. At best this connection is minimal. If Congress wanted the ATS to extend to foreign corporations it would have said so in the law. Case law tells us that because of the separation of powers in the United States, courts must be cautious when deciding ATS cases; judges are not well-suited to make foreign relations decisions. Congress is better suited to decide the public policy implications of extending liability of the ATS. For 13 years this litigation has caused significant diplomatic tensions with Jordan, the type the ATS sought to avoid. For these reasons, the Supreme Court held that foreign corporations may not be defendants in suits brought under the ATS.

Discussion Questions

1. What are the dangers of being, as Chief Justice Roberts suggested, "the moral custodian of the world"?

2. In *Kiobel*, the Court stated that there is a presumption against imposing the laws of the United States (the ATS) on other countries unless the law specifically says so. To hold otherwise, the Court said, would be dangerous for U.S. citizens abroad. How so?

3. The dissent in *Jesner* says the majority is confusing a "custom or norm" with enforcement of a legal claim. Meaning, international customs and norms tells us what conduct is and is not acceptable in the global community but that each country must determine how to enforce those norms. Identify the custom or norm in *Jesner*.

Critical Thinking

In Chapter 15, you will learn that, increasingly, courts are treating corporations like people, with free speech rights, religious rights, even a race. Should obligations come with those rights? For example, if an individual can be sued in the United States for human rights abuses abroad, why shouldn't a corporation be sued for the same violations?

International Customs and Law

- International law is a collection of principles, including treaties, customs, and natural law theories.

- The United Nations is a global body of nations working together to ensure

peace, security, and cooperation among member nations.

- The UN Commission on Human Rights developed the UDHR, a set of rights to which all human beings are entitled.

DOING BUSINESS AROUND THE WORLD

LO 11.3   Discuss the treaties and organizations that ensure stable global markets.

You are the manager of a sales team for a U.S. pharmaceutical company, and your company entered the Japanese market a year ago. You have developed a great relationship (because of your cultural competency) with your contact in the Japanese government, who is head of the public hospital system in that country. Over the course of the past year, you have visited Japan three times, each time meeting with your colleague and enjoying a meal together. Sadly, you learn that your Japanese colleague's mother has died. Because of your cultural competence, you understand that in Japan it is customary to give a monetary gift called *koden* to help defray the funeral expenses.[17] However, you are also aware of the law: Would following this time-honored Japanese tradition be considered a bribe?

Foreign Corrupt Practices Act

Just as different cultures have different perspectives on human rights, different cultures also have different perspectives on business methods and customs. For example, in many Asian countries use of an indirect communication style is a component of the important concept of "saving face," whereas in Germany communication style is very direct, to the point of bluntness. In Japan, it is customary to bring a small gift to any business meeting and present it to the most senior member of the team. But what about other gifts or payments? Would the pharmaceutical sales manager be in violation of the law by paying *koden*?

The **Foreign Corrupt Practices Act (FCPA)** was passed in 1977 and prohibits American companies from paying bribes or giving "anything of value" to a foreign official to win an "improper advantage" in business. The anti-bribery provision of the FCPA was amended in 1989 to apply to foreign businesses and persons who "cause, directly or through agents, and act in furtherance of such corrupt payment to take place within the territory of the United States."[18]

Foreign companies whose stock is listed in the United States must also comply with the accounting provisions of the FCPA, which are meant to work together with the anti-bribery provisions and require companies to maintain certain records and internal accounting controls. The two provisions work together to prevent, for example, improper payments

Alien Tort Statute (ATS): Statute that gives U.S. federal courts jurisdiction to hear "any civil action by an alien for a tort only, committed in violation of the law of nations or a Treaty of the United States."

Foreign Corrupt Practices Act (FCPA): Prohibits American companies from paying bribes or giving "anything of value" to a foreign official to win an "improper advantage" in business.

facilitation payments: A
small payment given to
low-level government
officials to speed up
routine governmental
actions.

U.S. Department of
Justice (DOJ): Has
civil and criminal
enforcement powers for
violations of the anti-
bribery and accounting
provisions of the FCPA.

from being hidden somewhere deep inside balance sheets. In some countries, it is custom-ary to pay small amounts, called **facilitation payments**, to low-level government officials to speed up routine governmental actions. Under the FCPA, facilitation payments are not meant to influence a decision but just to speed up a process, such as processing paperwork filed to get a license, and are one of the few exceptions to the law.[19]

FCPA investigations and cases are brought by the **U.S. Department of Justice (DOJ)** and the U.S. Securities and Exchange Commission (SEC). Although both agencies usually work together on cases, they have different jurisdictions. The DOJ has civil and criminal enforcement powers for violations of the anti-bribery and accounting provisions of the law. The SEC has civil enforcement power for violations of the anti-bribery provisions and accounting provisions as well, but its jurisdiction is limited to issuers (publicly traded companies), officers, directors, and employees.

For example, in December 2016, TEVA Pharmaceutical Industries, an Israeli company and the world's largest manufacturer of generic drugs, agreed to pay $965 million to settle charges that its Russian and Ukrainian subsidiaries paid bribes or gave "things of value" to government officials in order to corruptly influence approving the TEVA registration to market and sell its products in those countries.[20] Of the $965 million, $236 million went to the SEC in disgorgement (giving back) of interest and $283 million to the DOJ in a deferred prosecution agreement. TEVA resolved the bribery charges with the Israeli State Attorney's Office for $22 million in criminal penalties. According to the Israeli govern-ment, the settlement and fine were based on TEVA already paying a fine to the United States. Also, TEVA fired the workers involved in the bribery, implemented a robust compli-ance program to empower employees to act more ethically, and created an organizational structure designed to reduce similar conduct.[21]

CASE STUDY 11.2

Is an Unpaid Internship a "Thing of Value"?

In the TEVA Pharmaceutical case, the investigation revealed that TEVA executives in Russia were offer-ing substantial discounts on its products sold to the Russian government in order to increase sales throughout the country via government-owned busi-nesses. The "thing of value" in that case, despite lay-ers of people and businesses, is clear (the discounts) as is the "improper advantage." But must a thing of value have an obvious monetary value? What if the improper advantage is something everyone in the industry does? Is it still improper?

For years, banks on Wall Street hired, both in paid and unpaid internships, the sons and daugh-ters of prominent foreign government officials in the hopes that these decisions would lead to better and more lucrative relationships in those countries. In 2013, the SEC opened an investigation into whether several major banks tried to win business by hiring

the children of Chinese government officials. Many thought the SEC investigation was too aggressive; the banking industry worldwide relies on relationships and hiring well-connected people is one way to build those relationships. Moreover, how can you prove that hiring one person actually led to winning a deal?

The SEC answered these questions in 2015 when it settled bribery charges for almost $15 mil-lion with Bank of New York Mellon (BNY Mellon). The SEC accused the bank of giving three intern-ships to the sons and nephew of two high-ranking officials at a Middle Eastern sovereign wealth fund in exchange for more business from the fund. Accord-ing to the investigation, one official made a personal request that BNY Mellon provide two internships. He described the internships as an "opportunity" for BNY Mellon and that if BNY Mellon did not pro-vide the internships, the official would secure the internships at a competing bank. The other official asked for an internship for his son in the European offices of BNY Mellon. Internal BNY Mellon documents describe this official as "crucial to both retaining and gaining new business" for the bank. The bank provided three internships, one of which was unpaid, to the three sovereign fund relatives. None of the interns met their most basic requirement for interns—that they be enrolled in a degree program—nor the minimum grade point average (GPA) requirements. Yet they were never interviewed or evaluated by BNY Mellon employees before they were hired. All three worked at the bank for approximately six months, longer than a typical internship.

In 2016, JPMorgan Chase, America's largest bank, agreed to pay $264 million to settle charges that between 2006 and 2013 it hired almost 100 interns and full-time employees at the request of Chinese and other Asian government officials in exchange for growing its banking business in that part of the world. According to the complaint, investment bankers at JPMorgan Chase's Asia subsidiary created a client-referral hiring program they called the "Sons & Daughters Program" to leverage the promise of a well-paying job in order to win or retain business. Nonreferral candidates had to submit to a rigorous hiring process and compete for a limited number of positions. Referral hire candidates bypassed the firm's normal hiring process, did not compete against others based on merit, and were less qualified than nonreferral candidates. Referral-hire candidates were hired based on their direct or potential

links to banking revenue that could be generated from the referring client in exchange for the hire. Referral hires that made the bank a lot of money were offered longer-term jobs. Bank employees even created a spreadsheet tracking the amount of money generated from each referral hire. During this period, JPMorgan Chase entered into transactions with referring clients totaling more than $100 million. The complaint also alleges that because JPMorgan Chase employees knew this practice violated the FCPA, they purposely provided inaccurate or incomplete information to the legal department for compliance review of the candidates in order to get them hired. No referral hire was ever denied a job at the bank.

Discussion Questions

1. Who are the stakeholders in the decision whether to award an internship (paid or otherwise) to the relative of a big client? What is at stake for each?

2. What rationalizations might bank employees have used to justify breaking the law?

Critical Thinking

If you were the hiring manager at a big bank and a very good client asked that you place her daughter in an internship at your bank, how would you respond? Are there people at the bank with whom you would discuss this? What are the objections you would face (if any) from your boss? What objections would you face from the client? Can you see a solution?

The **Organization for Economic Cooperation and Development (OECD)** was founded in 1961 to promote global economic and social well-being. Eighteen European countries, the United States, and Canada were the founding members and committed to economic development around the world. Today, the OECD has 34 member democracies with market economies and works closely with emerging economies like China, India, and Brazil and developing economies in Africa, Asia, Latin America, and the Caribbean. The OECD provides governments of member countries a forum in which to collaborate with 70 nonmember economies to promote growth and sustainable development and where members can discuss shared experiences, coordinate standards, and seek advice.[22] The OECD is also a pioneer in corporate social responsibility (CSR) and values-cased leadership. In 1976 it established a set of guidelines for MNCs addressing business conduct in human rights, supply chain management, anti-corruption, labor relations, and environmental impact. All OECD member countries and 11 observer countries have endorsed the guidelines.[23]

Organization for Economic Cooperation and Development (OECD): Founded in 1961 to promote global economic and social well-being.

Anti-Bribery
Convention: Adopted
by the OECD to assure
a "functional equivalence
among measures
taken by the parties
to sanction bribery of
foreign public officials"
without each country
having to change their
legal system.

OECD Working Group on
Bribery: A process by
which member countries
conduct year-round
reviews of other member
countries' commitment
to and compliance with
the convention.

Because the FCPA made paying bribes illegal, many U.S. companies worried that they would be at a disadvantage in global business competing with companies from countries without similar laws. In 1998, in response to these concerns, the OECD adopted its **Anti-Bribery Convention** and created the **OECD Working Group on Bribery**.[ii] The goal of the convention is to "assure a functional equivalence among the measures taken by the parties to sanction bribery of foreign public officials" without each country having to change their legal system.[24] The 30 OECD members and seven nonmember countries have made bribing foreign public officials in international business a crime. The Working Group Bribery Peer-Review Monitoring Process is a process by which member countries conduct year-round reviews of other member countries' commitment to and compliance with the convention.

Protectionism and the General Agreement on Tariffs and Trade

Imagine you are the leader of a small, developing country. Your country relies heavily on imports because it does not have the technology or skilled labor to grow domestic industries. As the leader, you decide that if you pass laws that favor what small, fledgling industries you have, you can strengthen and grow those industries and rely less on imports.

CASE STUDY 11.3

Walmart de Mexico

In 2018 the OECD Working Group on Bribery completed its Phase 4 evaluation of Mexico's implementation of the convention. According to the report, Mexico needs to "urgently implement" reforms that ensure adequate resources for fighting bribery, such as enacting whistleblower protections for public and private sector workers, nominating a special anti-corruption prosecutor, and appointing more judges. The recommendations follow one of the largest foreign bribery investigations in U.S. history: a 6-year investigation of Walmart in Mexico, China, India, and Brazil. Almost 20% of all Walmart stores are located in Mexico, and the company is the largest private employer in the country. In 2012, the DOJ alleged Walmart de Mexico paid more than $24 million in bribery payments to Mexican officials to expedite construction of stores in the country. A *New York Times* investigation revealed that Walmart de Mexico was a willing corrupter, paying not only facilitation payments to speed up routine approvals but also bribes to thwart public votes and open debates and circumvent regulatory procedures that safeguard construction sites. For example, as a result of eight bribes totaling $341,000, Walmart de Mexico was able to build a Sam's Club in a densely populated section of Mexico City without a construction permit, an environmental permit, an urban impact assessment, or a traffic permit. According to the *New York Times* investigation, Walmart executives understood the seriousness of the conduct, and the company's own investigation found documentation of hundreds of suspected payments that showed Walmart de Mexico executives knew about the bribes and had taken steps to hide them from headquarters in Arkansas. Despite its findings, Walmart shut down its own investigation in 2006, and in 2008 the CEO of Walmart de Mexico, who it is alleged was behind much of the bribery schemes, was promoted to vice chairman of Walmart. U.S. prosecutors reached a tentative resolution with the company, including $300 million in fines; however, prosecutors want Walmart to admit to their misconduct. In June 2019, Walmart agreed to pay $282 million to settle FCPA charges brought by both the SEC and the Justice Department. The global settlement ended all FCPA investigations of the company in Mexico, Brazil, China, and India. As part of the settlement, Walmart Brazil pled guilty to FCPA charges.

ii OECD Anti-Bribery Peer Monitoring Country Reports are available at http://www.oecd.org/daf/anti-bribery/countryreportsontheimplementationoftheoecdanti-briberyconvention.htm

According to the *Wall Street Journal*, federal investigators found evidence of FCPA violations by Walmart in India too. Most of the illegal payments were under $200, with some as low as $5, but collectively totaled millions of dollars. Investigators claimed the payments were made to help move goods through customs or to secure real estate deals. Because fines under the FCPA are often tied to how much profit was realized by the bribe, it is unlikely that Walmart will be issued a substantial fine.

Discussion Questions

1. Identify potential motivations and rationalizations of Walmart de Mexico executives in deciding to make bribery payments, and deciding to hide the payments from headquarters in Arkansas.

2. Some have been critical of the $300 million fine as too light of a penalty for Walmart's misconduct. However, Walmart also spent almost $900 million in legal fees, costs associated with its own internal investigation, and a global overhaul of its compliance processes. Should those costs be considered when determining punishment? Why or why not?

Critical Thinking

Another issue that some say is holding up resolution of this case and payment of the $300 million fine (in addition to Walmart's reluctance to admit any wrongdoing) has to do with the U.S. government's food assistance program. Walmart is the largest recipient of food stamp spending in the United States. If the retailer pleads guilty to a federal crime, it may become ineligible to accept food stamps.

Using teleological and deontological approaches, analyze how the parties should resolve the criminal case in terms of fines and admissions.

One way to do this is to tax imported products that will hurt the growth of your small industries. This makes imported products more expensive than domestic products and gives your industries a chance to make money and expand. This type of government policy is called **protectionism** because it restrains international trade in order to protect local businesses and jobs from foreign competition.

There are several different types of protectionist policies. For example, tariffs are a tax on imported goods and services. A **tariff** immediately raises the prices of imported goods, making them less competitive compared to domestic goods. This method can work well for countries with a lot of imports. However, tariffs can make domestic industries less efficient and innovative because they are not subject to global competition.

An **import quota** is a limit on the number of products that can be imported over a period of time. The purpose is to limit the supply of a specific product, which would give domestic businesses a chance to meet the local demand. An import quota would also protect against **dumping**, when an exporter sells a large volume of goods in a foreign country at a lower price than it charges its own domestic market. For example, in 2016 Indian rubber company Reliance Industries filed a complaint with the Indian Department of Commerce against companies from Korea, Russia, South Africa, Iran, and Singapore for dumping. Reliance alleged that the companies sold a rubber product that is indistinguishable from their domestic rubber product at prices well below the price at which they sell their products in their own countries. Reliance claims the dumping injured the domestic market in terms of lost profits, return on capital, and deterioration in margins.[25]

A **subsidy** is a benefit given to an individual, business, or institution—usually by the government. It is typically a cash payment to relieve a burden (**direct subsidy**) or a tax benefit to incentivize behavior that is generally thought to be in the best interest of society (**indirect subsidy**). For example, in the United States if someone is temporarily out of work and looking for a job, they might be eligible to receive money from the government

protectionism: Restrains international trade in order to protect local businesses and jobs from foreign competition.

tariff: A tax on imported goods and services.

import quota: A limit on the number of products that can be imported over a period of time.

dumping: Occurs when an exporter sells a large volume of goods in a foreign country at a lower price than it charges its own domestic market.

subsidy: A benefit given to an individual, business, or institution—usually by the government.

direct subsidy: A cash payment to relieve a burden.

indirect subsidy: A tax benefit to incentivize behavior that is generally thought to be in the best interest of society.

(unemployment benefits) to help them financially during this time. Or consider that electric cars are more environmentally friendly than traditional gas cars, so encouraging people to buy electric cars would be good for society. Both the federal government[iii] and 45 states plus the District of Columbia offer tax credits and other incentives to encourage people to buy electric cars.[26] Similarly, China offers subsidies to help grow their automotive industry. There are advantages of subsidies; they can make doing business domestically cheaper and encourage behavior that is good for society. However, subsidies can also make the subsidized business or industry less efficient and might encourage relationships between subsidized businesses or industries with politicians who have the power to continue those subsidies.

There are advantages and disadvantages of protectionism. Tariffs, quotas, and subsidies allow domestic companies to grow their businesses and hire domestic workers; however, this is usually a short-term benefit. Long term, many feel protectionism weakens the competitiveness of industries because without the pressure of competition there is no need to innovate and make a product or service better. Ultimately, this will lead to outsourcing jobs because local businesses are less competitive, which in turn may lead to layoffs.

In March 2018, President Trump imposed a 10% tariff on foreign aluminum and a 25% tariff on foreign steel. Several countries have negotiated exemptions from the tariff including Mexico, Canada, South Korea, Argentina, Australia, and Brazil. It is unclear whether the tariffs have helped the U.S. steel and aluminum industries, but what is clear is that U.S. manufacturers of parts that use aluminum and steel were not happy about the tariffs. Two U.S. companies and a trade association sued the U.S. government to overturn the tariffs.

LAW AND SOCIETY 11.1

American Institute for International Steel and Sim-Tex Et Al. V. United States, Slip Op. 19-37, United States Court of International Trade (March 25, 2019)

Facts: The American Institute for International Steel (AIIS) is a steel-related trade organization that supports both tariff and nontariff barriers in the promotion of free trade in steel. Sim-Tex is a Texas-based distributor of alloy steel pipe products used in the production and distribution of oil and gas and a member of AIIS. Sim-Tex directly and indirectly (through traders) imports approximately 40,000 to 45,000 tons per month from Korea, Taiwan, Brazil, Germany, and Italy.

Both organizations filed suit challenging the constitutionality of Section 232 of the Trade Expansion Act (TEA) as an improper delegation of legislative power to the president in violation of the separation of powers and checks and balances guaranteed by the Constitution. AIIS and Sim-Tex claim Section 232 lacks any intelligible principle to limit the discretion of the president in imposing tariffs that, according to him, threaten to "impair the national security." Not only does Section 232 give the president unlimited discretion in how to counter a national security threat, it also allows the president to consider almost any effect on the U.S. economy as part of "national security." This, according to AIIS and Sim-Tex, is in direct violation of Article 1, Section 8 of the Constitution, which gives Congress the power to "lay and collect...duties (and)...to regulate Commerce with foreign Nations."

Issue: Is Section 232 of the TEA unduly broad in violation of the Constitution?

[iii] A tax credit of $7,500 begins to phase out for each manufacturer after they sell 200,000 eligible cars. See https://www.energy.gov/eere/electricvehicles/electric-vehicles-tax-credits-and-other-incentives

Decision: No, Section 232 of the TEA is not so broad that it violates the Constitution. According to Section 232 of the TEA, the secretary of commerce can initiate an investigation to "determine the effects on the national security" of any imports. The secretary of commerce must notify the secretary of defense of the investigation and consult with that person regarding the method of investigating and the policy issues raised. The secretary of commerce may also request from the Department of Defense an assessment of the defense requirements of any imports subject to the investigation. A report is produced of the investigation submitted to the president, including, if needed, a course of action. If the president agrees with the report, they then determine the "nature and duration of the action" in order to adjust the imports so that there is no threat to national security. This analysis must include impact on the economic welfare of domestic industries, unemployment, loss of skills or investment, or other "serious effects resulting from displacement of any domestic products."

Since 1935, no act has been struck down as lacking in intelligible principles. In fact, the U.S. Supreme Court has upheld the delegation of authority by Congress to the president in the TEA as having sufficient guidelines because Section 232 established clear preconditions to action: the investigation by the secretary of commerce with consultation from the secretary of defense and their finding that an item is being imported in such quantities as to threaten national security. The discretion afforded the president is not unlimited as the plaintiffs suggest. Section 232 makes it clear that the president can only act if "he deems necessary to adjust the imports" and must articulate specific factors to be considered in exercising his authority under the law. While the law does afford the president some discretion, there are boundaries. Case law tells us that our review here is limited to whether there is constitutional power, not if the president abused the discretion given him under that power. In this case, Section 232 of TEA grants the president authority to limit imports if a determination has been made such imports threaten national security.

Law and Management Questions

1. What is the national security threat at issue in this case? In answering this, think about the goal of tariffs.

2. In 2018, the Department of Commerce opened an investigation into whether car and auto imports can be considered a national security threat under Section 232. The president has said he may impose a 20% tariff on cars imported from the European Union. Who are the stakeholders in this decision? Think of the auto manufacturing supply chain.

Protectionist policies are alive and well in the 21st century. For example, in January 2017, President Trump signed an executive order withdrawing the United States from the Trans-Pacific Partnership (TPP), a multilateral agreement including Canada, Mexico, Japan, Australia, New Zealand, Chile, Peru, Malaysia, Singapore, Vietnam, and Brunei that would have reduced tariffs for American imports and exports with those countries.[iv] Globally, the G20 countries (the leaders of the world's 19 wealthiest countries plus the European

---

[iv] President Obama negotiated the TPP; however, because it was never approved by Congress, and many feel it never would have been, it never went into effect in the United States. Bradner, E. (2017, January 23). *Trump's TPP withdrawal: 5 things to know*. Retrieved from http://www.cnn.com/2017/01/23/politics/trump-tpp-things-to-know/index.html

General Agreement on Tariffs and Trade (GATT): Signed by 23 countries; agreement that states that each member must confer most-favored-nation status to every other member, prohibits many import and export restrictions, and eliminates tariffs on imports from developing countries.

most-favored-nation status: The principle that all members must be treated equally in terms of tariffs.

Union) pursue their own protectionist policies through import quotas and subsidies for domestic goods and services.[27]

Protectionism has a long history. The practice was popular as far back as the 18th century and allowed local economies around the world to grow. However, this growth came at a cost to international trade; protectionism plus retaliatory trade policies essentially halted international trade in the years leading up to and during the Great Depression.[28] In 1944, the United Nations Monetary and Financial Conference was held in Bretton Woods, New Hampshire. At that conference, among other accomplishments, 15 countries focused on negotiating a trade agreement that would eliminate trade restrictions affecting $10 billion in trade. The agreement, the **General Agreement on Tariffs and Trade (GATT)**, went into effect in 1948 and was signed by 23 countries. GATT had three main provisions; the most important of which was that each member must confer **most-favored-nation status** to every other member, meaning that all members must be treated equally in terms of tariffs. GATT also prohibited many import and export restrictions. The third provision was added in 1965 and sought to help developing countries by eliminating tariffs on imports from those countries.

GATT has been amended over the years. In the 1960s, an antidumping provision was added, and in the 1970s, more trade improvements were added. Talks between 1986 and 1994 resulted in the creation of the **World Trade Organization (WTO)**, which incorporated the provisions of GATT as its foundation. The WTO wears many hats: a global organization dealing with the rules of trade to ensure smooth and peaceful global trade agreements, a forum to negotiate trade agreements, and a place to resolve trade disputes. There are 164 member countries in the WTO led by a director general. All major decisions are made by the membership as a whole through their ambassador delegates. The WTO is headquartered in Geneva, Switzerland.

World Trade Organization (WTO): A global organization composed of 164 member countries, dealing with the rules of trade to ensure smooth and peaceful global trade agreements, a forum to negotiate trade agreements, and a place to resolve trade disputes.

The foundation of the WTO is the principles agreed to in GATT during the 1986 through 1994 talks, which serve as a rule book for international trade. With the addition of newer rules, the complete set is 30 agreements set out in about 30,000 pages dealing with topics ranging from custom duty rates, intellectual property (IP), dispute settlement, and trade policy review. The agreements bind member nations to ensure nondiscriminatory trading, guarantees that its exports will be treated fairly in member markets, and promises to do the same with imports into its own markets.[29]

Other Trade Agreements

North American Free Trade Agreement (NAFTA): A multilateral trade agreement between Canada, the United States, and Mexico whereby the three countries agreed to remove almost all tariffs among them, allowing for the free flow of goods across the borders.

Numerous bilateral and multilateral trade agreements are in force at any given time around the globe. For example, according to the Office of the United States Trade Representative, the United States has trade agreements with 20 countries, including Australia, Bahrain, Israel, Korea, and Peru. We also have multilateral trade agreements with the Dominican Republic and Central America. The world's largest free trade agreement was the **North American Free Trade Agreement (NAFTA)**, which went into effect in 1994. NAFTA was a multilateral trade agreement between Canada, the United States, and Mexico whereby the three countries agreed to remove almost all tariffs among them, allowing for the free flow of goods across the borders. The goal was to encourage economic cooperation between the countries, which would ultimately lead to better economic prosperity for all three in an environment where technology and economies were evolving and changing.

Many also say a goal of NAFTA was to improve political relations between the three countries following the theory "when goods don't pass international borders, soldiers will."[30]

Many say that NAFTA caused the United States to lose jobs because the treaty made it easier for U.S. companies to move to Mexico where the cost of doing business is much cheaper. This, in turn, led to lower wages in the United States. However, there are millions of U.S. jobs that depend on NAFTA; for example, U.S. auto manufacturers like Ford and GM employ far more people in the United States than in Mexico but rely on their lower-cost Mexican production facilities. And because of the elimination of tariffs, grocery prices in the United States were kept lower because of the tariff-free imports from Mexico, and gas prices were kept lower by importing oil from Canada and Mexico.[31] On November 30, 2018, the three countries signed a new agreement, the **United States–Mexico–Canada Agreement (USMCA)**, which is a more modern version of NAFTA, with some changes to the rules for the auto industry and dairy markets, and changes to labor and environmental standards.

Another multilateral agreement is the **Agreement on Trade-Related Aspects of Intellectual Property Rights (TRIPS)**, which was signed in 1995. TRIPS is the first global treaty to incorporate IP rights into the system of international trade for all members of the WTO. Any country that wishes to join the WTO must agree to the requirements in TRIPS. The agreement establishes minimum IP rights for WTO members, covering areas such as copyright, trademarks, service marks, industrial design, patents, trade secrets, and test data among others. TRIPS also includes enforcement rules and subjects disputes to the WTO dispute resolution process. The goal of the agreement is similar to the goals of the WTO: to facilitate international trade in a consistent and beneficial manner in terms of economies and public welfare.[32] Criticism exists, however, concerning how well TRIPS can achieve this goal given its demanding standards. For example, many developing countries feel the TRIPS strict IP standards favor developed countries and MNCs. These high standards—sometimes stricter than a developing countries' own IP laws—translate into higher drug prices and costs for agricultural products in developing countries, which in turn suppress development and hinder access to medicine in already struggling economies. On the other hand, strong IP laws will encourage investment in developing countries that will stimulate innovation and growth.[33]

A **free trade zone (FTZ)** is a type of **special economic zone** used as part of a larger economic growth strategy. According to the World Bank, a special economic zone like an FTZ is a geographically defined area administered by a single body offering incentives for businesses physically located in that zone, such as tariff- and duty-free importing and streamlined customs. Unlike trade agreements with one or more governments, FTZs can be domestic only and limited in geographic area within a country. The goal of FTZs, and special economic zones generally, is to help a country develop and diversify exports while protecting the businesses in that FTZ to help them create jobs and pilot new business strategies. For example, an FTZ might give tax breaks to the businesses operating within the zone, bringing costs down and encouraging foreign investment. However, because of the low costs, concerns have been raised about the impact of zones on working conditions, wages, and the environment. Because there are several FTZs located around the world, finding a lower cost production facility for a foreign company is not hard; thus, the competition to keep costs as low as possible makes the conditions ripe for worker abuses and poor working conditions. The most successful special economic zones (FTZs and other

United States–Mexico–Canada Agreement (USMCA): A more modern version of NAFTA, with some changes to the rules for the auto industry and dairy markets, and changes to labor and environmental standards.

Agreement on Trade-Related Aspects of Intellectual Property Rights (TRIPS): A multilateral agreement with the goal of facilitating international trade in a consistent and beneficial manner in terms of economies and public welfare.

free trade zone (FTZ): A type of special economic zone used as part of a larger economic growth strategy to help a country develop and diversify exports while protecting the businesses in that FTZ to help them create jobs and pilot new business strategies.

special economic zone: Usually part of a larger economic growth strategy to help a country develop and diversify exports while protecting domestic businesses.

types of zones) are located in Asia, Latin and Central America, and Eastern and Central Europe. The industries in these zones are typically labor-intensive production line work like apparel, textiles, and electronics. See Figure 11.2 for the advantages and disadvantages of FTZs.

Figure 11.2   Point–Counterpoint: Free Trade Zones

Pros

1. Gives local industries time and room to grow.
2. Creates local jobs and industries.

Cons

1. Competition among free trade zones (FTZs) globally encourages keeping costs low, impacting working conditions and wages.
2. Can lead to inefficient processes and low quality due to lack of competition.

ETHICS IN CONTEXT

Free Trade Zones

iStockphoto.com/Rawpixel

Frequently in FTZs, unions are the workers' best hope for securing adequate working conditions and rights, such as bathroom and water breaks, not being fired because of pregnancy, and protection from other forms of discrimination and abuse.

Moreover, the legal minimum wage in many FTZs is not enough to live on.

According to the World Bank, the Dominican Republic is one of the "global pioneers" in the use of FTZs. These zones have fueled economic growth in the Dominican Republic textile and apparel industries. An experiment is underway in the FTZ in the Dominican Republic to build and run the "model factory." In 2010, Joe Bozich, then CEO, and Donnie Hodge, then president of Knights Apparel, the leader in college-logo apparel in the United States, opened Alta Gracia in the Dominican Republic. The men worked with the Worker Rights Consortium and local union members to create a model factory that can pay workers a living wage, not just a minimum wage, provide benefits, operate humanely and with dignity, allow workers to unionize, and still be profitable. With a minimum wage of 80 cents an hour, many in the apparel industry viewed the Dominican Republic as too expensive relative to Asia. Bozich and Hodge worked with the Worker Rights Consortium, an independent organization formed by universities and college students, to determine a "living wage," calculated based on the local prices for goods and services that would meet the basic needs of a worker with two dependents. Alta Gracia's living wage was set at $497 per month, which exceeds the legal minimum wage in the FTZ ($148 per month) by almost 340% and does not include the value of the benefits provided. The *salario digno* (wage with dignity) allows workers to provide food, housing, and education for their families.

The Alta Gracia experiment was so ground-breaking that John Kline and Edward Soule, two business professors from Georgetown University, asked to study the factory over the course of years to track its progress in order to learn from the experiment. The professors published an initial report in 2011 as the factory got off the ground. Their most recent report from 2014 describes how workers are more productive, the turnover rate is far below the industry average (6% v. 67%) and that the factory broke even. All of these facts indicate the factory is moving from start-up mode to established model, and both predict profit in the very near future. HanesBrands purchased Knights Apparel in 2015, and Alta Gracia currently operates as a stand-alone, privately held company run by Hodge. Its brand is sold in over 800 college bookstores, makes sports apparel for the National Hockey League, and in 2017 partnered with the National Football League Dallas Cowboys to develop a new line of T-shirts. Professor Kline believes that if a small factory like Alta Gracia, which employs 140 people, can provide living wages and ethical working conditions, so can large apparel companies.

Discussion Questions

1. *Stakeholder theories*: Watch the student piece on Alta Gracia found on the companion website (**http://edge.sagepub.com/clark1e**), and identify the different stakeholders in the clothing supply chain and how they can exert pressure to make positive change.

2. *Ethical decision-making*: Visit your college or university bookstore. Do they sell Alta Gracia apparel? If so, pay attention to the amount of product, floor space, and marketing devoted to the brand. Is there enough attention drawn to the brand to impact buying decisions? Look at the product: What information on the tags tells you about the social mission of the brand?

3. *Ethical decision-making*: How does being privately held help Hodge and management at Alta Gracia stay loyal to its values and social mission?

Take a Position

Is it appropriate to prioritize social good over making a profit?

Another type of special economic zone is an **industrial zone**. These zones are targeted at specific economic activities like media or textiles, and infrastructure help is adapted to suit the needs of that particular industry. For example, the Moroccan port of Tangiers is using free zones to develop into a business hub. The Tangier Free Zone takes a multisector approach—not just exports but also sector development. The zone includes over 400 companies and has created 40,000 jobs. Dubai has established industrial zones targeting specific industries—for example, Dubai Media City (DMC). DMC was created to stimulate development of media and media technology.[34] Egypt also has an industrial zone focused on media—Media Production City—which offers incentives for producing drama and other forms of TV production.[35]

industrial zone: A type of special economic zone targeted at specific economic activity with infrastructure to suit the needs of that particular industry.

Doing Business Around the World

- Although different countries may have different views of the role of payments and gifts in international business, the FCPA prohibits American companies from paying bribes or giving anything of value to a foreign official to gain an advantage.

- OECD members have made bribing foreign public officials a crime in over 30 countries.

- Protectionist trade policies limit international trade in order to protect local businesses from foreign competition.

- The WTO was created to ensure smooth global trade agreements and a forum to resolve trade disputes.

SUMMARY

Cultural competence is one of the keys to a successful international business. Learning the language and understanding the political system of a country is important but not enough. Research tells us cultural competence also requires a mindset that can be developed by exposure to and interaction with different cultures.

Understanding the context in which you do business includes familiarity with international laws and treaties that impact markets. Global disputes may be resolved through local justice systems, which have different social norms and cultures, making enforcement complicated.

KEY TERMS

Agreement on Trade-Related Aspects of Intellectual Property Rights (TRIPS) 255
Alien Tort Statute (ATS) 245
Anti-Bribery Convention 250
cultural competence 241
cultural norms 242
cultural sensitivity 241
custom 243
customary international law (CIL) 243
direct subsidy 251
dumping 251
facilitation payments 248
Foreign Corrupt Practices Act (FCPA) 247
free trade zone (FTZ) 255

General Agreement on Tariffs and Trade (GATT) 254
import quota 251
indirect subsidy 251
industrial zone 257
International Bill of Human Rights 245
International Covenant on Civil and Political Rights 244
International Covenant on Economic, Social, and Cultural Rights 245
League of Nations 243
most-favored-nation status 254
natural law 243
North American Free Trade Agreement (NAFTA) 254
OECD Working Group on Bribery 250

Organization for Economic Cooperation and Development (OECD) 249
protectionism 251
special economic zone 255
subsidy 251
tariff 251
treaties 243
UN Commission on Human Rights 244
United Nations 243
United States–Mexico–Canada Agreement (USMCA) 255
Universal Declaration of Human Rights (UDHR) 244
U.S. Department of Justice (DOJ) 248
World Trade Organization (WTO) 254

REVIEW QUESTIONS

1. Explain the components of cultural competence.

2. What is the difference between a treaty and a custom? Identify examples of each.

3. What is the role of the United Nations in international business?

4. What is the FCPA, and how does it combat bribery?

5. Explain protectionism and the pros and cons of specific protectionist policies.

MANAGER'S CHALLENGE

Foreign Corrupt Practices Act

Ella's U.S.-based business and her new U.K. expansion are taking off: Sales are at record levels, customer demand is increasing, and production is running smoothly. She has asked her U.K. sales agent to look around for office space in the United Kingdom that would be suitable for another location. The sales agent has found the perfect spot to rent, and Ella agreed; the business will open its U.K. office in 2 months. While in the United Kingdom inspecting her new office space, the landlord mentions to Ella that his daughter is in the United States studying for a year and really needs a summer job. If Ella had any openings in her office, he would certainly be grateful for the placement. Ella politely brushed this request off and continued with her inspection. Two weeks later, the landlord sent Ella an e-mail confirming the rent but also stating that he cannot control fluctuations in the market price for office space, and the rent might need to be renegotiated sooner than anticipated. He then asked again if Ella had any openings for a summer job for his daughter.

Framing Questions

1. What provisions of the FCPA should Ella be thinking about when deciding whether she can hire her landlord's daughter?

2. Assuming Ella routinely hires summer workers, what information would she want from her landlord about his daughter?

Assignment

Draft a memo to your human resources (HR) department about the landlord's request, and outline a procedure by which your people can objectively evaluate his daughter and decide whether to hire her without violating the FCPA.

PART III

CONTEMPORARY BUSINESS ISSUES IN TODAY'S SOCIETY

CHAPTER 12: Social Media and Citizen Movements

CHAPTER 13: Big Data and Hacking

CHAPTER 14: Privacy in the Digital Age

CHAPTER 15: Corporate Personhood

CHAPTER 16: Globalization

SOCIAL MEDIA AND CITIZEN MOVEMENTS

Ethics in Context

Social Media Addiction

According to Facebook, its mission is to "give people the power to build community and bring the world closer together." Twitter's mission is to "give everyone the power to create and share ideas and information instantly without barriers." Based on these mission statements, and those of other social media companies, it sounds like power to use their platform lies in the hands of users. But most social media companies use the same psychological techniques used by casinos to trigger responses and form habits that make their social media apps indispensable to our lives. Later in the chapter, in the Ethics in Context section, we will examine how these techniques impact our use of social media and the ethical implications of purposeful manipulation.

iStockphoto.com/alexsl

INTRODUCTION

The ubiquity of social media in our lives has changed the way we do business, the way we are governed, and the way we voice our opinions and organize. It has also changed how we engage with others, how we treat other people, and how we make decisions. Although most readers of this text do not remember a time in their lives when there wasn't social media, the platform is a relatively new phenomenon. Facebook, the most dominant social media platform with 2.2 billion users worldwide, has been in existence for only 14 years. Snapchat,

Learning Objectives

Upon completion of this chapter, the reader should be able to do the following:

12.1 Understand the evolution of social media.

12.2 Critique how the business models of social media companies influence the impact of the platforms on society.

12.3 Analyze how social media equalizes brand power between large and small businesses.

12.4 Explore how social media is used to unite, organize, and sometimes sow discord.

12.5 Identify public safety issues with social media.

12.6 Analyze whether regulation is the most effective means of mitigating public safety.

with 187 million users, has been around for only 6 years. The law has not caught up with this new technology, and as a result, there are few rules that apply to social media companies and the activity that takes place on social media. The upside of few laws is that the social media industry has thrived. The downside of few rules is that courts, legislatures, and the public are not sure yet how to handle the many problems that occur as a result of social media.

THE EVOLUTION OF SOCIAL MEDIA

LO 12.1 Understand the evolution of social media.

social media: Forms of electronic communications (such as websites for social networking and microblogging) through which users create online communities to share information, ideas, personal messages, and other content (such as videos).

Social media includes websites for social networking and microblogging on which users create online communities to share information, ideas, personal messages, and other content such as videos and photos.[1] Most of us understand social media to be how we communicate with each other, get our news, find the best Chinese restaurant, look for jobs, look for dates, look for pets, look for makeup tips—essentially how we live our lives. Many people in most parts of the world feel the same way, as evidenced by the growth of social media around the globe (see Figure 12.1).[i]

From Bulletin Boards to Instagram

In the 1970s, computers and computer networks were more likely to be associated with "big brother" than independence. Moreover, the technology at the time was comparatively clunky and accessible to only a few tech-savvy people. In 1979, Tom Truscott and Jim Ellis, both graduate students at Duke University, developed Usenet as a way to share mailing lists and files among universities that were conducting similar research. Usenet ultimately grew to connect millions of people and computers to 20,000 different newsgroups at hundreds of thousands of sites around the world.[2]

bulletin board systems (BBSes): An early version of a chat room in which messages or other files were shared.

chat rooms: Contemporary version of a BBS that allows users to share messages or other files with others.

While Usenet was an effective method of sharing information, the development of **bulletin board systems (BBSes)** allowed people to share information and talk with each other. The early versions of BBSs limited access to one user at a time, usually run by hobbyists who hosted subject-specific boards, and many were used for illicit purposes like hacking, hosting virus code, and adult material. In the early 1980s, online services companies like CompuServe were the first companies to incorporate BBS, now called **chat rooms**, into their service. In 1985, GE developed Genie, the first competitor to CompuServe. Genie was a text-based service that offered games, shopping, mail, and forums. By 1992, America Online (AOL) had gone public and the Internet, including e-mail and chat rooms, became far more accessible in the United States.[3] AOL changed the culture and structure of the Internet; organization of social media was no longer centered on topics but on people. For the first time, members had searchable communities and profiles where users revealed personal information.

---

[i] This section is meant to be a sampling of social media sites throughout the industry's short lifetime, focusing on the major players that shape how we use and interact with social media. There are many other sites that contributed to this evolution that, in the interest of space, are not mentioned in this section.

Classmates.com came on the scene in 1995 and proved that the idea of reconnecting (through a virtual school reunion) was a compelling role for social media.[4] A similar concept, Six-Degrees.com, combined the features of many earlier social media sites and allowed users to not only create profiles but also connect as "friends," list their friends, and surf the friend lists of other users. Some believe this breakthrough was also the demise of SixDegrees.com: At the time, there were not many people online with large networks of friends who were also online; thus, the true value of the connections, to both users and SixDegrees.com, was not optimized.[5]

In 2002, social media sites began refining their approach; Friendster was launched promoting the value of common bonds between online friends. The next year LinkedIn was introduced as a more serious and professional approach to social media: businesspeople who wanted to connect with other professionals. Myspace also launched in 2003. Similar to Friendster, Myspace allowed users to incorporate things like videos and other features; the site was hipper and attracted many Friendster users.[6] In 2016 Microsoft bought LinkedIn for $26 billion, and today the platform has more than 610 million users in 200 countries.[7] Friendster, however, quickly declined and is now an online gaming site, while Myspace focuses mainly as a social networking site for bands and musicians.[8]

Perhaps the biggest development in the social media space came when Mark Zuckerberg and his friends launched Facebook in their dorm room at Harvard in 2004. Originally developed to profile fellow students, the site quickly spread across campuses and high schools in the United States and abroad. By 2006, the site was open to the public, and Facebook quickly became big business; U.S. investor Peter Thiel invested tens of millions, and a Hong Kong investor injected $60 million into the company. Aside from its explosive growth in these early years, what set Facebook apart from other social media sites of the time were its innovations. Not only could users easily create profiles, list friends, and search others' friends but the platform could easily accept applications, which allowed third-party developers the ability to create features that worked within the platform such as photo sharing, video streaming, feeds, and timelines. For the first time, social media was used for more than just posting information. Facebook and its competitors were spaces to network—meet other people, make connections, and share their networks and their lives. The applications possible on Facebook enhanced user profiles, allowed for commenting and direct messaging, and let users compare interests such as movies and travel.[9] The popularity of Facebook's "Like" button, both on the platform and in other places on the Internet, put Facebook everywhere whether you were on the site or not.

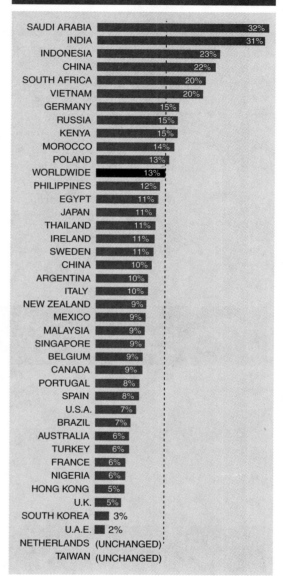

Figure 12.1 Annual Growth of Social Media Users Globally

SAUDI ARABIA	32%
INDIA	31%
INDONESIA	23%
CHINA	22%
SOUTH AFRICA	20%
VIETNAM	20%
GERMANY	15%
RUSSIA	15%
KENYA	15%
MOROCCO	14%
POLAND	13%
WORLDWIDE	13%
PHILIPPINES	12%
EGYPT	11%
JAPAN	11%
THAILAND	11%
IRELAND	11%
SWEDEN	11%
CHINA	10%
ARGENTINA	10%
ITALY	10%
NEW ZEALAND	9%
MEXICO	9%
MALAYSIA	9%
SINGAPORE	9%
BELGIUM	9%
CANADA	9%
PORTUGAL	8%
SPAIN	8%
U.S.A.	7%
BRAZIL	7%
AUSTRALIA	6%
TURKEY	6%
FRANCE	6%
NIGERIA	6%
HONG KONG	5%
U.K.	5%
SOUTH KOREA	3%
U.A.E.	2%
NETHERLANDS	(UNCHANGED)
TAIWAN	(UNCHANGED)

Source: Digital in 2018: World's Internet Users Pass the 4 Billion Mark by Simon Kemp; We Are Social and Hootsuite. https://wearesocial.com/blog/2018/01/global-digital-report-2018#.

subreddits: Online forums dealing with specific topics that are found on Reddit.

Redditors: The term used for Reddit users.

moderators: A Redditor with the authority to regulate content on a subreddit.

At the same time, social networking was gaining global momentum. Google's Orkut was the most popular platform in Brazil before it spread to India. The Japanese embraced Mixi, Sweden liked LunarStorm, Dutch users preferred Hyves, and Grono was popular among Polish users. Hi5 was adopted in many of the smaller countries in Latin America, South America, and Europe. Bebo covered the United Kingdom, New Zealand, and Australia; Cyworld dominated South Korea; and the Chinese QQ became the world's largest social networking site.[10]

A third wave of social media evolution began with the development of YouTube, Reddit, and Twitter. In February 2005, Steve Chen, Chad Hurley, and Jawed Karim founded YouTube as a video sharing site. On the site, users post videos, watch others' videos, like and comment, create their own YouTube channel, and subscribe to others' channels. Within the first year, users were uploading eight terabytes of data every day. In 2006, Google bought YouTube for $1.65 billion.[11] Currently, over 1 billion hours of YouTube videos are watched every day, and 400 hours of video are uploaded every minute—the equivalent of 65 years of video a day.[12]

Reddit launched in 2005 as a completely different type of social networking. Instead of organizing your posts into your own feed or timeline and following people and friends, Reddit is organized by subject communities (**subreddits**). And instead of liking or retweeting, Reddit users (**Redditors**) vote posts up or down with the most popular posts rising to the top and increasing in visibility. Perhaps the most unique feature of Reddit is the role of **moderators**. Each subreddit is moderated by a volunteer who can edit the appearance of posts, dictate the content of the subreddit, and ban Redditors from the community. The "Ask Me Anything" thread is the most popular feature where a well-known person agrees to answer any question asked by Redditors (see Figure 12.2).[13] In 2006, Reddit was bought by Condé Nast for between $10 million and $20 million. Today, Reddit is the third most popular website in the United States, valued at $1.8 billion.[14]

Developed as a microblogging site, Twitter differs from traditional Facebook-like social media in fundamental ways. First, on Twitter you can follow people or be followed without an expectation of reciprocity. Originally, Twitter users were limited to 140 characters for their tweets (posts), unlike traditional social media where post length is unlimited. The app was developed to allow photos, videos, retweets, likes, and comments (see Figure 12.3). In 2017, in part because of shrinking user numbers, Twitter increased the character limit for tweets to 280.[15]

As Facebook was growing in popularity, Google was growing nervous; it had several failed attempts at entering social networking. In 2011 the company launched Google+ as a "social destination at a level and scale that [they had] never attempted."[16]

Figure 12.2 President Barack Obama's Tweet in 2012 Announcing His AMA on Reddit

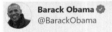

Barack Obama ✔
@BarackObama

Hey, everyone: I'll be taking your questions online today. Ask yours here: OFA.BO/gBof44 -bo

1:08 PM · Aug 29, 2012 · Twitter Web Client

4.9K Retweets   **1.5K** Likes

Source: Twitter/@BarackObama

Figure 12.3 Twitter Reaches the International Space Station

TJ Creamer ✔
@Astro_TJ

Hello Twitterverse! We r now LIVE tweeting from the International Space Station -- the 1st live tweet from Space! :) More soon, send your ?s

12:13 AM · Jan 22, 2010 · Twitter Web Client

4K Retweets   **1.2K** Likes

Source: Twitter/@Astro_TJ

According to former Google employees who worked on the launch, the site looked just like Facebook with very few original features. Google+ did not give Facebook users a reason to leave Facebook, and in 2014, Google pivoted the platform to focus on photo sharing and streaming, two successful features of Google+.[17] Figure 12.4 illustrates the most popular social media sites today.

Smartphones and Apps

With the development of the smartphone, social media moved from your computer into your hand and went with you everywhere. Although Facebook started as a platform accessed on computers, it quickly recognized the power of mobile devices. Similarly, Twitter was optimized as a mobile platform. The advent of mobile technology sparked a new wave of social media both among current players and also new entrants. With this new wave of mobile-first social media also came new technology: Rather than hosting platforms where people can connect and share, social media companies began using technology to make our interactions manageable, formal, and manipulable.

Two new entrants to the mobile social media market were Instagram and Snapchat. Instagram launched in 2010 as a method of communication solely through photos, with users able to like and comment on others' pictures. Its popularity was almost instantaneous,

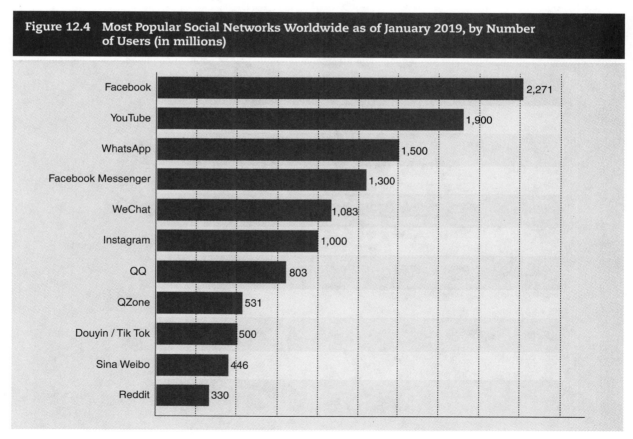

Figure 12.4   Most Popular Social Networks Worldwide as of January 2019, by Number of Users (in millions)

Facebook	2,271
YouTube	1,900
WhatsApp	1,500
Facebook Messenger	1,300
WeChat	1,083
Instagram	1,000
QQ	803
QZone	531
Douyin / Tik Tok	500
Sina Weibo	446
Reddit	330

Source: We Are Social and Hootsuite, via Statista.

and a mere 2 years later Facebook bought the app for $1 billion. At the time of purchase, Instagram had 30 million users on iPhone.[18] Currently Instagram has 1 billion active monthly users.[19] Picaboo, which later became Snapchat, was founded in 2011 as an app to share photos that would quickly disappear. One key differentiator was Snapchat's features: Users could edit, augment, or change photos in any way they wished. In this way, Snapchat didn't "conform to unrealistic notions of beauty or perfection but rather create[d] space to be funny, honest, or whatever else."[20] 190 million users snap daily.[21]

The majority of North American users engage with social media on their phones. As Figure 12.5 indicates, many regions of the globe predominantly engage with social media on their smartphones.

Figure 12.5   Social Media and Smartphone Usage Across the Globe

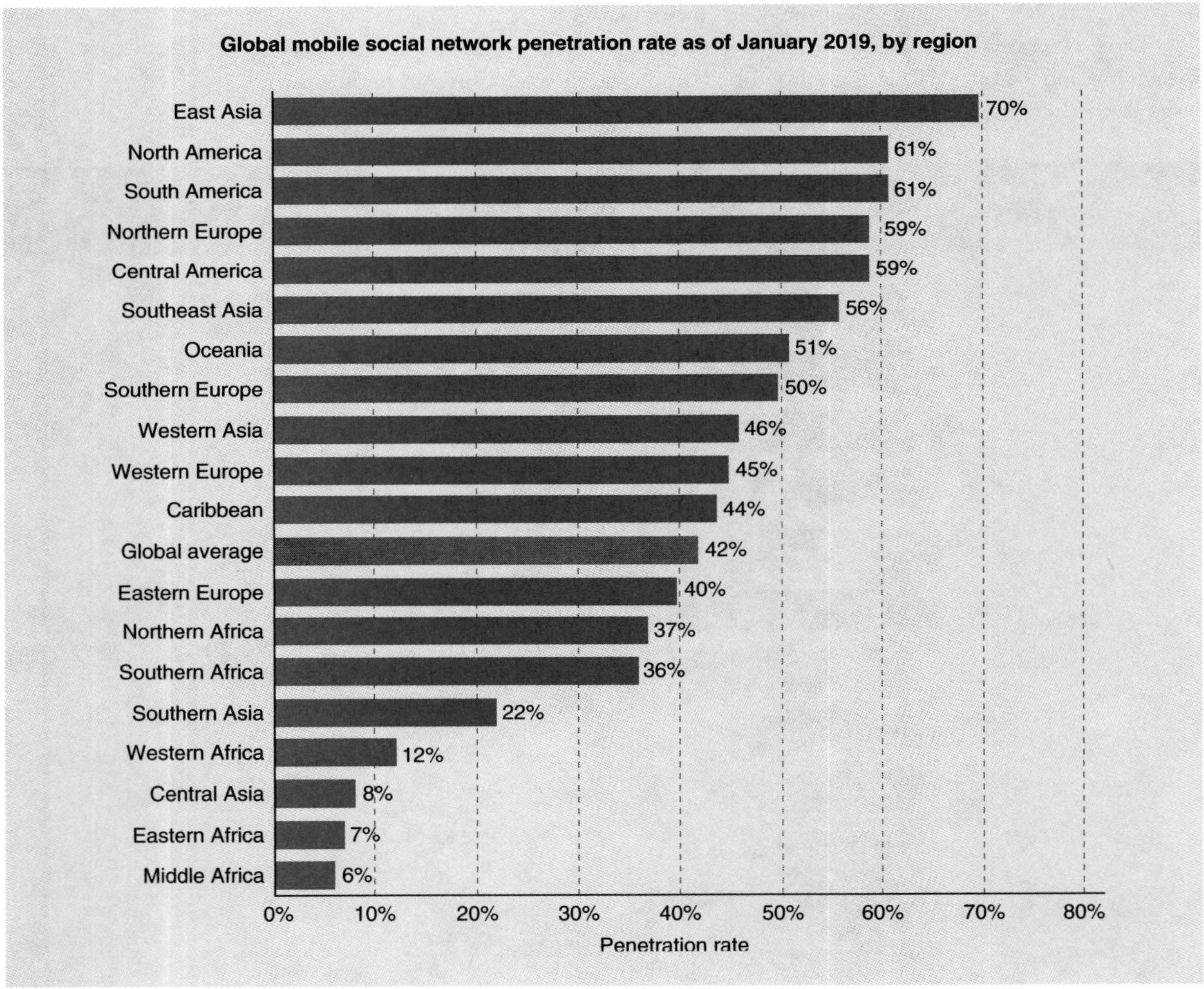

Global mobile social network penetration rate as of January 2019, by region

Region	Penetration rate
East Asia	70%
North America	61%
South America	61%
Northern Europe	59%
Central America	59%
Southeast Asia	56%
Oceania	51%
Southern Europe	50%
Western Asia	46%
Western Europe	45%
Caribbean	44%
Global average	42%
Eastern Europe	40%
Northern Africa	37%
Southern Africa	36%
Southern Asia	22%
Western Africa	12%
Central Asia	8%
Eastern Africa	7%
Middle Africa	6%

Source: "Global Digital 2019" reports, We Are Social and Hootsuite, via Statista.

KEY TAKEAWAYS

The Evolution of Social Media

- Social media evolved from file sharing to networking, posting, and sharing our lives.

- Almost all social media is consumed on mobile devices.

THE BUSINESS MODEL OF SOCIAL MEDIA

LO 12.2 Critique how the business models of social media companies influence the impact of the platforms on society.

One factor contributing to the explosive and ubiquitous growth of social media is the price tag for most users: It is free. Over time, some platforms such as Reddit and YouTube have created tiered levels of membership where users can pay for certain premium upgrades; however, the vast majority of users pay nothing. Broadly speaking, social media companies make money in two interrelated ways: selling advertising space and monetizing the vast amounts of data they collect on users. The business transaction taking place on social media isn't you watching cute puppy videos; it is getting advertisers in front of the users watching the cute puppy videos. In many ways this is similar to the traditional marketing strategies used by old-school media companies: A television network knows the demographic that watches their latest crime drama and will sell advertising space to companies that want to reach that specific demographic. But on social media, there are more users and more data—thus, more opportunity to make money.

Selling Ad Space

Like a television network, advertisers on social media want the space with the most viewers, or **engagement**. This is measured using the new metrics of social media, such as "likes" "shares," "reposts," and "retweets." The more likes and shares a post gets, the more valuable the space for advertisers and the more money the social media company makes. Figure 12.6 illustrates this very simple model.

engagement: A term used to describe the amount of traffic of a social media post measured by "likes," "shares,""reposts,"and "retweets."

This is a successful model. In the first quarter of 2019, Facebook earned almost $15 billion from advertising revenue, almost all of it from mobile.[22] Twitter has a similar advertising model and in the first quarter of 2019 earned $679 million from advertising revenue out of $787 million total revenue for the quarter.[23] For many social media companies, attracting and retaining advertisers is their primary focus. For example, in its first quarter 2019 letter to shareholders, Twitter stated that going forward it is focused on "delivering better relevance, making it easier for advertisers to declare their objective, initiate their campaign, and measure their success."[24]

Figure 12.6 General Business Model for Social Media

Popular Posts → More Likes and Shares → More User Engagement → More Ads → More Clicks on Ads → More Advertiser Sales → More Revenue for Social media Company

Exactly how social media companies allow advertisers to target certain audiences can differ from company to company. Facebook has mastered its business model and optimized it for maximum returns: They have no cost for content because users and companies generate the content, no marketing costs because users speak with each other about their experience, and minimal costs to sell the advertising space because their ad service is do-it-yourself.[25] Through Facebook's **Ads Manager**, businesses create and manage their ads, find tools to help them target specific audiences, track results, and make changes all without ever interacting with a person at Facebook.[26] Twitter operates a little differently by giving companies three ways to advertise on the platform: They can promote a tweet that will appear in a person's timeline, promote an entire account, or promote a trend. Moreover, Twitter charges advertisers based on the amount of engagement their ads generate, charging either per click or per retweet. The company uses a similar model with its video advertising but also includes in-stream advertising where a company will pay to roll a short video advertisement before the user views the video they searched for. Companies can also bid on certain high-traffic space on the platform. Because the nature of Twitter is microblogging and quick scrolling, users do not linger on particular tweets, unlike Facebook where users can spend long periods of time reading lengthy posts and comments while ads are displayed to the side of their timeline. This difference means Twitter must develop ad space that does not interrupt the user experience and reduce engagement.[27]

> **Ads Manager:** Facebook's "do-it-yourself" ad service in which businesses create and manage their ads, find tools to target specific consumer audiences, and track results.

Alphabet's YouTube, on the other hand, offers tiered subscription options in addition to the free, ad-filled video streaming. For $10 per month, users can listen to ad-free music on YouTube Music Premium,[28] and for $12 per month, users can experience everything YouTube has to offer, ad-free with YouTube Premium.[29] Similarly, Microsoft's LinkedIn sells subscriptions to users that entitle them to increase their searches, send e-mails rather than just receive them, contact people outside of their networks, and see information on people who have looked at their profile. Because LinkedIn is a professional social networking site, it also sells recruitment services to professional recruiters and businesses.[30]

Selling Data

How social media companies monetize our data is another differentiator. Twitter licenses its public data in a bulk format called firehose. Companies do the work of analyzing that data and can sell it to third parties or use it to determine everything from sentiment about certain products to predicting inventory levels needed in different regions. For instance, U.S. football teams can track sentiment toward particular players in different parts of the country and use that data to stock player jerseys in sporting goods stores.[31] LinkedIn has partnered with a company that will scrape user data, anonymize and aggregate it, then sell it to third parties to develop more targeted advertising.[32] Facebook's expertise in collecting and sorting user data is driven by its pricing structure for advertisers: It charges companies for access to different targeted segments of their user base. But unlike Twitter and LinkedIn, Facebook doesn't sell user data to third parties; it does the hard work of finding the targets based on the companies' parameters and then shows the ads to that population. Mark Zuckerberg said, "What we allow for is advertisers to tell us who they want to reach, and then we do the placement . . . without that data ever changing hands and going to the advertiser."[33]

> **application programming interface (API):** An app development platform that makes third-party applications accessible to users.

Social Media, Our Data, and Trust

"There's a very common misperception about Facebook—that we sell data to advertisers . . . And we do not sell data to advertisers. We don't sell data to anyone," said Mark Zuckerberg, CEO of Facebook, on April 10, 2018.[34] As mentioned earlier, Facebook does the work of sorting through the data on its 2.2 billion users to get advertisers the specific audience they are paying for. However, in December 2009 the Federal Trade Commission (FTC), the federal agency charged with protecting consumers, charged Facebook with engaging in deceptive business practices when it changed its website, without warning or asking for consent from its users, so that their once private information was made public. Moreover, despite its claims that the company does not share users' personal data with advertisers, it allowed them access to personally identifiable information when a user clicked on an ad on their timeline. Facebook also shared user information with outside app developers. Even if the user deactivated or deleted their account app, developers still had access to photos and videos despite promising users it would never share their information in this manner. Facebook settled these charges, eight in all, with the FTC in 2011. As part of the settlement, the company agreed to privacy audits conducted by a third party every 2 years for 20 years, to obtain the express consent of its users before making changes that override a users' privacy preferences, and to get user consent before sharing their data with third parties.

In 2014 Facebook allowed a third-party app developer named Aleksandr Kogan to run a personality survey among Facebook users. Users had to download an app to take the survey and were told that the results would be used for academic purposes. Once users downloaded the app, the app scraped personal information from their profile. About 270,000 users took the survey. However, within Facebook's **application programming interface (API)**, the app development platform that makes third-party apps accessible to Facebook users, developers not only had access to the personal information of those who used the app but also the personal information of all of their friends. In total, Kogan gained access to over 80 million user profiles, which it sold to political consulting firm Cambridge Analytica—seemingly in violation of Facebook's 2011 consent decree with the FTC. The Trump presidential campaign and Vote Leave Campaign (U.K. pro-Brexit group) were among Cambridge Analytica's clients. With the user data, the firm was able to identify personality traits of American voters and create ads to influence their vote in the 2016 presidential election.

When Facebook learned of this data harvesting in 2015, it changed its API to prevent access to friends' data. But the company did not suspend the accounts of Cambridge Analytica or Kogan until 2018. This controversy led the FTC to open an investigation into whether Facebook violated its 2011 consent decree. In July 2019, Facebook agreed to pay a record-breaking $5 billion penalty and submit to new restrictions, which include multiple channels of compliance and accountability standards for decisions made about privacy.

Discussion Questions

1. Industry experts have noted that over the 14 years of Facebook, CEO Mark Zuckerberg has made numerous apologies. For a company started by a 20-year-old that experienced explosive growth in a short period of time, that is to be expected. Zuckerberg apologized in 2010, after the FTC charged it with deceptive business

(Continued)

(Continued)

practices, by writing an op-ed in the *Washington Post*, and again in 2018 after Cambridge Analytica admitted that "it was certainly a breach of trust." Twitter apologized in May 2019 for breaching user trust when it inadvertently shared user location data with third parties that were bidding on advertising space. What role does trust play in providing a social media platform? Is trust important to you when you use social media? Why or why not?

2. Most social media platforms are free to use; however, many feel that if companies like Facebook charged for its services, it would better protect our data. Zuckerberg's response to this suggestion was this: Giving people "the power to build community and bring the world closer together" can only happen if everyone can use the service, which means it must stay free. Can you think of other reasons why Facebook would not want to move to a subscription-based model? Explain.

Critical Thinking

What is Facebook, Twitter, and other publicly traded social media companies' duty to their shareholders? What is their duty to their stakeholders? When it comes to our data, should one group take precedence? Why or why not?

What Data Do Social Media Companies Collect?

Most social media users understand that we voluntarily share personal information when we create accounts on Facebook or Twitter, or any other social media platform. For example, when you create an account on Facebook, a user must reveal their name, gender, date of birth, and e-mail or phone number. Once we start using Facebook, the company gathers data about what we click on, what we "like," and what we share. Our data profile is constantly updated every time we add information like where we went to school, maiden names, and other social networks we engage with like alumni groups or clubs. Importantly, Facebook has a "user log" for each user that stores all of our activity "from today back to the very beginning."[35] This includes photos we were tagged in, the adding of friends, connections made over the years, and searches for other people and pages. Twitter has a similar collection strategy. When we tweet, or read our feed, Twitter is working behind the scenes collecting information such as the websites we visit that have Twitter content (regardless of whether we are logged into Twitter), information from friends, family, business contacts, and anyone else in your contacts, and it can track us from our phone to our laptop using our IP address. Twitter can determine what we like by collecting data on the tweets we read, like, and retweet, what language we speak, and our age.[36] Twitter also works with some of its advertising partners to collect similar data from their websites.[37]

Companies use this information in a variety of ways. For example, companies can use Twitter's streaming API to collect tweets based on keywords. In one study, researchers used Twitter handles for 20 companies in five different industries—fast-food, department stores, telecommunications, footwear, and consumer electronics—to collect tweets over 6 months. They were able to distill the data into very specific results: 15.7% of the tweets about fast-food were about promotions that stores were offering, and 66.7% of the tweets about Comcast contained negative sentiment.[38] In another study, advertisers wanted to learn how to effectively use digital billboards in the London Underground. Using the API and Twitter's **geotagging** feature, a function that allows Twitter users to tag their location when

geotagging: A feature that allows users to tag their location when they post content on social media.

they post a tweet, the company pulled the location of the specific Underground station and the time and content of each tweet posted at those stations. After a year of collecting this data, the company learned that almost 35% of tweets from the Holloway Road station were about sports, and almost 40% of the tweets posted between 6:00 p.m. and midnight on the weekends at the North Greenwich station were about music. This information can be used to create specific ads, such as a rotating digital billboard featuring a music-related ad in the North Greenwich station in the evening on weekends.[39] See Figure 12.7 on data collection.

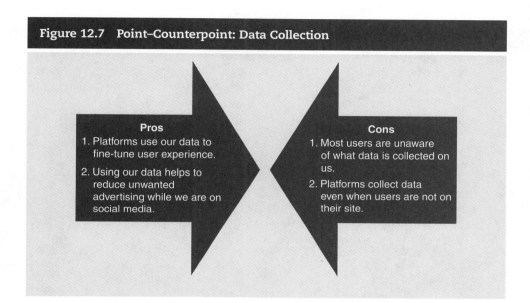

Figure 12.7   Point–Counterpoint: Data Collection

Pros
1. Platforms use our data to fine-tune user experience.
2. Using our data helps to reduce unwanted advertising while we are on social media.

Cons
1. Most users are unaware of what data is collected on us.
2. Platforms collect data even when users are not on their site.

variable ratio schedule: A strategy used by social media developers to entice app users to increase viewing time on their apps by creating a delay before showing results.

infinite scroll: A continuous scrolling of social media posts developed by Brian Raskin in 2006.

push notifications: Pop-up notifications of social media apps

social reciprocity: A psychological tactic utilized by social media developers to induce users to spend more time on social media by including "friend suggestions."

Social Media Addiction

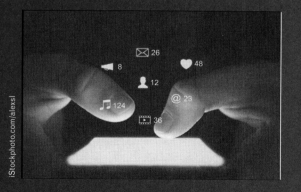

iStockphoto.com/alexsl

What do most of us do when we are waiting in line to order a coffee, getting on the bus, or walking home from class? We look at our phones and maybe check Instagram or Snapchat. Our urge to check our favorite social media app could border on addiction, and according to some engineers, that is exactly what social media companies want. Tristan Harris, a former design ethicist at Google, compares using social media apps on our phone to playing a slot machine: "When someone pulls a lever, sometimes they get rewarded and sometimes they don't." This is called a **variable ratio schedule,** and it is how slot machines keep users inserting quarters and smartphone users checking their favorite social media platform. According to Harris, on Twitter when you swipe your finger down, a spinning wheel indicates that it is possibly loading new tweets. Or maybe

(Continued)

ETHICS IN CONTEXT

(Continued)

it isn't. You don't know, but you are going to stick around to find out because now you're interested in seeing whether you have a reward: new tweets (Instagram uses the same spinning wheel). The same technique is used when you first check your Twitter from the mobile app: The screen is momentarily blue and the white bird is in the middle. This isn't due to slow Internet service; it is on purpose. The delay leaves users unsure of what they are going to see, and that entices us to stay to see what we get. Stick around enough times, and you have formed a habit. And once we have formed a habit, we no longer need a trigger like a notification or a sound to check our social media because we have developed an emotional need to check.

Once you are on your social media account, let's say it's Instagram, you must scroll to see posts. The **infinite scroll** was designed by Brian Raskin in 2006. Because you use your finger to quickly swipe down through content rather than click through content, according to Mr. Raskin, "You don't give your brain time to catch up with your impulses, you just keep scrolling." Facebook uses this because they know it is a guaranteed way to keep us scrolling longer, searching for something worth reading. And the longer we are on their app, the more data Facebook, and most other social media companies, collect about us that they then sell to advertisers and other third parties. Access to our data is valuable: Ad spending on social media doubled in 2 years to more than $3 billion in 2017.

By the time we check our social media to see if we have any likes or retweets, programmers have already determined the best time to release any likes based on our engagement history with the app. Some Instagram likes might be withheld in order to be released in a burst, which triggers more excitement than a slow release. That excitement keeps us coming back to check. Leah Pearlman is the cocreator of the Facebook Like button. According to Pearlman, she became addicted to Facebook because she based her self-worth on the number of likes she got on her posts. She knew she became addicted to the feedback when she realized that she checked her phone when she felt lonely or insecure.

Push notifications keep you coming back to social media apps because they speak to you directly to show you what you are missing. According to

Avery Hartmans, from *Business Insider*, Instagram's push notifications are one reason why the app is so addictive. If a user has enabled them, push notifications send an alert about many different kinds of activity happening on the platform, such as when someone you follow is filming live video or when someone posts an Instagram story. Push notifications have doubled user retention on iOS and increased user retention by almost 6 times on Android.

Although not as popular as Facebook, LinkedIn has a diverse membership and uses a different psychological tactic to keep us scrolling: **social reciprocity**. When someone sends an invitation to connect, directly below the invitation is a list of other people you could connect with. Our "unconscious impulse" to connect turns into a social obligation that earns LinkedIn profit as we spend more time on the platform making connections.

As the most popular social media platform, Facebook leverages its user size in a variety of ways. One of the most successful (for Facebook) is helping us log into other apps. Instead of creating a new user name and password for every app that we use, Facebook conveniently lets us log into them using our Facebook account (Google does this too). In this way, having a Facebook or Google account makes your life easier while at the same time allowing access to more of our data. Similarly, Facebook makes our lives easier by keeping track of our friends' birthdays and anniversaries so we don't have to. Instead of just a platform to connect with other people, Facebook has now become a vital component in helping us manage our lives.

What is the impact of the tactics used to keep us scrolling through social media posts? Former Google design ethicist Tristan Harris says, "Never before in history have a handful of people at a handful of technology companies shaped how a billion people think and feel every day. . . ."

According to Harris, and what he told Google, the constant bombardment is "weakening our relationships with each other [and] destroying our kids' ability to focus." According to a study conducted at the University of Pennsylvania, there is a link between reducing social media use and improvement in well-being. In the study, 143 undergraduate students were randomly assigned to one of two groups: One group continued to use social media as usual, and the other group was limited to 30 minutes of social media use a day—split 10 minutes each between Facebook, Instagram, and Snapchat. Researchers kept the students honest by looking at their phone usage data. Baseline readings were measured of all participants in areas like depression, loneliness, self-esteem, and autonomy. At the end of the 3 weeks, those in the reduced social media group experienced reductions in loneliness and depression, regardless of the levels in their baseline readings.

Why this connection exists is less clear. Oscar Ybarra, a psychology professor at the University of Michigan, suggests that even though people know that most lives on social media are heavily curated, there nevertheless is a social comparison happening. And the more we use social media, the more we compare ourselves to others on the platform. Amy Summerville, a psychology professor at Miami University in Ohio, suggests that FOMO (fear of missing out) is another driving force that has been linked with social media use. This type of regret, according to Summerville, is part of a larger need for inclusion and social standing.

Resisting the pull of these psychological forces to reduce our time spent on social media is no easy feat. Luckily, there is an app for that. Gabe Zichermann, known in Silicon Valley for "gamifying" apps, is developing an app called Onward that is designed to break the social media habit by tracking use and recommending a user do something else after a certain period of time. Ramsay Brown from Dopamine Labs made an app called Space that created a 12-second delay before any social media app would open. Space was rejected from the App Store. In 2018 Facebook launched a new tool that shows users how long they have been on their Facebook or Instagram apps. Users can set time limits and automatic reminders. Both Apple (on iPhones and iPads) and Google (on Pixel phones) have similar new features.

Discussion Questions

1. *Stakeholder theory*: Tech companies want to improve "user engagement" with their app. Mr. Raskin, the developer of infinite scroll, admits that he never meant to get users addicted and now feels guilty about it. According to Raskin, designers were motivated to create a successful product in order to get the next round of funding, or to increase their company's stock price. And the only way to do either was to show that your product was popular based on how long people spent in your app. Focusing on the incentive, says Raskin, motivated people to concentrate on new ways to keep users hooked. Who are the stakeholders affected by successful social media features? What is at stake for each? Why do you think Mr. Raskin, and other designers, did not factor in other stakeholders when they designed their features and apps?

2. *Ethical reasoning*: Mr. Brown, from Dopamine Labs, writes code using similar triggers as social media for financial services firms and fitness companies, hopefully getting users to save or invest more or exercise more. Both are laudable goals. Using a principles-based approach and a consequences-based approach, answer the following: Does it matter how designers get us to save more money or exercise more, knowing the same technology is used to keep us addicted to social media? Or does it just matter that we save more money and exercise more?

Take a Position

According to Facebook, its mission is to "give people the power to build community and bring the world closer together." Twitter's mission is to "give everyone the power to create and share ideas and information instantly without barriers." Based on these mission statements, and those of other social media companies, it sounds like the power of social media is in the users' hands. Yet, it is clear that most social media companies use psychological tactics to get users to use their platforms in a particular way for as long as possible. According to Harris, "It's not because anyone is evil or has bad intentions"; it's because the financial incentives are to get as much attention as possible.

Issue: Do social media companies have an ethical responsibility not to use psychological techniques to keep users hooked to their platforms? Explain your answer.

KEY TAKEAWAYS

The Business Model of Social Media

- The business model of most social media is driven by user engagement: The longer we stay on the platform, the more data is collected, the more valuable the space for advertisers.

- Data collected can be used to more efficiently target ads, but social media platforms must tell users what data is collected and how that data will be used.

- Features such as infinite scroll and push notifications are purposely designed to keep users on the platform and increase engagement regardless of the impact on the user.

HOW BUSINESSES USE SOCIAL MEDIA

LO 12.3 Analyze how social media equalizes brand power between large and small businesses.

According to the 2018 CMO Survey,[ii] spending on social media marketing increased more in 2017 than any other year in the past decade. Companies in the study spend almost 14% of their total marketing budgets on social media marketing and plan to increase that by over 66% in the next 5 years.[40] Using the data of billions of social media users has changed the way even the most traditional companies market their brand. For example, IBM, founded in 1911, currently has 433,000 employees—many of whom blog. In 2005, IBM began allowing all employees to blog with crowdsourcing blogging guidelines everyone agrees to follow. Today, including most major media platforms, IMB employees have 32,000 individual blogs—most of which are housed on IBM.com, in addition to the IBM formal digital marketing team. Rather than use its digital space for more traditional sales techniques, IBM is using social media to change the image of the company. It is no longer just a source of products; it is also a source of content and information. Not surprisingly, IBM content has not gone viral—on the IBM YouTube channel some videos only get hundreds of views. But the goal of their social media strategy is to showcase IBM employees as a valuable resource for customers, not to rack up likes.[41]

Compare that to Unilever's brand Dove. In 2004 Dove began its Dove Campaign for Real Beauty, a strategy designed to learn more about what women thought about beauty.[42] Dove was an early adopter of YouTube; its 2006 video "Evolution" went viral on the platform and its 2013 YouTube video "Real Beauty Sketches" became the most watched video ad of all time and the third most shared ad of all time.[43] Going viral is not always an advantage. In October 2017 Dove released a 3-second video ad for body wash on Facebook. The ad depicted a black woman taking off her shirt and transforming into a white woman who then took off her shirt and transformed into an Asian woman.[44] The image of using soap to transform a woman of color into a white woman raised historic racist images from ads suggesting people of color were dirty.[iii] The swift response to the ad prompted Dove to apologize on Facebook and remove the video.[45]

[ii] Conducted in partnership between Deloitte, Duke's Fuqua School of Business, and the American Marketing Association.

[iii] Author and colleague Sarah Dasher as graduate students at Boston University's Graduate School of Communications won the Page Society Case Competition with their work examining the cultural issues raised by the 2017 Dove video and fallout described in the article.

Big businesses are not the only players harnessing the power of social media to build their brand. Small businesses have created effective digital content for social media at very little expense. Consider Blendtec. Founded in 1976, this small Orem, Utah, company designs and sells commercial and residential kitchen equipment such as blenders, mixers, and kitchen mills. In 2006, founder Tom Dickson spent $50 to post a series of five videos to YouTube titled, "Will It Blend?" The series showed a Blendtec blender blending ordinary items such as marbles, glow sticks, and credit cards. Within days, the series had millions of views. Dickson was featured on *The Today Show*, *The Tonight Show* with Jay Leno, and the Discovery Channel.[46] Over the years, the "Will It Blend?" YouTube series has blended, among other things, toy cars, light bulbs, a garden hose, an iPhone, a Wii remote, a Kindle Fire, an Amazon Echo, and an Elf on the Shelf.[47]

iStockphoto.com/Kritchanut

The popularity of social media has spawned a new industry: influencing. A **social media influencer** is a user on social media who has credibility and influence in a specific industry or with a specific audience. They could be activists, bloggers, YouTubers, or celebrities. Not every social media user is an influencer; they need to have high engagement with their followers, a level of relatability or inspiration, and most importantly they need to have built trust with their followers. The influencer industry is projected to generate as much as $10 billion by 2020. Influencers will typically be paid to promote a product or service within their social media feed, often with "#sponsored" visible in the post.

Influencers can be valuable marketing channels for brands. Hopper HQ, an automated Instagram scheduler, estimates that Kylie Jenner makes approximately $1 million per sponsored Instagram post, Selena Gomez about $800,000, and soccer star Cristiano Ronaldo about $750,000. These are estimates because most individuals and brands do not disclose the exact costs of their sponsored ads. Mike Bandar, Hopper HQ cofounder, claims that "everyone has seen or responded to influencer marketing, whether we know it or not." Sure, these stars have hundreds of millions of followers, but does that mean their followers trust their brand recommendations? According to a 2015 survey by global measurement and analytics company Nielsen, over 80% of people trust the recommendations of friends and family, and 66% say they trust consumer opinions posted online. Moreover, according to a 2016 Collective Bias survey of over 14,000 adults, almost one third of consumers are more likely to buy a product endorsed by a noncelebrity blogger than a celebrity, and almost 20% find Facebook and YouTube the most influential channels impacting their in-store purchases.

As a result, brands frequently look to **micro-influencers**—someone on YouTube or Facebook who might not have 112 million followers like Kylie Jenner but who is nonetheless engaged with a devoted group of followers. That brand will contact the influencer, and if they strike a relationship, the influencer and brand will create content about the product or service to share with the influencer's followers on social media. The influencer typically gets paid for that promotion or sometimes gets free products or services from the brand. Because this industry is so new, and because it is impossible to know how many influencers are on social media, determining a fair price for promoting a product or service can be difficult.

social media influencer: A social media user with credibility and influence in a specific industry or with a specific audience to sway followers into purchasing sponsored items.

micro-influencers: Social media users who do not have enough followers to be categorized as social media influencers but are engaged with a devoted group of followers.

Got Influence?

Social media is more of an art than a science, and you have to hope that you charge a fair price without undervaluing your contributions.

Gretchen and her friend started producing YouTube videos about beauty and fashion in her bedroom when she was 15 years old. She thought it was fun and kept creating videos throughout high school, gradually building followers and catching the interest of some brands. When she went to college, Gretchen adapted her content to include day-in-the-life videos, dorm tours, and tips on decorating your dorm room. The interest from brands increased as well, and Gretchen found herself unable to manage doing her schoolwork, rowing on the crew team, and pursuing her business opportunities on social media. By the end of her sophomore year, Gretchen quit the crew team and hired a manager to help her balance her growing business and schoolwork. Today, at 21 years old, she has 137,000 Instagram followers and over 290,000 subscribers to her YouTube channel. For Gretchen, the trust she has built with her followers is the key to her success. She knows that consumers would rather try a product recommended by a friend than by a celebrity, so Gretchen tries to create content and run her vlog and social media as if she were talking with her best girlfriends or sister. Understanding her personal values has helped Gretchen navigate the business of social media influencing. Honesty and trust guide her business decisions about which brands to work with and what content to create to promote those brands.

While many social media influencers run their business in a manner similar to Gretchen, others do not. According to YouTube beauty vlogger Marlena Stell, based on her experience, some influencers just want to be famous and "they want to have a nice paycheck." This, she claims, leads to money being the decision-maker rather than ethics and values. For example, Manny Gutierrez is a beauty vlogger with almost 5 million YouTube subscribers. He has been accused of orchestrating a fake feud with a start-up eyelash company with the hope that the fake fight would lead to more sales for the company. Both have denied the accusation. The *New York Times* investigated the use of *social media bots*, autonomous programs that can interact with users, purchased by fledgling influencers to inflate their online following. According to the investigation, one company, Devumi, sold approximately 200 million Twitter followers to at least 39,000 customers, including famous athletes, chefs, and micro-influencers. The market has evolved to address this growing fraud. A company called Sylo can, for a fee, analyze the followers of an influencer and determine what percentage are bots. Facebook and YouTube have new disclosure rules for promoted posts and Instagram said it was cracking down on apps used by influencers to generate automated likes, comments, and follows on other users' accounts.

Discussion Questions

1. Major brands are starting to take influencer fraud more seriously. Kellogg's has created new rules for how they engage with influencers and have changed the metrics they use to determine influencer success in order to reduce gaming the system. Unilever announced that it would no longer work with influencers who purchased followers. Is this enough? Should large companies be doing more to reduce influencer fraud? What if you are not a Fortune 100 company, you are a start-up that wants to penetrate social media? What rules would you develop to reduce your involvement with influencer fraud?

2. A newer trend among aspiring influencers is the "fake-it-till-you-make-it" approach: They pretend that their posts are sponsored when in reality they are not. The idea is that the only way to attract brands and actual sponsorship deals is to pretend that you already have a lot of sponsorship deals. One aspiring influencer in justifying her deception told *New York Magazine*: Everyone "assume[s] everything is sponsored when it really isn't." What are the dangers of this type of fraud to consumers? To brands? Do you consider this type of deception worse than buying social media followers? Why or why not?

Critical Thinking

There are not many rules that apply to online marketing and the role of influencers. While government interest in social media has been focused on selling data and the role of outside influence, not much time has been devoted to influencer fraud. The FTC has issued guidelines for disclosure of sponsored content, but there has not been any noticeable enforcement of these rules against influencers. One exception is the $700,000 penalty issued against DJ Khaled and Floyd Mayweather Jr. for failing to disclose receipt of promotional payments for their post about initial coin offerings.

You are an industry analyst at the FTC who has been asked to draft disclosure regulations for influencers, brands, and platforms. What are the short-term and long-term consequences of disclosure regulations on the three groups? Based on your answer, draft a list of goals for the proposed regulation of each group.

KEY TAKEAWAYS

How Businesses Use Social Media

- Social media can equalize the reach between large and small businesses.

- Influencers are the new marketing engine for products and services, but like traditional marketing, consumers must be aware of deceptive claims by influencers.

SOCIETY, DEMOCRACY, AND SOCIAL MEDIA

LO 12.4 Explore how social media is used to unite, organize, and sometimes sow discord.

LO 12.5 Identify public safety issues with social media.

Almost 3.5 billion people around the world use social media.[48] If you want to gain followers for your movement or cause, social media is a good place to start. Social media has changed the face of modern organizing; activists and organizations do not need a lot of money or structure to gain members or get their message out. All they need are "likes" and retweets. Similarly, concerned citizens don't have to attend a rally or protest to feel involved; they can follow their favorite organization on Facebook and Twitter to learn of the latest news and events, to voice their support or disagreement, and to make donations.

There are conflicting opinions about the value of social media in terms of organizing and sustaining social and political movements. It is clear that social media is the place to go to quickly gain followers and momentum around issues. Motivated activists can organize demonstrations and protests quickly and cheaply without the structure required for traditional organizing. Likes and comments provide groups with instant feedback on their events and ideas. Social media users can quickly join a group just by liking the group page on Facebook or following them on Twitter and Instagram. In this way, social media provides unprecedented access to people and voices to galvanize a cause, create a common identity, and shape discourse.[49]

But the key to its success is also one of its greatest challenges. Because users can freely like any organization they choose, use hashtags, and post commentary, organizations often struggle to maintain a focused message. Ideologies can quickly blur when users repost and comment, slowly straying from the original message of the organization. Moreover, due to the commercial nature of most social media platforms, group activity does not win many advertisers. Facebook, Twitter, Instagram, and others are optimized for individual use, collecting data on our every move, not for collective solidarity.[50] The ease with which people can join an organization gives new meaning to the concept of "membership" but might also lull people into a false sense of activism, called slacktivism—when users feel they have achieved something merely by virtually joining a group.[51] Thus while social media can quickly organize members, their commitment is often shallow and unsustainable using social media alone. Lastly, organizing online is vulnerable to the type of behavior all social media users are vulnerable to, including trolling,[iv] doxxing,[52] and bullying.[53]

Examining how three successful activist organizations use social media illustrates how the platform can be used to build momentum and scale and also creates challenges and threats.

#OccupyWallStreet[v]

In September 2011, several hundred people descended on Zuccotti Park in Manhattan near the New York Stock Exchange (NYSE) to protest the dramatic income inequality in the United States, corporate greed, and the corrosive nature of money in politics. Largely organized via social media and inspired by Arab Spring,[vi] the group became known by their hashtag #OccupyWallStreet (OWS). Word spread quickly via social media as 6,500 occupiers were arrested in the first six months, and OWS groups were set up in more than 1,000 cities.[54] Labor unions and community groups joined the cause, and suddenly groups voicing their frustration with income inequality appeared in San Francisco, Boston, Los Angeles, Denver, and Chicago. Because social justice is a dynamic examination of fairness and equality issues, it makes sense that the issues evolve. For example, in the early days of OWS, most participants were young, white, and educated and also jobless and disenchanted with their prospects. Then the demographics of the group evolved to recognize the of role of race in income inequality. Soon large labor unions and community groups joined the cause, and OWS began lending its voice to other related social justice issues such as New York City's stop-and-frisk policy and the lack of safety for women and members of the LGBTQ community in public spaces.

The diffuse nature of joining OWS via social media presented challenges for the group in terms of keeping their message focused. However, the ease of joining also reflected the movement's values of "inclusiveness and direct participation, as well as its claims that it spoke for the 99%."[55] OWS used Facebook pages to gain support and generate momentum; however, organizers believe the true value of social media is to mobilize followers

slacktivism: A false sense of activism by users simply joining social media groups that advocate for a cause while failing to further contribute to the cause.

trolling: When a social media user deliberately produces provocative content to generate a negative response.

doxxing: To search, with malicious intent, for online information regarding an individual.

#OccupyWallStreet (OWS): A social media-organized activist group whose mission is to draw attention to income inequality, corporate greed, and the corrosive nature of money in politics.

social justice: A dynamic examination of fairness and equality issues in society.

[iv] Deliberately making unsolicited and controversial comments online with the intent to provoke. See https://www.urbandictionary.com/define.php?term=Trolling

[v] See Chapter 10 for a more detailed look at the OWS response to the financial crisis and their protests about financial systems in the United States.

[vi] A wave of peaceful protests and unrest that spread across the Arab-speaking world in 2010 and 2011. The events gained momentum and spread rapidly due to social media.

to participate in in-person events such as a local occupation: "Even if they went out to their local Occupy, brought them a casserole or something, that's miles beyond clicking a like on a Facebook page."[56] Turning virtual participation into physical participation fostered longer-lasting and sustainable support. Feedback was another important component of OWS social media use; according to organizers, "Success is purely based on how many 'Likes' . . . to me if you're getting ten thousand 'likes' a week on Facebook, it means whatever it is you're doing . . . is a success."[57]

iStockphoto.com/Starflamedia

#BlackLivesMatter

In response to the 2013 acquittal of George Zimmerman for the shooting death of Trayvon Martin, an unarmed African American teenager in Sanford, Florida, Patrisse Cullors, a community organizer from Los Angeles, California; Alicia Garza, a community activist; and Opal Tometi, a community organizer from New York City, formed **Black Lives Matter (BLM)**. The social justice ideals of BLM—the economic, political, and social empowerment of African Americans and the right "to live with dignity and respect"[58]—resonated across the country. BLM is an "ideological and political intervention."[59] Unlike the civil rights movements of the past, many feel BLM has focused its priorities on fighting for a fundamental "reordering of society where black lives are free from systemic dehumanization"[60] rather than changing specific laws. Like OWS, BLM has sparked a national conversation about the treatment of Black communities, inspiring other groups such as the Women's March, March for Our Lives, and #MeToo to raise their voices on issues of unfairness and inequality. BLM has grown into a national network, including more than 50 organizations with a shared vision of equality, intersectionality and inclusion, and ending police brutality. Like with OWS, social media allows BLM to shape its discourse and priorities, whereas traditional media tends to define the group more narrowly.

> **Black Lives Matter (BLM):** An activist group focused on the reordering of society to allow African Americans equal opportunities and the economic, political, and social empowerment of African Americans.

Among its priorities, BLM stresses the lack of a typical hierarchy, signaling inclusiveness and equality. Because of this, social media is crucial in helping a grassroots activist organization operate and provide members a "safe space" to speak and reflect on issues related to race and policing.[61] Another priority for BLM is in-person activism and civil disobedience. As a communication tool, social media allows organizers to share ideas and coordinate events locally and nationally. According to one BLM group member, "We cross-share events. We basically tell people, 'Hey this is going on here, this is going on there, the school board is happening here . . .' and because of the heavy use of social media with the demographic we have, the information spreads like wildfire."[62] A march that the group organized after the Alton Sterling and Philando Castile shootings quickly grew to over 1,500 people after it was posted on the group's Facebook, Twitter, and Instagram accounts.

Burnout is a problem for leaders in BLM; the work is challenging, stressful, and often tragic. For BLM leaders, social media is a source of support—having others to commiserate and share experiences with helps to boost morale and keep momentum. Social media "allows you to be like, 'Okay, I see what you are doing. How did you get through that? Alright, okay.

I'm gonna do that over here.' And it allows us to be a whole network without being right in front of each other's faces."[63] Social media also allows for quick and easy networking with other groups and coalitions such as LGBTQ, women, and immigrant groups. BLM has successfully used social media to connect with better-resourced white ally groups, crowdfund donations, and request specific resources, like ride-sharing to events or access to venue spaces.

Some challenges BLM has experienced include the ease with which groups can misappropriate BLM symbols even if they do not share the same ideology or mission. This can confuse the message the public sees about BLM. Moreover, everyone has an opinion on social media, and while this can help shape discourse, it can also lead to trolling that can shut down entire conversations. To protect against this, many in BLM monitor the comments sections of their social media; however, this diverts their energy away from activism. At times, the trolling has devolved into racial slurs and death threats. And because social media is always open, the risk for this behavior is constant.[64]

#JeSuisCharlie

Charlie Hebdo is a radical weekly magazine published in Paris, France, that often takes sarcastic, provocative, and—to many—offensive jabs at French government and culture. On January 7, 2016, two brothers stormed the magazine, shooting and killing 11 workers. The terrorist group Al-Qaeda claimed that the magazine was targeted because of caricatures depicting the Prophet Muhammad. When Joachim Roncin, an art director at a magazine in central Paris, learned of the shooting he said, "We all stopped everything."[65] Roncin decided to use the font of *Charlie Hebdo* in a simple image that said "Je Suis Charlie"—"I am Charlie"—that he posted on Twitter. Roncin's intent was an expression of solidarity. The hashtag #JeSuisCharlie was used more than 1.5 million times on the day of the attacks and 6 million times on Twitter, Instagram, and Facebook in the following week, making it one of the largest hashtags of solidarity in the world.[66]

The hashtag took on a larger meaning: Standing with *Charlie Hebdo* meant standing against terrorists; it represented a community. However, many felt alienated by the slogan, especially those that were often depicted in the magazine's satirical and sometimes offensive cartoons. Within a day of the attacks, a counter hashtag of #JeNeSuisPasCharlie"—"I am not Charlie"—became popular, driven mainly by users in France, the Middle East, Latin America, and Pakistan.[67] Although horrified by the attacks, French Blacks, Arabs, Muslims, and young people from the poor suburbs of Paris see the magazine as a mean-spirited, bullying voice of the majority. Shortly after the killings, #JeSuisAhmed peaked on Twitter, in memory of murdered police officer Ahmed Merabet, a practicing Muslim killed in the attacks.[68] For many, the #JeSuisCharlie hashtag "attributed some kind of nobility to the content of the newspaper,"[69] which people who found the cartoons racist objected to.

The popularity and controversy of the hashtag thrust a once poor, radical group of cartoonists into the global spotlight. Although in the wake of the shootings thousands subscribed to the magazine, many at the magazine felt that with the newfound popularity came heightened expectations; the magazine and those who worked there were seen as symbols of a global community, when in reality they were cartoonists traumatized by a horrific workplace shooting.[70]

#MeToo

Tarana Burke founded the **Me Too movement** in 2006 as a survivor network for black women and girls and other young women of color who were victims of sexual violence. The goal was, and still is, to give voice to victims, both women and men, build a community, and lead the way to finding solutions to sexual violence.[71] It wasn't until October 15, 2017, that the world heard "#MeToo" from a tweet posted by actress Alyssa Milano (see Figure 12.8).

The reaction was almost instantaneous on Facebook, Twitter, Instagram, Snapchat, and other social media platforms. On Facebook, the hashtag was shared in almost 12 million posts and reactions within the first 24 hours and on Twitter half a million times in 24 hours.[72] A year later, #MeToo has been used on Twitter more than 19 million times.[73] Rather than organizing online to lead to in-person activism, #MeToo became a way to express solidarity with and support for victims of sexual violence and harassment and as a visual illustration of the pervasiveness of sexual violence.

Similar to the challenges faced by OWS and BLM, Burke fears her symbol will be co-opted for a use that was not her intended use and the movement will lose meaning and efficacy. Because of the public nature of many cases of sexual assault and harassment on both social media and in mainstream media, Burke fears #MeToo will be seen as a cause for outing alleged perpetrators when the real purpose and goal is to focus on victims and to draw attention to the power structures that lead to and enable abuse.[74]

> **#MeToo movement:** A movement that began in 2006 as a survivor network for women and girls of color who were victims of sexual assault. The movement evolved in 2017 as a way to express solidarity with and support for all victims of sexual violence and harassment.

Figure 12.8   The Tweet That Made the #MeToo Movement Viral

Alyssa Milano ✓
@Alyssa_Milano

If you've been sexually harassed or assaulted write 'me too' as a reply to this tweet.

> Me too.
>
> Suggested by a friend: "If all the women who have been sexually harassed or assaulted wrote 'Me too.' as a status, we might give people a sense of the magnitude of the problem."

1:21 PM · Oct 15, 2017 · Twitter for iPhone

Source: Twitter/@Alyssa_Milano

#Hate

Much of the world communicates online and through social media, and those who want to communicate messages of hate can find an audience there. The Council on Foreign Relations describes hate speech online as a global problem (see Figure 12.9).

The same features that make social media a key organizing tool for OWS, BLM, and #MeToo can also be used by hate groups to organize and spread ideology. And because the business model of most social media platforms is based on engagement, the more likes, reposts, and retweets a post gets, the more valuable the traffic is for advertisers. The algorithms that determine the level of user engagement cannot distinguish between happy family reunions and hate speech. This, some say, leads to the promotion of inflammatory and often divisive dialogue.[75]

In 2018, Amnesty International and artificial intelligence (AI) start-up Element AI used 6,500 volunteers to analyze 288,000 tweets aimed at 800 female journalists and politicians from the United States and the United Kingdom. The groups labeled tweets that contained language that was abusive, hurtful, or hostile. Once the tweets were reviewed by humans, it used those results to build and test a machine-learning algorithm that could spot and report abusive content. The groups ran the algorithm on almost 15 million tweets, mentioning the same 800 women, and discovered that 7% of the tweets were found to be abusive, women of color were 34% more likely to be targets than white women, and black women specifically were 84% more likely than white women to be mentioned in abusive tweets.[76]

Recognizing the connection between social media and the prevalence of hate speech, Congressman José Serrano and Senator Robert Casey introduced the **Stop Harmful and Abusive Telecommunications Expression (HATE) Act** in 2018. According to Congressman Serrano, "Hate speech online is directly related to the rise of hate crimes in the U.S. and worldwide."[77] The bill would continue the work of the Department of Commerce's National Telecommunications and Information Administration's 1993 report on the role of telecommunication in hate crimes, updated for the 21st century. The report looked at the role of telecommunications in hate crimes at the time and recommended ways the government and citizens could combat the threats. The Stop HATE Act would authorize a new report focusing on social media and require the administration report to Congress periodically with updates.[78]

Stop Harmful and Abusive Telecommunications Expression (HATE) Act: Legislation that requires the Department of Commerce's National Telecommunications and Information Administration to include hate crimes involving social media with their periodic report to Congress.

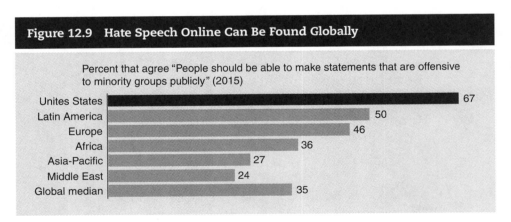

Figure 12.9   Hate Speech Online Can Be Found Globally

Percent that agree "People should be able to make statements that are offensive to minority groups publicly" (2015)

Unites States	67
Latin America	50
Europe	46
Africa	36
Asia-Pacific	27
Middle East	24
Global median	35

Source: "2015 Global Attitudes Survey." Pew Research Center, Washington, DC (June 23, 2015) https://www.pewresearch.org/global/2015/06/23/spring-2015-survey/.
Note: Displays the median among countries included in the survey.

An Algorithm for Hate?

According to YouTube, over 1.9 billion users visit the site each month, and worldwide people watch more than 1 billion YouTube hours a day. Users of the platform can subscribe to others' channels or simply search the site for videos without ever subscribing to another channel. Unlike Instagram and Twitter, where users see content from people they choose to follow, YouTube proactively provides content to users. For example, once you find a video on the site down the right side of the screen, YouTube will display a list of videos "up next." YouTube utilizes a recommender algorithm to suggest videos that might be of interest to the viewer, to keep us on the platform. The algorithm works. According to Google, their recommended videos account for more than 70% of viewing time on the platform. And the longer a user is on the platform, the more money Google makes selling ad space to run before and during videos.

According to YouTube, the algorithm recommends videos that are already showing high traffic. The problem is, the videos with the most traffic are often false, extreme, and divisive. Similar to the algorithm used on other social media platforms to assess high user engagement, YouTube's recommender algorithm cannot differentiate between white supremacist videos and cat videos in terms of measuring popularity. According to a *Wall Street Journal* investigation, when a user shows an interest in searching for a political video, the recommender algorithm suggests other political videos that are increasingly partisan and misleading and often feature conspiracy theories and extreme viewpoints. Former Google engineer Guillaume Chaslot worked on the recommender algorithm while at YouTube and helped the *Wall Street Journal* develop their investigation. According to Mr. Chaslot, Google uses an AI technique called a deep neural network. This technique makes connections between videos that for various reasons humans would not watch, using hundreds of signals coupled with what the viewer has watched. It then makes a recommendation.

For the investigation, Mr. Chaslot created a program that simulated a user on YouTube: It collected the top five results to a search and the top three recommended videos YouTube provided once the program clicked on each of the five videos. Then it collected the top three recommendations for each of the three recommended videos, ultimately reaching four clicks out from the original search. Using the top searched terms for November 2018, Chaslot's program was led to divisive and misleading videos. If the original search was a mainstream news source, the algorithm led it to far-right or far-left videos. If the program searched for information on the flu vaccine, anti-vaccine conspiracy theories were recommended. The algorithm suggested increasingly extreme videos even when the program returned to the home page. After searching for "9/11" then clicking on one CNN video and returning to the home page, the fifth and sixth recommended videos were about whether the United States actually carried out the attacks. One video claiming it was a military plane hitting one of the towers had 5.3 million views. YouTube was sharply criticized for recommending videos promoting a theory that the survivors of the Parkland, Florida, school shooting were actually hired "crisis actors." A researcher at Columbia University created a YouTube account and searched "crisis actor" and found that the "up next" recommendations led to 9,000 videos promoting this conspiracy theory and a related theory that the 2012 Newtown, Connecticut, school shooting was a hoax.

In 2019, YouTube was notified that its recommender algorithm had curated innocent videos of children swimming, playing, and doing gymnastics and, through a series of recommendations, made them available to viewers of erotic and sexual material. On their own, the videos were harmless, but together they conveyed a dangerous message. Once notified, YouTube immediately changed its recommender algorithm.

YouTube has been working on this algorithm and is developing one to recommend "more authoritative" news sources, and according to Johanna Wright, the product management leader for recommendations, "this is our responsibility . . . and we have more to do." YouTube and Google are both owned by Alphabet. Google's search algorithm produces results that are authoritative and not just popular. For example, the *Wall Street Journal* investigators searched "FBI Memo" shortly after Republicans released a memo detailing a warrant authorizing surveillance of a former Trump adviser. YouTube suggested several mainstream news sources and also videos from BPEarthWatch "dedicated to Watching

(Continued)

(Continued)

End Time Events that Lead to the Return of Our Lord Jesus Christ, Comets, Asteroids, Earth Quakes, Solar Flares and The End Time Powers"; Styxhexenhammer666, whose profile simply states, "I am God"; and Alex Jones, founder of Infowars and known conspiracy theorist. The same search on Google only resulted in mainstream news sources. However, Google has more experience recommending news sources because when breaking news hits, people write stories about it; they usually don't make videos. When the *Wall Street Journal* conducted more searches on YouTube several weeks later, it noted the algorithm recommended videos from more mainstream news sources.

Discussion Questions

1. Zeynep Tufekci, a professor at the University of North Carolina, likens YouTube's recommender algorithm to a restaurant that serves customers lots of fat, salt, and sugar because it knows that is what we crave. But when confronted about the health concerns of the menu, the restaurant merely states that it is giving us what we want. What role do users play in the damage created by the recommender algorithm?

2. Do YouTube and Alphabet have an ethical obligation to protect us from ourselves? Why or why not? Is this possible?

Critical Thinking

All of the major social media platforms have been touched by scandal. When asked about the prospect of government regulation of social media, Tim Cook, CEO of Apple, stated, "The free market is not working." Academics have suggested social media should be treated like a public utility: strictly regulated by the government. Others have warned that speech on social media cannot be treated as a public good—subject to political control; speech is an individual right. Many claim that no regulation can happen without dismantling the business model that incentivizes extremism and division. Sheryl Sandberg, COO of Facebook, stated, "We don't think it's a question of whether regulation, we think it's a question of the right regulation."

Who are the stakeholders in the analysis of whether social media should be regulated? What is at stake for each? What should the goals of regulation be? Minimizing hate speech? Protecting against abuse of our data? Something else?

KEY TAKEAWAYS

Society, Democracy, and Social Media

- A movement can quickly gain followers and organize using social media.

- The ubiquity of social media makes it difficult for movements to retain control of their messaging.

- Algorithms used on social media to recommend videos and create news feeds are driven by shocking and hateful material, thereby enabling a platform for division.

WHAT RULES APPLY TO SOCIAL MEDIA?

LO 12.5 Analyze whether regulation is the most effective means of mitigating public safety.

Due to the fact that social media is a rapidly developing phenomenon, there are not many laws that apply to what takes place on the platforms. The Communications Decency Act

(CDA) has been fundamental to the growth of social media and the tech industry in the United States. The CDA was passed as a response by Congress to some of the earliest legal challenges in the new and evolving world of social media. For example, CompuServe, one of the earliest social media companies, hosted an online general information service; members could access sites, and CompuServe hosted special interest forums. In 1991, a business claimed that a writer of one of the forums posted defamatory material and sued CompuServe. The court said that because CompuServe merely hosted the forum and comment section and did not review or otherwise edit the posted material, it could not be liable for defamation.[79]

In 1995, a different court reached a different conclusion in a suit against Prodigy, a web services company that had 2 million subscribers at the time. In that case, the court stated that because Prodigy moderated its message boards and deleted posts that were offensive, Prodigy was more like a publisher and should be responsible for defamatory content on its platform. At the time, Prodigy received over 60,000 posts a day and could not possibly moderate them all. But because the platform moderated some posts, the court said it was responsible for all of the posts.[80]

The CDA was passed in 1996 to address several issues, including protecting children online and making it illegal to knowingly send or show obscene content to minors. Section 230 of the CDA was drafted to address the conflicting results in the CompuServe and Prodigy cases. The section protects providers of interactive computer services from being treated as publishers of content posted by third parties. Protecting social media platforms will "encourage the unfettered and unregulated development of free speech on the Internet."[81] Online services would be free to develop their own standards for policing their platforms. Since the passage of Section 230 of the CDA, courts have interpreted what it means to be a passive host versus a publisher of content. In Law and Society 12.1, the families of victims of terrorism in Israel claim that Facebook's sophisticated algorithms that combine user data with preferences and user history amounts to Facebook creating its own content.

Force v. Facebook, 934 F.3d 53 (2019)

Facts: The plaintiffs in this case are the U.S. citizen victims and families of victims of terrorist attacks committed by Hamas in Israel. Hamas is a Palestinian Islamist organization in Gaza, which the United States and Israel have designated as a foreign terrorist organization. According to the families, between 2014 and 2016 Hamas used Facebook to post content that encouraged the attacks that killed or injured their family members. For example, Yaakov Fraenkel, a teenager, was kidnapped by Hamas in 2014 while walking home from school near Jerusalem and then was shot to death. On Facebook, Hamas advocated kidnapping Israeli soldiers (although Fraenkel was not a soldier). A 3-month-old baby was killed at a train station when a Hamas member drove a car into a crowd. This attack happened after Hamas encouraged in a Facebook post car-ramming attacks at train stations. The families allege the attackers viewed these posts, and after the attacks, Hamas used Facebook to celebrate the deaths.

The families claim the perpetrators were able to view these posts despite the fact that such posts violate Facebook's policies for use because Facebook failed to remove "openly maintained" pages and content of Hamas leaders. Not only did Facebook not remove the posts but also, according to the families,

(Continued)

(Continued)

Facebook's algorithm directed the content to the personalized news feeds of the perpetrators of the attacks. In so doing, according to the families, Facebook enables Hamas to disseminate its message to its intended audience "to carry out the essential communication components of [its] terror attacks."

The families sued, claiming Facebook was liable for damages for aiding and abetting Hamas in furtherance of terrorism, conspiring with Hamas in furtherance of terrorism, and providing Hamas material support. The district court held that under Section 230 of the CDA, Facebook could not be liable as a publisher of information provided by a third party. The families appealed saying their claims against Facebook are not dependent on Facebook being a publisher.

Issue: Do the plaintiffs' claims depend on Facebook being a publisher and therefore barred by §230?

Decision: Yes, the plaintiffs' claims depend on Facebook being a publisher of content, and therefore, their claims are barred by Section 230. The legislative history of Section 230 of the CDA tells us that the goal of the law was "to keep government interference in the medium (the Internet) to a minimum" and to "preserve the vibrant and competitive free market . . . for the Internet." Because the amount of information communicated online is "staggering," liability for that content would stifle growth and innovation. To overrule *Stratton v. Oakmont*, Congress passed Section 230, shielding publishers of third-party content from liability for that content. A publisher is "one that makes public."

Here, the plaintiffs want to hold Facebook liable for giving Hamas a forum in which to bring Hamas content to interested users. This activity fits squarely within the activities of a publisher, as does Facebook's alleged failure to delete content. The plaintiffs claim that they are not treating Facebook as a publisher because the platform uses algorithms to suggest content to users as a result of their "matchmaking"—matching users with specific content

based on the users' history, existing social connections on Facebook, and using other behavioral and demographic data. The court is not persuaded that Facebook is not a publisher in this context as well. Arranging and distributing third-party content is an essential result of publishing; imposing liability for organizing content would mean that simply placing third party content on a home page would lead to liability, because content on a home page tends to recommend that content to users. Deciding what format in which to display the content (chat room, blogs, news feeds, etc.) would also risk liability. Nor does matchmaking render Facebook a "provider" of information. A provider in this context means a person who is responsible, in whole or in part, for the creation or development of information. And developing information includes directly or materially contributing to what made the content itself unlawful. Facebook does not edit, or suggest edits, to content. Moreover, the algorithms used to make matches is content neutral; it uses objective factors that apply to all content. It simply makes content more visible and available, another essential part of publishing. As a result, the plaintiffs' claims are premised on Facebook being a publisher of third-party content, and publishers of third-party content are immune from liability for that content under Section 230 of the CDA.

Dissent: First, let's not forget the CDA was passed to encourage computer service providers to protect minors from online porn and to empower parents to decide the content their children receive, and today we hold that same provision shields those same providers from connecting terrorists to one another. Moreover, the CDA says that "no provider . . . shall be treated as *the* publisher . . . of any information provided by another information content provider" (emphasis added). Thus, Section 230 is not blanket protection for publishers in the abstract but whether they are a publisher of the specific content provided. Next, it strains the English language to say that in targeting and recommending content to users, and forging new social networks, that

Facebook is acting as a publisher of information. Facebook has developed sophisticated algorithms based on mountains of data it has collected on its billions of users both on and off its platform. Facebook then unleashes these algorithms to generate friend, group, and event suggestions based on what it perceives to be the user's preferences. For example, if a user searches for news on Hamas, Facebook might suggest the user become friends with Hamas terrorists on Facebook, or join a Hamas-related group, or attend a Hamas-inspired event. In short, the platform extends the reach of Hamas by using its (Facebook's) own content. Thus, the plaintiffs don't seek to punish Facebook for the content of others' posts or for bringing Hamas terrorists together but for Facebook's own content: that it thinks you—specifically—will like this content, group, or event.

Law and Management Questions

1. The court says that if merely organizing content led to liability for the substance of that content, most computer service providers would face liability. If that were true, would that justify protecting them from liability? Why or why not?

2. If you were head of social media marketing for a business, how would this decision impact your marketing strategy?

Courts have also recognized the quickly changing and relatively unchartered territory of social media and how this new media and form of communication impacts more traditional areas of law. For example, in commenting on privacy in a case dealing with a public employer's search of an employee's text messages on an employer-provided pager, the Supreme Court cautioned, "The judiciary risks error by elaborating too fully on the Fourth Amendment implications of emerging technology before its role in society has become clear."[82] But the size and breadth of social media use has led courts to understand that although "the Cyber Age is a revolution of historic proportions," because it is so new "we cannot appreciate yet its . . . vast potential to alter how we think, express ourselves, and define who we want to be."[83]

What Rules Apply to Social Media?

- Section 230 of the CDA exempts social media platforms from all liability for any content posted by third parties.

- Courts urge caution when applying traditional legal theories to social media because social media's role in society is still evolving.

KEY TAKEAWAYS

SUMMARY

We will see throughout this text how social media has impacted important areas of our lives, from undercover police friending you on Facebook, to elected officials blocking constituents from their social media pages, to getting fired for what you post on Facebook, to social media as the new public square from which we cannot be excluded. In some cases, courts apply old-fashioned legal principles to this relatively new forum, and in other cases, courts pioneer new thinking. In each instance, you will be asked to draw your own conclusions about the role of courts, law, and our own ethics in the wild world of social media.

KEY TERMS

#OccupyWallStreet (OWS) 280
Ads Manager 270
application programming interface (API) 271
Black Lives Matter (BLM) 281
bulletin board systems (BBS) 264
chat rooms 264
doxxing 280
engagement 269

geotagging 272
infinite scroll 274
Me Too movement 283
micro-influencers 277
moderators 266
push notifications 274
Redditors 266
slacktivism 280
social justice 280

social media 264
social media influencer 277
social reciprocity 274
Stop Harmful and Abusive Telecommunications Expression (HATE) Act 284
subreddits 266
trolling 280
variable ratio schedule 273

REVIEW QUESTIONS

1. How did the advent of the smartphone change our relationship with social media?

2. What kind of strategies do social media and app designers use to keep us looking at our social media accounts?

3. How do most social media companies make money? What are some of the different models?

4. What are the different strategies used by activist organizations to harness the power of social media? What are some of the challenges they face with social media?

5. How do the business models of most social media companies perpetuate division, misinformation, and hateful speech online?

MANAGER'S CHALLENGE

Access to User Data

You have developed an app, and a small business selling ad space on the app, to link local and state elected officials with constituents of all political parties. A voter can use the app to see what their elected official is working on as well as their voting records, bill sponsorship, and public events in the community. Elected officials and their offices gain valuable information about their constituents, like demographic data, income, where they work, and what issues constituents are interested in based on attendance at public events and search time on different areas of the app. Your programmer has told you that she can include a feature that allows constituents to sign in using their Facebook or Google accounts. This will then give you access to all of the data the social media giants collect on your users, and it gives Facebook and Google access to your user data.

Framing Questions

1. Based on Facebook's experience handling user data, what particular issues should you think about when deciding whether to add the new feature to your app?

2. What information do you want from your advertisers before you sell them space and data collected from your app?

Assignment

Draft two sections of your user agreement that would give users adequate notice of what information you share with your advertisers and that you might share with Facebook and Google.

BIG DATA AND HACKING

Learning Objectives

Upon completion of this chapter, the reader should be able to do the following:

13.1 List the major drivers of technology and their impact.

13.2 Describe the impact of the digital divide on society.

13.3 Define *big data*, and explain how organizations use data analytics in their business planning and operations.

13.4 Identify the primary challenges faced by organizations in managing and protecting data of stakeholders from hackers.

13.5 Understand the mosaic of laws that apply to data usage.

13.6 Explain the ethical issues related to data usage.

Ethics in Context

Big Data and Insurance

Today, automobiles are a treasure trove of big data, often used to monitor speed, braking frequency, time and location of the trip, and more across multiple users. On the one hand, the purpose of big data is often to form real-time or predictive analyses across a wide range of factors, which makes it helpful for insurance companies aiming to predict the likelihood and severity of a potential future incident. In this manner, insurance policies might provide fairer, more accurate rates based on relevant factors, such as driving history or vehicle safety ratings. But, on the other hand, the data can be used to discriminate by, for example, charging young men higher premiums because the data indicate that they—generally—drive less safely than other categories of drivers. Later in the chapter, in the Ethics in Context section, we will examine the ethical implications of this technology.

iStockphoto.com/metamorworks

INTRODUCTION

The digital age has transformed the ways in which organizations do business and how society communicates, works, and thinks. Rapid advances in technology allow organizations to collect and use large sets of data that were previously beyond the reach of even the most sophisticated analysts. In this chapter, we examine the digital revolution and its impact on business and society. We consider some of the potential advantages and consequences of data-driven decision-making, illustrating that while it can offer strategic opportunities for business and sometimes benefits for individuals, there are also costs which raise important societal issues.

THE DIGITAL REVOLUTION

LO 13.1 List the major drivers of technology and their impact.

It may sound like an exaggerated claim to talk about a "digital revolution." Yet consider the frenzy of technological advances, starting with the emergence of the iPhone. It is doubtful that even the late Steve Jobs, the CEO of Apple at the time, could have foreseen how the digital revolution would unfold. Indeed, new companies and inventions reshaped how people and machines interact and redefined how people interact with each other. In 2007 alone, storage capacity for computing skyrocketed, Twitter was launched and quickly became the most popular microblogging site, Google bought YouTube and launched Android, and Amazon released the Kindle. All in one year! In this section, we examine what drives technology and the impact of the digital revolution on organizations and the public at large.

Drivers of Technology

Economist Joseph Schumpeter introduced the idea of a three-part trilogy of technological change, often viewed as chronological stages, involving *invention*, *innovation*, and *diffusion*.[1]

- *Invention:* In essence technological change is the invention of technologies (including processes) and their commercialization via research and development (producing emerging technologies). It is the result of a conscious effort to do things differently.

- *Innovation:* This stage refers to continual improvement of technologies (in which they often become less expensive). It is moving from the old or obsolescent to the new and more productive.

- *Diffusion:* In this stage new products and processes spread throughout industry or society, which sometimes involves disruption in the way we used to use something. The impact of new technology occurs at the diffusion stage, and its impact is a result of how the economy changes as a result.

Another driver of technological change is convergence. According to the World Economic Forum (WEF), developments in previously disjointed fields such as artificial intelligence (AI) and machine learning, robotics, nanotechnology, 3D printing, and genetics and biotechnology are all building on and amplifying one another. Smart systems—now found in factories, farms, and homes—will help tackle problems ranging from supply chain management to climate change.

According to the WEF, cloud technology and big data are two of the top industry drivers of change and disruptions to business models identified by the senior executives in its Future of Jobs Survey, ranked according to the share of respondents who expected each trend to be among the top trends impacting their industry by 2020 (see Figure 13.1).[2]

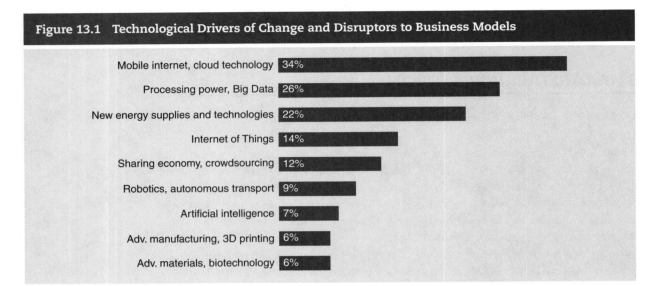

Figure 13.1 Technological Drivers of Change and Disruptors to Business Models

Mobile internet, cloud technology	34%
Processing power, Big Data	26%
New energy supplies and technologies	22%
Internet of Things	14%
Sharing economy, crowdsourcing	12%
Robotics, autonomous transport	9%
Artificial intelligence	7%
Adv. manufacturing, 3D printing	6%
Adv. materials, biotechnology	6%

Source: Future of Jobs Survey, World Economic Forum.

Cloud technology and big data are also on the minds of the board of directors in today's corporations. The EY Center for Board Matters found, in a 2019 survey of 365 public company directors on disruptive technology, that only about half of directors believe their boards have the appropriate resources to address the disruption caused by emerging technology. And only about 67% of respondents indicated that oversight of emerging technologies lies with the full board, rather than the company's management.[3]

There is no question that technology has impacted business and society in many positive ways. But it is also hard to ignore its negative consequences. Here, we tee up some positives and negatives—many of which you may have already discussed in class or in campus residence halls and coffee shops.

Positive Impacts on Society

Technology has improved agriculture: Modern agricultural technology allows a small number of farmers to grow vast quantities of food in a short period with less labor input, which results in high yields and higher returns. It has also resulted in more efficient agricultural production, resulting in year-round crops due to more resistant seeds and stronger pesticides. Consulting firm McKinsey & Company reports that technology is rapidly reshaping agricultural resources too with the potential to unlock around $900 billion to $1.6 trillion in savings throughout the global economy by 2035, an amount equivalent to the current gross domestic product of Canada or Indonesia.[4]

Technology has improved transportation: Transportation is one of the basic areas of technological activity. Both society and businesses have benefited from the new transportation methods. Driverless cars and space travel are front-page news, and technology has drastically improved our everyday use of air and water transportation and made the importing and exporting of goods easier and faster. Energy efficiency, sometimes called the "fifth fuel" after coal, gas, nuclear, and renewables, will play an important role in helping the world meet its demand for power and mobility.[5]

Technology has improved communication: Both society and organizations depend on communication to transfer information. Information is sent faster, more reliably, and to a larger audience. It has also opened doors for new ways of communicating—chat rooms, discussion forums, texting, videoconferencing, etc.—all of which helps reduce our carbon footprint and increase our productivity.

Technology has improved education and learning: Education is the backbone of every economy. People need well and organized educational infrastructures so they can learn how to interpret information. From grade schools to doctoral programs, learning institutions integrate educational technologies into their curriculum as you likely see in your own classroom. Machine learning can anticipate your needs and wants through the digital traces you leave behind.

Technology has improved security: Security-tracking systems have improved the ability to monitor and apprehend criminals and solve so-called cold cases through new DNA testing. In early 2019, authorities in Sacramento, California, announced they finally solved a 40-year-old cold case by arresting a man, known as the Golden State Killer, who terrified the state back in the 1970s and 1980s. To do so, they used a powerful new tool called genetic genealogy, a mixture of high-tech DNA analysis, high-speed computer technology, and traditional genealogy. Its advocates claim it's opened up a new frontier in criminology.[6]

Can you think of any other positive effects?

Threats to Society

Big data, and its prevalence, requires us to consider not only what we *can* do but what we *should* do. Ethicists often say that "ought implies can"—which means that if you ought to do something then it is possible to actually do it. This encapsulates the ethical challenges facing us in big data—issues such as machine-made mistakes, unintended consequences, bias, loss of security, and privacy. These issues are certainly on the minds of many with countries and states alike ushering in new regulations (discussed next). Kai-Fu Lee, considered the oracle of AI in China, believes that it will change the world more than anything in history—more than the invention of electricity it so relies on. A few changes to consider are as follows:

Resource depletion: The increased demand for new technologies and advancement of current technologies results in ever more pressure on earth's natural resources in a variety of ways. According to the consulting firm McKinsey Global Institute, this technological innovation—including the adoption of robotics, AI, Internet of things (IoT) technology, and data analytics—along with macroeconomic trends and changing consumer behavior, is transforming the way resources are consumed and produced. From the consumption of wind and solar energy, to coal, copper, and iron, natural resources are at risk for becoming depleted.[7]

Increased population: Technology has helped us live longer by improving health facilities and aiding in the research for complex medical treatments and cures. This is good news for developed countries, but the strain of overpopulation has its downsides. It took hundreds of years for the world to reach 1 billion people, but in little over two centuries this figure multiplied sevenfold. Why? Overpopulation is primarily due to the falling mortality rate resulting from advances in both medicine and food production. The effects of this overpopulation include environmental degradation, depletion of natural resources, increased unemployment, and cost of living.[8]

Environmental impact: Although industry may be more efficient, it does not necessarily translate into less pollution of air and waterways. Concerns over pollution and climate change are forcing businesses and governments to think hard about how they produce and use energy. We discuss environmental sustainability more in Chapter 7.

Privacy implications: Improving security across society, based on digital devices, can impact an individual's privacy. Companies tracking big data can pick out specific details about an individual's shopping habits, preferences, or tendencies. However, when they collect and analyze digital traces, companies do not always take responsibility or ask permission for such monitoring. Going back to solving the Golden State Killer cold case, there are many ethical questions being raised by civil rights groups and bioethicists about the reliability of crime scene DNA so long after the crime and the lack of standards and protocol in this new field. Another issue being raised is whether genealogy website users have become genetic informants on their relatives, many of whom did not send their DNA to a lab.[9]

Biased decision-making: Making decisions on the basis of big data can create unfair discrimination and even exacerbate existing social inequalities by reflecting and amplifying existing race, sex, and other biases. We explore these security and bias more in Chapter 14.

Lack of personal connection: While many agree their lives have been enhanced by technology, many also believe it is less satisfying due to the lack of face-to-face human interaction. A world where a text or a tweet can be sent without having to face the person can lead to more and more anonymity. But there are also ways to communicate that are completely anonymous, like Tor. Tor is a free global network consisting of some 7,000 relays designed to conceal a user's location and usage from anyone conducting network surveillance or traffic analysis.[10] The most common impact of anonymity is harassment, cyberbullying, and racism. The human cost in terms of ruined reputations, loss of trust, and general deterioration in morals is thought to be in the billions of dollars each year.[11]

Can you think of any other negative effects? Figure 13.2 compares the positive and negative characteristics of technology.

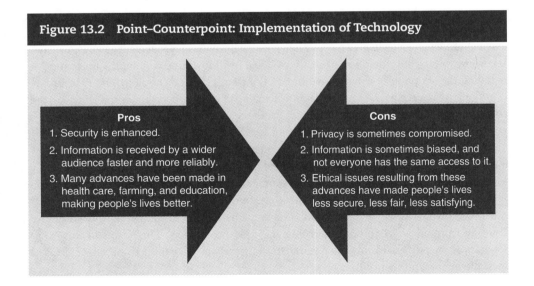

Figure 13.2   Point–Counterpoint: Implementation of Technology

Pros
1. Security is enhanced.
2. Information is received by a wider audience faster and more reliably.
3. Many advances have been made in health care, farming, and education, making people's lives better.

Cons
1. Privacy is sometimes compromised.
2. Information is sometimes biased, and not everyone has the same access to it.
3. Ethical issues resulting from these advances have made people's lives less secure, less fair, less satisfying.

RFID Transponders and Paying Your Toll

Driving on some U.S. highways became a much different experience with the innovation of new, automated toll collection systems using transponders (e.g., E-ZPass) hung on a car's front windshield. Electronic toll collection technology was first deployed in the Dallas–Fort Worth metro area of the United States in 1989. Today one integrated electronic toll collection system links the highways of 16 states through the use of radio frequency identification (RFID) tags in transponders installed in vehicles that communicate with reader equipment in open toll lanes by connecting to the account of the transponder's owner. If it is in good standing, the toll will be charged. If not, the owner of the car will receive a ticket. The technology has other benefits; in fact, it is so effective at managing traffic that some cities have placed reader equipment in locations far away from highway tolls. In New York, government agencies have set up transponder readers around the state to collect driving data. As part of its Midtown in Motion program, city transportation officials set up 100 microwave readers, 32 traffic video cameras, and 149 transponder readers around the city to measure traffic volumes throughout the day. As a result, it can be used to improve traffic flow in addition to reducing emissions from cars that were used to having to stop and idle while waiting for their turn to pay the toll. Location data can reveal private details about drivers' lives, and many states monitor our speed as we travel past the toll readers with some sending speeders warning letters and in a few cases temporarily suspending the driver's transponder. Likewise, the potential exists for the data to be used in intrusive ways, such as when the transponder is used for purposes other than toll collection.[12]

For many, the unease with the collection of our personal information is this: What if it gets out? And this is not just as a result of a security breach but also if the information is purposely used in a harmful way. In 2012, the Port Authority of New York and New Jersey had just increased tolls on area bridges and tunnels, and officials were being questioned by elected representatives about the need for and impact of such hikes. When Frank Lautenberg, the late senator from New Jersey, inquired, the Port Authority deputy chief responded, "Respectfully, Senator, you only started paying tolls recently. . . . In fact, I have a copy of your free EZ Pass [records]; you took 284 trips for free in the last two years you had the pass."[13]

Discussion Questions

1. Like Utah, Pennsylvania, and many other states in the United States, New Jersey law states that drivers' private E-ZPass records can be obtained only by government officials through a court order or subpoena. Yet officials were able to not only obtain Senator Lautenberg's records but also use them against him publicly. What recourse or penalty should there be for misuse by the government of our private data? Would that have worked in the Port Authority episode?

2. What should the developer or supplier of these transponders, Austrian company Kapsch TrafficCom AG, disclose to customers about the use of the data it collects?

Critical Thinking

Consider what is in the best interests of customers, society, and the business and government entities that use the data gathered by these transponders. Are there any other stakeholders here?

Assignment

You have been asked by the mayor to draft a memo outlining the stakeholders in this decision and what specifically is at stake for them if the data was used for information gathering of a more personal nature (i.e., other than toll collection).

CASE STUDY 13.1

CHAPTER 13 • BIG DATA AND HACKING   297

KEY TAKEAWAYS

The Digital Revolution

- Technology is driven by a combination of invention, innovation, diffusion, and convergence.

- There are many positive outcomes for both business and society with recent

technological innovation, but there are also negative consequences to consider.

THE DIGITAL DIVIDE

LO 13.2 Describe the impact of the digital divide on society.

Not all people have the same access to data. This is as obvious as it is troubling. The differential access to ways of thinking about and using data can potentially exacerbate power imbalances in the digital era. Since the mid-1990s the U.S. National Telecommunications and Information Administration (NTIA), a branch of the Department of Commerce, has been publishing reports on the general public's access to and usage of the Internet. NTIA defines the **digital divide** as "the divide between those with access to new technologies and those without" and declared it as one of the "leading economic and civil rights issues." Its most recent report considers the "**sharing economy**" where people are buying, selling, and trading goods and services with each other. Examples include ride-hailing services, lodging, and e-commerce. In its 2019 report, NTIA data show two thirds of U.S. Internet users are not participating in the sharing economy. Furthermore, geography plays an important role in the sharing economy participation (see Figure 13.3). While 35% of Internet users in metropolitan areas reported using such services, only 19% of those in nonmetropolitan regions engaged in sharing economy activities. Moreover, there was a 50 percentage point difference between the highly urban territory, with the highest level of participation (68% of Internet users in the District of Columbia) and the primarily rural state with the lowest rate (18% in South Dakota).[14]

Two additional issues exist with regard to the digital divide: economic disparities and educational disparities.

digital divide: The divide between those with access to new technologies and those without.

sharing economy: An economy where people are constantly buying, selling, and trading goods and services with each other.

Economic Disparities

More than half of the world's population still does not have access to Internet, with Asia and Africa having the lowest rates of access, according to a recent United Nations Educational, Scientific, and Cultural Organization (UNESCO) report.[15]

Of the 7.6 billion people in the world, 3.58 billion, or 48%, are using the Internet—a significant jump from 2016, when 3.4 billion people, or 45.9% of the world's population, were estimated to be online.

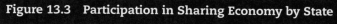

Figure 13.3   Participation in Sharing Economy by State

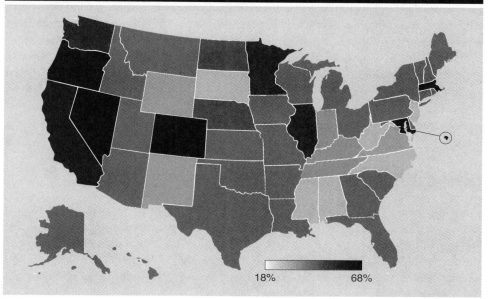

18%   68%

Source: National Telecommunications and Information Administration, U.S. Department of Commerce, "NTIA Data: Two-thirds of U.S. Internet Users Do Not Participate in the Sharing Economy," August 21, 2019 by Amy Robinson and Rafi Goldberg.

Europe has the world's highest rate of connectivity, with nearly 80% of people online, while Africa has the lowest percentage of Internet user penetration, with only 21.8% of the population having Internet access. But Asia had the highest percentage of people without access, making up 62% of all people in the world not online.

These offline populations typically live in sparsely populated, rural areas and suffer from low-income levels and weak or nonexistent enabling infrastructure (such as electricity and high-capacity fixed telecom networks).

The digital expansion we discussed previously tends to exclude those who find themselves in a lower economic class. For example, 12% fewer women used the Internet than men worldwide, and this disparity is more pronounced in low- and lower-middle income countries, like Africa. This digital gender gap is unlikely to close on its own. According to the UNESCO report, its root causes are due to social, economic, and cultural barriers. To combat this gap, it notes an initiative—#SheMeansBusiness—focused on empowering women to use the Internet as a tool for economic growth and entrepreneurship. #SheMeansBusiness was created to inspire and empower women to start businesses; it offers training, resources, and a community for women entrepreneurs.

From a global perspective, a major threat remains very relevant to technology and its impact on society. And that threat is as developed countries adopt new and advanced technologies, the gap between those countries and underdeveloped countries grows, causing them to lag further and further behind.

Educational Disparities

The digital divide also impacts children's ability to learn and grow in low-income school districts. Without Internet access, students are unable to cultivate necessary tech skills in order to understand today's dynamic economy. A 2018 Pew Research Center study indicates one in five students say they are unable to finish their homework due to an inability to either connect to the Internet or, in some cases, find a computer. This aspect of the digital divide—sometimes referred to as the "homework gap"—can be an academic burden for teens who lack access to digital technologies at home. Black teens, as well as those from lower-income households, are especially likely to face these school-related challenges as a result.[16]

Digital Readiness

digital readiness: The degree to which people succeed or struggle when they use technology to navigate their environments, solve problems, and make decisions.

For many years concerns about the digital divide centered primarily on whether people had access to digital technologies. Now, another issue has cropped up—**digital readiness**—the degree to which people succeed or struggle when they use technology to navigate their environments, solve problems, and make decisions. Figure 13.4 shows the results of a Pew Research Center study on how the level of digital readiness also impacts the ability of certain subgroups (e.g., age, gender, income) to thrive.

However, concerns about digital readiness have given way to an increasingly difficult problem to see or even grasp. Today, digital data are captured through a variety of devices that have the ability to monitor an individual's everyday life. These data are often processed by algorithms, which both drive and support managers' decisions. This algorithmic decision-making occurs when data are collected through digitized devices carried by individuals such as smartphones and technologies with built-in sensors—and subsequently processed by algorithms, which are then used to make (data-driven) decisions.[17]

The data trail we leave is used by companies and presents a number of strategic opportunities for managers from managing employee productivity to personalizing products and services for clients and customers. All these efforts are based on developing algorithms that are capable of making predictions about individuals by recognizing complex patterns in huge data sets compiled from multiple sources.

KEY TAKEAWAYS

The Digital Divide

- The sharing economy has become a way of life around the world with people constantly exchanging information, ideas, products, and services.

- Access to technology and one's readiness to use it has created a digital divide in terms of economic and educational disparities.

Figure 13.4　Digital Readiness

The five groups along a spectrum from least ready to most ready

% of U.S. adults each group			More Likely To Have These Characteristics
Relatively hesitant 52%	**14%**	**The Unprepared** They have relatively lower levels of tech adoption and do not use the Internet for learning, need help setting up new tech devices, and are not familiar with "ed tech" terms. The Unprepared do not have confidence in their computer skills and are not sure they can find trustworthy information online.	• Women • Ages 50 and older • Lower income households • Lower levels of formal education
	5%	**Traditional Learners** They are active learners and have technology, but are not as likely to use the Internet for pursuing learning and have concerns about whether to trust online information.	• Women • Minorities • Ages 50 and older • Lower income households
	33%	**The Reluctant** They have higher levels of digital skills than the Unprepared, but they have low levels of awareness of new education technology concepts. This translates into relatively low use of the Internet for learning.	• Men • Ages 50 and older • Lower income households • Lower levels of formal education
Relatively more prepared 48%	**31%**	**Cautious Clickers** They have high levels of tech ownership as well as confidence in their online skills and abilities to find trustworthy information. But they are less familiar with online learning terms and less apt than the Digitally Ready to use online tools for learning.	• Higher income households • Some college experience • In their 30s and 40s
	17%	**Digitally Ready** They are ardent learners for personal enrichment. They have technology and are confident about their digital skills and abilities to find trustworthy online information. They also know the most about online learning resources.	• Higher income households • Higher education level • In their 30s and 40s

Source: Pew Research Center.

BIG DATA AND THE ORGANIZATION

LO 13.3 Define *big data*, and explain how organizations use data analytics in their business planning and operations.

Nothing is more central to achieving the promises of big data than a workforce of capable individuals prepared to tackle the opportunities and challenges of analytics. Likewise, there are widespread deficiencies in managers' ability to supervise and take action on the results of analytic projects. What all businesses need is data analysts who are sensitive to the downsides of data as well as its upsides, to enable them to avoid harmful consequences of analytics while still achieving the benefits.[18]

What Is Big Data?

In the early 2000s, industry analyst Doug Laney articulated the now-mainstream definition of big data as the three Vs:[19]

- *Volume:* Organizations collect data from a variety of sources, including business transactions, social media, and information from sensor or machine-to-machine data. In the past, storing it would've been a problem—but new technologies (such as Hadoop) have eased the burden. Hadoop is a digital open source data processing framework that facilitates using a vast network of many computers to solve problems using big data.

- *Velocity:* Data streams in at an unprecedented speed and must be dealt with in a timely manner. RFID tags, sensors, and smart metering are driving the need to deal with torrents of data in near-real time.

- *Variety:* Data comes in all types of formats—from structured, numeric data in traditional databases to unstructured text documents, e-mail, video, audio, stock ticker data, and financial transactions.

Big data is big business. In 2017, it accounted for $35 billion a year in revenue, and experts expect the growth to continue.[20] Journalist Daniel Newman, writing in *Forbes* about the digital transformation trends of 2019, notes the following:

Recent data has shown we have created 90% of the world's data in the past year, research is also showing that we are only using 1% of the data effectively. With improved processing power that can increase machine learning, we are going to see digital leaders investing in making more of all of their data and this will be done with machine learning and AI (artificial intelligence) and I believe that 1% figure will grow to 3 or 4% by 2020; which may seem small but is a massive increase in data utilization.[21]

Reaching this goal relies on a very interconnected world. The *Internet of things (IoT)* is a term first coined by bloggers to describe the network of physical devices, vehicles, home appliances, and other items embedded with electronics, software, sensors, actuators, and network connectivity that enable these objects to connect and exchange large amounts of data. Each thing is uniquely identifiable through its embedded computing system but is able to interoperate within the existing Internet infrastructure. Most of the digitized devices that collect such individual level activity data fall under the IoT, and it is growing at an unprecedented pace because each of us are "walking data generators."[22] A *Harvard Business Review* analysis estimated that the IoT will consist of about 30 billion objects by 2020. It also estimated that the global market value of IoT will reach $7.1 trillion by 2020. Sources of big data include virtually all mobile devices but also aerial sensory technology, software logs, cameras, microphones, RFID readers, and wireless sensor networks to name a few.

Data Analytics and the Organization

It is perhaps no surprise that a new field has cropped up just to deal with the vast number of uses of big data. Data scientists, as they are called today, build models to predict behaviors. They routinely use big data, or data sets that are so large, diverse, and complex that sophisticated techniques are needed for discovery of insights that were not previously possible to discern.

There are many current forms and use of data analytics in practice—descriptive, diagnostic, predictive, and prescriptive. The last step, for some data scientists, includes a preemptive set of analytics.[23] While the tasks become harder through these phases, the business value of the information to the organization also increases (see Figure 13.5).[24]

Figure 13.5 The Phases of Data Analytics: As the Difficulty Level Increases, the Value to the Business Also Increases

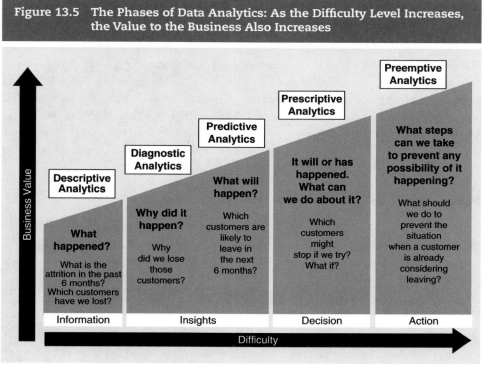

Source: Adapted from aziyatiyusoff.com.

For example, in November 2019, Google announced a partnership with Ascension, a provider of multiple health centers across the southern United States. It has plans to roll this partnership out across various states and eventually globally. Although both acknowledged privacy concerns, they say the agreement is compliant with U.S. federal law and that health data collected and used will be kept secure.[25]

Descriptive Analytics

The descriptive phase begins the process and attempts to describe the situation largely by using sociometric data (e.g., posts, clicks, views), which has been automatically recorded, for analytical use by an organization. It tries to answer the question: What has happened? In the partnership between Google and Ascension, Google is providing the cloud computing services and Ascension the health data. Google has hired its own health care executives to facilitate a full description of what the data tells them has historically been the best and worst health care problems. It's goal is to provide doctors with new tools going forward.

Diagnostic Analytics

The diagnostic phase attempts to answer this question: Why did it happen? Managers try to gain greater insights into consumer or employee behavior so they can learn from these trends. For example, Google is tracking whether someone refills a prescription and hopes to use the data to manage care and keep patients healthy. It is also testing the use of AI to examine health records and find patterns that Google says might help doctors and other providers. Google is also planning to use data from Fitbit watches, having announced a deal to buy the company.[26]

Predictive Analytics

The predictive phase looks to analyze the current data and compare it to data the company does not yet have by using such techniques as statistical gathering, data mining, predictive modeling, and machine learning techniques. It tries to answer this question: What will happen? It is also concerned with learning how to anticipate failures. Because this data is so powerful and can carry a large amount of authority, many managers focus on thinking about this question: What should happen? For example, Google and Ascension are trying to spot a potentially worsening medical condition.

Prescriptive Analytics

In the prescriptive phase, businesses are trying to determine what is the best possible outcome and generate various "what if?" scenarios to, ideally, create multiple futures with various causes. Ultimately, Google and Ascension want to prevent unnecessary emergency room visits, surgeries, and long hospital stays through a series of data-driven scenarios.

Preemptive Analytics

Here, the goal is to develop a set of action items to prevent unintended consequences—a main focus of the preemptive phase. Using this data, Google and Ascension are hoping to prescribe certain narratives and courses of action so patients can take greater ownership of their own health care based on certain patient profiles.

Big Data and the Organization

- There are five phases of the data analytics process in practice: descriptive, diagnostic, predictive, prescriptive, and preemptive.

- Big data consists of information with high volume, velocity, and variety.

DIGITAL SECURITY AND SAFETY

LO 13.4 Identify the primary challenges faced by organizations in managing and protecting data of stakeholders from hackers.

One of the most serious potential threats to an organization's well-being is the extent to which businesses and consumers rely on the interconnectedness of their digital assets on a day-to-day basis. Any disruption or breach of security has the potential to have a significant (and unexpected) financial and resource impact on firms that extensively rely on computer systems as part of their business model. **Digital security** refers to an organization's efforts to protect its digital assets from outsiders. **Digital safety** is when individuals or companies practice safeguarding user personal safety against security risks to private information and property associated with using the Internet—and the self-protection from computer crime in general.[27]

One of the biggest threats is malware and data breaches. **Malware** is a shorthand term for malicious software that is used to gain access to information stored on a computer or computer network. This personal information, such as credit card data, Social Security number, driver's license number, or passport number, is stolen and sold for fraudulent use. Malware is a category of software that is used to describe a broad array of malicious programs including Trojan horses, viruses, worms, ransomware, spyware, adware, and scareware. See Figure 13.6 for a full description of these types of malware and Chapter 14 for a full definition of *personal information*.

Media stories of data breaches caused by malware are becoming a relatively common occurrence. Since 1992, the nonprofit Privacy Rights Clearinghouse has kept a database of breaches from across a broad variety of organizations, including financial institutions, credit bureaus, retail, education, media, government, and health care. On its website (www.privacyrights.org), consumers can ask questions, submit complaints, or search its database for specific companies according to type of organization, or type of breach. Over 12 billion records have been breached.[28] Some famous companies who have reported substantial data breaches include Equifax, Yahoo, Home Depot, Target, AT&T, Bank of America, LinkedIn, eHarmony, Zappos, and Sony.

According to legal research firm BakerHostetler's 2019 Data Security Incident Response Report, based on its analysis of more than 750 data security incidents, the top causes of data breeches in order are phishing (37%), network intrusion (30%), inadvertent disclosure (12%), stolen or lost devices or records (10%), and system misconfiguration (4%). The health-care industry tops the list at 25%, followed by finance and insurance and

digital security: An organization's efforts to protect its digital assets from outsiders.

digital safety: When individuals or companies practice safeguarding user personal safety against security risks to private information and property associated with using the Internet—and the self-protection from computer crime in general.

malware: A shorthand term for malicious software that is used to gain access to information stored on a computer or computer network.

Figure 13.6 Types of Malware

- **Trojan horse:** Appears harmless but hides malicious function

- **Virus:** Copies itself and spreads from one computer to another without the user's knowledge

- **Worm:** Is installed in "back door" of infected computer, which allows perpetrator to control the computer

- **Spyware:** Monitors your computer and reveals collected information to a hacker, such as what webpages are visited, and monitors everything you do with your mouse and keyboard

- **Ransomware:** Infects a data system, and a hacker holds user's data hostage

- **Scareware/Rogueware:** Dupes users into thinking fake antivirus software will remove any viruses

- **DoS attack:** Overloads a network with information, causing the computer not to function properly

then business and professional services—each at 17%. By revenue, $10 million- to $100 million-dollar companies were impacted most frequently (27%), followed by $101 million- to $500 million-dollar companies (23%). On the brighter side, 74% of breaches were internally discovered. Typically, companies responded or offered the following most often:

- Notification was provided in 53% of incidents over a 4-year period (2015–2018), even though not all incidents require notification.

- 70% of companies that notified individuals of a security breach offered credit monitoring—which BakerHostetler recommends when Social Security numbers or driver's licenses are affected.[29]

CASE STUDY 13.2

Ransomware That Made Managers "WannaCry"

Ransomware's Origins

Malware that holds data for ransom has been around for years. In 1991, a biologist spread PC Cyborg, the first ever ransomware, by sending floppy disks via surface mail to other researchers. Soon after, a series of "police" ransomware packages appeared that purported to be warnings from government agents about the victims' illicit activities and demanded payment of fines. Most experts identify CryptoLocker, a ransomware program that infected over half a million computers in 2013, as the beginning of a new day in data kidnapping. It spread via attachments to spam messages and acted to seal up user files until users paid cash in return for the decryption keys.

Although ransomware attacks were typically the subject of isolated media reports over the past decade, the modern era of ransomware was hatched by a worldwide cyberattack of a cryptoworm called WannaCry in 2017. The WannaCry ransomware cryptoworm infected more than 230,000 computers in 150 countries in a single day by targeting computers running the Microsoft Windows operating system, encrypting (hiding) data, and demanding ransom payments in the electronic currency called bitcoin. The initial brunt of the attack affected hospitals in the United Kingdom, causing them to halt care of noncritical cases. Nissan Motor Manufacturing and Renault also stopped production in an attempt to stop the spread of the ransomware. Although researchers discovered a kill switch had been built in by its creators just days after its release, economists estimate losses from the cyberattack were over $4 billion before the ransomware was stopped. A similar instance, called Petya, attacked banks, utilities, and airlines across the United Kingdom and Western Europe.[30]

Discussion Questions

1. In most ransomware attacks, the amount of money demanded is relatively small (as low as $300). Why do you think hackers would use such a low figure?

2. Modern hackers demand their payment in bitcoin. Does this raise any issues about regulation of electronic currency such as bitcoin? Should the government monitor bitcoin users and accounts? What would be the result if the government began to regulate bitcoin or the technology behind it?

3. It was clear the hackers were exploiting vulnerability in the Windows operating system. Does Microsoft have an ethical obligation to pay some of the losses suffered by its users? Why or why not?

Critical Thinking

The dilemma for managers in affected organizations is straightforward: Do we pay or not? Some favor paying simply because there is a sort of "honor among thieves" that will result in an outcome that allows you to get on with your business and take steps to be sure it doesn't happen again. Others argue that there is no guarantee that the data will be released and paying only supports this sort of behavior, promotes it, and ultimately makes it even more of a threat to everyone. Which argument is most compelling and why? How do you balance the reality of running a business with long-term ethical practices that are important to your company? What other considerations should a management team sift through when deciding this issue?

Cyberterrorism

While some experts believe that any attack on a computer or computer system constitutes cyberterrorism, most insist that the term must be reserved for true acts of terrorism facilitated by computers, computer systems, and/or the Internet. The National Conference of State Legislatures, which provides guidance for policymakers in a variety of areas, provides a useful working definition of **cyberterrorism**: the use of information technology by terrorist groups and individuals to further their agenda. Cyberterrorism can be accomplished by methods that were discussed previously such as malware, viruses, worms, denial-of-service (DoS) attacks, and cyberterrorism threats via electronic means.

> cyberterrorism: The use of information technology by terrorist groups and individuals to further their agenda.

In 2014, a federal grand jury indicted five military officers from China on charges of economic espionage and trade secret theft. The U.S. Justice Department alleged that the group had hacked computer systems of American companies such as Alcoa and U.S. Steel Corp. for purposes of taking commercial advantage and private financial gain. Although it is highly unlikely that any of these defendants would ever be brought to trial, the indictments were the first step in the U.S. government's campaign to expose cybercrimes committed with the backing of a foreign power.

Increasingly, governments all over the world are focused on what they call true cyberterrorism—such as an attack on the electric grid or water supply. Terrorist groups are increasingly adopting the power of modern communications technology for planning, recruiting, propaganda, fundraising and funds transfer, information gathering, and the like.

Cybercrimes are committed either by using the computer as an *instrument* of crime by an individual or when a criminal *targets* a computer or network. Using the Internet for criminal purposes is sometimes referred to as netcrime. The legal definition of cybercrime has expanded rapidly over the past decade. Cybercrime could be considered any use of communication network (e.g., the Internet or smartphones) to cause harm to a victim's computer, network, personal safety, reputation, or mental well-being.

Hacking is yet another security problem for business and society alike. A **hacker** is a person who illegally gains access to and sometimes tampers with information in a computer system. **Hacktivists** are individuals or groups who hack into government or corporate computer networks and then release information to try to embarrass the organizations or gain leverage against the organizations. Some examples of these groups are Anonymous and Hacker's List. Cambridge Analytica came to symbolize the dark side of social media in the wake of the 2016 U.S. presidential election and is the subject of a recent movie on Netflix.[31]

hacker: A person who illegally gains access to and sometimes tampers with information in a computer system.

hacktivists: Individuals or groups who hack into government or corporate computer networks and then release information to try to embarrass the organizations or gain leverage against the organizations.

LAW AND SOCIETY 13.1

Michael *Terpin* v. AT&T Mobility, 2019 U.S. Dist. LEXIS 121905

Facts: Michael Terpin is a crypto investor and well known in the cryptocurrency field. He lives in Puerto Rico and maintains a residence in California. On June 11, 2017, Terpin's cell phone suddenly stopped working because his cell number had been hacked. Hackers tried and failed 11 times to change Terpin's AT&T password in AT&T stores but were successful when they tried to change it remotely. The hack gave the criminals control of Terpin's phone number, which allowed them to divert his personal information, including telephone calls and text messages, and to gain access to his accounts that use his telephone number for authentication. With Terpin's phone number, the hackers accessed his cryptocurrency accounts and also impersonated him on Skype to convince his client to send him cryptocurrency and the diverted cryptocurrency to themselves. Later that day, AT&T was able to cut off the hacker's access to Terpin's phone number, but by that time substantial funds had been stolen.

On June 13, 2017, Terpin met with AT&T representatives in Puerto Rico who promised to put Mr. Terpin's account on a higher security level with protections like requiring a six-digit passcode (known only to Terpin and his wife) for anyone to access or change the account or transfer the number to another phone.

Terpin's phone again stopped working on January 7, 2018. He learned that an employee at an AT&T store in Norwich, Connecticut, helped an imposter with a SIM card swap, which is a ploy to get a provider to transfer the target's phone number to a SIM card controlled by the criminal. Once they get the number, criminals can use it to reset the victim's passwords and break into their online accounts. Through the SIM card swap, criminals obtained control of Terpin's phone number. Terpin contacted AT&T to have his phone number cancelled, but the company did not cancel it promptly. As a result, criminals intercepted Terpin's personal information, including telephone calls and text messages, and gained access to his cryptocurrency accounts. As a result, between January 7 and 8, Terpin alleges criminals stole almost $24 million worth of cryptocurrency from him.

Terpin sued AT&T for, among many counts, a declaration that its user agreement is unconscionable and contrary to public policy; violations of California's consumer protection laws; Business and Professions Code and unfair competition law; negligence; and breach of contract. AT&T filed a motion to dismiss Terpin's complaint, stating he does not have enough facts to allege legal violations.

Issue: Does Terpin have enough facts to support the allegations in his complaint?

Decision: Yes and no. A complaint must contain enough facts to raise a right to relief; that right to relief cannot be speculative but must be plausible. AT&T claims Terpin's complaint should be dismissed because he cannot show that the conduct by AT&T actually caused his injury. According to AT&T, Terpin cannot show this because the intervening criminal conduct of the hackers was the real cause of his injury. According to California law, a criminal act is a superseding cause and therefore breaks the chain of causation unless the criminal conduct involves a particular and foreseeable injury on a foreseeable person. Here, Terpin provides facts that show his injury was foreseeable to AT&T. For example, Terpin claims he informed AT&T in June 2017 that he was the victim of a SIM card swap and that AT&T put his account on a higher level of security with special protection. Thus, AT&T was on notice that Terpin's account was vulnerable. Despite this, Terpin was again a victim of a SIM card swap in January 2018 allegedly as a result of the involvement by AT&T. Terpin has enough facts in his complaint to allege his injury was foreseeable to AT&T. What Terpin does not do in his complaint, however, is connect how the SIM card swap led to him losing $24 million; he does not include any facts about how the hackers gained access to his cryptocurrency accounts. Because of this, we will dismiss this claim but allow Terpin to correct the errors and refile it.

Terpin also has enough facts to allege unauthorized disclosure of customer proprietary information in violation of the Federal Communications Act. AT&T divulged his phone number, account information, and his private communications to hackers in the January 2017 SIM card swap.

Regarding Terpin's claims for violation of California law, these must also be dismissed because California law does not apply to criminal conduct that took place outside of the state. Although Terpin claims he owns a home in California, he lives in Puerto Rico, was in Puerto Rico at the time of the incidents, and met with an AT&T representative in Puerto Rico. The second hack took place in Connecticut. Owning property in a state does not mean the laws of that state apply to criminal conduct that took place in another state. Terpin may correct the errors in this claim, if he can, and refile.

Law and Management Questions

1. Why do you think Terpin did not file this lawsuit in Puerto Rico (which operates within the U.S. constitutional system)?

2. Hacks are not uncommon in the cryptocurrency space; SIM card swaps are a common way for hackers to get access to cryptocurrency accounts. But SIM cards are easily purchased and swapped out for a variety of legitimate purposes. Whose responsibility is it to ensure the safety of SIM cards: SIM card sellers, SIM card manufacturers, cell phone service providers, and/or cell phone manufacturers?

Experts encourage companies to develop an incident–response plan for these attacks. These plans complement the effort to prevent access to information but also focuses on what to do when a breach occurs. Some companies reduce criminal intrusion to their sites by paying hackers, often called white hatters to identify weaknesses in the company's information systems.

Cyberstalking is a prime example of the use of computers and the Internet to facilitate a traditional offline crime. **Cyberstalking** generally refers to the use of the Internet, e-mail, or other electronic communications devices to stalk another person—where stalking in the traditional sense means to engage in repeated harassing or threatening behavior. This includes following a person, appearing at a person's home or workplace, making harassing telephone calls, or leaving written messages or objects that places the victim in reasonable fear of death or bodily injury. **Cyberbullying** is using the Internet, cell phones, or other devices to send or post text or images intended to hurt or embarrass another person. Those engaged in cyberbullying typically post pornographic, threatening, or harassing information online or send it directly to their victim.

cyberstalking: Generally refers to the use of the Internet, e-mail, or other electronic communications devices to stalk another person—where stalking in the traditional sense means to engage in repeated harassing or threatening behavior.

cyberbullying: Using the Internet, cell phones, or other devices to send or post text or images intended to hurt or embarrass another person.

KEY TAKEAWAYS

Digital Security and Safety

- Data security and privacy remain major challenges for managers, organizations, and societies.

- There exists a variety of laws and ethical issues in using big data that continually need assessment by managers.

LEGAL AND ETHICAL ASPECTS OF BIG DATA

LO 13.5   Understand the mosaic of laws that apply to data usage.
LO 13.6   Explain the ethical issues related to data usage

Legal Issues and the Use of Big Data

There is no one law that is completely on point in addressing data privacy; protection is found in a mosaic of laws that apply to certain issues under certain conditions. Here are some laws in this mosaic:

- *Federal Trade Commission (FTC) Act*: A federal consumer protection law that prohibits unfair or deceptive practices that has been applied to online and offline privacy policies.

- *Electronic Communications Privacy Act (ECPA)*: Prohibits intentional interception of e-mails, blogs, and social media as a means of communications; allows an employer to monitor e-mails sent and received on its servers.

- *Stored Communications Act (SCA):* Prohibits the intentional unauthorized access of a third party to an Internet service provider facility in order to obtain access to an electronic communication.

- *The Fourth Amendment to the U.S. Constitution*: Secures the right of the people to be free of unreasonable searches and seizures.

- *General Data Protection Regulation (GDPR):* The European Union has recently placed strict regulations on businesses in regard to using big data. This law, GDPR, prevents companies from collecting any data that can be connected to an identifiable person. According to *Forbes*, GDPR is the start of a more global trend that will hold companies accountable for how they treat privacy and personal data.[32] More discussion of GDPR appears in Chapter 14.

One aspect deserving attention relates to how different countries and regulators balance the trade-off between privacy and security. For instance, they might choose to privilege the maximization of societal welfare or, instead, to pay attention to minorities who are penalized by the discriminations of algorithmic decision-making. Data privacy laws and regulations—how citizens perceive the value of privacy—are country-specific and are related to cultural and historical issues.[33]

Ethical Issues and the Use of Big Data

As we have mentioned often in this chapter and textbook, there are ethical implications to certain managerial practices, and the collection and use of big data is no exception. While machine learning is capable of looking at patterns in data, this AI is not able to detect bias. Also, the context of the situation is not appreciated by the data or the machine on its own—that is, the special circumstances that make someone not behave as predicted by the data, the anomaly if you will. Likewise, computers do not have the ability to process tacit knowledge, or the kind of emotional and intuitive information that is part of a person's consciousness. After all, this type of information is acquired through human interaction and shared activities. So, is it even possible for a machine to make ethical decisions that rely on this type of information? If not, what can the company do to help ensure ethics are being followed in the use of big data? For example, would ethics codes or training work?

Despite these lingering questions, the technological revolution has, in some cases, delegated increasingly important and higher-order business decisions to big data. The short-term efficiency benefits may be outweighed by corporate irresponsibility in instances where value judgments are necessary.

Therefore, an important way of looking at the issues created by big data is to use an ethical lens, learned in Chapter 3, where we consider individuals' right to maintain their privacy, freedom, and independence, against businesses' right to discriminate in the process of securing a sale by using big data analytics. We suggest that such dilemmas can be addressed using the teleological or deontological approaches to ethics (or both).

Recall, the teleological approach suggests ethical behavior maximizes societal welfare while minimizing social harm. According to this approach, a company may be right in being algorithm driven—as in an insurance company applying higher premiums to those who, according to the data analytics, are more at risk of having car accidents. However, the deontological approach bases ethical decisions on universal ethical principles and moral values such as honesty, promise-keeping, fairness, loyalty, and rights (e.g., to safety, privacy) so that the process or means by which an individual does something, rather than the outcome, is the focus of decision-making (e.g., lying is dishonest as it is one's duty to be honest regardless of whether this might lead to some ultimate good); therefore, the end never justifies the means. According to this latter approach, discriminations by insurance companies should not take place if a minority is adversely and unfairly treated—never mind if following an algorithm maximizes positive consequences for society. Take a look at the Manager's Challenge at the end of the chapter.

Big Data and Insurance

iStockphoto.com/metamorworks

Automobile insurer Progressive's Snapshot tracker device technology has the ability to capture multiple driver details.[34] U.S.-based Progressive is known as a leader in analyzing data to price its policies by capturing billions of driving and other data. For example, Progressive also uses Apache Hadoop, the open-source software, to review months' worth of online advertising data in a few hours.

Progressive began to offer Snapshot to drivers in 2008, on an opt-in basis, and marketed the device to customers as a means to lower their insurance premiums. Information regarding your driving habits—when you drive, how much, how you accelerate and brake, mileage, and locations (via GPS)—is reviewed by a team at Progressive.[35] Your insurance rates are adjusted accordingly—up to a 30% discount according to Progressive's marketing.

Snapshot plugs directly into your vehicle's diagnostic port (the OBD-II) or via use of a mobile app, and the collected data is sent wirelessly back to Progressive at the end of each trip. How and what information is used varies from state to state. The data could result in lower or higher rates and, to some, could be used to discriminate (e.g., by charging young men higher premiums because the data

indicate that they—generally—drive less safely than other categories of drivers).[36] This potential has led to the European Union ruling that different premiums for men and women, purely on the grounds of gender, are incompatible with the principle of unisex pricing included in EU gender equality legislation.[37] Such legislation does not exist in the United States.

Despite the fact that gender differences may be clear from the analysis of a vast data set, it is also used for specific individual policies. While young men in general may drive more recklessly and be more prone to accidents, an individual young man may not be. Likewise, there are other issues with the data. A user noted, "I started my car after tinkering under the hood in the middle of the night once, and it registered that I was 'driving' at 11:00 p.m., a high-risk period." Snapshot is engaged when you start your car to record the time of day data.

Discussion Questions

1. *Stakeholder–shareholder theories*: Who are the stakeholders affected by these types of usage-based insurance programs? Are there conflicts of interest in the way Progressive works with its customers to determine insurance rates?

2. *Ethical decision-making*: Using a principles-based approach and a consequences-based approach, answer this question: What is the problem with companies using big data to set insurance rates?

Take a Position

Issue: Should Progressive use big data for individual policies? Should the United States government follow the EU law?

Legal and Ethical Aspects of Big Data

- Privacy protection is found in a mosaic of laws that apply to certain issues under certain conditions.

- Countries and regulators balance the trade-off between privacy and security.

- There are lingering questions about whether machines can make ethical decisions, but we as humans can use ethical frameworks to work side by side.

SUMMARY

There has been a sea change ushered in by the digital age transforming the ways we communicate, work, live, and even think. Big data allows organizations to collect and use large sets of data that were previously beyond their reach. There are multiple advantages and disadvantages of data-driven decision-making, and both raise ethical and societal issues that are ultimately the responsibility of the organizations (e.g., governments and businesses) that collect such data.

KEY TERMS

cyberbullying 310
cyberstalking 310
cyberterrorism 307
digital divide 298

digital readiness 300
digital safety 305
digital security 305
hacker 308

hacktivists 308
malware 305
sharing economy 298

REVIEW QUESTIONS

1. Technology is driven by a combination of factors. What are they?

2. What are some of the positive outcomes for both business and society with recent technological innovation? What are some negative consequences to consider? Can you relate these to the ethical issues discussed in this chapter?

3. What are the five phases of the data analytics process in practice?

4. Big data can be described as information with three V's. What are they?

5. Name some of the laws governing big data.

Big Data and Codes of Ethics

Real Time Corporation (RTC) is a company whose business model depends on gathering data through users' GPS devices in smartphones, combined with built-in gyroscopes and accelerometers, to parse streams of photos that users take and thus pinpoint their locations. As RTC continues to develop its data gathering and analysis tools, the management team realizes that the potential dark side of big data suggests the need for a code of ethical principles.

Framing Questions

1. Should RTC notify users in real time that it is collecting data from customers' smartphones? If it does, what would be the impact on the RTC business model? Would users object? Why or why not?

2. Some privacy experts advocate a "privacy by design" approach. This means that organizations should incorporate privacy protections into everything they do. How could RTC implement a privacy by design approach?

3. Is it necessary to have a code of ethics that is specifically tied to big data? Can't RTC simply follow its existing general ethical code (e.g., Our business values respect for privacy)? Why or why not?

Assignment

Prepare a draft code of big data ethics for RTC in preparation for a management team discussion at an upcoming meeting. Think about the following: What specific behavioral statements should it include? Should it be aspirational or punitive?

PRIVACY IN THE DIGITAL AGE

Ethics in Context

Profits Versus Privacy Protection

Recently companies like Facebook, Twitter, and Instagram have come under fire about their use of personal data as a central aspect of their business plan. All three of these companies have altered their privacy terms multiple times to give the company greater ability to use personal data for profit. To be sure, technology gives businesses access to a great deal of informa-

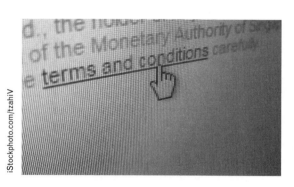

iStockphoto.com/tzahiV

tion. However, managers' strong attraction to using big data can be at odds with the protection of individuals' rights to their own information. Later in the chapter, in the Ethics in Context section, we will examine the tension between profits and privacy.

Learning Objectives

Upon completion of this chapter, the reader should be able to do the following:

14.1 Articulate the difference between privacy and security and how personal information is involved.

14.2 Explain the responsibilities that individuals, governments, and companies have in the protection of privacy.

14.3 Describe the right to be forgotten, the right to erasure, and the practice of surveillance as well as when and where they apply.

14.4 Explain the various best practices of personal information that managers need to be aware of.

INTRODUCTION

Privacy is an important management issue that continues to challenge organizations. Much is focused on the problems resulting from the decisions organizations make about using or reusing personal information.[1] Today, the decentralized technology environment contributes to a large variety of additional privacy problems. In this chapter, we focus on three key issues: data privacy, surveillance, and the right to be forgotten or erasure.

WHAT IS THE RIGHT TO PRIVACY?

LO 14.1 Articulate the difference between privacy and security and how personal information is involved.

The concept of one's privacy has been at issue since the late 1800s when in the United States lawyer Louis Brandeis (who would later become a Supreme Court justice) wrote a *Harvard Law Review* article discussing the privacy rights of Prince Albert of England, who wished to prevent the publication of his personal sketches. In this article, Brandeis describes privacy as "the right to be let alone."[2]

Times have certainly changed things, but the idea expressed in "the right to be let alone" has endured. Today, **privacy** is a multidimensional concept that is dependent on context and also varies with a person's life experiences. As Professor Lillian BeVier writes, "Privacy is a chameleon-like word, used denotatively to designate a wide range of wildly disparate interests—from confidentiality of personal information to reproductive autonomy—and connotatively to generate goodwill on behalf of whatever interest is being asserted in its name."[3] Lew McCreary wrote about privacy in the past tense in 2008 in a *Harvard Business Review* article because "individuals can no longer feel confident that the details of their lives—from identifying numbers to cultural preferences—will be treated with discretion rather than exploited."[4]

> **privacy:** A multidimensional concept relating broadly to confidentiality of personal information.

With these ideas in mind, in this chapter we will be guided by a general use of the term—or the right for one's personal information to be protected from public scrutiny—and apply it to a variety of contexts.

Certainly, security is one aspect of privacy. **Security** is about protecting personal information, while privacy is broader and encompasses the permission and use of personal information. Privacy is difficult to achieve without security. However, organizations can successfully secure the personal information in their custody and still make bad decisions about how the personal information they have collected is subsequently used.[5]

> **security:** The act of protecting personal information.

Personal information means information that identifies; relates to; describes; is capable of being associated with; or could reasonably be linked, directly or indirectly, with a particular consumer or household—for example, identifiers such as a real name, alias, postal address, unique personal identifier, online identifier, Internet protocol address, e-mail address, account name, Social Security number, driver's license number, passport number, or other similar identifiers.[i]

> **personal information:** Information that identifies, relates to, describes, is capable of being associated with, or could reasonably be linked, directly or indirectly, with a particular consumer or household.

Given the vast amount of personal information generated by millions of consumer transactions each day, there can be serious privacy problems resulting from the storage, analysis, use, or sharing of this information. However, there are also many benefits to collecting and using such information. As a result, such opportunities need to be considered alongside the ethical challenges that may result and managers will need to become accustomed to dealing with both of these aspects.

---

[i]*Personal information* is defined in Section 1798.140(o) (1) of the CCPA; see https://www.socalinternetlawyer.com/california-consumer-privacy-act-personal-information-definition. For more information, see the CCPA law found at https://leginfo.legislature.ca.gov/faces/billTextClient.xhtml?bill_id=201720180AB375

The Fourth Amendment secures our right to be free from unreasonable searches and seizures by the government. The Law and Society section addresses the issue of search of personal data, but the data came from cell phone towers, not the person himself. Is that an unreasonable search?

Data Privacy and the Constitution: *United States v. Carpenter,* 819 F.3d 880 (2016)

Facts: In April 2011, police arrested four men suspected of committing a string of armed robberies at RadioShack and T-Mobile stores in the Detroit, Michigan, area and in Ohio. One of the men confessed and supplied police with the cell phone numbers of the 15 men involved in the robberies. In May the Federal Bureau of Investigation (FBI) applied for three orders from a magistrate, pursuant to the Stored Communications Act (SCA), to obtain records including cell site information from the wireless carriers of the men. Under the SCA the FBI had to show that there were reasonable grounds to believe the contents of an electronic communication are relevant and material to an ongoing criminal investigation. Based on this standard, the FBI received the warrants and later charged Carpenter with six counts of aiding and abetting robbery that affected interstate commerce.

At trial, seven accomplices testified that Carpenter organized most of the robberies, often supplied the guns, and served as a lookout. Carpenter waited in a stolen car across the street from the target, and at his signal, the robbers would enter the store, herd customers and employees to the back, and steal merchandise. After each robbery, the team met nearby to dispose of the guns and getaway vehicles and to sell the stolen goods.

An FBI expert also testified about the cell site data provided by Carpenter's wireless carrier. According to his testimony, cell phones work by establishing a radio connection with nearby cell towers. In urban areas like Detroit, cell towers typically cover a half mile to

2 miles, and carriers store call detail records form these towers. The cell tower data for Carpenter's cell phone show that he was within a half mile to 2 miles of the location of each robbery around the time the robberies happened. For example, MetroPCS records show that on December 13, 2010, at 10:24 a.m. Carpenter was within a half mile to 2 miles of a RadioShack when his phone received a call that lasted 4 minutes. Police records show that at 10:35 a.m. RadioShack was robbed. The jury convicted Carpenter on all counts and sentenced him to four mandatory minimum prison sentences of 25 years, each served consecutively.

Carpenter challenged the court's refusal to dismiss the cell tower data from evidence. Carpenter claimed the heightened Fourth Amendment standard of probable cause applied to the FBI warrant application; however, the court held that the search of the carrier's data was not a search under the Fourth Amendment.

Issue: Is there a privacy interest in location data supplied by cell phone tower records?

Decision: There is no privacy interest in location data supplied by cell phone tower records. The Fourth Amendment protections apply to the areas enumerated in the amendment but also to those areas where there is a certain expectation of privacy. The privacy expectation must meet two criteria for protection: First, the person exerting it must have an actual subjective expectation of privacy; also, that expectation must be one that society is prepared to recognize.

(Continued)

(Continued)

The issue here is about the privacy expectation in information related to personal communications. On this point, federal courts have held that although the content of personal communications is private, the information necessary to get those communications from Point A to Point B is not. The U.S. Supreme Court has held that police's installation of a pen register (a device used to track the phone numbers a person dialed from their home) was not a search because the caller could not reasonably expect the numbers to remain private. Similarly, while the content of a letter is private, the information on the outside of the envelope is not. The same distinction applies here: The cell tower data say nothing about the content of any calls; instead, they include routing information that the carriers collected in the normal course of their business. Carriers keep records of this data to help it identify weak spots in its coverage and to determine when roaming charges will apply. Thus, the cell site data, like the outside of an envelope and a phone number, is information that facilitates communication and not part of the content of the communication. The trial court's decision is affirmed.

Law and Management Questions

1. Police learned much more than just phone numbers from the cell tower data; it learned of Carpenter's physical location. Explain how this information is different than just routing information.

2. Our cell phones contain far more information on us than what apps we have and our contacts. That's why most cell phone makers allow us to install passwords. However, learning what is on a suspect's cell phone could be valuable information to law enforcement. Explain the tension between a cell phone maker like Apple and police when the police want access to a suspect's encrypted iPhone.

KEY TAKEAWAYS

What Is the Right to Privacy?

- The right to privacy varies in terms of context, place, and circumstances, but everyone has a fundamental right to be left alone.

- There is a difference between privacy and security; privacy involves the permission to use personal information, and security involves the responsibility to protect it. However, they need to work in tandem to be effective.

COLLECTING PERSONAL INFORMATION: BENEFITS AND HARMS

artificial intelligence (AI): Machine-based learning involving adaptive mechanisms that enable computers to learn from example, experience, and analogy.

LO 14.2   Explain the responsibilities that individuals, governments, and companies have in the protection of privacy.

Today's consumers are looking for products or services to be easy, fast, and smart. What's more, **artificial intelligence (AI)** is dominating the delivery of these products and services.

AI is machine-based learning involving adaptive mechanisms that enable computers to learn from example, experience, and analogy.[6] These learning capabilities improve over time, creating a truly intelligent system.

Companies often struggle with finding the balance between enjoying the benefits of technology and keeping control of its possible threats. Gathering, mining, and employing data provides a business with opportunities to improve private and public life as well as the environment—for example, think of the development of smart cities. A more lengthy discussion of big data appears in Chapter 13.

The extensive use of increasingly more data—often personal, often sensitive—and the growing reliance on algorithms to analyze them in order to shape choices and to make decisions (i.e., AI) are at the root of the harmful effects of collecting personal information. What's more, some experts believe there has been a gradual reduction of human involvement in these automatic processes and that they, too, pose pressing issues of fairness, rights, and responsibility—concepts from Chapter 3.

These harmful effects can and should be addressed. Perhaps this concern is why the European Union plans to test ethical guidelines for the responsible and beneficial use of AI in a pilot project planned for the summer of 2019.[7] Developing and deploying data science while also ensuring the personal **right to privacy**—as well as the values necessary for shaping open and tolerant information societies—is a great opportunity for managers. Consider for a moment the risks and benefits of information technology in Figure 14.1.

right to privacy: The right for one's personal information to be protected from public scrutiny.

Responsibilities of Individuals, Companies, and Governments

Individuals everywhere willingly provide a large amount of information—whether it be to their social media accounts, to their friends, schools, or civic organizations—and this information is then used or reused. It might come as no surprise that they bear some

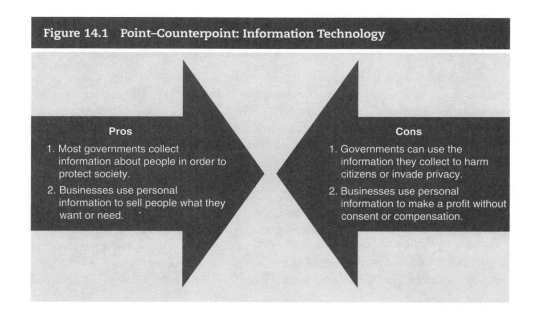

Figure 14.1 Point–Counterpoint: Information Technology

Pros

1. Most governments collect information about people in order to protect society.

2. Businesses use personal information to sell people what they want or need.

Cons

1. Governments can use the information they collect to harm citizens or invade privacy.

2. Businesses use personal information to make a profit without consent or compensation.

responsibility to providing this information. However, some basic privacy principles exist in the areas of an individual's ability to access, correct, delete and download their own personal information.[8] However, these are not so easily accomplished. For example, Jeffrey Toobin, in an article in the *New Yorker*, explained that Facebook always allows people to delete the content they create—a photo or a post, for example. Since Facebook allows users to "tag" other people in photographs and videos to indicate their identity, the author wondered if Facebook grants a user the right to remove their own posts and does that extend to others' posts about you. Users can untag themselves, but they can't remove the actual photos. If Facebook were to remove those tagged photos, videos, or entire posts, its Community Operations team would consider that request.[9]

There is a lot at stake for companies too in terms of personal information. For example, noted privacy researchers Kathleen Greenaway and Yolande Chan showed that an organization's information privacy behaviors can help a firm achieve legitimacy and can provide a strategic advantage to an organization.[10] Others believe that companies leverage algorithms and big data to create invasive personal ads and inappropriately use customer information.[11] The latter has become known as **datification**—or the technologies and work practices by which people and organizations are sorted and classified, scored and ranked on various dimensions, and prescribed or predicted, often with the aim of manipulation.[12]

> **datification:** The technologies and work practices by which people and organizations are sorted and classified, scored and ranked on various dimensions, and prescribed or predicted, often with the aim of manipulation.

In fact, there are two issues of concern for managers arising from the way organizations process personal information: information reuse and unauthorized access to personal information. Typically, information reuse involves organizations making legal decisions about new uses for the personal information they have collected, while unauthorized access represents activities that violate either laws or corporate policies. Both activities, information reuse and unauthorized access, can potentially threaten an individual's ability to maintain a condition of limited access to his or her personal information, harm individuals, and subsequently threaten the organization's legitimacy in its interactions with consumers, shareholders, and regulators.[13]

While companies see the importance in collecting and analyzing data of consumers, many countries, including the United States, have few laws regarding individuals' privacy rights. Furthermore, calls for better privacy protection face fragmented laws and regulations, which are often country-specific.[14]

For example, in the United States, the Federal Trade Commission (FTC) recommends that businesses offer consumers greater disclosure and simple the ability to **opt out**, but there is no legislation enacted by Congress that enforces these practices. This lack of collaboration between the FTC and Congress creates a gap between what personal information citizens expect to be protected and what businesses are actually doing in regard to collecting data.

> **opt out:** Companies make available information about how they collect, use, and share personal information and allow individuals to opt out if they desire.

In 2012, the White House proposed the Consumer Privacy Bill of Rights and in 2015 proposed the Consumer Privacy Act; however, Congress enacted neither into law. Without success on the federal level, states began to consider the issue on their own. On June 28, 2018, the California state legislature passed a law known as the California Consumer Privacy Act (CCPA), which aims to provide Californian citizens and residents with more information about how companies collect their personal data, outlining several rights to personal information (see Figure 14.2). Fines are enforced

Figure 14.2 CPAA Basic Rights

- Right to know all data collected by a business on you

- Right to say no to the sale of your information

- Right to delete your data

- Right to be informed of what categories of data will be collected about you prior to its collection and to be informed of any changes to this collection

- Right to know the categories of third parties with whom your data is shared

- Right to know the categories of sources of information from whom your data was acquired

- Right to know the business or commercial purpose of collecting your information

- Private right of action when companies breach your data

by the California attorney general and can reach up to $7,500 per violation (in the case of intentional violations).[15] Unintentional violations remain subject to a $2,500 maximum fine. As of this writing, some 12 other states in the United States are considering similar laws.[16]

Unlike the uncertainty of personal information collection in the United States, the European Union has recently placed strict regulations on businesses in regard to using big data. This law, called the General Data Protection Regulation (GDPR), prevents companies from collecting and processing any data that can be connected to an identifiable person without prior consent.[17] In addition, individuals have the ability to block companies from collecting their data and using it for profiling purposes.[18] Implemented in May 2018, the GDPR has also imposed conditions on how the information is stored, and for how long.[19] If something similar were to be enacted in the United States, businesses like the University of Arizona (UA), Case Study 3.1 in Chapter 3, would be forced to reconsider their collection of student data.

One of the key differences of the GDPR and the CCPA is the data collection consent aspect. GDPR specifically requires consumers to **opt in**, or to consent to data collection before the site collects the data. The CCPA offers consumers only the right to *opt out*, where companies make available information about how they collect, use, and share personal information and allow individuals to opt out if they desire. While there are pros and cons to each approach, experts generally agree that opt-in privacy rules create a greater sense of control over personal information.[20] In a recent 2-year study by the Pew Research Center, a nonpartisan fact tank that informs the public about the issues, attitudes, and trends shaping the world, 91% of adults agree or strongly agree that consumers have lost control of how personal information is collected and used by companies.[21]

opt in: Consumers must consent to data collection before the site collects the data.

Lastly, there is some measure of nationalism being reflected in global data privacy laws—as India, China, Russia, Canada, and Brazil have all adopted privacy laws in 2018.[22]

Profits Versus Privacy Protection

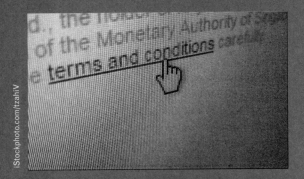

iStockphoto.com/tzahiV

In 2019 the *Wall Street Journal* conducted an investigation of Facebook's use of sensitive personal information it obtained from applications developed by other providers—like health, real estate, or sexual information—which is independent of the app's functionality.

Founded in 2004, Facebook's mission is "to give people the power to build community and bring the world closer together. People use Facebook to stay connected with friends and family, to discover what's going on in the world and to share and express what matters to them."

Facebook has been under a great deal of scrutiny from U.S. and European regulators for how it treats the information of users and nonusers (e.g., for giving companies special access to users records well after it said it prevented it). The investigation revealed that Facebook collects intensely personal information from many commonly used smart phone apps—even if the user has no connection to Facebook—and in many cases immediately shares it with Facebook.

At the heart of the issue is an analytics tool Facebook offers to these app developers, which allows them to see statistics about their users' activities—and to target those users with Facebook advertisements. These ads are the primary way Facebook generates revenue.

Facebook said some of the data sharing uncovered by the *Wall Street Journal*'s testing appeared to violate its business terms, which instructs app developers not to send it "health, financial information, or other categories of sensitive information." One of the app developers said it doesn't send "critical user data" and that the data it does send Facebook is "depersonalized" to keep it private and secure. The *Wall Street Journal*'s testing, according to the article, showed sensitive information was in fact sent with what is called a unique advertising identifier, which can easily be matched to a person's device and/or their online profile. The *Wall Street Journal* tested 70 apps and found 11 sent Facebook potentially sensitive information.

Discussion Questions

1. *Stakeholder–shareholder theories:* Who are the stakeholders affected by Facebook's practice? Does the collection benefit these stakeholders or not?

2. *Ethical decision-making:* Discuss the question of how much information companies should (or is ethically permissible to) collect about their stakeholders. Using a principles-based approach and a consequences-based approach, answer the following questions: Who is responsible for protecting personal information data? Does any one party bear more responsibility than others due to greater ease in protecting data? Does ease matter in terms of responsibility?

Take a Position

Issue: Is there a conflict between the economic benefits of Facebook collecting and/or selling data and its obligation to protect the personal information data of its users?

Sources: Facebook Investor Relations. (n.d.). *What is Facebook's mission statement?* Retrieved from https://investor.fb.com/resources; Schechner, S., & Secada, M. (2019, February 22). You give apps sensitive personal information. Then they tell Facebook. *The Wall Street Journal.* Retrieved from https://www.wsj.com/articles/you-give-apps-sensitive-personal-information-then-they-tell-facebook-11550851636

KEY TAKEAWAYS

Collecting Personal Information: Benefits and Harms

- Managers have a significant role in using and abusing personal information and need to be mindful of the benefits and harms of AI and the increasing occurrence of datification.

- Individuals, companies, and governments all play an important

role in proper use and protection of personal information can be subject to various laws regulating the use.

- Managers must be aware of both the ethical and legal ramifications of using personal information.

RIGHT TO BE FORGOTTEN, RIGHT TO ERASURE, AND SURVEILLANCE

LO 14.3 Describe the right to be forgotten, the right to erasure, and the practice of surveillance as well as when and where they apply.

Both the popularity of search engines for retrieving information and consumers' desire for obtaining products and services online fast have created an overreliance on sensitive and personal data. Because of this reality, search engines have been portrayed as both champions of freedom and as agents of surveillance.[23] They both facilitate gathering vast amounts of online data and help people acquire knowledge, engage in debate, and participate in democratic processes. But, as discussed previously, they can pose a risk to privacy. One of the effects of this movement toward life online is that people are finding it difficult to escape their past, avoid embarrassment, or experience favorable treatment when information about them is put to unexpected use.[24] As a result, governments have moved to create the right to be forgotten and the right to erasure that both companies and individuals need to understand.

The Right to Be Forgotten

The right to be forgotten can be understood as peoples' right to request the removal of information from the Internet or other repositories because it violates their privacy or is no longer relevant. This right assumed greater prominence in the digital era when people began finding it increasingly difficult to escape information that had accumulated over many years, resulting in expressions such as "the net never forgets," "everything is in the cloud," "reputation bankruptcy," and "online reputation."[25] According to Jeffrey Rosen, professor of law at George Washington University, the intellectual roots of the right to be forgotten could be found in French law, which recognized *le droit à l'oubli*—or the "right of oblivion"—a right that allowed a convicted criminal who had served his time and been rehabilitated to object to the publication of the facts of his conviction and incarceration.[26]

> **right to be forgotten:** A person's right to request the removal of information from the Internet or other repositories because it violates their privacy or is no longer relevant.

Although the right to be forgotten was rooted in expunging criminal records, the rise of the Internet has given the concept a new, more complex meaning. Search engines enable users to access information on just about any topic with considerable ease. The ease with which information can be shared, stored, and retrieved through online search raises issues of both privacy and freedom of expression. On the one hand, when opening a bank account, joining a social networking website, or booking a flight online, a consumer voluntarily discloses vital personal information such as name, address, and credit card numbers. Consumers are often unsure of what happens to their data and are concerned that it might fall into the wrong hands—that is, that their privacy will be violated.

On the other hand, by facilitating the retrieval of information, search engines enhance individuals' freedom to receive and impart information. Any interference with search engine activities could therefore pose a threat to the effective enjoyment of these rights.[27] As Van Alsenoy, a researcher at the Interdisciplinary Center for Law and Information Communication Technology, argued, "In a world where search engines are used as the main tool to find relevant content online, any governmental interference in the provisioning of these services presents a substantial risk that requires close scrutiny."[28]

Since the 1990s, both the European Union and its member states (such as Spain) have enacted laws addressing the right to privacy and, by extension, the right to be forgotten.

A fundamental right of individuals to protect their data was introduced in the European Union's original data protection law, passed in 1995. Specifically, the European Data Protection Directive 95/46 defined the appropriate scope of national laws relating to personal data and the processing of those data. According to Article 3(1), Directive 95/46 applied "to the processing of personal data wholly or partly by automatic means, and to the processing otherwise than by automatic means of personal data which form part of a filing system or are intended to form part of a filing system."[29] Article 2(b) of the EU Data Protection Directive 95/46 defined the processing of personal data as follows:

> [It is] any operation or set of operations which is performed upon personal data, whether or not by automatic means, such as collection, recording, organization, storage, adaptation or alteration, retrieval, consultation, use, disclosure by transmission, dissemination or otherwise making available, alignment or combination, blocking, erasure or destruction.

Individual countries within the European Union also enacted their own laws, which were sometimes stronger than those of the EU. For example, in Spain, the protection of data was a constitutional right. The Spanish Constitution recognized the right to personal privacy, secrecy of communications, and the protection of personal data. These rights were protected through the Data Protection Act (the "act"), passed in 1999, which incorporated the 1995 European Directive on data protection, and was enforced by the Spanish Data Protection Agency, or Agencia Española de Protección de Datos (AEPD). Created in 1993, this agency was relatively inactive until the passing of the act, which gave it more powers and a mandate to enforce privacy rules in a wide range of situations.[30]

The Spanish agency exercised its powers broadly. For example, in 2013, it fined telecom firm Telefónica, S.A., €20,000 for twice listing an individual's phone number in local phone books without the individual's prior consent. In 2008, the agency fined a marketing company 600 euros for using "recommend this to a friend" icons on websites, saying that senders of recommendation e-mails had to first request the recipient's permission. The agency had also successfully required anyone using security cameras to clearly mark their presence with a recognizable icon. Supporters of this move have highlighted the importance of transparency in protecting one's privacy.[31]

Over time, however, differences in the way that each EU country interpreted privacy rights led to an uneven level of protection for personal data, depending on where an individual lived or bought goods and services. This led the European high court to take a second look, in 2013, at the original law.[32] A European Commission memo at that time noted that the right "is about empowering individuals, not about erasing past events or restricting freedom of the press."[33] The changes were intended to give citizens more control over their personal data, making it easier to access and improve the quality of information they received about what happened to their data once they decided to share it. An unanswered question, however, was the latitude given to national courts and regulators across Europe to set the parameters by which these requests could be made.[34]

U.S. courts had taken a very different approach to privacy and to the right to be forgotten. A few U.S. laws recognized the right to be forgotten; the Fair Credit Reporting Act of 1970, for example, gave individuals the right to delete certain negative information about their credit—such as late payments, tax liens, or judgments—7 years from the date of the delinquency. But, for the most part, fundamental differences in legal philosophy made this right less likely to become widely supported in the United States. In an article published in the *Atlantic* in May 2014, Matt Ford suggested that in the U.S. context, one person's right to be forgotten logically imposed a responsibility to forget upon someone else, a notion that was alien to American law. The First Amendment to the Constitution barred the government from interfering with free speech. Law professor Rosen argued that the First Amendment would make a right to be forgotten virtually impossible not only to create but to enforce. For example, the U.S. Supreme Court ruled in 1989 that penalizing a newspaper for publishing truthful, lawfully obtained information from the public record was unconstitutional.[35]

Case 14.1 deals with the origins and effects of the European Union's adoption of the law in 2015 for its 28 member states. It is noteworthy that Google, the company responsible for receiving and deciding which requests are eligible for the right to be forgotten, is continuing to argue with regulators over the scope of the law. For example, Google is in a dispute with French authorities over whether search results had to be removed from EU searches only or from all global searches. Google also recently lost a dispute in the United Kingdom in 2019 regarding whether information about a businessman's criminal conviction was in the public interest—one of the key criteria for the information to remain accessible on the Internet.

Google and the Right to Be Forgotten[ii]

In 2009, Mario Costeja Gonzalez, a self-employed attorney living in a small town outside Madrid, Spain, casually "googled" himself and was startled by what came up on his computer screen. Prominently displayed in the search results was a brief legal notice that had appeared more than a decade earlier in a local newspaper, *La Vanguardia*, which listed property seized and being auctioned by a government agency for nonpayments of debts. Among the properties was a home jointly owned by Costeja and his wife.

Costeja immediately realized this information could damage his reputation as an attorney. Equally troubling, the information was no longer factual. He had paid his debt nearly a decade earlier. Abanlex, Costeja's small law firm, depended on the Internet to gain much of its new business, which was often generated by a Google search. Potential clients might choose not to hire him, based on the old auction notice. His mind then turned to the possible effects of this kind of information on other people's livelihoods. "There are people who cannot get a job because of content that is irrelevant," he thought.[36] "I support freedom of expression and I do not defend censorship. [However, I decided] to fight for the right to request the deletion of data that violates the honor, dignity and reputation of individuals."[37]

The next week, Costeja wrote to *La Vanguardia* and requested that it remove the article about his debt notice because it had had been fully resolved a number of years earlier and reference to it now was therefore entirely irrelevant.[38] In doing so, he was making use of his rights under Spain's strong data protection policies, which recognized the protection and integrity of personal data as a constitutional right under Section 18 of the nation's Data Protection Act.[39] In response, the newspaper informed him it had recently uploaded to the Internet all its past archives, dating back to 1881, to allow them to be searched by the public. It also noted that the auction notice had originally been publicly posted in order to secure as many bidders as possible. The newspaper refused Costeja's request, stating the information was obtained from public records and had thus been published lawfully.[40]

To be sure, the real problem for Costeja was not that the notice had appeared in *La Vanguardia*'s digital library but that it had shown up in the results of the most widely used search engine in the world, Google, where potential clients might use it to judge his character.[41] Following this reasoning, Costeja then wrote to Google Spain, the firm's Spanish affiliate, only to be told that the parent company, Google Inc., was the entity responsible for the development of search results.[42] Costeja was taken aback by this development. "The resources Google has at their disposal aren't like those of any other citizens," he reflected.[43] Costeja felt he would be at a disadvantage in a lawsuit against an industry giant like Google.

In March 2010, after his unsuccessful attempts with the newspaper and Google Spain, Costeja turned to the AEPD, the government agency responsible for enforcing the Data Protection Act. "Google in Spain asked me to address myself to its headquarters in the U.S., but I found it too far and difficult to launch a complaint in the U.S., so I went to the agency in Spain to ask for their assistance. They said I was right, and the case went to court," he explained.[44] In a legal filing, Costeja requested, first, that the agency issue an administrative order requiring *La Vanguardia* either to remove or alter the pages in question (so that his personal data no longer appeared) or to use certain tools made available by search engines in order to shield the data from view. Second, he requested that the agency require Google Spain or Google Inc. to remove or conceal his personal data so that it no longer appeared in the search results and in the links to *La Vanguardia*. Costeja stated that his debt had been fully resolved.[45]

With these steps, a small-town Spanish lawyer had drawn one of the world's richest and best-known companies, Google, into a debate over the right to be forgotten.

Google, Inc.

Google Inc. is a technology company that builds products and provides services to organize information. Google's mission is to organize the world's information and make it universally accessible and useful. It employs more than 55,000 people and has revenues of $45 billion. The company also has 70

[ii] By Cynthia E. Clark, Bentley University. Copyright © 2015 by the author. Used by permission.

offices in more than 40 countries. The company's main product, Google Search, provides information online in response to a user's search. Google's other well-known products provide additional services.

Search Technology

In its core business, Google conducted searches in three stages: crawling and indexing, applying algorithms, and fighting spam.

Crawlers, programs that browsed the web to create an index of data, looked at webpages and followed links on those pages. They then moved from link to link and brought data about those webpages back to Google's servers. Google would then use this information to create an index to know exactly how to retrieve information for its users. Algorithms were the computer processes and formulas that took users' questions and turned them into answers. At the most basic level, Google's algorithms looked up the user's search terms in the index to find the most appropriate pages. For a typical query, thousands, if not millions, of webpages might have helpful information. Google's algorithms relied on more than 200 unique signals or "clues" that made it possible to guess what an individual was really looking for. These signals included the terms on websites, the freshness of content, the region, and the page rank of the webpage. Lastly, the company fought spam through a combination of computer algorithms and manual review. Spam sites attempted to game their way to the top of search results by repeating keywords, buying links that passed Google's Page Rank process, or putting invisible text on the screen. Google scouted out and removed spam because it could make legitimate websites harder to find. While much of this process was automated, Google did maintain teams whose job was to review sites manually.[46]

Policy on Information Removal

Google's policy on the general removal of information was the following:

> Upon request, we'll remove personal information from search results if we believe it could make you susceptible to specific harm, such as identity theft or financial fraud. This includes sensitive govern-

ment ID numbers like U.S. Social Security numbers, bank account numbers, credit card numbers, and images of signatures. We generally don't process removals of national ID numbers from official government websites because in those cases we consider the information to be public. We sometimes refuse requests if we believe someone is attempting to abuse these policies to remove other information from our results.[iii]

Apart from this general policy, Google Inc. also removed content or features from its search results for legal reasons. For example, in the United States, the company would remove content with valid notification from the copyright holder under the Digital Millennium Copyright Act (DMCA), which was administered by the U.S. Copyright Office. The DCMA provided recourse for owners of copyrighted materials who believed that their rights under copyright law had been infringed upon on the Internet.[iv] Under the notice and takedown procedure of the law, a copyright owner could notify the service provider, such as Google, requesting that a website or portion of a website be removed or blocked. If, upon receiving proper notification, the service provider promptly did so, it would be exempt from monetary liability.

Google regularly received such requests from copyright holders and those that represented them, such as the Walt Disney Company and the Recording Industry Association of America. Google produced and made public a list of the domain portions of URLs that had been the subject of a request for removal and noted which ones had been removed. As of July 2015, it had removed more than 600,000 URLs out of more than 2.4 million requests.[v]

Likewise, content on local versions of Google was also removed when required by national laws.

[iii] See http://www.google.com/insidesearch/howsearchworks/policies.html.

[iv] Information about Digital Millennium Copyright Act (DMCA) notice procedure is available at fosterinstitute.com/legal-forms/dmca-notice.

[v] Information about the removal process is available online at https://transparencyreport.google.com/copyright/overview.

(Continued)

(Continued)

For example, content that glorified the Nazi Party was illegal in Germany, and content that insulted religion was illegal in India.[vi] The respective governments, via a court order or a routine request as described previously, typically made these requests. Google reviewed these requests to determine if any content should be removed because it violated a specific country's law.

When Google removed content from search results for legal reasons, it first displayed a notification that the content had been removed and then reported the removal to www.chillingeffects.org, a website established by the Electronic Frontier Foundation and several law schools. The Chilling Effects database[vii] collected and analyzed legal complaints and requests for removal of a broad set of online materials. It was designed to help Internet users know their rights and understand the law. Researchers could use the data to study the prevalence of legal threats and the source of content removals. This database also allowed the public to search for specific takedown notifications.[47]

Google removed content quickly. Its average processing time across all copyright infringement removal requests submitted via its website was approximately six hours. Different factors influenced the processing time, including the method of delivery, language, and completeness of the information submitted.

The Lawsuit and Court Decision

The main focus of Costeja's complaint before the AEPD was his request that *La Vanguardia* remove the debt notice from its archives. In doing so, he was claiming his constitutional right to protect the integrity of his personal data. Costeja's request had two parts: that (1) *La Vanguardia* be required either to remove or alter the pages in question or to use certain tools made available by search engines in order to protect the data and (2) that Google Spain or Google Inc. be required to remove or conceal the personal data relating to him so that the data no longer appeared in search results.

In July 2010, just 2 months after Costeja's original request, the AEPD ordered Google Spain and Google Inc. to take "all reasonable steps to remove the disputed personal data from its index and preclude further access," upholding that part of the complaint.[viii] However, the AEPD rejected Costeja's complaint as it related to *La Vanguardia* because it considered that the publication of the information in question was legally justified.[48]

A year later, Google filed an appeal against the decision by the AEPD before the Audiencia Nacional in the highest national court in Madrid, Spain. In March 2012, this court referred the case to the European Court of Justice, the EU high court, for a preliminary ruling.[49]

In their briefs, Google Spain and Google Inc.'s argument hinged on the meaning of "personal data" and "crawling." Crawling, as noted previously, was the use of software programs to find multiple websites that responded to requests for information online.[ix] These programs were configured to look for information on the Internet, according to a set of criteria that told them where to go and when.[50] Once the relevant webpages had been copied and collected, their content was analyzed and indexed.[51] Google compared its search engine index to an index at the back of a textbook in that it included information about words and their locations.[x]

Specifically, Google argued before the European Court of Justice that because it crawled and indexed websites "indiscriminately" (that is, without a deliberate intent to process personal data as such), no processing of personal data within the meaning of

[vi] See https://www.google.com/insidesearch/how searchworks/policies.html.

[vii] Chilling Effects database underwent a name change in 2015 and is now known as Lumen.

[viii] Audiencia Nacional. Sala de lo Contencioso, Google Spain SL y Google Inc., S.L. c. Agencia de Protección de Datos, paragraph 1.2, at http://www.poderjudicial.es/search/doAction?action=contentpdf&databasematch=AN&reference=6292979 &links=%22725/2010%22&optimize=20120305&publicinterface=true.

[ix] See http://answers.google.com/answers/thread view/id/33696.html.

[x] More information about crawling is available online at http://www.google.com/intl/en/insidesearch/howsearchworks/crawling-indexing.html.

Article 2(b) of the EU Data Protection Directive 95/46 actually took place. This absence of intent, the company argued, clearly distinguished Google's activities as a search engine provider from the processing of personal data as interpreted by the court.

Google's other main argument was that the publisher of the information should be the sole controller of data, not the search engine. After all, its attorneys argued that Google's intervention was purely accessory in nature; it was merely making information published by others more readily accessible. If a publisher, for whatever reason, decided to remove certain information from its website, this information would (eventually) be removed from Google's index and would no longer appear in its search results. As a result, Google's counsel argued, the role of a search engine should be thought of as an "intermediary."

In May 2014, the European Court of Justice ruled against Google. The court found the Internet search provider was responsible for the processing of personal data that appeared on webpages published by third parties. It further required Google to remove links returned in search results based on an individual's name when those results were deemed to be "inadequate, irrelevant or no longer relevant, or excessive." At the heart of the court's logic was the process that Google used to produce its search results. The official ruling explained the court's rationale:

> The court points out in this context that processing of personal data carried out by such an operator enables any Internet user, when he makes a search on the basis of an individual's name, to obtain, through the list of results, a structured overview of the information relating to that individual on the internet. The court observes, furthermore, that this information potentially concerns a vast number of aspects of his private life and that, without the search engine, the information could not have been interconnected or could have been only with great difficulty.[xi]

In essence, the court ruled that an activity, "whether or not by automatic means," could be considered to be the "processing of personal data" within the meaning of Article 2(b), even if no intention to process such data existed.[52] The court's ruling applied to any search engine operators that had a branch or a subsidiary in any of the 28 member states of the EU.[53]

Costeja's lawyer, Joaquín Muñoz, was pleased with the ruling. "When you search for something in Google, they don't scour the entire Internet for you and then give you a result. They've stored links, organized them, and they show them based on a criteria they've decided upon."[54] As for Costeja, he expressed satisfaction with the result of his 4-year legal crusade. Speaking of the court's decision, he said, "I think this is the correct move. You have to provide a path for communication between the user and the search engine. Now that communication can take place."[55]

Google's Application of the Ruling

For its part, Google—although disappointed with the ruling—set about complying with it. Soon after the court decision, it removed Costeja's disputed information from its search results. But the company also took more general action.

The court's decision recognized Google as a data controller, or the operator of the search engine and the party responsible for its data. As such, the court said, Google was required to police its links and put into place a mechanism to address individual concerns. Accordingly, shortly after the ruling was announced, Google set up an online form for users (from the European Union only) to request the right to be forgotten. The company website stated that each request would be evaluated individually and that Google would attempt to "balance the privacy rights of the individual with the public's interest to know and the right to distribute information."[xii]

[xi] Court of Justice. Judgment in Case C-131/12 Google Spain SL, *Google Inc. v. Agencia Española de Protección de Datos, Mario Costeja González.*

[xii] See the Personal Information Removal Request Form at https://support.google.com/legal/contact/lr_eudpa?product=websearch.

[xii] See the European privacy requests search removals FAQs at http://www.google.com/transparencyreport/removals/europeprivacy/faq/?hl=en#how_does_googles_removals.

(Continued)

(Continued)

Once an individual had filled out the form, he or she received a confirmation. Each request was assessed on a case-by-case basis. Occasionally, Google would ask for more information from the individual. Once Google had made its decision, it notified the individual by e-mail, providing a brief explanation if the decision was against removal. If so, the individual could request that a local data protection authority review Google's decision.

In evaluating a request, Google looked at whether the results included outdated or inaccurate information about the individual. It also weighed whether or not the information was of public interest. For example, Google generally retained the information if it related to financial scams, professional malpractice, criminal convictions, or a government official's public conduct.[xiii]

At the same time, Google invited eight independent experts to form an advisory council expressly to "advise it on performing the balancing act between an individual's right to privacy and the public's interest in access to information."[56] The committee included three professors (two of law and one of ethics), a newspaper editorial director, a former government official, and three privacy and freedom of speech experts (including one from the United Nations). Google's CEO and chief legal officer served as conveners. The committee's job was to provide recommendations to Google on how to best implement the EU court's ruling.

The majority recommendation of the advisory council, published on February 6, 2015, was that the right to be forgotten ruling should apply only within the 28 countries in the European Union.[57] As a practical matter, this meant that Google was only required to apply removals to European domains, such as Google.fr or Google.co.uk, but not Google.com, even when accessed in Europe. Although over 95% of all queries originating in Europe used European domains, users could still access information that had been removed via the Google.com site.

The report also explained that once the information was removed, it was still available at the source site (e.g., the newspaper article about Costeja in *La Vanguardia*). Removal meant merely that its accessibility to the general public was reduced because searches for that information would not return a link to the source site. A person could still find the information, since only the link to the information had been removed, not the information itself.

The advisory council also recommended a set of criteria Google should use in assessing requests by individuals to "delist" their information (that is, to remove certain links in search results based on queries for that individual's name). How should the operator of the search engine best balance the privacy and data protection rights of the subject with the interest of the general public in having access to the information? The authors of the report felt that whether the data subject experienced harm from such accessibility to the information was relevant to this balancing test. Following this reasoning, they identified four primary criteria for evaluating delisting requests:

1. First, what was the data subject's role in public life? Did the individuals have a clear role in public life (CEOs, politicians, sports stars)? If so, this would weigh against delisting.

2. Second, what type of information was involved? Information that would normally be considered private (such as financial information, details of a person's sex life, or identification numbers) would weigh toward delisting. Information that would normally be considered to be in the public interest (such as data relevant to political discourse, citizen engagement, or governance) would normally weigh against delisting.

3. Third, what was the source of the information? Here, the report suggested that journalistic writing or government publications would normally not be delisted.

4. Finally, the report considered the effect of time, given that as circumstances change, the relevance of information might fade. Thus, the passage of time might favor delisting.

[xiii] See the European privacy requests search removals FAQs at http://www.google.com/transparencyreport/removals/europeprivacy/faq/?hl=en#how_does_googles_removals.

The advisory council also considered procedures and recommended that Google adopt an easily accessible and easy-to-understand form for data subjects to use in submitting their requests.

The recommendations of the advisory council were not unanimous. Jimmy Wales, the cofounder of Wikipedia and one of the eight group members, appended a dissenting comment to the report. "I completely oppose the legal situation in which a commercial company is forced to become the judge of our most fundamental rights of expression and privacy, without allowing any appropriate procedure for appeal by publishers whose work in being suppressed," Mr. Wales wrote. "The recommendations to Google contained in this report are deeply flawed due to the law itself being deeply flawed."[58]

Discussion Questions

1. In what ways has technology made it more difficult for individuals to protect their privacy?

2. Do you believe an individual should have the right to be forgotten—that is, to remove information about themselves from the Internet? If so, should this right be limited, and if so, how?

3. How does public policy with respect to individual privacy differ in the United States and Europe, and what explains these differences?

Critical Thinking

Google created an advisory council in 2009 to oversee the delisting of information, or the right to be forgotten. Its criteria included a set of four primary criteria mentioned in the case. Assume the role of an EU government official, and evaluate whether those criteria are still valid today. Would your position change if you were an official with the U.S. government, where Google is based? If you were a Google executive, how should you balance the privacy rights of the individual with the public's interest to know and the right to distribute information?

In considering these positions, think about whether Google, a public company, should be responsible for modifying its search results in response to individual requests. If so, what criteria should it use in doing so? Are there limits to the resources the company should be expected to use to comply with such requests?

Right to Erasure

Somewhat similarly, GDPR has a feature called the **right to erasure**, which means the data subject has the right to request erasure of personal data concerning him or her in certain circumstances (i.e., Article 17) with the company having 30 days to respond to a consumer request. GDPR has outlined a set of criteria for users of personal information. They are as follows:

right to erasure: A person's right to request erasure of personal data concerning him or her in certain circumstances.

- The processing is based on consent, and the data subject has withdrawn consent.

- The data subject objects to the processing, and there are no overriding legitimate grounds for the processing, or the data subject objects to the processing for direct marketing purposes.

- The personal data was processed unlawfully.

- Erasure is required for compliance with a legal obligation in the European Union or member state law to which the controller of the data is subject.

- The personal data have been collected in relation to the offer of information society services to a child.

These points were used as template for CCPA, which has a similar right to erasure article that states "a consumer shall have the right to request that a business delete any personal information about the consumer which the business has collected from the consumer."[59] Unlike GDPR, the company has 45 days to respond to consumer request under the CCPA.

How to Manage Erasure

With the enactment of these laws comes a manager's need to understand how to effectively honor the mandates. One of the main challenges is to manage consumers who are increasingly looking for products or services to be easy and fast to navigate but also intelligent.

For example, many consumers want and like the data tools to be able to learn their style, make suggestions, and even anticipate their next move or request. As discussed earlier, AI drives this ability.

This situation requires that companies consider how they can achieve this consumer desire without embedding AI-driven smart technology or "smarts." The first question for companies to ask themselves is whether this can be done without the collection of personal information at all.

This question is often achieved by two things:

1. Regularly tracking the behavior of the individual consumer

2. Extending this practice to aggregate the behaviors of all of the company's consumers to be able to offer suggestions and to continuously improve and enhance the consumers' experience[60]

Following these considerations, experts suggest the company determine if consumer tracking is, in fact, necessary for the service. If it is not, then consent may not be required. And if consent is not required, then it may be the case that the right to erasure would not apply. In the event the company's product or service does require the personal information in order to operate, the company can then consider aggregating to data to make sure it cannot be directly connected to a single person.[61] Aggregation involves developing overarching themes from the personal information without direct and personal identification.

Surveillance

Surveillance is becoming a central aspect of any society. It can take multiple forms—government, citizen, self, and corporate surveillance all play a role. The Pew Research Center has conducted polls on peoples' views of surveillance, and most are divided about what is acceptable. Most believe, however, it is acceptable to monitor others but not themselves (see Figure 14.3).[62]

Professor Saher Selod coined the term *radicalized surveillance* to refer to the hyper monitoring of bodies by relying on radical cues that include observable characteristics as well as culture attributes—like clothing, language, and nationality.[63] She and others have become concerned about its increasing deployment globally. Let's explore this phenomenon further.

Government surveillance is a global phenomenon as a number of countries place limits on the movement of persons in and out of countries. Some require certain people to register with a government entity prior to being granted the ability to travel. In the

government surveillance:
A global phenomenon as a number of countries place limits on the movement of persons in and out of countries.

Figure 14.3 American Beliefs About Surveillance

Most Americans believe it is acceptable to monitor others, except U.S. citizens

% of U.S. adults who say it is acceptable or unacceptable for the American government to monitor communications from . . .

	Acceptable	Unacceptable
American citizens	40%	57%
Citizens of other countries	54	44
American leaders	60	38
Leaders of other countries	60	37
Terrorism suspects	82	15

Source: Pew Research Center.

United States, the National Security Entry-Exit Registration System (NSEERS) requires noncitizen men from 25 countries to register with it in order to be cleared to enter or exit the United States. Of the 25, only one (North Korea) is not an ally of the United States. These men are required to be fingerprinted, photographed, and interrogated as part of the registration. NSEERS is used to create the country's no-fly list.

Governments have also intervened to restrict their citizens' access to information and various Internet and social media sites (e.g., China, North Korea, Pakistan, Iran, and Singapore). The intention is to suppress political dissent or certain ideological views. In France, following the terrorist attack in Paris, the government passed the Intelligence Act of July 24, 2015. The new law allowed the French government to access cell phones and computers as well as various Internet subscriber information. Similarly, the United States passed the Patriot Act in 2001 following the attacks on 9/11, allowing the FBI to search telephone, e-mail, and financial records without a court order. Following a lack of congressional approval, parts of the Patriot Act expired on June 1, 2015. With the passage on June 2, 2015, the expired parts were restored and renewed through 2019. However, Section 215 of the law was amended to stop the National Security Agency (NSA) from continuing its mass phone data collection program. Instead, phone companies will retain the data, and the NSA can obtain information about targeted individuals with permission from a federal court. Many governments seem to place a greater emphasis on using data to protect against perceived threats rather than protecting an individual's right to his or her personal information.

Citizen surveillance involves the province, city, or state putting the responsibility on the citizen to monitor their surroundings. An example is the "If you see something, say something" posters that are common in most any airport or public space globally. China's vast and unprecedented national surveillance system, built with help from its thriving technology industry, including well-known companies Alibaba and Baidu, is designed to rate the trustworthiness of its citizens by analyzing their social behaviors and collecting fiscal and government data. Its Social Credit System, which will be mandatory for Chinese

citizen surveillance: A province, city, or state puts the responsibility on the citizen to monitor their surroundings.

citizens' to participate in 2020, uses other people's information, personal identity, facial recognition, and robotic observations to produce a "citizen score."[64] Good behavior results in benefits such as people with high credit scores don't need to pay deposits when checking in at hotels and can obtain a visa to Europe more quickly than others.[65]

Citizen surveillance often results in self-surveillance—the act of keeping out of the line of sight on cameras—although that may be hard in China, which has some 200 million surveillance cameras.[66] Others have taken to wearing more colorful clothes, even colorful hijabs, or head covering worn by some Muslim women, to change the perception of one's self in the hopes of discrediting the radicalized surveillance.[67]

Finally, there is corporate surveillance. In many areas of the globe, companies have the right to monitor employee e-mails at work. On the one hand, businesses need to ensure the time employees spend on the job is productive, since wasting time can result in significant economic losses. On the other hand, there are aspects of an employees' life that should remain private even though the company needs to store and use this information (e.g., government issued identification numbers, driver's license numbers, or even someone's marital status).

Another aspect of corporate surveillance is data companies—Alibaba, Choicepoint, Google, Facebook—selling information or products to a government in an effort to keep watch on its citizens. It is big business for many. Companies like Rohde & Schwarz, Evolv Technologies, and Liberty Defense use millimeter technology to provide full body scans of airport travelers. Using AI to analyze images, screeners can "see" through clothes, ignore skin, and red-flag suspicious shapes and objects.[68] However, Marc Rotenberg, president of the Electronic Privacy Information Center, says these machines invade peoples' privacy and feels that organizations like the Transportation Security Administration (TSA) do not understand peoples' dislike of them.[69] Winning these government contracts can be very lucrative for the data company.

self-surveillance: The act of keeping out of the line of sight on cameras.

corporate surveillance: A company's right to monitor employee e-mails at work.

KEY TAKEAWAYS

Right to be Forgotten, Right to Erasure, and Surveillance

- Because personal information is important to protect, a host of mandates have been put forth globally, such as the right to be forgotten and the right to erasure.

- The practice of surveillance has become widespread with some countries doing so in order to gain economic and social control over their citizenry.

WHAT CAN MANAGERS DO?

LO 14.4   Explain the various best practices of personal data that managers need to be aware of.

There are a number of precautions managers can take with regard to minimizing the negative impacts of managing personal data. In this section, we explore various best practices offered by governments, industry, and consulting groups.

Best Practices

While companies themselves stress best practices, other organizations do so as well. For example, the Computer Ethics Institute (CEI) serves as a resource for identifying, assessing, and responding to ethical issues associated with the advancement of information technologies in society. It created the "Ten Commandments of Computer Ethics" to serve as a guide for both companies and individuals; the list has been translated into over a dozen languages (see Figure 14.4).[70]

The FTC offers a best practice guide for businesses in how to protect personal information. On a fundamental level, the FTC acknowledges that in today's technologically driven environment, most companies keep sensitive personal information—names, Social Security numbers, credit card, or other account data—that identifies customers or employees. According to the FTC, a sound data security plan is built on five key principles (see Figure 14.5).[71]

Risk Mitigation

According to Andrew Shaxted, senior director of FTI Consulting Inc., a global business advisory firm, companies must employ organizational governance at multiple levels by

---

Figures 14.4   Ten Commandments of Computer Ethics

Providing a moral compass for the ocean of information technology

1. Thou Shalt Not Use a Computer To Harm Other People.

2. Thou Shalt Not Interfere With Other People's Computer Work.

3. Thou Shalt Not Snoop Around in Other People's Computer Files.

4. Thou Shalt Not Use a Computer To Steal.

5. Thou Shalt Not Use a Computer To Bear False Witness.

6. Thou Shalt Not Copy or Use Proprietary Software for Which You Have Not Paid.

7. Thou Shalt Not Use Other People's Computer Resources Without Authorization or Proper Compensation.

8. Thou Shalt Not Appropriate Other People's Intellectual Output.

9. Thou Shalt Think About the Social Consequences of the Program You Are Writing or the System You Are Designing.

10. Thou Shalt Always Use a Computer in Ways That Insure Consideration and Respect For Your Fellow Humans.

**Computer Ethics Institute • 1388 17th Street NW • Suite 215 • Washington DC 2044E 202-29156-7147
E-mail: info@Pcomputerethicsinstitute.org**

Source: Ramon C. Barquin, PhD, Computer Ethics Institute, Washington, DC (www.computerethics institute.org)

Note: The Ten Commandments of Computer Ethics was first presented in Dr. Ramon C. Barquin's paper, "In Pursuit of a 'Ten Commandments' for Computer Ethics."

Figure 14.5   Key Principles of Data Security

1. **TAKE STOCK.** Know what personal information you have in your files and on your computers.

2. **SCALE DOWN.** Keep only what you need for your business.

3. **LOCK IT.** Protect the information that you keep.

4. **PITCH IT.** Properly dispose of what you no longer need.

5. **PLAN AHEAD.** Create a plan to respond to security incidents.

Source: Federal Trade Commission.

creating three levels of security: (1) an incident response group, as a first line of defense; (2) an identity and access working group; and (3) a policy and governance working group so that data privacy and risk protection are properly controlled and implemented throughout the business.[72]

Increasingly, these working groups make presentations to the board of directors, with cybersecurity one of the top issues in corporate governance today. Spencer Stuart, a global executive search and board advisory firm, noted in a recent survey that corporate boards are grappling with how to ensure that the risks and opportunities emerging from a diverse set of digital forces—ranging from AI, automation, and robotics to cybersecurity, data science, and e-commerce—are fully understood by directors and factored into a business's strategy. The report notes many boards are considering adding a board member with digital expertise.[73]

Privacy Policies

Although company privacy policies are extraordinarily common, they still serve an important role in personal information protection. Privacy policies outline the situation between a company and its consumers and serves as the organization's top-level privacy document. According to European Union's GDPR Knowledge Database, the key elements of a sound privacy policy are the following:[74]

- *Purpose of the policy:* Begin with a statement about why this policy is being used and its importance for the company (i.e., the company's privacy vision).

- *Definitions of key terms:* Next, define key terms like *personal data*, *privacy*, and s*ecurity* for the company. This chapter defines these terms, and the GDPR legislation offers a glossary for additional help.

- *Principles and purposes of processing:* It's important to define the company's protocol for processing personal data as well as why and when personal data can be processed. Make sure to list the key requirements in order to be compliant with the policy.

- *Key roles and their responsibilities:* Lastly, define the set of stakeholders necessary for compliance with the policy and their specific roles and responsibilities.

Use Protocols

Many experts agree that companies must take the time to establish protocol for handling customer data and customer requests for erasure. First, managers need a continuous and careful review of its reasons for the retention of personal information and create a records' retention schedule, taking great care to document the business justifications for a given retention period. Second, firms need to ensure personal information is being deleted regularly according to the retention schedule—and to be consistent in the reasons the company provides for similar consumer requests for erasure. Third, firms should review the business processes involving personal information and determine systematically when deletion is required by law.

What Can Managers Do?

- Managers have options like best practice, privacy policies, risk mitigation, and use protocols for helping to protect personal data.

- Individuals, companies, and governments all play an important role in proper use and protection of personal information, and each party requires diligence and care.

KEY TAKEAWAYS

SUMMARY

Both privacy and security, and their interconnectedness, continue to be an important management issue. Organizations need to spend considerable time determining the best way to use, store, and reuse personal information. Multiple mandates exist around the world governing certain rights to one's personal information. In this chapter, we focus on several issues resulting from government surveillance: the right to be forgotten and the right to erasure.

KEY TERMS

artificial intelligence (AI) 318
biometric data 338
citizen surveillance 333
corporate surveillance 334
datification 320

government surveillance 332
opt in 321
opt out 320
privacy 316
right to be forgotten 323

right to erasure 331
right to privacy 319
security 316
self-surveillance 334

1. What are the differences and similarities of privacy and security? What is a right to privacy?

2. Who bears the responsibility for protecting personal information? The individual? The company? The government?

3. What is the GDPR law? What laws exist in the United States to protect privacy?

4. What is surveillance, and what types of surveillance are typically employed?

5. What is the right to be forgotten? The right to erasure?

6. How can companies and individuals be mindful of these in their daily life?

MANAGER'S CHALLENGE

14.1: Biometric Data, Ethics, and the Law

You are the regional manager for a large parent company that manages multiple day care centers for children, which is called WeeCare. Your boss thinks it's both secure and cool to use biometric data for employees when they clock in for work each day. By requiring employees to sign in for work through fingerprint or retinal data—so-called biometric data—our boss can easily track employees as they arrive to and leave from work. Such a practice is becoming a mainstream way to verify employee hours and check workers in and out of facilities for security reasons. According to a recent *Wall Street Journal* article, among companies in the United States, Europe, and Canada surveyed in 2018 by Gartner Research, 6% said they track employees by using biometric data.

Some of your employees have shown outright frustration for this new process, given it can take longer if the fingerprint is not readable, while others are concerned about what WeeCare is going to do with their personal information data.[75]

The relevant law is the Biometric Information Privacy Act (Public Act 095-994; BIPA). BIPA imposes requirements on companies that collect bibliometric data.[76] Specifically, BIPA regulates the privacy and protection of biometric information (which is defined by the statute as a retina or iris scan, fingerprint, voiceprint, or scan of hand or face geometry). Under BIPA, companies that collect this information are generally required to inform the individual that his or her biometric information is going to be collected; indicate the purpose of the collection; describe the length of time the biometric information is to be collected, stored, and used; develop a written, publicly available policy that establishes a retention schedule; and obtain a written release from the individual before collecting any biometric data or sharing collected biometric data with a third party. See http://www.ilga.gov/legislation/ilcs/ilcs3.asp?ActID=3004&ChapterID=57.

Framing Questions

1. How can you get your employees to use the biometric system of check in? What arguments would you include?

2. How would you speak to the ethics and the legalities of this situation?

Assignment

As regional manager, write a memo to your employees to explain the benefits of the new process and address the concerns they have as well. Restate the issue or problem they see, the rationale for the company's preferred policy, and a call to action (i.e., what you would like to see happen next) to conclude the memo.

14.2: Safety or Ethics?

You are an airline executive, and you are reviewing your company's boarding procedure. As discussed previously, in the United States, you are fully aware of NSEERS, which requires noncitizen men from 25 countries to register with it in order to be cleared to enter or exit the United States. These men are required to be fingerprinted, photographed, and interrogated as part of the registration. NSEERS is used to create the country's no-fly list. You are also well versed in the SPOT program—Screening of Passengers by Observation Techniques—which sometimes occurs at the gate as people are boarding. You rely on your gate ticket agents to use SPOT as well as to keep the line moving so the plane can leave on time. You've increasingly received complaints from gate agents and passengers alike that the SPOT program is discriminatory. You and others wonder if the screening should continue to be based on language, clothing, or skin color. Or should there be a different basis for making these decisions?

Framing Questions

1. How do people judge something as discriminatory? As preserving safety?

2. What type of surveillance is this?

Assignment

Write a memo to the CEO addressing the arguments for preserving passenger and crew safety that is also sensitive to the law and the ethics of profiling passengers. What arguments would you include? How will you convince your team one way or another?

> biometric data: Retina or iris scans, fingerprints, voiceprints, or scans of hand or face geometry.

CORPORATE PERSONHOOD

Learning Objectives

Upon completion of this chapter, the reader should be able to do the following:

15.1 State the concept and development of corporate personhood, and assess its implications for business and society.

15.2 Explain the regulation of business by Congress through the Commerce Clause.

15.3 Identify Congress's power to regulate business through the Tax and Spend Clause.

Ethics in Context

Sin Taxes

Congress has the power to regulate business through the Tax and Spend Clause. Congress can also regulate people by imposing taxes on a business, especially when that business sells tobacco products, e-cigarettes, or soda.

Should the government tax businesses to encourage us to make better decisions? Is that an effective strategy to get people to make healthier choices? Later in the chapter, in the Ethics in Context section, we will explore the ethical implications of sin taxes.

iStockphoto.com/Ta Nu

INTRODUCTION

The Constitution is probably not the first thing that comes to mind when one thinks of business. We have already seen the impact of different amendments, such as the First Amendment, on our individual rights and on business. One of the many goals of our Founding Fathers was to create a government that could raise money without stifling innovation and growth. We can see this in the Commerce Clause and the Tax and Spend Clause in the Constitution. And that makes sense: Regulating commerce between states and laying and collecting taxes are powers of the federal government that directly impact businesses. More recently, businesses have been embarking on strategies that involve rights and values more traditionally reserved for human beings, like the right to free speech, expanding their role as citizens in our society. In Chapter 2 on corporate social responsibility (CSR), we explored the role corporations play in the environments where they operate. Here, we look at the evolving role of corporations in society more broadly.

CORPORATE PERSONHOOD

LO 15.1 State the concept and development of corporate personhood, and assess its implications for business and society.

In Chapter 1, you learned that corporations have duties to their shareholders and that a corporation is a separate legal entity. But does a corporation have rights like people? The idea of **corporate personhood**, a corporation as a person with similar rights and values, has long existed in America despite corporations never being mentioned in the Constitution as being part of "we the people." In 2011, then presidential candidate Mitt Romney told people at the Iowa State Fair that "corporations are people, my friend."[1] The next year, former GE CEO Jack Welch and his wife Suzy explained in a *Wall Street Journal* opinion piece that "of course corporations are people. What else would they be? Buildings don't hire people. Buildings don't design cars that run on electricity."[2]

> **corporate personhood:** The idea that a corporation is viewed as a person with similar rights and values.

Whether a corporation has rights similar to people is a debate that dates back to the 19th century to a case called *Santa Clara County v. S. Pac. R. Co.*[3] In that case, the railroad was protesting state taxes under the Fourteenth Amendment's Equal Protection Clause. The Equal Protection Clause was adopted in 1868 to grant emancipated slaves full citizenship: "No state shall . . . deprive any person of life, liberty, or property without due process of law, nor deny to any person . . . the equal protection of the laws."[4] The theory of corporate personhood, the legitimacy of which is disputed by historians, was that in drafting the Fourteenth Amendment, Congress specifically used the word *person* rather than *citizen* so as to include corporations within the protections of the amendment.[5] The Court in *Santa Clara County* accepted that argument. However, over the years not all justices have agreed with this theory. In 1819 Supreme Court chief justice Marshall described a corporation as "an artificial being, invisible, intangible, and existing only in contemplation of law" yet able to effect the "charitable or other useful . . . goals of their creators."[6] In 1986, Chief Justice Rehnquist explained that "to ascribe to such artificial entities [corporations] an 'intellect' or 'mind' for freedom of conscience purposes is to confuse metaphor with reality."[7]

Nevertheless, over time the *Santa Clara County* decision has been relied upon to bestow rights on corporations that look increasingly like the rights we human beings are afforded in the Constitution. For example, in the 1970s in *Belotti v. First National Bank of Boston*, the Supreme Court struck down a Massachusetts law that banned for-profit corporate spending to influence ballot referenda. The Court stated that the corporate identity of the speaker did not deprive it of First Amendment rights. Importantly, in *Belotti* the Court stated this protection did not apply to corporate spending in elections because of the very real danger of corruption. The dissent cautioned against giving corporations the same rights as people and warned that they could overwhelm elections with massive spending.

How *Citizens United* and *Hobby Lobby* Shaped the Corporate Personhood Debate

Two contemporary U.S. Supreme Court cases have expanded the rights of for-profit corporations. Although corporations have enjoyed certain constitutional rights such as freedom to contract and due process, among others, it wasn't until 2010 when the U.S. Supreme Court decided *Citizens United v. The Federal Election Commission* that the public began to take notice. *Citizens United* was the first of three cases that gave new shape and definition to the question of whether corporations can have rights and values similar to people and more importantly, what that could mean for regular people every day.

Before the 2008 presidential primary elections, Citizens United (CU), a nonprofit group, produced a documentary titled *Hillary: The Movie*. The movie was critical of Hillary Clinton's time in service to the United States both as a senator and as first lady. CU had planned to run television ads promoting the movie before the Democratic National Convention and in anticipation of a Clinton nomination, before the presidential election. However, campaign laws threatened to shut the movie down before it opened: The Bipartisan Campaign Reform Act (BCRA) of 2002 restricts using general corporate funds to broadcast electioneering communications in order to sway how a viewer should vote. The law also requires disclosure of the identities of those who contributed more than $1,000 toward the production of the electioneering communication.

CU claimed the regulations violated their First Amendment right to free speech. The Federal Election Commission, on the other hand, claimed the restrictions were constitutional because they were related to the compelling government interest of preventing fraud in elections and protecting the public interest in transparency in the democratic process.

The U.S. Supreme Court, in a 5–4 decision, found for CU. The majority reaffirmed that "speech is an essential mechanism of democracy, for it is the means to hold officials accountable to the people." Corporations have long possessed First Amendment protections, which include protection for political speech. The Court explained that political speech does not lose protection simply because the speaker is a corporation: "The identity of the speaker is not decisive in determining whether speech is protected." Like people, corporations contribute to the discussion and debate in the marketplace of ideas that the First Amendment protects. The dissent saw things differently. In the context of democratic elections "the distinction between corporate and human speakers is significant" because corporations "cannot vote or run for office . . . and because they may be managed by nonresidents, their interests may conflict in fundamental respects with the interests of eligible voters." Regulating speech based on the identity of the speaker is nothing new; courts have recognized limits on the speech of public school students, prisoners, members of the armed forces, foreigners, and government employees. According to the dissent, here the speakers "are not natural persons, much less members of our political community"; they "have no consciences, no beliefs, no feelings, no thoughts, no desires . . . they are not themselves members of 'We the People' by whom and for whom our Constitution was established." Figure 15.1 illustrates the path of money in elections. The role of political action committees (PACs) and super PACs ensures an unlimited source of funds without having to reveal the identity of the donors. Because of *Citizens United*, corporations have similar rights as people to contribute and can donate money to PACs without revealing the identity of the donors.

Perhaps the most controversial case to date in the trend of "enabling corporate entities to assume an increasing number of personal attributes and liberties"[9]

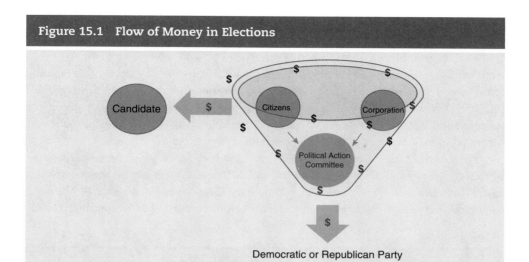

Figure 15.1   Flow of Money in Elections

Candidate

Citizens

Corporation

Political Action Committee

Democratic or Republican Party

is *Burwell v. Hobby Lobby*,[i] decided by the U.S. Supreme Court in 2014. This case involves the Patient Protection and Affordable Care Act, or Affordable Care Act (ACA) contraceptive mandate: Employers with 50 or more full-time employees must offer health insurance coverage that provides preventive care and screenings for women, including all Food and Drug Administration (FDA)-approved contraceptives, free of charge. Both Conestoga Wood and Hobby Lobby are closely held corporations owned and run by religious families. The companies objected on religious grounds to mandatory coverage of certain contraceptives that prevent an already fertilized egg from developing. They sued, claiming the coverage mandate violated their rights under the **Religious Freedom Restoration Act (RFRA)**, which prohibits the "government [from] substantially burdening a person's exercise of religion."[10] The government contended that neither the corporation nor the owners could sue under the RFRA because they are for-profit businesses, and although the owners may be religious, the law provides exemptions only for religious organizations like churches and other houses of worship.

The Court found for Hobby Lobby and Conestoga Wood. As closely held businesses, they were entitled to the religious protection guaranteed by the RFRA. Because the RFRA protects "persons," Congress meant to include corporations because "person" includes, among other things, "corporations, companies, [and] associations."[11] A corporation "is simply a form of organization used by human beings to achieve desired ends . . . when rights, whether constitutional or statutory, are extended to corporations, the purpose is to protect the rights of these people." As a result, the ACA requirement that businesses cover contraceptives that prohibit development of a fertilized egg imposes a substantial burden on the companies' exercise of religion because doing so violates the "sincerely held religious beliefs of the companies' owners."

The dissent warned that "closely held is not synonymous with 'small' . . . [and] Hobby Lobby's case demonstrates that RFRA claims are indeed pursued by large corporations employing thousands of persons of different faiths whose ownership is not diffuse." Moreover,

> **Religious Freedom Restoration Act (RFRA):** Prohibits the government from substantially burdening a person's exercise of religion.

---

[i] In order to resolve inconsistent circuit decisions, the U.S. Supreme Court agreed to hear two cases: *Hobby Lobby v. Sebelius*, 723 F.3d 1114 (10th Cir. 2013) and *Conestoga Wood Specialties Corp. v. Secretary of the U.S. Department of Health and Human Services*, 724 F3d. 377 (3d Cir. 2013).

no decision of the Supreme Court has recognized a for-profit corporation's "qualification for a religious exemption from a generally applicable law." The reason for this makes sense: "Religious organizations exist to foster the interests of persons subscribing to the same religious faith." For-profit corporations, on the other hand, are operated by workers not typically of the same religion, and they use labor to make a profit rather than spread their religious beliefs. By law, workers' religious beliefs cannot be part of the employment relationship in a for-profit business. Thus, to allow a religion-based exemption to a for-profit employer would "operat[e] to impose the employer's religious faith on the employees."[12]

The Court in *Citizens United* made it clear that corporations have First Amendment rights when it comes to political speech and money, and in *Hobby Lobby* we learned they could exercise religion. In the Law and Society 15.1 section, the Court addresses the issue of whether a corporation can assume the racial identity of its owner for purposes of a discrimination claim.

LAW AND SOCIETY 15.1

Race and Corporations: *Carnell Construction Corp. v. Danville Redevelopment & Housing Authority*, 745 F.3d 703 (2014)

Facts: The town of Danville, Virginia, wanted to build a large, low-income housing complex. The project was funded in part by a $20 million grant from the U.S. Department of Housing and Urban Development. The Danville Redevelopment & Housing Authority (DRHA) solicited bids for construction, and Carnell submitted a bid, representing itself as a certified minority business enterprise because its owner is African American. Carnell won the bid and entered into a contract with DRHA to clear the project site. As work progressed, both parties became dissatisfied with the other's performance, and the relationship soured. Carnell complained of racial discrimination to the DRHA director, claiming Carnell was "being singled out as a minority contractor," and was "expected to work . . . for free" on "excessive" project changes. After attempts to resolve the conflict failed, DRHA informed Carnell they would not renew its contract for work on the project and Carnell was to remove its equipment and employees from the work site by the following month.

Carnell complied and requested reimbursement for instances of unpaid work, but DRHA refused, and Carnell sued, alleging racial discrimination in terminating the contract. DRHA claimed that Carnell could not sue for racial discrimination in terminating the contract because as a corporation, Carnell did not have a "race, color, or national origin" and thus was not protected by the antidiscrimination laws.

Issue: Can a corporation acquire the racial identity of its owner and sue for race discrimination?

Decision: Yes, a corporation can assume the racial identity of its owner for purposes of a race discrimination claim. Because our Court has never addressed this issue, we look to other federal appellate courts that have considered the question and have allowed race discrimination claims brought on behalf of minority-owned businesses to move forward. The law states that "no person" shall be subjected to discrimination based on race, color, or national origin in any program receiving federal funding. "Person" includes corporations. It would be inconsistent to deny Carnell the right to sue on the grounds that it "has no racial identity and therefore cannot be the direct target of discrimination" but at the same time allow shareholders of a corporation to sue for an injury to the corporation and not to them. If a corporation is certified under state law as a minority owned enterprise, then the racial identity of its owner can be imputed to the corporation and the corporation can move forward with a discrimination claim separate and apart from its minority owner.

Law and Management Questions

1. If a corporation can assume the racial identity of its owner, what other characteristics of its owner might it be able to assume? Can you describe a situation similar to Carnell where the owner is a woman? What was the result?

2. How might attributing a religion or race to a corporation limit the growth potential of that company? Expand its growth potential? Which do you think is more likely and why?

Public Accommodation

Although businesses seem to be attaining rights more similar to we human beings, businesses are in business to make money. A business is considered a **place of public accommodation** if it sells its goods or services to the public, which means most places where we live our lives that are not home are considered places of public accommodation. The coffee shop you stopped at before class, the movie theater you went to last weekend, and your dentist's office are all places of public accommodation. Federal and state laws require places of public accommodation to offer their goods and services equally to all members of the public. Many state laws prohibit discrimination in public accommodations based on categories such as race, religion, and gender. Only Alabama, Georgia, Mississippi, North Carolina, and Texas do not have public accommodation laws for nondisabled people. Twenty-two states prohibit discrimination in public accommodations based on sexual orientation.

> **place of public accommodation:** A business that sells goods or services to the public.

CASE STUDY 15.1

Public Accommodations and the First Amendment: Can Business Be Art?

The U.S. Supreme Court tells us in the *Hobby Lobby* case that under certain circumstances, a business can assume the religion of its owners. And public accommodation laws prohibit businesses from discriminating in the provision of goods or services. For a business in Colorado, the Masterpiece Cakeshop, the owner's religion and public accommodation laws collided.

Jack Phillips owns Masterpiece Cakeshop. The bakery offers a variety of baked goods for sale from cookies and brownies to elaborate custom-made cakes. Phillips, a devout Christian, has owned and operated the bakery for 24 years. In 2012 Charlie Craig and Dave Mullins visited the Masterpiece Cakeshop to order a cake for the men's upcoming wedding. Phillips explained to the couple that he did not "create" wedding cakes for same-sex weddings but would make them birthday cakes, shower cakes, or sell them cookies or brownies. Phillips said that he does not create wedding cakes for same-sex weddings because of his religious opposition to same-sex marriage. He felt that to create a cake for something that directly conflicted with his religion would be an endorsement of the relationship and participation in the ceremony.

The men filed a complaint with the Colorado Civil Rights Commission, claiming that Phillips's refusal to serve them violated the Colorado Anti-Discrimination Act (CADA). CADA prohibits discrimination based on, among other things, sexual orientation in the "full and equal enjoyment of the goods, services, facilities, privileges, advantages, or accommodations of a place of public accommodation." Both the administrative law judge and

(Continued)

(Continued)

the Colorado Civil Rights Commission found that Phillips had refused to sell weddings cakes to six other same-sex couples on the same basis as his refusal to sell to Craig and Mullins, and his refusal to sell to Craig and Mullins violated CADA. In his appeal, Phillips claimed that applying CADA this way would require him to create a cake for a same-sex wedding, which violates his First Amendment right to free speech by compelling him to exercise his artistic talent to express a message with which he did not agree. Moreover, requiring him to create a cake for a same-sex wedding would violate his right to the free exercise of religion, which is also protected by the First Amendment. When the appeals court upheld the decision of the Civil Rights Commission, Phillips asked the U.S. Supreme Court to hear his case.

The Supreme Court confirmed that gay persons and gay couples must be able to exercise their freedom on terms equal to others in society and this equality must be given great weight. So, too, must religious views. The Court stated religious objections do not allow a business to deny protected persons equal access to goods and services under a religion-neutral public accommodations law like CADA. However, according to the Supreme Court, the Colorado Civil Rights Commission did not enforce CADA in a religion-neutral manner in Phillips's case. At several points during the commission hearings, commissioners made clear their view that religious beliefs should not be present in business or in public life. The commissioner stated that freedom of religion has been used throughout history to justify all kinds of discrimination from slavery to the Holocaust. This, according to the commissioner, was "one of the most despicable pieces of rhetoric that people can use—to use their religion to hurt others." These comments, according to the Supreme Court, were inappropriate and disparaging, showing a lack of concern for Phillips's free exercise rights and describing his religious beliefs as merely rhetorical, insubstantial, even insincere. The role of Colorado's Civil Rights Commission is as a fair and neutral enforcement body of Colorado's antidiscrimination laws. These statements, said the Court, cast doubt on the fairness and impartiality of the commission in deciding the complaint.

As further evidence, the Court pointed to three cases similar to Masterpiece Cakeshop that came before the commission but had different outcomes. In those cases, the commission considered the refusal of bakers to create cakes with images that conveyed disapproval of same-sex marriages, along with religious text. In each case, the commission found that the bakers did not violate CADA in refusing service because the requested cakes included words and images the bakers deemed derogatory. However, in Phillips's case, the commission said that any words or images on Craig and Mullins's cake would be attributed to the couple, not to the bakery. Moreover, the commission found it relevant that in each of the three cases the bakers were willing to sell the customer other products, including those with Christian themes, but it dismissed Phillips's willingness to sell birthday cakes, shower cakes, cookies, or brownies to gay and lesbian couples as irrelevant. Because Phillips did not receive a fair and neutral hearing at the Colorado Civil Rights Commission, the Court reversed the decision of the Colorado Court of Appeals.

But what about the art? In *Masterpiece Cakeshop*, the Supreme Court never decided whether making a wedding cake was a form of protected expression or what would happen if that protected expression collided with public accommodation laws. It may get another chance with Sweetcakes by Melissa. Melissa and Aaron Klein, both Christians, owned Sweetcakes by Melissa in Gresham, Oregon. Unlike Masterpiece Cakeshop, Sweetcakes by Melissa only sold custom-ordered cakes; it did not sell other baked goods. Each cake was a product of a lengthy consultation with the engaged couple after which Melissa would make a sketch based on the couple's preferences, styles, and themes. In 2013, Rachel Cryer and her mother went to Sweetcakes by Melissa to order a cake for Rachel's wedding. When Aaron asked for the names of the bride and groom, Rachel told him it was for two brides. Aaron apologized and said that because of their religious beliefs, he and his wife could not make a custom-designed cake for that purpose. Rachel and her wife, Laurel Bowman, filed a complaint alleging the Kleins' refusal to serve them based on their sexual orientation violated public accommodation laws.

To the Kleins, their cakes were artistic expressions; therefore, they argued, under the First Amendment they could not be compelled to use their artistic talent for an expression with which they do not agree. The Oregon Court of Appeals found that the Kleins' wedding cakes are the result of a collaborative process and are not original art; they are based on customer preferences and ongoing dialogue together with Melissa's designs and judgment as inspiration. The process is not simply the Kleins executing precise instructions from their customers, nor is it an original creation. It is not enough that the Kleins believe their cakes are fundamentally pieces of art; First Amendment protection also involves how it will be perceived and experienced by others. Their cakes, even though custom made, are meant to be eaten, and the Kleins did not present to the court any evidence to show that people attending a wedding would think any wedding cake that the Kleins would create was art rather than food.

Given that the Kleins' business did not involve fully protected expression because their work was a combination of original expression and someone else's expression, the court had to determine whether the public accommodations law furthered a government interest important enough to justify an incidental burden on speech. If it did, then an incidental burden on First Amendment rights would be tolerated as long as the burden was no more than what was necessary. The U.S. Supreme Court has consistently held that states have a compelling interest in ensuring equal access to goods and services and in preventing the indignity of discrimination. The Oregon court stated that Oregon law is focused on ensuring equal access to products like wedding cakes when a seller chooses to sell them to the general public; it is not focused on the design

or decoration of the cake. Thus, the court found that the Kleins violated Oregon public accommodation laws when they refused to sell a cake to Rachel Cryer. In October 2018, the Kleins asked the U.S. Supreme Court to hear their case, and in June 2019, the U.S. Supreme Court vacated the decision of the Oregon Court of Appeals and remanded back to that court to consider the case again in light of the Supreme Court's decision in *Masterpiece Cakeshop*.

Discussion Questions

1. If the U.S. Supreme Court takes the Kleins' case and then decides a custom-made cake is art protected by the First Amendment, can you think of other industries, businesses, goods, or services that could be considered art that also would be entitled to protection?

2. Based on your answer to Question 1, what impact might First Amendment protection have on the business and the public as a place of public accommodation?

Critical Thinking

In his concurrence in *Masterpiece Cakeshop*, Justice Thomas argued the case is not about religion and should be decided purely on First Amendment speech grounds. In their dissent, Justices Ginsburg and Sotomayor argued that there was no evidence an objective observer thinks wedding cakes convey a message of the baker. If the Klein case gets to the U.S. Supreme Court, identify and explain two arguments why the case should be decided based just on speech and two arguments why religion should also factor into the decision. Then identify facts to explain the dissent's point that reasonable observers do not consider a wedding cake to be the speech of the baker.

We first read about the Americans with Disabilities Act (ADA) in Chapter 9 regarding employees with disabilities. The ADA also requires that places of public accommodation be accessible to those with disabilities and legal challenges. Typically the focus has been on accessibility to physical spaces: stores, public restrooms, restaurants, and the like. Resolution of these issues may involve physical solutions like lower countertops, elevators, and ramps.

Most stores also have an online presence. In fact, traditional retail's e-commerce grew faster (8–12%) than brick-and-mortar sales (2.8%) in the first quarter of 2017. The Starbucks mobile app is so popular it accounts for almost 30% of total sales at rush hour.[13]

We know a Starbucks coffee shop is a place of public accommodation, but what about the app? Businesses as varied as Warby Parker, Domino's Pizza, Winn-Dixie, and Harvard University have been sued for allegedly not having ADA accessible websites or apps. Since January 2015, at least 750 lawsuits have been filed on this issue. As varied as the businesses being sued, so, too, are the court decisions on this issue. Courts are split on whether a commercial website qualifies as a place of public accommodation.

CASE STUDY 15.2

Is A Website a Place of Public Accommodation?

In 2017 a California man sued Domino's Pizza, claiming the Domino's website and mobile app could not be accessed by people who were blind or of low vision and used screen reader software. Because of this, the man could not access the menu and other apps within the site. Although the ADA was passed before the advent of e-commerce, regulations from the U.S. Department of Justice (DOJ; one of the federal agencies that enforces the ADA) could provide guidance on whether websites are places of public accommodation. The court said that because the DOJ had not issued regulations specifically addressing website accessibility under the ADA, it would violate Domino's due process rights to find them in violation of the law for conduct the government hasn't yet determined violates the law.

That same year, a Florida court ruled that grocery store chain Winn-Dixie violated the ADA because its website was not accessible to the visually impaired. Although customers could not buy groceries through the website, they could obtain coupons and link them to discount cards used in the stores, refill prescriptions for in-store pick-up, and find store locations. Thus, according to the court, Winn-Dixie's website was heavily integrated with its physical store locations and must meet accessibility standards.

Harvard University and MIT were sued for failing to provide adequate closed-captioning in their online lectures, courses, and other educational materials on sites like YouTube, iTunes U, and their shared nonprofit edX that offers dozens of massive open online courses (MOOCs) free to the public. In 2016 a Massachusetts federal court ruled that providing adequate closed-captioning would not require a change to the schools' existing service or program but instead would allow "meaningful access" to the service Harvard and MIT offers the public.

In the Harvard case, the plaintiffs were not claiming Harvard's website was a place of public accommodation. Rather, they were claiming that Harvard is a place of public accommodation and its websites are benefits or services offered by Harvard to the public. The California court in the Domino's case made a similar point: The ADA must be narrowly construed to apply only to websites with a connection to a brick-and-mortar presence.

Courts are split on whether the ADA applies to all websites or just those associated with a physical location. For example, in 2010 Melissa Earll, who is deaf, could not successfully register with eBay as a seller in eBay's marketplace because the registration process included a telephone verification. Ms. Earll repeatedly communicated with eBay via e-mail and chat explaining her difficulty but could not register as a seller using alternative verification. Ms. Earll sued claiming eBay's seller verification system violated the ADA because it was unusable by the hearing impaired. The California court ruled that a place of public accommodation must include some connection between the good or service and an actual physical place. Because eBay's services are not connected to an actual physical place, eBay is not a place of public accommodation.

Yet, in Massachusetts a case against Netflix ended differently. In that case Lee Nettles, who is deaf, claimed that Netflix provided closed captioning for only a small portion of the titles available on its streaming service Watch Instantly. Nettles also claimed the small number of films that are captioned are not categorized the same way as uncaptioned films, making it impossible for deaf or hard of hearing people to use Netflix's personalized film recommendations. The court agreed with Nettles' claim that Watch Instantly falls within one of several ADA-listed places of public accommodation, such as "place of exhibition and entertainment," "place of recreation," "sales and rental establishment," and "service establishment" because providing subscription service Internet-based streaming is like operating a video rental store. Moreover, applicable case law established that a place of public accommodation is not limited to an actual structure. Nor did the court agree with Netflix's argument that Watch Instantly could not be a place of public accommodation because it is accessed only in private homes, not in public spaces. According to the court, the ADA covers services "of" a public accommodation not services "at" or "in" a public accommodation. Thus, while a home itself is not a place of public accommodation, entities that provide services in the home such as plumbers, pizza delivery, and moving companies may qualify as places of public accommodation.

The DOJ has been in the process of drafting accessibility guidelines for websites for several years, but there is no sign of any coming soon. Because of this, courts have relied on the general guidelines of the ADA in making very fact-intensive, feature-by-feature decisions. As we have seen, these are subject to interpretation and have led to inconsistent decisions.

Discussion Questions

1. Public accommodations laws were based on the premise that if all citizens are to have equal rights, everyone must be entitled to enjoy the goods and services of business on an equal basis. Given the difficulties people with disabilities experience shopping in stores, can they ever enjoy the goods and services offered by places of public accommodations on an equal basis if they cannot equally access or use the business's website? Explain your answer.

2. The ADA was written before e-commerce developed and does not mention Internet accessibility. Although some agency guidelines explain that the ADA should be read as keeping up with technology, many courts, such as the court in California in the eBay case, have enforced the law strictly. How would you change the ADA to address accessibility to websites?

Critical Thinking

If you were starting a business that was entirely Internet based, how would you create your website and interface? Identify outside experts you might consult and their needed expertise.

KEY TAKEAWAYS

Corporate Personhood

- Corporate personhood is the theory that a corporation is a person with similar rights and values as human beings.

- The *Citizens United* and *Hobby Lobby* cases expanded the idea of corporate personhood by establishing broad First Amendment rights in terms of speech and religion.

REGULATION OF BUSINESS THROUGH THE COMMERCE CLAUSE

LO 15.2   Explain the regulation of business by Congress through the Commerce Clause.

Commerce Clause: Article I, Section 8, Clause 3 of the U.S. Constitution; gives Congress the power to "regulate commerce with foreign nations, and among the several states, and with the Indian tribes."

Article I, Section 8, Clause 3 of the U.S. Constitution, referred to as the Commerce Clause, gives Congress the power to "regulate commerce with foreign nations, and among the several states, and with the Indian tribes." The Commerce Clause is one of the greatest sources of federal power and one of the most important limitations imposed by the Constitution on state power. It arose to address an issue giving rise to the Constitution itself: no federal commerce power under the Articles of Confederation.

Evolution of the Commerce Clause

For the first century of its existence, the Commerce Clause was used to stop discriminatory state laws where states would, for example, tax commerce from other states coming in at rates higher than it would tax domestic commerce. Once the industrial revolution changed our economy and how quickly we could manufacture and transport goods, Congress embarked on an era of federal regulation under the Commerce Clause. Generally, Congress can regulate the channels of interstate commerce, the instrumentalities of interstate commerce including people or things, and anything that has a substantial effect on interstate commerce.

What Is Commerce?

commerce: All forms of commercial intercourse, including buying and selling as well as the interchange of commodities.

This seems obvious, yet the term *commerce* is not defined in the Commerce Clause and has had various interpretations by courts over the years. In 1845 in *Gibbons v. Ogden*, Chief Justice Marshall defined commerce within the Commerce Clause as not just "buying or selling, or the interchange of commodities" but also all forms of "commercial intercourse."[14]

What Is Commerce Among States?

interstate commerce: Any commercial transaction or traffic that crosses state lines or may involve more than one state.

Usually referred to as interstate commerce, commerce among states is any commercial transaction or traffic that crosses state lines or may involve more than one state. While that may seem like an easy concept, courts have interpreted interstate commerce narrowly and broadly over the years sometimes using "commerce" to address a social or ethical issue. For example, in *Swift & Co. v. United States*, the Supreme Court found that a price-fixing scheme among meat packers in Chicago was a restraint on interstate trade because the local meat-packing industry was part of a larger "current of commerce among the states." Similarly, in *Heart of Atlanta Motel v. United States*, the Court determined that a local hotel's refusal to rent rooms to African Americans in violation of the Civil Rights

Act falls within the power of Congress because Congress's power to regulate interstate commerce "also includes the power to regulate the local incidents thereof . . . which might have a substantial and harmful effect upon that commerce."[15] However, in *United States v. Lopez*, the Supreme Court found that the Gun-Free School Zones Act of 1990, which prohibited the possession of a gun within 1,000 feet of a school, was unconstitutional because the law "neither regulates a commercial activity nor contains a requirement that the possession be connected in any way to interstate commerce."[16]

The Commerce Clause and Marijuana

Congress has often used its powers under the Commerce Clause to regulate activities within states, leading to ongoing controversies between state power and federal power. A recent example of this struggle is the growing acceptance among the states of medical and recreational use of marijuana. As Figure 15.2 shows, 33 states allow for medical marijuana use; however, marijuana remains illegal under federal law. This inconsistency has set the stage for clashes between states and the federal government with citizens and businesses in the middle.

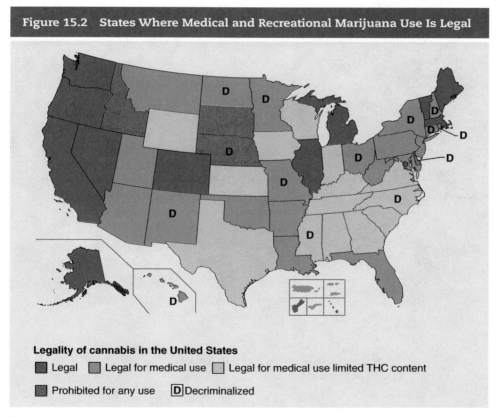

Figure 15.2   States Where Medical and Recreational Marijuana Use Is Legal

Legality of cannabis in the United States

- ■ Legal
- ■ Legal for medical use
- □ Legal for medical use limited THC content
- ■ Prohibited for any use
- |D| Decriminalized

Source: Data obtained from National Conference of State Legislatures. Graphic derived from Blank USA, w territories.svg by Lokal_Profil and Blank US Map (states only).svg by Theshibboleth. Licensed under CC BY-SA 2.5.

Gonzales v. Raich, 545 U.S. 1 (2005)

Facts: The federal Controlled Substances Act (CSA) criminalizes the possession, manufacture, or distribution of marijuana. Sale and possession of marijuana was also illegal under California law, but in 1996 the state passed the Compassionate Use Act (CUA), which provides an exemption from criminal prosecution for people who have a medical recommendation from their physician, and they (or their primary caregivers) possess or cultivate marijuana for the patient's own personal use. Angel Raich and Diane Monson live in California and used medical marijuana pursuant to the requirements of the CUA. Raich's doctor believes that without cannabis, Raich's excruciating pain could prove fatal. Monson cultivates her own marijuana, and on August 15, 2002, county deputy sheriffs and federal Drug Enforcement Administration (DEA) agents came to Monson's home. After an investigation, the county deputy sheriff determined that she was cultivating and using marijuana in accordance with the CUA. Nevertheless, after a 3-hour standoff, the DEA agents seized and destroyed Monson's six cannabis plants. Raich and Monson sued, claiming enforcement of the CSA in this case exceeded the scope of Congress's power to regulate commerce because their marijuana use was personal and within the state of California, thus not part of interstate commerce.

Issue: Is it within Congress's authority under the Commerce Clause to prohibit the in-state manufacture and possession of marijuana for medical purposes pursuant to California law?

Decision: Yes, Congress has the authority under the Commerce Clause to prohibit the in-state manufacture and possession of marijuana pursuant to the CUA. Our case law consistently upholds Congress's power to regulate purely local activities that are part of an economic "class of activities" that have a substantial effect on interstate commerce. Here, Raich and Monson are cultivating a commodity for which there is an already established, albeit illegal, interstate market. The primary purpose of the CSA is to control the supply and demand of controlled substances in both the legal and illegal markets.

It is not difficult to see how a nationwide exemption for all homegrown marijuana would have a substantial impact on the interstate market for the substance. This would certainly frustrate the federal interest in eliminating commercial transactions in the interstate market. Thus, there is a rational basis to believe that failure to regulate the intrastate manufacture and possession of marijuana would leave a gaping hole in the CSA.

Dissent: We agree that we must look beyond Raich and Monson's own activities to determine an impact on the market; otherwise, individuals would always claim their personal activities have no impact on interstate commerce. However, the Court's definition of economic activity threatens to sweep all of productive human activity into reach of federal regulators. Everyone agrees that the marijuana at issue in this case was never in the stream of commerce and possession itself is not an economic activity. They have simply grown marijuana in their own homes, for their own use, without buying, acquiring, selling, or bartering a thing of value. There is simply no evidence that homegrown medical marijuana users constitute a sizable enough class to have a discernable, let alone substantial, impact on the national illicit drug market or otherwise threaten the CSA regime.

Law and Management Questions

1. Given the prevalence of e-commerce and apps, are most businesses, no matter their size, engaged in interstate commerce? If you were starting a small business, how would the *Raich* case inform your strategy?

2. What does the dissent mean when it says the decision "threatens to sweep all of productive human activity into reach of federal regulators"? Do you agree with this statement? Explain your answer?

Contributing to the illicit interstate market for marijuana is not the only commerce at issue when it comes to medical or recreational use of marijuana. The legal marijuana industry grew to $10.4 billion in 2018.[17] If and when black market sales become legal it could be worth $50 billion by 2026. Colorado and Washington both legalized recreational marijuana in 2012. In 2015, Colorado saw a $2.39 billion boost in its economy, and the marijuana industry is credited with creating over 18,000 jobs. Washington has collected almost $70 million in taxes related to marijuana sales and expects to collect more than $1 billion in the next 3 years.[18] California, the sixth largest economy in the world, became the biggest market to open when in 2016 residents passed Proposition 64, legalizing recreational marijuana.[19]

If Not the Commerce Clause, Then What?

As with many nascent markets, much confusion surrounds the market for legal marijuana: It is legal in several states but still illegal under federal law. This creates obstacles for legal marijuana businesses when it comes to using banks; depositing illegal money with banks subjects the banks to federal scrutiny and potential prosecution. Private investment has stepped in to fill the capital void left by traditional banks. Investors poured over $10 billion into cannabis in North America in 2018. For example, Privateer Holdings, backed by Peter Thiel's Founders Fund, has raised over $122 million since 2010 for its portfolio, which includes marijuana growers; Bob Marley's marijuana brand Marley Natural; and Leafly, an online review platform similar to Yelp. And this is a global market: Luxembourg will become the first EU country to legalize recreational marijuana, Israel allows exports of medical marijuana, and Canada and Uruguay fully legalized and created a regulatory scheme for marijuana. Australia, Germany, Ireland, and Jamaica have approved measures to legalize medical marijuana.

Based on this growth, it would seem the effect on interstate commerce in the United States would be substantial and ripe for federal regulation. However, despite the Supreme Court's decision about the Commerce Clause in *Gonzales v. Raich*, federal enforcement of the CSA has been scarce, and now a majority of states allow some use of marijuana. As a result, states and interest groups opposed to legalizing marijuana have resorted to novel and creative legal challenges. In 2015, ranch owners in Pueblo County, Colorado, sued Colorado governor John Hickenlooper and the owner of a cultivation facility claiming the facility blocks their view of Greenhorn Valley and Pikes Peak. The owners claim that under the Racketeer Influenced and Corrupt Organizations (RICO) Act, they have standing to sue to stop the organized criminal conduct. The owners also claim the Colorado law is invalid under the Supremacy Clause because it conflicts with a federal law (the CSA). A federal district court dismissed the suit against most of the defendants on several grounds: Private individuals do not have standing to make a Supremacy Clause challenge, and government officials and offices cannot be sued under RICO because as the government they cannot form criminal intent.

Neighboring Nebraska and Oklahoma used a rare procedure to challenge the Colorado law: They asked the U.S. Supreme Court to allow them to file a suit directly with the justices. The Supreme Court has original jurisdiction to hear disputes between states, but the Court rarely takes these types of cases—typically only to resolve water rights disputes. Nebraska and Oklahoma do not challenge the decriminalization of possession or use of marijuana. They claim that other parts of the law conflict with federal law and impact their states through increased demand on their criminal justice systems because residents of Nebraska and Oklahoma travel to Colorado to buy marijuana and then bring it back to their home states. According to their lawsuit, Colorado exports thousands of pounds of marijuana to 36 states: "If this entity were based south of the border, the federal government would prosecute it as a drug cartel."

Colorado claimed that the Nebraska and Oklahoma suit was counterproductive because they were asking the Court to strike down a regulatory

(*Continued*)

(Continued)

scheme that channels the drug away from dangerous black markets and into a closely monitored legal market. Moreover, the U.S. solicitor general argued that Nebraska and Oklahoma are complaining that third parties are committing crimes in their states, yet they are not alleging that Colorado authorized any individual to transport marijuana to their states. Both states still have the authority to pass their own laws that make trafficking, selling, and possession of marijuana a crime; thus, the Colorado law does not infringe on their sovereignty. On March 21, 2016, the U.S. Supreme Court declined to hear the case, but Nebraska and Oklahoma consolidated their case with the ranchers' case and refiled in the Tenth Circuit Court of Appeals in Denver, which heard oral argument in January 2017. The court has yet to make a decision.

Discussion Questions

1. Out-of-state interest groups like for-profit prisons, rehabilitation centers, and Washington, D.C.-based Safe Streets Alliance funded the ranchers' lawsuit as well as two others (one was settled, and one was dismissed) challenging Colorado's law. What do these groups have to gain by funding lawsuits like this?

2. Over half of Colorado voters voted in favor of legalizing recreational marijuana in 2012. Thinking back to the *Citizens United* case, how could the involvement of out-of-state, corporate-funded interest groups impact the democratic process in Colorado?

Critical Thinking

As the legal challenges to Colorado's law move through the courts, many wonder how the Trump administration will treat this issue. The Obama administration ultimately adopted a hands-off approach, but much is unknown about Trump's strategy. A bill recently introduced in the Colorado legislature reflects an unusual strategy in case of a change in policy or enforcement by the federal government: All current legal growers and manufacturers could immediately reclassify their operations as medical marijuana instead of recreational marijuana. This sounds like a solution, but medical marijuana is not taxed as heavily as recreational marijuana. How would that impact Colorado? Does this sound like a sustainable solution? What, in your opinion, would be the best long-term solution to the confusing legal reality of marijuana in this country? Explain your answers.

The Dormant Commerce Clause

The Commerce Clause traditionally has been seen as a grant of federal power and a restriction on state power. If Congress has the power to regulate economic activity that has a substantial effect on interstate commerce, that means states cannot pass laws that burden interstate commerce. This prohibition is referred to as the **Dormant Commerce clause**, and for James Madison, this was the more important aspect of the Commerce Clause. The Commerce Clause, according to Madison, grew out of "the abuse of the importing States in taxing the non-importing."[20] Figure 15.3 highlights the differences between the Commerce Clause and the Dormant Commerce Clause. In 1994 the Supreme Court found that a Massachusetts tax on milk products, in conjunction with in-state farm subsidies, violated the Dormant Commerce Clause because it impeded interstate commerce by making milk produced out of state more expensive. Although all milk was subjected to the tax, the subsidy program for Massachusetts producers offset the cost of the tax, making in-state milk cheaper than milk produced out of state.

Dormant Commerce Clause: States cannot pass laws that burden interstate commerce, since Congress has the power to regulate economic activity that has a substantial effect on interstate commerce.

Discrimination is a key component of a Dormant Commerce Clause analysis: Did a state law discriminate between transactions on the basis of an interstate element? In Law and Society 15.3, although the court had to answer whether Puerto Rico was discriminating against Walmart when the commonwealth amended its tax code, the real issue was whether Puerto Rico's new tax law was a desperate attempt to escape declaring bankruptcy.

Figure 15.3   Comparison of the Interstate and Dormant Commerce Clause

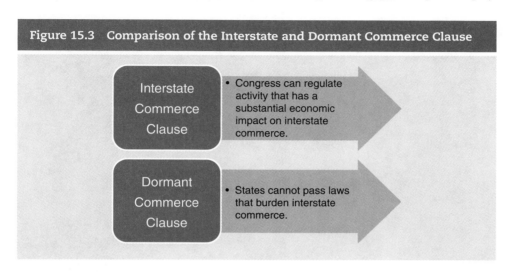

Interstate Commerce Clause
- Congress can regulate activity that has a substantial economic impact on interstate commerce.

Dormant Commerce Clause
- States cannot pass laws that burden interstate commerce.

Wal-Mart Puerto Rico, Inc. v. Juan Zaragoza-Gomez, 834 F. 3d 110 (August 24, 2016)

LAW AND SOCIETY 15.3

Facts: The Commonwealth of Puerto Rico is in dire financial straits. It is being crushed by a public debt that is larger than its gross national product; its credit rating is junk status, and it has started to default on its debt obligations. In an effort to raise more tax revenue, Puerto Rico's legislature amended its alternative minimum tax (AMT). Typically, the AMT assessed a corporate taxpayer is calculated, in part, on a tentative minimum tax that is based on the value of goods and services sold or otherwise provided to the corporate taxpayer by a related entity located outside of Puerto Rico. Prior to the 2015 amendment, this tax was a 2% flat rate, but the 2015 amendment raised the rate to 6.5% for taxpayers with $2.75 billion or more in gross sales in Puerto Rico.

Walmart Puerto Rico (P.R.) is the largest private employer in Puerto Rico: 14,300 people work in its 48 stores. Walmart P.R. earns about $3 billion in sales annually in Puerto Rico. In 2013 Walmart P.R.'s total tax liability to Puerto Rico was $18.6 million. But in 2016, after the amendment, Walmart P.R.'s tax liability was $46.5 million, $32.9 million of which was attributable to the amended AMT. Walmart P.R alleges that if enforced, the AMT would make its tax liability 132% of the company's total annual income because the tax is not keyed to the company's income but its volume of transactions from outside of Puerto Rico. Because of this, Walmart P.R. estimates its annual effective tax rate will be over 300%. Walmart P.R. is the only retailer that meets the sales threshold for the top tax rate of 6.5%, and it is alleged the "Walmart tax" was directed specifically to raise money from the retailer. Walmart P.R. sued to stop enforcement of the new AMT alleging the tax violated the Dormant Commerce Clause.

Issue: Does the new AMT violate the Dormant Commerce Clause?

(Continued)

(Continued)

Decision: Yes, Puerto Rico's amended AMT violates the Dormant Commerce Clause. A state may not tax a transaction more heavily when it crosses state lines than when it occurs entirely within the state. Here, the original intent of the AMT was to prevent multistate corporations doing business in Puerto Rico from shifting profits off the island by purchasing inventory from related mainland entities at artificially inflated prices. However, Puerto Rico conceded that the amended tax is simply a revenue-raising measure, and we find it was directed at multistate retailers like Walmart P.R. It is indisputable that the amended AMT discriminates against interstate commerce: It taxes only cross-border transactions between a Puerto Rico corporate taxpayer and home office outside of Puerto Rico. If every state were to adopt the amended AMT structure, multistate corporations doing business across state lines would be disadvantaged relative to those doing business only within the state. Although Puerto Rico has a legitimate interest in preventing profit-shifting, there was no

reason to believe that Walmart P.R. was participating in this abusive tactic. Moreover, the secretary cannot show that there are no other ways to achieve their legitimate purpose; he all but admits that a unitary tax system that uses a formula to distribute a multistate corporation's income to different jurisdictions would be an acceptable alternative to the amended AMT. For these reasons, the amended AMT does not survive Dormant Commerce Clause scrutiny.

Law and Management Questions

1. Governments will often offer tax incentives to entice corporations to locate in their community. Over time, how might large tax breaks for corporations impact a community or state's budget? What typically is expected to offset the loss of revenue from corporate taxes?

2. What might the impact have been had Walmart P.R. lost this case and have to pay the increased tax?

KEY TAKEAWAYS

Regulation of Business Through the Commerce Clause

- The commerce at issue in the Commerce Clause has been interpreted broadly to include purely local activities that might have a substantial effect on interstate commerce.

- The Dormant Commerce Clause prohibits states from passing laws that burden interstate commerce.

REGULATION THROUGH THE TAX AND SPEND CLAUSE

Tax and Spend Clause: Grants Congress the power to tax and spend for the general welfare of the people.

LO 15.3 Identify Congress's power to regulate business through the Tax and Spend Clause.

Like the Commerce Clause, the **Tax and Spend Clause** addresses one of the most important and broadest powers of Congress. According to Article I, Section 8, Congress has the power to tax and spend for the general welfare of the people. That means Congress can create a tax to raise revenue and spend that revenue in any way it believes will serve the general welfare. No tax or spending program has been declared unconstitutional because it does not serve the general welfare; Congress has broad discretion in making these decisions. James Madison and Alexander Hamilton disagreed on the breadth of this authority: Madison believed Congress should be able to tax and spend only on enumerated powers in the Constitution like building the army or navy. Hamilton, on the other hand, thought Congress should have broad authority to tax and spend on anything that serves the general welfare. Why should we care about this debate? Ask yourself whether Congress should spend money to provide disaster relief for people, like after Hurricane Katrina. James Madison would say no.

The debate was settled in 1936 in *U.S. v. Butler*, where farmers were paid not to grow crops in order to stabilize prices: Keep supply low, and raise prices to incentivize farmers to keep growing. Although the Court said the payments made pursuant to the Agricultural Adjustment Act were an unconstitutional invasion into state power, the broad discretion of Congress to tax and spend for the general welfare not limited to the enumerated powers in the Constitution was confirmed.

Values, Justice, Taxes, and Commerce

Our federal government has limited powers; states and the people have the rest. However, the extent of the enumerated powers of the federal government is continually questioned. And while it might not look like it, many of these issues stem directly from debates about values and justice—for example, access to health care: Many feel it is a human right while others feel that securing health insurance is a choice. The answer, for now, lies in the Tax and Spend Clause.

National Federation of Independent Businesses v. Sebelius, 567 U.S. 519 (2012)

Facts: In 2010 Congress passed the ACA in order to increase the number of Americans who had health insurance and thereby decrease the cost of health care. Cost-shifting is a problem in the health care market: Everyone will need health care at some point, but if they don't have insurance many can't pay for it. Because laws require that hospitals provide some level of service to people regardless of their ability to pay, hospitals end up not getting paid in full for the services they provide, and those costs get passed on to insurers who pass them on to customers in the form of higher premiums. In order to prevent this shift, the ACA has an individual mandate provision that requires people to buy health insurance, and those who do not must make a "shared responsibility payment" to the Internal Revenue Service (IRS) when they pay their taxes.

The National Federation of Independent Business, along with 26 states, sued, claiming the individual mandate, among other provisions of the ACA, was an unconstitutional exercise of the Commerce Clause. The government claimed the individual mandate was a valid exercise of the Commerce Clause, and even if it wasn't, the individual mandate was a valid exercise of the Tax and Spend Clause.

Issue: Was the individual mandate provision of the ACA a valid exercise of Congress's powers under the Commerce Clause and/or the Tax and Spend Clause?

(Continued)

LAW AND SOCIETY 15.4

(Continued)

Decision: The individual mandate was not a valid exercise of Congress's power under the Commerce Clause, but it was a valid exercise of its power under the Tax and Spend Clause. The Constitution gives Congress the power to *regulate* commerce. Regulation assumes there is commercial activity to regulate. Although over time courts have construed Congress's power under this clause expansively, every decision describes an existing activity that must be addressed. The Framers knew the difference between doing something and doing nothing; that is why they gave Congress power to regulate commerce, not compel it. Congress already has broad powers to regulate what people do; to allow it to regulate people precisely because they are doing nothing would give it too much power. The individual mandate in the ACA does not describe an existing commercial activity; instead, it requires people to *become* active in commerce by buying health insurance because not doing so effects interstate commerce.

Although the Commerce Clause does not support the individual mandate, that does not mean it might not be supported by another provision of the Constitution. The government claims the individual mandate may be upheld under the Tax and Spend Clause. For this argument, the government asks us to see the individual mandate not as ordering people to buy health insurance but as imposing a tax on those who do not. Under the ACA, if a person does not buy health insurance there are no legal ramifications; the only consequence is that she must make an additional payment to the IRS when she pays her taxes. Thus, the individual mandate can be seen as a condition—not buying health insurance—that triggers a tax, just like buying gas or earning income. The amount a person must pay is determined based on her taxable income, number of dependents, and joint filing status. Moreover, for most people, the amount they pay will be far less than paying for insurance (by law it can never be more), and the payment is collected by the IRS through the normal means of collecting taxes.

While it is true the individual mandate is intended to affect people's behavior, many provisions of our tax code are designed to effect behavior: Federal and state taxes comprise more than half the price of cigarettes not just to raise money but to encourage people to quit smoking. Similar tax schemes have been upheld for taxes on selling marijuana and sawed-off shotguns. Thus, the individual mandate may be upheld as a lawful exercise of Congress's power under the Tax and Spend Clause.

Law and Management Questions

1. Many Americans do not eat a healthy diet, and the health impacts of that cost more than the impact of people not having health insurance. If the government had won this case on its Commerce Clause argument, how might it solve the problem of our unhealthy diet?

2. What facts did the Court rely on to consider the individual mandate a taxable activity?

Our tax codes contain many value judgments. For example, to encourage donating to charities, donors get a tax break on their contributions. To incentivize reducing energy consumption, tax credits are available to homeowners for things like energy-efficient doors and windows. Tax codes can also discourage behavior. A **sin tax** is a tax on socially harmful behavior like smoking, drinking alcohol, and gambling. Taxing consumption in these areas usually has two goals: curbing the behavior and raising revenue. Both are easier said than done. Although economic policy is based on rational decision-making, humans are frequently irrational due to our lack of self-control, inattention, and sometimes due to our mistaken beliefs about certain types of consumption ("fat free means I can eat as much as I want"). Moreover, if one goal of a sin tax is to curb behavior, the more successful it is the

sin tax: A tax on socially harmful behavior such as smoking, drinking, or gambling.

less money it will raise. Figure 15.4 highlights these conflicts. Because of this, sin taxes are frequently considered unsustainable revenue sources—perhaps good for a short-term revenue boost but not a long-term solution to a state's budget problems.

One criticism of sin taxes is that they are regressive. A **regressive tax** means that although applied uniformly, the taxes take a larger percentage of income from low-income people than from high-income people. A **progressive tax** would take a larger percentage from high-income people than from lower-income people based on a person's ability to pay. Businesses that sell goods that are subject to a sin tax frequently pass the extra cost on to consumers. But sin taxes can also impact the behavior of the business.

regressive tax: A tax that while applied uniformly takes a larger percentage of income from low-income people than from higher-income people.

progressive tax: A tax that takes a larger percentage of income from high-income people than from lower-income people based on a person's ability to pay.

Figure 15.4   Point–Counterpoint: Sin Taxes

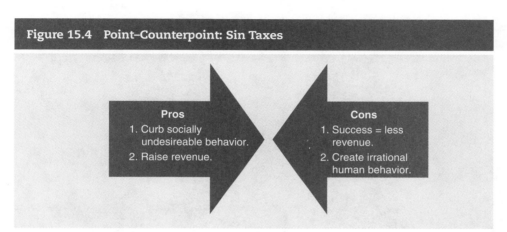

Pros
1. Curb socially undesireable behavior.
2. Raise revenue.

Cons
1. Success = less revenue.
2. Create irrational human behavior.

Sin Taxes

Tobacco is the leading cause of preventable death in the United States. According to the Centers for Disease Control and Prevention (CDC), 40% of all cancer cases and 30% of all cancer deaths are linked to smoking. Smoking rates dropped 6% between 2005 (21%) and 2015 (15%). Evidence shows people smoke less when cigarettes are more expensive—especially teens—so some of the drop may be attributable to the 2009 tax increase of 62 cents per pack. While a decline in the number of people who smoke is good news, the impact of the taxes is not equal. For example, in Britain where almost 80% of the cost of a pack of cigarettes is tax, the lowest income residents spent 34% of their disposable income on indirect taxes—2.9% on tobacco—while the wealthiest spent just 14% of their income on indirect taxes—0.1% on tobacco. In the United States, according to the CDC 25% of those below the poverty level smoke compared to 14% of those at or above the poverty level.

About 60% of U.S. adults who smoke e-cigarettes (vaping) also smoke cigarettes. Many feel e-cigarettes provide an alternative to traditional cigarettes and are a viable option for those trying to quit. Others are concerned because e-cigarettes still contain addictive nicotine and other chemicals, the long-term impact of which are unknown, and are troubled by

iStockphoto.com/Ta Nu

(Continued)

ETHICS IN CONTEXT

the probability of kids who vape becoming smokers. Some communities have turned to sin taxes for e-cigarettes. In 2017, Pennsylvania became the first state to tax e-cigarettes: Retailers pay a 40% tax on their inventory. Since the tax went into effect, more than 100 of the 400 vape shops in the state have closed, and the tax has raised over $13 million. Many worry that because vaping is an alternative to smoking and has helped smokers quit, the higher price of e-cigarettes and decreased number of retailers will hurt the downward trend in smoking because fewer people will be able to afford this alternative. Almost 70% of low-income Pennsylvanians who receive health insurance through the state's Medicare program smoke cigarettes. A viable alternative to smoking will save lives and save the state money that would otherwise be spent treating smoking-related diseases. California's Proposition 56 increased the tax rate on noncigarette tobacco products, including e-cigarettes, to 27.3%. A year later, that went up to 65% of the wholesale cost. Some fear the price of e-cigarettes in California is so high that smoking traditional cigarettes is a cheaper, albeit more dangerous, alternative. Critics say this imbalance does not make sense if the goal of the tax is to encourage people to stop smoking.

Given the complexities of human decision-making, sin taxes are not a clearly effective policy. Countries around the world have begun taxing sugary drinks in an effort to stem the growing rate of obesity. In 2016 the World Health Organization urged countries to tax sugary drinks like soda and sports drinks. In the United States, seven cities have taxed sugary drinks with mixed results. In 2014, Berkeley, California, became the first U.S. city to implement a tax. One year later, research showed a 10% drop in sales of sugar-sweetened drinks in the city. Philadelphia, Pennsylvania, also passed a sugary drink tax in 2017. A small study looked at the short-term impact of the tax by tracking buying patterns before the tax and the first two months after the tax. The results indicate that Philadelphia residents were 40% less likely to report drinking sugary drinks and 64% less likely to drink energy drinks. In response, some soda manufacturers have increased their product offerings to include more diet sodas and waters.

Research also indicates the Philadelphia tax has a disparate impact on low-income residents. While many residents can travel outside of the city to buy low-cost sugary drinks, many low-income residents do not have that option. Moreover, grocery stores in areas of the city that are food deserts (low-income neighborhoods that have no direct access to a real grocery store) struggle to survive under the best of circumstances; shoppers choosing to shop in the suburbs to avoid the tax will buy the rest of their groceries there, which means fewer shoppers in the city, and could lead to fewer stores and fewer options to buy alternatives to soda.

More cities and states are considering a sugary drink tax. In November 2018, residents of Boulder, Colorado, voted to keep their sugary drink tax, but voters in Washington State voted to ban cities and counties from imposing a new tax on sugary drinks and other groceries, although the sugary drink tax in Seattle will remain. Californians will vote in 2020 whether to overturn a ban on sugary drink taxes. The ban was implemented after the cities of Albany, Berkeley, Oakland, and San Francisco each passed a tax in the past 4 years.

Other countries are also weighing the impacts of a sugary drink tax. Mexico imposed a 10% tax on sugary drinks in 2014, resulting in a 5.5% decrease in sales of sugary beverages in 2014 and a 9.7% drop in 2015. The biggest decrease came from lower-income residents. South Africa has the highest levels of obesity in sub-Saharan Africa, and the government has set a goal of reducing obesity by 10% by 2020. One part of their strategy is a tax of 2.1 cents per gram of sugar on beverages. South Africa is the first African country to tax sugary drinks, although a tax on soft drinks and mineral water was imposed in 2002 to raise revenue. In April 2018, Ireland gained EU approval to impose a tax on sugary drinks in order to tackle obesity and other sugar-related diseases. Ireland joins France, Hungary, and Finland, which all have similar taxes.

In 2016 Britain announced a sugary drink tax that went into effect in 2018. Unlike other countries, including the United States, the goal of the British tax is not to decrease consumption; it is to decrease the amount of sugar in drinks. The tax incentivizes manufacturers to reformulate their recipes by charging two separate rates based on the total sugar content. The results were obvious before the tax went into effect: Coca-Cola changed its recipe for Fanta, and Nestle reduced the sugar content in San Pellegrino soda by 40%. Restaurant chains Pizza Hut and TGI Fridays have limited the availability of some fountain drinks in order to avoid paying the tax. The incentive to reformulate has been so successful that the government cut the revenue projections for the tax in half. It is too soon to tell if this tax model will actually reduce obesity and overall sugar consumption or just the sugar content in a few popular drinks. Because consumers can get sugar in other foods and drinks, a sugary drink tax is an unproven strategy for reducing obesity.

Discussion Questions

1. *Stakeholder theory:* Who are the stakeholders impacted by a government's decision to tax tobacco products? What is at stake for them? Who are the stakeholders impacted by a government's decision to tax sugary drinks? What is at stake for them? Looking at the sugary drink tax in Philadelphia and Britain, what stakeholder concerns are best addressed in each law?

2. *Ethical decision-making:* While there is some evidence that a tax on sugary drinks may reduce consumption, there is scant evidence that taxes on sugary drinks actually reduces obesity and other sugar-related illnesses. Moreover, governments have found that when consumption of a good is taxed in one community, consumers simply buy that product in another community that does not have the tax. Using a principles-based approach and a consequences-based approach answer, answer the following questions: Should the government intervene in human behavior? Even behavior that may harm their health? Is the British law a better solution? Explain your answer.

Take a Position

Many feel that drinking sugary drinks and smoking mostly hurt the user, not the general public. Plus, many people enjoy soda and other sugary drinks.

Issue: Should the government get involved in discouraging behavior through a sin tax? Or should the government focus on nonmonetary strategies like education instead? Explain your answers.

KEY TAKEAWAYS

Regulation Through the Tax and Spend Clause

- Congress has broad power to lay and collect taxes for the general welfare.

- Many tax laws are based on value judgments.

- Sin taxes discourage socially harmful behavior by making the behavior more expensive. But sin taxes can have a disparate impact on lower-income populations.

SUMMARY

Businesses are regulated by the government through the Commerce Clause and the Tax and Spend Clause. Even issues that do not seem to touch upon business may fall within the reach of the Commerce Clause. More recently, rights usually attributed to people have been evolving as corporate rights, such as free speech and religion. The expansion of corporate personhood impacts not only businesses and business strategy but also the communities in which businesses are located and larger society.

KEY TERMS

commerce 350
Commerce Clause 350
corporate personhood 341
Dormant Commerce Clause 354

interstate commerce 350
place of public accommodation 345
progressive tax 359
regressive tax 359

Religious Freedom Restoration Act
  (RFRA) 343
sin tax 358
Tax and Spend Clause 356

REVIEW QUESTIONS

1. How did the *Citizens United*, *Hobby Lobby*, and *Carnell Construction* cases shape the corporate personhood theory?

2. What is a place of public accommodation, and what are a business's obligations to its customers under the ADA?

3. Explain the two aspects of the Commerce Clause.

4. What is a sin tax? Explain the pros and cons of using a sin tax to curb socially undesirable behavior like smoking or drinking sugary drinks.

MANAGER'S CHALLENGE

Dormant Commerce Clause

Olivia is the tax assessor for Old Westbrook, a small town. There are several charities in Old Westbrook, and Olivia established a tax system that exempted in-town charities from real estate taxes but denied this benefit to Old Westbrook charities that served mostly out-of-state residents. Camp Heatherwood is a charity located in Old Westbrook, and 95% of its campers come from out of state. The head of Camp Heatherwood called Olivia to discuss the new tax system.

Framing Questions

1. Why would Olivia treat charities that serve mostly in-state residents differently than those that serve mostly out-of-state residents?

2. Why would Camp Heatherwood not like this tax system?

3. Does Camp Heatherwood have a legal challenge to the new tax system?

Assignment

You are Olivia's assistant. Given your answer to Question 1, draft a memo to Olivia suggesting different policies that might accomplish those goals.

GLOBALIZATION

Ethics in Context

Think and Act Globally

There is a tendency for leaders to say, "Governments should always do what is in the national interest." But this often results in a "tragedy of the commons" where a shared resource is used, depleted, or spoiled in a country's own self-interest to the detriment of the common good. How, then, do we face, ethically, issues such as the global use of environmental resources like water, which has no national borders?

Later in the chapter, in the Ethics in Context section, we use stakeholder and ethical lenses to examine this question.

iStockphoto.com/tomazl

Learning Objectives

Upon completion of this chapter, the reader should be able to do the following:

16.1 Explain globalization and its impact on the world economy.

16.2 State the major institutions in the arena of international trade as well as barriers to free trade.

16.3 Identify the human aspects of globalization.

INTRODUCTION

The world is becoming smaller due to the increasing comingling of regional economies and recent advances in technology. Organizations must consider their role as global citizens in the new world economy. In this chapter, we will examine globalization by looking at recent trends in the global marketplace and identifying challenges and opportunities for managing in an increasingly global context.

GLOBALIZATION AND ITS IMPACT

LO 16.1   Explain globalization and its impact on the world economy.

Just by looking around you, it's easy to see the increasing integration of nation states. Very often this integration is achieved through the flow of economic, cultural, social, and informational resources—some of them provided by students like you. In fact, you might think of yourself as somewhat of a global citizen, even practicing **global citizenship** by exercising the rights, responsibilities, and obligations that arise from being part of a global community.

In general, we refer to **globalization** as the increasing movement of goods, services, and capital across national borders. It's likely no surprise that international trade and financial flows work together to integrate the world economy, leading to the spread of technology, culture, and politics. The KOF Globalization Index measures the economic, social, and political dimensions of globalization—all of which have been on the rise since the 1970s, especially after the end of the Cold War in the late 1980s. KOF has an interactive map of the rise in globalization since the 1970s by country; a link to this is provided on the companion resource site.[1]

There are multiple other trends hastening this movement. Some recent trends include increases in the working population, the interactivity through social media in emerging economies, the gig economy and independent workers, and even climate change. It is further accelerated by political upheavals (e.g., Hong Kong's pro-democracy demonstrations, Brexit) and by sociocultural processes such as increasing cross-border migration, the erosion of traditions, growing individualization, and the emergence of pluralist societies with differing values, cultures and ways of life.[2] Many of these topics we discuss separately in this textbook.

As a result, **multinational corporations (MNCs)** operate in a complex and uncertain environment, especially when dealing with gaps in regulation and ill-defined rules of appropriate business conduct. The United Nations defines an MNC simply as a firm that controls assets abroad. Today, there are over 100,000 MNCs operating in the modern global economy. In fact, most global commerce is carried out by a small number of powerful firms. According to *Fortune*, the most profitable MNCs in 2019 are shown in Figure 16.1.

Globalization has both positive and negative impacts. For example, globalization quite simply opens up the global marketplace, and this can help firms in emerging markets increase consumer demand for their products. As these firms widen their footprint, they then lower their costs per unit of product. In turn, this broadening of scope can attract new investors and attract **foreign direct investment (FDI)**. FDI is when a company, individual, or fund invests money in another country, buying shares of stock in or loaning money. Expanding foreign trade is often seen as another benefit because products often found only in developed countries can be found elsewhere across the globe. Companies and countries can export their goods to other countries through international trade, and they can also tap into human and natural resources that are scarce locally. For example, Starbucks operates in some 50 countries and has provided jobs and income for hundreds of thousands of people worldwide as well as benefits to suppliers and customers.[3] Another positive is the

global citizenship: Exercising the rights, responsibilities, and obligations that arise from being part of a global community.

globalization: The increasing movement of goods, services, and capital across national borders.

multinational corporations (MNCs): Businesses that have assets in more than one country.

foreign direct investment (FDI): A company, individual, or fund invests money in another country, buying shares of stock or loaning money.

Figure 16.1 The Most Profitable Multinational Corporations in 2019

Rank	Name	Revenues ($M)	Revenue Percent Change	Profits ($M)	Assets ($M)	Profits Percent Change	Employees	Change in Rank	Country/ Territory
1	Walmart	$514,405.00	2.8%	$6,670.00	$219,295.00	-32.4%	22,00,000	-	U.S.
2	Sinopec Group	$414,649.90	26.8%	$5,845.00	$3,29,186.30	280.1%	619,151	1	China
3	Royal Dutch Shell	$396,556.00	27.2%	$23,352.00	$3,99,194.00	79.9%	81,000	2	Netherlands
4	China National Petroleum	$392,976.60	20.5%	$2,270.50	$6,01,899.90	-	1,382,401	-	China
5	State Grid	$387,056.00	10.9%	$8,174.80	$572,309.50	-14.3%	917,717	-3	China
6	Saudi Aramco	$355,905.00	35.3%	$110,974.50	$358,872.90	46.9%	76,418	-	Saudi Arabia
7	BP	$303,738.00	24.2%	$9,383.00	$282,176.00	176.9%	73,000	1	Britain
8	ExxonMobil	$290,212.00	18.8%	$20,840.00	$346,196.00	5.7%	71,000	1	U.S.
9	Volkswagen	$278,341.50	7.0%	$14,322.50	$523,672.30	9.3%	664,496	-2	Germany
10	Toyota Motor	$272,612.00	2.8%	$16,982.00	$469,295.60	-24.6%	370,870	-4	Japan

Source: Fortune, Global 500 Ranking, 2019. https://fortune.com/global500/2019/search/

ability of people from different backgrounds to interact with one another. Thus, attitudes and values about society, religion, and technology can be transformed by cultural diffusion brought by globalization.

Yet, these benefits of globalization are also challenges. According to the World Economic Forum (WEF), technological progress is a key driver of how people improve their income levels and their standard of living. However, these new technologies, and the new knowledge that results, do not necessarily develop everywhere or at the same time. Therefore, the way technology spreads across countries is central to how global growth is generated and shared across countries.[4] The WEF advises policymakers to ensure that the benefits from globalization and technological innovation are shared widely across the population, while preventing exploitation of the newly acquired technology to gain excessive control of a market to the detriment of consumers.

Because the manufacturing of new technology is often outsourced to countries where the costs of manufacturing goods and wages are lower than in home countries, job insecurity can result. Accountants, programmers, editors, and scientists have lost jobs due to outsourcing to cheaper locations like India.[5] The WEF also notes that some believe globalization benefits the interests of the richest countries, with most of the profits flowing back to them. And although globalization is helping to create more wealth in some developing countries, it is not helping to close the gap between the world's poorest and wealthiest nations.[6] As such, income inequality is a concern. **Bottom of the pyramid (BOP),** also called base of the pyramid, is an economic term that refers to the poorest two thirds of the economic human pyramid, a group of more than 4 billion people living in abject poverty (see Figure 16.2). More broadly, it refers to a framework of economic development that promises to simultaneously alleviate widespread poverty while providing growth and profits for MNCs.[7] Alleviating poverty was identified by the UN Global

bottom of the pyramid (BOP): An economic term that refers to the poorest two thirds of the economic human pyramid, a group of more than 4 billion people living in abject poverty; also known as base of the pyramid.

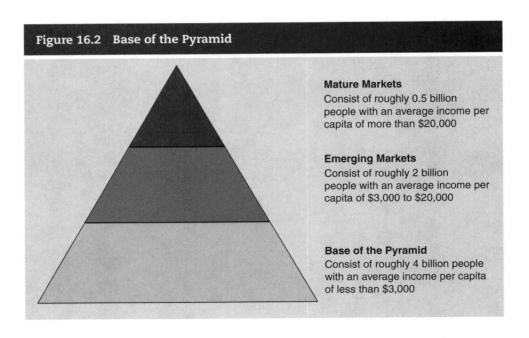

Figure 16.2 Base of the Pyramid

Mature Markets
Consist of roughly 0.5 billion people with an average income per capita of more than $20,000

Emerging Markets
Consist of roughly 2 billion people with an average income per capita of $3,000 to $20,000

Base of the Pyramid
Consist of roughly 4 billion people with an average income per capita of less than $3,000

Compact discussed in Chapter 7. Inequality doesn't just exist in emerging economies; it exists in all economies.

Similarly, not all industries benefit because commerce can and does move elsewhere. For example, steel companies in the United Kingdom once thrived, providing work for thousands of people, but when China began producing cheaper steel, U.K. steel plants closed down and thousands of jobs were lost.[8]

Turning back to Starbucks, in 2016 it faced clashes with Western values and the law in countries like South Africa and Saudi Arabia. In Riyadh, Saudi Arabia, signs were posted asking male drivers to come in for women who wanted coffee. Messages about this were tweeted and posted on Facebook, according to CNN.[9] Starbucks explained its post with "This was the only such Starbucks store in Saudi Arabia. During construction, the store could only accommodate and serve single men, and a poster was placed at the store entrance as required by local law."[10] While this incident is certainly the result of globalization, it also presents an ethical issue. Such gender segregation violates human rights and denies respect to those involved, and thus, internationally it is viewed as morally wrong. Most business ethics violations are not blatant but are made out of complicity.[11] **Complicity** is when one "facilitates, assists, legitimizes, encourages abuse of internationally accepted ethical standards."[12] Is Starbucks complicit? This question also begs the issue, discussed in Chapter 3, of global hypernorms.

Hypernorms are the result of a convergence of religious, political, and philosophical thought across a number of countries and cultures.[13] Examples include a country's citizenry being allowed to participate in some way in the direction of the country's political affairs and the common humanity that should be afforded all people. Figure 16.3 illustrates the positive and negative impacts of globalization.

complicity: The act of facilitating, assisting, legitimizing, and encouraging abuse of internationally accepted ethical standards.

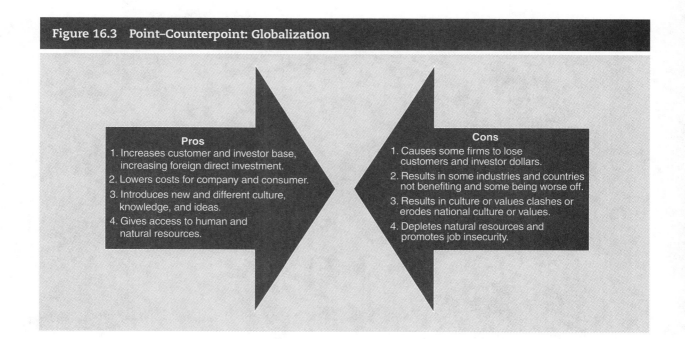

Figure 16.3   Point–Counterpoint: Globalization

Pros
1. Increases customer and investor base, increasing foreign direct investment.
2. Lowers costs for company and consumer.
3. Introduces new and different culture, knowledge, and ideas.
4. Gives access to human and natural resources.

Cons
1. Causes some firms to lose customers and investor dollars.
2. Results in some industries and countries not benefiting and some being worse off.
3. Results in culture or values clashes or erodes national culture or values.
4. Depletes natural resources and promotes job insecurity.

Yahoo!, Inc. v. La Ligue Contra le Racisma et L'Antisemitisma, 433 F.3d 1199 (9th Cir. 2006)

Facts: France enacted a law making it illegal and punishable with both civil and criminal penalties to display or sell Nazi artifacts. Nazi material was being made available through Yahoo's online auction service hosted out of the United States (although Yahoo France complied with the French law). In April 2000, La Ligue Contre Le Racisme et L'Antisemitisme (LICRA) and L'Union des Etudiants Juifs de France (UEJF) filed suit in a French court, claiming that Yahoo violated the French Penal Code, which prohibits exhibition or sale of racist materials. The French court found it had jurisdiction, held Yahoo liable, and ordered Yahoo to use all means necessary to prevent French users from accessing its auction site. It further ordered Yahoo "to remove from 'all browser directories accessible in the territory of the French Republic'" the "negationists" heading, as well as all links "bringing together, equating, or presenting directly or indirectly as equivalent sites about the Holocaust and sites by Holocaust deniers."

Yahoo then brought suit in a federal district court in California seeking a declaration that the French court's order was unenforceable. The California court found that it had jurisdiction over the two French organizations, and decided that there was an actual controversy, which was causing a real and immediate threat to Yahoo. However, the court also held that the enforcement of the French order in the United States would violate the First Amendment of the U.S. Constitution.

This decision was overturned by the Court of Appeals for the Ninth Circuit, which concluded that the district court erred in finding that it had personal jurisdiction over the French organizations. Jurisdiction in a U.S. court could only be obtained, and Yahoo's First Amendment claim heard, if the French parties sought enforcement of the French judgment in the United States—and that had not yet happened.

Yahoo appealed this decision. In the first Ninth Circuit Court of Appeals decision, the three-judge panel used the familiar test to determine jurisdiction: whether sufficient minimum contacts existed such that trying the case in that forum would not offend fair play and justice.

This would be the case if LICRA and UEJF had purposefully directed their activities with the forum, the claims arose out of, or related to, LICRA and UEJF forum-related activities, and the exercise of jurisdiction would be reasonable. Here, because LICRA and UEJF took action to enforce their rights under French law and because Yahoo makes no allegation that could lead a court to conclude that there was anything wrong in the organization's conduct, the district court did not properly exercise personal jurisdiction over LICRA and UEJF.

Issue: Did California courts have jurisdiction over the French organizations?

Decision: Yes, California did have jurisdiction over the French organizations. Nevertheless, the case was dismissed for other reasons. There were several opinions issued in the appeal.

The Majority (Judge W.A. Fletcher, joined by Chief Judge Schroeder and Judges Hawkins, Fisher, Gould, Paez, Clifton, and Bea)

A majority of eight judges concluded that the U.S. district court properly exercised personal jurisdiction over the defendants because the French court order required Yahoo to take actions in California (where Yahoo was headquartered), and the order was under threat of substantial penalty. "The case before us is the classic polar case for specific jurisdiction described in *International Shoe*, in which there are very few contacts but in which those few contacts are directly related to the suit." The court reviewed the French organizations' actions under the applicable *International Shoe* test, holding that a court in California could exercise personal jurisdiction over LICRA based on its sending a cease and desist letter to Yahoo in California, serving process on Yahoo, and obtaining and serving a French court order. Together, these contacts were enough to confer jurisdiction. Under the *Calder v. Jones* test, the first two requirements are that LICRA and UEJF (1) committed an intentional act (2) expressly aimed at the forum state. Both requirements are satisfied here: LICRA intentionally filed suit in the French court, and the suit was expressly aimed at California. The suit sought, and the French court granted, orders directing Yahoo to perform significant acts in California. Although the effect of the order would be felt in France, that does not change the fact that significant acts were to be performed in California. The servers that support yahoo.com are located in California, and compliance with the French court's orders necessarily would require Yahoo to make some changes to those servers. Lastly, to the extent that any financial penalty might be imposed, the impact of that penalty would be felt by Yahoo at its corporate headquarters in California. Therefore, the federal court had jurisdiction over the French organizations.

Despite the majority's conclusion that jurisdiction existed, the action was dismissed by a majority of six—only three of whom found jurisdiction. Three judges (Chief Judge Schroeder and Judges W.A. Fletcher and Gould) concluded "that the suit is unripe"—that is, not ready for litigation. When their votes were combined with "those of three dissenting judges who conclude that there is no personal jurisdiction over LICRA and UEJF, there are six votes to dismiss Yahoo's suit."

The Concurrence (Judges Ferguson, O'Scannlain, and Tashima)

Dismissal was appropriate because personal jurisdiction was *not* present. LICRA did not expressly aim its French litigation activities at California as

required to find jurisdiction under *Calder*. An intentional act aimed exclusively at a location other than the forum state, which results in harm to a plaintiff in the forum state, does not satisfy the "express aiming" requirement under *Calder*.

The LICRA and UEJF suit sought French court orders directing Yahoo to perform significant acts in France, such as preventing surfers calling from France from viewing anti-Semitic services on their computer screen; identifying the geographical origin of a visiting site from the caller's IP address, which should enable it to prevent surfers calling from France from accessing services and sites that when displayed on a screen installed in France is liable to be deemed an offense in France and/or to constitute a manifestly unlawful act; and taking all measures to dissuade and make impossible any access by a surfer calling from France to disputed sites and services of which the title and/or content constitutes a threat to internal public order. Thus, there is no evidence that LICRA and UEJF had any intention to expressly aim their suit at California.

Judge O'Scannlain's Separate Concurrence (Joined by Judges Ferguson and Tashima)

Dismissal was appropriate; however, under *Calder* the rule of jurisdiction applies to intentional tortious actions directed at the forum state. Here, neither LICRA nor UEJF has ever carried on business or any other activity through which they have availed themselves of the benefits and protections of California's laws, nor should either party have reasonably anticipated that it would be haled into court in California to answer for the legitimate exercise of its rights in France.

Moreover, despite the majority opinion, the personal jurisdiction requirement is not merely a rule of civil procedure; it is a constitutional constraint on the powers of a state, as exercised by its courts, in favor of the due process rights of the individual. Case law does not support the majority's unprecedented

(*Continued*)

(Continued)

holding that by litigating a bona fide claim in a foreign court and receiving a favorable judgment, a foreign party automatically assents to being haled into court in the other litigant's home forum.

Law and Management Questions

1. Does a U.S. court have jurisdiction over a foreign organization that obtains a judgment against a U.S. defendant in a foreign court?

2. *Ethical consideration:* Yahoo's French subsidiary, and eventually Yahoo itself, took all Nazi paraphernalia from the site, complying with French law. What does this say about the values of the French people? The values of Yahoo? Was Yahoo motivated by the obligation to comply with a court order or by the adherence to the values of the French people? Or by the value of doing business in the French market?

3. The litigation took approximately six years and involved multiple appeals and some related criminal proceedings. What does this tell us about the actual costs of complex cyber litigation?

KEY TAKEAWAYS

Globalization and Its Impacts

- Globalization is an undeniable force for both business and society that managers must face head-on.

- International trade and financial flows work together to integrate the world economy, leading to the spread of technology, culture, and politics.

- There are as many benefits to globalization as there are challenges. Managers must consider fully each when bringing their firm to multiple new marketplaces.

INTERNATIONAL TRADE

LO 16.2 State the major institutions in the arena of international trade as well as barriers to free trade.

International trade rules and regulations have been in the news a great deal in the past decade, underscoring the importance of trade with countries like China, the United States, Canada, and Mexico. Next, we will discuss the major trade agreements affecting the business and society relationship. First, let's consider the institutions that oversee global commerce.

The World Bank, the International Monetary Fund (IMF), and the World Trade Organization (WTO) are the three main institutions that set the rules by which international commerce is transacted.

The IMF, created in 1945, is an organization of 189 countries, focusing mainly on global monetary cooperation—the system of exchange rates and international payments that enables countries (and their citizens) to transact with each other. In doing so, it tries to promote high employment and sustainable economic growth—and to reduce poverty around the world.[14]

The World Bank is a global source of funding and knowledge for developing countries and oversees some 12,000 projects. It's composed of five institutions that share a commitment to reducing poverty, increasing shared prosperity, and promoting sustainable development. The International Development Association and the International Bank for Reconstruction and Development provide financing, policy, and technical advice to developing countries. The International Finance Corporation, the Multilateral Investment Guarantee Agency, and the International Centre for Settlement of Investment Disputes focus on strengthening the private sector in developing countries.[15]

Lastly, no business can operate across national boundaries without complying with rules set by the WTO. The funds the WTO provides are used mainly for roads, dams, power plants, and pipelines. It is an organization designed to open trade and provides a forum for governments to negotiate trade agreements and settle trade disputes. It does so by operating a system of trade rules designed to ensure trade flows as smoothly, predictably, and freely as possible. A link to its website, which provides an interactive map of its members, can be found on the companion resource site. However, not all countries are in favor of free trade and instead seek some form of isolationism, or a policy to be absent from alliances and other international political and economic relations. A good example of this policy is Brexit, or the decision of the United Kingdom to exit the European Union. The Manager's Challenge section, later in this chapter, illustrates this type of policy.

> isolationism: A policy to be absent from alliances and other international political and economic relations.

Globalization and Brexit

The United Kingdom left the European Union on January 31, 2020, after three deadline extensions in 2019. This comes as a result of a referendum vote on March 26, 2016, where 52% of voters chose to leave the European Union. This decision is commonly known as "Brexit." British prime minister David Cameron resigned promptly after the vote, paving the way for Theresa May to become prime minister followed by Boris Johnson in 2019. Critics predict an economic slump for the United Kingdom. The Brexit decision marks a strong and highly visible move away from globalism and toward a traditional nation-state economic approach. Critics of the European Union applaud the Brexit decision as a means to strengthen the British economy, keep high-paying jobs for their citizens, and preserve their cultural identity. Opponents see the Brexit decision as a move toward isolationism, which will put European nations at a disadvantage when competing against the U.S. and Asian markets. Johnson favors a conventional trade deal with the European Union, which absolves the United Kingdom of some of the EU rules in exchange for no longer having a seamless trading system. Johnson believes he can eventually negotiate a deeper trade deal with the

United States instead.[16] Clearly, this decision is expected to change the international business landscape for decades to come.

Discussion Questions

1. Why did the British voters choose to exit the European Union?

2. What do you think will be some of the biggest impacts of this decision on the remaining EU nations?

3. How do you think the post-Brexit landscape will benefit individuals currently employed in the United Kingdom?

Critical Thinking

Critics of globalization claim that it puts certain nations and employees at a competitive disadvantage, while proponents of globalization claim that it can lead to greater prosperity and quality of life. What are the strongest arguments on each side of this issue? Which argument on each side of the issue is most compelling? Why?

CASE STUDY 16.1

Lowering trade barriers is one of the most obvious ways of encouraging trade. These barriers include customs tariffs and measures such as import bans or quotas that restrict quantities selectively. A tariff[i] is a duty or tax that is levied on goods brought into a country. Tariffs can be used to discourage foreign competitors from entering a market. Quotas place a limit on the amount of a product that can leave or enter a country. Similarly, a **boycott**, a government-imposed prohibition on the purchase and importation of certain goods from other countries, can be a barrier. Barriers to trade also include cultural and political factors and red tape. Selling products from one country to another country is sometimes difficult when the culture of two countries differs, significantly causing issues such as a loss of cultural distinctiveness and cultural dominance by more powerful nations as well as the spread of what is called a commodity culture where everyone and everything looks the same. Political violence may change attitudes toward foreign firms at any time. Red tape can involve a lack of sufficient information for traders to know how and why various licenses are required and granted. Or it can be in the form of technical barriers such that the standards and procedures are discriminatory or otherwise create obstacles to trade.[17]

Two developments in 2019 illustrate how tensions can arise when dealing with trade negotiations. In December 2019, the United States, Canada, and Mexico drafted a revision of the former trade agreement called the North American Free Trade Agreement, or NAFTA. The new trade agreement, signed by all three countries, called United States–Mexico–Canada Agreement, or USMCA, is designed to safeguard North American economic integration by, among other things, including new provisions aimed at creating more manufacturing jobs. For example, a greater proportion of material used in cars and trucks will now need to originate in North America in order to avoid tariffs.[18]

The significance of this trade agreement is big. According to the U.S. Census Bureau, trade with Canada is balanced, with about $300 billion in goods going each way, while the United States has a trade deficit with Mexico (see Figure 16.4). Specifically, Mexico sent $346 billion in cars, auto parts, and other goods to the United States, compared with $265 billion in farm products, auto parts, and other goods going from the United States to Mexico.

According to the *Wall Street Journal*, USMCA has the following hallmarks:

- Puts new rules in place surrounding Mexican workers and their ability to unionize

- Sets up increased restrictions on duty-free trade of vehicles: a specified proportion of an automobile will need to be produced by workers with higher wages, and a greater proportion of the vehicle components will have to originate in North America

- Creates rules mandating the free flow of data between the United States, Canada, and Mexico

- Protects current export markets in agriculture in the United States

- Eliminates protections of Big Pharma from the development of generic imitators[19]

boycott: Government-imposed prohibition on the purchase and importation of certain goods from other countries.

---

[i]For more on doing business around the globe, see Chapter 11.

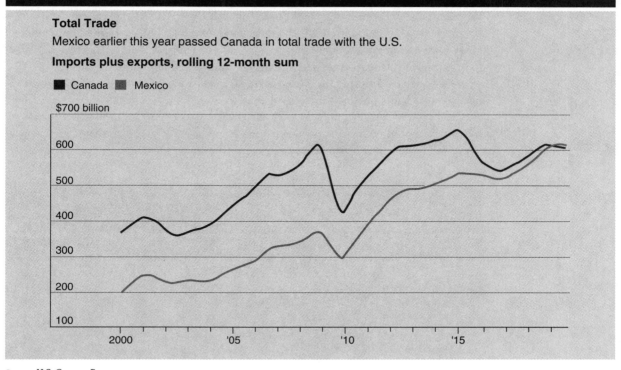

Figure 16.4 Imports Between the United States, Mexico, and Canada

Total Trade

Mexico earlier this year passed Canada in total trade with the U.S.

Imports plus exports, rolling 12-month sum

■ Canada ■ Mexico

Source: U.S. Census Bureau.

Note: Not adjusted for inflation.

For the better part of a year, the U.S. and Chinese governments have been trying to finalize a new trade agreement. A core feature for the United States is to obtain commitments by the Chinese government to eliminate pressure on international companies, wanting access to Chinese markets, to license or otherwise transfer technology to the Chinese.[20] Additionally, U.S. negotiators have asked their Chinese counterparts to commit to some agricultural purchases up front, according to the *Wall Street Journal* report. The Chinese government wants to tie the size of the up-front commitment to how much tariff relief the United States would be willing to extend immediately. Both sides in the negotiation are at odds over whether—and by how much—the United States would agree to lift tariffs on Chinese imports. This represents the Chinese government's core demand and is linked to its offers on other issues.[21] According to the report, the biggest holdup in the U.S.–China negotiations is the U.S. demand that China guarantee its pledge to buy more American soybeans, poultry, and other agricultural products. Also at issue are tariffs. Trade between the United States and China has fallen in recent years as both sides applied tariffs on billions of dollars' worth of goods being imported from the other. In December 2019, however, the United States held off planned 15% tariffs on Chinese goods (e.g., cell phones, computers, and toys) while China canceled planned retaliatory tariffs, including a 25% tariff on U.S.-made cars.[22] This first phase truce is an encouraging sign to many who want to see a new trade deal between the two countries.[23]

Countries often compete for trade and investment. The WEF Global Competitiveness Index defines *competitiveness* as "the set of institutions, policies and factors that determine the level of productivity of a country." The index, published since 1979, maps the competitiveness landscape of 141 economies using 103 indicators organized into 12 themes. These themes range from strength of a countries' institutions, infrastructure, health, skills, and labor market to its financial systems, market size, business dynamism, and innovation capability.

See Figure 16.5 for the latest list. Each year the WEF produces a Global Competitiveness Report that is designed to be used as a tool to help governments, the private sector, and civil society work together to boost productivity and generate prosperity. The WEF has argued that by comparing countries, leaders can better gauge areas that need strengthening and build a coordinated response.[24]

Figure 16.5   The World's 10 Most Competitive Countries: The Global Competitive Index—2019

Rank	Country	Last Year's Rank
1	Singapore	2
2	United States	1
3	Hong Kong	7
4	The Netherlands	6
5	Switzerland	4
6	Japan	5
7	Germany	3
8	Sweden	9
9	United Kingdom	8
10	Denmark	10

Source: World Economic Forum, The Global Competitiveness Report 2019 Ranking out of 141 Economies.

KEY TAKEAWAYS

International Trade and Barriers

- There are three important supranational institutions in the arena of international trade: the WTO, the IMF, and the World Bank.

- There are several barriers to trade that prevent the type of free trade these organizations are working to promote.

HUMAN ASPECTS OF GLOBALIZATION

LO 16.3   Identify the human aspects of globalization.

While it's clear globalization affects countries, it's perhaps less clear how it affects people, their lives, and their livelihoods. While all four of the basic aspects of globalization from the IMF—trade, investment movement, knowledge transfer, and migration—have a human element, the latter focuses directly on the movement of people as a result of globalization.[25] According to the United Nations Department of Economic and Social Affairs (UN DESA), as of 2019, the increase in the global number of international migrants continues to outpace growth of the world's population.[26]

There is little doubt the ability to move to a new job in a new location can be a benefit to your career. Many countries are, in fact, nations of immigrants. In fact, U.S. president John F. Kennedy wrote a book called *A Nation of Immigrants* when he was a senator in 1959; its purpose was to underscore the importance of immigration to the growth of the country. It later became a platform for an open immigration policy in the United States.

According to UN DESA, the United States has the highest number of immigrants (foreign-born individuals), with 48 million—5 times that of Saudi Arabia (11 million) and 6 times more than in Canada (7.6 million). See Figure 16.6.

Consistently, most international migrants move between countries located within the same region—perhaps due to fewer language and cultural barriers. One out of every seven

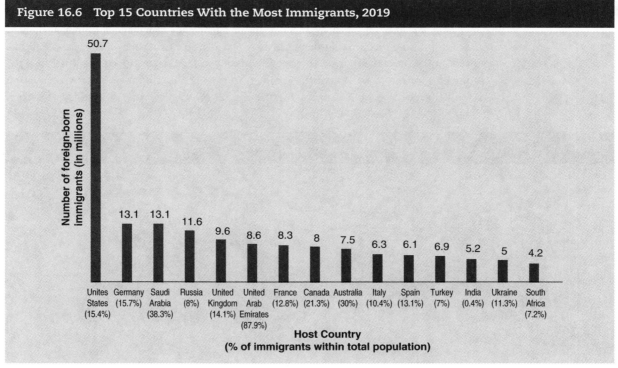

Figure 16.6   Top 15 Countries With the Most Immigrants, 2019

Source: Data from United Nations Population Division. (2019, August). International migrant stock 2019. Retrieved from https://www.un.org/en/development/desa/population/migration/data/estimates2/estimates19.asp

international migrants is below the age of 20 years, and three out of every four international migrants are of working age (20–64 years).[27]

Immigration is sometimes challenging for both the immigrant as well as the host country, with each trying to adapt. Perceptions can often be a hurdle to adapting. Another can be an immigrant's willingness to adopt the host country's customs. However, according to a 2018 Pew Research Center survey, most say immigrants strengthen their countries rather than burden them. Yet, attitudes are mixed on immigrants' willingness to adopt local customs. According to the Pew survey, a median of 49% among countries surveyed say immigrants want to be distinct from the host country's society, while a median of 45% say immigrants want to adopt the host country's customs and way of life.[28] Why do you think there is such a split?

Consider the pros and cons of cultural globalization (see Figure 16.7). Are there reasons to adopt local customs and reasons to not adopt? Do you think the concepts of cultural sensitivity and competency discussed in Chapter 11 would help mitigate some of these issues?

Moving to better your life is one thing, but what if you had to move for a decent job because none were offered in your area, or you had to move because of war, famine, or persecution?

According to the UN report in 2019, forced displacements across international borders continue to rise. Between 2010 and 2017, the global number of refugees and asylum seekers increased by about 13 million, accounting for close to a quarter of the increase in the number of all international migrants. Northern Africa and Western Asia hosted around 46% of the global number of refugees and asylum seekers, followed by sub-Saharan Africa (21%).

Sometimes these immigrants arrive without proper documentation. Majorities in most immigrant destination countries surveyed by the Pew Research Center in 2018 support the deportation of people who are in their countries illegally. In the United States, public opinion is divided on the issue.[29] Perhaps this is due to the topic being front and center over the past few years. In May 2019, the Trump administration issued a new immigration plan aimed at pushing for more border security, especially on the border of Mexico, which followed on the heels of attempts to close the border with Mexico entirely resulting in separating children from their families. Changes to the legal immigration system include the administration's goal of focusing on merit and skills rather than family ties or humanitarian

Figure 16.7   Point–Counterpoint: Cultural Globalization

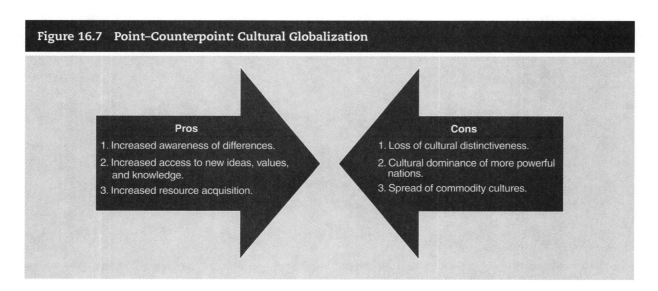

Pros
1. Increased awareness of differences.
2. Increased access to new ideas, values, and knowledge.
3. Increased resource acquisition.

Cons
1. Loss of cultural distinctiveness.
2. Cultural dominance of more powerful nations.
3. Spread of commodity cultures.

needs, building a wall along the southern border focusing on 33 key places it believes are high-frequency areas for human trafficking and drug activity, and simplifying the visa process.[30] There has been much debate and little progress since the announcement of the new plan. With an election in the United States in 2020, many candidates have unveiled their own immigration plans, so the topic is very much in flux.

Expansion of global activity has strained natural resources. According to the UN, water scarcity has been growing globally at more than twice the rate of population increase. As a result, some regions of the world are reaching their limit at which water can be sustainably delivered to citizens.[31] Does the market for bottled water exacerbate this scarcity?

Think and Act Globally

iStockphoto.com/tomazl

FIJI Water LLC is a U.S.-based company marketing a colorful, recognizable bottled water brand in more than 60 countries. Fiji's bottling plant is located in the Fiji Islands, and according to its website, the water is the leading export from Fiji and the number one imported bottled water to the United States. Its website also describes its process:

On a remote Pacific island, 1,600 miles from the nearest continent, equatorial trade winds purify the clouds that begin FIJI® Water's journey through one of the world's last virgin ecosystems. As tropical rain falls on a pristine rain forest, it filters through layers of volcanic rock, slowly gathering the natural minerals and electrolytes that give FIJI Water its soft, smooth taste. The water collects in a natural artesian aquifer, deep below the Earth's surface, shielded from external elements by confining layers of rock. Natural pressure forces the water towards the surface, where it's bottled at the source, free from human contact until you unscrew the cap. Untouched by man®. Earth's Finest Water®.[32]

But earlier this decade, the company was singled out as a primary example of "water insanity" because the product was shipped from a remote island in the South Pacific to its main markets thousands of miles away.[33] In response to this protest, the company launched a new promotion campaign under a slogan "Every drop is green" only to be immediately accused by environmentalist groups and government watchdogs of engaging in greenwashing activities.[ii] In an interview on U.S.-based National Public Radio (NPR), a guest put it simply: "No one in this country needs water from Fiji."[34]

Fiji Water is economically powerful on the island nation, and according to some, it controls about 20% of its exports.[35] While benefiting the island of Fiji, the production of water is also costly to the country due to how it is extracted. The water comes from an aquifer—a naturally formed underground chamber consisting of layers of permeable volcanic rock that bears water, overlain by protective rock that limits the entry of contaminants into the confined aquifer and pressurizes the chamber. In order to access the water, the rock barrier must be penetrated by a borehole or the creation of a well.[36]

Fiji Water has enjoyed a tax-free status, granted when the company was founded in 1995.

(Continued)

[ii]See Chapter 7 on environmentalism for more information on greenwashing.

(Continued)

But as the company became successful, the government enacted a water resource tax of 15 Fiji cents (or about 8.5 U.S. cents) and said it would take back Fiji Water's wells and rights to provide the water if it did not pay the new tax.[37]

According to NPR, in Fiji itself, 53% of the people who live in Fiji don't have access to clean, safe water, which means that Americans can easily get clean water from Fiji more simply than Fijians can.[38]

Discussion Questions

1. *Stakeholder–shareholder theories:* Who are the stakeholders affected by Fiji's exporting water? What is the tragedy of the commons? How is it related to the effect of economic activity on the natural environment globally and in each country (using the Fiji Water example)?

2. *Ethical decision-making:* How can we address, ethically, issues such as the global use of environmental resources like water, which have no national borders? Who or what should govern these resources?

Take a Position

Issue: Consider the consequences of Fiji Water's operations for the natural environment. What should the company do to minimize the negative impact on the natural environment locally and globally?

KEY TAKEAWAYS

Human Aspects of Globalization

- Globalization affects countries but also people, their lives, and their livelihoods.

- Most immigrants move between countries located within the same region—perhaps due to fewer language and cultural barriers.

- Immigration policies affect a country's labor market and ability to be competitive globally.

- Cultural globalization has both pros and cons.

SUMMARY

Globalization presents many countries with unprecedented opportunity for economic, humanitarian, and civic growth. However, not all countries share in the upsides and are often exploited or left behind. Moreover, although the benefits of globalization are many, its impact on societies and natural resources cannot be ignored.

KEY TERMS

bottom of the pyramid (BOP) 366
boycott 372
complicity 367

foreign direct investment (FDI) 364
global citizenship 364
globalization 364

isolationism 371
multinational corporations (MNCs) 364

REVIEW QUESTIONS

1. What is globalization?

2. What are the major institutions (political, economic, legal) that govern the globalization process?

3. Why is there discontent with the way globalization is proceeding?

4. What are the effects of globalization on business? What are the effects of business on globalization?

5. Explain why Brexit is an example of a movement toward isolationism.

MANAGER'S CHALLENGE

Managing International Assignments

MNCs are increasing their use of international assignments of key personnel. Often, these assignments are based on the need for a scarce skill set, career development, or the launching of a new product or venture. However, these assignments can be difficult to manage effectively, with a failure rate of nearly half of all assignments. The Society for Human Resource Management (SHRM) suggests that an international assignment will have a significantly better chance for success if the candidate not only has job-related expertise but also the psychological resources to adjust to living in a new culture and setting as well as the social skills to build a network with local stakeholders.

Framing Questions

1. What competencies do you think are necessary for employees to have to be effective candidates for international assignments?

2. Why do you think there is such a high failure rate for international appointments?

3. What steps should management take to develop the necessary skill sets for employees to adjust to international assignments?

Assignment

Prepare a two-page employee development plan that will serve to provide employees with the necessary skill set to thrive in an international assignment.

GLOSSARY

#OccupyWallStreet (OWS) [Chapter 12, p. 280]: A social media-organized activist group whose mission is to draw attention to income inequality, corporate greed, and the corrosive nature of money in politics.

actual malice [Chapter 5, p. 96]: Must prove if a public official or personality is suing for defamation; the defendant published a statement that was either (1) false and published it anyway or (2) acted with a reckless disregard for the truth.

Ads Manager [Chapter 12, p. 270]: Facebook's "do-it-yourself" ad service in which businesses create and manage their ads, find tools to target specific consumer audiences, and track results.

Age Discrimination in Employment Act (ADEA) [Chapter 9, p. 201]: Passed in 1967, prohibits discrimination based on age (40 years old and older). Allows for disparate treatment, disparate impact, and harassment claims.

aggregate limits [Chapter 4, p. 72]: Restrictions on how much money a donor may contribute in total to all candidates and committees.

agreement [Chapter 5, p. 105]: An element of a contract; includes making a definite offer and that offer was accepted.

Agreement on Trade-Related Aspects of Intellectual Property Rights (TRIPS) [Chapter 11, p. 255]: A multilateral agreement with the goal of facilitating international trade in a consistent and beneficial manner in terms of economies and public welfare.

Alien Tort Statute (ATS) [Chapter 11, p. 245]: Statute that gives U.S. federal courts jurisdiction to hear "any civil action by an alien for a tort only, committed in violation of the law of nations or a Treaty of the United States."

Americans with Disabilities Act (ADA) [Chapter 9, p. 204]: A federal law that prohibits discrimination against an otherwise qualified individual based on his or her disability, including disparate treatment, disparate impact, harassment, and failure to accommodate.

Anti-Bribery Convention [Chapter 11, p. 250]: Adopted by the OECD to assure a "functional equivalence among measures taken by the parties to sanction bribery of foreign public officials" without each country having to change their legal system.

application programming interface (API) [Chapter 12, p. 271]: An app development platform that makes third-party applications accessible to users.

appropriation of name or likeness [Chapter 5, p. 100]: Also known as the right of publicity; occurs when someone uses another's name or likeness without their permission for personal benefit.

arbitration [Chapter 8, p. 179]: A private proceeding using a neutral third party to render a binding decision in a dispute.

artificial intelligence (AI) [Chapter 14, p. 318]: Machine-based learning involving adaptive mechanisms that enable computers to learn from example, experience, and analogy.

bait and switch [Chapter 6, p. 122]: A technique used by companies to lure the consumer into buying a product of a higher price by initially advertising a product at a low price but in actuality selling a different product at a higher price.

bargaining unit [Chapter 8, p. 179]: A group of employees who do similar work and share similar issues and concerns when it comes to working conditions.

base limits [Chapter 4, p. 72]: Restriction on donations to a specific candidate.

best efforts [Chapter 10, p. 216]: A contractual agreement that the underwriter does not guarantee the price for the securities but markets and sells the securities on behalf of the company for a commission.

bill [Chapter 4, p. 68]: A draft of a proposed law.

biometric data [Chapter 14, p. 338]: Retina or iris scans, fingerprints, voiceprints, or scans of hand or face geometry.

Bipartisan Campaign Reform Act (BCRA) of 2002 [Chapter 4, p. 72]: A federal law that regulates the financing of political campaigns.

Black Lives Matter (BLM) [Chapter 12, p. 281]: An activist group focused on the reordering of society to allow African Americans equal opportunities and the economic, political, and social empowerment of African Americans.

bottom of the pyramid (BOP) [Chapter 16, p. 366]: An economic term that refers to the poorest two thirds of the economic human pyramid, a group of more than 4 billion people living in abject poverty; also known as base of the pyramid.

bounty program [Chapter 8, p. 168]: A monetary award for whistleblowers in order to incentivize reporting of wrongdoing.

boycott [Chapter 16, p. 372]: Government-imposed prohibition on the purchase and importation of certain goods from other countries.

breach [Chapter 5, p. 111]: Of a contract; when a party to a contract does not fulfill one or more of its promises.

breach of duty [Chapter 5, p. 102]: An element of negligence; the defendant failed to act as a reasonable person with care in a circumstance.

broad view (CSR) [Chapter 2, p. 32]: View of CSR in which the starting point is a socially defined goal rather than a business objective.

bubble [Chapter 10, p. 222]: Term used by economists to describe a long-lasting deviation of the price of some assets from their fundamental value (e.g., housing bubble).

bulletin board systems (BBSes) [Chapter 12, p. 264]: An early version of a chat room in which messages or other files were shared.

business ethics [Chapter 3, p. 45]: Applying personal values to business decisions.

capacity [Chapter 5, p. 105]: An element of a contract; one's authority under law to engage in certain actions or undertakings.

chat rooms [Chapter 12, p. 264]: Contemporary version of a BBS that allows users to share messages or other files with others.

choice of law clause [Chapter 5, p. 109]: A clause in a contract where the parties agree what state's law will apply to the agreement.

circular economic theory [Chapter 7, p. 147]: Describes an economy that goes beyond the pursuit of waste prevention and waste reduction to inspire technological, organizational, and social innovation across and within value chains.[i]

citizen interest organizations [Chapter 7, p. 160]: An individual or group with the authority to file enforcement lawsuits by virtue of citizen suit provisions.

citizen surveillance [Chapter 14, p. 333]: A province, city, or state puts the responsibility on the citizen to monitor their surroundings.

claim [Chapter 1, p. 4]: A legal entitlement or a right to be treated in a certain way.

classical insider trading [Chapter 6, p. 131]: The illegal act of an individual that owes a fiduciary duty to the company—usually an employee or director—learns nonpublic information and breaches its fiduciary duty by trading the securities of the company.

collective bargaining agreement (CBA) [Chapter 8, p. 179]: Negotiated with the employer, a contract that covers all of the terms of employment for the members of a bargaining unit, such as pay, hours, conditions for promotion, employee discipline, raises, termination, health insurance, benefits, and vacation time.

commerce [Chapter 15, p. 350]: All forms of commercial intercourse, including buying and selling as well as the interchange of commodities.

Commerce Clause [Chapter 15, p. 350]: Article I, Section 8, Clause 3 of the U.S. Constitution; gives Congress the power to "regulate commerce with foreign nations, and among the several states, and with the Indian tribes."

committee [Chapter 4, p. 68]: A legislative suborganization in the U.S. Congress or state legislature that handles subject matter.

Communications Decency Act (CDA) [Chapter 5, p. 96]: Passed in 1996, the CDA was an attempt made by U.S. Congress to regulate pornography on the Internet.

compensatory damages [Chapter 5, p. 91]: Money awarded to the plaintiff, or injured person, that is intended to restore them to the position they were in before the injury.

compliance-based approach [Chapter 3, p. 59]: The goal is to protect and punish legal violations.

complicity [Chapter 16, p. 367]: The act of facilitating, assisting, legitimizing, and encouraging abuse of internationally accepted ethical standards.

concerted activities [Chapter 8, p. 179]: The right of all employees guaranteed under the NLRA, regardless of union membership, to act together to improve their working conditions for mutual aid and protection.

conflict of interest (COI) [Chapter 3, p. 62]: When a manager has to choose between his or her interests and the interest of another group.

consideration [Chapter 5, p. 105]: An element of a contract; bargaining that leads to an exchange.

constructive insiders [Chapter 6, p. 131]: Attorneys, accountants, consultants, and other third parties who have a temporary fiduciary duty to the company because of their jobs.

Consumer Financial Protection Bureau (CFPB) [Chapter 6, p. 125]: An agency created to regulate consumer financial transactions, including credit cards, home mortgages, and bank accounts.

contract [Chapter 5, p. 105]: A promise that the law will enforce.

corporate governance [Chapter 1, p. 6]: The rules, processes, and procedures as outlined by an organization's board of directors to ensure accountability, fairness, and transparency among all parties with a claim on the organization.

corporate hypocrisy [Chapter 2, p. 36]: When a firm deceptively claims to be what it is not or to be doing something it is not.

corporate personhood [Chapter 15, p. 341]: The idea that a corporation is viewed as a person with similar rights and values.

---

[i]Deloitte. (n.d.). *Circular economy: From theory to practice*. Retrieved from https://www2.deloitte.com/content/dam/Deloitte/fi/Documents/risk/Circular%20economy%20FINAL%20web.pdf

corporate social advocacy [Chapter 4, p. 75]: When a CEO or other high-level executive of a business speaks directly with the public and/or an elected official about a current social topic that is outside the scope of their core business. CAS has the potential to influence legislation and policy in the same manner as lobbying.

corporate social irresponsibility [Chapter 2, p. 36]: When the firm causes some social harm and should be held in contempt for the harm.

corporate social responsibility (CSR) [Chapter 2, p. 24]: Actions that appear to further some social good, beyond the interests of the firm and that which is required by law.

corporate surveillance [Chapter 14, p. 334]: A company's right to monitor employee e-mails at work.

cultural competence [Chapter 11, p. 241]: A person's effectiveness in drawing upon their knowledge, skills, and personal traits in order to successfully work with people from a different culture, whether that happens among culturally diverse workers or customers at home or in a different country.

cultural norms [Chapter 11, p. 242]: The standards we live by and are shared by people within a social group.

cultural sensitivity [Chapter 11, p. 241]: The desire to learn and understand different cultures. This leads to the development of cultural competence.

custom [Chapter 11, p. 243]: A state practice that people of that state would consider illegal to break.

customary international law (CIL) [Chapter 11, p. 243]: Customs that are accepted universally as international law.

cyberbullying [Chapter 13, p. 310]: Using the Internet, cell phones, or other devices to send or post text or images intended to hurt or embarrass another person.

cyberstalking [Chapter 13, p. 310]: Generally refers to the use of the Internet, e-mail, or other electronic communications devices to stalk another person—where stalking in the traditional sense means to engage in repeated harassing or threatening behavior.

cyberterrorism [Chapter 13, p. 307]: The use of information technology by terrorist groups and individuals to further their agenda.

dark money [Chapter 4, p. 72]: Money donated by a business to a nonprofit or a trade association that will then contribute to a candidate the donor supports but will not have to reveal the identity of the donor when making the contribution.

datification [Chapter 14, p. 320]: The technologies and work practices by which people and organizations are sorted and classified, scored and ranked on various dimensions, and prescribed or predicted, often with the aim of manipulation.

debt instruments [Chapter 6, p. 126]: Assets that have a fixed rate of return (e.g., bonds and mortgages).

defamation [Chapter 5, p. 93]: Intentional tort; defamatory statement that is false, communicated to someone other than the plaintiff, and causes injury.

deontological [Chapter 3, p. 56]: An ethical approach focusing on duties—like justice or rights—and therefore the means not the ends.

digital divide [Chapter 13, p. 298]: The divide between those with access to new technologies and those without.

digital readiness [Chapter 13, p. 300]: The degree to which people succeed or struggle when they use technology to navigate their environments, solve problems, and make decisions.

digital safety [Chapter 13, p. 305]: When individuals or companies practice safeguarding user personal safety against security risks to private information and property associated with using the Internet—and the self-protection from computer crime in general.

digital security [Chapter 13, p. 305]: An organization's efforts to protect its digital assets from outsiders.

direct democracy [Chapter 4, p. 68]: When people are allowed to vote directly on a law.

direct initiative [Chapter 4, p. 69]: A petition with a required number of signatures supporting an issue can be put on the ballot for a vote.

direct subsidy [Chapter 11, p. 251]: A cash payment to relieve a burden.

disability [Chapter 9, p. 205]: A physical or mental impairment that substantially limits a major life activity.

discrimination [Chapter 9, p. 191]: Acting on our biases and stereotypes in decision-making.

disparate impact [Chapter 9, p. 195]: Legal claim under Title VII, ADEA, and ADA; when a rule or policy doesn't look discriminatory, but in practice it discriminates against a group of people based on a protected trait.

disparate treatment [Chapter 9, p. 195]: Legal claim under Title VII, ADEA, and ADA; intentionally treating someone less favorably because of their protected trait.

diversity [Chapter 9, p. 189]: A reflection of all differences in people, not just the categories protected by law—race, gender, color, national origin, religion, age, and disability—but also including culture, background, and experience.

Dodd–Frank Act (DFA) [Chapter 6, p. 125]: Under this act, it is unlawful for any provider of consumer financial products or services to engage in any unfair, deceptive, or abusive act or practice.

Dormant Commerce Clause [Chapter 15, p. 354]: States cannot pass laws that burden interstate commerce, since

Congress has the power to regulate economic activity that has a substantial effect on interstate commerce.

doxxing [Chapter 12, p. 280]: To search, with malicious intent, for online information regarding an individual.

dumping [Chapter 11, p. 251]: Occurs when an exporter sells a large volume of goods in a foreign country at a lower price than it charges its own domestic market.

duty of due care [Chapter 5, p. 102]: An element of negligence; a level of responsibility to act as a reasonable person with care in a circumstance.

economic strikes [Chapter 8, p. 179]: Usually involving economic issues like higher wages or better working conditions.

employee [Chapter 8, p. 164]: Employment status where the worker works for one employer, at the direction of his or her employer, and may receive benefits like health insurance, access to a retirement fund, and paid leave as well as have taxes withheld from his or her pay.

employment at will [Chapter 8, p. 167]: Unless there is a contract that says otherwise, employees are hired at will—they can leave for any reason and can be fired for any reason or no reason. Employment at will is one of the oldest employment theories in the United States.

engagement [Chapter 12, p. 269]: A term used to describe the amount of traffic of a social media post measured by "likes," "shares," "reposts," and "retweets."

environmental ethics [Chapter 7, p. 144]: The discipline in philosophy that studies the moral relationship of human beings to, and also the value and moral status of, the environment and its nonhuman contents.

environmental justice [Chapter 7, p. 140]: The fair treatment of all people with respect to the development, implementation, and enforcement of environmental laws, regulations, and policies.

environmentalism [Chapter 7, p. 140]: The study of the interaction between various components within the environment to look for solutions for environmental problems.

Equal Employment Opportunity Commission (EEOC) [Chapter 9, p. 195]: Created by Title VII, it is a federal agency with the authority to investigate claims of employment discrimination, mediate disputes, and sue on behalf of injured parties.

Equal Pay Act [Chapter 9, p. 195]: Passed in 1963, it requires that men and women be paid equally for equal work. Pay includes salary, bonuses, stock options, vacation and holiday pay, travel reimbursements, and the like.

equal work [Chapter 9, p. 195]: Means the job content (not job title) is substantially similar in skill, effort, and responsibility.

equity [Chapter 6, p. 126]: An ownership percentage of a venture.

ethical climate [Chapter 3, p. 62]: Employees' shared perceptions of the ethical practices and procedures of a firm.

ethical dilemma [Chapter 3, p. 48]: A conflict between two right moral values.

ethical temptation [Chapter 3, p. 47]: A conflict between a clear right behavior and clear wrong behavior.

ethics [Chapter 3, p. 45]: The expectations of conduct regarding how a person should behave, based on moral principles or values.

facilitation payments [Chapter 11, p. 248]: A small payment given to low-level government officials to speed up routine governmental actions.

factual cause [Chapter 5, p. 102]: An element of negligence; the defendant's conduct caused the plaintiff's injury.

Fair Debt Collection Practices Act [Chapter 6, p. 125]: Regulates communications between creditors and debtors and prohibits creditors from making false, deceptive, or misleading statements.

Fair Labor Standards Act (FLSA) [Chapter 8, p. 173]: Passed in 1938, regulates child labor, establishes a minimum wage, and requires premium pay for overtime.

False Claims Act (FCA) [Chapter 8, p. 168]: Federal law protecting a person or entity who reports, with evidence, fraud against any federal program or contractor. A whistleblower under the FCA can sue the wrongdoer on behalf of the U.S. government and recover up to 25% of any court award.

Family and Medical Leave Act (FMLA) [Chapter 8, p. 183]: Law designed to support working families in times of serious medical conditions.

federal tipped minimum wage [Chapter 8, p. 176]: Required by the FLSA, the employer must pay at least $2.13 per hour in direct wages. If an employee's tips combined with the employer's direct wages of at least $2.13 per hour do not equal the minimum hourly wage, the employer must make up the difference. States may have their own tipped minimum wage.

fiduciary duty [Chapter 1, p. 6]: The trust that *one* party will act in the best interests of another, owing them a duty of loyalty and care.

financial firms [Chapter 10, p. 214]: Sometimes called brokerage houses—firms that act on behalf of investors in buying and selling securities.

fintech [Chapter 10, p. 217]: Term used to refer to innovations in the financial and technology crossover space and typically refers to companies or services that use technology to provide financial services to businesses or consumers.

firm commitment agreement [Chapter 10, p. 216]: When the underwriter purchases all the issued securities at a negotiated price and then resells the shares to the public.

Foreign Corrupt Practices Act (FCPA) [Chapter 11, p. 247]: Prohibits American companies from paying bribes or giving "anything of value" to a foreign official to win an "improper advantage" in business.

foreign direct investment (FDI) [Chapter 16, p. 364]: A company, individual, or fund invests money in another country, buying shares of stock or loaning money.

foreseeable harm [Chapter 5, p. 102]: An element of negligence; it was foreseeable that the defendant's conduct could cause this type of harm.

forum selection clause [Chapter 5, p. 109]: A section of a contract that states that the parties agree that any litigation will be resolved in a specific state (forum).

free riders [Chapter 8, p. 179]: Those workers who benefit from the services of the union but do not join the union or pay dues.

free trade zone (FTZ) [Chapter 11, p. 255]: A type of special economic zone used as part of a larger economic growth strategy to help a country develop and diversify exports while protecting the businesses in that FTZ to help them create jobs and pilot new business strategies.

General Agreement on Tariffs and Trade (GATT) [Chapter 11, p. 254]: Signed by 23 countries; agreement that states that each member must confer most-favored-nation status to every other member, prohibits many import and export restrictions, and eliminates tariffs on imports from developing countries.

geotagging [Chapter 12, p. 272]: A feature that allows users to tag their location when they post content on social media.

global citizenship [Chapter 16, p. 364]: Exercising the rights, responsibilities, and obligations that arise from being part of a global community.

global financial crisis [Chapter 10, p. 220]: An 18-month economic downturn from 2007 to 2009 that the IMF concluded was the most severe recession since the Great Depression in the 1930s.

global financial system [Chapter 10, p. 210]: A set of formal and informal agreements that are intended to promote economic stability and access to money for investment and new venture financing.

globalization [Chapter 16, p. 364]: The increasing movement of goods, services, and capital across national borders.

government surveillance [Chapter 14, p. 332]: A global phenomenon as a number of countries place limits on the movement of persons in and out of countries.

green management [Chapter 7, p. 142]: Describes an organization's efforts to incorporate environmentalism and sustainability into its business model and practices.

grievance [Chapter 8, p. 179]: A procedure for internal dispute resolution involving an employee, union representation, and the employer's management team.

hacker [Chapter 13, p. 308]: A person who illegally gains access to and sometimes tampers with information in a computer system.

hacktivists [Chapter 13, p. 308]: Individuals or groups who hack into government or corporate computer networks and then release information to try to embarrass the organizations or gain leverage against the organizations.

harassment [Chapter 9, p. 199]: Includes unwelcome conduct that is based on a protected category. Becomes discrimination prohibited by law when enduring the conduct becomes a condition of the job or is so severe or pervasive that it creates a work environment that a reasonable person would find intimidating or abusive.

hypernorms [Chapter 3, p. 49]: The result of a convergence of religious, political, and philosophical thought across a number of countries and cultures.

implicit bias [Chapter 9, p. 191]: Stereotypes and attitudes that affect our understanding in an unconscious way.

implied warranties [Chapter 6, p. 121]: When a merchant creates a warranty through actions or words that describe the product as having certain qualities.

import quota [Chapter 11, p. 251]: A limit on the number of products that can be imported over a period of time.

inclusion [Chapter 9, p. 189]: A workplace that makes all people feel welcome and helps them thrive.

independent contractor [Chapter 8, p. 164]: Employment status where the worker can work for more than one company at the same time, does not receive benefits or paid time off, and does not have taxes withheld from his or her pay. Also, most employment laws do not apply to independent contractors.

independent contractor agreement [Chapter 8, p. 164]: Contract establishing independent contractor status for the worker. The agreement usually lays out the terms of the work and usually includes a statement that the agreement is not an employment contract.

indirect initiative [Chapter 4, p. 69]: A petition with a required number of signatures supporting the issue can go to the legislature for a vote.

indirect subsidy [Chapter 11, p. 251]: A tax benefit to incentivize behavior that is generally thought to be in the best interest of society.

industrial zone [Chapter 11, p. 257]: A type of special economic zone targeted at specific economic activity with infrastructure to suit the needs of that particular industry.

infinite scroll [Chapter 12, p. 274]: A continuous scrolling of social media posts developed by Brian Raskin in 2006.

initial public offering (IPO) [Chapter 6, p. 126]: The first time securities are issued to the public markets.

initiative [Chapter 4, p. 69]: A proposal for a new law or constitutional amendment.

injury [Chapter 5, p. 102]: An element of negligence; a physical injury or measurable loss.

insider trading [Chapter 6, p. 131]: The illegal act of buying or selling of securities for a profit based on information not available to the public.

integrity-based approach [Chapter 3, p. 59]: Combines the concern for the law with an emphasis on managerial responsibility for ethical behavior.

intentional tort [Chapter 5, p. 92]: Harm caused by deliberate conduct.

Internal Revenue Service [Chapter 8, p. 168]: Federal agency that enforces the IRC. The IRS has a bounty program for whistleblowers who report persons who fail to pay their taxes. Whistleblowers can collect up to 30% of what the IRS collects.

International Bill of Human Rights [Chapter 11, p. 245]: Composed of the UDHR; the International Covenant on Civil and Political Rights; and the International Covenant on Economic, Social, and Cultural Rights.

International Covenant on Civil and Political Rights [Chapter 11, p. 245]: Encompasses rights established in the UDHR and everyday rights such as the right to life; equality before the law; the right to individual liberties such as religion, expression, and assembly; the right to work; and the right to education.

International Covenant on Economic, Social, and Cultural Rights [Chapter 11, p. 245]: Encompasses rights such as the right to work for fair wages, to a safe work environment, to social security, to an adequate standard of living, to the highest achievement of physical and mental health, and to participate in cultural life and the benefits of science.

international financial institutions [Chapter 10, p. 211]: Institutions created after World War II by one or more nations to facilitate development and ensure financial stability.

intersectionality [Chapter 9, p. 192]: Identities do not exist independently from each other, and our multidimensional identities shape our experiences of bias and discrimination.

interstate commerce [Chapter 15, p. 350]: Any commercial transaction or traffic that crosses state lines or may involve more than one state.

intrusion into seclusion [Chapter 5, p. 100]: Occurs when one intrudes into another's private affairs and that intrusion would be highly offensive to a reasonable person.

isolationism [Chapter 16, p. 371]: A policy to be absent from alliances and other international political and economic relations.

JOBS Act [Chapter 6, p. 129]: A law that created exemptions to existing securities regulations in order to ease the process of obtaining capital, especially for small- to medium-sized companies.

Kyoto Protocol [Chapter 7, p. 154]: Treaty protocols requiring developed countries to reduce their emissions in two phases.

law [Chapter 3, p. 45]: A society's codification of public opinion and belief.

lawful strikes [Chapter 8, p. 179]: Strikes based upon economic issues or unfair labor practices.

League of Nations [Chapter 11, p. 243]: Precursor to the United Nations; intended to promote international cooperation and work toward peace and security.

legal purpose [Chapter 5, p. 105]: An element of a contract; the contract must be compliant with the law of the land and public policy.

legislative referendum [Chapter 4, p. 69]: When the state legislature sends a proposed bill straight to the public for a vote.

legitimacy [Chapter 1, p. 17]: Some form of acceptance of a stakeholder's claim or of the group itself.

leveraging [Chapter 10, p. 222]: In the context of investing, borrowing money to invest with the objective of producing a higher level of return.

limitation of liability clause [Chapter 5, p. 109]: A section of a contract that limits the amount of exposure a company faces in the event of a lawsuit.

lobbying [Chapter 4, p. 70]: Influencing or advocating on an issue making its way through the legislative process.

Lobbying Disclosure Act [Chapter 4, p. 71]: Legislation that is meant to bring increased accountability to federal lobbying practices and that requires certain compliance with registration, contribution reporting, and disclosure.

Main Street [Chapter 10, p. 213]: In the context of finance, Main Street is sometimes called the real economy because it is shorthand for individuals, as well as owners of small- and medium-sized businesses, who generate savings primarily through their own labor (rather than generating income primarily through investing) and then seek ways to invest their savings in ways that provide a return on their investment.

malware [Chapter 13, p. 305]: A shorthand term for malicious software that is used to gain access to information stored on a computer or computer network.

market [Chapter 6, p. 116]: One in which buyers view two products as close substitutes.

market-based incentives [Chapter 7, p. 157]: Approach in which businesses have certain choices as to how they may reach their pollution reduction goals, including pollution allowances that can be traded, bought, and sold.

material [Chapter 6, p. 127]: Information that would be important to an average investor.

Me Too movement [Chapter 12, p. 283]: A movement that began in 2006 as a survivor network for women and girls of color who were victims of sexual assault. The movement evolved in 2017 as a way to express solidarity with and support for all victims of sexual violence and harassment.

micro-influencers [Chapter 12, p. 277]: Social media users who do not have enough followers to be categorized as social media influencers, but are engaged with a devoted group of followers.

minimum wage [Chapter 8, p. 173]: Minimum hourly wage required by FLSA, currently $7.25 per hour. States may have a different minimum wage.

misappropriation theory [Chapter 6, p. 131]: Postulates that a person who uses insider information in trading securities has committed securities fraud against the source of the information.

moderate view (CSR) [Chapter 2, p. 32]: Social responsibility is a balance between being a good corporate citizen and creating economic value.

moderators [Chapter 12, p. 266]: A Redditor with the authority to regulate content on a subreddit.

monopoly [Chapter 6, p. 116]: Occurs when a company or its products dominate a particular market.

moral hazard [Chapter 10, p. 222]: An information failure where one party to a transaction has greater material knowledge than the other party.

moral intuition [Chapter 3, p. 55]: The sudden appearance in one's consciousness of a moral judgment, including an affective valence (good-bad, like-dislike), without any conscious awareness of having gone through steps of searching, weighing evidence, or inferring a conclusion.

moral reasoning [Chapter 3, p. 56]: A conscious mental activity that consists of transforming given information about people in order to reach a moral judgment.

morals [Chapter 3, p. 45]: One's own determination of right and wrong.

mortgage [Chapter 6, p. 125]: A loan secured by real estate.

most-favored-nation status [Chapter 11, p. 254]: The principle that all members must be treated equally in terms of tariffs.

multinational corporations (MNCs) [Chapter 16, p. 364]: Businesses that have assets in more than one country.

narrow view (CSR) [Chapter 2, p. 32]: Focusing on profits as a sole source of social responsibility.

National Labor Relations Act (NLRA) [Chapter 8, p. 178]: Passed in 1935, guarantees the right of employees to organize, form unions, and bargain collectively with their employers. The law ensures that workers have a choice on whether to belong to a union or not, and promotes collective bargaining to insure peaceful industry-labor relations. It also requires employers to bargain in good faith with unions.

National Labor Relations Board (NLRB) [Chapter 8, p. 179]: Created by the NLRA to arbitrate deadlocked labor-management disputes, guarantee democratic union elections, and penalize employers for unfair labor practices.

natural law [Chapter 11, p. 243]: A set of instinctual beliefs that some acts are right and some acts are wrong.

negligence [Chapter 5, p. 102]: Careless conduct and accidents that cause injury to another person or to property. Elements of negligence include (1) duty of due care, (2) breach of duty, (3) factual cause, (4) foreseeable harm, and (5) injury.

negligent design [Chapter 5, p. 103]: A type of product liability; the product was designed poorly so that it was unreasonably risky.

negligent failure to warn [Chapter 5, p. 103]: A type of product liability; the business did not warn consumers of the reasonable dangers associated with the normal use, and even foreseeable misuse, of the product.

negligent manufacturing [Chapter 5, p. 103]: A type of product liability; something happened during the manufacturing of the product, such as a failure to inspect, that caused a dangerous product to leave the manufacturing facility.

nondisclosure agreement (NDA) [Chapter 5, p. 109]: A contract, or a clause in a larger contract, that prohibits one or both parties from speaking about certain things typically under the threat of financial penalty.

North American Free Trade Agreement (NAFTA) [Chapter 11, p. 254]: A multilateral trade agreement between Canada, the United States, and Mexico whereby the three countries agreed to remove almost all tariffs among them, allowing for the free flow of goods across the borders.

OECD Working Group on Bribery [Chapter 11, p. 250]: A process by which member countries conduct year-round reviews of other member countries' commitment to and compliance with the convention.

Office of the Whistleblower [Chapter 8, p. 168]: Office within the SEC created by the DFA to enforce whistleblower provisions of the law.

opt in [Chapter 14, p. 321]: Consumers must consent to data collection before the site collects the data.

opt out [Chapter 14, p. 320]: Companies make available information about how they collect, use, and share personal information and allow individuals to opt out if they desire.

Organization for Economic Cooperation and Development (OECD) [Chapter 11, p. 249]: Founded in 1961 to promote global economic and social well-being.

otherwise qualified [Chapter 9, p. 205]: An employee has the requisite skills, education, and experience for the position and can perform the essential functions of the job with, or without, a reasonable accommodation.

outsourcing [Chapter 4, p. 79]: When the government contracts with a private business to complete municipal work.

pay gap [Chapter 9, p. 192]: Disparities in pay.

payday loans [Chapter 10, p. 229]: Controversial financing method that requires a borrower to pay a loan back with interest in one lump sum on her next payday.

per se standard [Chapter 6, p. 115]: Conduct that is inherently anticompetitive and harmful to the market is analyzed under this standard to determine whether an action is an unreasonable restraint.

personal information [Chapter 14, p. 316]: Information that identifies, relates to, describes, is capable of being associated with, or could reasonably be linked, directly or indirectly, with a particular consumer or household.

place of public accommodation [Chapter 15, p. 345]: A business that sells goods or services to the public.

popular referendum [Chapter 4, p. 69]: When the public can vote to repeal a law after it has been passed.

portable benefits [Chapter 8, p. 166]: Benefits that move with a worker from job to job.

post-effective period [Chapter 10, p. 217]: The time after the SEC declares the registration statement effective, allowing for the sales of securities through the company's underwriters.

power [Chapter 1, p. 17]: The ability or potential of a group to influence another and to secure a desired outcome.

pre-emption bills [Chapter 8, p. 173]: Laws passed by states to roll back or abolish state increases to the minimum wage.

prefiling or quiet period [Chapter 10, p. 216]: The period of time between when the company decides to go public and when the registration statement is publicly filed with the SEC.

price discrimination [Chapter 6, p. 118]: Offering products at different prices to competitors.

price gouging [Chapter 6, p. 122]: A seller steeply increases the price of goods or services, usually after a demand or supply shock.

primary market [Chapter 6, p. 126]: Original and reissuance of securities by a business to raise capital.

privacy [Chapter 14, p. 316]: A multidimensional concept relating broadly to confidentiality of personal information.

private company [Chapter 10, p. 215]: A company that has only sold securities to early investors that are not offered on the public markets.

private placements [Chapter 6, p. 126]: The limited groups of investors that issuers sell securities to (e.g., venture capitalists or institutional investors).

product liability [Chapter 5, p. 103]: Businesses that manufacture and sell products are responsible for injuries caused by their products if the product has (1) negligent design, (2) negligent manufacturing, or (3) negligent failure to warn.

progressive tax [Chapter 15, p. 359]: A tax that takes a larger percentage of income from high-income people than from lower-income people based on a person's ability to pay.

prospectus [Chapter 10, p. 216]: A document that discloses financial details about the company, such as risk factors, a business plan, and/or pending or threatened litigation.

protectionism [Chapter 11, p. 251]: Restrains international trade in order to protect local businesses and jobs from foreign competition.

public disclosure of embarrassing facts [Chapter 5, p. 100]: Revealing truthful information that the public has no legitimate need to know.

public markets [Chapter 6, p. 126]: Markets open to the general investing community.

public policy exceptions to employment at will [Chapter 8, p. 167]: Exceptions to the at will employment doctrine for reasons that harm the public interest, such as refusing to break the law, refusing to commit perjury, exercising a legal right, and serving on a jury.

public–private partnership (3P) [Chapter 4, p. 79]: A relationship between a public sector agency—either federal, state, or local—and a private business with a contract containing agreed-upon terms and conditions. Both parties share the resources, risks, and rewards of a project.

publication [Chapter 5, p. 96]: In libel, print communication.

punitive damages [Chapter 5, p. 91]: Damages, in addition to compensation for the injury, that are intended to punish the defendant for reprehensible conduct and deter others from engaging in the same type of conduct.

push notifications [Chapter 12, p. 274]: Pop-up notifications of social media apps.

reasonable accommodation [Chapter 9, p. 205]: Requirement under the ADA for an employer to work with a disabled employee to find an accommodation that would enable the employee to perform the essential functions of the job.

reasonable factor other than age [Chapter 9, p. 202]: A non-age factor that is objectively reasonable to an employer.

reasonably accommodate a religious observance or practice [Chapter 9, p. 200]: Requirement under Title VII of employers to work with employees to find an accommodation for a conflict between a workplace rule and a religious belief, practice, or observance.

Redditors [Chapter 12, p. 266]: The term used for Reddit users.

referendum [Chapter 4, p. 68]: A vote by registered voters on whether to approve or reject an existing law.

regressive tax [Chapter 15, p. 359]: A tax that while applied uniformly takes a larger percentage of income from low-income people than from higher-income people.

Regulation CF [Chapter 6, p. 129]: Entrepreneurs and other small businesses can raise up to $1 million from any investors using an online platform by selling restricted securities, and maximum investments vary depending on income.

Regulation D [Chapter 6, p. 128]: Exempts small transactions from the registration requirements of the 1933 Securities Act.

Religious Freedom and Restoration Act (RFRA) [Chapter 15, p. 343]: Prohibits the government from substantially burdening a person's exercise of religion.

respondeat superior [Chapter 5, p. 103]: A theory that states an employer is liable for the negligence of its employees if the employee was acting within the scope of her employment at the time of the injury.

restricted securities [Chapter 6, p. 128]: Securities that cannot be resold on a public market.

retaliation [Chapter 8, p. 168]: "Getting back at" a person. It could include firing or demoting or in any way discouraging someone from reporting violations of law or enforcing their rights.

revolving door [Chapter 4, p. 70]: Reference to the circumstance where former public officials take jobs with the companies that used to lobby their office, or when former lobbyists or corporate officials take jobs with the government agencies they used to lobby.

right to be forgotten [Chapter 14, p. 323]: A person's right to request the removal of information from the Internet or other repositories because it violates their privacy or is no longer relevant.

right to erasure [Chapter 14, p. 331]: A person's right to request erasure of personal data concerning him or her in certain circumstances.

right to privacy [Chapter 14, p. 319]: The right for one's personal information to be protected from public scrutiny.

right-to-work laws [Chapter 8, p. 179]: Present in states that prohibit union security agreements.

road show [Chapter 10, p. 217]: Occurs during the waiting period when the company's executives and underwriters travel around the United States to present the company to investment banks and institutional investors.

Rule 10b-5 [Chapter 6, p. 131]: Prohibits fraud in the purchase or sale of securities; the SEC can pursue civil and criminal claims against violators.

Rule 504 [Chapter 6, p. 128]: Transactions where no more than $5 million is being raised, there is no advertising, and only restricted securities are sold is exempt from registration requirements.

Rule 506 [Chapter 6, p. 128]: Sets limitations on the type of investor that can buy the security but no limit on the dollar amount of the offering.

rule of reason [Chapter 6, p. 115]: Conduct that is illegal only if it has an anticompetitive effect.

Sarbanes–Oxley Act (SOX) [Chapter 4, p. 68]: Federal law that increases transparency in public company reporting requirements. The law protects employees of publicly traded companies who report violations by their employers of SEC regulations.

secondary market [Chapter 6, p. 126]: The purchase and sale of issued securities between investors.

Section 18(a) [Chapter 6, p. 131]: Allows anyone who bought or sold securities in reliance on a false or misleading filing to sue for money damages.

Section 230 [Chapter 5, p. 96]: Part of the CDA; protects providers and users of interactive computer services from liability for what others say and do online.

Section 5 of the Federal Trade Commission (FTC) Act [Chapter 6, p. 121]: An advertisement is deceptive if it contains an important misrepresentation or omission that is likely to mislead a reasonable consumer.

Securities Exchange Act of 1934 (or Exchange Act) [Chapter 6, p. 127]: Regulates the secondary market for securities.

securities [Chapter 6, p. 126]: Includes equities and debt instruments and other types of tradeable financial assets.

securities fraud [Chapter 2, p. 29]: Deception that induces an investor to make a purchase or sale decision based on a false or deceptive statement.

security [Chapter 14, p. 316]: The act of protecting personal information.

self-surveillance [Chapter 14, p. 334]: The act of keeping out of the line of sight on cameras.

sexual harassment [Chapter 9, p. 199]: Harassment based on gender; includes unwelcome sexual advances, requests for sexual favors, and other verbal of physical conduct of a sexual nature.

shareholder [Chapter 1, p. 4]: A person, group, or organization owning one or more shares of stock in a corporation.

shareholder theory [Chapter 1, p. 6]: A shareholder-oriented view of the firm's responsibilities claims that managers should spend capital, given to them by shareholders initially, in ways that have been authorized by shareholders and act in the shareholders' interests.

sharing economy [Chapter 13, p. 298]: An economy where people are constantly buying, selling, and trading goods and services with each other.

sin tax [Chapter 15, p. 358]: A tax on socially harmful behavior such as smoking, drinking, or gambling.

single publication theory [Chapter 5, p. 96]: States that the alleged defamatory statement was communicated once—when it was published in the newspaper.

slacktivism [Chapter 12, p. 280]: A false sense of activism by users simply joining social media groups that advocate for a cause, while failing to further contribute to the cause.

social justice [Chapter 12, p. 280]: A dynamic examination of fairness and equality issues in society.

social media [Chapter 12, p. 264]: Forms of electronic communications (such as websites for social networking and microblogging) through which users create online communities to share information, ideas, personal messages, and other content (such as videos).

social media influencer [Chapter 12, p. 277]: A social media user with credibility and influence in a specific industry or with a specific audience to sway followers into purchasing sponsored items.

social reciprocity [Chapter 12, p. 274]: A psychological tactic utilized by social media developers to induce users to spend more times on social media by including "friend suggestions."

Social Security [Chapter 8, p. 173]: A financial safety net for retired, disabled, and disadvantaged workers funded by a tax on workers' earnings.

Social Security Act [Chapter 8, p. 173]: A law to create a federal financial safety net for elderly, unemployed, and disadvantaged workers.

special economic zone [Chapter 11, p. 255]: Usually part of a larger economic growth strategy to help a country develop and diversify exports while protecting domestic businesses.

stake [Chapter 1, p. 4]: A kind of interest in or claim on something of value.

stakeholder [Chapter 1, p. 4]: Any identifiable group or individual who can affect the achievement of an organization's objectives or who is affected by the achievement of an organization's objectives.

stakeholder salience [Chapter 1, p. 16]: A stakeholder group's ability to stand out or apart from something else by possessing power, legitimacy, and urgency.

stakeholder theory [Chapter 1, p. 5]: Creating value for society beyond a pure monetary benefit for shareholders, sometimes referred to as there being a moral obligation to work toward addressing the needs of customers, employees, suppliers, and the local community as well as shareowners, and keeping these needs and interests in balance.

statements of employment particulars [Chapter 8, p. 167]: Written employment agreements in the EU, covering topics like pay, title, and expected hours of work.

stereotype [Chapter 9, p. 191]: Framework through which we judge other people based on their social category, such as age, gender, or ethnicity.

Stop Harmful and Abusive Telecommunications Expression (HATE) Act [Chapter 12, p. 284]: Legislation that requires the Department of Commerce's National Telecommunications and Information Administration to include hate crimes involving social media with their periodic report to Congress.

strikes [Chapter 8, p. 179]: Mass work stoppages usually in response to employee grievances.

subprime mortgage [Chapter 10, p. 224]: Mortgages that allow borrowers to have initial lower payments that increase over time.

subreddits [Chapter 12, p. 266]: Online forums dealing with specific topics that are found on Reddit.

subsidy [Chapter 11, p. 251]: A benefit given to an individual, business, or institution—usually by the government.

sustainability [Chapter 7, p. 140]: The ability of ecosystems and processes to endure through future generations.

tariff [Chapter 11, p. 251]: A tax on imported goods and services.

Tax and Spend Clause [Chapter 15, p. 356]: Grants Congress the power to tax and spend for the general welfare of the people.

teleological [Chapter 3, p. 56]: An ethical approach focusing on the outcomes or consequences of a decision, the ends not the means.

theory [Chapter 1, p. 5]: A set of propositions or concepts that seeks to explain or predict something.

tip pooling [Chapter 8, p. 177]: An arrangement whereby servers pool their tips at the end of a shift and share them with other staff.

tipped employee [Chapter 8, p. 176]: Someone who works in a job in which they customarily and regularly receive more than $30 a month in tips.

tippees [Chapter 6, p. 132]: Those who receive nonpublic information from insiders and then trade.

tipper [Chapter 6, p. 132]: The insider.

Title VII of the Civil Rights Act [Chapter 9, p. 195]: Prohibits discrimination based on race, religion, sex, national origin, or color in all facets of employment.

tombstone ad [Chapter 10, p. 217]: A simple ad containing basic information about the offering: the amount and type of security, the underwriter, and the price.

tort [Chapter 5, p. 91]: A civil wrong that causes harm to another.

tortious interference with a prospective business advantage [Chapter 5, p. 98]: A tort based on unlawful conduct in competition. Elements of this claim are as follows: (1) the plaintiff had a business relationship with a third party, (2) the defendant knew about the relationship, (3) the defendant maliciously interfered with that relationship, and (4) the interference caused injury to the relationship between the plaintiff and the third party.

treaties [Chapter 11, p. 243]: Consensual agreements between the countries who sign them.

triple bottom line [Chapter 2, p. 29]: Financial, social, and environmental results, taken together as an integrated whole, constitute a company's triple bottom line.

trolling [Chapter 12, p. 280]: When a social media user deliberately produces provocative content to generate a negative response.

Truth in Lending Act (TLA) [Chapter 6, p. 125]: Requires lenders disclose all of the loan information clearly, including the amount financed, the total of payments, the finance charge, and the APR.

UN Commission on Human Rights [Chapter 11, p. 244]: Established in 1947 with the goal of developing a set of rights to which all human beings on the planet are entitled.

underwriter [Chapter 10, p. 216]: Usually an investment bank, advises the company throughout the IPO process, helping the company determine its value and its initial share price.

undue hardship [Chapter 9, p. 205]: Under the ADA, an accommodation is not reasonable if it creates an undue hardship for the employer; this may include cost of the accommodation relative to the finances, size, and operation of the business; the location of the business's facilities; and the composition and functions of its workforce.

unfair labor practices [Chapter 8, p. 179]: Practices that violate the NLRA, such as retaliating against an employee for joining a union.

Uniform Commercial Code (UCC) [Chapter 6, p. 120]: A set of uniform rules to govern commercial transactions.

union [Chapter 8, p. 179]: An organized group of workers who work together to make decisions about the terms and conditions of work.

union security agreements [Chapter 8, p. 179]: Agreements between unions and businesses whereby the union can require eligible employees to join or that the employer will collect dues on behalf of the union.

United Nations [Chapter 11, p. 243]: A global body made up of many nations seeking to work together to ensure international peace and security, provide humanitarian aid, promote sustainable development, uphold international law, and protect human rights.

United States–Mexico–Canada Agreement (USMCA) [Chapter 11, p. 255]: A more modern version of NAFTA, with some changes to the rules for the auto industry and dairy markets, and changes to labor and environmental standards.

Universal Declaration of Human Rights (UDHR) [Chapter 11, p. 244]: A declaration of "inalienable entitlements of all people, at all times, in all places."

unlawful strike [Chapter 8, p. 179]: The purpose of which violates the NLRA.

unreasonable restraints [Chapter 6, p. 116]: Include conduct that restrains competition.

U.S. Department of Justice [Chapter 11, p. 248]: Has civil and criminal enforcement powers for violations of the anti-bribery and accounting provisions of the FCPA.

U.S. Securities and Exchange Commission (SEC) [Chapter 10, p. 233]: An independent agency consisting of five commissioners appointed by the president of the United States.

variable ratio schedule [Chapter 12, p. 273]: A strategy used by social media developers to entice app users to increase viewing time on their apps by creating a delay before showing results.

waiting period [Chapter 10, p. 217]: The time between public filing of the registration statement with the SEC and the effective date of the IPO.

Wall Street [Chapter 10, p. 213]: Individuals and global firms that make the financial markets function by generating revenue primarily using financial markets rather than labor.

warranty [Chapter 6, p. 120]: A legally binding promise that goods will meet certain standards.

warranty of fitness for a particular purpose [Chapter 6, p. 121]: Promises the product will be fit for that purpose as long as the seller knows that the buyer is relying on the seller's skill or judgment with regard to whether the product is fit for that purpose.

warranty of merchantability [Chapter 6, p. 121]: Promises the goods will be fit for the ordinary purposes for which they are used.

whistleblower [Chapter 8, p. 167]: A person, often an employee or former employee, who reports illegal or fraudulent activity by an employer, government, or organization.

workers' compensation [Chapter 8, p. 172]: Type of insurance program that compensates employees for lost wages and medical care after sustaining an injury or illness that is work related.

World Trade Organization (WTO) [Chapter 11, p. 254]: A global organization composed of 164 member countries, dealing with the rules of trade to ensure smooth and peaceful global trade agreements, a forum to negotiate trade agreements, and a place to resolve trade disputes.

NOTES

CHAPTER 1

1. Boesso, G., & Kumar, K. (2009). An investigation of stakeholder prioritization and engagement: Who or what really counts. *Journal of Accounting & Organizational Change, 5*, 62–80; Jones, T. M., Felps, W., & Bigley, G. A. (2007). Ethical theory and stakeholder-related decisions: The role of stakeholder culture. *Academy of Management Review, 32*, 137–155.

2. Eesley, C., & Lenox, M. J. (2006). Firm responses to secondary stakeholder action. *Strategic Management Journal, 27*, 765–781.

3. Freeman, R. E. (1984). *Strategic management: A stakeholder approach*. Boston, MA: Pitman.

4. Freeman, R. E., & Reed, D. L. (1983). Stockholders and stakeholders: A new perspective on corporate governance. *California Management Review, 25*, 19.

5. Ibid.

6. Clarkson, M. B. E. (1995). A stakeholder framework for analyzing and evaluating corporate social performance. *The Academy of Management Review, 20*, 92–127.

7. Smith, H. J. (2003). The shareholders vs. stakeholders debate. *MIT Sloan Management Review, 44*, 85–91.

8. See Donaldson, T., & Preston, L. E. (1995). The stakeholder theory of the corporation: Concepts, evidence, and implications. *Academy of Management Review, 20*, 65–91; Evan, W. M. & Freeman, R. E. (1993). A stakeholder theory of the modern corporation: Kantian capitalism. In T. Beauchamp & N. Bowie (Eds.), *Ethical theory and business* (pp. 75–93). Englewood Cliffs, NJ: Prentice Hall; Hansmann, H., & Kraakman, R. (2001). The end of history for corporate law. *Georgetown Law Journal, 89*, 439–468.

9. Donaldson & Preston (1995); Marcoux, A. M. (2003). A fiduciary argument against stakeholder theory. *Business Ethics Quarterly, 13*, 1–24.

10. Clark, C. E. (2018). Value, accountability and corporate boards. Paper presented at the 2018 Trans-Atlantic Business Ethics Conference, Rutgers University, New Brunswick, NJ.

11. Donaldson & Preston (1995).

12. Jones et al. (2007).

13. Armitage, S., Hou, W., Sarkar, S., & Talaulicar, T. (2017). Corporate governance challenges in emerging economies. *Corporate Governance: An International Review, 25*, 148–154.

14. Smith (2003).

15. Freeman, R. E. (2008). Ending the so-called "Friedman-Freeman" debate. *Business Ethics Quarterly, 18*, 162–166.

16. Devinney, T. M., Mcgahan, A. M., & Zollo, M. (2013). A research agenda for global stakeholder strategy. *Global Strategy Journal, 3*, 325–337.

17. Friedman, M. (1962/1982). *Capitalism and freedom*. Chicago, IL: University of Chicago Press. See also Smith, 2003.

18. Hasnas, J. (1998). The normative theories of business ethics: A guide for the perplexed. *Business Ethics Quarterly, 8*, 1–38.

19. Anabtawi, I., & Stout, L. (2008). Fiduciary duties for activist shareholders. *Stanford Law Review, 60*, 1255–1308.

20. Jensen, M. C., & Meckling, M. (1976). Theory of the firm: Managerial behavior, agency costs and ownership structure. *Journal of Financial Economics, 3*, 305–360.

21. Hasnas (1998).

22. Hansmann & Kraakman (2001).

23. Bradley, M., Schipani, C. A., Sundaram, A. K., & Walsh, J. P. (1999). The purposes and accountability of the corporation in contemporary society: Corporate governance at a crossroads. *Law and Contemporary Problems, 62*, 9–86.

24. Marcoux (2003).

25. Clark, C. E., Steckler, E. L., & Newell, S. (2016). Managing contradiction: Stockholder and stakeholder views of the firm as paradoxical opportunity. *Business and Society Review, 121*, 123–159.

26. Jensen, M. C. (2002). Value maximization, stakeholder theory, and the corporate objective function. *Business Ethics Quarterly, 12*, 235–256; Bratton, W. W., & Wachter, M. L. (2010). The case against shareholder empowerment. *University of Pennsylvania Law Review, 15*, 653–728.

27. Marcoux (2003).

28. Boatright, J. R. (1994). Fiduciary duties and the shareholder-management relation: Or, what's so special about shareholders. *Business Ethics Quarterly 4*, 393–407.

29. Stout, L. A. (2001). Bad and not-so-bad arguments for shareholder primacy. *Southern California Law Review, 75*, 1189.

30. Smith (2003).

31. Ibid.

32. Boatright, J. R. (2006). What's wrong—and what's right— with stakeholder management. *Journal of Private Enterprise, 21*, 106–130.

33. Boatright (2006, p. 108).

34. Freeman (1984).

35. Smith (2003).

36. Clark (2018).

37. Jensen, M. C. (2002). Value maximization, stakeholder theory, and the corporate objective function. *Business Ethics Quarterly, 12*, 235–256; Jensen, M. C. (2008). Non-rational behavior, value conflicts, stakeholder theory, and firm behavior. *Business Ethics Quarterly, 18*, 167–171.

38. Rasche, A., & Esser, D. E. (2006). From stakeholder management to stakeholder accountability. *Journal of Business Ethics, 65*, 251–267.

39. Jensen (2008).

40. Zott, C., & Amit, R. (2007). Business model design and the performance of entrepreneurial firms. *Organization Science, 18*, 181–199.

41. Harrison, J. S., & Wicks, A. C. (2013). Stakeholder theory, value, and firm performance. *Business Ethics Quarterly, 23*, 7–124.

42. Porter, M. E., & Kramer, M. R. (2011). Creating shared value. *Harvard Business Review, 89*, 62–77.

43. Freeman & Reed (1983).

44. Phillips, R. (2003). Stakeholder legitimacy. *Business Ethics Quarterly, 13*, 25–41.

45. Baron, D. P. (1995). Integrated strategy: Market and nonmarket components. *California Management Review, 37*, 47–65.

46. Ibid.

47. Bevan, D., & Werhane, P. (2010). Stakeholder theorising and the corporate-centric world. *Dans Management & Avenir, 3*, 127–141.

48. McKay, B., Maloney, J., & Chaker, A. (2018, November 9). Juul to stop sales of most flavored e-cigarettes in retail stores. *The Wall Street Journal.* Retrieved from https://www .wsj.com/articles/juul-to-stop-sales-of-most-flavored-e-cigarettes-in-retail-stores-1541784238

49. Juul. (n.d.). Our mission. Retrieved from https://www.juul .com/mission-values

50. McKay, B. (2018, November 15). Youth use of e-cigarettes jumped 78%, government study shows. *The Wall Street Journal.* Retrieved from https://www.wsj.com/articles/ youth-use-of-e-cigarettes-jumped-78-government-study-shows-1542310284

51. McKay et al. (2018).

52. Ibid.

53. Maloney, J. (2018, November 13). Juul says it will quit social media. *The Wall Street Journal.* See also https://newsroom .juul.com/2018/11/13/juul-labs-action-plan

54. McKay et al. (2018).

55. Ibid.

56. Abbott, B., & Maloney, J. (2019, September 7). People urged to stop vaping following more deaths, hundreds of illnesses. *The Wall Street Journal.* Retrieved from https://www.wsj .com/articles/authorities-investigating-450-vaping-ill nesses-and-a-third-death-11567794441?mod=article_inline

57. Eesley & Lenox (2006); Boesso & Kumar (2009).

58. Bevan & Werhane (2010).

59. Phillips (2003).

60. Neville, B. A., Bell, S. J., & Whitwell, G. J. (2011). Stakeholder salience revisited: Refining, redefining, and refueling an underdeveloped conceptual tool. *Journal of Business Ethics, 102*, 357–378.

61. Clark, C. E., Bryant, A. P., & Griffin, J. J. (2017). Firm engagement and social issue salience, consensus, and contestation. *Business & Society, 56*, 1136–1168. See also Eesley & Lenox (2006).

62. Clark et al. (2017); Eesley & Lenox (2006).

63. Eesley & Lenox (2006); Pfeffer, J. (1981). *Power in organizations.* Boston, MA: Pitman.

64. Suchman, M. C. (1995). Managing legitimacy: Strategic and institutional approaches. *Academy of Management Review, 20*, 571–610.

65. Jones et al. (2007).

66. Freeman, R. E., Velamuri, S. R., & Moriarty, B. (2006). Company stakeholder responsibility: A new approach to CSR. *Business Roundtable Institute for Corporate Ethics, 19.*

67. The Coca-Cola Company. Retrieved from https://www .coca-colacompany.com/stories/stakeholder-enga gement

68. Freeman et al. (2006).

69. Freeman, R. E., Harrison, J. S., Wicks, A. C., Parmar, B. L., & De Colle, S. (2010). *Stakeholder theory: The state of the art.* Cambridge, UK: Cambridge University Press.

70. Freeman et al. (2006).

71. Vielkind, J., & Honan, K. (2019, August 18). The missing piece of Amazon's New York debacle: It kept a burn book. *The Wall Street Journal.* Retrieved from https://www.wsj .com/articles/the-missing-piece-of-amazons-new-york-debacle-it-kept-a-burn-book-11567003239?mod=searchr esults&page=1&pos=1

CHAPTER 2

1. Smith, R. E. (2012, July 1). Defining corporate social responsibility: A systems approach for socially responsible capitalism. *University of Pennsylvania Scholarly Commons.*

2. McWilliams, A., & Siegel, D. S. (2011). Creating and capturing value: Strategic corporate social responsibility, resource-based theory, and sustainable competitive advantage. *Journal of Management, 37,* 1480–1495.

3. Acquier, A., Gond, J.-P., & Pasquero, J. (2011). Rediscovering Howard R. Bowen's legacy: The unachieved agenda and continuing relevance of social responsibilities of the businessman. *Business & Society, 50,* 607–646. See also Armstrong, J. S. (1977). Social irresponsibility in management. *Journal of Business Research, 5,* 185–213.

4. See Friedman, M. (1970, September 13). The social responsibility of business is to increase its profits. *The New York Times Magazine,* 32–33, 122, 124, 126.

5. Massachusetts Institute of Technology. (2011). Sustainability: The "embracers" seize the advantage. *MIT Sloan Management Review.* Retrieved from http://c0426007.cdn2 .cloudfiles.rackspacecloud.com/MIT-SMR-BCGsustain-ability-the-embracers-seize-advantage-2011.pdf

6. Carroll, A. B. (1999). Corporate social responsibility—evolution of a definitional construction. *Business and Society, 38,* 268–295.

7. McWilliams, A., Siegel, D., & Wright, P. (2006). Corporate social responsibility: Strategic implications. *Journal of Management Studies, 43,* 1–18.

8. Tidey, A. (2014). *Rich and poor worried about income gap.* CNBC. Retrieved from https://www.cnbc.com/ burson-marsteller-corporate-perception-indicator/#

9. Keys, T., Malnight, T. W., & van der Graaf, K. (2009, December). Making the most of corporate social responsibility. *McKinsey Quarterly.* Retrieved from https:// www.mckinsey.com/featured-insights/leadership/ making-the-most-of-corporate-social-responsibility

10. Werther, W. B., & Chandler, D. (2005). Strategic corporate social responsibility as a global brand insurance. *Business Horizons, 48,* 317–324. Retrieved from http://dx.doi .org/10.1016/j.bushor.2004.11.009

11. Godfrey, P. C. (2005). The relationship between corporate philanthropy and shareholder wealth: A risk management perspective. *Academy of Management Review, 30,* 777–798.

12. KPMG. (2017). *The road ahead: The KPMG survey of corporate responsibility reporting.* Retrieved February 14, 2018, from https://assets.kpmg.com/content/dam/kpmg/xx/ pdf/2017/10/kpmg-survey-of-corporate-responsibility-reporting-2017.pdf

13. GRI. (n.d.). *About GRI.* Retrieved from https://www.glob-alreporting.org/Information/about-gri/Pages/default.aspx

14. Hasnas, J. (1998). The normative theories of business ethics: A guide for the perplexed. *Business Ethics Quarterly, 8,* 19–42

15. Friedman (1970).

16. Vogel, D. J. (2005). Is there a market for virtue?: The business case for corporate social responsibility. *California Management Review, 47,* 19–45.

17. Ibid.

18. Gunningham, N., Kagan, R. A., & Thornton, D. (2006, July 28). Social license and environmental protection: Why businesses go beyond compliance. *Law and Social Inquiry, 29,* 307, 321.

19. Matten, D., & Moon, J. (2008). "Implicit" and "explicit" CSR: A conceptual framework for a comparative understanding of corporate social responsibility. *Academy of Management Review, 33,* 404–424.

20. Ibid., p. 410.

21. See Skarmeas, D., & Leonidou, C. N. (2013). When consumers doubt, watch out! The role of CSR skepticism. *Journal of Business Research, 66,* 1831–1838; Lange, D., & Washburn, N. T. (2012). Understanding attributions of corporate social irresponsibility. *Academy of Management Review, 37,* 300–326.

22. Wagner, T., Lutz, R. J., & Weitz, B. A. (2009). Corporate hypocrisy: Overcoming the threat of inconsistent corporate social responsibility perceptions. *Journal of Marketing, 73,* 77–91.

23. Masaka, D. (2008). Why enforcing corporate social responsibility (CSR) is morally questionable. *Electronic Journal of Business Ethics and Organizational Studies, 13,* 13–21. Retrieved from http://ejbo.jyu.fi/pdf/ejbo_vol13_no1_ pages_13-21.pdf

24. Banerjee, S. B. (2014). A critical perspective on corporate social responsibility: Towards a global governance framework. *Critical Perspectives on International Business, 10,* 84–95. Retrieved from https://doi.org/10.1108/ cpoib-06-2013-0021

25. Pichai, S. (2018, June 7). *AI at Google: Our principles*. Retrieved from https://www.blog.google/technology/ai/ai-principles

26. Shane, S., Metz, C., & Wakabayashi, D. (2018, May 30). How a Pentagon contract became an identity crisis for Google. *The New York Times*. Retrieved from https://www.nytimes.com/2018/06/01/technology/google-pentagon-project-maven.html

CHAPTER 3

1. American Marketing Association. (n.d.). *About AMA*. Retrieved from https://www.ama.org/about-ama

2. IESBA Staff. (2018, June 1). *IESBA overview of the revised and restructured code of ethics*. Retrieved from http://www.ifac.org/news-events/2018-06/iesba-overview-revised-and-restructured-code-ethics

3. Paine, L. S. (1994). Law, ethics and managerial judgment. *Journal of Legal Studies in Business, 12,* 160.

4. Deloitte Insights. (2018). *2018 Deloitte millennial survey*, p. 29. Retrieved from https://documents.deloitte.com/insights/2018DeloitteMillennialSurvey

5. KPMG. (n.d.). *2019 chief compliance officer survey*. Retrieved from https://advisory.kpmg.us/articles/2019/2019-cco-survey-gated.html.html

6. Kidder, R. M. (2005). *Moral courage: Taking action when your values are put to the test*. New York, NY: William Morrow.

7. Ibid.

8. Leavitt, K., & Sluss, D. M. (2015). Lying for who we are: An identity-based model of workplace dishonesty. *Academy of Management Review, 40,* 587–610.

9. Kidder (2005).

10. Donaldson, T., & Dunfee, T. W. (1999). *Ties that bind: A social contracts approach to business ethics*. Boston, MA: Harvard Business School Press.

11. Clark, C., & Brown, J. (2015). Multinational corporations and governance effectiveness: Towards a more integrative board. *Journal of Business Ethics, 132,* 565–577.

12. Donaldson, T., & Dunfee, T. (1999). When ethics travels. *California Management Review, 41,* 45–63.

13. Koehn, D. (2010). *Living with the dragon: Thinking and acting ethically in a world of unintended consequences*. New York, NY: Routledge.

14. ECI. (2018, December). *Interpersonal misconduct in the workplace: What it is, how it occurs and what you should do about it*. Retrieved from https://www.ethics.org/wp-content/uploads/2019/01/Global_Business_Ethics_Survey_2018_Q4_Final.pdf

15. Wang, Q., Dou, J., & Jia, S. (2016). A meta-analytic review of corporate social responsibility and corporate financial performance: The moderating effect of contextual factors. *Business & Society, 55,* 1083–1121.

16. JUST Capital. (2019). Overall rankings February 2019. Retrieved from https://justcapital.com

17. Gentile, M. C. (2010). *Giving voice to values: How to speak your mind when you know what's right*. New Haven, CT: Yale University Press.

18. Messick, D. M., & Bazerman, M. H. (2001). Ethical leadership and the psychology of decision making. In J. Dienhart, D. Moberg, & R. Duska (Eds.), *The next phase of business ethics: Integrating psychology and ethics* (pp. 213–238). Bingley, UK: Emerald Group Publishing Limited.

19. Ibid. Also, 90% choose New York, but it's Rome.

20. The University of Arizona. (n.d.). *About us—you and the university, that is*. Retrieved from https://www.arizona.edu/about

21. College Factual. (n.d.). *University of Arizona*. Retrieved from https://www.collegefactual.com/colleges/university-of-arizona/academic-life/graduation-and-retention

22. Davenport, D. K. (2018, March). *Arizona universities: Student success*. Retrieved from https://www.azauditor.gov/sites/default/files/18-102_Report.pdf

23. University Communications. (2017, October 4). *UA retention at an all-time high*. Retrieved from https://uanews.arizona.edu/story/ua-retention-rates-exceed-abor-goals

24. Blue, A. (2018, March 7). *Researcher looks at digital traces*. Retrieved September 3, 2018, from https://uanews.arizona.edu/story/researcher-looks-digital-traces-help-students

25. Ibid.

26. Ibid.

27. Meyer, D. (2018, March 13). An American university is spying on students. *Fortune*. Retrieved from http://fortune.com/2018/03/13/university-arizona-catcard-big-data-dropouts

28. Blue (2018).

29. The University of Arizona. (n.d.). *CatCard FAQ*. Retrieved from https://catcard.arizona.edu/faq

30. Jess, S. (2018, April 3). *CatCard research raises privacy concerns*. Retrieved from https://www.azpm.org/s/55217-catcard-research-raises-privacy-concerns

31. The University of Arizona. (n.d.). *UA acceptable use of computers and networks*. Retrieved from http://policy.arizona.edu/information-technology/acceptable-use-computers-and-networks

32. The University of Arizona. (n.d.). *UA electronic privacy policy*. Retrieved September 3, 2018, from http://policy.arizona.edu/information-technology/electronic-privacy-policy

33. Blue (2018).

34. Statista. (n.d.). *IT services: Big data market forecast*. Retrieved September 3, 2018, from https://www.statista.com/statistics/254266/global-big-data-market-forecast.

35. Meyer (2018).

36. Ibid.

37. Ibid.

38. Sedley, D. (2011). *Introduction to Meno and Phaedo by Plato* (D. Sedley & A. Long, Eds. & Trans.). Cambridge, UK: Cambridge University Press.

39. Rousseau, J.-J. (2003). *Emile*. Amherst, NY: Prometheus Books.

40. Haidt, J. (2001). The emotional dog and its rational tail: A social intuitionist approach to moral judgment. *Psychological Review, 108*, 814. See also, Haidt, J. (2006). *The happiness hypothesis: Finding modern truth in ancient wisdom*. New York, NY: Basic Books.

41. OpinionFront. (n.d.). *Who eats horsemeat? These facts will definitely surprise you*. Retrieved from https://opinionfront.com/who-eats-horse-meat; see also https://www.theatlantic.com/technology/archive/2017/06/horse-meat/529665

42. Haidt (2001).

43. Schwartz, M. S. (2016). Ethical decision-making theory: An integrated approach. *Journal of Business Ethics, 139*, 755–776.

44. Smith, H. (2009). *The world's religions*. New York, NY: HarperOne.

45. Rachels, J., & Rachels, S. (2010). *The elements of moral philosophy*. New York, NY: McGraw Hill.

46. Koehn (2010).

47. Rachels & Rachels (2010)

48. Koehn (2010).

49. Kidder (2005)

50. Rachels & Rachels (2010)

51. Ibid.

52. Paine, L. S. (1994). Managing for organizational integrity. *Harvard Business Review 72*, 2.

53. Victor, B., & Cullen, J. B. (1988). The organizational bases of ethical work climates. *Administrative Science Quarterly, 33*, 101–125.

54. Shin, Y. (2012). CEO ethical leadership, ethical climate, climate strength, and collective organizational citizenship behavior. *Journal of Business Ethics, 108*, 299–312.

55. Davis, M., & Johnston, J. (2009). Appendix C: Conflict of interest in four professions: A comparative analysis. In Institute of Medicine (US) Committee on Conflict of Interest in Medical Research, Education, and Practice; Lo, B., & Field, M. J. (Eds.), *Conflict of interest in medical research, education, and practice*. Washington, DC: National Academies Press. Retrieved from https://www.ncbi.nlm.nih.gov/books/NBK22946

56. Hayward, M. L. A., & Boeker, W. (1998). Power and conflicts of interest in professional firms: Evidence from investment banking. *Administrative Science Quarterly, 43*, 1–22.

57. Boatright, J. R. (2009). Conflicts of interest in financial services. *Business and Society Review, 105*, 201–219.

58. See Clark, C., & Van Buren, H. J. Compound conflicts of interest in the U.S. proxy system. *Journal of Business Ethics, 116*, 355–371; Clark C. & Newell, S. (2013). Institutional work and complicit decoupling across the U.S. capital markets: The work of rating agencies. *Business Ethics Quarterly, 23*, 1–30.

CHAPTER 4

1. Fortune 500. (2002). *A database of 50 years of FORTUNE's list of America's largest corporations*. Retrieved from https://archive.fortune.com/magazines/fortune/fortune500_archive/full/2002

2. Beltran, L. (2002, July 22). *WorldCom files largest bankruptcy ever*. CNN/Money. Retrieved from https://money.cnn.com/2002/07/19/news/worldcom_bankruptcy

3. Green, S. (2004). A look at the causes, impact and future of the Sarbanes-Oxley Act. *Journal of International Business and Law, 3*. Retrieved from http://scholarlycommons.law.hofstra.edu/jibl/vol3/iss1/2

4. California 2016 Ballot Propositions. (n.d.). Retrieved from https://ballotpedia.org/California_2016_ballot_propositions

5. History.com Editors (2009, November 16). *Eisenhower warns of military-industrial complex*. Retrieved from https://www.history.com/this-day-in-history/eisenhower-warns-of-military-industrial-complex

6. Drutman, L. (2015, April 20). How corporate lobbyists conquered American democracy. *The Atlantic*. Retrieved from

https://www.theatlantic.com/business/archive/2015/04/
how-corporate-lobbyists-conquered-american-democ-
racy/390822

7. Drutman, L. (2015, April 16). *The business of America is lobby-ing*. New York, NY: Oxford University Press.

8. Schouten, F. (2009, May 19). Several Bush officials work in areas related to former jobs. *USA Today*. Retrieved from https://usatoday30.usatoday.com/news/washington/2009-05-19-newjobs_N.htm

9. Dillet, R. (2016, April 15). David Plouffe to talk at Disrupt NY about his move from the White House to Uber strate-gic advisor. *TechCrunch*. Retrieved from https://techcrunch.com/2016/04/15/david-plouffe-to-talk-at-disrupt-ny-about-his-move-from-the-white-house-to-uber-strategic-adviser

10. Constine, J. (2017, January 10). Uber's David Plouffe will run politics for the Chan Zuckerberg Initiative. *TechCrunch*. Retrieved from https://techcrunch.com/2017/01/10/yes-z-can

11. Wadman, P. (2014, April 4). How our campaign finance system compares to other countries. *The American Pros-pect*. Retrieved from https://prospect.org/article/how-our-campaign-finance-system-compares-other-countries

12. Khazan, O. (2013, September 30). Why Germany's politics are much saner, cheaper, and nicer than ours. *The Atlantic*. Retrieved from https://www.theatlantic.com/international/archive/2013/09/why-germany-s-politics-are-much-saner-cheaper-and-nicer-than-ours/280081

13. Kokalitcheva, K. (2016, July 13). Government lobbyists are more nimble than ever. *Fortune*. Retrieved from http://fortune.com/2016/07/13/government-lobbyists-social-media

14. McGregor, J. (2016, September 7). Starbucks is brewing up feel-good digital civics lessons to go with its coffee. *The Washington Post*. Retrieved from https://www.washingtonpost.com/news/on-leadership/wp/2016/09/07/starbucks-now-offers-stories-about-citizen-do-gooders-to-go-with-your-coffee/?utm_term=.83d463b10df9

15. Dodd, M. S., & Supa, D. W. (2014). Conceptualizing and measuring "corporate social advocacy" communication: Examining the impact on corporate financial performance. *Public Relations Journal, 8*. Retrieved from https://www.prsa.org/Intelligence

16. Bronner, S. (2016, March 23). Disney, Marvel threaten to skip filming in Georgia if governor signs "anti-gay bill." *Entrepreneur*. Retrieved from https://www.entrepreneur.com/article/272922

17. Ellis R., & Grinberg, E. (2016, March 28). *Georgia gov Nathan Deal to veto "religious liberty" bill*. Retrieved from http://www.cnn.com/2016/03/28/us/georgia-north-carolina-lgbt-bills

18. Jarvie, J. (2019, May 15). Stacey Abrams weighs in on abor-tion bans, boycotts and California. *Los Angeles Times*. Retrieved from https://www.latimes.com/politics/la-na-stacey-abrams-abortion-film-boycott-georgia-california-20180515-story.html

19. Livingston, G. (2016, September 26). *Among 41 nations, U.S. is the outlier when it comes to paid parental leave*. Retrieved from http://www.pewresearch.org/fact-tank/2016/09/26/us-lacks-mandated-paid-parental-leave

20. The National Council for Public-Private Partnerships. (n.d.). *Automated traffic photo enforcement, Washington DC, 2000 NCPPP Project award winner*. Washington, DC: Author. Retrieved from http://www.ncppp.org/resources/case-studies/public-safety/automated-traffic-photo-enforcement-washington-dc

21. Semuels, A. (2016, May 12). New Balance bought its own commuter rail station. *The Atlantic*. Retrieved from https://www.theatlantic.com/business/archive/2015/05/new-balance-bought-its-own-commuter-rail-station/392711

22. Garfield, L. (2018, July 28). San Francisco Bay Area cit-ies are cracking down on free food at tech companies— Here's why that's a good idea, according to a startup cofounder. *Business Insider*. Retrieved from https://www.businessinsider.com/san-francisco-bay-area-ban-free-food-at-tech-companies-cafeterias-why-2018-7/commerce-on-business-insider

23. Mumford, M., Schanzenbach, D. W., & Nunn, R. (2016, October 20). *The economics of private prisons*. Retrieved from http://www.hamiltonproject.org/papers/the_economics_of_private_prisons

24. Yates, S. Q. (2016, August 18). *Phasing out our use of private prisons, deputy attorney general, Department of Justice* [Memo]. Retrieved from https://www.justice.gov/archives/opa/blog/phasing-out-our-use-private-prisons

25. Mumford et al. (2016).

26. Olsen, L. (2017, August 19). Private prisons boom in Texas and across America under Trump's immigration crack-down. *Houston Chronicle*. Retrieved from https://www.houstonchronicle.com/news/houston-texas/houston/article/Private-prisons-boom-in-Texas-and-across-America-11944652.php

27. CoreCivic 2017 Annual Report Form 10-K. (2018, February 22). Retrieved from http://ir.corecivic.com/static-files/6e38a54c-cdea-4ff9-ba06-f24d38a6ad60

CHAPTER 5

1. Bloomberg (2019, May 21). Johnson & Johnson loses one baby powder cancer case and wins another. *Los Angeles*

Times. Retrieved from https://www.latimes.com/business/
la-fi-johnson-baby-powder-talc-cancer-20190521-story
.html

2. Loftus, P. (2019, May 31). Johnson & Johnson hit with $300 million in punitive damages in talc case. *The Wall Street Journal*. Retrieved from https://www.wsj.com/articles/johnson-johnson-hit-with-300-million-in-punitive-damages-in-talc-case-11559339141

3. Helmut, K. (2013). Harmonising tort law in the European Union: Advantages and difficulties. *Elite Law Journal, 1*. Retrieved from https://eltelawjournal.hu/wp-content/uploads/2014/03/ELJ_Separatum_koziol.pdf

4. Jiang, H. (2015, August 19). Chinese tort law between tradition and transplants. In M. Bussani & A. Sebok (Eds.), *Comparative tort law: Global perspectives*. Cheltenham, UK: Edward Elgar Publishing. Retrieved from https://ssrn.com/abstract=2705916

5. RM Warner Law. (2015, April). *UK defamation: Legal overview*. Retrieved from http://kellywarnerlaw.com/uk-defamation-laws

6. *Sandals Resort Intl. v. Google*, 86 A.D.3d 32, 42 (2011).

7. Id. at 43.

8. *Cheryl Jacobus v. Donald Trump*, 55 Misc.3d 470 (2017).

9. *Enigma Software Grp v. Bleeping Computer*, 194 F. Supp.3d 263 (S.D.N.Y. 2016).

10. *Avepoint, Inc. v. Power Tools, Inc.*, 981 F.S Supp.2d 496 (2013).

11. *Broadspring v. Congoo*, 2014 U.S.Dist. LEXIS 116070, p. 5.

12. Gardner, E. (2012, August 29). Kim Kardashian settles lawsuit over look-alike in Old Navy ad (Exclusive). *The Hollywood Reporter*. Retrieved from https://www.hollywoodreporter.com/thr-esq/kim-kardashian-settles-lawsuit-look-alike-old-navy-gap-366522

13. *Herrick v. Grindr*, 306 F. Supp.3d 579, 585 (2018).

14. Rottman, G., & Rowland, L. (2013, August 1). *New proposal could singlehandedly cripple free speech online*. Retrieved from https://www.aclu.org/blog/national-security/privacy-and-surveillance/new-proposal-could-singlehandedly-cripple-free

15. Dogauchi, H. (2005). Formation of contracts. In *Outline of contract law in Japan*. Retrieved from http://www.law.tohoku.ac.jp/kokusaiB2C/overview

16. Pecht, G. (n.d.). *2015 litigation trends annual survey*. Retrieved from http://www.nortonrosefulbright.com/files/20150514-2015-litigation-trends-survey_v24-128746.pdf

17. Apple Media Services Terms and Conditions, G, i. Retrieved from https://www.apple.com/legal/internet-services/itunes/au/terms.html

CHAPTER 6

1. *Standard Oil Co. of New Jersey v. U.S.*, 221 U.S. 1 (1911).

2. *U.S. v. Apple, Inc.*, 952 F. Supp. 2d 638 (S.D.N.Y. 2013).

3. Ahmed, A. (2011, May 16). Nasdaq drops bid to buy NYSE Euronext. *The New York Times*. Retrieved from https://dealbook.nytimes.com/2011/05/16/nasdaq-drops-its-bid-to-buy-nyse-euronext

4. Freeman, M. (2019, July 18). Qualcomm slapped with $271 million fine by European regulator for predatory pricing. *The San Diego Tribune*. Retrieved from https://www.sandiegouniontribune.com/business/technology/story/2019-07-18/qualcomm-slapped-with-271-million-fine-by-european-regulator-for-predatory-pricing

5. Jolly, J. (2019, July 5). Competition regulator pauses Amazon's deal with Deliveroo. *The Guardian*. Retrieved from https://www.theguardian.com/business/2019/jul/05/competition-regulator-pauses-amazon-deal-with-deliveroo

6. Friedman, M. (1970, September 13). The social responsibility of business is to increase its profits. *The New York Times*.

7. Ibid.

8. Federal Trade Commission. (n.d.). *About the FTC; our vision*. Retrieved August 14, 2019, from https://www.ftc.gov/about-ftc

9. Federal Trade Commission. (2012, May 16). *Skechers will pay $40 million to settle FTC charges that it deceived consumers with ads for "toning shoes."* Retrieved from https://www.ftc.gov/news-events/press-releases/2012/05/skechers-will-pay-40-million-settle-ftc-charges-it-deceived

10. *POM Wonderful, LLC v. FTC*, 777F.3d 478 (D.C. Cir. 2015).

11. Federal Trade Commission. (2017, June). *State of Georgia obtains court order permanently halting electronics buyback scheme*. Retrieved from https://www.ftc.gov/news-events/press-releases/2017/06/ftc-state-georgia-obtain-court-order-permanently-halting

12. California Penal Code § 396.

13. U.S. Food and Drug Administration. (2018, March 29). *Laws enforced by FDA*. Retrieved August 15, 2019, from https://www.fda.gov/regulatory-information/laws-enforced-fda

14. U.S. Food and Drug Administration. (2019, September 30). *Food safety modernization act*. Retrieved August 15, 2019, from https://www.fda.gov/food/guidance-regulation-food-and-dietary-supplements/food-safety-modernization-act-fsma

15. Dodd–Frank Act, Title X, Subtitle C, Sec. 1036; PL111-203 (July 21, 2010).

16. Stempel, J. (2018, February 26). *Facebook settles lawsuit over 2012 IPO for $35 million*. Retrieved August 11, 2019, from https://www.reuters.com/article/us-facebook-settlement/facebook-settles-lawsuit-over-2012-ipo-for-35-million-idUSKCN1GA2JR

17. *United States v. O'Hagan*, 521 US 642 (1997).

18. *Salman v. U.S.*, 137 S.Ct. 420 (2016).

19. Id. at 427–428.

CHAPTER 7

1. Schlosberg, D. (2007). *Defining environmental justice: Theories, movements, and nature*. New York, NY: Oxford University Press.

2. See, e.g., Hofer, C., Cantor, D. E., & Dai, J. (2012). The competitive determinants of a firm's environmental management activities: Evidence from US manufacturing industries. *Journal of Operations Management, 30*, 69–84.

3. Greenwashing. (n.d.). In *Oxford English dictionary* (vol. 8).

4. Motavalli, J. (2011, February 12). *A history of greenwashing: How dirty towels impacted the green movement*. DailyFinance. Retrieved from https://web.archive.org/web/20150923212726/http://www.dailyfinance.com/2011/02/12/the-history-of-greenwashing-how-dirty-towels-impacted-the-green

5. Ibid.

6. Sullivan, J. (2009, August 1). "Greenwashing" gets his goat: Environmental activist coined the famous term. *Times Herald-Record*.

7. Stanford Encyclopedia of Philosophy. (2015, July 21). *Environmental ethics*. Retrieved from https://plato.stanford.edu/entries/ethics-environmental

8. Landrum, S. (2017, March 17). Millenials driving brands to practice socially responsible marketing. *Forbes*. Retrieved from https://www.forbes.com/sites/sarahlandrum/2017/03/17/millennials-driving-brands-to-practice-socially-responsible-marketing/#43deb1b64990

9. Horovitz, B. (2015, April 10). Starbucks: 99% ethically sourced java. *USA Today*. Retrieved from https://www.usatoday.com/story/money/2015/04/10/starbucks-fast-food-restaurants-dining-coffee-ethically-sourced/25571937

10. Starbucks Investor Relations. (2018, November 1). *Starbucks reports Q4 and full year fiscal 2018 results*. Retrieved from https://investor.starbucks.com/press-releases/financial-releases/press-release-details/2018/Starbucks-Reports-Q4-and-Full-Year-Fiscal-2018-Results/default.aspx

11. Bruntland Commission, United Nations General Assembly (1987). *Our common future*, p. 43.

12. The World Bank. (n.d.). *World development indicators*. Retrieved from http://datatopics.worldbank.org/world-development-indicators

13. Deloitte. (n.d.). *Circular economy: From theory to practice*. Retrieved from https://www2.deloitte.com/content/dam/Deloitte/fi/Documents/risk/Circular%20economy%20FINAL%20web.pdf

14. Tuladhar, A. (2018, February 6). Circular economy: A zero-waste model for the future. *Fair Observer*. Retrieved from https://www.fairobserver.com/world-news/circular-economy-zero-waste-recycling-environment-davos-economic-forum-news-14318

15. International Organization for Standardization. *ISO 14005:2019: Environmental management systems—Guidelines for a flexible approach to phased implementation* [Abstract]. Retrieved from https://www.iso.org/standard/72333.html

16. International Organization for Standardization. (2018, March). *Contributing to the UN sustainable development goals with ISO standards*. Retrieved from https://www.iso.org/files/live/sites/isoorg/files/store/en/PUB100429.pdf

17. United Nations Global Compact. (n.d.). Retrieved from https://www.unglobalcompact.org

18. United Nations Global Compact. (n.d.). *Delisted participants*. Retrieved from https://www.unglobalcompact.org/participation/report/cop/create-and-submit/expelled

19. Glantz, S. A. (2017, September 15). The UN Global Compact (finally) throws the tobacco industry out. *University of California San Francisco Center for Tobacco Control Research and Education*. Retrieved from https://tobacco.ucsf.edu/un-global-compact-finally-throws-tobacco-industry-out

20. Kelly, A. (2009, March 26). Money "wasted" on water projects in Africa. *The Guardian*. Retrieved from https://www.theguardian.com/society/katineblog/2009/mar/26/water-projects-wasted-money; Liddle, E. S., & Fenner, R. (2017, April 1). Water point failure in sub-Saharan Africa: The value of a systems thinking approach. *Waterlines*. Retrieved from https://www.developmentbookshelf.com/doi/full/10.3362/1756-3488.16-00022

21. The 169 commandments. (2015, March 26). *The Economist*. Retrieved from https://www.economist.com/leaders/2015/03/26/the-169-commandments

22. Kumar, R. (2017, January 30). Why the SDG critics are wrong. Devex.

23. ClimatePath. (n.d.). *The science of climate change*. Retrieved from https://www.climatepath.org/science

24. Cook, J., Oreskes, N., Doran, P. T., Anderegg, W. R., Verheggen, B., Maibach, E. W., & Nuccitelli, D. (2016). Consensus on consensus: a synthesis of consensus estimates on human-caused global warming. *Environmental Research Letters, 11*.

25. IPCC. (2014). Climate change 2014: Synthesis report. Retrieved from https://www.ipcc.ch/report/ar5/syr

26. Leahy, S. (2019, January 21). Greenland's ice is melting four times faster than thought—what it means. *National Geographic*. Retrieved from https://www.nationalgeographic.com/environment/2019/01/greeland-ice-melting-four-times-faster-than-thought-raising-sea-level

27. ClimatePath (n.d.).

28. Mooney, C. (2014, October 22). There's a surprisingly strong link between climate change and violence. *The Washington Post*.

29. Duke, R. (2019, May 19). Leaving the Paris Agreement is a bad deal for the United States. *Foreign Policy*. Retrieved from https://foreignpolicy.com/2019/05/19/leaving-the-paris-agreement-is-a-bad-deal-for-the-united-states

30. Pearson, S., & Lewis, J. T. (2019, September 24). Brazil's Bolsonaro defends right to develop Amazon. *The Wall Street Journal*. Retrieved from https://www.wsj.com/articles/brazils-bolsonaro-defends-right-to-develop-amazon-11569338624

31. Hamrick, K., & Gallant, M. (2018, August). *Voluntary carbon markets outlooks and trends: January to March 2018* [PDF]. Retrieved from https://www.forest-trends.org/wp-content/uploads/2019/04/VCM-Q1-Report-Final.pdf; also, nearly $200 million was spent in the voluntary carbon offset market in 2016, the most recent data year.

32. Zwick, S. (2019, October 8). *Carbon offsetting: The frequently asked questions*. Retrieved from https://www.ecosystemmarketplace.com/articles/carbon-offsetting-the-frequently-asked-questions

33. European Union. (n.d.). *European Environment Agency*. Retrieved from https://europa.eu/european-union/about-eu/agencies/eea_en

34. Decision No 1386/2013/EU of the European Parliament and of the Council of 20 November 13 on a General Union Environment Action Programme to 2020 "Living well, within the limits of our planet." Retrieved from https://eur-lex.europa.eu/legal-content/EN/TXT/?uri=CELEX:32013D1386

35. The Life and Legacy of Rachel Carson. (n.d.). Silent spring. Retrieved from https://www.rachelcarson.org/SilentSpring.aspx

36. Macdonald, J. (2019, October 16). Is tap water safe to drink in London and the UK? Tripsavvy. Retrieved from https://www.tripsavvy.com/is-london-tap-water-safe-1583358

37. Slaymaker, T., & Bain, R. (2017, March 17). Water in development: Working in development: Access to drinking water around the world—in five infographics. *The Guardian*. Retrieved from https://www.theguardian.com/global-development-professionals-network/2017/mar/17/access-to-drinking-water-world-six-infographics

38. 733 U.S.C. § 1251 et seq.

39. Sanchez, E., McCarthy, J., & Gralki, P. (2019, August 22). *7 organizations you can support to protect the Amazon rainforest*. Retrieved from https://www.globalcitizen.org/en/content/organizations-donate-amazon-rainforest

40. Colgate. (n.d.). *Make every drop count*. Retrieved from https://smiles.colgate.com/page/content/everydropcounts

41. Colgate-Palmolive. (n.d.). *Living our values*. Retrieved from https://www.colgatepalmolive.com/en-us/core-values

CHAPTER 8

1. Pryce-Jones, J. (2010). *Happiness at work: Maximizing your psychological capital for success*. Hoboken, NJ: Wiley-Blackwell.

2. U.S. Department of the Treasury. (2012, February). *General explanations of the administration's fiscal year 2013 revenue proposals* (p. 148). Retrieved from http://www.treasury.gov/resource-center/tax-policy/Documents/General-ExplanationsFY2013.pdf, figures in table: http://www.treasury.gov/resource-center/tax-policy/Documents/General-Explanations-FY2013- Tables.pdf

3. Cordray, R. (2009, February 18). *Report of the Ohio attorney general on the economic impact of misclassified workers for state and local governments in Ohio*. Retrieved from https://iiiffc.org/images/pdf/employee_classification/OH%20AG%20Rpt%20on%20Misclass.Workers.2009.pdf

4. *Petermann v. Intl Brotherhood of Teamsters*, 174 Cal.App. 2d 184 (1959).

5. Council of the European Union. (2019, October 7). *Better protection of whistle-blowers: New EU-wide rules to kick in 2021* [Press release]. Retrieved from https://www.consilium.europa.eu/en/press/press-releases/2019/10/07/

better-protection-of-whistle-blowers-new-eu-wide-rules-to-kick-in-in-2021

6. Dalby, D., & Bowers, S. (2019, April 18). *LuxLeaks, Panama Papers spur EU to better protect whistleblowers.* International Consortium of Investigative Journalists. Retrieved from https://www.icij.org/investigations/panama-papers/lux-leaks-panama-papers-spur-eu-to-better-protect-whistleblowers

7. Organization for Economic Cooperation and Development. (2017, December 12). The role of whistleblowers and whistleblower protection. In *The detection of foreign bribery.* Retrieved from www.oecd.org/corruption/the-detection-of-foreign-bribery.htm

8. Title 29, Chapter 8, U.S. Code § 202(a).

9. Charlton, E. (2018, December 20). *These countries have the highest minimum wage.* Retrieved from https://www.weforum.org/agenda/2018/12/these-countries-have-the-highest-minimum-wages

10. BBC News. (2018, December 12). *Spain's minimum wage to jump 22% in new year.* Retrieved from https://www.bbc.com/news/world-europe-46539748

11. Blake, J. (2018, April 13). *The fight for $15 takes on the Jim Crow economy.* Retrieved from https://www.cnn.com/2018/04/13/us/fight-for-15-birmingham/index.html

12. Connley, C. (2019, May 25). *Amazon, Facebook and 8 other companies that have committed to raising their minimum wage.* Retrieved from https://www.cnbc.com/2019/05/24/glassdoor-10-companies-that-have-committed-to-raising-minimum-wage.html

13. Allegretto, S. A., & Cooper, D. (2014). Twenty-three years and still waiting for change: Why it's time to give tipped workers the regular minimum wage. Economic Policy Institute and Center for Wage and Employment Dynamics, Briefing Paper #379. Retrieved from https://www.epi.org/files/2014/EPI-CWED-BP379.pdf

14. 29 U.S.C. §§151-169.

15. *NLRB v. American Medical Response, Inc.*, 438 F. 3d 188 (2009).

16. Livingston, G. (2018, September 24). *Stay-at-home moms and dads account for about one-in-five U.S. parents.* Washington, DC: Pew Research Center.

17. Dishamn, L. (2016, December 28). How paid parental leave changed in 2016. *Fast Company.* Retrieved from https://www.fastcompany.com/3066856/the-future-of-work/how-paid-parental-leave-changed-in-2016

18. Tepper, T. (2015, December 3). Facebook workers just got a better paid parental leave. *Time.* Retrieved from http://time.com/money/4129990/facebook-paid-parental-leave

19. Isaacs, J., Healy, O., & Peters, H. E. (2017, May). *Paid family leave in the United States.* Retrieved from https://www.urban.org/sites/default/files/publication/90201/paid_family_leave_0.pdf

20. Miller, C. C. (2018, January 24). Walmart and now Starbucks: Why more big companies are offering paid family leave. *The New York Times.* Retrieved from https://www.nytimes.com/2018/01/24/upshot/parental-leave-company-policy-salaried-hourly-gap.html

21. National Partnership for Women & Families. (n.d.). *Are you familiar with the FMLA?* Retrieved from http://www.nationalpartnership.org/our-work/workplace/fmla.html

22. Klerman, J. A., Daley, K., & Pozniak, A. (2013, September 13). *Family and Medical Leave in 2012: Executive summary, prepared for the Department of Labor.* Retrieved from https://www.dol.gov/asp/evaluation/fmla/FMLA-2012-Executive-Summary.pdf

23. *U.S. v. Jones*, 132 S. Ct. 945 (2012).

CHAPTER 9

1. Dezso, C. L., & Ross, D. G. (2011, March 9). Does female representation in top management improve firm performance? A panel data investigation (Robert H. Smith School Research Paper No. RHS 06-104). Retrieved from https://ssrn.com/abstract=1088182

2. Richard, O., McMillan, A., Chadwick, K., & Dwyer, S. (2003). Employing an innovation strategy in racially diverse workforces: Effects on firm performance. *Group & Organization Management, 28*, 107–126.

3. Lilly. (n.d.). *Diversity & inclusion.* Retrieved from https://www.lilly.com/who-we-are/diversity-and-inclusion

4. SodaStream. (n.d.). *About SodaStream.* Retrieved from https://corp.sodastream.com/about

5. Hunt, V., Yee, L., Prince, S., & Dixon-Fyle, S. (2018, January). *Delivering through diversity.* Retrieved from https://www.mckinsey.com/business-functions/organization/our-insights/delivering-through-diversity

6. Ibid.

7. Lorenzo, R., Voight, N., Tsusaka, M., Krentz, M., & Abouzahr, K. (2018, January 23). *How diverse leadership teams boost innovation.* Retrieved from https://www.bcg.com/en-us/publications/2018/how-diverse-leadership-teams-boost-innovation.aspx

8. Roberson, Q., M. (2006). Disentangling the meanings of diversity and inclusion in organizations. *Group & Organization Management, 212*, 233.

9. Lyons, S. (2019, September 9). The benefits of creating a diverse workforce. *Forbes*. Retrieved from https://www.forbes.com/sites/forbescoachescouncil/2019/09/09/the-benefits-of-creating-a-diverse-workforce/#7199bc28140b

10. Hauser, C. (2016, October 14). Black doctor says Delta flight attendant rejected her; sought "actual physician." *The New York Times*. Retrieved from https://www.nytimes.com/2016/10/15/us/black-doctor-says-delta-flight-attendant-brushed-her-aside-in-search-of-an-actual-physician.html

11. Ibid.

12. Chugh, D. (2018). *The person you meant to be, how good people fight bias*. New York, NY: HarperCollins.

13. Crenshaw, K. (1989). *Demarginalizing the intersection of race and sex: A black feminist's critique of antidiscrimination doctrine, feminist theory and antiracist politics*, 1989 U. Chi. Legal F. 139, 1989.

14. Hegewisch, A. (2018, September 13). *The gender wage gap: 2017; Earnings differences by gender, race, and ethnicity*. Retrieved from https://iwpr.org/publications/gender-wage-gap-2017/

15. Hernandez-Ojeda Alvirez, H., & Ruiz Gutiérrez, L. R. (2019, March 4). *Mexico: Employment & labour law 2019*. Retrieved from https://iclg.com/practice-areas/employment-and-labour-laws-and-regulations/mexico

16. L&E Global. (2016, October 28). Anti-discrimination laws in France. Retrieved from https://knowledge.leglobal.org/anti-discrimination-laws-in-france

17. Glazer, E. (2018, August 31). At Wells Fargo discontent simmers among female executives. *The Wall Street Journal*. Retrieved from https://www.wsj.com/articles/at-wells-fargo-discontent-simmers-among-female-executives-1535707801

18. *Griggs v. Duke Power*, 401 U.S. 424, 436 (1971).

19. *Price Waterhouse v. Ann Hopkins*, 400 U.S. 228 (1989).

20. *Nichols v. Azteca Restaurant Enterprises, Inc.*, 256 F. 3d 864 (9th Cir.) (2001).

21. *Rene v. MGM Grand Hotel, Inc.*, 305 F. 3d 1061 (9th Cir.) (2002).

22. *Stephens v. R.G. & G.R. Funeral Homes*, 884 F. 3d 560 (6th Cir.) (2018).

23. Ryzik, M. (2019, May 21). In a test of their power, #MeToo's legal forces take on McDonald's. *The New York Times*.

Retrieved from https://www.nytimes.com/2019/05/21/business/mcdonalds-female-employees-sexual-harassment.html

24. U.S. Equal Employment Opportunity Commission. (n.d.). *Harrassment*. Retrieved from https://www.eeoc.gov/laws/types/harassment.cfm

25. *Oncale v. Sundowner Offshore Services, Inc.*, 523 U.S. 75, 80 (1998).

26. U.S. Equal Employment Opportunity Commission. (n.d.). *Sexual harassment*. Retrieved from https://www.eeoc.gov/laws/types/sexual_harassment.cfm

27. Lerouge, L. (2010–2011). Moral harassment in the workplace: French law and European perspectives. *Competitive Labor Law & Policy Journal, 109*.

28. Id.

29. U.S. Equal Employment Opportunity Commission (n.d.).

30. *Clotier v. Costco*, 390 F. 3d. 126 (2004).

31. Lipnic, V. A. (2018, June). *The state of age discrimination and older workers in the U.S. 50 years after the Age Discrimination in Employment Act (ADEA)*. Retrieved from https://www.eeoc.gov/eeoc/history/adea50th/report.cfm

32. U.S. Equal Employment Opportunity Commission. (2018, June 26). *EEOC acting chair Lipnic releases report on the state of older workers and age discrimination 50 years after the ADEA* [Press release]. Retrieved from https://www.eeoc.gov/eeoc/history/adea50th/report.cfm

33. Ibid.

34. *Smith v. City of Jackson*, 544 U.S. 228 (2005).

35. Id. at 231.

36. Id. at 242.

37. Americans with Disabilities Act. (n.d.). *ADA: Findings, purpose, and history*. Retrieved from https://www.adaanniversary.org/findings_purpose

38. Ibid.

39. Tamako, H. (2007). Equality of opportunity or employment quotas?—A comparison of Japanese and American employment policies for the disabled. *Social Science Japan Journal, 10*, 41–57.

40. 42 U.S.C. 126 §12112(a).

41. 42 U.S.C. 126 §12102, (4)(D).

42. 42 U.S.C. 126 §12111, (8).

43. 42 U.S.C. 126 §12111, 9 (A)(B).

44. 42 U.S.C. 126 §12111, 10 (A)(B).

45. U.S. Bureau of Labor Statistics. (2020, February 21). *Economic news release*. Retrieved from https://www.bls.gov/news.release/empsit.t18.htm

CHAPTER 10

1. McKinsey Global Institute. (2018, September). *How secure is the global financial system a decade after the crisis?* [Podcast]. Retrieved from https://www.mckinsey.com/industries/financial-services/our-insights/how-secure-is-the-global-financial-system-a-decade-after-the-crisis

2. World Economic Forum. (2013, August 23). *The role of financial services in society: A multistakeholder compact*. Retrieved from https://www.weforum.org/reports/role-financial-services-society-multistakeholder-compact

3. Cassis, Y. (2006). *Capitals of capital: A history of international financial centres, 1780–2005*. Cambridge, UK: Cambridge University Press.

4. The World Bank. (2019, October). *Country program snapshots*. Retrieved from https://www.worldbank.org/en/region/eca/brief/country-program-snapshots

5. International Monetary Fund. (n.d.). *About the IMF*. Retrieved from https://www.imf.org/en/About

6. Grameen Bank—Bank for the Poor. (n.d.). *FAQ*. Retrieved from https://www.grameen-info.org/faq

7. Ibid.

8. Grameen America. (n.d.). *Corporate partners*. Retrieved from https://www.grameenamerica.org/corporate-partners

9. Yunus, M. (2007). *Creating a world without poverty*. New York, NY: Public Affairs Press.

10. Page, T. (2018, April 9). Finance isn't just for fat cats. *The New York Times*.

11. Kar, S. (2018). *Financializing poverty: Labor and risk in Indian microfinance*. Stanford, CA: Stanford University Press.

12. Grameen America, Inc. (n.d.). *About us*. Retrieved from https://www.grameenamerica.org

13. Grameen America. (n.d.). *Lifting America: The campaign for her future*. Retrieved from https://liftingamerica.grameenamerica.org

14. Kaplan, S., & Rauh, J. (2010). Wall Street and Main Street: What contributes to the rise in the highest incomes? *The Review of Financial Studies, 23*, 1004–1050.

15. See Desjardins, J. (2016). *All of the world's stock exchanges by size*. Retrieved from http://money.visualcapitalist.com/all-of-the-worlds-stock-exchanges-by-size

16. Anthony, L. (2011, February 25). *Gunjumping restrictions on communications related to IPOs*. Retrieved from http://lawcast.com/2011/02/25/gunjumping-restrictions-on-communications-related-to-ipos

17. Sraders, A. (2020, February 11). *What is Fintech? Uses and examples in 2020*. Retrieved from https://www.thestreet.com/technology/what-is-fintech-14885154

18. Elezaj, R. (2018, December 7). *4 ways mobile apps are transforming the banking sector*. Retrieved from http://info.localytics.com/blog/4-ways-mobile-apps-are-transforming-the-banking-sector

19. Ibid.

20. Ibid.

21. McCarthy, N. (2018, June 8). 1.7 billion adults worldwide do not have access to a bank account. *Forbes*. Retrieved from https://www.forbes.com/sites/niallmccarthy/2018/06/08/1-7-billion-adults-worldwide-do-not-have-access-to-a-bank-account-infographic/#460a53634b01

22. Sapienza P., & Zingales, L. (2012). A trust crisis. *International Review of Finance, 12*, 123–131.

23. Davis, B. (2009, April 9). What's a global recession? *The Wall Street Journal*.

24. Blinder, A. (2013). *After the music stopped*. New York, NY: Penguin Press.

25. Pace, G. (2008). *NYC restaurants slammed by crisis*. Retrieved from http://www.nbcnews.com/id/27106533/ns/business-local_business/t/nyc-restaurants-slammed-financial-crisis/#.W_RCu5NKjIU

26. Financial Crisis Inquiry Report (FCIR). (2011, January). *Final report of the National Commission on the Causes of the Financial and Economic Crisis in the United States*.

27. Ibid.

28. Jennings, M. M. (2010). The Goldman standard and shades of gray. *Corporate Finance Review, 15*, 35–41. See also Clark, C., & Newell, S. (2016). Institutional work and complicit decoupling across the U.S. capital markets: The work of rating agencies. *Business Ethics Quarterly, 23*, 1–30.

29. McKinsey Global Institute (2018).

30. Shiller, R. (2005). *Irrational exuberance* (2nd ed.). Princeton, NJ: Princeton University Press.

31. U.S. Department of Housing and Urban Development. (2009, January 20). *Subprime lending report: Unequal burden: Income and racial disparities in subprime lending*. Retrieved from https://archives.hud.gov/reports/subprime/subprime.cfm

32. Simkovic, M. (2013). Competition and crisis in mortgage securitization. *Indiana Law Journal, 88*, 213. Retrieved from http://ssrn.com/abstract=1924831

33. U.S. Securities and Exchange Commission. (2010, April 16). *SEC charges Goldman Sachs with fraud in structuring and marketing of CDO tied to subprime mortgages* [Press release]. Retrieved from http://www.sec.gov/news/press/2010/2010-59.htm

34. Blinder (2013, p. 70).

35. FCIR (2011, p. 4).

36. Ibid., p. 9

37. Bernanke, B. (2008). *Mortgage delinquencies and foreclosures.* Retrieved from http://www.federalreserve.gov/newsevents/speech/Bernanke20080505a.htm

38. Schoen, E. J. (2017). The 2007–2009 financial crisis: An erosion of ethics: A case study. *Journal of Business Ethics. 146,* 805–830.

39. FCIR (2011, p. 16).

40. Friedman, T. (2009, March 10). This is not a test. *The New York Times.* Retrieved from https://www.nytimes.com/2009/03/11/opinion/11friedman.html

41. Morgenson, G. (2011, April 14). In financial crisis, no prosecutions of top figures. *The New York Times.*

42. Gould-Wartofsky, M. (2015). *The occupiers: The making of the 99 percent movement.* New York, NY: Oxford University Press.

43. Sanchez, R. (2016, September 16). Occupy Wall Street five years later. CNN.com.

44. Berman, J. (2013, January 29). Occupy Wall Street actually not at all representative of the 99 percent, report finds. *HuffPost.* Retrieved from http://www.huffingtonpost.com/2013/01/29/occupy-wall-street-report_n_2574788.html

45. Miron, J. (2008). *Commentary: Bankruptcy, not bailout, is the right answer.* Retrieved from http://www.cnn.com/2008/POLITICS/09/29/miron.bailout

46. Blinder (2013, pp. 208–209).

47. PBS. (2009, February 17*). Frontline: Inside the meltdown.* Retrieved from https://www.pbs.org/wgbh/pages/frontline/meltdown

48. The Pew Charitable Trusts. (2012, July). *Payday lending in America: Who borrows, where they borrow, and why.* Retrieved from https://www.pewtrusts.org/~/media/legacy/uploadedfiles/pcs_assets/2012/pewpaydaylendingreportpdf.pdf

49. Zingales, L. (2015). Does finance benefit society? *National Bureau of Economic Research Working Paper Series,* 20894.

50. Bankrate. (2020, March 20). *Current credit card interest rates.* Retrieved from https://www.bankrate.com/finance/credit-cards/current-interest-rates.aspx

51. Weinberger, E. (2018, October 19). CFPB expected to cut payday repayment tests in rule overhaul. *Bloomberg News.* Retrieved from https://www.bna.com/cfpb-expected-cut-n57982093184

52. Cowley, S. (2019, February 6). Consumer protection bureau cripples new rules for payday loans. *The New York Times.* Retrieved from https://www.nytimes.com/2019/02/06/business/payday-loans-rules-cfpb.html

53. Consumer Financial Protection Bureau. (2014, March). *CFPB data point: Payday lending.* Retrieved from https://files.consumerfinance.gov/f/201403_cfpb_report_payday-lending.pdf

54. Editorial. (2008, February 14). Payday parasites. *The Washington Post.* Retrieved from http://www.washingtonpost.com/wp-dyn/content/article/2008/02/13/AR2008021303100.html?noredirect=on

55. The Pew Charitable Trusts. (2013, October 30). Payday lending in America: Policy solutions. Retrieved from https://www.pewtrusts.org/en/research-and-analysis/reports/2013/10/29/payday-lending-in-america-policy-solutions

56. Morse, A. (2011). Payday lenders: Heroes or villains? *Journal of Financial Economics, 102,* 28–44.

57. Edmiston, K. D. (2010). *Report on payday lending for the Federal Reserve Bank of Kansas City.* Retrieved from https://www.kansascityfed.org/publicat/econrev/pdf/11q1Edmiston.pdf

58. Organization for Economic Cooperation and Development. (n.d.). *Where: Global reach.* Retrieved from http://www.oecd.org/about/members-and-partners

59. Maiden, B. (2019, July 18). *House panel passes climate risk disclosure bill.* Retrieved from https://www.corporatesecretary.com/articles/compliance/31710/house-panel-passes-climate-risk-disclosure-bill

60. Financial Stability Board. (n.d.). *Work of the FSB.* Retrieved from https://www.fsb.org/work-of-the-fsb

61. Field, M. (2019, October 14). G20 Bankers warned on digital coins. *The Daily Telegraph.*

62. Financial Stability Board. (2018, November 16). *2018 list of global systemically important banks.* Retrieved from https://www.fsb.org/wp-content/uploads/P161118-1.pdf

63. Board of Governors of the Federal Reserve System. (2019, June). *Dodd-Frank Act stress test 2019: Supervisory stress test results.* Retrieved from https://www.federalreserve.gov/publications/files/2019-dfast-results-20190621.pdf

64. Ibid.

65. Cowen, T. (2016, September 20). Let's think again about Dodd-Frank. *Bloomberg Opinion.* Retrieved from https://www.bloomberg.com/opinion/articles/2016-09-20/let-s-think-again-about-dodd-frank

66. Schoen, J. W. (2017, February 6). Despite critics' claims, Dodd-Frank hasn't slowed lending to business or

consumers. *CNBC*. Retrieved from https://www.cnbc .com/2017/02/06/despite-critics-claims-dodd-frank-hasnt-slowed-lending-to-business-or-consumers.html

CHAPTER 11

1. The Wharton School, University of Pennsylvania. (2005, January 26). *How culture affects work practices in Latin America*. Retrieved from https://knowledge.wharton.upenn.edu/ article/how-culture-affects-work-practices-in-latin-america

2. Lamson, M. (2018, July 3). 10 tips to develop your firm's cultural competence. *Inc*. Retrieved from https://www.inc .com/melissa-lamson/cultural-competence-your-most-valuable-business-asset.html

3. Johnson, J. P., Lenartowicz, T., & Apud, S. (2006). Cross-cultural competence in international business: Toward a definition and a model. *Journal of International Business Studies*, *37*, 525–543.

4. Ibid., p. 530.

5. Id. at 531.

6. European Consumer Centre France. (2019, July). *Main sales periods*. Retrieved from https://www.europe-consom-mateurs.eu/en/consumer-topics/buying-goods-services/ vat-seasonal-sales/vat-sales-in-france/main-sales-periods

7. Siek, W. (2019, September 26). *Cultural norms: Do they matter?* Retrieved from https://www.globalcognition.org/ cultural-norms

8. Ibid.

9. Ibid.

10. United Nations. (n.d.). *Overview*. Retrieved from http:// www.un.org/en/sections/about-un/overview/index.html

11. United Nations. (n.d.). *Introductory note*. Retrieved from http://www.un.org/en/sections/un-charter/introductory-note/index.html

12. United Nations. (n.d.). *The drafters of the Universal Declaration of Human Rights*. Retrieved from http://www.un.org/ en/sections/universal-declaration/drafters-universal-declaration-human-rights/index.html

13. Gardner, R. (1988, December 10). Eleanor Roosevelt's legacy: Human rights. *The New York Times*.

14. United Nations. (2015). *Universal Declaration of Human Rights: Introduction*. Retrieved from https://www.un.org/ en/udhrbook/pdf/udhr_booklet_en_web.pdf

15. United Nations. (n.d.). *Human rights law*. Retrieved from http://www.un.org/en/sections/universal-declaration/ human-rights-law/index.html

16. Ibid.

17. Former Deep Japan Writer. (2015, July 19). *What to do at a Japanese funeral: Funeral etiquette*. Retrieved from http:// www.deepjapan.org/a/4124

18. U.S. Department of Justice. (2017, February 3). *Foreign Corrupt Practices Act: An overview*. Retrieved from https://www.justice.gov/criminal-fraud/foreign-co rrupt-practices-act

19. Criminal Division of the U.S. Department of Justice and the Enforcement Division of the U.S. Securities and Exchange Commission. (2012, November 14). *A resource guide to the U.S. Foreign Corrupt Practices Act* (p. 25). Retrieved from https://www.justice.gov/sites/default/files/ criminal-fraud/legacy/2015/01/16/guide.pdf

20. *United States of America v. TEVA Pharmaceuticals Industries*, 16-20968-CR, U.S. Dist. Ct. Dist. of So. Florida (December 22, 2016).

21. Soloman, S. (2018, January 15). Teva to pay NIS 75 million to Israeli authorities to settle foreign bribe claims. *Times of Israel*.

22. Organization for Economic Cooperation and Development. (n.d.). *Who we are*. Retrieved from http://www.oecd .org/about

23. Makandar, N. B. M. (2018). Special economic zones and corporate social responsibility. *International Journal of Advance Research and Development*, *3*, 212–213.

24. Robinson, A. S. (2013). Developments in anti-corruption law in Mexico: Ley Federal Anticorrupciones en Contrataciones Publicas. *Law and Business Review of the Americas*, *19*, 81, 85. Retrieved from https://scholar.smu.edu/lbra/vol19/iss1/7

25. Government of India, Department of Commerce. (2016, September 16). *Initiation of anti-dumping investigation concerning imports of "polybutadiene rubber or PBR" originating in or exported from Korea PR, Russia, South Africa, Iran, and Singapore*. Retrieved from https://commerce.gov.in/writereaddata/tra deremedies/MOC636099736810350897_PBRInitiation%20 notification.pdf

26. Hartman, K., & Dowd, E. (2017, September 26). *State efforts to promote hybrid and electric cars*. Retrieved from http://www.ncsl.org/research/energy/state-electric-vehicle-incentives-state-chart.aspx

27. DiLieto, G., & Treisman, D. (2017, July 11). Three charts on: G20 countries' stealth trade protectionism. *The Conversation*. Retrieved from https://theconversation.com/ three-charts-on-g20-countries-stealth-trade-protection ism-80678

28. Brown, C. (2009, November 3). *Self-enforcing trade: Developing countries and WTO dispute settlement* (p. 11). Washington, DC: Brookings Institution Press.

29. World Trade Organization. (n.d.). *WTO in brief*. Retrieved from https://www.wto.org/english/thewto_e/whatis_e/inbrief_e/inbr03_e.htm

30. Holodny, E. (2017, February 5). Trump wants to renegotiate NAFTA—Here's what you need to know. *Business Insider*. Retrieved from http://www.businessinsider.com/what-is-nafta-is-it-good-for-america-2017-2

31. Gillespie, P. (2016, November 15). *NAFTA: What is it, and why Trump hates it*. Retrieved from http://money.cnn.com/2016/11/15/news/economy/trump-what-is-nafta/index.html

32. World Trade Organization. (n.d.). *Overview: The TRIPS agreement*. Retrieved from https://www.wto.org/english/tratop_e/trips_e/intel2_e.htm#generalprovisions

33. Dutfield, G. (2001, January 10). TRIPS and its impact on developing countries. *SciDevNet*. Retrieved from http://www.scidev.net/global/policy-brief/trips-and-its-impact-on-developing-countries.html

34. Dubai Media City. (n.d.). *MENA'S largest integrated media hub*. Retrieved from http://dmc.ae

35. Oxford Business Group. (2019). Egypt's industrial zones attract new producers. Retrieved from https://oxfordbusinessgroup.com/analysis/room-build-industrial-zones-attract-new-manufacturing-capacity

CHAPTER 12

1. Social media. (n.d.). *Merriam-Webster.com Dictionary*. Retrieved from https://www.merriam-webster.com/dictionary/social%20media

2. Hauben, M., & Hauben, R. (1998, August). Netizens: On the history and impact of Usenet and the Internet. *First Monday, 3*. Retrieved from https://firstmonday.org/ojs/index.php/fm/article/view/605/526

3. Web Designer Depot. (2009, October 7). *The history and evolution of social media*. Retrieved from https://www.webdesignerdepot.com/2009/10/the-history-and-evolution-of-social-media

4. Shah, S. (2016, May 14). The history of social networking. *Digital Trends*. Retrieved from https://www.digitaltrends.com/features/the-history-of-social-networking

5. Boyd, D., & Ellison, N. (2007). Social network sites: Definition, history, and scholarship. *Journal of Computer-Mediated Communication, 13*, 210–230. https://doi.org/10.1111/j.1083-6101.2007.00393.x

6. Shah (2016).

7. LinkedIn. (n.d.). *About LinkedIn*. Retrieved from https://about.linkedin.com

8. Shah (2016).

9. Boyd & Ellison (2007).

10. Ibid.

11. Fitzpatrick, L. (2010, May 31). A brief history of YouTube. *Time*. Retrieved from http://content.time.com/time/magazine/article/0,9171,1990787,00.html

12. Nicas, J. (2017, February 27). YouTube tops 1 billion hours of video a day, on pace to eclipse TV. *The Wall Street Journal*. Retrieved from https://www.wsj.com/articles/youtube-tops-1-billion-hours-of-video-a-day-on-pace-to-eclipse-tv-1488220851

13. Nicol, W. (2018, July 19). *What is Reddit? A beginner's guide to the front page of the Internet*. Retrieved from https://www.digitaltrends.com/web/what-is-reddit

14. Elkins, K. (2018, July 25). *The first thing Alexis Ohanian bought after he sold Reddit for millions at age 23*. Retrieved from https://www.cnbc.com/2018/07/25/the-1st-thing-alexis-ohanian-bought-after-he-sold-reddit-for-millions.html

15. Pardes, A. (2017, September 9). A brief history of the ever-expanding tweet. *Wired* Retrieved from https://www.wired.com/story/a-brief-history-of-the-ever-expanding-tweet

16. Fiegerman, S. (2015, August 2). Inside the failure of Google+, a very expensive attempt to unseat Facebook. *Mashable*. Retrieved from https://mashable.com/2015/08/02/google-plus-history

17. Ibid.

18. Rusli, E. M. (2012, April 9). Facebook buys Instagram for $1 billion. *The New York Times*. Retrieved from https://dealbook.nytimes.com/2012/04/09/facebook-buys-instagram-for-1-billion

19. Clement, J. (2019, December 3). *Number of monthly Instagram users from January 2013 to June 2018 (in millions)*. Retrieved from https://www.statista.com/statistics/253577/number-of-monthly-active-instagram-users

20. Bernazzani, S. (2017, February 10). *A brief history of snapchat*. Retrieved from https://blog.hubspot.com/marketing/history-of-snapchat

21. Versai, A. (2019, April 29). 190 million daily snap users make Q1 2019 profitable for Snapchat. *Technowize Magazine*. Retrieved from https://www.technowize.com/190-million-daily-snap-users-make-q1-2019-profitable-for-snapchat

22. Facebook Investor Relations. (2019, April 24). *Facebook reports first quarter results*. Retrieved from https://investor.fb.com/investor-news/press-release-details/2019/Facebook-Reports-First-Quarter-2019-Results/default.aspx

23. *Twitter announces first quarter 2019 results*. (2019, April 23). Retrieved from https://s22.q4cdn.com/826641620/files/doc_financials/2019/q1/Q1-2019-Earnings-Release.pdf

24. Ibid.

25. Sherman, L. (2018, April 16). Why Facebook will never change its business model. *Forbes*. Retrieved from https://www.forbes.com/sites/lensherman/2018/04/16/why-facebook-will-never-change-its-business-model/#b65684364a7a

26. Facebook for Business. (n.d.). *Reach out to future customers and fans*. Retrieved from https://www.facebook.com/business/ads

27. Gadkari, P. (2013, November 7). How does Twitter make money? *BBC News*. Retrieved from https://www.bbc.com/news/business-24397472

28. YouTube. (n.d.). *YouTube music*. Retrieved from https://www.youtube.com/musicpremium

29. YouTube. (n.d.). *YouTube premium*. https://www.youtube.com/premium

30. Investopedia. (2019, September 22). *How does Linkedin make money?* Retrieved from https://www.investopedia.com/ask/answers/120214/how-does-linkedin-lnkd-make-money.asp

31. Gadkari (2013).

32. Wagner, K. (2017, January 18). LinkedIn wants more ad dollars, so it's offering up more user data to advertiser. *Vox*. Retrieved fromhttps://www.vox.com/2017/1/18/14308060/linkedin-datasift-partnership-advertising

33. Gilbert, B. (2018, April 11). How Facebook makes money from your data, in Mark Zuckerberg's words. *Business Insider*. Retrieved from https://www.businessinsider.com/how-facebook-makes-money-according-to-mark-zuckerberg-2018-4

34. Crook, J. (2018, April 10). *Mark Zuckerberg: "We do not sell data to advertisers."* Retrieved from https://techcrunch.com/2018/04/10/mark-zuckerberg-we-do-not-sell-data-to-advertisers

35. Korosec, K. (2018, March 21). This is the personal data that Facebook collects—and sometimes sells. *Fortune*. Retrieved from http://fortune.com/2018/03/21/facebook-personal-data-cambridge-analytica

36. Twitter. (n.d.). Privacy policy. Retrieved from https://twitter.com/en/privacy#update

37. Ibid.

38. McCourt, A. (2018, April 3). Social media mining: The effects of big data in the age of social media. *Media Freedom & Information Access Clinic*.

39. Ibid.

40. The CMO Survey. (2018, August). *Highlights and insights report*. Retrieved from https://cmosurvey.org/wp-content/uploads/sites/15/2018/08/The_CMO_Survey-Highlights_and_Insights_Report-Aug-2018.pdf

41. Wasserman, T. (2012, October 15). IBM has become a publisher. Is it any good? *Mashable*. Retrieved from https://mashable.com/2012/10/15/ibm-content-social

42. Bahadur, N. (2014, January 21). Dove "Real Beauty" campaign turns 10: How a brand tried to change the conversation about female beauty. *HuffPost*. Retrieved from https://www.huffpost.com/entry/dove-real-beauty-campaign-turns10_n_4575940?guccounter=1&guce_referrer=aHR0cHM6Ly93d3cuZ29vZ2xlLmNvbS8&guce_referrer_sig=AQAAALXoR6iK41FOUojbh8lhU6W_sm0WR2JudMzcq5Z7HEoZ80lE2pJtzg2yCBvUKYDOHvvaZQrRfhQVNOPpYlelskmtcd2_o0QGKrq4KOMnHwtnaQH_BPZ_XgQK81zRSGdIgn1nOY_ijdi1_E2ZBYZRGUuIsIYaQck8cRVfDWNvdNZ

43. Murphy, S. (2013, May 20). Viral Dove campaign becomes most watched ad ever. *Mashable*. Retrieved from https://mashable.com/2013/05/20/dove-ad-most-watche

44. Zed, O. (2019, April 16). How Dove's real beauty campaign won, and nearly lost, its audience. *PRWeek*. Retrieved from https://www.prweek.com/article/1582147/doves-real-beauty-campaign-won-nearly-lost-its-audience

45. Astor, M. (2017, October 8). Dove drops an ad accused of racism. *The New York Times*. Retrieved from https://www.nytimes.com/2017/10/08/business/dove-ad-racist.html

46. Blendtec. (n.d.). *An unfaltering dedication to innovation*. Retrieved from https://www.blendtec.com/pages/about

47. YouTube. (n.d.). *Blendtec's will it blend?* Retrieved from https://www.youtube.com/user/Blendtec/videos

48. Kemp, S. (2019, January 30). *Digital 2019: Global Internet use accelerates*. Retrieved from https://wearesocial.com/blog/2019/01/digital-2019-global-internet-use-accelerates

49. Kavada, A. (2015). Creating the collective: Social media, the Occupy Movement and its constitution as a collective actor. Information, Communication & Society, *18*, 872–886, 873.

50. Mundt, M., Ross, K., & Burnett, C. M. (2018, November 1). Scaling social movements through social media: The case of Black Lives Matter. *Social Media + Society*, *4*, 3.

51. Ibid. (p. 10).

52. McNealy, J. (2018, May 16). What is doxxing, and why is it so scary? *The Conversation*. Retrieved from https://theconversation.com/what-is-doxxing-and-why-is-it-so-scary-95848?utm_medium=email&utm_campaign=Wednesday%20516%20Test%201&utm_content=Wednesday%20516%20Test%201+CID_e774fad2a1a7

b415ee8a93d5c858971b&utm_source=campaign_monitor_us&utm_term=What%20is%20doxxing%20and%20why%20is%20it%20so%20scary

53. Mundt et al. (2018, p. 12).

54. Costanza-Chock, S. (2012). Mic check! Media cultures and the occupy movement. *Social Movement Studies, 11*, 375–385.

55. Kavada (2015).

56. Ibid.

57. Ibid.

58. Miller, R. W. (2016, July 11). Black Lives Matter: A primer on what it is and what it stands for. *USAToday*. Retrieved from https://www.usatoday.com/story/news/nation/2016/07/11/black-lives-matter-what-what-stands/86963292

59. Black Lives Matter. (n.d.). *Herstory*. Retrieved from https://blacklivesmatter.com/about/herstory

60. Roberts, F. L. (2018, July 13). How black lives matter changed the way Americans fight for freedom. Retrieved from https://www.aclu.org/blog/racial-justice/race-and-criminal-justice/how-black-lives-matter-changed-way-americans-fight

61. Mundt (2018).

62. Ibid.

63. Ibid.

64. Ibid. (p. 11).

65. Devichand, M. (2016, January 3). How the word was changed by the slogan "Je Suis Charlie." *BBC News*. Retrieved from https://www.bbc.com/news/blogs-trending-35108339

66. Dearden, L. (2016, January 7). Charlie Hebdo attack survivor says "Je suis Charlie" slogan has been "misused" in year since atrocity. *The Independent*. Retrieved from https://www.independent.co.uk/news/world/europe/charlie-hebdo-attack-survivor-says-je-suis-charlie-slogan-has-been-misused-in-year-since-atrocity-a6801111.html

67. Devichand (2016).

68. Dearden (2016).

69. Devichand (2016).

70. Ibid.

71. Me Too. (n.d.). *History & vision*. Retrieved from https://metoomvmt.org/about/#history

72. Burke, T. (2018). #MeToo founder Tarana Burke on the rigorous work that still lies ahead. *Variety*.

Retrieved from https://variety.com/2018/biz/features/tarana-burke-metoo-one-year-later-1202954797

73. Anderson, M., & Toor, S. (2018, October 11). *How social media users have discussed sexual harassment since #MeToo went viral*. Retrieved from https://www.pewresearch.org/fact-tank/2018/10/11/how-social-media-users-have-discussed-sexual-harassment-since-metoo-went-viral

74. Ibid.

75. Leetaru, K. (2018, December 14). Should social media be allowed to profit from terrorism and hate speech? *Forbes*. Retrieved from https://www.forbes.com/sites/kalevleetaru/2018/12/14/should-social-media-be-allowed-to-profit-from-terrorism-and-hate-speech/#587f283c92c8

76. Amnesty International. (2018, March). *Toxic Twitter: A toxic place for women*. Retrieved from https://www.amnesty.org/en/latest/research/2018/03/online-violence-against-women-chapter-1

77. Congressman José E. Serrano Website. (2019, March 28). *Congressman Serrano and Senator Casey introduce the Stop HATE Act to address the rise in hate crimes through social media* [Press release]. Retrieved from https://serrano.house.gov/media-center/press-releases/congressman-serrano-and-senator-casey-introduce-stop-hate-act-address

78. Ibid.

79. *Cubby, Inc. v. CompuServe*, 776 F.Supp. 135 (S.D.N.Y. 1991).

80. *Stratton Oakmont v. Prodigy*, 1995 WL 323710.

81. Electronic Frontier Foundation. (n.d.). *CDA 230: Legislative history*. Retrieved from https://www.eff.org/issues/cda230/legislative-history

82. *City of Ontario v. Quon*, 130 S.Ct. 2619, 2629 (2010).

83. *Packingham v. North Carolina*, 137 S.Ct. 1730, 1736 (2017).

CHAPTER 13

1. Ziemnowicz, C. (2013). Joseph A. Schumpeter and innovation. In E. G. Carayannis (Ed.), *Encyclopedia of creativity, invention, innovation and entrepreneurship*. New York, NY: Springer.

2. Leopold, T. A., Ratcheva, V., & Zahidi, S. (2016). *The future of jobs*. Retrieved from http://reports.weforum.org/future-of-jobs-2016/drivers-of-change/

3. Corporate Board Member & Ernst & Young. (2019). *How boards are governing disruptive technology*. Retrieved from https://assets.ey.com/content/dam/ey-sites/ey-com/en_us/

topics/cbm/ey-how-boards-are-governing-disruptive-technology.pdf

4. Woetzel, J., Sellschop, R., Chui, R., Ramaswamy, S., Nyquist, S., Robinson, H., . . . Ross, R. (2017, February). *How technology is reshaping supply and demand for natural resources.* Retrieved from https://www.mckinsey.com/business-functions/sustainability/our-insights/how-technology-is-reshaping-supply-and-demand-for-natural-resources

5. Choudhry, H., Lauritzen, M., Somers, K., & Van Niel, J. (2015, November). *Technologies that could transform how industries use energy.* Retrieved from https://www.mckinsey.com/business-functions/operations/our-insights/technologies-that-could-transform-how-industries-use-energy

6. Kroft, S. (2018, October 21). Inside the genetic genealogy being used to solve crimes. *60 Minutes.* Retrieved from https://www.cbsnews.com/news/genetic-genealogy-tracing-family-trees-to-catch-killers-60-minutes

7. Woetzel et al. (2017).

8. Sustainability For All. (n.d.). *Causes and consequences of overpopulation.* Retrieved from https://www.activesustainability.com/sustainable-development/causes-consequences-overpopulation/

9. Kroft (2018).

10. Dredge, S. (2013, November 5). What is Tor? A beginner's guide to the privacy tool. *The Guardian.* Retrieved from https://www.theguardian.com/technology/2013/nov/05/tor-beginners-guide-nsa-browser

11. The Onion Router. (2015, October 1). *The negative impact of Internet anonymity.* Retrieved from http://www.mediafactory.org.au/2015-media6-deepweb/2015/10/01/the-negative-impact-of-internet-anonymity

12. Hill, K. (2013, September 12). E-ZPasses get read all over New York (not just at toll booths). *Forbes.* Retrieved from http://www.forbes.com/sites/kashmirhill/2013/09/12/e-zpasses-get-read-all-over-new-york-not-just-at-toll-booths/#49e70a2f3cfc

13. Cushing, T. (2015, January 21). Chris Christie, Port Authority official abused E-ZPass data for their own ends. Retrieved from https://www.techdirt.com/articles/20150120/10430629761/chris-christie-port-authority-official-abused-e-zpass-data-their-own-ends.shtml

14. Robinson, A. (2019, August 21). *NTIA data: Two-thirds of U.S. Internet users do not participate in the sharing economy.* Retrieved from https://www.ntia.doc.gov/blog/2019/ntia-data-two-thirds-us-internet-users-do-not-participate-sharing-economy

15. UNESCO. (2017). *The state of broadband.* Retrieved from https://www.itu.int/dms_pub/itu-s/opb/pol/S-POL-BROADBAND.18-2017-PDF-E.pdf

16. Pew Research Center. (2018). *Nearly one-in-five teens can't always finish their homework because of the digital divide.* Retrieved from https://www.pewresearch.org/fact-tank/2018/10/26/nearly-one-in-five-teens-cant-always-finish-their-homework-because-of-the-digital-divide

17. Newell, S., & Marabelli, M. (2015). Strategic opportunities (and challenges) of algorithmic decision-making: A call for action on the long-term societal effects of "datification." *The Journal of Strategic Information Systems, 24,* 3–14.

18. Topi, H., & Markus, L. (2015). Educating data scientists in the broader implications of their work. *Journal of the Washington Academy of Sciences, 101,* 39–48.

19. SAS. (n.d.). *Big data: What it is and why it matters.* Retrieved from https://www.sas.com/en_us/insights/big-data/what-is-big-data.html

20. Statista. (n.d.). Big data market size revenue forecast worldwide from 2011 to 2027 [Graph]. Retrieved from https://www.statista.com/statistics/254266/global-big-data-market-forecast

21. Newman, D. (2018, September 11). Top 10 digital transformation trends for 2019. *Forbes.* Retrieved from https://www.forbes.com/sites/danielnewman/2018/09/11/top-10-digital-transformation-trends-for-2019/#2008e73a3c30

22. McAfee, A., & Brynjolfsson, E. (2012). Big data: The management revolution. *Harvard Business Review, 90,* 60–68.

23. Bresnick, J. (2015). *Healthcare big data analytics: From description to prescription.* Retrieved from https://healthitanalytics.com/news/healthcare-big-data-analytics-from-description-to-prescription

24. Yusoff, A. (2017, July 19). *Ten best infographics of big data—Descriptive, predictive, and prescriptive methods.* Retrieved from https://aziyatiyusoff.com/2017/07/19/ten-best-infographics-of-big-data-descriptive-predictive-and-prescriptive-methods

25. Lerman, R. (2019, November 12). Google's health care ambitions now involve patient data. *ABC News.* Retrieved from https://abcnews.go.com/Health/wireStory/googles-health-care-ambitions-now-involve-patient-data-66952224

26. Ibid.

27. Scheff, S. (2014, November 21). Online safety: What does it mean to you? *HuffPost.* Retrieved from https://www.huffpost.com/entry/online-safety-what-does-i_b_6179918

28. Privacy Rights Clearinghouse. (n.d.). *Data breaches.* Retrieved from https://www.privacyrights.org/data-breaches

29. BakerHostetler. (2019). *2019 Data security incident response report: Managing enterprise risks in a digital world: Privacy, cybersecurity, and compliance collide.* Retrieved from https://

f.datasrvr.com/fr1/419/17257/2019_BakerHostetler_DSIR_Final.pdf?cbcachex=990603

30. Scheff (2014). See also Brandom, R. (2017, June 27). A new ransomware attack is infecting airlines, banks, and utilities across Europe. *The Verge*. Retrieved from https://www.theverge.com/2017/6/27/15879480/petrwrap-virus-ukraine-ransomware-attack-europe-wannacry

31. Amer, K., & Noujaim, J. (Directors). (2019, January 26). *The great hack* [Documentary]. Retrieved from https://www.netflix.com/Title/80117542

32. Newman (2018).

33. Culnan, M. J., & Williams, C. C. (2009). How ethics can enhance organizational privacy: Lessons from the Choicepoint and TJX data breaches. *MIS Quarterly, 33*, 673–687.

34. Stauffer, E. (2018). *Progressive Snapshot review*. Retrieved from https://www.expertinsurancereviews.com/usage-based-insurance/progressive-snapshot

35. Manna, J. (2014, June 21). *What every driver needs to know about Progressive Snapshot*. Retrieved from https://blog.joemanna.com/progressive-snapshot-review

36. Norling, D. (2019, June 19). *The inconsistent correlations between gender and car insurance rates*. Retrieved from https://channels.theinnovationenterprise.com/articles/inconsistent-correlations-between-gender-car-insurance-rates

37. Collinson, P. (2017, January 14). How an EU gender equality ruling widened inequality. *The Guardian*. Retrieved from https://www.theguardian.com/money/blog/2017/jan/14/eu-gender-ruling-car-insurance-inequality-worse

CHAPTER 14

1. Greenaway, K. E., & Chan, Y. E. (2005). Theoretical explanations of firms' information privacy behaviors. *Journal of the Association for Information Systems, 6*, 171–198.

2. Brandeis, L., & Warren, S. D. (1890, December 15). The right to privacy. *Harvard Law Review, 4*, 193–220.

3. BeVier, L. R. (1995). Information about individuals in the hands of government: Some reflections on mechanisms for privacy protection. *William & Mary Bill of Rights Journal, 4*, 455, 458.

4. McCreary, L. (2008). What was privacy? *Harvard Business Review, 86*, 123–130.

5. Culnan, M. J., & Williams, C. C. (2009). How ethics can enhance organizational privacy: Lessons from the Choicepoint and TJX data breaches. *MIS Quarterly, 33*, 673–687.

6. Negnevitsky, M. (2005). *Artificial intelligence: A guide to intelligent systems* (2nd ed.). Boston, MA: Addison-Wesley.

7. Murawski, J. (2019, April 8). EU to test AI ethics guidelines. *The Wall Street Journal*. Retrieved from https://www.wsj.com/articles/eu-to-test-ai-ethics-guidelines-11554741165?mod=article_inline

8. Compliance Week. (2019, March 28). *Forget me not: Business challenges over rights to erasure and threats to AI* [Webcast]. Retrieved from https://www.complianceweek.com/webcasts/forget-me-not-business-challenges-over-rights-to-erasure-and-threats-to-ai/26991.article

9. Ibid.

10. Greenaway & Chan (2005).

11. Marwick, A. E. (2018). Privacy at the margins: Understanding privacy at the margins—Introduction. *International Journal of Communication, 12*, 9.

12. Galliers, R. D., Newell, S., Shanks, G., & Topi, H. (2017). Datification and its human, organizational and societal effects. *The Journal of Strategic Information Systems, 26*, 185–190. See also Markus, M. L. (2017). Datification, organizational strategy, and IS research: What's the score? *The Journal of Strategic Information Systems, 26*, 233–241.

13. Culnan & Williams (2009).

14. MacDonald, D. A., & Streatfeild, C. M. (2014). Personal data privacy and the WTO. *Houston Journal of International Laws, 625*, 625–653. See also Otjacques, B., Hitzelberger, P., & Feltz, F. (2007). Interoperability of e-government information systems: Issues of identification and data sharing. *Journal of Management Information Systems, 23*, 29–51.

15. For more information, see the CCPA law found at https://leginfo.legislature.ca.gov/faces/billTextClient.xhtml?bill_id=201720180AB375

16. Compliance Week (2019).

17. Ibid.

18. Meyer, D. (2018, March 13). An American university is spying on students. *Fortune* Retrieved from http://fortune.com/2018/03/13/university-arizona-catcard-big-data-dropouts

19. Regulation (EU) 2016/679 (General Data Protection Regulation). (2018, May 28). Retrieved from https://advisera.com/eugdpracademy/gdpr

20. Ibid.

21. McQuinn, A. (2017, October 6). *The economics of "opt-out" versus "opt-in" privacy rules*. Retrieved from https://itif.org/publications/2017/10/06/economics-opt-out-versus-opt-in-privacy-rules

22. Pew Research Center. (2016, September 21). The state of privacy in post-Snowden America. Retrieved from https://www.pewresearch.org/fact-tank/2016/09/21/the-state-of-privacy-in-america

23. Compliance Week (2019).

24. Van Alsenoy, B., Kuczerawy, A., & Ausloos, J. (2013, September 6). Search engines after Google Spain: internet@liberty or privacy@peril? ICRI Working Paper Series. Retrieved from http://ssrn.com/abstract=2321494

25. Derechoaleer. (2014, May 30). *The unforgettable story of the seizure to the defaulter Mario Costeja González that happened in 1998.* Retrieved from http://derechoaleer.org/en/blog/2014/05/the-unforgettable-story-of-the-seizure-to-the-defaulter-mario-costeja-gonzalez-that-happened-in-1998.html

26. Ford, M. (2014, May 13). Will Europe censor this article? *The Atlantic.* Retrieved from https://www.theatlantic.com/international/archive/2014/05/europes-troubling-new-right-to-be-forgotten/370796

27. Van Alsenoy et al. (2013).

28. Ibid.

29. Ibid.

30. Information Policy. (2010, June 24). Data protection in Spain. Retrieved from www.i-policy.org/2010/06/data-protection-in-spain.html

31. Román, D. (2014, June 26). Spanish agency behind the Google ruling lauded by some, hated by others. *The Wall Street Journal.* Retrieved from https://www.wsj.com/articles/spanish-agency-behind-the-google-ruling-lauded-by-some-hated-by-others-1403795717?cb=logged0.03531818146039811

32. Mizroch, A. (2014, May 13). What is the "right to be forgotten?" *The Wall Street Journal.* Retrieved from https://www.wsj.com/articles/what-is-the-right-to-be-forgotten-1400011724

33. European Commission. (2013, October 22). LIBE Committee vote backs new EU data protection rules. Retrieved from http://europa.eu/rapid/press-release_MEMO-13-923_en.htm

34. Mizroch (2014).

35. Ford (2014).

36. Buck, T. (2014, May 30). Google privacy campaigner praises search engine for bowing to EU. *Financial Times.* Retrieved from https://www.ft.com/content/18e1a5e4-e7d6-11e3-9af8-00144feabdc0

37. Reuters. (2014, May 30). The man who sued Google to be forgotten. *Newsweek.* Retrieved from https://www.newsweek.com/man-who-sued-google-be-forgotten-252854

38. European Parliament.(2014, May 13). *Judgment of the court.* Retrieved from http://curia.europa.eu/juris/document/document.jsf?docid=152065&doclang=EN

39. Derechoaleer (2014).

40. Ford (2014).

41. Derechoaleer (2014).

42. Van Alsenoy et al. (2013).

43. Kassam, A. (2014, May 13). Spain's everyday Internet warrior who cut free from Google's tentacles. *The Guardian.* Retrieved from http://www.theguardian.com/technology/2014/may/13/spain-everyman-google-mario-costeja-gonzalez

44. Reuters (2014).

45. Court of Justice, Judgment in Case C-131/12 Google Spain SL, *Google Inc. v. Agencia Española de Protección de Datos, Mario Costeja González.*

46. Information about Google Search is available online at www.google.com/insidesearch/howsearchworks/index.html

47. Lumen. (n.d.). *About us.* Retrieved from www.chillingeffects.org/pages/about

48. Román (2014).

49. Van Alsenoy et al. (2013).

50. Cutts, M. (2010, March 4). *How search works,* s30–s44. Retrieved from http://www.youtube.com/watch?v=BNHR6IQJGZs

51. Van Alsenoy et al. (2013).

52. European Parliament. (2014, May 13). *Judgment of the court.* Retrieved from http://curia.europa.eu/juris/document/document.jsf?docid=152065&doclang=EN

53. European Commission. *Fact sheet on the right to be forgotten.* Retrieved from http://ec.europa.eu/justice/data-protection/files/factsheets/factsheet_data_protection_en.pdf

54. Kassam (2014).

55. Buck (2014).

56. Floridi, L., Kauffman, S., Kolucka-Zuk, L., La Rue, F., Leutheusser-Schnarrenberger, S., Piñar, J.-L., . . . Wales, J. (2015, February 6). *The Advisory Council to Google on the right to be forgotten.* Retrieved from https://drive.google.com/file/d/0B1UgZshetMd4cEI3SjlvV0hNbDA/view?pli=1

57. Scott, M. (2015, February 6). Limit "right to be forgotten" to Europe, panel tells Google. *The New York Times.* Retrieved from https://bits.blogs.nytimes.com/2015/02/06/

limit-right-to-be-forgotten-to-europe-panel-says/?mtrref=www.google.com&gwh=105CE54FACECD88BFAF3A954F63976FC&gwt=pay&assetType=REGIWALL

58. Ibid.

59. California Legislative Information. Retrieved from https://leginfo.legislature.ca.gov/faces/billTextClient.xhtml?bill_id=201720180AB375

60. Compliance Week (2019).

61. Ibid.

62. Pew Research Center (2016).

63. Selod, S. (2018). Gendered racialization: Muslim American men and women's experience with racialized surveillance. *Ethnic and Racial Studies, 42,* 552–569.

64. Mitchell, A., & Diamond, L. (2018, February 2). China's surveillance state should scare everyone. *The Atlantic.* Retrieved from https://www.theatlantic.com/international/archive/2018/02/china-surveillance/552203

65. Hatton, C. (2015, October 26). *China "social credit": Beijing sets up huge system.* BBC News. Retrieved from https://www.bbc.com/news/world-asia-china-34592186

66. Mozur, P. (2018, July 8). Inside China's dystopian dreams: A.I., shame and lots of cameras. *The New York Times.* Retrieved from https://www.nytimes.com/2018/07/08/business/china-surveillance-technology.html

67. Selod (2018).

68. Stewart, J. (2018). Super-fast airport scanners are coming—eventually. *Wired Magazine.* Retrieved from https://www.wired.com/story/super-fast-airport-scanners

69. Jensen, B. (2016). TSA defends full-body scanners at airport checkpoints. *USA Today.* Retrieved from https://www.usatoday.com/story/news/2016/03/02/tsa-defends-full-body-scanners-airport-checkpoints/81203030

70. Computer Ethics Institute. (n.d.). Retrieved from https://computerethicsinstitute.org/home.html

71. Federal Trade Commission. (n.d.). Retrieved from https://www.ftc.gov/tips-advice/business-center/privacy-and-security/data-security

72. Compliance Week (2019).

73. Spencer Stuart. (n.d.). *The digital dilemma.* Retrieved from https://www.spencerstuart.com/-/media/2019/february/digitalexpertboard-013019.pdf

74. Bhatia, P. (n.d.). *Contents of the data protection policy according to GDPR.* Retrieved from https://advisera.com/eugdpracademy/knowledgebase/contents-of-the-data-protection-policy-according-to-gdpr

75. Chen, T.-P. (2019, March 27). Workers push back as companies gather fingerprints and retina scans. *The Wall Street Journal.* Retrieved from https://www.wsj.com/articles/workers-push-back-as-companies-gather-fingerprints-and-retina-scans-11553698332

76. Winston & Strawn. (2019, January 30). *Landmark ruling on the Illinois Biometric Information Privacy Act.* Retrieved from https://www.winston.com/en/thought-leadership/landmark-ruling-on-the-illinois-biometric-information-privacy-act.html

CHAPTER 15

1. James, F. (2011, August 11). Romney's "corporations are people" a gift to political foes. Retrieved from https://www.npr.org/sections/itsallpolitics/2011/08/11/139551684/romneys-corporations-are-people-getting-lots-of-mileage

2. Welch, J., & Welch, S. (2012, July 15). It's true: Corporations are people. *The Wall Street Journal.* Retrieved from https://www.wsj.com/articles/SB10001424052702303740704577524823306803692

3. *Santa Clara County v. S. Pac. R. Co.,* 118 U.S. 394 (1886).

4. *Trustees of Dartmouth College v. Woodward,* 17 U.S. 518, 527 (1918).

5. Torres-Spelliscy, C. (2014, April 7). *The history of corporate personhood.* Retrieved from https://www.brennancenter.org/our-work/analysis-opinion/history-corporate-personhood

6. Raskin, J. (2009, September 10). *Corporations aren't people.* Retrieved from https://www.npr.org/templates/story/story.php?storyId=112714052

7. Ibid.

8. *Citizens United v. Fed. Election Comm'n* (2010).

9. Leonhardt, T. C. (2016). *Hobby Lobby, Carnell Construction, and the theoretical deficit of second-class personhood: The indecipherable calculus of corporate rights,* 94 N.C. L. Rev. 648 (2016). Retrieved from http://scholarship.law.unc.edu/nclr/vol94/iss2/5

10. *Burwell v. Hobby Lobby Stores, Inc.* (2014), p. 767.

11. Id. at 768.

12. Id. at 769.

13. Soper, T. (2017, July 27). *Mobile payments now account for 30% of Starbucks transactions as company posts $5.7B in revenue.*

Retrieved from https://www.geekwire.com/2017/mobile-payment-now-accounts-30-starbucks-transactions-company-posts-5-7b-revenue

14. Duignan, B. (2016, April 29). Commerce clause. *Encyclopedia Brittanica*. Retrieved from https://www.britannica.com/topic/commerce-clause

15. *Heart of Atlanta Motel v. United States*, 379 U.S. 241, 258 (1961).

16. *United States v. Lopez*, 514 U.S. 549, 551 (1995).

17. Flaccus, G. (2018, December 27). *Legal marijuana industry toasts banner year*. Retrieved from https://www.apnews.com/0bd3cdbae26c4f99be359d6fe32f0d49

18. Anderson, M. (2016, November 5). *The trend toward legalizing recreational marijuana*. Retrieved from https://www.npr.org/2016/11/05/500816719/the-trend-toward-legalizing-recreational-marijuana

19. Robinson, M. (2017, January 3). The legal weed market is growing as fast as broadband Internet in the 2000s. *Business Insider*. Retrieved from https://www.businessinsider.com/arcview-north-america-marijuana-industry-revenue-2016-2017-1

20. *West Lynn Creamery v. Healy*, 512 U.S. 186, 193 (1994).

CHAPTER 16

1. Gygli, S., Haelg, F., Potrafke, N., & Sturm, J.-E. (2019). The KOF Globalisation Index—Revisited. *Review of International Organizations*, *14*, 543–574. Retrieved from https://kof.ethz.ch/en/forecasts-and-indicators/indicators/kof-globalisation-index.html

2. Scherer, A. G., Palazzo, G., & Matten, D. (2009). Introduction to the special issue: Globalization as a challenge for business responsibilities. *Business Ethics Quarterly*, *19*, 327–347.

3. Gray, A. (2017, January 10). *What is globalization anyway?* Retrieved from https://www.weforum.org/agenda/2017/01/what-is-globalization-explainer

4. Aslam, A., Jaumotte, F., Eugster, J., Ho, G., Osorio-Buitron, C., & Piazza, R. (2018, April 11). *This is the major impact globalization has had on productivity*. Retrieved from https://www.weforum.org/agenda/2018/04/globalization-helps-spread-knowledge-and-technology-across-borders

5. King. S. D. (2017). *Grave new world: The end of globalization, the return of history*. New Haven, CT: Yale University Press.

6. Gray (2017).

7. Winn, M., & Kirchgeorg, M. (2015). Bottom of the pyramid. *Encyclopedia Brittanica*. Retrieved from https://www.britannica.com/topic/Bottom-of-the-Pyramid

8. Gray (2017).

9. Hanks, H. (2016). *Women welcome at a Saudi Arabia Starbucks shop after temporary ban*. Retrieved from https://www.cnn.com/2016/02/07/world/saudi-starbucks-women-ban-feat/index.html

10. Ibid.

11. Kobrin, S. J. (2009). Private political authority and public responsibility: Transnational politics, transnational firms, and human rights. *Business Ethics Quarterly*, *19*, 349–374.

12. UN Global Compact for Business. (n.d.). *Principle 2: Human rights*. Retrieved from https://www.unglobalcompact.org/what-is-gc/mission/principles/principle-2

13. Donaldson, T., & Dunfee, T. W. (1999). *Ties that bind: A social contracts approach to business ethics*. Boston, MA: Harvard Business School Press.

14. International Monetary Fund. (n.d.). *About the IMF*. Retrieved from https://www.imf.org/en/About

15. The World Bank. (n.d.). *Who we are*. Retrieved from https://www.worldbank.org/en/who-we-are

16. Colchester, M., & Hannon, P. (2019, December 13). After thumping victory, Boris Johnson focuses on swift Brexit, boots to public spending. *The Wall Street Journal*. Retrieved from https://www.wsj.com/articles/after-thumping-victory-boris-johnson-focuses-on-swift-brexit-boost-to-public-spending-11576236384?emailToken=981d4cb96726bc938b31ee3847ef4429+HRQV8FCLR5WesmytrKJt3Gf4SxodGgCocvTvcVDp28NJB9C45rJ4ujjfZ+I6JIdG+uvUGFsR5jyVOxYbh1ouDEMk2H+Wh7vPem5j7hQMr2Xcm3z+9xT9vKiOMtczSibULSefq57DShHNFMeNsqoPw/aQOc0PttetmXrluSYLOs%3D&reflink=article_email_share

17. World Trade Organization. (n.d.). *Technical barriers to trade*. Retrieved from https://www.wto.org/english/tratop_e/tbt_e/tbt_e.htm

18. Andrews, N., Mauldin, W., & Harrup, A. (2019, December 10). Revised trade pact set for likely approval by Congress in 2020. *The Wall Street Journal*. Retrieved from https://www.wsj.com/articles/house-democrats-reach-agreement-with-trump-administration-on-usmca-trade-deal-11575989670

19. Ibid.

20. Reuters. (2019, December 16). *FACTBox—What is actually in the U.S.-China "Phase One" trade deal?* Retrieved from https://www.cnbc.com/2019/12/16/reuters-america-factbox-what-is-actually-in-the-u-s-china-phase-one-trade-deal.html

21. Deng, C., Wei, L., & Mauldin, W. (2019, November 4). U.S.-China trade talks hit snag over farm purchases. *The Wall Street Journal*. Retrieved from https://www.wsj.com/articles/u-s-china-trade-talks-hit-snag-over-farm-purchases-11573671418?mod=article_inline

22. Reuters (2019).

23. Cheng, E. (2019, December 16). *Despite the US-China trade agreement, key details are unclear*. Retrieved from http://nbr.com/2019/12/16/despite-the-us-china-trade-agreement-key-details-are-unclear

24. World Economic Forum. (n.d.). *Global competitiveness report 2019: How to end a lost decade of productivity growth*. Retrieved from https://www.weforum.org/reports/how-to-end-a-decade-of-lost-productivity-growth

25. IMF Staff. (2002, January). *Globalization: Threat or opportunity?* Retrieved from https://www.imf.org/external/np/exr/ib/2000/041200to.htm

26. United Nations Department of Economic and Social Affairs. (2019, September 17). *The number of international migrants reaches 272 million, continuing and upward trend in all world regions, says UN*. Retrieved from https://www.un.org/development/desa/en/news/population/international-migrant-stock-2019.html

27. United Nations Department of Economic and Social Affairs (2019).

28. Gonzalez-Barrera, A., & Connor, P. (2019, March 14). *Around the world, more say immigrants are a strength than a burden*. Retrieved from https://www.pewresearch.org/global/2019/03/14/around-the-world-more-say-immigrants-are-a-strength-than-a-burden

29. Ibid.

30. Alcindor, Y. (2019, May 16). What's in Trump's immigration proposal. *PBS NewsHour*. Retrieved from https://www.pbs.org/newshour/politics/whats-in-trumps-immigration-proposal

31. United Nations. (n.d.). *Water facts: Water scarcity*. Retrieved from https://www.unwater.org/water-facts/scarcity

32. Fiji Water. (n.d.). *About us: More than water*. Retrieved from https://www.fijiwater.com/company.html

33. Dietvorst, C. (2011, October 6). *Fiji: US bottled water exporter finally pays up*. Retrieved from https://www.ircwash.org/news/fiji-us-bottled-water-exporter-finally-pays

34. NPR. (2010, December 1). *A bottled-water drama in Fiji* [Transcript]. Retrieved from https://www.npr.org/2010/12/01/131733493/A-Bottled-Water-Drama-In-Fiji

35. Olson-Sawyer, K. (2019, November 4). *Fiji water and its parent company leave locals high and dry*. Retrieved from https://www.watercalculator.org/footprints/fiji-water-locals-dry

36. Fiji Water. (n.d.). *FAQ*. Retrieved from https://www.fijiwater.com/faqs.html

37. Dietvorst (2011).

38. NPR (2010).

Abacus, 225
Abrams, Stacey, 77
Actual malice, 96
Ads Manager, 270, 380
Ad space selling, 269–270. *See also* Social media
Affordable Care Act (ACA), 343
Age Discrimination in Employment Act (ADEA), 194, 201–202, 380
Aggregate limits, 72, 380
Agreement, 105, 380
Agreement on Trade-Related Aspects of Intellectual Property Rights (TRIPS), 255, 380
Agricultural Adjustment Act, 357
AI-driven smart technology. *See* Smarts
Alcoholics Anonymous (AA), 132
Alibaba, 333–334
Alien Tort Statute (ATS), 245, 380
Alsenoy, Van, 324
Alternative financing, 229–233. *See also* Payday loans
Amazon, 20–21, 38, 64, 81–82, 116–118, 183, 203, 293
    corporate social responsibility (CSR), 38
    e-books, 116
    investment in Deliveroo, 117
    pricing policies, 116
    stakeholders demands, 20–21
    Amazon Watch, 160
    American Civil Liberties Union (ACLU), 74, 204
    American Heart Association, 43
    American Institute for International Steel and Sim-Tex Et Al. v. United States (2019), 252
    American International Group (AIG), 220
    American Marketing Association, 45
    American Recovery and Reinvestment Act of 2009, 227
    American Society of Civil Engineers, 80
    Americans with Disabilities Act (ADA), 204, 347, 380
    America Online (AOL), 264
    Amnesty International, 284
    Andersen, Arthur, 234
    Annual percentage rate (APR), 125, 230
    Anthem Health, 64
    Anti-Bribery Convention, 250, 380
    Anticompetitive behaviour, 115–120
    Anti-Corruption and Civil Rights Commission (ACRC), 169
    Anti-price gouging, 123
    Antitrust law, 114
    Antitrust regulation, 115–120
    Clayton Act, 117–118
    Federal Trade Commission Act, 117
    Monopolies, 116
    Robinson–Patman Act, 118
    Sherman Antitrust Act, 115–117
    Sherman Antitrust Act, 115–117
    Unreasonable Restraints of Trade, 116
App culture, 82
Apple, 71, 76, 82, 107, 109, 116, 193, 212, 275, 286, 293, 318
Application programming interface (API), 271, 380
Appropriation of name. *See* Likeness
Apps, 267–269. *See also* Social media
Arbitration, 179, 380
Artificial intelligence (AI), 284, 293, 318, 380
AT&T, 305
Auto title loan, 230

Back-of-the-house workers, 177
Baidu, 333
Bait and switch, 122, 380
Bandar, Mike, 277
Bank of America, 305
Bargaining unit, 179, 380
Base limits, 72, 380
Base of the pyramid, 366
Bear Stearns, 226
Bellwether index, 50
Belotti v. First National Bank of Boston, 341
Benioff, Marc, 76–78
Bentham, Jeremy, 57
Best efforts, 216, 380
"Best places to work" award, 63
Big data, 302–305
    data analytics, 303–304
    definition, 302
    ethical issues, 311–312
    insurance and, 292, 312
    legal issues, 310–311
    variety, 302
    velocity, 302
    volume, 302
Bigley, Gregory, 17
Bill, 68, 380
Biometric data, 338, 380
Biometric Information Privacy Act, 338
Bipartisan Campaign Reform Act (BCRA) of 2002, 72, 342, 380
Bitcoin, 307. *See also* Cryptocurrency
Black Car Fund (BCF), 166
Black Lives Matter (BLM), 281–282, 380
Blinder, Alan, 229

Blue Cross Blue Shield, 70
BNP, 214
Boatright, John, 10
Boston Consulting Group, 189
Bottom of the pyramid (BOP), 366, 380
Bounty program, 168, 380
Boycott, 372, 380
BPEarthWatch, 285
Braun et al. v. Wal-Mart Stores, Inc. (2014), 175–176
Breach, 111, 380
Breach of duty, 102, 381
Brexit, 371
Broadspring, Inc. v. Congoo (2014), 99
Broad view (CSR), 32, 381
Brokerage firms, 214
Brokerage houses, 214
Brown, Ramsay, 275
Bubble, 222, 381
Bulletin board systems (BBSes), 264, 381
Burns, Kevin, 16
Burwell v. Hobby Lobby, 343
Business ethics, 45, 381
Business Roundtable, 11

Calder v. Jones test, 369
California Consumer Privacy Act (CCPA), 320
Cambridge Analytica, 271, 308
Cannes Summit, 235
Capacity, 105, 381
Carbon Disclosure Project (CDP), 145
Carbon offset, 154. *See also* Climate change
Carnell Construction Corp. v. Danville Redevelopment & Housing Authority, (2014), 344
Carnival Cruise Line, 63
Case–Shiller Real Estate Index, 222
Categorical imperative, 58
Cause marketing, 39
Centers for Disease Control and Prevention (CDC), 359
Challenger, Andy, 63
Chamber of Commerce, 72
Chan, Priscilla, 71
Chan, Yolande, 320
Chat rooms, 264, 381
Chicago Booth/Kellogg School Financial Trust Index, 218
Choice of law clause, 109, 381
Choicepoint, 334
Circular economic theory, 147–148, 381
Citigroup, 107
Citizen interest organizations, 160, 381
Citizens United, 72
Citizens United v. The Federal Election Commission, 342
Citizen surveillance, 333–334, 381
Civil Rights Act, 60, 110, 194, 351
Civil Rights Commission, 346

Claim, 4, 381
Clark, Cynthia E., 6
Classical insider, 131
Classical insider trading, 131, 381
Classmates.com, 265
Clayton Act, 115, 117–118
Clayton Antitrust Act, 115
Clean Air Act (CAA), 157
Clean Water Act (CWA), 157
Climate change, 151–155
    awareness of, 152
    carbon offset, 154
    effects of, 151
    Global Response, 153
    Kyoto Protocol, 153–154
    Paris Agreement, 153–154
    rate of warming, 152
    society and, 153
Climate Change Dispatch, 152
Climate Risk Disclosure Act, 234
CMO Survey, 276
CNBC/Burson-Marsteller Corporate Perception Indicator, 27
Coca-Cola, 18–19
Code of ethics, 46 (figure)
    for the International Federation of Accountants, 46 (figure)
    of the American Marketing Association, 46 (figure)
Colgate-Palmolive, 162
Collateralized debt obligation (CDO), 223
Collective bargaining agreement (CBA), 179, 381
Colorado Anti-Discrimination Act (CADA), 345
Commerce, 350, 381
Commerce clause, 350, 381
    business regulation, 350–355
    commerce, 350
    Dormant Commerce clause, 354–355
    interstate commerce, 350
    Marijuana and, 351–354
Commercial banks, 217
Committee, 68, 381
Commodity culture, 372
Communications Decency Act (CDA), 96, 203, 286, 381
Communications Workers of America (CWA), 203
Community microfinancing, 238
Compassionate Use Act (CUA), 352
Compensatory damages, 91, 381
    goal of, 91
Competition and Markets Authority (CMA), 117
Compliance-based approach, 59, 381
Complicity, 367, 381
CompuServe, 287
Computer ethics, 335 (figure)
Computer Ethics Institute (CEI), 335
Concerted activities, 179–180, 381
Conference of the Parties (COP), 153

Conflict of interest (COI), 62, 381
Consequences-based approach to ethics, 57–58
Consideration, 105, 381
Constructive insiders, 131, 381
Consumer Financial Protection Bureau (CFPB), 120, 125, 231, 381
Consumer Privacy Act, 320
Consumer Privacy Bill of Rights, 320
Consumer protection, 120–125, 134–135
    credit transactions, 125
    deceptive sales practices, 121–122
    FDA food safety processes, 124
    food and drug safety, 124
    warranties, 120
Consumer Protection Act, 228
Contract, 104–108, 381
    agreement, 105
    breach, 111
    capacity, 105
    choice of law clause, 109
    consideration, 105
    elements of, 105–107
    forum selection clause, 109
    legal purpose, 105
    limitation of liability clause, 109
    limit liability risk, 108–111
    nondisclosure agreements (NDA), 109–111
    public safety and, 110–111
Controlled Substances Act (CSA), 352
CoreCivic, 84–86. *See also* Private prisons
Corporate Citizenship Conference, 77
Corporate governance, 6, 381
Corporate hypocrisy, 36, 381
Corporate money, 73
    role in elections, 73
Corporate, normative theories of, 5
Corporate personhood, 340–349, 381
    Citizens United case, 342
    Hobby Lobby case, 342
    money flow in elections, 343 (figure)
    public accommodation, 345
    race and, 344
    role of political action committees (PACs), 342
Corporate philanthropy, 39
Corporate social advocacy (CSA), 75, 382
Corporate social irresponsibility, 36, 382
Corporate social responsibility (CSR), 23–24, 249, 382
    advantages of, 38
    benefits, 36–37
    branding, 27
    as a business strategy, 35
    cause marketing, 39
    corporate hypocrisy, 36
    corporate philanthropy, 39
    costs, 36–37

    definition, 24
    disadvantages of, 38
    economic pillar, 25
    ethical pillar, 26
    explicit framework, 33–34
    explicit *vs.* implicit, 34 (table)
    good corporate citizenship (broad view), 33
    implicit framework, 33–34
    law and society, 29
    legal pillar, 25
    limitations, 36–37
    Maven project and, 41
    multiple benefits, 36
    opponents of, 37
    origins, 24
    philanthropic pillar, 26
    pillars, 24–26
    profit first (narrow view), 32
    pros/cons, 37 (figure)
    reasons, 27
    reporting, 28–29
    reputation, 27
    schools of thought, 31–34, 34 (figure)
    shared value (moderate view), 32
    social irresponsibility, 36
    socially responsible business practices, 40
    as a strategy, 27–31
    strategic partnerships, 39
    strategies, 39–40
    sustainable development and, 29
    trends, 39–40
    views, 31–34
    volunteerism, 40
Corporate surveillance, 334, 382
Corporate volunteer, employee participation, 43
Corporate welfare, 21
Council on Environmental Quality, 156
Credit default swap, 223
Creditors, protection of, 120–125
    credit transactions, 125
    deceptive sales practices, 121–122
    FDA food safety processes, 124
    food and drug safety, 124
    warranties, 120
Credit transactions, 125
Crenshaw, Kimberlé, 192
Crowdfunding, 128–129
    caution and, 129–130
Cryptocurrency, 235–236
Cultural competence, 241–242, 382
    cultural norms, 242
    skill component, 242
    tacit knowledge, 242
    work in progress, 242 (figure)

Cultural norms, 242, 382
Cultural revolution, 92
Cultural sensitivity, 241, 382. *See also* Cultural competence
Custom, 243, 382
Customary international law (CIL), 243, 382
Cyber age, 289
Cyberbullying, 310, 382
Cyberterrorism, 307–308, 382

Dark money, 72, 382
Data analytics, 303–304
   descriptive, 304
   diagnostic, 304
   phases, 303 (figure)
   predictive, 304
   preemptive, 304
   prescriptive, 304
Data collection, 272–273
   pros/cons, 273 (figure)
Data metrics, 43
Data privacy, Constitution and, 317–318
Data Protection Act, 324, 326
Data Security
   incident response report, 305
   principles of, 336 (figure)
Data selling, 270–271
Datification, 320, 382
Debt instruments, 125–126, 382
Deceptive sales practices
   Bait and Switch, 122
   pricing and price gouging, 122–123
Defamation, 93–101, 382
   injury for, 93
   invasion of privacy, 100–101
   public figures and, 112–113
   prospective business advantage, 98
   social media and, 94–98
   tortious interference, 99–100
Democracy, 279
Democratic National Convention, 342
Deontological, 56, 382
Deontological ethics, 56
Depression, 220
Diageo, 4
Digital divide, 298–301, 382
   digital readiness, 300
   economic disparities, 298–299
   educational disparities, 300
Digital Millennium Copyright Act (DMCA), 327
Digital readiness, 300–301, 301 (figures), 382
Digital revolution, 283–297
   biased decision-making, 296
   diffusion, 293
   drivers, 283–284

environmental impact, 296
implementation of technology, 296 (figure)
improved communication, 295
improved education and learning, 295
improved security, 295
improved transportation, 294–295
increased population, 295–296
innovation, 293
invention, 293
lack of personal connection, 296
positive impacts on, 294–295
privacy implications, 296
resource depletion, 295
threats to, 295–296
Digital safety, 305, 382
Digital security, 305–306, 382
   cyberbullying, 310
   cybercrimes, 308
   cyberstalking, 310
   cyberterrorism, 307–308
   denial-of-service (DoS) attacks, 307
   hacker, 308
   hacktivists, 308
   malware, 306 (figure), 307
   ransomware, 306
   safety, 305–306
   viruses, 307
   worms, 307
Dimon, Jamie, 20
Direct democracy, 68, 382
Direct initiative, 69, 382
Direct subsidy, 251, 382
Disability, 205, 382
Discrimination, 191, 382
   Age Discrimination in Employment Act, 201–202
   Americans with Disabilities Act, 204–205
   Civil Rights Act, Title VII, 195,-201
   Equal Pay Act, 195
   grooming codes and, 208
   legal prohibitions, 194–205
   stereotypes and, 196–198
Disparate impact, 195, 382
Disparate treatment, 195, 382
Diverse workforce. *See* Workforce diversity
Diversity, 189, 382
Dodd–Frank Act (DFA), 125, 168, 227–228, 382
   credit ratings agencies, 235
   fiduciary duty of broker–dealers, 234
   hedge funds, 234
   secret investigations, 234
Dodd–Frank Wall Street Reform, 228
Dollar General Literacy Foundation, 28. *See also* Corporate social responsibility (CSR)
Domino's Pizza, 348

Donaldson, Tom, 8, 49
Dormant Commerce Clause, 354–355, 382
   interstate clause comparison, 355 (figure)
   key component, 355
Doxxing, 280, 383
Dress code, 200
Drug Enforcement Administration (DEA), 352
Dumping, 251, 383
Dunfee, Tom, 49
Durban Platform for Enhanced Action, 154
Duty of due care, 102, 383

Earth Summit, 153
E-cigarettes, 15–16, 359–360
eBay, 240, 348
Eco-branding, 145–146
Economic disparities, 298–299
Economic strikes, 179, 182, 383
Edelman Trust Barometer, 27, 218
Eeoc v. Abercrombie & Fitch Stores, Inc. (2015), 201
EHarmony, 305
Ehling v. Monmouth-Ocean Hosp. Service Corp, 101
Eighth Amendment, 86–87
Elections, 72–73
   dark money, 72
   role of corporate money, 73
Electronic Communications Privacy Act (ECPA), 310
Electronic Privacy Information Center, 334
Eli Lilly, 188
E-Mail campaign, 135 (figure)
Emergency Economic Stabilization Act of 2008, 226
Employee, 164, 383
Employee privacy, 184–185
   GPS tracking apps, 185
   monitoring employee's personal social media, 184–185
Employment
   employment relationship, 164–167
   public policy exception, 167–169
   whistleblowers, 167–169
   at will, 167–171, 383
Engagement, 269, 383
Environmental activists
   bright greens, 141
   dark greens, 141
   light greens, 141
Environmental code of ethics, 145
Environmental conduct code, 144–146
   compliance, 144
   global concerns, 144
   implementation, 145
   marketing, 144
   measures, 145
   purpose of, 144 (figure)
   risk mitigation, 144

Environmental Defense Fund, 160
Environmental ethics, 144, 383
   business role, 162
Environmentalism, 139–140, 383
   definitions, 140
   environmental activists, 141
   environmental justice, 140
   policy objectives, 140–142
Environmental justice, 140–141, 383
Environmental Protection Agency (EPA), 140, 156
Environment regulation and protection, 155–160
   air quality, 157
   citizen interest organizations, 160
   limiting government impact, 156–157
   market-based incentives, 157–158
   objectives, 155–156
   sources of environmental policy, 155
   U.S. Clean Air Act, 157–158
   U.S. Clean Water Act, 158
   U.S. Water Quality Regulation, 158
   water quality, 157
Equal Employment Opportunity Commission (EEOC), 195, 178, 383
Equal Pay Act, 195, 383
Equal Protection Clause, 341
Equal work, 195, 383
Equifax, 305
Equity, 126, 383
Ethical climate, 62, 383
Ethical dilemma, 48–51, 383
   hypernorms, 49
   individual *vs.* community, 48
   justice *vs.* mercy, 48
   short term *vs.* long term, 48
   truth *vs.* loyalty, 48
   University of Arizona, 53–54
Ethical temptation, 47–48, 383
Ethics, 45, 338, 383
   codes of ethics, 46 (figure)
   compliance-based approach, 59
   conflicts of interest, 62–63
   consequences-based approach, 57–58
   definition, 45
   deontological, 56
   ethical climate, 62
   ethical dilemma, 46, 48–51
   ethical reasoning, 44
   ethical temptation, 46–48
   global business ethics, 49
   integrity-based approach, 59
   law and, 45, 66
   moral intuition, 55, 65
   moral reasoning, 56
   morals and, 45

organizational ethics, 59–64
origin of, 55–59
principles-based approach, 58
profitability and, 66
profits *vs.* ethics, 44
rationalizations and, 51–52
summary of ethical theories, 57 (figure)
teleological, 56
virtue-based approach, 58
Ethics of virtue, 58
Ethics Resource Center (ERC), 50
EU Data Protection Directive, 324
European Central Bank, 235
European Environment Agency, 155–156
Every drop counts campaign, 162
Evolv Technologies, 334
Explicit framework (CSR), 33–34
ExxonMobil, 29–31

Facebook, 15, 71, 74, 81–83, 96–98, 101, 127–128, 173, 180,
    183–184, 188, 191, 203–204, 235, 263, 265–272, 274–283,
    286–291, 315, 320, 322, 334, 367
  application programming interface (API), 271
  score, 184
  use of sensitive personal information, 322
Facilitation payments, 248, 383
Factual cause, 102, 383
Fair Credit Reporting Act, 325
Fair Debt Collection Practices Act, 125, 383
Fair Labor Standards Act (FLSA), 173–176, 383
Fair Pay Act, 193
False Claims Act (FCA), 168, 383
Family and Medical Leave Act (FMLA), 383
FDA Food Safety Processes, 124
Federal Arbitration Act, 106
Federal Bureau of Prisons, 84
Federal Communications Act, 309
Federal Deposit Insurance Corporation (FDIC), 236
Federal tipped minimum wage, 176, 383
Federal Trade Commission (FTC), 54, 115, 271, 320
Federal Trade Commission (FTC) Act, 115, 117, 310
FedEx, 4
Felps, Will, 17
Fiduciary, 9
Fiduciary duty, 6, 383
Fifth fuel, 294
FIJI Water LLC, 377
Finance
  global financial system, 210–211
  microfinance, 211–213
  roles in society, 210–211
  stakeholders, 211 (figure)
Financial crisis. *See* Global financial crisis
Financial firms, 214, 383

Financial industry, public perceptions, 218–219
  capital and payment system access, 219
  financial data collection, 219
  financial resilience, 219
  safeguard savings, 219
Financial Institutions Reform, Recovery, and Enforcement Act
    (FIRREA), 221
Financial market regulation, 233–237
  Dodd–Frank Act (DFA), 233
  enforcement, 233–235
  expanded jurisdiction, 233–235
  financial stability oversight, 235–237
Financial Stability Board (FSB), 235
Financial stability oversight
  early warning, 236
  identifying financial risk in firms, 236
  risk analysis, 236
Financial Stability Oversight Council (FSOC), 236
Fintech, 217, 383
Firehose, 270
Firm-centric approach, 14
Firm commitment agreement, 216, 384
First Amendment, 72–73
  public accommodations and, 345–347
Food and Drug Administration (FDA), 15, 343
Food and Drug Safety, 124
Food, Drug, and Cosmetic Act, 124
Food Safety Modernization Act, 124
Force v. Facebook, (2019), 287–289
Foreign Corrupt Practices, 258
Foreign Corrupt Practices Act (FCPA), 247–250, 259, 384
Foreign direct investment (FDI), 364, 384
Foreseeable harm, 102, 384
Fortune 500 corporations, 23, 35
Forum selection clause, 109, 384
Fourth Amendment, 311, 317
Fraenkel, Yaakov, 287
Freedom of Information Act (FOIA), 234
Free Exercise Protection Act, 76
Freeman, Edward, 4
Free riders, 179, 182, 384
Free trade zone (FTZ), 240, 255–257, 384
  in Dominican Republic, 256
  legal minimum wage in, 257
  pros/cons, 256 (figure)
French Labor Code, 195, 199, 368
Friedman, Milton, 24, 120
Friendster, 265

G20 bankers, 235
Gender pay equity, 193–194
Gender wage gap, 192
General Agreement on Tariffs and Trade (GATT), 250–254, 384
General Data Protection Regulation (GDPR), 54, 311, 321

Genetic genealogy, 295
Gentile, Mary, 51
Geo Group, 84
Geology.com, 99
Geotagging, 272, 384. *See also* Twitter
Gibbons v. Ogden (1845), 350
Gigs and side hustles, 165–166
Gino, Francesca, 190
GiveDirectly, 39
Giving voice to values (GVV) framework, 51–52
Gladiator school, 86
Glassdoor ratings, 44, 63–64
Global citizenship, 364, 384
Global Competitive Index, 374 (figure)
Global Competitiveness Report, 374
Global financial crisis, 219–229, 384
    debates, 228–229
    Dodd–Frank Act, 227–228
    "epicenter" of, 222
    government bailouts, 226
    housing bubble, 222
    leveraging, 222–224
    moral hazard, 222
    mortgage loans, 224–226
    regulatory oversight, 226
    root causes, 220–221
    subprime, 224–226
    unethical lending practices, 224–226
Global financial system, 210–211, 384
Globalization, 363–364, 384
    Brexit and, 371
    complicity, 367
    cultural globalization, 376 (figure)
    foreign direct investment (FDI), 364
    global citizenship, 364
    human aspects of, 375–377
    impact, 364–370
    international trade, 370–374
    multinational corporations (MNCs), 364
    negative impacts, 367
    positive impacts, 367
    profitable multinational corporations, 365 (figure)
    pros/con, 367 (figure)
Global reporting initiative (GRI), 29, 145
Golden State Killer, 295–296
Goldman Sachs, 203, 214, 225–226, 233
Gold rush bubble, 222
Gomez, Selena, 277
Gonzales v. Raich, (2005), 352–353
Gonzalez, Mario Costeja, 326
Google, 4, 41, 82, 203, 267, 285, 291, 330, 325, 334
    application of the ruling, 329–330
    lawsuit and court decision, 328–329
    policy on information removal, 327–328

    right to be forgotten and, 326–331
    search technology, 327
Google+, 266–267
Government bailouts, 226
Government surveillance, 332, 384. *See* Surveillance
GPS tracking apps, 185. *See also* Employee privacy
Grameen Bank, 211–212. *See also* Microfinance
Great depression, 173, 214, 254
Greater Pennsylvania Carpenters Pension Fund (Fund), 29
Great recession, 220
Greenaway, Kathleen, 320
Green management, 139, 142–146, 384
    competitive advantage and, 142–146
Greenwashing, 139, 143
Grievance, 179, 384
Grooming code, 200, 208. *See also* Dress code
Gun-free school zones, 351

Hacker, 308, 384
Hacktivists, 308, 384
Haidt, Jonathan, 55
Hallinan, Joseph T., 53
Hamilton, Alexander, 357
HanesBrands, 257
Harassment, 198–200, 384
    vs. sexual harassment, 199 (figure)
Harris, Tristan, 274
Harvard University, 348
#Hate, 284
Hate speech online, 284 (figure)
Hebdo, Charlie, 282
Herrick, Matthew, 103
High Flyers Corp., 36
Holmes–Rahe stress scale, 182
Home Depot, 305
"Hospitality Included" pricing model, 177
Housing bubble, 222
HQ2 decision, 20
Huber v. Wal-Mart Stores, (2007), 206
Humphrey, John, 244
Hypernorms, 49, 384. *See also* Ethical dilemmas

IBISWorld, 203
Implicit bias, 191, 384
Implicit framework (CSR), 33–34
Implied warranties, 121, 384
Import quota, 251, 384
Incarceration rates, 84
Inclusion, 189, 384
Independent contractor, 164, 384
Independent contractor agreement, 164, 384
Indirect initiative, 69, 384
Indirect subsidy, 251–252, 384
Industrial revolution, 147

Industrial zone, 257, 385
Infinite scroll, 274, 385
Influencers, 122
Initial public offering (IPO), 126, 215–216, 385
  best efforts agreements, 216
  fintech, 217
  firm commitment agreement, 216
  marketing of securities, 216
  post-effective period, 217
  prefiling or quiet period, 216
  road show, 217
  underwriter, 216
  waiting period, 217
Initiative, 69, 385
  direct initiative, 69
  indirect initiative, 69
Injury, 102, 385
  compensatory damages, 91
  intentional tort, 92–101
  negligence, 102
  punitive damages, 91
  risk of, 91–102
  tort, 91
In re Zappos.com Inc. Customer Data Security Breach Litigation, 106
Insider trading, 131–132, 385
  classical, 131
  constructive, 131
Instagram, 264–267, 274–275, 278–279, 285. *See also* Social media
Institute for Women's Policy Research, 192–193
Insurance, big data, 312
Integrity-based approach, 59, 385
Intelligence Act, 333
Intentional tort, 92, 385
Interdisciplinary Center for Law and Information Communication Technology, 324
Intergovernmental Panel on Climate Change (IPCC), 151
Internal revenue, 186
Internal Revenue Code (IRC), 168
Internal Revenue Service (IRS), 168, 385
International Bank for Reconstruction and Development, 371
International Bill of Human Rights, 245, 385
International Centre for Settlement of Investment Disputes, 371
International Court of Justice, 243
International Covenant on Civil and Political Rights, 244–245, 385
International Covenant on Economic, Social, and Cultural Rights, 245, 385
International Customs and Law, 243
International Development Association, 371
International Federation of Accountants, 46
International Finance Corporation, 371
International financial institutions, 211, 385
International human rights, state enforcement, 245–246

International Integrated Reporting Council (IIRC), 29
International Monetary Fund (IMF), 211, 370
International Shoe, 368–369
International torts, defamation, 93
International trade, 370–374
Intersectionality, 192, 385
Interstate commerce, 350, 385
Intrusion into seclusion, 100, 385
Invasion of privacy, 100–101
  appropriation of name or likeness, 100–101
  intrusion into seclusion, 100
  public disclosure of embarrassing facts, 100
Investment banks, 217
Investment quality, 221
Investors protection, 126–132
  private and small transactions, 128–129
  Securities Exchange Act of 1934 (Exchange Act), 130–131
  securities transactions, 126–127
Isolationism, 371, 385

Jenner, Kylie, 277
Jesner v. Arab Bank, 246
#JeSuisCharlie, 282
JOBS Act, 129–130, 385
Jobs survey, future of, 293
Johnson, Boris, 371
Jones, Thomas, 17
JPMorgan Chase, 20, 107, 214
J-SOX, 234
Judiciary Act, 245
JUST Capital, 50
Juul Labs, 15

Kardashian, Kim, 101
Karl Knauz Motors, Inc. d/b/a Knauz BMW and Robert Becker, 180
Katrina Hurricane, 357
Kennedy, John F., 375
Kidder, Rushworth, 47
Kiobel v. Royal Dutch Petroleum, 245
Knight v. Donald J. Trump, 74
Koehn, Daryl, 50, 58
KOF Globalization Index, 364
KPMG, 28
Kraninger, Kathleen, 231
Kyoto Protocol, 153–154, 385

Lautenberg, Frank, 297
Lawful strikes, 179, 182, 385
Laws, 45, 68–69, 338, 385
  bill, 68
  definition, 45
  ethics and, 45
  initiative, 69

morals and, 45
referendum, 68–69
League of Nations, 243, 385
Legal purpose, 105, 385
Legislative referendum, 69, 385
Legitimacy, 17, 69, 385
    forms of, 18 (table)
Lehman Brothers, 220
Les soldes, 241
Leverage, 224 (figure)
Leveraging, 222–224, 385
    power of, 223
Liability clause, limitation of, 109, 385
Liar loans, 225
Libel tourism, 93
Liberty Defense, 334
Likeness, 100
LinkedIn, 64, 203, 265, 270–271, 274, 305
Litigation costs, 108
Loans. *See* Payday loans
Lobbying, 67, 70, 385
    aggregate limits, 72
    business involvement, 70–71
    dark money, 72
    elections, 72–73
    evolution, 69–74
    first amendment, 71
    revolving door, 70
    social media and, 73–74
    technology lobbyists, 71
Lobbying Disclosure Act, 71, 385
Locke, John, 56
Lockheed Martin, 79
Loeb, Nick, 107
Lund, Susan, 209, 222

Mackey, John, 35
#MadeinCHINA, 96
Madison, James, 354, 357
Main street, 213, 385
    banks, 214
    brokerage houses, 214
    financial firms, 214
    initial public offering (IPO), 215–216
    issuing securities, 214–215
    public perceptions of the financial industry, 218–219
    vs. wall street, 213–219
Malware, 305, 306 (figure), 386
Marijuana, Commerce clause and. 351–354
Market, 116, 386
Market-based incentives, 157, 386
Market stakeholders, 12, 13 (figure)
Marriott, 4
Martin, Trayvon, 281

Massive open online courses (MOOCs), 348
Material, 127, 386
Maternity paid leave, 182 (figure)
Matten, Dirk, 33
May, Theresa, 371
McCreary, Lew, 316
McCutcheon v. Federal Election Commission (2014), 72–73
McDonald, 198–199, 209, 228–229
McKinsey Center for Business and Environment, 148
McKinsey & Company, 27
McKinsey Global Institute, 222, 295
Merrill Lynch, 226
Me Too movement, 283, 386
Mexican Federal Labor Law (MFLL), 195
Meyer, Danny, 177
Michael Terpin v. AT&T Mobility (2019), 308–309
Microfinance, 211–213
    in Action, 212
    in America, 212
    community microfinancing, 238
Micro-influencers, 277, 386
Microsoft, 4, 107
Migratory Bird Treaty Act, 243
Millennium development goals (MDGs), 149
Mill, John Stuart, 57
Minimum wage, 173, 174 (figure), 177, 386
    tipped employees, 176 (figure)
Minneci et al. v. Pollard (2012), 87
Misappropriation theory, 131, 386
Misclassification, 165
Misrepresentation, fraud and, 127–128
Moderate view (CSR), 32, 386
Moderators, 266, 386
Monopoly, 116, 386
Moody's rating company, 63
Moon, Jeremy, 33
Moral hazard, 222, 386
Moral intuition, 55, 65, 386
Moral reasoning, 56, 386
Morals, 45, 386
    definition, 45
    ethics and, 45
    law and, 45
Morgan Stanley, 226
Mortgage, 125, 386
    foreclosures, 223 (figure)
    loans, 224–226
    pick-a-pay, 225
Most-favored-nation status, 254, 386
Motivations, 46–53
    ethical dilemma, 48–51
    ethical temptations, 47–48
    rationalizations and, 51–52
Multilateral Investment Guarantee Agency, 371

Multinational corporations (MNCs), 364, 386
Myspace, 265

Narrow view (CSR), 32, 386
Nasdaq. *See* New York Stock Exchange (NYSE)
National Collegiate Athletic Association (NCAA), 114
National Commission on the Causes of the Financial and
    Economic Crisis (NCCFC), 222
National Environmental Policy Act (NEPA), 156
National Fair Housing Alliance, 204
National Federation of Independent Businesses v. Sebelius,
    (2012), 357
National Football League, 257
National Hockey League, 257
National Labor Relations Act (NLRA), 110, 178, 386
National Labor Relations Board (NLRB), 179, 386
National Public Radio (NPR), 377
National Security Agency (NSA), 333
National Security Entry-Exit Registration System
    (NSEERS), 333
National Telecommunications and Information
    Administration (NTIA), 298
National Whistleblower Center, 170
Natural law, 243, 386
Natural Resources Defense Council, 160
Nazi artifacts, penalties for display and selling, 368
Negligence, 102, 386
    breach of duty, 102
    duty of due care, 102
    factual cause, 102
    foreseeable harm, 102
    injury, 102
Negligent design, 103, 386
Negligent failure to warn, 103–104, 386
Negligent manufacturing, 103, 386
Netflix, 107, 308
Newman, Daniel, 302
New York Stock Exchange (NYSE), 68, 117, 214
Nichols v. Azteca Restaurant Enterprises, Inc, 197
Nondisclosure agreement (NDA), 90, 109, 386
    public safety and, 110–111
Nonmarket stakeholders, 12, 13 (figure)
Non-Proliferation of Nuclear Weapons Treaty, 243
Nordisk, Novo, 14
North American Free Trade Agreement (NAFTA), 254, 386, 372
No-tipping policy, 177

Obama, Barack, 73, 266
#OccupyWallStreet (OWS), 227, 280–281, 380
Oil Pollution Act (OPA), 159
Oil Spill, 159
Omnicom Group, 63
Online job postings, 188
    bias, 202–204

Online reputation, 323
Open Skies Treaty, 243
Opt in, 321, 387
Opt out, 320, 387
Organizational ethics, 59–64
Organization for Economic Cooperation and Development
    (OECD), 169, 234, 249, 387
    Anti-Bribery Peer Monitoring Country Reports, 250
    Working Group on Bribery, 250, 387
Otherwise qualified, 205, 387
Outsourcing, 79, 387
Oxley, Michael, 68

Packingham v. North Carolina, 74
Paine, Lynn Sharp, 45, 59
Paribas, 214
Paris Agreement, 153–155
Parker, Warby, 348
Patient Protection and Affordable Care Act, 343
Patriot Act, 333
Payday loans, 209, 229–233, 387
    auto title loans, 230
    defenders of, 232
    "legalized parasitism", 232
    parasites or providers, 232–233
    payday loan regulation, 230–231
    rates and fees charged by lenders, 230
Pay disparity, 192
Pay gap, 192, 387
Paypal (payment app), 217
Pearlman, Leah, 274
Pence, Mike, 76
Performance-based incentives, 20
Per se standard, 115, 387
Personal data, managers practices, 334–337
    best practices, 335
    computer ethics, 335 (figure)
    principles of data security, 336 (figure)
    privacy policies, 336
    protocols, 337
    risk mitigation, 335–336
Personal information, 305, 316, 318–321, 387
    artificial intelligence (AI), 318–319
    benefits, 318
    companies responsibilities, 319–321
    datification, 320
    Facebook data sharing, 322
    global data privacy laws, 321
    governments responsibilities, 319–321
    harms, 318
    individuals responsibilities, 319–321
    opt in, 321
    opt out, 320
    profits *vs.* privacy protection, 322

right to privacy, 319
uncertainty of, 321
Personal power zone, 123
Peterson v. Hewlett Packard, (2004), 60–62
Peter Thiel's Founders Fund, 353
Petya, 307
Pew Charitable Trusts, 232
Pew Research Center, 300, 300, 332, 376
Phillips, Jack, 345
Pick-a-pay mortgages, 225
Place of public accommodation, 345, 387
Policy
  business involvement, 70–71
  business role in, 68–69
  ethical dimensions, 84–86
  private prisons, 84–86
Political action committees (PACs), 72
Political violence, 372
Popular referendum, 69, 387
Portable benefits, 166, 387
Post-effective period, 217, 387
Power, 17, 387
Pre-emption bills, 173, 387
Prefiling or quiet period, 216, 387
Price discrimination, 118, 387
Price gouging, 122–123, 387
  pros/con, 123 (figure)
PriceWaterhouseCoopers (PwC), 40, 196–198
Price Waterhouse v. Ann Hopkins, 196
Primary market, 126, 387
Prime time, 123
Principle of justice, 58
Principle of rights, 58
Principles-based approach to ethics, 58
Privacy, 316, 387
  definition, 316
  invasion of, 100–101
  personal information, 316
  right to privacy, 316–317
  security, 316
  social media and, 101
  vs. security, 316
Privacy Rights Clearinghouse, 305
Private and small transactions
  crowdfunding, 128–129
  Regulation A+, 128
  Regulation D, 128
Private company, 215, 387
Private placements, 126, 387
Private prisons, 67, 84–86
  advocates of, 84
  Eighth Amendment and, 86
  operating costs, 85
  turnover rate, 85
Product liability, 103, 387

Profits *vs.* privacy protection, 315, 322
Progressive tax, 359, 387
Project Maven, 41
ProPublica, 203
Prospectus, 216, 387
Protectionism, 250–254, 387
  advantages and disadvantages of, 252
Proxy cost of carbon, 30
Public accommodation, 345–348
  First Amendment and, 345–347
  website, 348–349
Publication, 96, 388
Public disclosure of embarrassing facts, 100, 387
Public figures, defamation and, 112–113
Public markets, 126, 387
Public policy, 75–79
  corporate social advocacy (CSA), 75
  exceptions to employment at will, 167, 387
Public–private partnerships (3P), 79–81, 387
  advantages, 80
  drawbacks, 80
  pro/con, 80 (figure)
Public Safety, 90
Punitive damages, 91, 388
  pros/con, 92 (figure)
  vs. compensatory damages, 92 (figure)
Push notifications, 274, 388

Racketeer Influenced and Corrupt Organizations (RICO) Act, 353
Ramirez v. Exxon Mobil Corp. (2018), 29–31
Ram, Sudha, 53
Ransomware, 306–307
Rationalizations, 46–53
  examples, 52 (table)
  locus of loyalty, 52
  locus of responsibility, 52
  materiality, 52
  standard practice or status quo, 52
Real economy, 213. *See also* Main street
Reasonable accommodation, 205, 388
Reasonable factor other than age, 202, 388
Reasonably accommodate a religious observance or practice, 200, 388
Recognized duties, 133
Recording Industry Association of America, 327
Redditors, 266, 388
Red tape, 372
Reed, David, 4
Referendum, 68–69, 388
  legislative, 69, 385
  popular, 69
Regressive tax, 359, 388
Regulation
  anticompetitive behavior, 115–120
  antitrust regulation, 115–120

definition, 114
Regulation A+, 128
Regulation by embarrassment, 140
Regulation by publicity, 140
Regulation CF, 129, 388
Regulation D, 128, 388
Regulatory oversight, 226
Religious Freedom Restoration Act (RFRA), 76–77, 343, 388
Rene v. MGM Grand Hotel, Inc, 197
Reporting frameworks, 145 (figure)
Reproductive technology, 107
Reputation bankruptcy, 323
Respondeat superior, 103, 388
theory of, 103
Rest, James, 56
Restricted securities, 128, 388
Retail investors, 214
Retaliation, 168, 199, 388
Revolving door, 70, 388
RFID transponders, 297
Right of publicity, 100
Right to be forgotten, 323–331, 388
Google and, 326–331
Right to erasure, 331–332, 388
managing, 332
Right to privacy, 319, 388
Right-to-work laws, 179, 182, 388
Risk mitigation, 335–336
Road show, 217, 388
Robinson-Patman Act, 115, 118
Rohde & Schwarz, 334
Romney, Mitt, 73
Roosevelt, Eleanor, 244
Roosevelt, Franklin D., 243
Rosen, Jeffrey, 323
Rotenberg, Marc, 334
Rousseau, Jean-Jacques, 55
Rule 10b-5, 131, 388
Rule 504, 128, 388
Rule 506, 128, 388
Rule of reason, 115, 388
Russell 1000 index, 50

Salesforce.com, 76
Salman v. United States, 132
Same-sex marriages
disapproval of, 346
wedding cakes, 345
Sandals Resorts, 95
Santa Clara County v. S. Pac. R. Co., 341
SAP, 64
Sarbanes–Oxley Act (SOX), 68, 168, 234, 388
Sarbanes, Paul, 68
Save Our Planet, 143
Schlosberg, David, 140

Seaton v. TripAdvisor (2013), 93–94
Secondary market, 126, 388
Section 5 of the Federal Trade Commission (FTC) Act, 121, 388
Section 18(a), 131, 388
Section 230, 96, 388
Securities, 125–126, 214, 389
Securities Act of 1933 (or Securities Act), 127, 131, 214–215, 217
Securities and Exchange Commission (SEC), 22, 68, 128, 168, 214, 248
Securities Exchange Act of 1934 (Exchange Act), 127, 388
disclosure under, 130–131
insider trading, 131–132
Securities fraud, 29, 389
Securities transactions, 126
Security, 316, 389
Sedley, David, 55
Self-surveillance, 334, 389
Sentencing Commission, 140
Sexual harassment, 199, 389
incidence of, 178
Shareholder, 3–4, 389
arguments, 9–10
Shareholder theory, 4, 6–7, 389
characteristics, 7 (table)
misrepresentations, 10 (table)
perspective or theory, 4
vs. stakeholder, 5–7
Sharing economy, 298, 389
#SheMeansBusiness, 299
Sherman Antitrust Act, 114–116
Sierra Club, 160
SIFI Banks, 237 (table)
Single publication, 96
Single publication theory, 96, 389
Sin taxes, 340, 358–361, 389
for e-cigarettes, 360
pros/con, 359 (figure)
on sugary drinks, 360–361
Six-Degrees.com, 265
Skill component, 242
Slacktivism, 280, 389
Smartphone, 267–269
Smarts, 332
Smith, H. Jeff, 11
Snapchat, 263, 267–268, 273, 275, 283
Social credit system, 333
Social justice, 280, 389
Socially responsible business practices, 40
Social media, 73–74, 264, 389
addiction, 263, 273–275
algorithm for hate, 285–286
annual growth, 265 (figure)
apps, 267–269
#BlackLivesMatter, 281–282
bots, 278

bulletin board systems (BBSes), 264
business model, 269–273
chat rooms, 264
data and, 271–272
data collection, 272–273
data selling, 270–271
defamation and, 94–98
democracy and, 279–284
doxxing, 280
evolution of, 264–269
Facebook, 265–267
Friendster, 265
general business model, 270 (figure)
Google, 267
Google+, 266–267
government access and, 74–75
#Hate, 284
hate speech online, 284 (figure)
how businesses use, 276–277
influencer, 277
influencer, 277, 389
Instagram, 264, 267
#JeSuisCharlie, 282
LinkedIn, 265
#MeToo (Me Too movement), 283
microblogging site, 266
micro-influencers, 277
monitoring, 184–185
Myspace, 265
number of users, 267 (figure)
#OccupyWallStreet (OWS), 280–281
Orkut (Google), 266
prevalence of, 94
privacy and, 101
public safety issues, 279
Reddit, 266
rules, 286–289
Selling Ad Space, 269–270
slacktivism, 280
smartphones, 267–269
Snapchat, 267
society and, 279–284
trolling, 280
trust and, 271–272
Twitter, 266
ubiquity of, 263
Social reciprocity, 274, 389
Social Security, 173, 389
Social Security Act, 173, 389
Social Security Trust Fund, 173
Society for Human Resource Management (SHRM), 379
Sons & Daughters Program, 249
Sony, 305
SpaceX, 64
Spanish Data Protection Agency, 324

Special economic zone, 255, 389
SPOT program—Screening of Passengers by Observation
    Techniques, 339
Spotted Owl Defense League, 160
Square (payment app), 217
Stake, 4–5, 389
Stakeholder, 3–5, 389
    arguments, 8–9
    commitment levels, 19 (table)
    definition, 4–5
    interests, 12, 14–18
    issues, 12
    legitimacy, 12, 17–18
    managing, 18–19
    market and non-market, 12–14
    multiple obligations, 10 (figure)
    perspective or theory, 4
    power, 12, 14–18
    salience, 16–17, 389
    single obligations, 10 (figure)
    types, 12–18
    vs. shareholder, 5–7
Stakeholder theory, 5–6, 8, 389
    bull's-eye, 9
    central idea of, 11
    characteristics, 7 (table)
    criticism of, 9
    defining, 8
    misrepresentations, 10 (table)
Standard Oil Company, 115
Standard Oil Trust, 115
Standard & Poor's ratings company, 63
Stanford Research Institute, 4
Starbucks, 35, 75, 229
State Farm, 203
Statements of employment particulars, 167, 389
Steffen, Alex, 141
Stereotype, 191, 389
    discrimination and, 196–198
Stock exchanges, 215 (table)
Stockholder, multiple obligations, 10 (figure)
Stop BEZOS Act, 38
Stop Harmful and Abusive Telecommunications Expression
    (HATE) Act, 284, 389
Stored Communications Act (SCA), 311, 317
Stout, Lynn, 9
Strategic partnerships, 39
Strike, 179, 182, 389
    economic, 179, 182, 383
    lawful, 182
    unlawful, 182
Student–Athletes, 114
    Antitrust law and, 118–120
Subprime mortgages, 224–226, 389
Subreddits, 266, 389

Subsidy, 251–252, 389
  direct, 251
  indirect, 252
Suchman, Mark, 17
Surge pricing, 123–124
Surveillance, 332–334
  American beliefs, 333 (figure)
  citizen, 333–334
  corporate, 334
  government, 332–333
  radicalized, 332
  self-surveillance, 334
Sustainability, 139–140, 389
Sustainability Accounting Standards Board (SASB), 145
Sustainability reporting guidelines, 29
Sustainable development, 140, 146–151
  circular economic theory, 147–148
  global standards for, 148–149
  criticism and responses, 150–151
  principles, 149
  sustainable development goals (SDGs), 146, 149–151
Systemically important financial institutions (SIFIs), 235

Tacit knowledge, 242
Tangier Free Zone, 257
Target, 203, 305
Tariff, 251, 389
Tax and Spend Clause, 356, 389
  business regulation, 356–361
  commerce, 357–359
  justice, 357–359
  progressive tax, 359
  regressive tax, 359
  sin tax, 358
  taxes, 357–359
  values, 357–359
Teleological, 56, 390
Teleological ethics, 56
TEVA Pharmaceutical Industries, 248
Theory, 5, 390
Tillerson, Rex, 30–31
Tipped employee, 176, 390
Tippees, 132, 390
Tipper, 132, 390
Tip pooling, 177, 390
Title VII of the Civil Rights Act, 195–202, 390
  disparate impact, 195
  disparate treatment, 195
  harassment, 198–200
  religion, 200
Tombstone ad, 217, 390
Tort, 91, 390

Tortious interference with a prospective business
    advantage, 98, 390
Tort Liability Law, 92
Trade agreements, 254–257
  Agreement on Trade-Related Aspects of Intellectual
      Property Rights (TRIPS), 255
  North American Free Trade Agreement (NAFTA), 254
  United States–Mexico–Canada Agreement
      (USMCA), 255
Trade Expansion Act (TEA), 252
Trans-Pacific Partnership (TPP), 253
Transportation Security Administration (TSA), 334
Treaties, 243, 390
Treaty of Versailles, 243
TripAdvisor, 94
Triple bottom line, 29, 390
Trolling, 280, 390
Troubled Asset Relief Program (TARP), 226–227
Trump, Donald, 20, 95, 253
Trump presidential campaign, 271
Truth in Lending Act (TLA), 125, 390
Twitter, 74, 76, 82, 96–98, 160, 162, 263, 266–267, 269–273,
    275, 279–283, 285, 293, 315

U.S. v. Jones, 185
U.K. Defamation Act, 93
UN Climate Change Conference, 154
UN Commission on Human Rights, 244, 390
Underwriter, 216, 390
Undue hardship, 205, 390
UN Environment Programme, 151
Unethical lending practices, 224–226
Unfair labor practices, 179, 182, 390
UN Framework Convention on Climate Change (UNFCCC),
    153–154
UN Global Compact (UNGC), 6, 19, 149
Uniform Commercial Code (UCC), 120, 390
Union, 179, 390
Union security agreements, 179, 182, 390
Union Square Hospitality Group (USHG), 177
United States–Mexico–Canada Agreement (USMCA), 243,
    255, 372, 390. *See also* North American Free Trade
    Agreement (NAFTA)
United States v. Carpenter, (2016), 317
United States v. McGee, (2014), 132
United States v. Lopez, 351
Universal Declaration of Human Rights (UDHR), 244, 390
University of Arizona, 53–54
UN Monetary and Financial Conference, 254
Unlawful, 179
Unlawful strike, 179, 182, 390
Unpaid internship, 248–249

Unreasonable restraints, 116, 390
UPS, 203
U.S. Department of Justice (DOJ), 248, 390
User data access, 290–291
U.S. Ex Rel. O'donnell v. Countrywide Financial Corp and Bank of America (2016), 221
U.S. Securities and Exchange Commission (SEC), 233, 390
U.S. v. Butler, 357

Values conflicts, 48
  individual *vs.* community, 48
  justice *vs.* mercy, 48
  short term *vs.* long term, 48
  truth *vs.* loyalty, 48
Variable ratio schedule, 273, 390
Venmo (payment app), 217
Vergara, Sofia, 107
Versailles, Treaty of, 243
Vibrant economy, 120
Virtue-based approach, 58
Volunteerism, 40
Volunteer-Match program, 40
Vote Leave campaign, 271

Waiting period, 217, 390
Wales, Jimmy, 331
Wall Street, 213, 391
Walmart, 40, 175, 206, 250–251
Wal-Mart Puerto Rico, Inc. v. Juan Zaragoza-Gomez, (2016), 355
Walt Disney Company, 327
Warranty, 120, 391
Warranty of fitness for a particular purpose, 121, 391
Warranty of merchantability, 121, 391
Watchdog groups, 160
WeeCare, 338
Weisenburger, Randall J., 63
Welch, Jack, 341
Westerveld, Jay, 143
#Whatdoctorslooklike, 191
Whistleblowers, 167–169, 291. *See also* Employment
  office of the, 168, 387
  moral courage of, 169
  vs. bounties, 168 (figure)
Whistleblower bounty, 163, 169–174
  pros/con, 170 (figure)
Whistleblowing, 168
Whole Foods, 35
Willow Village, 83
Winn-Dixie (grocery store chain), 348

Worker Rights Consortium, 257
Worker's compensation, 171–172, 391
Workforce
  BIAS, 190
  categories of, 189 (figure)
  discrimination, 190
  diversity, 189–190
  inclusion, 189–190
  intersectionality, 192
  managing tips, 190 (figure)
Workplace misconduct, 51 (figure)
Workplace protections, 171–183
  concerted activity, 178–180
  Fair Labor Standards Act, 173–176
  federal tipped minimum wage, 176
  free riders, 182
  lawful strike, 182
  leave, 182–183
  minimum wage, 173
  pre-emption bills, 173
  right-to-work laws, 182
  strike, 182
  tipped employee, 176
  unfair labor practices, 182
  unions, 178–180
  union security agreements, 182
  unlawful strike, 182
  worker's compensation, 171–172
World Bank, 147, 211, 218, 255, 370–371
World Economic Forum (WEF), 19, 150, 210, 219, 293, 366
World Health Organization, 157, 360
World Meteorological Organization, 151
World Trade Organization (WTO), 254, 370–371, 391
World Wildlife Federation, 6
World Wildlife Fund (WWF), 39
Wright, Johanna, 285

Yahoo, 305
Yahoo!, Inc. v. La Ligue Contra le Racisma le L'Antisemitisma (2006), 368
Ybarra, Oscar, 275
YouTube, 96, 98, 266, 269–270, 276–278, 285–286, 293, 348
Yunus, Muhammad, 211

Zappos, 106–107, 305
Zelle (payment app), 217
Zichermann, Gabe, 275
Zimmerman, George, 281
Zuckerberg, Mark, 71, 265, 271